Pillsbury

THE COMPLETE BOOK OF BAKING

VIKING

Cherry Squares p. 480

The Complete Book of Baking
Pillsbury Publications
The Pillsbury Company

Publisher: Sally Peters
Publication Manager: Diane B. Anderson
Senior Editor: Jackie Sheehan
Food Editor: Nancy Lilleberg
Associate Food Editors: Sharon Saldin, Grace Wells, Lola Whalen
Test Kitchen Coordinator: Pat Peterson
Contributing Editor: Patricia Miller
Nutrition Information: Pillsbury Technology
Art Direction and Design: Tad Ware & Company, Inc.
Production Coordinator: Michele Warren
Production Assistant: Terri Peterson
Food Stylist: Barb Standal
Text Photography: Studio 3
Cover Photography: Glenn Peterson Inc.

VIKING
Published by the Penguin Group
Penguin Books USA Inc, 375 Hudson Street,
New York, New York 10014, U.S.A.
Penguin Books Ltd, 27 Wrights Lane,
London W8 5TZ, England
Penguin Books Australia Ltd, Ringwood,
Victoria, Australia
Penguin Books Canada Ltd, 10 Alcorn Avenue,
Toronto, Ontario, Canada M4V 3B2
Penguin Books (N.Z.) Ltd, 182–190 Wairau Road,
Auckland 10, New Zealand

Penguin Books Ltd, Registered Offices:
Harmondsworth, Middlesex, England

First Published in 1993 by Viking Penguin,
a division of Penguin Books USA Inc.

10 9 8 7 6 5 4 3

Copyright© The Pillsbury Company, 1993
All Rights Reserved

ISBN 0-670-77147-3
CIP data available.

Printed in the United States of America

CONTENTS

BAKING FROM A TO Z

For years, one of our sayings at Pillsbury has been, "Nothing says lovin' like something from the oven." And there are countless ways to express your love — from golden loaves of fresh-baked bread to still-gooey chocolate chip cookies to luscious fruit-filled pies.

You'll find all those and more on these pages, where we've gathered together our best baking recipes, tips and techniques.

Whether you're a new baker or an old pro, you'll find helpful information in this chapter about baking ingredients, equipment, terms and techniques that will help you turn out delicious results every time.

*Pictured: **Chocolate Chunk Cookies** p. 33*

BAKING FROM A TO Z

When you learn to read, you begin by
mastering the ABCs. Learning to bake is much the
same, but you need to become familiar with the IETTs — Ingredients,
Equipment, Terms and Techniques. Once you feel comfortable
with these baking basics, you'll be confident in the kitchen,
no matter what recipe you choose.

SIX EASY STEPS TO BAKING SUCCESS

1. Read through the entire recipe before you begin . . . it takes the surprise factor out of baking. You'll know just what ingredients and equipment you'll need and how much time the recipe will take.

2. Review the techniques you'll be using. If something is unfamiliar, refer to this chapter for help.

3. Set out and measure the ingredients in advance. Set out the equipment you'll need, too.

4. Clean up as you go. It's confusing to bake in chaos. So put ingredient containers away, wipe up spills and place dirty dishes in the sink.

5. Keep distractions to a minimum so that you won't accidentally skip a step or leave out an ingredient.

6. Relax! Baking is a pleasure, not a chore. So take your time, enjoy what you're doing and let your creativity flow.

INGREDIENTS

Begin with the best ingredients and you will be off to a good start. Fresh ingredients will help ensure that the final product is a success. Here's a reference list of the most common baking ingredients:

BAKING POWDER

Double-acting is the most popular kind of baking powder. It reacts first with liquids and then with heat during baking. Because baking powder, over time, loses its ability to leaven baked goods, use it before the expiration date on the can.

- You can substitute ½ teaspoon of cream of tartar and ¼ teaspoon of baking soda for 1 teaspoon of baking powder.

- To determine if baking powder is still active, add 1 teaspoon to ⅓ cup of hot water. If it bubbles vigorously, it's still active and will give good baking results.

BAKING SODA

Baking soda reacts instantly with liquids and acidic ingredients such as molasses, sour cream and buttermilk. Baked goods with baking soda should be baked as soon after the liquid is added as possible. When an acid isn't included in the recipe, cream of tartar is sometimes used.

BUTTER - SEE FATS

CHOCOLATE

Chocolate and cocoa products come from cocoa beans.

Chocolate should be wrapped tightly in foil or resealable plastic bags and stored in a cool, dry place for up to 9 months. The best storage conditions are between 60° and 78°F., with less than 50% relative humidity.

A grayish coating or "bloom" may form on chocolate when it is stored in a too-warm place because the cocoa butter rises to the surface. Bloom does not affect the flavor or quality. When used in a recipe, the chocolate will regain its original color.

Chocolate comes in countless forms and varieties — all of them delicious. Because they differ in flavor and performance, be sure to use the type specified in the recipe.

- **Chips:** For best results use real chocolate chips, not chocolate-flavored ones. Chips are available in sizes from mini to chunks and in several flavors: semi-sweet, milk, mint and vanilla milk. Vanilla milk chips are similar to a white baking bar and melt well for glazes and fillings.

- **Chocolate syrup:** This syrup is a combination of cocoa, corn syrup and flavoring.

- **Milk:** This is sweet chocolate with milk added. It is available in bars, chips and other shapes.

- **Semi-sweet:** This is unsweetened chocolate with sugar, additional cocoa butter and flavorings added. It may be molded into blocks, chips or bars.

- **Sweet baking or cooking:** Also called German sweet chocolate, it's similar to semi-sweet, but has a higher sugar content. It is available in bars.

- **Unsweetened:** This is the basic type from which all others are made. It is molded into 1 or 2-ounce blocks and packed 4 to 8 in a package.

- **Unsweetened cocoa:** This is pure chocolate powder with no ingredients added. Powdered drink mixes containing cocoa powder, sugar, flavoring and sometimes milk solids, should not be used as a substitute for unsweetened cocoa.

- **White:** White chocolate isn't really chocolate at all. It's a blend of cocoa butter, sugar, milk and flavorings and is available in blocks, bars and other shapes. White baking bars contain the greatest amount of cocoa butter. Vanilla-flavored candy coating, also known as almond bark, contains more sugar than white baking bars.

COCONUT

- Coconut is the white, sweet meat of the fresh coconut. Ready-to-use forms are available in cans or plastic bags. **Flaked** coconut (longer and moister pieces) or **shredded** coconut (shorter and drier pieces) can be used interchangeably in recipes unless otherwise specified.

EGGS

Eggs provide structure and volume and can bind ingredients together.

Use large eggs in recipes for baked goods unless another size is specified.

Use clean, fresh eggs with no cracks for baking. Fresh eggs have yolks that are firm and rounded and whites that are thick and clear.

Eggs should be stored in the refrigerator to preserve their freshness and quality and to prevent the growth of bacteria.

When separating eggs, wash your hands and the shells first before you begin. See p. 23.

Egg whites can be frozen in a freezer container for later use. Thaw them before using.

Fat-free and cholesterol-free egg products are available in the supermarket refrigerator and freezer cases. They are made using egg whites and, depending on the brand, contain no fat or less fat than whole eggs. All are cholesterol-free. Egg products can replace whole eggs in many recipes. Use ¼ cup thawed egg product for each egg called for in the recipe. Do not substitute egg products for eggs in cream puffs or popovers because they won't puff or pop.

FATS

Fats tenderize, provide flavor, help bind ingredients together and produce browning in baked goods. The main types of fats used in baking are:

- **Butter:** Sweet flavored and made from cream, butter is available salted or unsalted in 1-pound blocks, quarter-pound (½-cup) sticks and whipped in tubs. Butter is interchangeable with margarine in most recipes, but is recommended for candy, puff pastry, and croissants. If whipped butter is used, it should be measured by weight, not volume; 8 ounces of whipped butter equals 1 cup.

- **Butter-margarine blends:** These blends of 60% margarine and 40% butter are available in sticks and tubs.

- **Margarine:** This is made from a variety of vegetable oils including corn and soybean. Margarine is available in sticks, in tubs and whipped. Because whipped and tub margarines are softer and contain a higher percentage of air, only stick margarine should be used in baking. Margarine is interchangeable with butter in most recipes.

- **Lard:** Lard is pork fat that has been processed and refined. It is softer and oilier than butter or margarine and creates a flaky texture in biscuits and pie crusts.

- **Reduced-calorie or lowfat butter or margarine:** These products contain at least 20% less fat than regular butter or margarine and have water and air added. THEY SHOULD NOT BE USED FOR BAKING.

- **Vegetable oils:** These oils are low in saturated fat, contain no cholesterol and are pressed from a variety of seeds or kernels such as canola, corn, safflower, sunflower and soybean. They are referred to as "oil" in our

recipes and are interchangeable. Olive oil should not be used in baking unless specified in the recipe.

- **Vegetable shortening:** This solid fat is made from vegetable oils that have been processed with air. Shortening is practically flavorless. It also is available in butter flavor. Our recipes call for "shortening."

FLAVORINGS

For best results, extracts, flavors and liqueurs should be added to ingredients at room temperature, or once a dish (such as custard or frosting) has been removed from the heat.

- **Extracts and flavors:** There are scores of extracts and flavors that can be added to baked goods, such as almond, lemon, mint, rum and orange. These extracts or flavors may be used in place of liqueurs, although the flavors may not be as true or intense. The most popular extract is vanilla. Pure vanilla extract is made from vanilla beans and alcohol. Imitation vanilla is made of synthetic flavors and coloring; it is about half as expensive as vanilla extract and may leave an unpleasant aftertaste.

- **Liqueurs:** These alcohol-based beverages may be used to add chocolate, fruit, mint, nut or coffee flavors to baked goods.

FLOUR

Flour provides the structure for baked goods. It is the finely ground meal produced during the grinding of various edible grains. The most common flours are made from hard and soft wheat, blended during milling to produce different kinds of flour.

Flour is enriched to restore the natural iron and B vitamins that are lost during milling. Enrichment causes no change in the flour's taste, color, texture, quality or caloric value.

Flour may be bleached or unbleached. Bleached flour goes through an aging process which improves its baking performance and whitens the flour. Unbleached flour is allowed to age naturally, and is creamy-white in color. Bleaching does not affect the nutritional value of flour.

Today's flour is pre-sifted more than 100 times during milling, so it is no longer necessary to sift it before measuring.

Store flour in an airtight container in a cool, dry place. It also may be kept in the refrigerator or freezer — just let it warm to room temperature before using. All purpose and bread flours should be used within 18 to 24 months of purchase; self rising flour should be used within 12 to 18 months. Because whole grain flours contain fat from the wheat germ, they become rancid more quickly and are best stored in the refrigerator or freezer. Use them within 1 year.

There are a number of different types of flour. Be sure to use the type specified in the recipe.

- **All purpose:** Milled from the inner part of the wheat kernel, it contains a blend of hard and soft wheat. This versatile flour is appropriate for all uses and is available bleached or unbleached. Our recipes have been developed with bleached all purpose flour but unbleached flour can be used instead.

- **Bread:** Especially milled for baking with yeast, this flour contains more protein which gives the bread structure and increases the elasticity of the dough, resulting in loaves with higher volume. See p. 421.

- **Cake:** Made from soft wheat, it produces tender, delicate cakes.

- **Cracked wheat:** In this flour, wheat kernels are fractured but not finely ground during milling. The flour contains "chunks" of the cracked kernel, giving baked products a coarser, crunchier texture.

- **Rye:** It is available in medium (the most common) light and dark rye flour. Because rye flour has less baking strength than all purpose or bread flour, it should be used in combination with them in baking.

- **Self rising:** Baking powder, which makes baked goods rise, and salt are added during milling. One cup contains 1½ teaspoons baking powder and ½ teaspoon salt. It is especially suited for biscuits, muffins, light cakes and pastries. It is not recommended for popovers, egg-leavened cakes, chocolate recipes, rich bar cookies or yeast breads. It is available bleached or unbleached.

- **Whole wheat or graham:** Milled from the entire wheat kernel, it has a higher nutritional value and contains more fiber than other flours. Baked products have a heavier, more compact texture. Because whole wheat flour has less baking strength than all purpose flour, it should be used in combination with all-purpose or bread flour.

FRUIT

Fruit is available fresh, frozen, canned, candied or dried.

Select fresh fruit that is ripe, full of flavor and free of blemishes. All fresh fruit should be washed before using.

See p. 211 for Dessert Garnishes made with fruit.

Some of the most popular fruits and the varieties best for baking are:

- **Apples:** Choose apples for baking that have tart flavor and firm texture: Jonathan, McIntosh, Winesap, Granny Smith, Rhode Island, Greening, Rome Beauty and Northern Spy. One pound of apples is equivalent to 3 medium apples or 3 cups of sliced apples.

- **Apricots:** Fresh, canned or dried may be used for baking. One pound of apricots is equivalent to 8 to 12 whole apricots or 2½ cups of sliced apricots.

- **Berries:** Strawberries, raspberries, blueberries, blackberries, gooseberries and boysenberries are available fresh or frozen. For fresh, wash just before using. To freeze berries, wash and drain on paper towels; arrange on baking sheet and freeze until solid. Transfer frozen berries to freezer bags. Frozen berries are available in the supermarket freezer case with or without sugar or syrup added. Use thawed or frozen as specified in the recipe.

- **Bananas:** Bananas can be used for baking and cooking at different stages of ripeness. Use green-tipped in cooked desserts, full-yellow in uncooked desserts or pies and, brown-speckled for breads and cookies. One pound of bananas is equivalent to 3 bananas. One sliced banana equals $2/3$ cup; 3 mashed bananas equal 1 cup.

- **Cherries:** Choose tart, firm varieties for baking like Montmorency, Early Richmond and English Morella. Popular sweet varieties are Bing, Queen Anne and Tartarian. One pound of cherries is equivalent to $2\frac{1}{3}$ cups of pitted cherries.

- **Cranberries:** Choose plump, firm, brightly colored berries. Store in the refrigerator or freezer. One 12-oz. pkg. fresh cranberries is equal to 3 cups.

- **Dates:** Available dried year-round and fresh from late summer through the winter. Dried and fresh are interchangeable in most recipes. Use scissors to cut dates. One pound dates is equal to $2\frac{3}{4}$ cups pitted and chopped dates.

- **Peaches:** Peaches are classified as freestone, meaning the pit separates easily from the flesh, or clingstone, meaning the fruit clings to the pit. Clingstone peaches are used for commercial products; freestone are more commonly found in the marketplace and are easiest to use for eating and baking. One pound of peaches is equivalent to 3 medium peaches or 3 cups of sliced peaches.

- **Pears:** Choose Bartlett for poaching, Bosc, Anjou and Comice for baking (when still firm). One pound of pears is equivalent to 3 medium pears or $3\frac{1}{2}$ cups of sliced pears.

- **Prunes:** High in fiber and sugar, prunes are dried plums. One pound dried pitted prunes is equal to $2\frac{1}{4}$ cups.

- **Pumpkin:** Canned pumpkin comes in 2 types: pumpkin (puree only) and pumpkin pie filling (sugar and seasonings added). Fresh pumpkin may replace canned pumpkin in recipes. A 5-pound pumpkin yields about $4\frac{1}{2}$ cups of cooked puree.

- **Raisins:** Available year-round, they are dark brown or golden in color. One pound of raisins equals 3 cups.

- **Rhubarb:** Choose crisp, plump, medium-sized stalks. Rhubarb leaves are poisonous and should not be eaten. One pound rhubarb is equal to 2 cups chopped and cooked rhubarb.

GRAINS

In addition to being milled for flour, grain derivatives are used as ingredients in recipes. Some types are:

- **Bulgur:** This is cracked, partially cooked wheat, which gives bread a chewy texture and nutty flavor. It is nutritionally identical to whole wheat. Use as is or as specified in recipe.

- **Oats:** A whole grain high in fiber; its bran may help lower cholesterol levels. Rolled oats are available in 3 varieties: old-fashioned, quick-cooking and instant. Old-fashioned and quick-cooking oats are interchangeable in recipes, unless otherwise specified. Instant oats are used primarily for breakfast cereal. Oat bran may be used in muffins or quick breads as an added ingredient or as a substitute for part of the flour or rolled oats. See Cook's Note p. 458.

- **Wheat germ:** These are flakes made from the sprouting part of the wheat kernel that are high in nutritional value and fiber. They may be used as a cereal or stirred into baked goods to add texture, vitamins and minerals. Due to its high fat content, wheat germ should be stored in the refrigerator or freezer. See Cook's Note p. 448.

MILK

Milk is a common liquid used in baking to moisten ingredients. It affects the consistency of the batter or dough. Use only the freshest milk and dairy products.

There are a number of milk products. Be sure to use the type specified in the recipe.

- **Buttermilk:** Despite its name, buttermilk contains no "butter." It is skim milk that has had bacteria cultures added to thicken it and give it a tangy flavor.

- **Evaporated:** This is whole milk that has been cooked to reduce the water content and is available in cans. It can be used as is, or reconstituted by adding ½ cup water to ½ cup evaporated milk to make 1 cup. It also is available as evaporated skimmed milk.

- **Half-and-half:** This is milk that contains 12% butterfat.

- **Regular:** This includes whole, 2%, 1% and skim. Milk containing differing percentages of butterfat may be used interchangeably in most recipes.

- **Sour cream:** Dairy sour cream is 18 to 20% fat, although low (light) and nonfat options now are available. Always use the type specified in the recipe. The milk has been treated with a lactic acid culture, which gives sour cream its characteristic tang and thick texture. Sour cream will curdle if it becomes too hot. Always add sour cream at the end of the cooking time and heat it only until it is warm, not hot. Never boil dairy sour cream.

- **Sweetened condensed:** This is milk that has been cooked to reduce the water content and has sugar added. This process makes the milk very sweet and thick. Do not substitute it for evaporated milk.

- **Whipping cream:** This is milk that contains from 32% (light) to 40% (heavy) butterfat. The high butterfat content allows it to be whipped, doubling in volume. Sugar is often added to whipped cream when it is used as a dessert topping. See p. 23.

- **Yogurt:** Yogurt is made from milk ranging from skim to half-and-half, which affects its fat content. The milk is treated with a bacteria culture which gives yogurt its tangy taste and thick texture. Yogurt is commercially available in a wide range of flavors, and also may be made at home with a yogurt maker. Yogurt adds flavor and moistness to recipes.

NUTS

All nuts are a good source of protein, contain no cholesterol but are high in fat and calories.

Store nuts in an airtight container in a cool, dry place or freeze them for up to 6 months. Unshelled nuts keep longer than shelled.

Each variety of nut has its own special characteristics, distinctive taste, aroma and use. Some of the most popular for baking are:

- **Almonds:** First cousin to the peach, almonds are flat, oval-shaped nuts with a brown skin that can be removed through blanching. Almond paste is made of ground blanched almonds, sugar and a liquid. Marzipan also is made of almonds, but is sweeter and finer-textured than almond paste. Almonds are available whole (shelled or in the shell), blanched, sliced or slivered.

- **Hazelnuts or filberts:** These are small, round, buttery nuts available whole (shelled or in the shell).

- **Macadamia:** Grown in Hawaii, these creamy, round nuts are especially popular in combination with coconut and pineapple. They are available shelled in jars or cans.

- **Peanuts:** Peanuts are actually a legume similar to garden peas. Peanuts are available in the shell or shelled, salted or unsalted, raw or roasted, and honey roasted.

- **Peanut butter:** Peanut butter is available in creamy and chunky varieties. Natural and old-fashioned peanut butters contain peanuts and peanut oil with no added sugar. The peanut oil separates out and must be stirred back in. To prevent separation, store these peanut butters in the refrigerator.

- **Pecans:** Grown primarily in the southern U.S., pecans are rich, buttery and have the highest fat content of any nut. They're versatile and available in the shell, shelled, halved and chopped.

- **Walnuts:** The most popular varieties of walnuts are English and black. English walnuts, the most common, are mild flavored and available year-round. Black walnuts have a stronger, richer flavor, are difficult to shell and are available only seasonally. Walnuts are available in the shell, shelled, halved and chopped.

SALT

Salt provides flavor, and in yeast breads, it controls the rate of growth of the yeast. The 2 most common types are:

- **Kosher salt:** A coarse-grained, additive-free salt sometimes used in baking. In our recipes, we refer to this as coarse salt.

- **Table salt:** A fine-grained salt used in cooking and at the table as a seasoning. Iodine is often added to table salt for dietary needs.

SPICES, HERBS AND SEEDS

Spices, herbs and seeds add that just-right touch of seasoning to baked goods. Store dried herbs, spices and seeds in a cool, dark, dry area in airtight containers. Seasonings lose flavor when exposed to heat and light, such as when stored over or near your kitchen range or in a countertop spice rack. Herbs and spices should be replaced annually. Store fresh herbs with cut stems in water in the refrigerator.

Herbs can be used either fresh or dried. One tablespoon of fresh herbs is equivalent to 1 teaspoon crushed or ½ teaspoon ground herbs. Here are some of the most popular for baking:

SPICES

- **Allspice:** This is called "4 spices" by the French because it tastes like a blend of cinnamon, cloves, nutmeg and juniper berry. It is available whole or ground.

- **Cardamom:** This is a 3-sided, creamy white pithy pod which contains 17 to 20 seeds. The seeds are pungent yet sweet. It is available in the pod, as shelled seeds or as ground seeds.

- **Cinnamon:** This is a mild, sweet spice which comes from the bark of a tree. It is available in stick, ground or as an oil.

- **Cloves:** Grown in Madagascar and Zanzibar, this pungent, oily spice is available whole, ground or as an oil.

- **Ginger:** This sweet yet slightly tangy spice comes from the root of a lily. Ginger is available fresh, ground and candied.

- **Nutmeg:** Nutmeg is the sweet, hard kernel of a fruit. Mace is from the same fruit and similar in flavor. Nutmeg is usually available in ground form but can be purchased whole.

- **Pumpkin pie spice:** This is a blend of cinnamon, ginger and nutmeg. To make your own, combine 4 teaspoons cinnamon, 1 teaspoon ginger, ½ teaspoon allspice, ½ teaspoon nutmeg and ½ teaspoon cloves.

- **Saffron:** Harvested from the autumn crocus, this golden-yellow spice is rare, costly, has a strong flavor and must be used sparingly. It imparts a yellow color to food.

HERBS

- **Basil:** This is a versatile, savory herb that is available in a wide range of varieties: Italian, lemon, spicy globe, cinnamon and opal.

- **Dill:** This is a member of the parsley family and has a tart, lemony flavor. It is available as dill weed and dill seed.

- **Mint:** This is usually used fresh in beverages or as a garnish.

- **Oregano:** This is a pungent herb that gives Italian food its distinctive flavor.

- **Parsley:** There are about 37 varieties of parsley. It's crisp, sharp flavor is often used in combination with other herbs.

- **Rosemary:** The leaves of this shrub-like herb have a strong, piney flavor and should be used sparingly.

- **Sage:** Sage is commonly used in poultry stuffing, but also works well in breads.

- **Thyme:** French and lemon are the most popular varieties of this pungent, aromatic herb.

SEEDS

- **Anise:** This is a comma-shaped seed that imparts a sweet licorice flavor.

- **Dill:** This is a flat seed from the dill plant. It adds a tart, lemony flavor.

- **Caraway:** This is an aromatic seed with a sharp, distinctive flavor.

- **Poppy:** This is a slate-blue, tiny seed from a variety of non-opium poppy grown in Holland.

- **Sesame:** This is a nutty-flavored seed used especially for topping baked goods.

- **Sunflower:** When cracked open, this seed contains a sweet, grayish, oval-shaped nut that adds crunch to baked goods.

SUGAR AND SWEETENERS

Sugar and sweeteners flavor and tenderize baked goods and give them a golden brown crust.

Sugar is processed from either sugar cane or sugar beets. There is no difference in quality or performance between cane or beet sugar.

Sugar should be stored in an airtight, moisture-proof container to prevent lumping.

There are a number of types of sugars and sweeteners. Be sure to use the type specified in the recipe.

- **Brown sugar:** This contains some molasses making it moist and firm. Both light and dark brown sugar are available. Dark brown sugar has a slightly stronger flavor because it contains more molasses. Brown sugar should be stored in a tightly sealed glass or plastic container in a cool, dry place to prevent it from drying out. To soften brown sugar that has dried out, add a piece of apple (placed in an open plastic bag) to the storage container. Seal tightly; remove the apple after 2 days.

- **Corn syrup:** This is a thick, sweet syrup available in 2 forms: light or dark. Dark corn syrup has a stronger flavor and is dark in color.

- **Granulated sugar:** This is a refined, white, all purpose sugar from which all the molasses has been removed.

- **Honey:** This is a very sweet, thick liquid made by bees from flower nectar. It contributes sweetness, moisture and a distinct flavor to baked goods. Use regular honey, not whipped, in recipes. If honey crystallizes, place the open jar in a pan of hot water until the honey turns liquid again.

- **Molasses:** This is a by-product of the sugar refining process and is available in 3 forms: light, dark and blackstrap. Light molasses is lightest in color and flavor; dark has a rich flavor; and blackstrap has a bitter flavor unsuitable for baking.

- **Powdered sugar:** Also known as confectioners' sugar, it is finely ground sugar which contains cornstarch for ease of mixing and blending. It may need to be sifted to remove lumps.

- **Superfine sugar:** This is sugar that is granulated to the finest crystals. It is ideal for making meringues and cakes.

YEAST

Yeast is bacteria that is activated by warm liquid and sugar. Because yeast is a living plant, accurate liquid temperatures are necessary for baking success and a thermometer offers the most accurate temperature control. Heat the liquid to the temperature specified in the recipe. The action of the bacteria produces gas bubbles which cause baked goods to rise. See p. 418 for Secrets for Baking with Yeast. One envelope of active dry yeast equals 2¼ teaspoons of bulk active dry yeast or ⅓ of a 2-ounce cake of compressed fresh yeast.

- **Active dry yeast (or regular):** These dehydrated granules are the most popular form of yeast. Active dry yeast is available in packets or jars.

- **Compressed fresh yeast:** This moist form of yeast is available in the refrigerator section of the grocery store. It must be stored in the refrigerator and used within 2 weeks.

- **Fast-acting (or quick-rising yeast):** These dehydrated granules reduce the rising time for dough by about half. Use this form interchangeably with regular yeast, and remember to reduce the rising time. Fast-acting yeast is available in packets or jars.

EMERGENCY SUBSTITUTIONS

For best results, use the ingredients called for in the recipe. But, if you run out of or run short of an ingredient, here are some substitutes that can fill in those gaps. Some substitutions may cause a change in texture or flavor, therefore, use these substitutions only when necessary.

EMERGENCY SUBSTITUTIONS

Ingredient	Substitute
Active dry yeast, 1 package	2¼ teaspoons dry or ⅓ cake compressed yeast, crumbled
Baking powder, 1 teaspoon	¼ teaspoon baking soda plus ½ teaspoon cream of tartar
Buttermilk, 1 cup	1 tablespoon vinegar or lemon juice plus enough milk to make 1 cup
Cake flour, 1 cup	1 cup all purpose flour minus 2 tablespoons
Cornstarch, 1 tablespoon	2 tablespoons flour
Dairy sour cream, 1 cup	1 cup plain yogurt
Flour (for thickening), 1 tablespoon	1½ teaspoons cornstarch
Half-and-half, 1 cup	⅞ cup (¾ cup plus 2 tablespoons) milk plus 3 tablespoons margarine or butter
Honey, 1 cup	1¼ cups sugar plus ¼ cup liquid
Lemon, 1 medium (fresh juice)	2 to 3 tablespoons bottled lemon juice
Orange, 1 medium (fresh juice)	¼ to ⅓ cup orange juice
Yogurt (plain), 1 cup	1 cup dairy sour cream
Self rising flour, 1 cup	1 cup all purpose flour plus 1½ teaspoons baking powder and ½ teaspoon salt
Semi-sweet chocolate, 1 ounce	1 ounce unsweetened chocolate plus 1 tablespoon sugar OR 3 tablespoons semi-sweet chocolate chips
Semi-sweet chocolate chips, (for melting) ½ cup	3 ounces semi-sweet chocolate
Unsweetened chocolate, 1 ounce	3 tablespoons unsweetened cocoa plus 1 tablespoon shortening or margarine

EQUIPMENT

Having a well-equipped kitchen will add to your baking enjoyment and success. You don't need to have a lot of equipment, or the most expensive, but a few basic, versatile and good-quality tools will allow you to create just about any recipe. Basic tools of the baking trade are:

- **Baking pans:** For best results, choose shiny metal ones. Aluminum and tin are the best metals for baking pans. However, insulated, dark-surfaced and nonstick pans are becoming increasingly popular. Foods baked in insulated pans require more baking time and take longer to brown. Foods baked in dark-surfaced pans require a shorter baking time and brown more quickly.

Pans come in standard sizes. It is essential to use the correct size of pan so that your baked goods will turn out well. The types and sizes of pans called for most often in this book are:

> 8-inch square pan
> 8 or 9-inch round cake pan
> 8x4-inch loaf pan
> 9x5-inch loaf pan
> 9-inch pie pan
> 9 or 10-inch springform pan
> 10-inch tart pan
> 10-inch tube pan
> 12-cup Bundt® pan*
> 13x9-inch pan
> 15x10x1-inch baking (or jelly roll) pan
> casserole or souffle dishes of
>   assorted sizes
> cookie sheets of assorted sizes
> muffin pans of assorted sizes

If the recipe calls for a pan you don't have, you can generally use what you do have, however, changing pan sizes will alter baking times. This chart will help you make practical pan-size substitutions:

PAN SUBSTITUTIONS

Recipe calls for:	Substitute:
8x4-inch loaf pan	Two 5½x3¼-inch loaf pans
9x5-inch loaf pan	Two 7½x3¾-inch loaf pans OR three 5½x3½-inch loaf pans
One 9-inch round cake pan	One 8-inch square pan
Two 9-inch round cake pans	Three 8-inch round cake pans
12-cup Bundt® pan	One 10-inch tube pan OR two 9x5-inch loaf pans
13x9-inch	Two 9-inch round cake pans OR two 8-inch round cake pans OR two 8-inch square pans

- **Blender, food processor:** A blender or food processor can speed some preparation steps by chopping, grinding and mixing. Choose one with variable speeds and parts that are easy to clean.

- **Bowls:** Choose a set of 4 nesting glass, stainless steel, plastic, or pottery bowls. Some sets are available with spouts for pouring. Plastic bowls may retain food odors, colors and oils.

- **Bread machine:** A nice-to-have, but not-necessary piece of equipment that mixes and bakes bread all in the same machine.

- **Custard cups:** These small glass cups may be used in the oven for baking single-serving desserts and custards. They also are handy for separating eggs, coloring small amounts of frosting and other baking uses.

- **Decorating bag:** This is also referred to as a pastry bag and is a waxed cloth, plastic or paper bag which comes with a variety of screw-on tips for decorating with frostings and icings. See Decorating Tips and Designs p. 185.

- **Eggbeater:** This is a hand-held rotary egg-beater that can be used in place of a wire whisk or electric mixer.

*Bundt® is a registered trademark of Northland Aluminum Products, Inc., Minneapolis, MN.

- **Electric mixer:** This appliance is used for mixing and whipping ingredients. A portable, hand-held mixer is great for light jobs. A free-standing electric mixer works best for bigger quantities and longer mixing times. Many freestanding mixers also come with bread dough hooks for making yeast bread.

- **Grater:** A utensil that has surfaces to produce fine to coarse shreds. It is available in plastic or metal.

- **Juicer:** This is a glass, metal or ceramic utensil for removing the juice from citrus fruits. Choose a juicer with holes for straining the juice from the pulp, a spout for pouring and a handle. Some juicers have a rim for placing over a measuring cup or bowl.

- **Knives:** An assortment of sharp, serrated and plain-edged knives, in sizes ranging from paring to butcher, will fit all your baking needs.

- **Measuring cups:** You will need 2 kinds: a glass measuring cup, which holds 1, 2 or 4 cups, for measuring all liquids, and a set of metal or plastic ¼, ⅓, ½ and 1 cup measuring cups for dry ingredients.

- **Measuring spoons:** Measuring spoons for ¼, ½, and 1 teaspoon and 1 tablespoon are available in metal or plastic for measuring small amounts of both dry and liquid ingredients.

- **Metal spatula:** These are used for leveling off ingredients. Rounded end spatulas are used for frosting cakes.

- **Mixing spoons:** Whether you prefer plastic, wood, or metal, have several mixing spoons of varying sizes on hand.

- **Pancake turner:** This is used to remove cookies from baking sheets or bars from pans. One with a short, wide blade works best.

- **Pastry brush:** Use these to spread glazes and grease pans. Choose brushes with soft natural or synthetic bristles that won't tear or mark dough.

- **Pastry cloth:** A sturdy, washable, canvas-like cloth to help prevent rolled doughs from sticking to countertops or tables.

- **Rolling pin:** This is used for rolling out doughs. Choose a smooth, non-porous finish, either wood, marble or plastic. Wooden rolling pins are lightweight, inexpensive and readily available. However, they can become permeated with oils and flour if the surface is nicked or damaged. To keep doughs from sticking, cover the rolling pin with a rolling pin cover. Marble rolling pins are heavy, and roll dough evenly and quickly. When chilled, dough does not stick to them.

- **Rolling pin cover:** This is also referred to as a stockinette cover. Made of a tube-knit cotton, it is stretched over a rolling pin. The cloth is then lightly floured and helps prevent rolled doughs from sticking.

- **Rubber scraper:** Choose a wide, slightly stiff blade and a strong handle for scraping the sides of the bowl during mixing. Keep one just for baking so that it won't pick up strong odors from other savory foods such as onions.

- **Strainer:** This is necessary for draining liquids and for rinsing fruit and is available in plastic or wire mesh.

- **Timer:** This is important for accurate baking times and is available in a number of styles. Choose one with a loud tone.

- **Wire racks:** For cooling baked goods, racks allow air to circulate around the food and keep crusts from getting soggy. They are available in several sizes.

- **Wire whisk:** This is used for mixing, beating egg whites and whipping cream and is available in a variety of sizes. Larger whisks are appropriate for bigger quantities and heavier mixtures.

HOW TO MEASURE INGREDIENTS

Knowing how to measure ingredients, and then measuring carefully, will help ensure that your baked goods will turn out just right.

Measuring liquids: Use a clear, standard liquid measuring cup with a pouring spout. This cup has measuring marks for ¼, ⅓, ½, ⅔, ¾ and 1 cup, as well as fluid ounces and milliliters. Place the measuring cup on a level surface and fill to the desired mark. Read the measurement at eye level for accuracy.

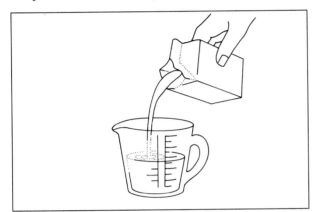

Measuring dry ingredients: Use standard dry measuring cups that come in sets of ¼, ⅓, ½ and 1 cup. Lightly spoon the ingredient into the measuring cup. Level it off with the straight edge of a spatula or knife.

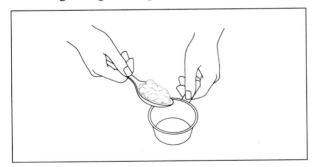

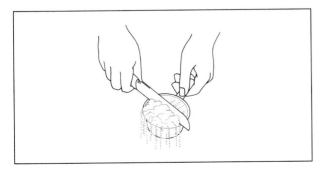

Measuring solid fats and brown sugar: Use standard dry measuring cups. Firmly press the ingredient into the cup and level it off with a spatula or knife.

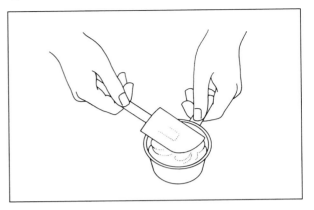

Measuring margarine or butter: The wrappers on stick butter or margarine are printed with measuring marks for each tablespoon, ¼ cup, ⅓ cup and ½ cup. Use a knife to cut the margarine or butter at the desired mark.

Here are some additional measures for margarine or butter:

⅛ stick = 1 tablespoon = ½ ounce
¼ stick = 2 tablespoons = 1 ounce
½ stick = 4 tablespoons = 2 ounces
1 stick = ½ cup = 4 ounces
2 sticks = 1 cup = 8 ounces
4 sticks = 2 cups = 16 ounces

Measuring dairy sour cream and yogurt: Use standard dry measuring cups. Spoon the ingredient into the cup and level it off with a spatula or knife.

Measuring small amounts of ingredients: Use standard measuring spoons for all ingredients. These spoons generally come in sets of ¼, ½, and 1 teaspoon and 1 tablespoon. For dry ingredients, fill the spoon and then level it off with a spatula or knife. For liquid ingredients, fill the spoon full.

EQUIVALENTS

Use these measuring equivalents if you halve or double a recipe:

> 3 teaspoons = 1 tablespoon
> 4 tablespoons = ¼ cup
> 5 tablespoons + 1 teaspoon = ⅓ cup
> 8 tablespoons = ½ cup
> 16 tablespoons = 1 cup
> 2 cups = 1 pint
> 2 pints = 1 quart
> 4 quarts = 1 gallon

TERMS

The language of baking clarifies what techniques and methods are needed for each recipe. Once you learn this language, you're on your way to mastering any recipe.

Bake: To cook in an oven with dry heat. The oven should always be heated for 10 to 15 minutes before baking.

Batter: A mixture of flour, liquid and other ingredients that is thin enough to pour.

Beat: To thoroughly combine ingredients and incorporate air with a rapid, circular motion. This may be done with a wooden spoon, wire whisk, rotary eggbeater, electric mixer or food processor.

Blanch: To partially cook food by plunging it into boiling water for a brief period, then into cold water to stop the cooking process.

Blend: To thoroughly combine 2 or more ingredients.

Boil: To heat a liquid until bubbles rise continually to the surface and break.

Caramelize: To heat sugar until it is melted and brown. Caramelizing sugar gives it a distinctive flavor.

Chop: To cut into small pieces using a sharp knife, appliance or scissors.

Coats spoon: When a thin, even film covers a metal spoon after it has been dipped into a cooked mixture and allowed to drain.

Combine: To stir together 2 or more ingredients until mixed.

Cool: To come to room temperature.

Cream: To beat 1 or more ingredients, usually margarine or butter, sugar and/or eggs, until the mixture is smooth and fluffy.

Crimp: To seal the edges of 2 layers of dough with the tines of a fork or your fingertips.

Cut in: To distribute solid fat throughout the dry ingredients using a pastry blender, fork or 2 knives in a scissors motion.

Dash: A measurement less than ⅛ teaspoon.

Dough: A soft, thick mixture of flour, liquids, fat and other ingredients.

Dot: To distribute small amounts of margarine or butter evenly over the surface of pie filling or dough.

Drizzle: To drip a glaze or icing over food from the tines of a fork or the end of a spoon.

Dust: To sprinkle lightly with sugar, flour or cocoa.

Flute: To make or press a decorative pattern into the raised edge of pastry.

Fold in: To gently combine a heavier mixture with a more delicate substance such as beaten egg whites or whipped cream without causing a loss of air. See p. 22.

Glaze: To coat with a liquid, thin icing or jelly before or after the food is cooked.

Grate: To shred with a hand-held grater or food processor.

Grease: To rub fat on the surface of a pan or dish to prevent sticking.

Grind: To produce small particles of food by forcing food through a grinder.

Knead: To fold, push and turn dough or other mixture to produce a smooth, elastic texture.

Lukewarm: A temperature of about 95°F. that feels neither hot nor cold.

Mix: To stir together 2 or more ingredients until they are thoroughly combined.

Mix until just moistened: To combine dry ingredients with liquid ingredients until the dry ingredients are thoroughly moistened, but the mixture is still slightly lumpy.

Partially set: To refrigerate a gelatin mixture until it thickens to the consistency of unbeaten egg whites.

Peel: To remove the skin of a fruit or vegetable by hand or with a knife or peeler. This also refers to the skin or outer covering of a fruit or vegetable.

Proof: To allow yeast dough to rise before baking. Or, to dissolve yeast in a warm liquid and set it in a warm place for 5 to 10 minutes until it expands and becomes bubbly.

Refrigerate: To chill in the refrigerator until a mixture is cool or a dough is firm.

Rind: The skin or outer coating of foods such as citrus fruit or cheese.

Rolling boil: To cook a mixture until the surface billows rather than bubbles.

Rounded teaspoon: To mound dough slightly in a measuring teaspoon.

Scald: To heat a mixture or liquid to just below the boiling point.

Score: To cut slits in food with a knife, cutting part way through the outer surface.

Softened: Margarine, butter, ice cream or cream cheese that is in a state soft enough for easy blending, but not melted.

Shred: To cut food into narrow strips using a grater or food processor fitted with a shredding disk.

Soft peaks: To beat egg whites or whipping cream to the stage where the mixture forms soft, rounded peaks when the beaters are removed.

Steam: To cook food on a rack or in a wire basket over boiling water.

Stiff peaks: To beat egg whites to the stage where the mixture will hold stiff, pointed peaks when the beaters are removed.

Stir: To combine ingredients with a spoon or whisk using a circular motion.

Toss: To mix lightly with a lifting motion, using 2 forks or spoons.

Whip: To beat rapidly with a wire whisk or electric mixer to incorporate air into a mixture in order to lighten and increase the volume of the mixture.

Zest: The colored outer peel of citrus fruit which is used to add flavor. The zest is often referred to as grated peel in recipes.

TECHNIQUES

You've become familiar with Ingredients, Equipment, How to Measure and Terms. Now it's time to brush up on Techniques. These are the methods or "how-tos" that will make your baking experience a success.

ADDING EGG YOLKS TO A HOT MIXTURE

Egg yolks will cook too quickly if added all at once to a hot mixture. This must be done gradually. To add egg yolks to a hot mixture:

1. Stir a spoonful of the hot mixture into the beaten egg yolks to condition them to the temperature of the hot mixture.

2. Add the egg yolk mixture to the remaining hot mixture and continue to stir over low heat until it thickens to the desired consistency.

BEATING EGG WHITES

Beaten egg whites incorporate air into baked goods or are used for meringues. They can be beaten with an electric mixer, hand-held rotary eggbeater or whisk. Bring egg whites to room temperature for best volume. (Use them within 30 minutes.) Be sure that both the bowl and beaters are clean and dry. Even a small amount of grease or oil, including specks of yolk, will prevent the whites from whipping properly. To beat egg whites:

1. Begin beating slowly, gradually increasing the speed as the egg whites begin to foam.

2. Beat the egg whites until they hold the desired shape, either soft or stiff peaks.

BROWNING BUTTER

Browned butter adds a rich, distinctive flavor to baked goods and frostings. To brown butter:

1. Place butter in a heavy saucepan over medium heat.

2. Melt butter, stirring occasionally. As the butter heats, it will foam.

3. Continue heating until butter becomes a rich caramel color, stirring frequently. Remove from heat.

FOLDING IN INGREDIENTS

Beaten egg whites or whipped cream are common ingredients that are folded into batters and other mixtures. They both contain air in the form of small bubbles, so folding, rather than mixing, is done to retain the air in the mixture. The egg whites and whipping cream are fragile, so use a light touch. To fold in egg whites or whipped cream:

1. Start with a large bowl containing the heavier mixture and place half of the egg whites or whipped cream on top of the mixture.

2. Using a circular motion with a rubber scraper, cut through the center of the mixture across the bottom of the bowl, gently lifting up and over.

3. After each fold, rotate the bowl slightly in order to incorporate the ingredients evenly.

4. Fold in the remaining egg whites or whipped cream until both mixtures are uniformly combined and no streaks remain.

HEATING THE OVEN

To help ensure accurate baking times, it is necessary to heat the oven for 10 to 15 minutes before baking.

KNEADING DOUGH

Kneading dough evenly distributes the ingredients, develops structure and makes the dough elastic so that it will rise and stay risen as the yeast works. Use a press, fold and turn motion. To knead dough:

1. Flatten the ball of dough with your hands and fold it in half toward you.

2. Press and push the dough away with the heels of your hands.

3. Rotate the dough a quarter turn and repeat these steps for 5 to 10 minutes or until the dough is smooth and elastic.

PREPARING THE PAN

Most recipes for baked goods call for the pan to be greased, or greased and floured. Prepare the pan before you begin making the recipe.

To grease a pan:

1. Use a solid vegetable shortening because it won't brown or add flavor to your baked goods. The recipes in this book have been tested with shortening unless otherwise specified.

2. With a paper towel or pastry brush, apply a thin, even layer of shortening to the pan. Grease generously, if specified in recipe, to ensure easy removal of baked items from the pan.

To grease and flour a pan:

1. Grease the pan. Then add a tablespoonful of flour to the pan and shake the pan so that flour sticks to all greased areas.

2. Turn the pan upside down and tap the bottom to remove excess flour.

                    OR

1. In a small bowl, blend ¼ cup shortening and ¼ cup all purpose flour until well mixed.

2. To grease and flour a pan, apply a thin, even layer of the shortening-flour mixture with a paper towel or pastry brush. (Store remaining mixture in an airtight container in the refrigerator.)

To paper-line a pan:

1. Line the pan with parchment paper or waxed paper cut to the appropriate size.

2. Grease the paper if specified in the recipe.

SEPARATING EGGS

A number of recipes call for the whites and yolks of eggs to be separated. Before you begin, wash your hands and the egg shells. You'll also need a bowl and 2 cups. To separate eggs:

1. Tap the side of the egg on the edge of a bowl or cup to crack the shell. Tip the egg so that the majority of its contents are in 1 half; pull the 2 halves of the shell apart.

2. Pass the yolk from shell half to shell half several times, allowing the white to slip off into a cup. Place the yolk in another cup.

3. Inspect the white for small amounts of yolk. If any yolk is present in the white, remove it with a spoon. Any yolk in the white will prevent the whites from beating into peaks.

4. Transfer the white to the bowl.

TOASTING NUTS AND COCONUT

Toasting nuts or coconut until golden brown adds a warm, rich flavor to these ingredients.

To toast nuts:

1. Heat the oven to 350°F. Spread nuts in a single layer on a cookie sheet. Bake for 5 to 10 minutes or until light golden brown to golden brown, stirring occasionally. (The baking time will vary, depending on the type of nut.) Watch them closely to avoid over-browning.

2. To toast in the microwave oven, spread nuts in a microwave-safe pan. Microwave on HIGH for 4 to 8 minutes or until light golden brown, stirring frequently.

To toast coconut:

1. Heat the oven to 350°F. Spread coconut evenly on a cookie sheet. Bake for 7 to 8 minutes or until light golden brown, stirring occasionally. Watch closely to avoid overbrowning.

2. To toast in the microwave oven, spread coconut in a microwave-safe pan. Microwave on HIGH for 4½ to 8 minutes, tossing the coconut with a fork after each minute.

WHIPPING CREAM

Whipped cream is used as an ingredient and as a topping in numerous recipes. Cream can be whipped with an electric mixer, hand-held rotary eggbeater or wire whisk. Before beginning, the cream, bowl and beaters should be very cold; chill them in the refrigerator or freezer for a few minutes. Whipping cream will double in volume when whipped. To whip cream:

1. Begin beating slowly to avoid splatters, then gradually increase speed as the cream thickens.

2. Beat until soft peaks form. Don't overbeat, or you'll end up with butter! If you whip cream too far ahead of time, it may separate. If this happens, stir it briefly with a wire whisk.

3. To sweeten whipped cream, gradually beat in 2 tablespoons of powdered sugar for each cup of whipping cream.

HIGH ALTITUDE BAKING

Baking at high altitudes, 3,500 feet above sea level or more, can be a challenge. For best results, follow the high altitude directions when they're included in the recipe. In addition, here are some general guidelines:

• Because there is generally lower humidity at high altitudes, flour tends to dry out more quickly and may absorb more liquid in a recipe. Store flour in an airtight container.

• At any altitude above sea level, the air pressure is lower. This lower air pressure allows baked foods to rise faster. Leavening agents such as yeast, baking powder and baking soda create larger gas bubbles that expand rapidly. The larger bubbles can weaken the structure of baked goods and cause cakes and breads to collapse unless recipe adjustments are made. In addition, too much sugar can weaken the structure of baked goods.

• Water boils at a lower temperature than at sea level (as elevation increases, the boiling point is reduced 2 degrees per 1,000 foot increase) so foods take longer to cook. Liquids evaporate faster at high altitudes so foods such as cooked frostings and candies will become harder more rapidly.

If no high altitude adjustments are given in a recipe, here are some suggestions to try:

• In cakes made with fats or oil, reduce the sugar called for in the recipe by 3 tablespoons per cup. If given a choice, use the largest pan size suggested.

• In cake or bar-type cookies, reduce the sugar called for in the recipe by 3 tablespoons per cup. If given a choice, use the largest pan size suggested.

• In yeast breads, use slightly less flour since flour is drier at high altitudes. Yeast breads will require a shorter rising time and should rise only until double in size to prevent them from collapsing during baking.

• Quick breads often need 2 to 4 tablespoons additional flour and a higher baking temperature.

FREEZING BAKED GOODS

It's wonderful to have a pie, dessert, cookies or cake baked and stored in the freezer for your family or unexpected guests. Many baked goods freeze and thaw beautifully. When freezing baked goods, note the following:

• The freezer temperature should be 0°F. or less.

• Use moisture-proof, vapor-proof wraps or containers such as plastic containers with tight-fitting lids, heavy-duty foil, freezer bags and freezer paper.

• Be sure that there's room for expansion when filling containers. When wrapping foods, press the air out and seal tightly.

Follow these guidelines to ensure that your baked goods retain their freshness and flavor in the freezer:

FREEZING GUIDELINES

Food	Special Tips	Storage Time	Thawing Hints
Breads: Yeast Breads, coffee cakes, muffins and quick breads.	Cool completely; do not frost or decorate. Place coffee cakes on foil-wrapped cardboard before freezing.	Up to 1 month	Unwrap slightly and thaw at room temperature for 2 to 3 hours. Serve at room temperature or reheat, wrapped in foil, at 350°F. for 15 to 20 minutes.
Cakes: Frosted or unfrosted. (Buttercream frosting freezes best; egg-white frostings and custard fillings do not freeze well.)	Cool cakes completely; place frosted cakes in the freezer to harden the frosting before covering. Place layer cakes in a cake container to prevent crushing. Angel and chiffon cakes are best left in the pan or placed in rigid containers to avoid crushing them. Cakes may be filled or frosted with whipped cream or whipped topping before freezing.	Unfrosted: Up to 6 months Frosted: Up to 3 months	Unfrosted: Thaw covered at room temperature for 2 to 3 hours. Frost or serve according to the recipe. Frosted: Thaw loosely covered overnight in the refrigerator.
Cheesecakes	If baked, cool completely before wrapping.	Up to 5 months	Thaw wrapped in the refrigerator for 4 to 6 hours.
Cookies	Package cookies in containers with tight-fitting lids. If cookies have been frosted before freezing, freeze them on a cookie sheet, then package the frozen cookies between layers of waxed paper in a rigid container.	Unfrosted: Up to 12 months Frosted: Up to 2 months	Thaw in the container at room temperature. If cookies should be crisp when thawed, remove them from the container before thawing.
Pies: Baked pumpkin or pecan pies and either baked or unbaked fruit pies.	Cool baked pies quickly. For unbaked pie, brush the bottom pastry with egg white before filling to prevent it from becoming soggy. Do not slit the top pastry. Cover pies with an inverted foil or paper plate and then wrap.	Baked: Up to 4 months Unbaked: Up to 3 months	Baked: Unwrap and heat at 325°F. for 45 minutes or until warm or room temperature. Unbaked: Unwrap, cut slits in the top pastry and bake at 425°F. for 15 minutes, then bake at 375°F. for 30 to 45 minutes or until the center is bubbly.
Pies: Chiffon. (Custard pies, cream pies and pies with meringue topping do not freeze well.)	Do not top with whipped cream or whipped topping. Refrigerate to set, then wrap as you would a fruit pie.	Up to 2 months	Unwrap and thaw in the refrigerator 2 to 3 hours. Top as desired.

COOKIES

Cookies! They're America's favorite sweet treat — ideal with a mug of cold milk, a cup of hot coffee, a tall glass of lemonade or just by themselves.

In this chapter, you'll find easy-to-make drop cookies, tender cutouts for melt-in-your-mouth appeal, intriguing shapes of all sorts and special cookies to celebrate the seasons of the year. You'll also find bars from elegant to hearty that can be toted anywhere from a wedding shower to a backyard barbecue.

Pictured: **Fudgy Brownies** *p. 98,* **Oatmeal Coconut Fun Chippers** *p. 36,* **Salted Peanut Chews** *p. 88*

COOKIES

Cookies are a wonderful way to learn about baking
or to become reacquainted with the joys of making treats from scratch.
Choose a recipe to suit a special occasion or one just right for everyday
snacking. The basics are easy and the results are delightful.

KINDS OF COOKIES

*Although cookies come in all shapes, sizes and
flavors, there are just six basic kinds. The recipes
in this chapter are grouped by these kinds:*

BAR

Bar cookies are made from a soft dough that is
spread in a pan. They can be layered or filled,
chewy or crisp. (Recipes begin on p. 83.)

BROWNIES

Brownies are probably the most popular bar
cookie. Soft and chewy, they can be made
in a wide variety of flavors. (Recipes begin
on p. 98.)

CUT-OUT

Made from a stiff dough, these cookies are
rolled into a thin or thick sheet. The rolled
dough can be cut into just about any shape
with a cookie cutter or with a sharp knife and
pattern. (Recipes begin on p. 72.)

DROP

One of the easiest cookies to make, drop
cookies are made from a softer dough that is
dropped from a spoon in mounds onto a
cookie sheet. (Recipes begin on p. 33.)

MOLDED, SHAPED AND PRESSED

To make these cookies, a stiff dough is molded
into shapes such as crescents, logs or balls.
They can be pressed flat with a fork or the
bottom of a glass. Cookies can also be made
using a cookie press or gun. (Recipes begin
on p. 53.)

SLICED

Also known as refrigerator cookies, these are
made from a stiff dough that is shaped into a
long, smooth roll and chilled. To bake, slices
are cut from the roll. These cookies can be
either thin and crisp or thick and crunchy.
(Recipes begin on p. 47.)

SECRETS TO SUCCESSFUL COOKIES

*Every batch of cookies you bake will be a success
once you learn these few simple secrets!*

SECRETS FOR ANY COOKIES

**Use either margarine or butter inter-
changeably in most recipes.** They give cookies
good flavor and crisp texture. Solid vegetable
shortening, used in some recipes, makes a
crunchier cookie. Tub, soft, whipped, liquid or
reduced-fat or -calorie butters or margarines
should not be used because the additional air
and water in them may result in thin, flat
cookies.

Measure accurately with standard measuring cups and spoons. The correct amount of ingredients will help ensure that cookies and bars aren't dry, crumbly or so soft that they spread too much during baking.

Heat the oven for 10 to 15 minutes before baking cookies.

Use shiny aluminum pans and cookie sheets. They will brown cookies lightly and evenly. Dark cookie sheets may absorb heat and cause cookies to overbrown on the bottom. If you use insulated cookie sheets, remember that cookies will not brown as much on the bottom and they may take slightly longer to bake.

Grease pans and cookie sheets with shortening. If the recipe calls for the pans or sheets to be greased, shortening works best. Butter tends to brown too quickly, and oils or spray-on coatings can sometimes cause sticking.

Place dough on cool cookie sheets. This will prevent the dough from melting and spreading before baking. Space them carefully to avoid unattractive run-together cookies.

Leave at least 2 inches around all sides of the cookie sheets or pans in the oven. This space allows the hot air to circulate properly. For best results, bake only 1 sheet or pan of cookies at a time on the center rack of the oven.

Cool cookies or pans of bars on wire racks. Place cookies in a single layer so that air can circulate around them. Steam from the cooling cookies evaporates and prevents them from becoming soggy.

SECRETS FOR BAR COOKIES AND BROWNIES

Use the proper size of pan. Bars or brownies baked in a pan that is too large can be dry and overbaked; if it's too small, they might be underbaked.

Bake bars in a foil-lined pan for easy removal and freezing. Line the pan with foil so that it extends up the sides and over the edges of the

pan. When the recipe calls for a greased pan, grease the foil. After baking and cooling, lift the bars from the pan using the extended foil edges. With a long knife, cut into bars; or wrap with additional foil and freeze.

Cool bars in the pan before cutting. Cutting when cool prevents the bars or brownies from crumbling. However, some recipes may call for cutting bars while warm.

Cut bars into decorative shapes. Cut bars on the diagonal to form diamonds (see diagram) or cut with a cookie cutter, such as a heart or star shape. Bar scraps can be cut into small cubes and layered with pudding or ice cream in dessert dishes.

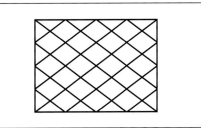

Cutting Bars into Diamonds

Remove the corner bar first. Removal of the remaining bars or brownies will be easier.

SECRETS FOR CUT-OUT COOKIES

Dust rolling pin and smooth surface with flour. This will prevent dough from sticking. If you use a rolling pin cover on the rolling pin and a pastry cloth, rub a small amount of flour into them. Too much flour will make cookies tough and dry. See p. 80.

Roll only part of the chilled dough at a time. Keep the remaining dough in the refrigerator.

Roll the dough to the appropriate thickness. Thinner dough makes a crisper cookie; thicker dough makes a softer, chewier cookie.

Check the thickness with a ruler. Cookies will bake evenly when the dough is rolled to a uniform thickness.

Use a pancake turner to transfer cookies. This will prevent unbaked cookies from stretching and tearing and baked cookies from breaking.

SECRETS FOR DROP COOKIES

Use the same amount of dough for each cookie. You can use either a teaspoon or tablespoon, depending on what size cookie you want.

Drop the dough onto the cookie sheet by pushing it from a teaspoon with a rubber scraper or another teaspoon. See p. 32.

Space the cookies carefully. This prevents the cookies from baking together. If you're trying a new recipe, you may want to "test bake" 2 or 3 cookies to see how much they spread.

SECRETS FOR SLICED COOKIES

Mold the dough into rolls as specified in the recipe.

Wrap the rolls of cookie dough in waxed paper, foil or plastic wrap. Twist the ends to seal them tightly. Refrigerate the dough until it is firm.

Use a thin sharp knife for slicing cookies. Remove the storage wrap before slicing.

Refrigerate rolls up to 1 week. You can also wrap them in foil and freeze for up to 6 months.

SECRETS FOR MOLDED, SHAPED AND PRESSED COOKIES

Refrigerate dough before shaping if necessary for easier handling.

Dust hands lightly with flour. This prevents the dough from sticking to your hands. Roll each cookie smoothly between your palms. Take time when molding fancy shapes so that all the cookies look the same.

Flatten cookies with your thumb, a fork or the bottom of a glass. Dip them in either flour or sugar to prevent sticking.

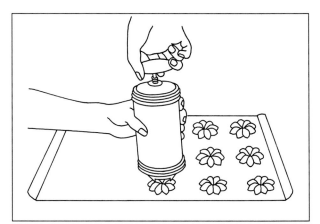

Using a Cookie Press

When making pressed cookies . . .

- Use room-temperature margarine or butter.
- Test for consistency by pressing a small amount of dough through the press. If the dough is too soft, refrigerate it briefly or add 1 to 2 tablespoons of flour. If the dough is too stiff, add 1 egg yolk.
- Use a cool, ungreased cookie sheet.
- Hold the cookie press so that it rests on the cookie sheet. Force the dough onto the sheet until the dough appears at the edge of the mold. Lift the press when you've completely formed the shape.
- If you don't own a cookie press, dough can be pressed through a decorating bag fitted with a ¼ to ½-inch diameter star tip.

HOW TO TELL WHEN COOKIES ARE DONE

Cookies are best when they've been baked just the right time — not too long and not too short. Here are some easy ways to tell when cookies are done.

Check cookies at the minimum baking time. Even 1 minute can make a difference! Continue checking them every minute until done. Immediately remove cookies from the sheets with a pancake turner, unless the recipe calls for them to cool on the sheet. If cookies stick to the sheet, they may have cooled too long. Return them to the oven briefly.

Cookies are done when . . . they are firmly set or browned according to recipe directions. When you touch them lightly with your finger, almost no imprint will remain. Bake cookies according to recipe directions for the correct amount of browning.

Bake brownies according to recipe directions.
- Cake-like brownies are done when they just begin to pull away from the sides of the pan, when a toothpick inserted in the center comes out clean, or when they are set in the center.
- Fudgy brownies do not have a specific doneness test. Bake the brownies within the time range stated in the recipe. Baking at the minimum time will produce very moist brownies. Baking at the maximum time will produce a moist brownie, but one that is not as "wet" as the one baked at the minimum time. Experiment to obtain the results that you prefer. Our recipes carry a DO NOT OVERBAKE statement. Overbaking brownies (baking beyond the maximum time) can result in dry, hard brownies, especially around the pan edges.

KEEPING COOKIES FRESH AND FLAVORFUL

If cookies last long enough to take them off the cooling rack, here are some tips for keeping them at their fresh-from-the-oven best.

Store different kinds of cookies in separate containers.

Cookie jars are only for short-term storage.

Store soft cookies in a container with a tight-fitting cover. Place sheets of waxed paper between layers so cookies won't stick together. Frosted or filled cookies should be stored in a single layer.

Store crisp cookies in a container with a loose-fitting cover. However, if you live in a humid climate, containers should be tightly covered. If crisp cookies soften, place them on a cookie sheet and warm them in a 300°F. oven for 3 to 5 minutes.

Store bars and brownies in the baking pan. Cover the pan tightly with plastic wrap or foil or slip it into a plastic bag and seal with a twist tie. Some frostings or fillings may require refrigeration.

Line cardboard containers with foil or plastic wrap. This will prevent the cookies from absorbing any cardboard flavor or aroma.

MAILING COOKIES

When sending cookies to loved ones far away, a few simple packing precautions will help keep the cookies from becoming crumbs.

Choose cookies that can withstand the trip. Bars, drop cookies and soft, moist cookies travel well.

Use a cardboard box or metal container. Line the container with plastic wrap, waxed paper or foil to preserve flavors.

Wrap fragile cookies in bottom-to-bottom pairs. Use foil, waxed paper or plastic wrap.

Cushion cookies with crumpled waxed paper. Place it on the top and bottom of the container and between each layer of cookies. Pack cookies tightly enough to avoid shifting.

Place the cookie container in a sturdy box. The shipping box should be slightly larger so that bubble wrap, foam pellets, shredded paper or crumpled newspaper can be packed around the cookie container. Don't use popcorn or cereal for cushioning because it may attract insects or rodents and absorb odors during shipping.

Mark the box "perishable" to encourage careful handling. You may also want to send cookies first class to ensure priority handling and prompt delivery.

NUTRITION IN THIS CHAPTER

Nutrition per serving means the calculation was done on 1 cookie or 1 bar.

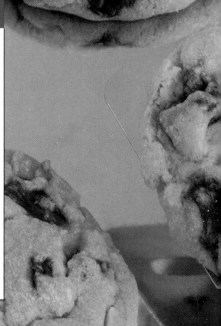

STEP 1. Beat brown sugar, sugar, margarine and shortening until light and fluffy. Blend in vanilla and egg. Mix in flour, baking soda and salt.

STEP 2. By hand, stir in coarsely chopped chocolate and nuts until evenly distributed.

STEP 3. Drop mounds of dough onto ungreased cookie sheets, placing dough about 2 inches apart to allow for spreading during baking.

CHOCOLATE CHIP COOKIES

⁓

- ³/₄ **cup firmly packed brown sugar**
- ¹/₂ **cup sugar**
- ¹/₂ **cup margarine or butter, softened**
- ¹/₂ **cup shortening**
- 1¹/₂ **teaspoons vanilla**
- 1 **egg**
- 1³/₄ **cups all purpose flour**
- 1 **teaspoon baking soda**
- ¹/₂ **teaspoon salt**
- 1 **(6-oz.) pkg. (1 cup) semi-sweet chocolate chips**
- ¹/₂ **cup chopped nuts or shelled sunflower seeds, if desired**

Heat oven to 375°F. In large bowl, combine brown sugar, sugar, margarine and shortening; beat until light and fluffy. Add vanilla and egg; blend well. Stir in flour, baking soda and salt; mix well. Stir in chocolate chips and nuts. Drop dough by teaspoonfuls 2 inches apart onto ungreased cookie sheets. Bake at 375°F. for 8 to 10 minutes or until light golden brown. Cool 1 minute; remove from cookie sheets.
Yield: 4 dozen cookies.

HIGH ALTITUDE:
Above 3500 Feet: No change.

NUTRITION PER SERVING:
Calories 100; Protein 1g; Carbohydrate 11g; Fat 6g; Sodium 70mg.

VARIATIONS:

CHOCOLATE CHIP COOKIE BARS: Prepare dough as directed in recipe. Spread in ungreased 13x9-inch pan. Bake at 375°F. for 15 to 25 minutes or until light golden brown. Cool completely. Cut into bars.
Yield: 36 bars.

CHOCOLATE CHUNK COOKIES: Prepare dough as directed in recipe, substituting 8 oz. coarsely chopped semi-sweet chocolate for chocolate chips. Drop dough by tablespoonfuls 3 inches apart onto ungreased cookie sheets. Bake at 375°F. for 9 to 12 minutes or until light golden brown. Immediately remove from cookie sheets.
Yield: 3 dozen cookies.

(Recipe continued on next page.)

Chocolate Chunk Cookies

(Recipe continued from previous page.)

CHOCOLATE CHIP ICE CREAM COOKIE-WICHES: Prepare dough as directed in recipe. Drop by heaping teaspoonfuls 3 inches apart onto ungreased cookie sheets. Bake at 375°F. for 9 to 14 minutes or until light golden brown. Cool 1 minute; remove from cookie sheets. Cool completely. To assemble each cookie-wich, place scoop of favorite flavor ice cream on bottom side of 1 cookie; flatten ice cream slightly. Place another cookie, bottom side down, on top of ice cream. Gently press cookies together in center to form ice cream sandwich. Quickly wrap in foil. Freeze.
Yield: 12 cookie-wiches.

CHOCOLATE CHOCOLATE CHIP COOKIES: Prepare dough as directed in recipe, substituting 1 cup margarine or butter, softened, for the ½ cup margarine and ½ cup shortening. Decrease vanilla to 1 teaspoon. Add ¼ cup unsweetened cocoa with flour. Drop dough by teaspoonfuls 2 inches apart onto ungreased cookie sheets. Bake at 375°F. for 7 to 11 minutes or until set.
Yield: 4 dozen cookies.

JUMBO CANDY COOKIES: Prepare dough as directed in recipe, omitting ½ cup sugar, 1 cup semi-sweet chocolate chips and ½ cup chopped nuts. Increase vanilla to 2 teaspoons. Stir 1 cup candy-coated chocolate pieces and ½ cup shelled sunflower seeds into dough. Refrigerate if necessary for easier handling. Shape dough into 2-inch balls. Place 4 inches apart on ungreased cookie sheets. Press an additional ½ cup candy-coated chocolate pieces into balls to decorate tops of cookies. Bake at 350°F. for 15 to 20 minutes or until light golden brown. Cool 2 minutes; remove from cookie sheets.
Yield: 14 cookies.

MAXI CHIPPERS: Prepare dough as directed in recipe. For each cookie, use ⅓ cup of dough; place 4 inches apart on ungreased cookie sheets. Bake at 375°F. for 12 to 18 minutes or until light golden brown. Cool 1 minute; remove from cookie sheets.
Yield: 10 cookies.

MINI CHIPPERS: Prepare dough as directed in recipe. Drop dough by ½ teaspoonfuls 1 inch apart onto ungreased cookie sheets. Bake at 375°F. for 5 to 7 minutes or until light golden brown. Immediately remove from cookie sheets.
Yield: 12½ dozen cookies.

SOFT AND CHEWY CHOCOLATE CHIP COOKIES

Try this big batch recipe for soft and chewy cookies. For extra chocolaty cookies, use the larger amount of chocolate chips.

1¼ **cups sugar**
1¼ **cups firmly packed brown sugar**
1½ **cups margarine or butter, softened**
 2 **teaspoons vanilla**
 3 **eggs**
4¼ **cups all purpose flour**
 2 **teaspoons baking soda**
½ **teaspoon salt**
 1 **to 2 (12-oz.) pkg. semi-sweet chocolate chips***

Heat oven to 375°F. In large bowl, beat sugar, brown sugar and margarine until light and fluffy. Add vanilla and eggs; blend well. Add flour, baking soda and salt; mix well. Stir in chocolate chips.** Drop dough by rounded tablespoonfuls 2 inches apart onto ungreased cookie sheets.

Bake at 375°F. for 8 to 10 minutes or until light golden brown.
Yield: 6 dozen cookies.

TIPS:
* If desired, half of the dough can be made with butterscotch, peanut butter, vanilla milk or mint chocolate chips instead of semi-sweet chocolate chips.
**At this point, dough can be frozen. Wrap tightly and freeze up to 2 months. To bake, thaw at room temperature for 1 to 2 hours. Bake as directed above.

HIGH ALTITUDE:
Above 3500 Feet: Decrease sugar, brown sugar and margarine to 1 cup each. Bake as directed above.

NUTRITION PER SERVING:
Calories 110; Protein 1g; Carbohydrate 16g; Fat 5g; Sodium 95mg.

CHOCOLATE CHIP COOKIES SUPREME

We've created a new, contemporary recipe for chocolate chip cookies. You'll enjoy the combination of rum extract and white chocolate in these chewy, moist cookies.

  1 **cup sugar**
  1 **cup firmly packed brown sugar**
1½ **cups margarine or butter, softened**
  2 **teaspoons vanilla**
 ½ **teaspoon rum extract**
  2 **eggs**
  3 **cups all purpose flour**
1½ **cups oat bran**
  1 **teaspoon baking powder**
  1 **teaspoon baking soda**
 ¼ **teaspoon salt**
  1 **(6-oz.) pkg. (1 cup) semi-sweet chocolate chips**
  1 **(6-oz.) pkg. white baking bars, chopped, or 1 cup vanilla milk chips**
  1 **cup chopped walnuts or pecans**

Heat oven to 375°F. In large bowl, beat sugar, brown sugar and margarine until light and fluffy. Add vanilla, rum extract and eggs; blend well. Stir in flour, oat bran, baking powder, baking soda and salt; mix well. Stir in chocolate chips, white baking bar and walnuts. (Dough will be stiff.) Drop dough by rounded tablespoonfuls 2 inches apart onto ungreased cookie sheets.

Bake at 375°F. for 9 to 15 minutes or until light golden brown. Cool 1 minute; remove from cookie sheets.
Yield: 4 dozen cookies.

HIGH ALTITUDE:
Above 3500 Feet: Decrease granulated sugar to ½ cup; increase flour to 3½ cups. Bake as directed above.

NUTRITION PER SERVING:
Calories 180; Protein 2g; Carbohydrate 21g; Fat 10g; Sodium 115mg.

SUPREME CHOCOLATE MINT CHIP COOKIES

Cocoa flavors the dough and mint chocolate chips are the surprise in these easy drop cookies.

COOKIES
  4 **cups all purpose flour**
  1 **cup unsweetened cocoa**
  1 **teaspoon baking soda**
 ½ **teaspoon salt**
1½ **cups sugar**
  1 **cup firmly packed brown sugar**
1½ **cups margarine or butter, softened**
  3 **eggs**
  1 **(10-oz.) pkg. (1½ cups) mint chocolate chips**

GLAZE
  2 **cups sugar**
 ½ **cup unsweetened cocoa**
 ½ **cup margarine or butter**
 ½ **cup milk**
  1 **teaspoon vanilla**

Heat oven to 350°F. Lightly grease cookie sheets. In large bowl, combine flour, 1 cup cocoa, baking soda and salt. In another large bowl, beat sugar, brown sugar and margarine until light and fluffy. Add eggs; blend well. Stir in flour mixture; mix well. Stir in mint chips. Drop dough by tablespoonfuls 3 inches apart onto greased cookie sheets; flatten slightly.

Bake at 350°F. for 8 to 10 minutes or until set. Cool 1 minute; remove from cookie sheets. Cool completely.

In medium saucepan, combine all glaze ingredients except vanilla. Bring to a boil; boil 1 minute. Stir in vanilla; cool slightly.* Beat until smooth and of glaze consistency. Spread glaze on cooled cookies. Let stand until glaze is set.
Yield: 6 dozen cookies.

TIP:
* To cool frosting quickly, place saucepan on ice in large bowl. If glaze becomes too thick, reheat slightly for spreading consistency.

HIGH ALTITUDE:
Above 3500 Feet: Increase flour to 4 cups plus 2 tablespoons. Bake as directed above.

NUTRITION PER SERVING:
Calories 150; Protein 2g; Carbohydrate 21g; Fat 7g; Sodium 105mg.

OATMEAL COCONUT FUN CHIPPERS

~

This thick, chewy oatmeal cookie can be made with quick-cooking or old-fashioned rolled oats. Cookies made with old-fashioned rolled oats have a moister, coarser texture.

1½ cups firmly packed brown sugar
 1 cup margarine or butter, softened
 1 tablespoon milk
 1 tablespoon vanilla
 2 eggs
2¼ cups all purpose flour
 2 teaspoons baking powder
 1 teaspoon baking soda
 ½ teaspoon salt
 2 cups rolled oats
 1 cup coconut
 1 (10-oz.) pkg. multi-colored candy-coated chocolate chips or 1½ cups semi-sweet chocolate chips

Heat oven to 375°F. In large bowl, beat brown sugar and margarine until light and fluffy. Add milk, vanilla and eggs; blend well. Stir in flour, baking powder, baking soda and salt; mix well. Stir in oats, coconut and chocolate chips. Drop dough by rounded tablespoonfuls 2 inches apart onto ungreased cookie sheets.

Bake at 375°F. for 9 to 13 minutes or until light golden brown. Cool 1 minute; remove from cookie sheets. Cool completely.
Yield: 4 dozen cookies.

HIGH ALTITUDE:
Above 3500 Feet: Decrease brown sugar to 1¼ cups; increase flour to 2½ cups. Bake as directed above.

NUTRITION PER SERVING:
Calories 130; Protein 2g; Carbohydrate 18g; Fat 6g; Sodium 110mg.

OATMEAL RAISIN COOKIES

~

Every mouth-watering bite of these crispy-chewy oatmeal cookies is full of good tasting nuts and raisins.

 ¾ cup sugar
 ¼ cup firmly packed brown sugar
 ½ cup margarine or butter, softened
 ½ teaspoon vanilla
 1 egg
 ¾ cup all purpose flour
 ½ teaspoon baking soda
 ½ teaspoon cinnamon
 ¼ teaspoon salt
1½ cups quick-cooking rolled oats
 ½ cup raisins
 ½ cup chopped nuts

Heat oven to 375°F. Grease cookie sheets. In large bowl, beat sugar, brown sugar and margarine until light and fluffy. Add vanilla and egg; blend well. Stir in flour, baking soda, cinnamon and salt; mix well. Stir in rolled oats, raisins and nuts. Drop dough by rounded teaspoonfuls 2 inches apart onto greased cookie sheets.

Bake at 375°F. for 7 to 10 minutes or until edges are light golden brown. Cool 1 minute; remove from cookie sheets.
Yield: 3½ dozen cookies.

HIGH ALTITUDE:
Above 3500 Feet: Increase flour to 1 cup. Bake as directed above.

NUTRITION PER SERVING:
Calories 70; Protein 1g; Carbohydrate 10g; Fat 3g; Sodium 55mg.

CHEWY DATE DROPS

Dates have always been recognized as a good high-energy food because of their carbohydrate, iron and protein content. Store dates tightly covered at room temperature or in the refrigerator for longer storage.

- 2 **cups chopped dates**
- ½ **cup sugar**
- ½ **cup water**
- ½ **cup sugar**
- 1 **cup firmly packed brown sugar**
- 1 **cup margarine or butter, softened**
- 1 **teaspoon vanilla**
- 3 **eggs**
- 4 **cups all purpose flour**
- 1 **teaspoon baking soda**
- 1 **teaspoon salt**
- 1 **cup chopped walnuts or pecans**

In medium saucepan, combine dates, ½ cup sugar and water. Cook over medium heat until thickened, stirring occasionally. Cool.

Heat oven to 375°F. Grease cookie sheets. In large bowl, beat brown sugar, ½ cup sugar and margarine until light and fluffy. Add vanilla and eggs; blend well. Stir in flour, baking soda and salt; mix well. Stir in date mixture and nuts. Drop dough by rounded teaspoonfuls 2 inches apart onto greased cookie sheets.

Bake at 375°F. for 8 to 10 minutes or until light golden brown. Immediately remove from cookie sheets.
Yield: 6 dozen cookies.

HIGH ALTITUDE:
Above 3500 Feet: Decrease sugar beaten with margarine to ¼ cup. Bake as directed above.

NUTRITION PER SERVING:
Calories 100; Protein 1g; Carbohydrate 15g; Fat 4g; Sodium 80mg.

COCONUT MACAROONS

Coconut macaroons are a delicious, chewy variation of the classic almond macaroon cookie. The combination of few ingredients and the drop cookie method makes them a snap to prepare.

- 2 **egg whites**
- ⅓ **cup sugar**
- 2 **tablespoons all purpose flour**
  Dash salt
- ¼ **teaspoon almond extract**
- 2 **cups coconut**

Heat oven to 325°F. Grease and lightly flour cookie sheet. In medium bowl, beat egg whites lightly. Add sugar, flour, salt and almond extract; blend well. Stir in coconut. Drop dough by tablespoonfuls 2 inches apart onto greased and floured cookie sheet.

Bake at 325°F. for 13 to 17 minutes or until set and lightly browned. Immediately remove from cookie sheet.
Yield: 1 dozen cookies.

HIGH ALTITUDE:
Above 3500 Feet: No change.

NUTRITION PER SERVING:
Calories 90; Protein 1g; Carbohydrate 12g; Fat 4g; Sodium 20mg.

COOK'S NOTE

MACAROONS

Macaroons originated in Italy and can be traced to a monastery where they have been made since 1791. Brought to France in the 16th century, the macaroons of many French towns are famous, including the best known ones made in Nancy. During the 17th century, macaroons were baked by the Carmelite nuns who followed the principle: "Almonds are good for girls who do not eat meat." During the Revolution, two nuns who hid in the town of Nancy made and sold macaroons. They became known as the "Macaroon Sisters," and in 1952 the street on which they had operated was named after them.

CHOCOLATE CHERRY SURPRISE COOKIES

For chocolate and cherry lovers, this is a delicious adaptation of the famous German Black Forest torte.

COOKIES

- ³/₄ cup sugar
- ¼ cup firmly packed brown sugar
- ½ cup margarine or butter, softened
- ½ teaspoon almond extract
- 1 egg
- 1³/₄ cups all purpose flour
- ½ cup unsweetened cocoa
- ½ teaspoon baking soda
- ¼ teaspoon salt
- ½ cup milk
- ½ cup chopped walnuts or pecans
- 18 to 20 maraschino cherries, halved, drained
- 18 to 20 large marshmallows, halved

FROSTING

- 3 cups powdered sugar
- 3 tablespoons margarine or butter, melted
- ½ teaspoon vanilla
- 3 oz. semi-sweet chocolate, melted
- 5 to 6 tablespoons water

Heat oven to 375°F. In large bowl, combine sugar, brown sugar, ½ cup margarine, almond extract and egg; blend well. In small bowl, combine flour, cocoa, baking soda and salt; blend well. Add to sugar mixture alternately with milk, mixing well after each addition. Stir in walnuts. Drop dough by rounded tablespoonfuls 2 inches apart onto ungreased cookie sheets. Firmly press cherry half, cut side down, into top of each cookie.

Bake at 375°F. for 6 to 8 minutes. Firmly press marshmallow half, cut side down, over cherry on top of each hot cookie. Bake an additional 2 minutes or until marshmallows are puffed. Cool 1 minute; remove from cookie sheets. Cool completely.

In small bowl, combine all frosting ingredients, adding enough water for desired spreading consistency. Blend until smooth. Frost top of each cookie with about 2 teaspoonfuls frosting, covering marshmallow completely. Garnish if desired.

Yield: 3 dozen cookies.

HIGH ALTITUDE:
Above 3500 Feet: Increase flour to 2 cups. Bake as directed above.

NUTRITION PER SERVING:
Calories 150; Protein 2g; Carbohydrate 25g; Fat 6g; Sodium 85mg.

TEXAN-SIZED ALMOND CRUNCH COOKIES

Big, tender, crunchy cookies to tempt young and old, this recipe was a finalist in the 30th Pillsbury BAKE-OFF® Contest.

- 1 cup sugar
- 1 cup powdered sugar
- 1 cup margarine or butter, softened
- 1 cup oil
- 1 teaspoon almond extract
- 2 eggs
- 3½ cups all purpose flour
- 1 cup whole wheat flour
- 1 teaspoon baking soda
- 1 teaspoon cream of tartar
- 1 teaspoon salt
- 2 cups coarsely chopped almonds
- 1 (6-oz.) pkg. almond brickle baking chips
  Sugar

Heat oven to 350°F. In large bowl, beat 1 cup sugar, powdered sugar, margarine and oil until well blended. Add almond extract and eggs; blend well. Add all purpose flour, whole wheat flour, baking soda, cream of tartar and salt; mix well. Stir in almonds and brickle chips. If necessary, cover with plastic wrap and refrigerate dough about 30 minutes for easier handling.

Shape large tablespoonfuls of dough into balls. Roll in sugar. Place 5 inches apart on ungreased cookie sheets. With fork dipped in sugar, flatten each in crisscross pattern.

Bake at 350°F. for 12 to 18 minutes or until light golden brown around edges. Cool 1 minute; remove from cookie sheets.

Yield: 3½ dozen (4-inch) cookies.

HIGH ALTITUDE:
Above 3500 Feet: No change.

NUTRITION PER SERVING:
Calories 230; Protein 3g; Carbohydrate 22g; Fat 15g; Sodium 130mg.

CHOCOLATE-GLAZED FLORENTINES

Although the name implies that these cookies originated in Florence, Italy, and the candied fruit and almonds are typical of Italian cooking, Austrian bakers also claim to have invented them.

COOKIES
- ⅓ cup margarine or butter
- ⅓ cup honey
- ¼ cup sugar
- 2 tablespoons milk
- ¼ cup all purpose flour
- ⅓ cup finely chopped candied orange peel
- ⅓ cup chopped candied cherries
- ⅓ cup slivered almonds

GLAZE
- 4 oz. semi-sweet chocolate
- 1 teaspoon shortening

Heat oven to 325°F. Generously grease and flour cookie sheets. Melt margarine in medium saucepan over medium heat; remove from heat. Stir in honey, sugar and milk; stir in flour. Cook over medium heat for 3 to 6 minutes or until slightly thickened, stirring constantly. Remove from heat; stir in candied peel, cherries and almonds. Drop mixture by teaspoonfuls 3 inches apart onto greased and floured cookie sheets.

Bake at 325°F. for 8 to 13 minutes or until edges are light golden brown. (Edges will spread and centers will remain soft.) Cool 1 minute; carefully remove from cookie sheets. (If cookies harden on cookie sheet, return to oven for 30 to 60 seconds to warm.) Cool completely.

Line large cookie sheet with waxed paper. Turn cookies upside down on waxed paper-lined cookie sheet. In small saucepan, melt glaze ingredients; stir to blend. Spread over flat surface of each cookie to within ¼ inch of edge. When set but not hard, use fork to make wavy lines in chocolate, if desired. Let stand until set. Store between sheets of waxed paper in airtight container in refrigerator.
Yield: 2½ dozen cookies.

NUTRITION PER SERVING:
Calories 80; Protein 1g; Carbohydrate 11g; Fat 4g; Sodium 30mg.

GERMAN CHOCOLATE CAKE MIX COOKIES

These easy-to-make chewy chocolate cookies are on our list of most requested recipes. The cookies puff during baking and then settle when removed from the oven, forming a pretty crinkled top.

- 1 (18.25-oz.) pkg. pudding-included German chocolate cake mix
- 1 (6-oz.) pkg. (1 cup) semi-sweet chocolate chips
- ½ cup rolled oats
- ½ cup raisins
- ½ cup oil
- 2 eggs, slightly beaten

Heat oven to 350°F. In large bowl, combine all ingredients; blend well. Drop dough by rounded teaspoonfuls 2 inches apart onto ungreased cookie sheets.

Bake at 350°F. for 8 to 10 minutes or until set. Cool 1 minute; remove from cookie sheets.
Yield: 4½ dozen cookies.

HIGH ALTITUDE:
Above 3500 Feet: Add ¼ cup flour to dry cake mix. Bake as directed above.

NUTRITION PER SERVING:
Calories 80; Protein 1g; Carbohydrate 11g; Fat 4g; Sodium 60mg.

COOK'S NOTE

GIVING COOKIES AS GIFTS

Try some of these packaging ideas for sharing homemade cookies with relatives and friends.
- Use decorative paper sacks or freezer bags and tie them with colorful ribbons.
- Decorate coffee or shortening cans with wrapping paper or colorful adhesive paper.
- Pack cookies in a wide-mouth canning jar. Cover the lid with fabric and secure it by screwing on the outer ring.
- Weave ribbons through fruit or vegetable baskets lined with colored cellophane or plastic wrap for a more festive look.
- Purchase decorated tins.

Brown Sugar Shortbread Puffs

These rich, buttery cookies can be made large or small.

- 1 **cup firmly packed brown sugar**
- 1¼ **cups margarine or butter, softened**
- 1 **teaspoon vanilla**
- 1 **egg yolk**
- 2¼ **cups all purpose flour**

Heat oven to 350°F. In large bowl, beat brown sugar and margarine until light and fluffy. Add vanilla and egg yolk; blend well. Add flour; stir until mixture forms a smooth dough. Drop dough by rounded teaspoonfuls 2 inches apart onto ungreased cookie sheets.

Bake at 350°F. for 10 to 15 minutes or until lightly browned and set.
Yield: 4 dozen cookies.

TIP:
To make larger puffs, drop dough from a ¼-cup ice cream scoop. Bake until lightly browned and set.

HIGH ALTITUDE:
Above 3500 Feet: No change.

NUTRITION PER SERVING:
Calories 80; Protein 1g; Carbohydrate 9g; Fat 5g; Sodium 50mg.

Pumpkin Cookies with Penuche Frosting

For easy shaping of these spice cookies, try a small ice cream scoop with a release bar. A number 80 or 90 scoop works well, yielding about 1 rounded teaspoonful of dough for each cookie.

COOKIES
- ½ **cup sugar**
- ½ **cup firmly packed brown sugar**
- 1 **cup margarine or butter, softened**
- 1 **cup canned pumpkin**
- 1 **teaspoon vanilla**
- 1 **egg**
- 2 **cups all purpose flour**
- 1 **teaspoon baking powder**
- 1 **teaspoon baking soda**
- 1 **teaspoon cinnamon**
- ¼ **teaspoon salt**
- ¾ **cup chopped walnuts or pecans**

PENUCHE FROSTING
- 3 **tablespoons margarine or butter**
- ½ **cup firmly packed brown sugar**
- ¼ **cup milk**
- 1½ **to 2 cups powdered sugar**

Heat oven to 350°F. In large bowl, beat sugar, ½ cup brown sugar and 1 cup margarine until light and fluffy. Add pumpkin, vanilla and egg; blend well. Add flour, baking powder, baking soda, cinnamon and salt; mix well. Stir in walnuts. Drop dough by rounded teaspoonfuls 2 inches apart onto ungreased cookie sheets.

Bake at 350°F. for 10 to 12 minutes or until light golden brown around edges. Immediately remove from cookie sheets. Cool completely.

In medium saucepan, combine 3 tablespoons margarine and ½ cup brown sugar. Bring to a boil. Cook over medium heat 1 minute or until slightly thickened, stirring constantly. Cool 10 minutes. Add milk; beat until smooth. Beat in enough powdered sugar for desired spreading consistency. Frost cooled cookies. Let stand until frosting is set.
Yield: 5 dozen cookies.

HIGH ALTITUDE:
Above 3500 Feet: No change.

NUTRITION PER SERVING:
Calories 100; Protein 1g; Carbohydrate 12g; Fat 5g; Sodium 75mg.

Pumpkin Cookies with Penuche Frosting

PEANUT AND CANDY JUMBLES

Children will enjoy helping with these chunky, chewy cookies and munching on the extra candy and peanuts!

  1   **cup firmly packed brown sugar**
  ½   **cup margarine or butter, softened**
  ½   **cup creamy peanut butter**
  1   **tablespoon vanilla**
  1   **egg**
  1   **cup all purpose flour**
  ½   **cup whole wheat flour**
  1   **teaspoon baking soda**
  ¾   **cup salted peanuts**
  ¾   **cup candy-coated chocolate pieces**

Heat oven to 375°F. In large bowl, beat brown sugar, margarine and peanut butter until light and fluffy. Add vanilla and egg; blend well. Stir in all purpose flour, whole wheat flour and baking soda; mix well. Stir in peanuts and candy-coated chocolate pieces. Drop dough by rounded tablespoonfuls 2 inches apart onto ungreased cookie sheets.

Bake at 375°F. for 6 to 10 minutes or until light golden brown. Immediately remove from cookie sheets. Cool completely.
Yield: 3 dozen cookies.

HIGH ALTITUDE:
Above 3500 Feet: Decrease brown sugar to ¾ cup. Bake as directed above.

NUTRITION PER SERVING:
Calories 130; Protein 3g; Carbohydrate 14g; Fat 7g; Sodium 105mg.

SPANISH PEANUT COOKIES

One of many peanut varieties, Spanish peanuts are generally used with their edible red skins. The peanuts add unique flavor and crunch to these easy-to-make cookies.

  1   **cup firmly packed brown sugar**
  ¾   **cup margarine or butter, softened**
  ¼   **cup creamy peanut butter**
  2   **teaspoons vanilla**
  1   **egg**
  1¾ **cups all purpose flour**
  1   **teaspoon baking soda**
       Dash salt
  1   **cup Spanish peanuts**

Heat oven to 375°F. In large bowl, beat brown sugar, margarine and peanut butter until light and fluffy. Add vanilla and egg; blend well. Stir in flour, baking soda and salt; mix well. Stir in peanuts. Drop dough by heaping teaspoonfuls 2 inches apart onto ungreased cookie sheets.

Bake at 375°F. for 8 to 12 minutes or until light golden brown. Cool 1 minute; remove from cookie sheets.
Yield: 3½ dozen cookies.

HIGH ALTITUDE:
Above 3500 Feet: Decrease brown sugar to ¾ cup; increase flour to 1¾ cups plus 2 tablespoons. Bake as directed above.

NUTRITION PER SERVING:
Calories 100; Protein 2g; Carbohydrate 10g; Fat 6g; Sodium 95mg.

FROSTED CASHEW COOKIES

"Beurre noisette" is the French term for "brown butter." Using medium heat and browning the butter just until it's a light hazelnut color will add the desired rich flavor to these special cookies.

COOKIES
- 1 cup firmly packed brown sugar
- ½ cup butter or margarine, softened
- ½ teaspoon vanilla
- 1 egg
- 2 cups all purpose flour
- ¾ teaspoon baking powder
- ¾ teaspoon baking soda
- ⅓ cup dairy sour cream
- ¾ cup coarsely chopped salted cashews

BROWN BUTTER FROSTING
- ½ cup butter (do not substitute margarine)
- 2 cups powdered sugar
- 3 tablespoons half-and-half or milk
- ½ teaspoon vanilla

Heat oven to 375°F. Lightly grease cookie sheets. In large bowl, beat brown sugar and ½ cup butter until light and fluffy. Add ½ teaspoon vanilla and egg; blend well. Add flour, baking powder, baking soda and sour cream; mix well. Stir in cashews. Drop dough by rounded teaspoonfuls 2 inches apart onto greased cookie sheets.

Bake at 375°F. for 8 to 10 minutes or until golden brown. Immediately remove from cookie sheets. Cool completely.

Heat ½ cup butter in medium saucepan over medium heat until light golden brown. Remove from heat. Stir in powdered sugar, half-and-half and ½ teaspoon vanilla; beat until smooth. Frost cooled cookies.

Yield: 4 dozen cookies.

HIGH ALTITUDE:
Above 3500 Feet: No change.

NUTRITION PER SERVING:
Calories 100; Protein 1g; Carbohydrate 13g; Fat 5g; Sodium 70mg.

CHERRY POPPY SEED TWINKS

Just drop the dough onto the cookie sheet for this easy, filled thumbprint cookie.

- 1 cup powdered sugar
- 1 cup margarine or butter, softened
- 1 teaspoon vanilla
- 1 egg
- 2 cups all purpose flour
- 2 tablespoons poppy seed
- ½ teaspoon salt
- ½ cup cherry preserves

Heat oven to 300°F. In large bowl, beat powdered sugar and margarine until light and fluffy. Add vanilla and egg; blend well. Stir in flour, poppy seed and salt; mix well. Drop dough by rounded teaspoonfuls 1 inch apart onto ungreased cookie sheets. With finger, make indentation in center of each cookie. Fill each with about ½ teaspoon of the preserves.

Bake at 300°F. for 20 to 25 minutes or until edges are light golden brown. Immediately remove from cookie sheets.

Yield: 2½ dozen cookies.

HIGH ALTITUDE:
Above 3500 Feet: No change.

NUTRITION PER SERVING:
Calories 120; Protein 1g; Carbohydrate 14g; Fat 7g; Sodium 110mg.

Cocoa-Mallow Cookie-Wiches

Marshmallow creme is a thick whipped mixture that is available in jars. No melting is necessary to make the creamy filling in these yummy chocolate sandwich cookies.

COOKIES
- 1 cup sugar
- ½ cup margarine or butter, softened
- 1 teaspoon vanilla
- 1 egg
- 1 cup milk
- 2 cups all purpose flour
- ½ cup unsweetened cocoa
- 1½ teaspoons baking soda
- ½ teaspoon baking powder
- ½ teaspoon salt

FILLING
- 2 cups powdered sugar
- 1 cup marshmallow creme
- ¼ cup margarine or butter, softened
- ¼ cup shortening
- 3 to 4 teaspoons milk
- 1 teaspoon vanilla

Heat oven to 375°F. Grease cookie sheets. In large bowl, combine sugar, ½ cup margarine, 1 teaspoon vanilla and egg; blend well. Stir in 1 cup milk. Add remaining cookie ingredients; mix well. Drop dough by rounded teaspoonfuls 2 inches apart onto greased cookie sheets.

Bake at 375°F. for 7 to 9 minutes or until edges appear set. Cool 1 minute; remove from cookie sheets. Cool completely.

In large bowl, combine all filling ingredients; beat until light and fluffy, about 2 minutes. Place flat sides of 2 cookies together with 1 tablespoon filling, sandwich-style. Store in tightly covered container.
Yield: 30 sandwich cookies.

HIGH ALTITUDE:
Above 3500 Feet: No change.

NUTRITION PER SERVING:
Calories 170; Protein 2g; Carbohydrate 24g; Fat 7g; Sodium 170mg.

Heavenly Chocolate Brownie Cookies

One of the best little cookies you'll ever eat. This recipe requires the use of parchment paper which is readily available at a supermarket or specialty food store.

- 4 oz. semi-sweet chocolate, chopped
- 2 oz. unsweetened chocolate, chopped
- ⅓ cup margarine or butter
- ¾ cup sugar
- 1½ teaspoons instant coffee granules or crystals
- 2 eggs
- ½ cup all purpose flour
- ¼ teaspoon baking powder
- ¼ teaspoon salt
- ¾ cup milk chocolate chips
- ¾ cup chopped walnuts or pecans

In small saucepan over low heat, melt semi-sweet chocolate, unsweetened chocolate and margarine, stirring constantly until smooth. Remove from heat; cool.

Heat oven to 350°F. Cover cookie sheets with parchment paper. In large bowl, beat sugar, instant coffee and eggs at high speed for 2 to 3 minutes. Blend in melted chocolate. Stir in flour, baking powder and salt; mix well. Stir in milk chocolate chips and walnuts. Drop dough by teaspoonfuls 2 inches apart onto parchment-lined cookie sheets.

Bake at 350°F. for 7 to 11 minutes or until tops of cookies are cracked. DO NOT OVERBAKE. Cool 1 minute; remove from parchment paper.
Yield: 3 dozen cookies.

HIGH ALTITUDE:
Above 3500 Feet: No change.

NUTRITION PER SERVING:
Calories 110; Protein 1g; Carbohydrate 10g; Fat 7g; Sodium 40mg.

CHOCOLATE RAISIN SMILE COOKIES

To make the frosting faces, place the frosting in a resealable plastic freezer bag and snip off a corner to make a very small hole. Squeeze the frosting gently through the opening.

COOKIES
1½ cups sugar
1 cup firmly packed brown sugar
1½ cups margarine or butter, softened
2 teaspoons vanilla
3 eggs
3 cups all purpose flour
1 cup unsweetened cocoa
1 teaspoon baking soda
¼ teaspoon salt
2 cups raisins

FROSTING
1 cup powdered sugar
1 drop red food color
2 drops yellow food color
2 to 4 teaspoons milk

Heat oven to 350°F. In large bowl, beat sugar, brown sugar and margarine until light and fluffy. Add vanilla and eggs; blend well. Stir in flour, cocoa, baking soda and salt; mix well. Stir in raisins. Drop dough by rounded tablespoonfuls 2 inches apart onto ungreased cookie sheets.

Bake at 350°F. for 10 to 14 minutes or until slightly set. Cool 1 minute; remove from cookie sheets.

In medium bowl, combine all frosting ingredients, adding enough milk for desired decorating consistency. Using decorating bag, decorating bottle, plastic bag or small spoon, make smiling faces on cookies.
Yield: 5 dozen cookies.

HIGH ALTITUDE:
Above 3500 Feet: Decrease sugar to 1¼ cups; decrease brown sugar to ¾ cup. Increase flour to 3½ cups. Bake as directed above.

NUTRITION PER SERVING:
Calories 130; Protein 1g; Carbohydrate 20g; Fat 5g; Sodium 95mg.

VARIATION:

GIANT COOKIE SMILES: Prepare cookie dough as directed above. For each cookie, place ¼ cup of dough 3 inches apart on ungreased cookie sheets. Bake at 350°F. for 10 to 14 minutes or until slightly set. Continue as directed above.
Yield: 2½ dozen cookies.

CANDIED FRUIT DROPS

Candied fruit is available in the baking section of large supermarkets.

¾ cup firmly packed brown sugar
1 cup margarine or butter, softened
1 egg
1¾ cups all purpose flour
½ teaspoon baking soda
½ teaspoon salt
1 (8-oz.) pkg. (1½ cups) chopped dates
1 cup chopped green candied pineapple
1 cup chopped red candied cherries
1½ cups chopped pecans or walnuts

Heat oven to 350°F. In large bowl, beat brown sugar and margarine until light and fluffy. Add egg; blend well. Add flour, baking soda and salt; mix well. Stir in dates, candied fruit and pecans. Drop dough by teaspoonfuls 2 inches apart onto ungreased cookie sheets.

Bake at 350°F. for 10 to 12 minutes. Cool 1 minute; remove from cookie sheets. Cool completely.
Yield: 7 dozen cookies.

HIGH ALTITUDE:
Above 3500 Feet: Increase flour to 2 cups. Bake as directed above.

NUTRITION PER SERVING:
Calories 70; Protein 1g; Carbohydrate 9g; Fat 4g; Sodium 45mg.

CHEWY GRANOLA COOKIES

Granola is a mixture containing various combinations of grains, nuts and dried fruits. We've included a variety of these ingredients to create healthful, tasty cookies.

1½ cups all purpose flour
  3 cups rolled oats
  1 cup wheat germ
  1 teaspoon baking powder
  ½ teaspoon salt
  1 cup firmly packed brown sugar
  1 cup margarine or butter, softened
  ½ cup honey
1½ teaspoons vanilla
  2 eggs
  ½ cup raisins
  ½ cup chopped almonds
  ¼ cup sesame seeds
  ¼ cup shelled sunflower seeds

Heat oven to 375°F. Lightly grease cookie sheets. In medium bowl, combine flour, oats, wheat germ, baking powder and salt; mix well. In large bowl, beat brown sugar, margarine and honey until light and fluffy. Add vanilla and eggs; blend well. Add flour mixture; mix well. Stir in remaining ingredients. Drop dough by rounded teaspoonfuls 2 inches apart onto greased cookie sheets.

Bake at 375°F. for 7 to 8 minutes or until edges are light golden brown. Immediately remove from cookie sheets.
Yield: 5 dozen cookies.

TIP:
For large-sized cookies, place ¼ cup of dough 4 inches apart on greased cookie sheets. Using metal spoon, flatten into 3-inch circles. Bake at 375°F. for 12 to 14 minutes.
Yield: 2½ dozen cookies.

HIGH ALTITUDE:
Above 3500 Feet: No change.

NUTRITION PER SERVING:
Calories 100; Protein 2g; Carbohydrate 13g; Fat 5g; Sodium 65mg.

GRANOLA APPLE COOKIES

These soft-textured cookies are delicious glazed or unglazed. Store glazed cookies between sheets of waxed paper in a tightly covered container.

COOKIES
1½ cups firmly packed brown sugar
  ½ cup margarine or butter, softened
  ¼ cup milk
  1 tablespoon lemon juice
  1 teaspoon grated lemon peel
  1 egg
1½ cups all purpose flour
  1 cup whole wheat flour
  1 teaspoon baking soda
  1 teaspoon cinnamon or nutmeg
  ¼ teaspoon salt
1½ cups finely chopped apples
  1 cup granola

GLAZE
  ¾ cup powdered sugar
  2 to 3 teaspoons lemon juice

Heat oven to 375°F. In large bowl, beat brown sugar and margarine until light and fluffy. Add milk, 1 tablespoon lemon juice, lemon peel and egg; blend well. Stir in all purpose flour, whole wheat flour, baking soda, cinnamon and salt; mix well. Stir in apples and granola. Drop dough by heaping teaspoonfuls 2 inches apart onto ungreased cookie sheets.

Bake at 375°F. for 9 to 13 minutes or until light golden brown. Immediately remove from cookie sheets. Cool completely.

In small bowl, combine glaze ingredients, adding enough lemon juice for desired drizzling consistency. Drizzle over cooled cookies.
Yield: 3 dozen cookies.

HIGH ALTITUDE:
Above 3500 Feet: Decrease brown sugar to 1 cup. Bake as directed above.

NUTRITION PER SERVING:
Calories 140; Protein 2g; Carbohydrate 21g; Fat 6g; Sodium 80mg.

BASIC REFRIGERATOR COOKIES

Sometimes called icebox cookies, these golden cookies are formed into a log, wrapped and refrigerated. They are sliced into rounds just before baking.

- ¾ **cup sugar**
- ¾ **cup firmly packed brown sugar**
- 1 **cup margarine or butter, softened**
- 1½ **teaspoons vanilla**
- 2 **eggs**
- 3 **cups all purpose flour**
- 1½ **teaspoons baking powder**
- ¾ **teaspoon salt**
- 1 **cup finely chopped nuts**

In large bowl, combine sugar, brown sugar, margarine, vanilla and eggs; beat well. Stir in flour, baking powder and salt; blend well. Stir in nuts. Divide dough into 3 equal parts. Shape each into roll 1½ inches in diameter. Wrap each roll in plastic wrap; refrigerate at least 2 hours or until firm.

Heat oven to 425°F. Cut dough into ¼-inch slices. Place 1 inch apart on ungreased cookie sheets. Bake at 425°F. for 5 to 7 minutes or until light golden brown. Immediately remove from cookie sheets. Cool completely.
Yield: 7½ dozen cookies.

TIP:
Cookie dough can be kept up to 2 weeks in refrigerator or up to 6 weeks in freezer. Slice and bake frozen dough as directed above.

HIGH ALTITUDE:
Above 3500 Feet: Add 3 tablespoons milk with sugar mixture. Bake as directed above.

NUTRITION PER SERVING:
Calories 60; Protein 1g; Carbohydrate 7g; Fat 3g; Sodium 50mg.

VARIATIONS:

COCONUT REFRIGERATOR COOKIES:
Add 1 cup coconut with nuts.

LEMON REFRIGERATOR COOKIES:
Add 1 tablespoon grated lemon peel with flour.

ORANGE REFRIGERATOR COOKIES:
Add 1 tablespoon grated orange peel with flour.

SPICE REFRIGERATOR COOKIES:
Add 1 teaspoon cinnamon, ½ teaspoon nutmeg and ¼ to ½ teaspoon cloves with flour.

OATMEAL REFRIGERATOR COOKIES

The answer to fresh cookies on a moment's notice. Mix, shape, wrap and refrigerate up to 2 weeks, then slice and bake as needed.

- 1 **cup sugar**
- 1 **cup firmly packed brown sugar**
- 1 **cup margarine or butter, softened**
- 2 **eggs**
- 2 **cups all purpose flour**
- 1 **teaspoon baking powder**
- 1 **teaspoon baking soda**
- 1 **teaspoon salt**
- 2 **cups quick-cooking rolled oats**
- 1 **cup coconut**
- ½ **to 1 cup chopped nuts**

In large bowl, combine sugar, brown sugar, margarine and eggs; beat well. Add flour, baking powder, baking soda and salt; mix well. Stir in oats, coconut and nuts. Divide dough in half. Shape each half into roll 2 inches in diameter. Wrap each roll in plastic wrap; refrigerate at least 2 hours or until firm.

Heat oven to 375°F. Cut dough into ¼-inch slices. Place 2 inches apart on ungreased cookie sheets. Bake at 375°F. for 8 to 11 minutes or until golden brown. Immediately remove from cookie sheets. Cool completely.
Yield: 6 dozen cookies.

HIGH ALTITUDE:
Above 3500 Feet: No change.

NUTRITION PER SERVING:
Calories 80; Protein 1g; Carbohydrate 11g; Fat 4g; Sodium 80mg.

PINWHEEL DATE COOKIES

These mouth-watering cookies with their marvelous date filling have long been favorites of all the "kids" who raid cookie jars.

FILLING
- ¾ cup finely chopped dates
- ¼ cup sugar
- ⅓ cup water
- 2 tablespoons finely chopped nuts

COOKIES
- 1 cup firmly packed brown sugar
- ½ cup margarine or butter, softened
- 1 egg
- 1½ cups all purpose flour
- 1½ teaspoons baking powder
- ¼ teaspoon salt

In small saucepan, combine dates, sugar and water. Bring to a boil. Reduce heat; cover and simmer 5 minutes or until thick. Stir in nuts. Cool.

In large bowl, beat brown sugar, margarine and egg until light and fluffy. Stir in flour, baking powder and salt; mix at low speed until dough forms. Cover with plastic wrap; refrigerate 1 hour for easier handling.

On lightly floured surface, roll dough into 16x8-inch rectangle; carefully spread with date filling. Starting with 16-inch side, roll up jelly-roll fashion; cut in half to form two 8-inch rolls. Wrap each roll in plastic wrap; refrigerate at least 2 hours.

Heat oven to 375°F. Cut dough into ¼-inch slices. Place 2 inches apart on ungreased cookie sheets. Bake at 375°F. for 6 to 9 minutes or until light golden brown. Immediately remove from cookie sheets. Cool completely.

Yield: 4½ to 5 dozen cookies.

HIGH ALTITUDE:
Above 3500 Feet: Increase flour to 1½ cups plus 2 tablespoons. Bake as directed above.

NUTRITION PER SERVING:
Calories 50; Protein 1g; Carbohydrate 8g; Fat 2g; Sodium 35mg.

CRANBERRY AND ORANGE PINWHEELS

This refrigerator cookie dough features a pretty swirl of cranberry filling.

FILLING
- 1 tablespoon cornstarch
- ¾ cup whole berry cranberry sauce
- ¼ cup orange marmalade

COOKIES
- ¾ cup firmly packed brown sugar
- ½ cup margarine or butter, softened
- 1 egg
- 1¾ cups all purpose flour
- 1 teaspoon baking powder
- 1 teaspoon grated orange peel
- ¼ teaspoon salt
- ¼ teaspoon allspice

In small saucepan, combine all filling ingredients. Bring to a boil over medium heat, stirring constantly. Refrigerate until thoroughly chilled.

In large bowl, beat brown sugar, margarine and egg until light and fluffy. Stir in remaining ingredients; mix well. Cover with plastic wrap; refrigerate 1 hour for easier handling.

On lightly floured surface, roll dough into 16x8-inch rectangle. Spoon and spread cooled filling evenly over dough to within ½ inch of edges. Starting with 16-inch side, roll up jelly-roll fashion; cut in half to form two 8-inch rolls. Wrap each roll in plastic wrap; refrigerate at least 2 hours.

Heat oven to 375°F. Generously grease cookie sheets. Using sharp knife, cut dough into ½-inch slices. Place 2 inches apart on greased cookie sheets. Bake at 375°F. for 9 to 13 minutes or until light golden brown. Immediately remove from cookie sheets. Cool completely.

Yield: 3 dozen cookies.

HIGH ALTITUDE:
Above 3500 Feet: Increase flour to 2 cups. Bake as directed above.

NUTRITION PER SERVING:
Calories 80; Protein 1g; Carbohydrate 13g; Fat 3g; Sodium 60mg.

Cranberry and Orange Pinwheels, Granola Apple Cookies p. 46

BUTTERY ALMOND COOKIES

Butter provides the best results in these rich cookies topped with whole almonds.

- 1 cup sugar
- ½ cup butter or margarine, softened
- ½ cup shortening
- 1 tablespoon almond extract
- 1 egg
- 2¼ cups all purpose flour
- 2 teaspoons baking powder
- 3 oz. whole blanched almonds (about 48)
- 1 egg, beaten

In large bowl, beat sugar, butter and shortening until light and fluffy. Add almond extract and 1 egg; blend well. Stir in flour and baking powder. (Dough will be stiff.) Divide dough into 4 equal parts. On lightly floured surface, form each part into a roll 6 inches long and 1½ inches thick. Wrap each roll in plastic wrap; refrigerate for at least 1 hour or until firm.

Heat oven to 375°F. Lightly grease cookie sheets. Cut each roll into twelve ½-inch slices. Place on greased cookie sheets. Gently press 1 almond into center of each cookie. Brush beaten egg lightly over each cookie.

Bake at 375°F. for 10 to 12 minutes or until light golden brown. Immediately remove from cookie sheets. Cool completely. Store in tightly covered container.
Yield: 4 dozen cookies.

HIGH ALTITUDE:
Above 3500 Feet: No change.

NUTRITION PER SERVING:
Calories 90; Protein 1g; Carbohydrate 9g; Fat 5g; Sodium 35mg.

LICORICE SNAPS

Mix and shape, then slice and bake these uniquely flavored cookies. Anise seed comes from a small annual plant that is a member of the parsley family and gives these cookies their distinctive licorice flavor.

- ¾ cup sugar
- ¾ cup firmly packed brown sugar
- 1 cup margarine or butter, softened
- 1 egg
- 2 cups all purpose flour
- 1 tablespoon anise seed
- 1 teaspoon baking soda
- ½ teaspoon salt
- ½ teaspoon cloves
- ½ teaspoon cinnamon
- ½ cup chopped pecans

In large bowl, beat sugar, brown sugar and margarine until light and fluffy. Add egg; blend well. Stir in flour, anise seed, baking soda, salt, cloves and cinnamon; mix well. Stir in pecans. Cover with plastic wrap; refrigerate 30 minutes for easier handling. Divide dough in half. Shape each half into 10-inch long roll. Wrap each roll in plastic wrap; refrigerate 4 hours or overnight.

Heat oven to 375°F. Cut dough into ¼-inch slices. Place 1 inch apart on ungreased cookie sheets. Bake at 375°F. for 6 to 8 minutes or until light golden brown. Immediately remove from cookie sheets. Cool completely.
Yield: 6 to 6½ dozen cookies.

HIGH ALTITUDE:
Above 3500 Feet: Increase flour to 2¼ cups. Bake as directed above.

NUTRITION PER SERVING:
Calories 60; Protein 1g; Carbohydrate 7g; Fat 3g; Sodium 55mg.

SHORTBREAD TRIANGLES

The classic method of making shortbread is to press the dough into a shallow earthenware mold that is decoratively carved. In this updated version, the tender dough is quickly shaped into triangles, then sliced and baked.

- 2 **cups powdered sugar**
- 2 **cups margarine or butter, softened**
- 2 **egg yolks**
- 4 **cups all purpose flour**
- 1 **cup cornstarch**

In large bowl, combine powdered sugar and margarine; beat until light and fluffy. Add egg yolks; blend well. Add flour and cornstarch; mix well. Divide dough in half. Shape each half into roll 12 inches long and 1½ inches in diameter. Wrap in plastic wrap. Press sides of roll with palm of hand to make 3 even sides, forming triangular shape. Press roll against countertop to smooth and flatten sides. Refrigerate until firm.

Heat oven to 350°F. Cut dough into ¼-inch slices. Place on ungreased cookie sheets. Bake at 350°F. for 8 to 13 minutes or until lightly browned and set. Prick tops of cookies with fork; remove from cookie sheets. Cool completely.
Yield: 4 dozen cookies.

HIGH ALTITUDE:
Above 3500 Feet: No change.

NUTRITION PER SERVING:
Calories 70; Protein 1g; Carbohydrate 7g; Fat 4g; Sodium 40mg.

CHOCOLATE-NUT WAFERS

Cinnamon and chocolate are a pleasant flavor combination in this thin and crispy cookie. Be sure to cool the chocolate slightly before adding it to the other ingredients.

- 1 **cup sugar**
- ¾ **cup margarine or butter, softened**
- 2 **oz. unsweetened chocolate, melted**
- 1 **teaspoon vanilla**
- 1 **egg**
- 2¼ **cups all purpose flour**
- ¼ **teaspoon salt**
- ¼ **teaspoon baking soda**
- ¼ **teaspoon cinnamon**
- ½ **cup chopped nuts**

In large bowl, combine sugar, margarine, chocolate, vanilla and egg; blend well. Stir in remaining ingredients; blend well. Divide dough in half. Shape each into roll 2 inches in diameter. Wrap each roll in plastic wrap; refrigerate at least 3 hours or until firm.

Heat oven to 400°F. Cut dough into ¼-inch slices. Place 2 inches apart on ungreased cookie sheets. Bake at 400°F. for 6 to 8 minutes or until set. DO NOT OVERBAKE. Immediately remove from cookie sheets. Cool completely.
Yield: 5 to 6 dozen cookies.

HIGH ALTITUDE:
Above 3500 Feet: No change.

NUTRITION PER SERVING:
Calories 50; Protein 1g; Carbohydrate 6g; Fat 3g; Sodium 35mg.

COOK'S NOTE

COOKIES AS AN INGREDIENT

Everyone loves cookies, and they can add great flavor and texture to other desserts. Add crumbled cookies to a milk shake, sprinkle cookie bits over pudding, or prepare a crust for pie using cookie crumbs. See p. 269.

SPICED WHOLE WHEAT REFRIGERATOR COOKIES

Because of its firm chewy texture, this traditional icebox cookie is ideal for mailing. Pack the cookies snugly in rows in a sturdy box or metal container. If necessary, cushion cookies with crumpled waxed paper.

- ½ **cup sugar**
- ½ **cup firmly packed brown sugar**
- ½ **cup margarine or butter, softened**
- 2 **tablespoons water**
- 2 **teaspoons vanilla**
- 1 **egg**
- 1¾ **cups whole wheat flour**
- 1 **teaspoon baking powder**
- 1 **teaspoon cinnamon**
- ½ **teaspoon baking soda**
- ¼ **teaspoon salt**
- ¼ **teaspoon cloves**
- ½ **cup finely chopped pecans or walnuts**

In large bowl, beat sugar, brown sugar and margarine until light and fluffy. Add water, vanilla and egg; blend well. Add whole wheat flour, baking powder, cinnamon, baking soda, salt and cloves; mix well. Stir in pecans. Shape dough into two 6-inch long rolls. Wrap each roll in plastic wrap; refrigerate at least 2 hours or until firm.

Heat oven to 375°F. Using sharp knife, cut dough into ¼-inch slices. Place 2 inches apart on ungreased cookie sheets. Bake at 375°F. for 6 to 8 minutes or until set. Cool 1 minute; remove from cookie sheets. Cool completely.
Yield: 3½ dozen cookies.

HIGH ALTITUDE:
Above 3500 Feet: Decrease sugar to ⅓ cup; decrease brown sugar to ⅓ cup. Increase flour to 2 cups. Bake as directed above.

NUTRITION PER SERVING:
Calories 70; Protein 1g; Carbohydrate 9g; Fat 3g; Sodium 60mg.

CRISP AND CHEWY MOLASSES COOKIES

Store this cookie dough in the refrigerator for up to 5 days and bake cookies as desired. Either light or dark molasses can be used to make this favorite cookie.

- ¾ **cup sugar**
- ½ **cup margarine or butter, softened**
- ½ **cup molasses**
- 1 **egg**
- 2 **cups all purpose flour**
- 1½ **teaspoons baking soda**
- ½ **teaspoon cinnamon**
- ¼ **teaspoon cloves**
- ¼ **teaspoon nutmeg**
- ¼ **teaspoon ginger**

In large bowl, beat sugar and margarine until light and fluffy. Add molasses and egg; blend well. Stir in remaining ingredients; mix well. Cover with plastic wrap; refrigerate 30 minutes for easier handling. Shape dough into roll 9½ inches long. Wrap roll in plastic wrap; refrigerate at least 6 hours or up to 5 days.

Heat oven to 375°F. Cut dough into ½-inch slices; cut each slice into fourths. Place 2 inches apart on ungreased cookie sheets. Bake at 375°F. for 6 to 10 minutes or until set. Immediately remove from cookie sheets. Cool completely.
Yield: 5 dozen cookies.

HIGH ALTITUDE:
Above 3500 Feet: Decrease sugar to ½ cup; decrease molasses to ¼ cup. Bake as directed above.

NUTRITION PER SERVING:
Calories 45; Protein 1g; Carbohydrate 7g; Fat 2g; Sodium 50mg.

PEANUT BUTTER COOKIES

Easily prepared and always familiar because of the forked pattern, peanut butter cookies are delicious anytime.

½ **cup sugar**
½ **cup firmly packed brown sugar**
½ **cup margarine or butter, softened**
½ **cup peanut butter**
2 **tablespoons milk**
1 **teaspoon vanilla**
1 **egg**
1¾ **cups all purpose flour**
1 **teaspoon baking soda**
½ **teaspoon salt**
 Sugar

Heat oven to 375°F. In large bowl, beat sugar, brown sugar, and margarine until light and fluffy. Add peanut butter, milk, vanilla and egg; blend well. Stir in flour, baking soda and salt; mix well. Shape dough into 1-inch balls. Place 2 inches apart on ungreased cookie sheets. Flatten in crisscross pattern with fork dipped in sugar.

Bake at 375°F. for 10 to 12 minutes or until golden brown. Immediately remove from cookie sheets. Cool completely.
Yield: 3½ dozen cookies.

HIGH ALTITUDE:
Above 3500 Feet: No change.

NUTRITION PER SERVING:
Calories 80; Protein 1g; Carbohydrate 10g; Fat 4g; Sodium 95mg.

BUTTERSCOTCH CHIP PEANUT BUTTER COOKIES

Butterscotch chips add a unique flavor to these peanut butter cookies. They're a great addition to lunch boxes.

½ **cup sugar**
½ **cup firmly packed brown sugar**
¾ **cup margarine or butter, softened**
½ **cup chunky peanut butter**
1 **teaspoon vanilla**
1 **egg**
1¾ **cups all purpose flour**
1 **teaspoon baking soda**
½ **teaspoon salt**
1 **cup butterscotch chips**

Heat oven to 375°F. In large bowl, beat sugar, brown sugar, margarine and peanut butter until light and fluffy. Add vanilla and egg; blend well. Stir in flour, baking soda and salt; mix well. Stir in butterscotch chips. Shape dough into 1-inch balls. Place 2 inches apart on ungreased cookie sheets. Flatten slightly with fork dipped in flour or sugar.

Bake at 375°F. for 6 to 10 minutes or until golden brown. Immediately remove from cookie sheets. Cool completely.
Yield: 4 to 5 dozen cookies.

HIGH ALTITUDE:
Above 3500 Feet: Increase flour to 2 cups. Bake as directed above.

NUTRITION PER SERVING:
Calories 80; Protein 1g; Carbohydrate 8g; Fat 4g; Sodium 75mg.

PEANUT BLOSSOMS

Sometimes called Brown-Eyed Susans, these cookies crowned with a chocolate kiss are from the 9th Pillsbury Grand National Baking Contest, the early name of the BAKE-OFF® Contest.

1¾ cups all purpose flour
½ cup sugar
½ cup firmly packed brown sugar
1 teaspoon baking soda
½ teaspoon salt
½ cup shortening
½ cup peanut butter
2 tablespoons milk
1 teaspoon vanilla
1 egg
   Sugar
48 milk chocolate candy kisses

Heat oven to 375°F. In large bowl, combine flour, ½ cup sugar, brown sugar, baking soda, salt, shortening, peanut butter, milk, vanilla and egg; blend at low speed until stiff dough forms. Shape into 1-inch balls; roll in sugar. Place 2 inches apart on ungreased cookie sheets.

Bake at 375°F. for 10 to 12 minutes or until golden brown. Immediately top each cookie with a candy kiss, pressing down firmly so cookie cracks around edge; remove from cookie sheets. Cool completely.
Yield: 4 dozen cookies.

HIGH ALTITUDE:
Above 3500 Feet: No change.

NUTRITION PER SERVING:
Calories 100; Protein 2g; Carbohydrate 12g; Fat 5g; Sodium 65mg.

HAWAIIAN COOKIE TARTS

These melt-in-your-mouth cookies are perfect for party trays. They are like miniature pineapple pies.

COOKIES
1¾ cups all purpose flour
½ cup powdered sugar
2 tablespoons cornstarch
1 cup margarine or butter, softened
1 teaspoon vanilla

FILLING
1 cup pineapple preserves
½ cup sugar
1 egg
1½ cups coconut
   Powdered sugar

Heat oven to 350°F. In large bowl, combine flour, ½ cup powdered sugar and cornstarch; blend well. Add margarine and vanilla. By hand, blend until a soft dough forms. Shape dough into 1-inch balls. Place 1 ball in each of 36 ungreased miniature muffin cups; press in bottom and up sides of each cup.*

Spoon 1 teaspoon pineapple preserves into each dough-lined cup. In small bowl, combine sugar and egg. Using fork, beat until well blended. Stir in coconut until well coated with egg mixture. Spoon 1 teaspoon coconut mixture over pineapple preserves in each cup.

Bake at 350°F. for 23 to 33 minutes or until crusts are very light golden brown. Cool 20 minutes. To release cookies from cups, hold muffin pan upside down at an angle over wire rack. Using handle of table knife, firmly tap bottom of each cup until cookie releases. Cool completely. Just before serving, sprinkle with powdered sugar.
Yield: 3 dozen cookies.

TIP:
* If only 1 muffin pan is available, keep remaining cookie dough refrigerated until ready to bake.

NUTRITION PER SERVING:
Calories 130; Protein 1g; Carbohydrate 17g; Fat 6g; Sodium 55mg.

Peanut Blossoms

CHOCOLATY SHORTBREAD COOKIES

Store these tender chocolate cookies in a single layer, tightly covered.

  3/4 **cup sugar**
  1/2 **cup margarine or butter, softened**
  1/2 **cup shortening**
  1 **teaspoon vanilla**
  1 **egg**
2 1/4 **cups all purpose flour**
  1/4 **cup unsweetened cocoa**
  1/2 **teaspoon baking powder**
      Sugar

Heat oven to 325°F. In large bowl, beat 3/4 cup sugar, margarine and shortening until light and fluffy. Add vanilla and egg; blend well. Stir in flour, cocoa and baking powder; mix well. Shape dough into 1-inch balls. Place 2 inches apart on ungreased cookie sheets. Flatten slightly with bottom of glass dipped in sugar.

Bake at 325°F. for 8 to 13 minutes or until set. Cool 1 minute; remove from cookie sheets.
Yield: 3 dozen cookies.

HIGH ALTITUDE:
Above 3500 Feet: Increase flour to 2 1/2 cups. Bake as directed above.

NUTRITION PER SERVING:
Calories 100; Protein 1g; Carbohydrate 10g; Fat 6g; Sodium 40mg.

ORANGE BUTTER COOKIES IN CHOCOLATE

These marvelous, tender, chocolate-dipped cookies melt in your mouth. Store the cookies in a covered container with waxed paper between the layers.

COOKIES
  1 **cup sugar**
  3/4 **cup butter or margarine, softened**
  1 **teaspoon vanilla**
  1 **egg**
  2 **cups all purpose flour**
  1 **teaspoon baking powder**
  3/4 **teaspoon salt**
  2 **tablespoons grated orange peel**

GLAZE
  1 **(6-oz.) pkg. (1 cup) semi-sweet chocolate chips**
  1/4 **cup shortening**
  3 **tablespoons light corn syrup**

Heat oven to 375°F. In large bowl, beat sugar and butter until light and fluffy. Add vanilla and egg; blend well. Stir in flour, baking powder, salt and orange peel. Shape dough into 1-inch balls. Place 2 inches apart on ungreased cookie sheets. Flatten to 1/8 to 1/4-inch thickness with bottom of glass dipped in sugar.

Bake at 375°F. for 6 to 8 minutes or until edges are lightly browned. Cool 1 minute; remove from cookie sheets.

Line cookie sheets with waxed paper. In small saucepan, combine glaze ingredients. Cook over low heat, stirring constantly until smooth. Remove from heat. Pour glaze into glass measuring cup; set in pan of hot water. Dip half of each cookie into glaze; shake off excess chocolate. Place dipped cookies on waxed paper-lined cookie sheets. Refrigerate until glaze is set, about 10 minutes.
Yield: 6 dozen cookies.

HIGH ALTITUDE:
Above 3500 Feet: No change.

NUTRITION PER SERVING:
Calories 70; Protein 1g; Carbohydrate 7g; Fat 4g; Sodium 50mg.

No-Roll
Sugar Cookies

What an easy way to make a large batch of sugar cookies! For variety, try the variations.

1 cup sugar
1 cup powdered sugar
1 cup margarine or butter, softened
1 cup oil
1 teaspoon vanilla
2 eggs
4¼ cups all purpose flour
1 teaspoon baking soda
1 teaspoon cream of tartar
1 teaspoon salt

In large bowl, beat sugar, powdered sugar and margarine until light and fluffy. Add oil, vanilla and eggs; blend well. Stir in flour, baking soda, cream of tartar and salt; mix well. Cover with plastic wrap; refrigerate at least 2 hours or overnight for easier handling.

Heat oven to 375°F. Shape dough into 1-inch balls. Place 2 inches apart on ungreased cookie sheets. Flatten with bottom of glass dipped in sugar. Bake at 375°F. for 5 to 8 minutes or until set but not brown. Immediately remove from cookie sheets. Cool completely.

Yield: 9 to 10 dozen cookies.

HIGH ALTITUDE:
Above 3500 Feet: No change.

NUTRITION PER SERVING:
Calories 60; Protein 1g; Carbohydrate 6g; Fat 3g; Sodium 45mg.

VARIATIONS:

ALMOND SUGAR COOKIES: Add 1 teaspoon almond extract with the vanilla.

ORANGE SUGAR COOKIES: Add 2 teaspoons grated orange peel and 1 teaspoon cinnamon with the dry ingredients.

Whole Wheat
Sugar Cookies

Whole wheat flour and nutmeg add new flavor to the all-time favorite sugar cookie. Just shape the dough into balls, roll them in the sugar-cinnamon mixture and bake.

1 cup sugar
½ cup margarine or butter, softened
2 tablespoons milk
1 teaspoon grated lemon peel
1 teaspoon vanilla
1 egg
2 cups whole wheat flour
1 teaspoon baking powder
½ teaspoon baking soda
½ teaspoon salt
½ teaspoon nutmeg
2 tablespoons sugar
½ teaspoon cinnamon

In large bowl, beat 1 cup sugar and margarine until light and fluffy. Add milk, lemon peel, vanilla and egg; blend well. Add flour, baking powder, baking soda, salt and nutmeg; mix well. Cover with plastic wrap; refrigerate 1 hour for easier handling.

Heat oven to 375°F. In small bowl, combine 2 tablespoons sugar and cinnamon. Shape dough into 1-inch balls; roll in sugar-cinnamon mixture. Place 2 inches apart on ungreased cookie sheets.

Bake at 375°F. for 8 to 10 minutes or until light golden brown. Cool 1 minute; remove from cookie sheets. Cool completely.

Yield: 2 to 3 dozen cookies.

HIGH ALTITUDE:
Above 3500 Feet: No change.

NUTRITION PER SERVING:
Calories 70; Protein 1g; Carbohydrate 11g; Fat 3g; Sodium 85mg.

CARAMEL CREAM SANDWICH COOKIES

These rich butter cookies with delicate caramel flavor are a prizewinning recipe from the 6th Pillsbury BAKE-OFF® Contest held in 1955.

COOKIES
- ¾ cup firmly packed brown sugar
- 1 cup butter or margarine, softened
- 1 egg yolk
- 2 cups all purpose flour

FROSTING
- 2 tablespoons butter (do not substitute margarine)
- 1¼ cups powdered sugar
- ½ teaspoon vanilla
- 4 to 5 teaspoons milk

In large bowl, beat brown sugar and 1 cup butter until light and fluffy. Add egg yolk; blend well. Stir in flour; mix well. Cover with plastic wrap; refrigerate 15 minutes for easier handling.

Heat oven to 325°F. Shape dough into 1-inch balls. Place 2 inches apart on ungreased cookie sheets. Flatten to 1½-inch circles with fork dipped in flour. Bake at 325°F. for 10 to 14 minutes or until light golden brown. Immediately remove from cookie sheets. Cool completely.

Heat 2 tablespoons butter in medium saucepan over medium heat until light golden brown. Remove from heat. Stir in remaining frosting ingredients, adding enough milk for desired spreading consistency; blend until smooth. Spread 1 teaspoon frosting between 2 cooled cookies. Repeat with remaining frosting and cookies.*
Yield: 2½ dozen sandwich cookies.

TIP:
* If frosting becomes too stiff as it cools, add enough additional milk for desired spreading consistency.

HIGH ALTITUDE:
Above 3500 Feet: No change.

NUTRITION PER SERVING:
Calories 130; Protein 1g; Carbohydrate 16g; Fat 7g; Sodium 70mg.

NUTMEG COOKIE LOGS

Nutmeg is found in the fruit of a tropical evergreen called a nutmeg tree.

COOKIES
- ¾ cup sugar
- 1 cup margarine or butter, softened
- 2 teaspoons vanilla
- 2 teaspoons rum extract
- 1 egg
- 3 cups all purpose flour
- 1 teaspoon nutmeg

FROSTING
- 2 cups powdered sugar
- 3 tablespoons margarine or butter, softened
- ¾ teaspoon rum extract
- ¼ teaspoon vanilla
- 2 to 3 tablespoons half-and-half or milk
  Nutmeg

In large bowl, beat sugar, 1 cup margarine, 2 teaspoons vanilla, 2 teaspoons rum extract and egg until light and fluffy. Stir in flour and 1 teaspoon nutmeg; mix well. Cover with plastic wrap; refrigerate 30 to 45 minutes for easier handling.

Heat oven to 350°F. Divide dough into 6 pieces. On lightly floured surface, shape each piece of dough into long rope, ½ inch in diameter. Cut into 3-inch lengths; place on ungreased cookie sheets. Bake at 350°F. for 12 to 15 minutes or until light golden brown. Immediately remove from cookie sheets. Cool completely.

In small bowl, combine all frosting ingredients except nutmeg, adding enough half-and-half for desired spreading consistency. Spread on top and sides of cookies. If desired, mark frosting with tines of fork to resemble bark. Sprinkle lightly with nutmeg. Let stand until frosting is set. Store in tightly covered container.
Yield: 4½ to 5 dozen cookies.

HIGH ALTITUDE:
Above 3500 Feet: No change.

NUTRITION PER SERVING:
Calories 80; Protein 1g; Carbohydrate 11g; Fat 4g; Sodium 40mg.

Caramel Cream Sandwich Cookies

Meringue Mushrooms

These delightful, airy little cookies are wonderful to eat or use as a garnish for other desserts.

- 2 **egg whites, room temperature**
- ¼ **teaspoon cream of tartar**
- ½ **cup sugar**
- 1 **to 2 tablespoons unsweetened cocoa**
- 2 **oz. semi-sweet chocolate**

Heat oven to 200°F. Line 2 cookie sheets with foil or parchment paper. In small bowl, beat egg whites and cream of tartar at medium speed until soft peaks form. Add sugar 1 tablespoon at a time, beating at high speed until stiff glossy peaks form and sugar is dissolved. Spoon meringue into decorating bag with ¼-inch plain decorating tip (No. 10, 11 or 12). For mushroom caps, pipe about fifty 1-inch mounds on one foil-lined cookie sheet. Lightly sift cocoa over caps.

Bake at 200°F. for 45 to 60 minutes or until firm and very lightly browned. Remove from oven. Immediately turn caps over; with finger, make indentation in center of each cap. Cool completely. Brush off any excess cocoa.

On second foil-lined cookie sheet, pipe remaining meringue into 50 upright stems, about ¾-inch tall. Bake at 200°F. for 40 to 45 minutes or until firm. Immediately remove from cookie sheet; cool completely.

Melt chocolate in small saucepan over low heat, stirring constantly. To assemble each mushroom, spread a small amount of melted chocolate in indentation of cap; insert pointed end of stem into chocolate. Let stand until dry. Store loosely covered at room temperature.
Yield: 4 to 5 dozen cookies.

NUTRITION PER SERVING:
Calories 12; Protein 0g; Carbohydrate 2g; Fat 0g; Sodium 0mg.

VARIATION:

MINT WREATHS: *Omit cocoa and chocolate.* Add ¼ teaspoon mint extract and a few drops of green food color, if desired, to egg whites when adding last tablespoon of sugar. Spoon meringue into decorating bag with ¼-inch plain decorating tip. Pipe two 1½-inch circles of meringue, one on top of the other, on foil-lined cookie sheet. Repeat for remaining wreaths. Decorate with bits of red and green candied cherries. Bake at 200°F. for 45 minutes. Turn oven off; leave meringues in oven an additional 1 hour to dry. Carefully peel from foil. Cool completely.
Yield: 3 dozen cookies.

Mexican Wedding Cakes

These buttery shortbread cookies can be shaped either into balls or crescents.

- ½ **cup powdered sugar**
- 1 **cup butter or margarine, softened**
- 2 **teaspoons vanilla**
- 2 **cups all purpose flour**
- 1 **cup finely chopped or ground almonds or pecans**
- ¼ **teaspoon salt**
  Powdered sugar

Heat oven to 325°F. In large bowl, beat ½ cup powdered sugar, butter and vanilla until light and fluffy. Stir in flour, almonds and salt; mix until dough forms. Shape into 1-inch balls. Place 1 inch apart on ungreased cookie sheets.

Bake at 325°F. for 15 to 20 minutes or until set but not brown. Immediately remove from cookie sheets. Cool slightly; roll in powdered sugar. Cool completely. Reroll in powdered sugar.
Yield: 5 dozen cookies.

HIGH ALTITUDE :
Above 3500 Feet: No change.

NUTRITION PER SERVING:
Calories 60; Protein 1g; Carbohydrate 6g; Fat 4g; Sodium 40mg.

Cook's Note

A COOKIE WITH MANY NAMES

Swedish Tea Cakes or Butterballs, Russian Tea Cakes, Mexican Wedding Cakes . . . many different names describe this favorite holiday cookie. The shape may be in a crescent, a log or a ball. Cookies may be plain, dipped in melted chocolate or rolled in powdered sugar. For a variation, substitute 1 cup miniature semi-sweet chocolate chips for 1 cup finely chopped nuts.

Chocolate Almond Bonbons,
Mexican Wedding Cakes

CHOCOLATE ALMOND BONBONS

This Pillsbury BAKE-OFF® Contest finalist prepared her delicious chocolate cookies in the Grand Ballroom of the Waldorf-Astoria Hotel in December, l952, along with 99 other finalists.

4 oz. sweet baking chocolate
2 tablespoons milk
¼ cup sugar
¾ cup margarine or butter, softened
2 teaspoons vanilla
2 cups all purpose flour
¼ teaspoon salt
1 (3½-oz.) tube almond paste
Sugar

Heat oven to 350°F. In small saucepan over low heat, melt chocolate in milk, stirring occasionally until smooth. In large bowl, beat ¼ cup sugar and margarine until light and fluffy. Blend in chocolate mixture and vanilla. Stir in flour and salt; mix well. Using rounded teaspoonfuls of dough, shape into balls. Place 2 inches apart on ungreased cookie sheets. Make an indentation in center of each cookie. Fill each with scant ¼ teaspoon almond paste; press dough around filling to cover.

Bake at 350°F. for 9 to 11 minutes or until set. Remove from cookie sheets; roll in sugar. Cool completely.
Yield: 4 dozen cookies.

HIGH ALTITUDE:
Above 3500 Feet: No change.

NUTRITION PER SERVING:
Calories 70; Protein 1g; Carbohydrate 8g; Fat 4g; Sodium 45mg.

SNICKERDOODLES

The whimsical name of this favorite cookie, which originated in New England, is simply a nineteenth century nonsense word for a quickly made confection.

1½ **cups sugar**
 ½ **cup margarine or butter, softened**
 1 **teaspoon vanilla**
 2 **eggs**
2¾ **cups all purpose flour**
 1 **teaspoon cream of tartar**
 ½ **teaspoon baking soda**
 ¼ **teaspoon salt**
 2 **tablespoons sugar**
 2 **teaspoons cinnamon**

Heat oven to 400°F. In large bowl, beat 1½ cups sugar and margarine until light and fluffy. Add vanilla and eggs; blend well. Add flour, cream of tartar, baking soda and salt; mix well. In small bowl, combine 2 tablespoons sugar and cinnamon. Shape dough into 1-inch balls; roll balls in sugar-cinnamon mixture. Place 2 inches apart on ungreased cookie sheets.

Bake at 400°F. for 8 to 10 minutes or until set. Immediately remove from cookie sheets. Cool completely.
Yield: 4 dozen cookies.

HIGH ALTITUDE:
Above 3500 Feet: No change.

NUTRITION PER SERVING:
Calories 70; Protein 1g; Carbohydrate 12g; Fat 2g; Sodium 50mg.

VARIATION:

WHOLE WHEAT SNICKERDOODLES:
Use 1¾ cups all purpose flour and 1 cup whole wheat flour.

CHOCOLATE PIXIES

When melting chocolate, constant stirring is needed to keep the mixture smooth and to prevent scorching.

 ¼ **cup margarine or butter**
 4 **oz. unsweetened chocolate**
 2 **cups all purpose flour**
 2 **cups sugar**
 ½ **cup chopped walnuts or pecans**
 2 **teaspoons baking powder**
 ½ **teaspoon salt**
 4 **eggs**
    Powdered sugar

In large saucepan over low heat, melt margarine and chocolate, stirring constantly until smooth. Remove from heat; cool slightly. Stir in remaining ingredients except powdered sugar; mix well. Cover with plastic wrap; refrigerate at least 1 hour for easier handling.

Heat oven to 300°F. Shape dough into 1-inch balls; roll each in powdered sugar, coating heavily. Place 2 inches apart on ungreased cookie sheets. Bake at 300°F. for 13 to 18 minutes or until set. Immediately remove from cookie sheets. Cool completely.
Yield: 4 dozen cookies.

HIGH ALTITUDE:
Above 3500 Feet: Increase flour to 2¼ cups. Bake as directed above.

NUTRITION PER SERVING:
Calories 80; Protein 1g; Carbohydrate 12g; Fat 3g; Sodium 50mg.

COOK'S NOTE

COOKIE HISTORY

The first cookies were created quite by accident. Cooks used a small amount of cake batter to test their oven temperature before baking a large cake. These little test cakes were called "koekje," meaning "little cake" in Dutch.

CARAMEL PECAN STICKY BUN COOKIES

∽

The title says it all! These buttery rich cookies would be a great addition to any cookie tray. The recipe will be requested often.

COOKIES
- 1 cup margarine or butter, softened
- ½ cup sugar
- ½ cup dark corn syrup
- 2 egg yolks
- 2½ cups all purpose flour

FILLING
- ½ cup powdered sugar
- ¼ cup margarine or butter
- 3 tablespoons dark corn syrup
- ½ cup coarsely chopped pecans, toasted, p. 23
- 1 egg white, slightly beaten

In large bowl, beat 1 cup margarine and sugar until light and fluffy. Add ½ cup corn syrup and egg yolks; blend well. Stir in flour; mix well. Cover with plastic wrap; refrigerate 1 hour for easier handling.

In small saucepan, combine powdered sugar, ¼ cup margarine and 3 tablespoons corn syrup; bring to a boil. Remove from heat. Stir in pecans. Refrigerate at least 10 minutes.

Heat oven to 375°F. Lightly grease cookie sheets. Shape dough into 1½-inch balls. Place 2 inches apart on greased cookie sheets. Bake at 375°F. for 5 minutes. Remove from oven. Brush dough lightly with egg white. With spoon, carefully make deep indentation in center of each cookie; fill each with ½ teaspoon filling. Return to oven and bake an additional 6 to 9 minutes or until light golden brown. Cool 1 to 2 minutes; remove from cookie sheets. Cool completely.
Yield: 3 dozen cookies.

HIGH ALTITUDE:
Above 3500 Feet: Decrease margarine in cookies to ¾ cup; decrease dark corn syrup in cookies to ⅓ cup. Bake as directed above on *ungreased* cookie sheets.

NUTRITION PER SERVING:
Calories 140; Protein 1g; Carbohydrate 16g; Fat 8g; Sodium 80mg.

CHERRY WINKS

∽

Maraschino cherries are available in the canned fruit section of grocery stores. Purchase cherries without stems for this 1950 Pillsbury BAKE-OFF® Contest winning favorite.

- 1 cup sugar
- ¾ cup shortening
- 2 tablespoons milk
- 1 teaspoon vanilla
- 2 eggs
- 2¼ cups all purpose flour
- 1 teaspoon baking powder
- ½ teaspoon baking soda
- ½ teaspoon salt
- 1 cup chopped pecans or walnuts
- 1 cup chopped dates
- ⅓ cup chopped maraschino cherries, well drained
- 1½ cups coarsely crushed cornflakes cereal
- 15 maraschino cherries, quartered, drained

Heat oven to 375°F. Grease cookie sheets. In large bowl, combine sugar, shortening, milk, vanilla and eggs; beat well. Stir in flour, baking powder, baking soda, salt, pecans, dates and ⅓ cup chopped cherries; mix well. Cover dough with plastic wrap and refrigerate for easier handling.

Drop dough by rounded teaspoonfuls into cereal; thoroughly coat. Form into balls; place 2 inches apart on greased cookie sheets. Lightly press maraschino cherry piece into top of each ball. Bake at 375°F. for 10 to 15 minutes or until light golden brown.
Yield: 5 dozen cookies.

HIGH ALTITUDE:
Above 3500 Feet: No change.

NUTRITION PER SERVING:
Calories 90; Protein 1g; Carbohydrate 12g; Fat 4g; Sodium 55mg.

LEMON BUTTER COOKIES

These lemony morsels are more tender when made with butter, but margarine is an acceptable alternative.

- ½ **cup sugar**
- ½ **cup powdered sugar**
- ¾ **cup butter or margarine, softened**
- ¼ **cup oil**
- 1 **tablespoon grated lemon peel**
- 1 **tablespoon lemon juice**
- 1 **egg**
- 2½ **cups all purpose flour**
- ½ **teaspoon cream of tartar**
- ½ **teaspoon baking soda**
- ¼ **teaspoon salt**
- **Yellow decorator sugar**

In large bowl, beat sugar, powdered sugar, butter and oil until light and fluffy. Add lemon peel, lemon juice and egg; blend well. Stir in flour, cream of tartar, baking soda and salt; mix well. Cover with plastic wrap; refrigerate 1 hour for easier handling.

Heat oven to 350°F. Shape dough into 1-inch balls; roll in decorator sugar. Place 2 inches apart on ungreased cookie sheets. Bake at 350°F. for 7 to 12 minutes or until set. Immediately remove from cookie sheets.

Yield: 3½ dozen cookies.

HIGH ALTITUDE:
Above 3500 Feet: Decrease sugar to ⅓ cup; increase flour to 2¾ cups. Bake as directed above.

NUTRITION PER SERVING:
Calories 90; Protein 1g; Carbohydrate 11g; Fat 5g; Sodium 60mg.

WHITE-CAPPED MOCHA COOKIES

Use your choice of candy coating or white baking bar to create these delectable candy-filled party cookies.

COOKIES
- ½ **cup firmly packed brown sugar**
- ¼ **cup sugar**
- ½ **cup margarine or butter, softened**
- 1 **(8-oz.) pkg. cream cheese, softened, reserving 2 oz. for frosting**
- 2 **teaspoons instant coffee granules or crystals**
- 2 **teaspoons hot water**
- 1 **egg**
- 2 **cups all purpose flour**
- ¼ **cup unsweetened cocoa**
- 1 **teaspoon baking powder**
- 2 **to 3 oz. vanilla-flavored candy coating or white baking bar, cut into small pieces (about ¼-inch cubes)**

FROSTING
- 1 **cup powdered sugar**
- **Reserved 2 oz. cream cheese**
- 2 **to 3 teaspoons milk**

Heat oven to 350°F. In large bowl, beat brown sugar, sugar, margarine and 6 oz. of the cream cheese until light and fluffy. In small bowl, dissolve instant coffee in hot water. Add dissolved coffee and egg; blend well. Stir in flour, cocoa and baking powder; mix well. Shape level tablespoonfuls of dough around each piece of candy coating, covering completely. Place 2 inches apart on ungreased cookie sheets.

Bake at 350°F. for 8 to 11 minutes or until set. Cool 1 minute; remove from cookie sheets. Cool completely.

In small bowl, combine all frosting ingredients, adding enough milk for desired spreading consistency. Frost cooled cookies.

Yield: 4½ dozen cookies.

HIGH ALTITUDE:
Above 3500 Feet: Decrease baking powder to ½ teaspoon. Bake as directed above.

NUTRITION PER SERVING:
Calories 80; Protein 1g; Carbohydrate 10g; Fat 4g; Sodium 45mg.

GINGER SNAPS

Ginger cookies with a crackly sugar topping are a long-standing favorite cookie jar cookie. For chewy cookies, bake just until set. For crisper cookies, bake 2 to 3 minutes longer.

    1   cup sugar
    ¾   cup margarine or butter, softened
    ¼   cup molasses
    1   egg
    2¼ cups all purpose flour
    2   teaspoons baking soda
    1   teaspoon cinnamon
    ½   teaspoon salt
    ½   teaspoon ginger
    ½   teaspoon cloves
    ¼   teaspoon nutmeg
    ¼   cup sugar

In large bowl, beat 1 cup sugar, margarine, molasses and egg until light and fluffy. Stir in remaining ingredients except ¼ cup sugar; mix well. Cover with plastic wrap; refrigerate 1 hour for easier handling.

Heat oven to 350°F. Shape dough into 1-inch balls; roll in ¼ cup sugar. Place 2 inches apart on ungreased cookie sheets. Bake at 350°F. for 8 to 12 minutes or until set. (Cookies will puff up and then flatten during baking.) Cool 1 minute; remove from cookie sheets. Cool completely.

Yield: 4½ to 5 dozen cookies.

HIGH ALTITUDE:
Above 3500 Feet: Decrease baking soda to 1½ teaspoons. Bake as directed above.

NUTRITION PER SERVING:
Calories 60; Protein 1g; Carbohydrate 9g; Fat 2g; Sodium 85mg.

CRISP CHOCOLATE SNAPS

Chocolate lovers will find this eye-catching version of a cookie classic irresistible. Smaller-sized snaps can be made for holiday cookie trays.

    2   cups sugar
    1   cup firmly packed brown sugar
    1½ cups margarine or butter, softened
    2   teaspoons vanilla
    3   eggs
    6   oz. unsweetened chocolate, melted, cooled
    ½   teaspoon red food color, if desired
    4   cups all purpose flour
    2   teaspoons baking soda
    1   teaspoon salt
        Sugar

In large bowl, beat sugar, brown sugar and margarine until light and fluffy. Add vanilla, eggs, unsweetened chocolate and food color; blend well. Stir in flour, baking soda and salt; mix well. Cover with plastic wrap; refrigerate 1 to 2 hours for easier handling.

Heat oven to 350°F. Lightly grease cookie sheets. Shape dough into 1½-inch balls; roll in sugar. Place 3 inches apart on greased cookie sheets. Bake at 350°F. for 8 to 12 minutes or until set. (Cookies will puff up and then flatten during baking.) Cool 1 minute; remove from cookie sheets. Cool completely.

Yield: 6 dozen cookies.

HIGH ALTITUDE:
Above 3500 Feet: No change.

NUTRITION PER SERVING:
Calories 110; Protein 1g; Carbohydrate 15g; Fat 5g; Sodium 110mg.

Triple Chocolate Strip Cookies

~

Make dozens of chocolate cookies in minutes by baking the rich chocolate dough in logs and then cutting them into strips.

COOKIES
  2 cups all purpose flour
  ½ cup unsweetened cocoa
  ½ teaspoon baking soda
  ¼ teaspoon salt
  ¾ cup sugar
  ½ cup firmly packed brown sugar
  ¾ cup margarine or butter, softened
  2 eggs
  1 (12-oz.) pkg. (2 cups) semi-sweet
      chocolate chips

WHITE CHOCOLATE GLAZE
  2 oz. white chocolate or vanilla-flavored
      candy coating

CHOCOLATE GLAZE
  2 oz. semi-sweet chocolate, cut into pieces
  ½ teaspoon margarine or butter

Heat oven to 350°F. Lightly grease 2 cookie sheets. In medium bowl, combine flour, cocoa, baking soda and salt. In large bowl, beat sugar, brown sugar and ¾ cup margarine until light and fluffy. Add eggs; blend well. Stir in flour mixture; mix well. Stir in chocolate chips. Divide dough into 4 equal portions. Shape each portion into a 12-inch roll. Place 2 rolls 2 inches apart on each greased cookie sheet.

Bake at 350°F. for 14 to 18 minutes or until toothpick inserted in center of each roll comes out almost clean. Remove from cookie sheets; cool on wire racks 10 minutes.

In small heavy saucepan over low heat, melt white chocolate. Drizzle over 2 rolls. In same saucepan, melt semi-sweet chocolate and ½ teaspoon margarine. Drizzle over remaining 2 rolls. Let stand until glazes are set. Cut rolls diagonally into 1-inch strips.
Yield: 4 dozen cookies.

HIGH ALTITUDE:
Above 3500 Feet: No change.

NUTRITION PER SERVING:
Calories 130; Protein 1g; Carbohydrate 15g; Fat 7g; Sodium 65mg.

Split Seconds

~

You'll enjoy this unique method for making delicious shortbread cookies. Choose your favorite flavor of jelly or preserves to make this 1954 Pillsbury BAKE-OFF® Contest classic.

  ¾ cup margarine or butter, softened
  ⅔ cup sugar
  2 teaspoons vanilla
  1 egg
  2 cups all purpose flour
  ½ teaspoon baking powder
  ½ cup red jelly or preserves

Heat oven to 350°F. In large bowl, beat margarine and sugar until light and fluffy. Add vanilla and egg; blend well. Stir in flour and baking powder; mix well. Divide dough into 4 equal parts. On lightly floured surface, shape each part into 12x¾-inch roll; place on ungreased cookie sheets. Using handle of wooden spoon or finger, make depression about ½ inch wide and ¼ inch deep lengthwise down center of each roll. Fill each roll with 2 tablespoons jelly.

Bake at 350°F. for 15 to 20 minutes or until light golden brown. Cool slightly; cut diagonally into strips. Cool completely on wire racks.
Yield: 4 dozen cookies.

HIGH ALTITUDE:
Above 3500 Feet: No change.

NUTRITION PER SERVING:
Calories 70; Protein 1g; Carbohydrate 9g; Fat 3g; Sodium 40mg.

Split Seconds

THUMBPRINTS

Only a few ingredients are needed to make these tasty cookies.

- ½ **cup sugar**
- 1 **cup margarine or butter, softened**
- 1 **teaspoon vanilla**
- 2 **egg yolks**
- 2¼ **cups all purpose flour**
- 1 **teaspoon baking powder**
- ¼ **cup any flavor jam or preserves**

In medium bowl, beat sugar, margarine, vanilla and egg yolks until light and fluffy. Gradually add flour and baking powder; mix well. Cover with plastic wrap; refrigerate 30 minutes for easier handling.

Heat oven to 350°F. Shape dough into 1-inch balls; place 2 inches apart on ungreased cookie sheets. With thumb, make imprint in center of each cookie. Bake at 350°F. for 11 to 14 minutes or until light golden brown around edges. Spoon about ¼ teaspoon jam into each baked cookie. Cool completely.

Yield: 3½ dozen cookies.

HIGH ALTITUDE:
Above 3500 Feet: No change.

NUTRITION PER SERVING:
Calories 80; Protein 1g; Carbohydrate 9g; Fat 5g; Sodium 60mg.

VARIATIONS:

CUSTARD-FILLED THUMBPRINTS: Prepare and shape cookie dough as directed above; do not bake. In small saucepan, combine 1 tablespoon sugar, 1 tablespoon flour and ¼ teaspoon almond extract. Gradually add ½ cup whipping cream or half-and-half; cook over low heat until smooth and thickened, stirring constantly. In small bowl, blend 2 tablespoons hot mixture into 1 slightly beaten egg yolk. Return to saucepan; blend well. Cook just until mixture bubbles, stirring constantly. Cool. Spoon ½ teaspoon filling into each *unbaked* cookie. Bake as directed above. Omit jam. Store cookies in refrigerator.

LEMON-FILLED THUMBPRINTS: Prepare and bake cookies as directed above. Omit jam. In medium saucepan, combine 1 beaten egg, ⅔ cup sugar, 2 to 3 teaspoons grated lemon peel, 1 teaspoon cornstarch, ¼ teaspoon salt, 3 tablespoons lemon juice and 1 tablespoon margarine or butter. Cook over low heat until smooth and thickened, stirring constantly. Cool filling slightly. Spoon ¼ teaspoon filling into each *baked* cookie. Sprinkle with powdered sugar or coconut. Store cookies in refrigerator.

SPRITZ

Spritz are delightful Scandinavian cookies formed into fanciful shapes by forcing dough through a cookie press. The name comes from "spritzen," which is German for "to squirt or spray."

- 1 **cup powdered sugar**
- 1 **cup margarine or butter, softened**
- ½ **teaspoon vanilla**
- 1 **egg**
- 2⅓ **cups all purpose flour**
- ¼ **teaspoon salt**

Heat oven to 400°F. In large bowl, beat powdered sugar, margarine, vanilla and egg until light and fluffy. Stir in flour and salt; blend well. Fit cookie press with desired plate. Fill cookie press; press dough onto ungreased cookie sheets.

Bake at 400°F. for 5 to 7 minutes or until lightly browned on edges. Immediately remove from cookie sheets. Cool completely.

Yield: 5 dozen cookies.

HIGH ALTITUDE:
Above 3500 Feet: No change.

NUTRITION PER SERVING:
Calories 50; Protein 1g; Carbohydrate 5g; Fat 3g; Sodium 45mg.

VARIATIONS:

CHOCOLATE SPRITZ: Add 2 oz. melted unsweetened chocolate to powdered sugar mixture.

EGGNOG SPRITZ: Substitute 1 teaspoon rum flavoring for vanilla. Add ¼ teaspoon nutmeg with dry ingredients.

ORANGE SPRITZ: Add 1 tablespoon grated orange peel with dry ingredients.

Spritz

AUTUMN LEAF COOKIES

These tender, vivid and sassy autumn leaves start with an orange-flavored cream cheese dough that is rolled and cut into leaf shapes. With orange and chocolate frosting, it's easy to create an array of colorful, edible leaves.

COOKIES
- 1 cup sugar
- 1 cup margarine or butter, softened
- 1 (3-oz.) pkg. cream cheese, softened
- 2 tablespoons orange juice
- 1 teaspoon vanilla
- 1 egg
- 2 tablespoons grated orange peel
- 3½ cups all purpose flour
- 1 teaspoon baking soda
- 1 teaspoon cream of tartar
- ½ teaspoon salt

ICING
- 1 recipe Buttery Decorator Icing p. 184
- ⅓ cup semi-sweet chocolate chips, melted
- 8 drops red food color*
- 8 drops yellow food color*

In large bowl, beat sugar, margarine and cream cheese until light and fluffy. Add orange juice, vanilla, egg and orange peel; blend well. Stir in flour, baking soda, cream of tartar and salt. Cover with plastic wrap; refrigerate 2 hours or until firm.

Heat oven to 375°F. Using cloth-covered rolling pin and floured pastry cloth, roll out ¼ of dough at a time to ⅛-inch thickness. Keep remaining dough refrigerated. Cut with floured leaf design cookie cutter. Place cutouts 1 inch apart on ungreased cookie sheets.

Bake at 375°F. for 4 to 6 minutes or until edges are light golden brown. Immediately remove from cookie sheets; cool completely.

Prepare Buttery Decorator Icing as directed in recipe; divide into 2 small bowls. To 1 bowl of icing, add melted chocolate chips; beat until well blended. To other bowl of icing, add red and yellow food color; blend well. Spread cooled cookies with 1 of the icings; pipe veins on leaves with the other icing. To prevent icing from drying out, keep bowls of icing covered with wet paper towels.** Allow icing to set several hours before storing cookies.
Yield: 7 to 8 dozen cookies.

TIPS:
* For more vivid color, paste food color can be used.
** If any icing is left over, cover tightly with plastic wrap; store in refrigerator. Use within 2 weeks.

HIGH ALTITUDE:
Above 3500 Feet: No change.

NUTRITION PER SERVING:
Calories 80; Protein 1g; Carbohydrate 10g; Fat 4g; Sodium 60mg.

COOK'S NOTE

TENDER CUT-OUT COOKIES
To make tender cut-out cookies, roll out a portion of the dough at a time. Using a floured cookie cutter, cut the shapes very close together so there are very few dough scraps remaining. Reroll all the dough scraps at once, using enough flour to keep the dough from sticking. Handling the dough as little as possible and using only the amount of flour necessary to prevent sticking will result in tender cut-out cookies.

Vanilla Sandwich Cookies

A creamy, flavorful, extra-special mocha filling is sandwiched between crisp, tender cookie rounds.

COOKIES
- ½ cup sugar
- ½ cup margarine or butter, softened
- 1 tablespoon milk
- 1 teaspoon vanilla
- 1 egg
- 1¼ cups all purpose flour
- 1 teaspoon cream of tartar
- ½ teaspoon baking soda
- ¼ teaspoon salt
  Sugar

FILLING
- 2 tablespoons margarine or butter
- 1⅓ cups powdered sugar
- ⅓ cup unsweetened cocoa
- 4 teaspoons hot water
- 2 to 3 tablespoons coffee-flavored liqueur

In large bowl, beat sugar and ½ cup margarine until light and fluffy. Add milk, vanilla and egg; blend well. Stir in flour, cream of tartar, baking soda and salt; mix well. Cover with plastic wrap; refrigerate 3 hours or until firm.

Heat oven to 425°F. Using cloth-covered rolling pin and well-floured pastry cloth, roll out ⅓ of dough at a time to ⅛-inch thickness. Keep remaining dough refrigerated. Cut with floured 1½-inch round cookie cutter. Sprinkle tops with sugar. Place 1 inch apart on ungreased cookie sheets.

Bake at 425°F. for 3 to 5 minutes or until edges are light brown. Immediately remove from cookie sheets; cool completely.

In small bowl, combine all filling ingredients, adding enough liqueur for desired frosting consistency. Spread rounded ½ teaspoon filling between 2 cooled cookies.

Yield: 5 dozen sandwich cookies.

HIGH ALTITUDE:
Above 3500 Feet: Increase flour to 1¼ cups plus 2 tablespoons. Bake as directed above.

NUTRITION PER SERVING:
Calories 45; Protein 0g; Carbohydrate 6g; Fat 2g; Sodium 40mg.

Rolled Sugar Cookies

These simple cookies are so versatile. They can be cut into shapes to fit any occasion and can be sprinkled with sugar or decorated.

- 1 cup sugar
- 1 cup margarine or butter, softened
- 3 tablespoons milk
- 1 teaspoon vanilla
- 1 egg
- 3 cups all purpose flour
- 1½ teaspoons baking powder
- ½ teaspoon salt
  Sugar, if desired

In large bowl, combine 1 cup sugar, margarine, milk, vanilla and egg; blend well. Stir in flour, baking powder and salt; mix well. Cover with plastic wrap; refrigerate 1 hour for easier handling.

Heat oven to 400°F. On lightly floured surface, roll out ⅓ of dough at a time to ⅛-inch thickness. Keep remaining dough refrigerated. Cut with floured cookie cutter. Place 1 inch apart on ungreased cookie sheets; sprinkle with sugar.

Bake at 400°F. for 5 to 9 minutes or until edges are light brown. Immediately remove from cookie sheets.

Yield: 5 to 6 dozen cookies.

HIGH ALTITUDE:
Above 3500 Feet: Increase flour to 3 cups plus 2 tablespoons. Bake as directed above.

NUTRITION PER SERVING:
Calories 60; Protein 1g; Carbohydrate 7g; Fat 3g; Sodium 50mg.

MOLASSES JACK-O'-LANTERN COOKIES

A great recipe for a children's party.

COOKIES
- 1 cup sugar
- ½ cup margarine or butter, softened
- ⅓ cup molasses
- 1 egg
- 2 cups all purpose flour
- 2 teaspoons grated orange peel
- 1½ teaspoons baking soda
- 1 teaspoon cinnamon
- ½ teaspoon ginger
- ¼ teaspoon salt
- ¼ teaspoon cloves

ICING
- 1 recipe Buttery Decorator Icing p. 184
- 3 drops red food color
- 6 drops yellow food color
- 4 drops green food color
  - Miniature chocolate chips
  - Candy corn
  - Gumdrops

In large bowl, beat sugar and margarine until light and fluffy. Add molasses and egg; blend well. Stir in flour and remaining cookie ingredients; mix well. Cover with plastic wrap; refrigerate 1 to 3 hours for easier handling.

Heat oven to 350°F. On well-floured surface, roll half of dough at a time to ⅛-inch thickness. Keep remaining dough refrigerated. Cut with floured 3-inch pumpkin-shaped or round cookie cutter. Place 1 inch apart on ungreased cookie sheets. Bake at 350°F. for 6 to 9 minutes or until set. Immediately remove from cookie sheets.

In small bowl, combine half of Buttery Decorator Icing, 3 drops red food color and 3 drops of the yellow food color; blend well to make orange icing. Divide remaining icing mixture in half; place in 2 small bowls. Add 4 drops green food color to 1 bowl and remaining 3 drops yellow food color to second bowl; blend each well. To decorate cookies, frost each cookie with orange-colored icing. Use green and yellow icings, chocolate chips, candy corn and gumdrops to make faces on frosted cookies.

Yield: 24 cookies.

Molasses Jack-O'-Lantern Cookies

HIGH ALTITUDE:
Above 3500 Feet: Decrease sugar to ⅔ cup; increase flour to 2½ cups. Bake as directed above.

NUTRITION PER SERVING:
Calories 220; Protein 1g; Carbohydrate 35g; Fat 9g; Sodium 160mg.

LINZER STARS

Red jelly is sandwiched between tender cookies.

- ½ cup sugar
- ½ cup margarine or butter, softened
- 1 tablespoon milk
- 1 teaspoon vanilla
- 1 egg
- 1¼ cups all purpose flour
- 1 teaspoon cream of tartar
- ½ teaspoon baking soda
- ¼ teaspoon salt
  - Powdered sugar
- ½ cup cherry or red currant jelly

In large bowl, beat sugar and margarine until light and fluffy. Add milk, vanilla and egg; blend well. Stir in flour, cream of tartar, baking soda and salt; mix well. Cover with plastic wrap; refrigerate 3 hours for easier handling.

Heat oven to 425°F. Using cloth-covered rolling pin and well-floured pastry cloth, roll out ⅓ of dough at a time to ⅛-inch thickness. Keep remaining dough refrigerated. Cut with floured 3-inch star-shaped cookie cutter. Using 1-inch round cookie cutter, cut out center of half of dough stars to form cookie tops. Place stars 1 inch apart on ungreased cookie sheets. Return dough centers to remaining dough for rerolling.

Bake at 425°F. for 3 to 5 minutes or until edges are light golden brown. Cool 1 minute; remove from cookie sheets. Cool completely. To assemble cookies, sprinkle powdered sugar over tops of cut-out cookies. Spread ½ teaspoon jelly over bottom side of each whole cookie. Place sugar-topped cookie over jelly.

Yield: 4 dozen sandwich cookies.

HIGH ALTITUDE:
Above 3500 Feet: Increase flour to 1¼ cups plus 2 tablespoons. Bake as directed above.

NUTRITION PER SERVING:
Calories 50; Protein 1g; Carbohydrate 7g; Fat 2g; Sodium 45mg.

Grandma's Date-Filled Cookies

GRANDMA'S DATE-FILLED COOKIES

Only a few ingredients combine to create a soft, old-fashioned filled cookie. For the filling, chop up whole pitted dates or purchase chopped dates.

COOKIES
1½ cups firmly packed brown sugar
 1 cup margarine or butter, softened
 1 teaspoon vanilla
 3 eggs
3½ cups all purpose flour
 1 teaspoon baking soda

FILLING
 2 cups chopped dates
 1 cup sugar
 1 cup water

In large bowl, beat brown sugar and margarine until light and fluffy. Add vanilla and eggs; beat well. Stir in flour and baking soda; mix well. Cover with plastic wrap; refrigerate at least 2 hours for easier handling.

Meanwhile, in medium saucepan combine all filling ingredients. Bring to a boil; reduce heat and simmer 10 minutes, stirring frequently. Refrigerate until ready to use. (Mixture will thicken as it cools.)

Heat oven to 375°F. On well-floured surface, roll out ⅓ of dough at a time to ⅛-inch thickness. Keep remaining dough refrigerated. Cut with floured 2½-inch round cookie cutter. In half of cookies, cut and remove 1-inch round hole or desired shape from center.* Place whole cookies on ungreased cookie sheet. Spoon 1 teaspoon cooled filling onto center of each. Top with dough ring. Using fingertips or fork, press edges of dough to seal. Repeat with remaining dough and filling. Bake at 375°F. for 7 to 10 minutes or until light golden brown.
Yield: 3½ dozen cookies.

TIP:
* The center of a doughnut cutter or canape cutters can be used.

HIGH ALTITUDE:
Above 3500 Feet: No change.

NUTRITION PER SERVING:
Calories 150; Protein 2g; Carbohydrate 27g; Fat 5g; Sodium 90mg.

OLD-FASHIONED SUGAR COOKIES

This sensational cookie recipe of German origin is a Christmas Eve tradition in many families. Crushed caraway seed combined with tiny candy sprinkles add a wonderfully unique flavor.

COOKIES
    3   cups all purpose flour
    1   teaspoon baking powder
    1   teaspoon baking soda
   ⅛   teaspoon salt
    1   cup margarine or butter
    2   eggs
  1½   cups sugar
    1   teaspoon vanilla
   ½   teaspoon lemon extract

FROSTING
    2   cups powdered sugar
   ⅓   cup margarine or butter, softened
   ½   teaspoon vanilla
    1   to 2 tablespoons half-and-half or milk

TOPPING
   ¼   cup multi-colored candy sprinkles or
        chocolate sprinkles
   ½   to 1 teaspoon crushed caraway seed

In large bowl, combine flour, baking powder, baking soda and salt; mix well. Using fork or pastry blender, cut in 1 cup margarine until mixture is crumbly.

In small bowl, beat eggs. Gradually add sugar, 1 teaspoon vanilla and lemon extract, beating until light. Add to flour mixture in large bowl. Stir by hand until dough forms. (If necessary, knead dough with hands to mix in dry ingredients.) Cover with plastic wrap; refrigerate 1 hour for easier handling.

Heat oven to 375°F. On lightly floured surface, roll out ⅓ of dough at a time to ⅛-inch thickness. Keep remaining dough refrigerated. Cut with 2½ to 3-inch floured cookie cutters. Place 1 inch apart on ungreased cookie sheets.

Bake at 375°F. for 6 to 11 minutes or until edges are light golden brown. Immediately remove from cookie sheets. Cool completely.

In small bowl, combine all frosting ingredients, adding enough half-and-half for desired piping consistency; blend until smooth. In shallow bowl, combine topping ingredients. Using decorating bag fitted with large writing tip or small star tip, pipe several ¼ to ½-inch dollops of frosting on each cookie. Sprinkle immediately with topping to coat frosting dollops. Let stand until set.
Yield: 4 to 5 dozen cookies.

HIGH ALTITUDE:
Above 3500 Feet: Increase flour to 3¼ cups; decrease sugar to 1¼ cups. Bake as directed above.

NUTRITION PER SERVING:
Calories 100; Protein 1g; Carbohydrate 13g; Fat 4g; Sodium 75mg.

LEMON BLACK-EYED SUSAN COOKIES

    1   cup sugar
    1   cup margarine or butter, softened
    3   tablespoons lemon juice
    1   egg
    3   cups all purpose flour
  1½   teaspoons baking powder
   ¼   teaspoon salt
    1   egg yolk
    1   teaspoon water
        Few drops yellow food color
   ¾   cup semi-sweet chocolate chips

In large bowl, beat sugar and margarine until light and fluffy. Add lemon juice and egg; blend well. Stir in flour, baking powder and salt; mix well. Cover with plastic wrap; refrigerate 1 hour for easier handling.

Heat oven to 400°F. On lightly floured surface, roll half of dough at a time to ¼-inch thickness. Keep remaining dough refrigerated. Cut with floured 2 to 3-inch flower-shaped cookie cutter. Place 1 inch apart on ungreased cookie sheets. In small bowl, combine egg yolk and water; blend well. Stir in food color. Brush tops of cookies with egg yolk mixture.

Bake at 400°F. for 5 to 7 minutes or until edges are light golden brown. Immediately place chocolate chip in center of each cookie. Remove from cookie sheets.
Yield: 5½ dozen cookies.

HIGH ALTITUDE:
Above 3500 Feet: No change.

NUTRITION PER SERVING:
Calories 70; Protein 1g; Carbohydrate 9g; Fat 4g; Sodium 50mg.

CHOCOLATE VALENTINE COOKIES

Bake a batch of these special heart-shaped cookies for that special Valentine's Day party. A creamy cherry filling is sandwiched between chocolate cookies.

COOKIES
      1 cup sugar
      1 cup margarine or butter, softened
    1/4 cup milk
      1 teaspoon vanilla
      1 egg
  2 3/4 cups all purpose flour
    1/2 cup unsweetened cocoa
    3/4 teaspoon baking powder
    1/4 teaspoon baking soda

FROSTING
      2 cups powdered sugar
    1/2 cup margarine or butter, softened
         Red food color
      2 to 3 tablespoons maraschino cherry liquid
         or milk

In large bowl, beat sugar and 1 cup margarine until light and fluffy. Add milk, vanilla and egg; blend well. Stir in flour, cocoa, baking powder and baking soda; mix well. Cover with plastic wrap; refrigerate 1 hour for easier handling.

Heat oven to 350°F. On floured surface, roll out 1/3 of dough at a time to 1/8-inch thickness. Keep remaining dough refrigerated. Cut with floured 2 1/2-inch heart-shaped cookie cutter. Place half of the hearts 1 inch apart on ungreased cookie sheets. Cut a 1-inch heart-shape from the centers of remaining hearts. Place cut-out hearts on cookie sheets. Return small hearts to remaining dough for rerolling.

Bake at 350°F. for 9 to 11 minutes or until set. Immediately remove from cookie sheets; cool completely.

In small bowl, combine all frosting ingredients, adding enough cherry liquid for desired spreading consistency; blend until smooth. Frost bottom side of whole cookies. Place cut-out cookies over frosting.
Yield: 4 dozen sandwich cookies.

HIGH ALTITUDE:
Above 3500 Feet: Decrease baking powder to 1/4 teaspoon. Bake as directed above.

NUTRITION PER SERVING:
Calories 110; Protein 1g; Carbohydrate 14g; Fat 6g; Sodium 85mg.

SANDWICHED MINT SURPRISES

You'll notice that these cookies have no sugar in the dough. The sweetness comes from dipping the cookies in sugar and from the mints baked in the center.

      2 cups all purpose flour
      1 cup margarine or butter, softened
    1/3 cup half-and-half
      3 tablespoons unsweetened cocoa
    1/2 teaspoon vanilla
         Sugar
     36 thin pastel mint wafers

In large bowl, beat flour, margarine, half-and-half, cocoa and vanilla until well blended. Cover with plastic wrap; refrigerate 30 minutes for easier handling.

Heat oven to 375°F. Lightly grease cookie sheets. On lightly floured surface, roll half of dough to 1/8-inch thickness. Keep remaining dough refrigerated. Cut with lightly floured 2-inch round cookie cutter. Dip 1 side of each dough round in sugar. Place half of dough rounds, sugared side down, on greased cookie sheets. Place mint wafer in center of each dough round. Top each with second dough round, sugared side up. Press fork firmly around edges of each to seal.

Bake at 375°F. for 8 to 10 minutes or until set. Cool 1 minute; remove from cookie sheets.
Yield: 3 dozen cookies.

HIGH ALTITUDE:
Above 3500 Feet: No change.

NUTRITION PER SERVING:
Calories 100; Protein 1g; Carbohydrate 11g; Fat 6g; Sodium 75mg.

POPPY SEED SUGAR COOKIES

Orange and almond flavors and a poppy seed glaze combine to create a new version of the rolled sugar cookie. Cut them large for the cookie jar or small and dainty for parties.

COOKIES

1¼ cups sugar
⅔ cup margarine or butter, softened
1 teaspoon almond extract
1 teaspoon vanilla
1 teaspoon butter flavor, if desired
1 tablespoon orange juice
2 eggs
3 cups all purpose flour
2 tablespoons poppy seed
2 teaspoons baking powder
½ to 1 teaspoon salt

GLAZE

⅓ cup sugar
¼ teaspoon poppy seed
2 tablespoons orange juice
¼ teaspoon almond extract
¼ teaspoon vanilla
1 teaspoon butter flavor, if desired

In large bowl, beat 1¼ cups sugar, margarine, 1 teaspoon almond extract, 1 teaspoon vanilla and 1 teaspoon butter flavor until light and fluffy. Add 1 tablespoon orange juice and eggs; blend well. By hand, stir in flour, 2 tablespoons poppy seed, baking powder and salt until well blended. If necessary, refrigerate dough for easier handling or stir in small amount of flour until no longer sticky.

Heat oven to 350°F. On lightly floured surface, roll out ⅓ of dough at a time to ⅛ to ¼-inch thickness. Keep remaining dough refrigerated. Cut with 2½ to 3-inch cookie cutter of desired shape. Place 2 inches apart on ungreased cookie sheets.

Bake at 350°F. for 9 to 12 minutes or until light golden brown. While cookies are baking, combine all glaze ingredients; mix well. Immediately brush baked cookies with glaze, stirring glaze occasionally. Cool 1 minute; remove from cookie sheets. Let stand until glaze is set.

Yield: 2½ to 3 dozen cookies.

HIGH ALTITUDE:
Above 3500 Feet: No change.

NUTRITION PER SERVING:
Calories 110; Protein 2g; Carbohydrate 17g; Fat 4g; Sodium 120mg.

BROWN SUGAR CUTOUTS

These caramel-flavored cookies are wonderful just as they are; however, for a holiday cookie tray you may wish to decorate them with a simple vanilla icing.

1 cup margarine or butter, softened
1 cup firmly packed brown sugar
1 teaspoon vanilla
1 egg
2½ cups all purpose flour
½ teaspoon baking soda

In large bowl, beat margarine and brown sugar until light and fluffy. Add vanilla and egg; blend well. Stir in flour and baking soda; mix well. Cover with plastic wrap; refrigerate 1 to 2 hours for easier handling.

Heat oven to 375°F. On floured surface, roll out ⅓ of dough at a time to ⅛-inch thickness. Keep remaining dough refrigerated. Cut with floured 1¾ to 2-inch cookie cutter. Place 1 inch apart on ungreased cookie sheets.

Bake at 375°F. for 5 to 8 minutes or until light golden brown. Immediately remove from cookie sheets.

Yield: 4 dozen cookies.

HIGH ALTITUDE:
Above 3500 Feet: Increase flour to 3 cups. Bake as directed above.

NUTRITION PER SERVING:
Calories 80; Protein 1g; Carbohydrate 9g; Fat 4g; Sodium 60mg.

STEP-BY-STEP FEATURE ∾
How to Make Cut-Out Cookies

STEP 1. Dust a rolling pin and flat, smooth surface with flour. Use just enough flour to prevent sticking. Shape a portion of dough into a flattened ball.

STEP 2. With light strokes, roll from the center of the dough to the edges. Repeat until dough is of uniform desired thickness.

STEP 3. Cut out dough with floured cookie cutter, cutting shapes close together. Transfer cookies to an ungreased cookie sheet using a pancake turner.

WHOLE WHEAT GINGERBREAD BOYS AND GIRLS

Create a variety of gingerbread folks using various sized cookie cutters. Let imaginations run wild as children help to decorate them with frosting and small candies.

COOKIES

1½	**cups sugar**
1	**cup margarine or butter, softened**
⅓	**cup molasses**
1	**egg**
2¼	**cups all purpose flour**
1	**cup whole wheat flour**
2	**teaspoons baking soda**
½	**teaspoon salt**
2	**teaspoons ginger**
2	**teaspoons cinnamon**

FROSTING AND DECORATIONS

2	**cups powdered sugar**
⅓	**cup margarine or butter, softened**
½	**teaspoon vanilla**
1	**to 2 tablespoons half-and-half or milk**
	Assorted small candies, if desired

In large bowl, beat sugar and 1 cup margarine until light and fluffy. Add molasses and egg; blend well. Stir in all purpose and whole wheat flour, baking soda, salt, ginger and cinnamon; mix well. If necessary, cover with plastic wrap and refrigerate 1 hour for easier handling.

Heat oven to 350°F. On lightly floured surface, roll out ¼ of dough at a time to ⅛-inch thickness. Keep remaining dough refrigerated. Cut with floured 5-inch (or desired size) gingerbread boy and girl cookie cutters. Place 1 inch apart on ungreased cookie sheets. If desired, move arms and legs of unbaked cookies for different poses. Cut scraps of dough into hats, scarves, etc.; place on cookie sheet against or slightly overlapping cookies.

Bake at 350°F. for 6 to 9 minutes or until set. Cool 1 minute. Remove from cookie sheets. Cool completely.

(Recipe continued on next page.)

Whole Wheat Gingerbread Boys and Girls

(Recipe continued from previous page.)

In medium bowl, combine powdered sugar, ⅓ cup margarine, vanilla and enough half-and-half for desired spreading or piping consistency; blend until smooth. Frost and decorate as desired. Let stand until frosting is set. Store in loosely covered container.

Yield: 2½ dozen cookies.

HIGH ALTITUDE:
Above 3500 Feet: Decrease sugar to 1 cup; increase all purpose flour to 2¾ cups. Bake as directed above.

NUTRITION PER SERVING:
Calories 210; Protein 2g; Carbohydrate 33g; Fat 9g; Sodium 210mg.

FROSTED GINGERBREAD CUTOUTS

Cinnamon, ginger, cardamom and cloves flavor these cookies.

COOKIES
1½ cups sugar
 1 cup margarine or butter, softened
 3 tablespoons molasses
 1 egg
 2 tablespoons water or milk
3¼ cups all purpose flour
 2 teaspoons baking soda
 ½ teaspoon salt
 2 teaspoons cinnamon
1½ teaspoons ginger
 ½ teaspoon cardamom
 ½ teaspoon cloves

FROSTING
 ¾ cup water
 1 envelope unflavored gelatin
 ¾ cup sugar
 ¾ cup powdered sugar
 1 teaspoon baking powder
 1 teaspoon vanilla

In large bowl, beat 1½ cups sugar, margarine and molasses until light and fluffy. Add egg and 2 tablespoons water; blend well. Stir in flour, baking soda, salt, cinnamon, ginger, cardamom and cloves; mix well to form a smooth dough. Cover with plastic wrap; refrigerate 1 hour for easier handling.

Heat oven to 350°F. On floured surface, roll out ⅓ of dough to ⅛-inch thickness. Keep remaining dough refrigerated. Cut with floured 2½-inch cookie cutters. Place 1 inch apart on ungreased cookie sheets. Repeat with remaining dough. Bake at 350°F. for 9 to 11 minutes or until set. Immediately remove from cookie sheets. Cool completely.

In 2-quart saucepan, combine ¾ cup water and gelatin; let stand 5 minutes. Stir in ¾ cup sugar; bring to a boil. Reduce heat; simmer 10 minutes. Stir in powdered sugar; beat until foamy. Stir in baking powder and vanilla; beat at highest speed until thick, about 10 minutes. Spread frosting on cooled cookies or pipe frosting following outline of cookies. Allow frosting to set for several hours before storing.

Yield: 8 to 10 dozen cookies.

HIGH ALTITUDE :
Above 3500 Feet: No change.

NUTRITION PER SERVING:
Calories 45; Protein 1g; Carbohydrate 7g; Fat 2g; Sodium 50mg.

COOK'S NOTE

GINGERBREAD HISTORY

Stories about gingerbread have appeared since the beginning of written history. The earliest gingerbread was made from bread crumbs, honey and spices; gradually the crumbs and honey were replaced by flour and molasses.

Ginger, the predominant spice in gingerbread, was used during the Middle Ages both as a preservative and as a medicine for a variety of ills. Because gingerbread did not spoil as quickly as other baked goods did in those days, it was thought to be somewhat magical.

For hundreds of years in Europe, cookies were made by pressing gingerbread into molds before baking. Spicy little figures of people and animals, sometimes decorated with edible gold paint, were sold at medieval fairs. In the 17th century, gingerbread baking was a profession in itself and gingerbread bakers alone had the right to make it, except at Christmas time, when everyone could make it.

DATE MAPLE CREAM BARS

〰️

Cooking the filling for this luscious bar softens the dates and thickens the mixture. These bars have delicious old-fashioned flavor and will remind you of the date bars that your grandma used to make.

FILLING
- ¾ cup firmly packed brown sugar
- 1 tablespoon cornstarch
- 1½ cups finely chopped dates
- 1½ cups dairy sour cream
- 1 teaspoon maple extract
- 3 egg yolks

BASE AND TOPPING
- 1¼ cups all purpose flour
- 2 cups quick-cooking rolled oats
- ¾ cup firmly packed brown sugar
- ½ teaspoon baking soda
- ¾ cup margarine or butter

Heat oven to 350°F. Grease 13x9-inch pan. In medium saucepan, combine all filling ingredients. Cook over medium heat until slightly thickened, stirring constantly. Cool slightly.

In medium bowl, combine flour, rolled oats, ¾ cup brown sugar and baking soda; mix well. With pastry blender or fork, cut in margarine until mixture is crumbly. Reserve 1½ cups oat mixture for topping. Press remaining oat mixture evenly in bottom of greased pan.

Bake at 350°F. for 10 minutes. Spoon filling evenly over base. Sprinkle with reserved oat mixture. Return to oven and bake an additional 20 to 30 minutes or until light golden brown and set. Cool completely. Cut into bars.
Yield: 36 bars.

HIGH ALTITUDE:
Above 3500 Feet: No change.

NUTRITION PER SERVING:
Calories 150; Protein 2g; Carbohydrate 21g; Fat 7g; Sodium 70mg.

KWIK-KRUMB RAISIN BARS

〰️

This yummy bar, filled with the goodness of raisins and applesauce, is perfect with a hot cup of coffee or tea.

FILLING
- 2½ cups raisins
- 1 cup water
- 1 cup applesauce
- 1 teaspoon lemon juice
- ¼ teaspoon cinnamon

BASE AND TOPPING
- 2 cups rolled oats
- 1 cup all purpose flour
- ½ cup sugar
- ½ cup coconut
- ¾ cup margarine or butter

In medium saucepan, bring raisins and water to a boil. Reduce heat; simmer 15 minutes. Drain; stir in applesauce, lemon juice and cinnamon. Set aside.

Heat oven to 350°F. In large bowl, combine oats, flour, sugar and coconut. Using pastry blender or fork, cut in margarine until mixture resembles coarse crumbs. Reserve 2½ cups of crumb mixture for topping. Press remaining crumb mixture firmly in bottom of ungreased 13x9-inch pan. Spread evenly with filling. Sprinkle with reserved crumb mixture; press lightly.

Bake at 350°F. for 30 to 40 minutes or until light golden brown. Cool completely. Cut into bars.
Yield: 36 bars.

HIGH ALTITUDE:
Above 3500 Feet: No change.

NUTRITION PER SERVING:
Calories 120; Protein 1g; Carbohydrate 18g; Fat 5g; Sodium 45mg.

APRICOT ALMOND SQUARES

Delicate fruit flavor and a streusel topping make this bar a luscious choice for a party tray.

BASE

- 1 (18.5-oz.) pkg. pudding-included yellow or white cake mix
- ½ cup margarine or butter, melted
- ½ cup finely chopped almonds
- 1 cup apricot preserves

FILLING

- 1 (8-oz.) pkg. cream cheese, softened
- ¼ cup sugar
- 2 tablespoons all purpose flour
- ⅛ teaspoon salt
- 1 teaspoon vanilla
- 1 egg
- ⅓ cup apricot preserves
- ½ cup coconut

Heat oven to 350°F. Generously grease 13x9-inch pan. In large bowl, combine cake mix and margarine; mix at low speed until crumbly. Stir in almonds. Reserve 1 cup base mixture for filling. Press remaining mixture in bottom of greased pan. Carefully spread 1 cup preserves over base.*

In same bowl, beat cream cheese, sugar, flour, salt, vanilla and egg until well blended. Stir in ⅓ cup preserves at low speed. Carefully spread filling mixture over base. Combine reserved 1 cup base mixture and coconut; sprinkle over filling.

Bake at 350°F. for 30 to 40 minutes or until golden brown and center is set. Cool completely. Cut into bars. Store in refrigerator.

Yield: 36 bars.

TIP:

* For ease in spreading, preserves can be warmed slightly.

HIGH ALTITUDE:
Above 3500 Feet: No change.

NUTRITION PER SERVING:
Calories 160; Protein 2g; Carbohydrate 22g; Fat 8g; Sodium 150mg.

CARAMEL APPLE BARS

This is the perfect recipe when apples are plentiful. Caramel ice cream topping combines with apples and nuts for rich, moist bars.

CRUST

- 2 cups all purpose flour
- 2 cups quick-cooking rolled oats
- 1½ cups firmly packed brown sugar
- 1 teaspoon baking soda
- 1¼ cups margarine or butter, melted

FILLING

- 1½ cups caramel ice cream topping
- ½ cup all purpose flour
- 2 cups coarsely chopped apples
- ½ cup chopped walnuts or pecans

Heat oven to 350°F. Grease 15x10x1-inch baking pan. In large bowl, combine all crust ingredients; mix at low speed until crumbly. Press half of crumb mixture, about 2½ cups, in greased pan. Reserve remaining crumb mixture for topping. Bake at 350°F. for 8 minutes.

In small saucepan over medium heat, combine caramel topping and ½ cup flour. Bring to a boil, stirring constantly. Boil 3 to 5 minutes or until mixture thickens slightly, stirring constantly. Sprinkle apples and nuts onto warm base. Pour caramel mixture evenly over top. Sprinkle with reserved crumbs.

Return to oven and bake 20 to 25 minutes or until golden brown. Cool completely. Cut into bars.* Store in tightly covered container.

Yield: 48 bars.

TIP:
* For ease in cutting, refrigerate bars.

HIGH ALTITUDE:
Above 3500 Feet: Bake at 375°F. as directed above.

NUTRITION PER SERVING:
Calories 150; Protein 2g; Carbohydrate 22g; Fat 6g; Sodium 135mg.

Oatmeal Carmelitas

This time-tested favorite is an often-requested recipe that is easy to make and delicious to eat. Prepare it for your next potluck or bake sale.

CRUST
- 2 cups all purpose flour
- 2 cups quick-cooking rolled oats
- 1½ cups firmly packed brown sugar
- 1 teaspoon baking soda
- ½ teaspoon salt
- 1¼ cups margarine or butter, softened

FILLING
- 1 (12.5-oz.) jar (1 cup) caramel ice cream topping
- 3 tablespoons all purpose flour
- 1 (6-oz.) pkg. (1 cup) semi-sweet chocolate chips
- ½ cup chopped nuts

Heat oven to 350°F. Grease 13x9-inch pan. In large bowl, blend all crust ingredients at low speed until crumbly. Press half of crumb mixture, about 3 cups, in bottom of greased pan. Reserve remaining crumb mixture for topping. Bake at 350°F. for 10 minutes. Meanwhile, in small bowl combine caramel topping and 3 tablespoons flour; set aside. Sprinkle warm crust with chocolate chips and nuts. Drizzle evenly with caramel mixture; sprinkle with reserved crumb mixture.

Return to oven and bake an additional 18 to 22 minutes or until golden brown. Cool completely. Refrigerate 1 to 2 hours or until filling is set. Cut into bars.

Yield: 36 bars.

HIGH ALTITUDE:
Above 3500 Feet: No change.

NUTRITION PER SERVING:
Calories 200; Protein 3g; Carbohydrate 27g; Fat 9g; Sodium 160mg.

Oatmeal Chocolate Chip Bars

Healthful oats help give these lunch box bars their chewy cookie texture.

- 1½ cups firmly packed brown sugar
- 1 cup shortening
- 2 tablespoons molasses
- 2 teaspoons vanilla
- 2 eggs
- 3 cups quick-cooking rolled oats
- 1 cup all purpose flour
- 1 teaspoon baking soda
- 1 teaspoon salt
- ¾ cup chopped nuts
- 1 (12-oz.) pkg. (2 cups) semi-sweet chocolate chips

Heat oven to 350°F. Grease 15x10x1 or 13x9-inch pan. In large bowl, beat brown sugar and shortening until light and fluffy. Add molasses, vanilla and eggs; blend well. Stir in oats, flour, baking soda and salt; blend well. Stir in nuts and chocolate chips. Spread in greased pan.

Bake at 350°F. for 20 to 25 minutes or until light golden brown and center is set. Cool slightly. Cut into bars. Serve warm or cool.

Yield: 48 bars.

HIGH ALTITUDE:
Above 3500 Feet: No change.

NUTRITION PER SERVING:
Calories 140; Protein 2g; Carbohydrate 17g; Fat 8g; Sodium 75mg.

Cook's Note

BAKING BARS IN JELLY ROLL PANS

Follow specific recipe directions for pan sizes. Standard jelly roll pans are 15x10x1-inch. Using a jelly roll pan that does not have 1-inch sides may result in the recipe spilling out of the pan during baking.

POPPY SEED SQUARES

Delicate crumb layers that melt in your mouth surround a marvelous poppy seed filling. It's no wonder these bars were a favorite of our taste panel.

FILLING
- ⅓ **cup poppy seed, ground***
- ⅓ **cup almonds, ground***
- ⅓ **cup sugar**
- ⅓ **cup milk**
- 2 **tablespoons margarine or butter**
- ½ **teaspoon almond extract**
- 1 **egg white**

BASE
- 1¾ **cups all purpose flour**
- ¾ **cup powdered sugar**
- ⅓ **cup ground almonds**
- 1 **teaspoon baking powder**
- ¾ **cup margarine or butter**
- 1 **teaspoon almond extract**
- 1 **egg yolk**

To prepare filling, in small saucepan combine poppy seed, almonds, sugar and milk. Cook over medium heat 10 to 15 minutes or until thick and milk is absorbed. Cool 15 minutes. Stir in 2 tablespoons margarine, ½ teaspoon almond extract and egg white; blend well. Cool.

Heat oven to 350°F. In medium bowl, combine flour, powdered sugar, ⅓ cup ground almonds and baking powder. Using pastry blender or fork, cut in ¾ cup margarine until mixture resembles coarse crumbs. With fork, stir in 1 teaspoon almond extract and egg yolk. Press half of crumb mixture firmly in bottom of ungreased 9-inch square pan. Carefully spread with filling mixture. Sprinkle with remaining crumb mixture; pat lightly.

Bake at 350°F. for 25 to 33 minutes or until light golden brown. Cool completely. Cut into bars.
Yield: 25 bars.

TIP:
* Poppy seed and almonds can be ground together in blender at medium speed for 1 minute, scraping sides once.

HIGH ALTITUDE:
Above 3500 Feet: No change.

NUTRITION PER SERVING:
Calories 150; Protein 2g; Carbohydrate 14g; Fat 9g; Sodium 90mg.

SUNBURST LEMON BARS

These home-baked lemon bars, with a delicate crumb crust and mouth-watering lemon filling, have been a favorite for generations, particularly for family gatherings and potlucks.

CRUST
- 2 **cups all purpose flour**
- ½ **cup powdered sugar**
- 1 **cup margarine or butter, softened**

FILLING
- 4 **eggs, slightly beaten**
- 2 **cups sugar**
- ¼ **cup all purpose flour**
- 1 **teaspoon baking powder**
- ¼ **cup lemon juice**

FROSTING
- 1 **cup powdered sugar**
- 2 **to 3 tablespoons lemon juice**

Heat oven to 350°F. In large bowl, combine all crust ingredients at low speed until crumbly. Press mixture evenly in bottom of ungreased 13x9-inch pan. Bake at 350°F. for 20 to 30 minutes or until light golden brown.

Meanwhile, in large bowl combine all filling ingredients except lemon juice; blend well. Stir in ¼ cup lemon juice. Pour mixture over warm crust.

Return to oven and bake an additional 25 to 30 minutes or until top is light golden brown. Cool completely.

In small bowl, combine 1 cup powdered sugar and enough lemon juice for desired spreading consistency; blend until smooth. Spread over cooled bars. Cut into bars.
Yield: 36 bars.

HIGH ALTITUDE:
Above 3500 Feet: No change.

NUTRITION PER SERVING:
Calories 140; Protein 2g; Carbohydrate 22g; Fat 6g; Sodium 75mg.

Sunburst Lemon Bars

GINGERBREAD BARS

~

Enjoy these not-too-sweet bars with hot apple cider on a crisp autumn day. Store them tightly covered.

- ½ cup sugar
- ½ cup oil
- ½ cup molasses
- 1 egg
- 1½ cups all purpose flour
- ¾ teaspoon baking soda
- ½ teaspoon cinnamon
- ¼ teaspoon salt
- ¼ teaspoon nutmeg
- ¼ teaspoon cloves
- ¼ cup boiling water
- ½ cup granola
- ½ cup raisins
  Powdered sugar, if desired

Heat oven to 350°F. Grease 13x9-inch pan. In large bowl, beat sugar, oil and molasses until well blended. Add egg; blend well. Add flour, baking soda, cinnamon, salt, nutmeg and cloves; mix well. Add boiling water; blend well. Stir in granola and raisins. Spread in greased pan.

Bake at 350°F. for 20 to 30 minutes or until toothpick inserted in center comes out clean. Cool completely. Sprinkle with powdered sugar. Cut into bars.

Yield: 36 bars.

HIGH ALTITUDE:
Above 3500 Feet: Increase flour to 2 cups; increase boiling water to ½ cup. Bake as directed above.

NUTRITION PER SERVING:
Calories 80; Protein 1g; Carbohydrate 12g; Fat 4g; Sodium 45mg.

SALTED PEANUT CHEWS

~

Reminiscent of a popular candy bar, these are sure to be a favorite with everyone.

CRUST
- 1½ cups all purpose flour
- ⅔ cup firmly packed brown sugar
- ½ teaspoon baking powder
- ½ teaspoon salt
- ¼ teaspoon baking soda
- ½ cup margarine or butter, softened
- 1 teaspoon vanilla
- 2 egg yolks
- 3 cups miniature marshmallows

TOPPING
- ⅔ cup corn syrup
- ¼ cup margarine or butter
- 2 teaspoons vanilla
- 1 (12-oz.) pkg. (2 cups) peanut butter chips
- 2 cups crisp rice cereal
- 2 cups salted peanuts

Heat oven to 350°F. In large bowl, combine all crust ingredients except marshmallows at low speed until crumbly. Press firmly in bottom of ungreased 13x9-inch pan.

Bake at 350°F. for 12 to 15 minutes or until light golden brown. Remove from oven. Immediately sprinkle with marshmallows. Return to oven and bake an additional 1 to 2 minutes or until marshmallows just begin to puff. Cool while preparing topping.

In large saucepan, combine all topping ingredients except cereal and peanuts; heat just until chips are melted and mixture is smooth, stirring constantly. Remove from heat; stir in cereal and peanuts. Immediately spoon warm topping over marshmallows; spread to cover. Refrigerate until firm. Cut into bars.

Yield: 36 bars.

HIGH ALTITUDE:
Above 3500 Feet: No change.

NUTRITION PER SERVING:
Calories 210; Protein 5g; Carbohydrate 23g; Fat 11g; Sodium 200mg.

AUSTRIAN CREAM CHEESE BARS

When the occasion is special, you'll enjoy this layered candy-like bar.

CRUST
1½ cups all purpose flour
1 cup firmly packed brown sugar
½ teaspoon cinnamon
⅔ cup margarine or butter, softened

TOPPING
1 (8-oz.) pkg. cream cheese, softened
¾ cup sugar
2 tablespoons all purpose flour
2 eggs
1 (6-oz.) pkg. (1 cup) semi-sweet chocolate chips

GLAZE
1 (6-oz.) pkg. (1 cup) semi-sweet chocolate chips
½ to ¾ cup chopped pecans or walnuts, toasted, p. 23

Heat oven to 350°F. In large bowl, combine all crust ingredients. Beat at medium speed about 2 minutes or until crumbly and well blended. Press mixture into ungreased 13x9-inch pan. Bake at 350°F. for 12 minutes. Remove from oven.

In small bowl, beat cream cheese, sugar, 2 tablespoons flour and eggs at medium speed until smooth, about 2 minutes. Stir in 1 cup chocolate chips. Pour over partially baked crust.

Return to oven and bake an additional 15 to 20 minutes or until topping is almost set. Remove from oven; immediately sprinkle 1 cup chocolate chips over top. Return to oven for 1 minute to melt chips. Gently spread melted chips over top. Sprinkle with pecans; lightly press into glaze. Refrigerate 1 hour. Cut into bars. Store in refrigerator.
Yield: 36 bars.

HIGH ALTITUDE:
Above 3500 Feet: Increase flour in crust to 1¾ cups. Bake as directed above.

NUTRITION PER SERVING:
Calories 190; Protein 2g; Carbohydrate 21g; Fat 11g; Sodium 60mg.

ROCKY ROAD CRESCENT BARS

Marshmallows, peanuts and chocolate chips top a creamy peanut butter filling and bake into a tempting sweet treat.

1 (8-oz.) can refrigerated crescent dinner rolls
½ cup sugar
¾ cup peanut butter
1 (8-oz.) pkg. cream cheese, softened
½ cup corn syrup
1 teaspoon vanilla
1 egg
1½ cups miniature marshmallows
¾ cup salted peanuts or other nuts, chopped
1 (6-oz.) pkg. (1 cup) semi-sweet chocolate chips

Heat oven to 375°F. Unroll dough into 2 long rectangles. Place in ungreased 13x9-inch pan; press over bottom to form crust. Firmly press perforations to seal. Bake at 375°F. for 5 minutes.

In medium bowl, combine sugar, peanut butter and cream cheese; blend until smooth. Stir in corn syrup, vanilla and egg; mix well. Pour mixture over partially baked crust; spread evenly. Sprinkle with marshmallows, peanuts and chocolate chips.

Return to oven and bake an additional 25 to 30 minutes or until filling is firm to touch. Cool completely. Refrigerate 1 to 2 hours. Cut into bars. Store in refrigerator.
Yield: 36 bars.

NUTRITION PER SERVING:
Calories 150; Protein 3g; Carbohydrate 15g; Fat 9g; Sodium 125mg.

CHEWY APPLESAUCE BARS

Muesli cereal is a blend of grains, fruits and nuts that has been a tradition in many parts of Europe for centuries. It adds texture, flavor and whole grain goodness to these breakfast bars.

BARS
- 1 cup firmly packed brown sugar
- ½ cup margarine or butter, softened
- 1 cup applesauce
- 1 egg
- 1½ cups all purpose flour
- 1 teaspoon baking soda
- 1 teaspoon cinnamon
- ¼ teaspoon salt
- ¼ teaspoon cloves
- ¼ teaspoon nutmeg
- 2 cups muesli cereal

GLAZE
- 2 tablespoons margarine or butter
- ¼ cup firmly packed brown sugar
- 1 teaspoon powdered sugar

Heat oven to 350°F. Grease and flour 13x9-inch pan. In large bowl, beat 1 cup brown sugar and ½ cup margarine until light and fluffy. Add applesauce and egg; blend well. Stir in flour, baking soda, cinnamon, salt, cloves and nutmeg; mix well. Stir in cereal. Spread mixture in greased and floured pan.

Bake at 350°F. for 25 to 30 minutes or until toothpick inserted in center comes out clean.

To prepare glaze, melt 2 tablespoons margarine in small saucepan over low heat. Stir in ¼ cup brown sugar. Cook about 1 minute or until mixture bubbles, stirring constantly. Remove from heat. Stir in powdered sugar. Quickly drizzle glaze over top of warm bars. Cool completely. Cut into bars.
Yield: 24 to 36 bars.

HIGH ALTITUDE:
Above 3500 Feet: No change.

NUTRITION PER SERVING:
Calories 100; Protein 1g; Carbohydrate 16g; Fat 4g; Sodium 100mg.

CHOCOLATY CARAMEL PECAN BARS

These indulgent candy-like bars won rave reviews from our taste panel of home economists. A buttery, tender crust is topped with caramel, pecans and chocolate. What could be more inviting?

CRUST
- ½ cup powdered sugar
- ½ cup margarine or butter, softened
- 1 tablespoon whipping cream
- 1 cup all purpose flour

FILLING
- 24 vanilla caramels, unwrapped
- ⅓ cup whipping cream
- 2 cups pecan halves

TOPPING
- 1 teaspoon margarine or butter
- ½ cup milk chocolate chips
- 2 tablespoons whipping cream

Heat oven to 325°F. Grease 9-inch square pan. In medium bowl, combine powdered sugar, ½ cup margarine and 1 tablespoon whipping cream; blend well. Add flour; mix until crumbly. With floured hands, press evenly in greased pan. Bake at 325°F. for 15 to 20 minutes or until firm to touch.

Meanwhile, in medium saucepan combine caramels and ⅓ cup whipping cream. Cook over low heat until caramels are melted and mixture is smooth, stirring occasionally. Remove from heat. Add pecans; stir well to coat. Immediately spoon over baked crust; spread carefully to cover.

In small saucepan over low heat, melt 1 teaspoon margarine and chocolate chips, stirring constantly. Stir in 2 tablespoons whipping cream. Drizzle over filling. Refrigerate 1 hour or until filling is firm. Cut into bars.
Yield: 24 bars.

NUTRITION PER SERVING:
Calories 200; Protein 2g; Carbohydrate 18g; Fat 14g; Sodium 75mg.

RASPBERRY-FILLED WHITE CHOCOLATE BARS

There is no sugar added to spreadable fruit. You'll find it in the jam and jelly section of most large grocery stores. It's delicious baked in these special occasion bars.

- ½ cup margarine or butter
- 1 (12-oz.) pkg. (2 cups) vanilla milk chips or 2 (6-oz.) pkg. white baking bars, chopped
- 2 eggs
- ½ cup sugar
- 1 cup all purpose flour
- ½ teaspoon salt
- 1 teaspoon amaretto liqueur or almond extract
- ½ cup raspberry spreadable fruit or jam
- ¼ cup sliced almonds, toasted, p. 23

Heat oven to 325°F. Grease and flour 9-inch square pan or 8-inch square baking dish. Melt margarine in small saucepan over low heat. Remove from heat. Add 1 cup of the vanilla milk chips. Let stand; do not stir.

In large bowl, beat eggs until foamy. Gradually add sugar, beating at high speed until lemon-colored. Stir in vanilla milk chip mixture. Add flour, salt and amaretto; mix at low speed until just combined. Spread half of batter (about 1 cup) in greased and floured pan. Bake at 325°F. for 15 to 20 minutes or until light golden brown.

Stir remaining 1 cup vanilla milk chips into remaining half of batter; set aside. Melt spreadable fruit in small saucepan over low heat. Spread evenly over warm, partially baked crust. Gently spoon teaspoonfuls of remaining batter over fruit spread. (Some fruit spread may show through batter.) Sprinkle with almonds.

Return to oven and bake an additional 25 to 35 minutes or until toothpick inserted in center comes out clean. Cool completely. Cut into bars.
Yield: 16 to 24 bars.

HIGH ALTITUDE:
Above 3500 Feet: No change.

NUTRITION PER SERVING:
Calories 170; Protein 2g; Carbohydrate 21g; Fat 9g; Sodium 100mg.

WHITE CHOCOLATE ALMOND BARS

For ease in preparation, the batter is mixed in the same saucepan used to melt the white baking bar.

- 2 oz. white baking bar, chopped
- ½ cup margarine or butter
- ¾ cup sugar
- 2 eggs
- 1 teaspoon almond extract
- ⅔ cup all purpose flour
- ½ teaspoon baking powder
- ¼ teaspoon salt
- ½ cup chopped almonds
- 1 tablespoon powdered sugar

Heat oven to 350°F. Grease and lightly flour bottom only of 8 or 9-inch square pan. Melt white baking bar in medium saucepan over very low heat, stirring constantly until smooth. Add margarine; stir until melted. Remove from heat; stir in sugar. Beat in eggs 1 at a time. Add almond extract. Add flour, baking powder, salt and almonds to chocolate mixture; mix well. Spread in greased and floured pan.

Bake at 350°F. for 25 to 35 minutes or until golden brown and center is set. Cool completely. Sprinkle with powdered sugar. Cut into bars.
Yield: 24 bars.

TIPS:
White baking bar melts slower than regular chocolate.
A wire whisk works well when blending the chocolate and margarine.

HIGH ALTITUDE:
Above 3500 Feet: Decrease sugar to ⅔ cup; increase flour to ¾ cup. Bake as directed above.

NUTRITION PER SERVING:
Calories 110; Protein 2g; Carbohydrate 11g; Fat 6g; Sodium 80mg.

PEANUT BRITTLE BARS

You'll enjoy the contrast between salty and sweet in these easy-to-make bars. The surprise is the nut-like flavor the whole wheat flour contributes to the crust.

BASE
1½ cups all purpose flour
½ cup whole wheat flour
1 cup firmly packed brown sugar
1 teaspoon baking soda
¼ teaspoon salt
1 cup margarine or butter

TOPPING
2 cups salted peanuts
1 cup milk chocolate chips
1 (12.5-oz.) jar (1 cup) caramel ice cream topping
3 tablespoons all purpose flour

Heat oven to 350°F. Grease 15x10x1-inch baking pan. In large bowl, combine all base ingredients except margarine; mix well. Using pastry blender or fork, cut in margarine until crumbly. Press evenly in greased pan. Bake at 350°F. for 8 to 14 minutes or until golden brown.

Sprinkle peanuts and chocolate chips over warm base. In small bowl, combine caramel topping and 3 tablespoons flour; blend well. Drizzle evenly over chocolate chips and peanuts. Return to oven and bake an additional 12 to 18 minutes or until topping is set and golden brown. Cool completely. Cut into bars.
Yield: 48 bars.

HIGH ALTITUDE:
Above 3500 Feet: No change.

NUTRITION PER SERVING:
Calories 150; Protein 3g; Carbohydrate 17g; Fat 8g; Sodium 150mg.

ORIGINAL RECIPE
PUMPKIN BARS

Deliciously spiced and topped with cream cheese frosting, these traditional bars are great teamed with a mug of hot apple cider.

BARS
2 cups all purpose flour
2 cups sugar
2 teaspoons baking powder
1 teaspoon baking soda
1 teaspoon cinnamon
1 teaspoon nutmeg
½ teaspoon salt
½ teaspoon cloves
1 cup oil
1 (16-oz.) can (2 cups) pumpkin
4 eggs
½ cup chopped nuts
½ cup raisins

FROSTING
2 cups powdered sugar
⅓ cup margarine or butter, softened
1 (3-oz.) pkg. cream cheese, softened
1 tablespoon milk
1 teaspoon vanilla

Heat oven to 350°F. Grease 15x10x1-inch baking pan. In large bowl, combine all bar ingredients except nuts and raisins; beat at low speed until moistened. Beat 2 minutes at medium speed. Stir in nuts and raisins. Pour into greased pan.

Bake at 350°F. for 25 to 30 minutes or until toothpick inserted in center comes out clean. Cool completely.

In small bowl, combine all frosting ingredients; beat until smooth. Frost cooled bars. Cut into bars. Store in refrigerator.
Yield: 48 bars.

HIGH ALTITUDE:
Above 3500 Feet: Decrease baking soda to ½ teaspoon. Bake at 375°F. for 30 to 35 minutes.

NUTRITION PER SERVING:
Calories 150; Protein 2g; Carbohydrate 20g; Fat 8g; Sodium 85mg.

Light and Spicy Pumpkin Bars

LIGHT AND SPICY PUMPKIN BARS

The combination of whole wheat flour, brown sugar and sweet spices gives these pumpkin bars a delicious rich flavor.

BARS
- 1 cup all purpose flour
- 1 cup whole wheat flour
- 1½ cups firmly packed brown sugar
- 2 teaspoons baking powder
- 1 teaspoon baking soda
- 1 teaspoon cinnamon
- ½ teaspoon nutmeg
- ½ teaspoon cloves
- ¼ teaspoon salt
- ½ cup oil
- ½ cup apple juice
- 1 (16-oz.) can (2 cups) pumpkin
- 2 eggs

FROSTING
- 1½ cups powdered sugar
- 2 tablespoons margarine or butter, softened
- ½ teaspoon vanilla
- 2 to 3 tablespoons plain yogurt

Heat oven to 350°F. Grease and flour 15x10x1-inch baking pan. In large bowl, beat all bar ingredients at low speed until moistened. Beat 2 minutes at medium speed. Spread in greased and floured pan.

Bake at 350°F. for 20 to 30 minutes or until toothpick inserted in center comes out clean. Cool completely.

In medium bowl, combine all frosting ingredients, adding enough yogurt for desired spreading consistency; beat until smooth. Frost cooled bars; sprinkle with nutmeg, if desired. Refrigerate to set frosting. Cut into bars.

Yield: 48 bars.

HIGH ALTITUDE:
Above 3500 Feet: Increase all purpose flour to 1⅓ cups; decrease baking powder to 1 teaspoon. Bake as directed above.

NUTRITION PER SERVING:
Calories 90; Protein 1g; Carbohydrate 15g; Fat 3g; Sodium 60mg.

GLAZED FRUITCAKE SQUARES

This fruitcake-like bar is festive, easy and delicious.

BARS
- 2 cups powdered sugar
- ½ cup margarine or butter, softened
- ¼ cup brandy*
- 2 eggs
- 2 cups all purpose flour
- 3 teaspoons baking powder
- 1 teaspoon salt
- 2 cups chopped candied fruit
- 1 cup coarsely chopped walnuts

GLAZE
- 1 cup powdered sugar
- 1 tablespoon margarine or butter, softened
- 1 to 2 tablespoons brandy**

Heat oven to 375°F. Grease 15x10x1-inch baking pan. In large bowl, combine powdered sugar, ½ cup margarine, ¼ cup brandy and eggs; mix well. By hand, stir in remaining bar ingredients; press in greased pan.

Bake at 375°F. for 15 to 25 minutes or until light golden brown. Cool. In small bowl, combine all glaze ingredients, adding enough brandy for desired drizzling consistency; beat until smooth. Drizzle glaze over top. When glaze is set, cut into bars.
Yield: 48 bars.

TIPS:
* To substitute for brandy in bars, use ¼ cup water or orange juice and 1 teaspoon brandy extract.
** To substitute for brandy in glaze, combine 1 to 2 tablespoons water with ½ teaspoon brandy extract.

HIGH ALTITUDE:
Above 3500 Feet: No change.

NUTRITION PER SERVING:
Calories 110; Protein 1g; Carbohydrate 16g; Fat 4g; Sodium 110mg.

WHOLE WHEAT ZUCCHINI BARS

When zucchini is plentiful, you can shred and freeze it in amounts just right for these wholesome bars.

BARS
- 3 eggs
- 1½ cups sugar
- 1 cup oil
- 1½ cups whole wheat flour
- ½ cup all purpose flour
- 1 teaspoon baking powder
- ½ teaspoon salt
- 1 teaspoon cinnamon
- 2 cups shredded zucchini
- 1 cup dried currants or raisins

GLAZE
- 1 cup powdered sugar
- ¼ teaspoon cinnamon
- 2 tablespoons margarine or butter, melted
- 2 tablespoons milk

Heat oven to 350°F. Grease 13x9-inch pan. In large bowl, beat eggs. Add sugar and oil; beat well. In medium bowl, combine whole wheat flour, all purpose flour, baking powder, salt and 1 teaspoon cinnamon. Add flour mixture to egg mixture; mix well. Stir in zucchini and currants. Spread in greased pan.

Bake at 350°F. for 40 to 50 minutes or until toothpick inserted in center comes out clean. Cool completely.

In small bowl, combine all glaze ingredients until smooth. Spread evenly over cooled bars. Cut into bars.
Yield: 36 bars.

HIGH ALTITUDE:
Above 3500 Feet: No change.

NUTRITION PER SERVING:
Calories 130; Protein 1g; Carbohydrate 17g; Fat 7g; Sodium 50mg.

THREE LAYER BARS

No flour is used to make these rich, delicious bars. They boast a chewy crust full of nuts and coconut and a creamy pudding filling that's lightly glazed with milk chocolate.

CRUST
- ½ cup margarine or butter
- ¼ cup unsweetened cocoa
- 2 teaspoons vanilla
- 1 egg, slightly beaten
- 2 cups graham cracker crumbs
- ½ cup powdered sugar
- ½ cup shredded coconut
- ½ cup chopped nuts

FILLING
- ½ cup margarine or butter
- ½ cup milk
- 1 (3-oz.) pkg. vanilla pudding and pie filling mix (not instant)
- 3 cups powdered sugar

TOPPING
- 1 (8-oz.) bar milk chocolate, cut up
- 1 tablespoon graham cracker crumbs

Heat oven to 350°F. Grease 13x9-inch pan. In medium saucepan, combine ½ cup margarine and cocoa. Cook over low heat until melted. Remove from heat. Add vanilla and egg; mix well. Stir in remaining crust ingredients; mix well. Press mixture in bottom of greased pan. Bake at 350°F. for 10 minutes. Cool.

Melt ½ cup margarine in medium saucepan over low heat. Blend in milk and pudding mix; cook until mixture thickens slightly, about 5 minutes, stirring constantly. Remove from heat. Beat in 3 cups powdered sugar until smooth. Spread over crust. Refrigerate 20 to 30 minutes or until set.

Melt chocolate in small saucepan over low heat, stirring constantly. Spread evenly over filling. Sprinkle with 1 tablespoon graham cracker crumbs. Refrigerate 10 to 15 minutes to set chocolate. Cut into bars. Store in refrigerator.

Yield: 36 bars.

NUTRITION PER SERVING:
Calories 170; Protein 2g; Carbohydrate 22g; Fat 9g; Sodium 120mg.

PEANUT BUTTER RIBBON BARS

Brownie mix helps to make these special bars easy to make. They have a creamy peanut butter flavor.

FILLING
- 1 (3-oz.) pkg. cream cheese, softened
- ⅓ cup peanut butter
- ¼ cup sugar
- 1 teaspoon vanilla
- 1 egg

BARS
- 1 (21½-oz.) pkg. fudge brownie mix
- ⅓ cup water
- ⅓ cup oil
- 1 egg

GLAZE
- 1 oz. semi-sweet chocolate, cut into pieces
- 2 teaspoons shortening

Heat oven to 350°F. Generously grease bottom of 13x9-inch pan. In small bowl, combine all filling ingredients; beat at medium speed until smooth. Set aside.

In large bowl, combine all bar ingredients; beat 50 strokes with spoon. Spread half of batter in greased pan. Drop filling by tablespoonfuls over batter. Spoon remaining batter over filling. Marble by pulling knife through batter in wide curves. Bake at 350°F. for 30 to 35 minutes or until set.

In small saucepan over low heat, melt chocolate and shortening, stirring constantly. Drizzle glaze over bars. Refrigerate at least 1 hour. Cut into bars. Store in refrigerator.

Yield: 36 bars.

HIGH ALTITUDE:
Above 3500 Feet: Add ¼ cup flour to dry brownie mix. Bake as directed above.

NUTRITION PER SERVING:
Calories 120; Protein 2g; Carbohydrate 16g; Fat 6g; Sodium 80mg.

CHARMIN' CHERRY BARS

Scarlet cherries, coconut and walnuts top a buttery crust in this 1951 Junior Winner from the 3rd Pillsbury BAKE-OFF® Contest.

CRUST
- 1 cup all purpose flour
- ¼ cup powdered sugar
- ½ cup margarine or butter, softened

FILLING
- ¼ cup all purpose flour
- ¾ cup sugar
- ½ teaspoon baking powder
- ¼ teaspoon salt
- 2 eggs
- ½ cup maraschino cherries, well drained, chopped
- ½ cup coconut
- ½ cup chopped walnuts

Heat oven to 350°F. In small bowl, combine 1 cup flour and powdered sugar. Using fork or pastry blender, cut in margarine until mixture resembles coarse crumbs. Press crumb mixture firmly in bottom of ungreased 9-inch square pan. Bake at 350°F. for 10 minutes.

Meanwhile, in same small bowl combine ¼ cup flour, sugar, baking powder and salt. Add eggs; beat well. Stir in cherries, coconut and walnuts. Spread over partially baked crust.

Return to oven and bake an additional 25 to 30 minutes or until golden brown. Cool completely. Cut into bars.
Yield: 25 bars.

HIGH ALTITUDE:
Above 3500 Feet: No change.

NUTRITION PER SERVING:
Calories 120; Protein 2g; Carbohydrate 14g; Fat 6g; Sodium 75mg.

SO-EASY SUGAR COOKIES

The name says it all — and they're so good, they'll become a family favorite! Instead of rolling out the dough, it's baked in a pan, then cut into squares.

- ¾ cup sugar
- ⅓ cup margarine or butter, softened, or shortening
- ⅓ cup oil
- 1 tablespoon milk
- 1 to 2 teaspoons almond extract
- 1 egg
- 1½ cups all purpose flour
- 1½ teaspoons baking powder
- ¼ teaspoon salt
- 1 tablespoon sugar

Heat oven to 375°F. In large bowl, beat ¾ cup sugar, margarine, oil, milk, almond extract and egg until light and fluffy. Stir in flour, baking powder and salt; blend well. Spread evenly in ungreased 15x10x1-inch baking pan; sprinkle with 1 tablespoon sugar.

Bake at 375°F. for 10 to 12 minutes or until light golden brown. Cool 5 minutes. Cut into bars.
Yield: 48 bar cookies.

FOOD PROCESSOR DIRECTIONS:
Place ¾ cup sugar, margarine, oil, milk, almond extract and egg in food processor bowl with metal blade. Cover; process until light and fluffy. Add flour, baking powder and salt. Cover; process using on/off turns just until flour is well blended. (Do not overprocess or cookies will be tough.) Continue as directed above.

HIGH ALTITUDE:
Above 3500 Feet: Decrease baking powder to 1 teaspoon. Bake as directed above.

NUTRITION PER SERVING:
Calories 50; Protein 1g; Carbohydrate 6g; Fat 3g; Sodium 35mg.

So-Easy Sugar Cookies

FUDGY BROWNIES

The ultimate in fudgy brownies!

BROWNIES
- 4 oz. unsweetened chocolate
- ½ cup margarine or butter
- 2 cups sugar
- 4 eggs
- 2 teaspoons vanilla
- 1 cup all purpose flour
- ¼ teaspoon salt

GLAZE
- 2 oz. white baking bar, chopped, ⅓ cup vanilla milk chips, or ⅓ cup semi-sweet chocolate chips
- 3 teaspoons oil

Heat oven to 350°F. Grease 13x9-inch pan. In small saucepan over low heat, melt chocolate and margarine, stirring constantly until smooth. Remove from heat; cool slightly.

In medium bowl, beat sugar, eggs and vanilla until light and fluffy. Add flour, salt and chocolate mixture; blend well. Spread in greased pan. Bake at 350°F. for 30 to 38 minutes. DO NOT OVERBAKE. Cool completely.

In small saucepan, melt glaze ingredients over low heat, stirring constantly until smooth. Drizzle glaze over brownies. Let stand until glaze is set. Cut into bars.
Yield: 36 bars.

HIGH ALTITUDE:
Above 3500 Feet: No change.

NUTRITION PER SERVING:
Calories 110; Protein 2g; Carbohydrate 16g; Fat 6g; Sodium 55mg.

CHOCO-LITE BROWNIES

- ⅔ cup all purpose flour
- ¾ cup sugar
- ⅓ cup unsweetened cocoa
- ¼ teaspoon baking powder
- ¼ teaspoon salt
- ⅓ cup margarine or butter, melted
- 2 teaspoons vanilla
- 2 eggs, slightly beaten
  Powdered sugar

Heat oven to 350°F. Grease and flour bottom only of 8-inch square pan. In large bowl, combine flour, sugar, cocoa, baking powder and salt; blend well. Add margarine, vanilla and eggs; stir just to combine. Pour into greased and floured pan.

Bake at 350°F. for 18 to 23 minutes or until set. DO NOT OVERBAKE. Sprinkle with powdered sugar. Cool completely. Cut into bars.
Yield: 24 bars.

HIGH ALTITUDE:
Above 3500 Feet: Increase flour to ¾ cup. Bake as directed above.

NUTRITION PER SERVING:
Calories 70; Protein 1g; Carbohydrate 10g; Fat 3g; Sodium 70mg.

CHOCOLATE CHUNK PECAN BROWNIES

This culinary inspiration was developed for chocoholics. It's a moist, nut-textured, intensely flavored brownie to satisfy that chocolate craving.

- 1 cup margarine or butter
- 2 cups sugar
- 2 teaspoons vanilla
- 4 eggs, slightly beaten
- 1 cup all purpose flour
- ½ cup unsweetened cocoa
- ½ teaspoon salt
- 8 oz. semi-sweet chocolate, coarsely chopped
- 1 cup chopped pecans

Heat oven to 350°F. Grease 13x9-inch pan. In medium saucepan over low heat, melt margarine. Add sugar, vanilla and eggs; blend well. Stir in flour, cocoa and salt; mix well. Add chocolate and pecans. Pour into greased pan.

Bake at 350°F. for 30 to 40 minutes or until set. Cool completely. Cut into bars.
Yield: 36 bars.

HIGH ALTITUDE:
Above 3500 Feet: No change.

NUTRITION PER SERVING:
Calories 160; Protein 2g; Carbohydrate 19g; Fat 10g; Sodium 105mg.

CHOCOLATE SYRUP BROWNIES

These brownies are baked in a square pan. It's the perfect size for smaller households.

BROWNIES
½ cup margarine or butter, softened
½ cup sugar
2 eggs
½ cup chocolate syrup
2 teaspoons vanilla
¾ cup all purpose flour
¼ teaspoon salt

FROSTING
1 cup powdered sugar
2 tablespoons chocolate syrup
1 tablespoon margarine or butter, softened
2 to 4 teaspoons milk

Heat oven to 350°F. Grease 8-inch square pan. In large bowl, combine ½ cup margarine and sugar; beat until light and fluffy. Add eggs, ½ cup chocolate syrup and vanilla; beat well. Stir in flour and salt. Pour into greased pan.

Bake at 350°F. for 25 to 30 minutes or until toothpick inserted in center comes out clean. Cool completely.

In small bowl, combine all frosting ingredients, adding enough milk for desired spreading consistency; beat until smooth. Spread over cooled brownies. Cut into bars.

MICROWAVE DIRECTIONS:
Grease 10x6-inch (1½-quart) microwave-safe dish. Prepare brownies as directed above. Pour into greased dish. Microwave on MEDIUM for 8 minutes, rotating dish ½ turn halfway through cooking. Microwave on HIGH for 2 to 3 minutes or until center is set. Cool completely on flat surface.

Prepare frosting and frost as directed above. Cut into bars.
Yield: 12 to 16 bars.

HIGH ALTITUDE:
Above 3500 Feet: Increase flour to 1 cup. Bake as directed above. For microwave, cook in greased 9-inch round microwave-safe dish. Microwave on MEDIUM for 8 minutes, rotating dish every 2 minutes. Microwave on HIGH for 1 to 2 minutes or until center is set.

NUTRITION PER SERVING:
Calories 170; Protein 2g; Carbohydrate 24g; Fat 7g; Sodium 130mg.

FAVORITE FUDGE BROWNIES

These brownies have a cake-like texture but a rich and fudgy flavor. Allow the chocolate to cool slightly after melting to help prevent dry brownies.

BROWNIES
5 oz. unsweetened chocolate, cut into pieces
¾ cup margarine or butter
1 tablespoon vanilla
2¼ cups sugar
4 eggs
1⅓ cups all purpose flour
1½ cups coarsely chopped nuts

FROSTING
1½ cups powdered sugar
2 tablespoons unsweetened cocoa
¼ cup margarine or butter, softened
2 tablespoons milk
½ teaspoon vanilla
Pecan or walnut halves, if desired

Heat oven to 375°F. Grease 13x9-inch pan. In small saucepan over low heat, melt chocolate and ¾ cup margarine, stirring constantly until smooth. Remove from heat. Stir in 1 tablespoon vanilla; set aside.

In large bowl, combine sugar and eggs; beat about 7 minutes or until sugar is dissolved. Add flour, chocolate mixture and nuts to egg mixture; stir just until blended. Pour batter into greased pan.

Bake at 375°F. for 25 to 35 minutes. DO NOT OVERBAKE. Cool completely.

In small bowl, combine all frosting ingredients except pecans; blend until smooth. Frost cooled bars; refrigerate 1 hour. Cut into bars; garnish each bar with a pecan half.
Yield: 24 bars.

HIGH ALTITUDE:
Above 3500 Feet: No change.

NUTRITION PER SERVING:
Calories 280; Protein 4g; Carbohydrate 34g; Fat 17g; Sodium 95mg.

GOURMET MINT BROWNIES

A mint-flavored cream cheese filling is swirled through a chocolate brownie.

FILLING
- 1 (8-oz.) pkg. cream cheese, softened
- ¼ cup sugar
- 1 egg
- 1 teaspoon mint extract
- 4 drops green food color

BROWNIES
- 1 cup margarine or butter
- 4 oz. unsweetened chocolate, cut into pieces
- 2 cups sugar
- 2 teaspoons vanilla
- 4 eggs
- 1 cup all purpose flour

FROSTING
- 2 tablespoons margarine or butter
- 2 tablespoons corn syrup
- 2 tablespoons water
- 2 oz. unsweetened chocolate, cut into pieces
- 1 teaspoon vanilla
- 1 cup powdered sugar

Heat oven to 350°F. Grease and flour 13x9-inch pan. In small bowl, beat cream cheese and ¼ cup sugar until smooth. Add 1 egg, mint extract and food color; mix well. Set aside.

In large saucepan, melt 1 cup margarine and 4 oz. chocolate over very low heat, stirring constantly. Remove from heat; cool slightly. Stir in 2 cups sugar and 2 teaspoons vanilla. Add 4 eggs 1 at a time, beating well after each addition. Stir in flour; mix well. Spread in greased and floured pan. Carefully spoon filling over brownie mixture. Lightly swirl filling into brownie mixture.

Bake at 350°F. for 45 to 50 minutes or until set. Cool completely.

In heavy saucepan, bring 2 tablespoons margarine, corn syrup and water to a rolling boil. Remove from heat. Add 2 oz. chocolate; stir until melted. Stir in 1 teaspoon vanilla and powdered sugar; beat until smooth. Frost cooled bars. Cut into bars. Store in refrigerator.
Yield: 36 bars.

HIGH ALTITUDE:
Above 3500 Feet: No change.

NUTRITION PER SERVING:
Calories 180; Protein 2g; Carbohydrate 20g; Fat 11g; Sodium 95mg.

PECAN BLONDIES

The term "blondie" refers to a brownie containing no chocolate. Our version of blond brownies is moist and chewy, with a rich melt-in-your-mouth flavor.

- 1½ cups firmly packed brown sugar
- ½ cup margarine or butter, softened
- 2 teaspoons vanilla
- 2 eggs
- 1½ cups all purpose flour
- 1 teaspoon baking powder
- ½ teaspoon nutmeg
- ¼ teaspoon salt
- ½ cup chopped pecans
- 1 tablespoon powdered sugar

Heat oven to 350°F. Grease 13x9-inch pan. In large bowl, beat brown sugar and margarine until light and fluffy. Add vanilla and eggs; blend well. Add flour, baking powder, nutmeg and salt; mix well. Spread in greased pan. Sprinkle with pecans.

Bake at 350°F. for 18 to 28 minutes or until set and golden brown. Cool completely. Sprinkle with powdered sugar; cut into bars.
Yield: 36 bars.

HIGH ALTITUDE:
Above 3500 Feet: Increase flour to 1¾ cups. Bake as directed above.

NUTRITION PER SERVING:
Calories 90; Protein 1g; Carbohydrate 13g; Fat 4g; Sodium 60mg.

VARIATION:

DATE PECAN BLONDIES: Stir 1 cup chopped dates into batter before spreading in pan.

Gourmet Mint Brownies, Pecan Blondies

CHEWY BUTTERSCOTCH BROWNIES

The marvelous coconut-pecan base adds special appeal to these luscious change-of-pace brownies. They are sure to satisfy a sweet tooth.

BASE
- ¼ cup margarine or butter
- 1 cup flaked coconut
- ½ cup firmly packed brown sugar
- ½ cup chopped pecans

BROWNIES
- 1 cup firmly packed brown sugar
- ½ cup margarine or butter, softened
- ½ teaspoon vanilla
- 1 egg
- 1½ cups all purpose flour
- ½ teaspoon baking soda
- ¼ teaspoon salt
- ½ cup miniature marshmallows
- ½ cup chopped pecans
- 1 cup miniature marshmallows, if desired

GLAZE
- 1 tablespoon margarine or butter
- ½ cup powdered sugar
- ¼ cup firmly packed brown sugar
- 2 to 4 teaspoons milk

Heat oven to 350°F. Grease 13x9-inch pan. In small saucepan, melt ¼ cup margarine. Stir in remaining base ingredients. Press mixture in bottom of greased pan.

In large bowl, beat 1 cup brown sugar and ½ cup margarine until light and fluffy. Add vanilla and egg; blend well. Stir in flour, baking soda and salt; mix well. Add ½ cup marshmallows and ½ cup pecans; blend well. Spoon brownie mixture over base; gently spread with wet hands.

Bake at 350°F. for 20 to 27 minutes or until golden brown. Sprinkle with 1 cup marshmallows. Bake an additional 2 minutes. Cool completely.

In small saucepan, melt 1 tablespoon margarine. Stir in powdered sugar, ¼ cup brown sugar and enough milk for desired drizzling consistency. Drizzle glaze over brownies. Cut into bars.
Yield: 48 bars.

HIGH ALTITUDE:
Above 3500 Feet: Decrease brown sugar in brownies to ¾ cup.

NUTRITION PER SERVING:
Calories 110; Protein 1g; Carbohydrate 14g; Fat 5g; Sodium 65mg.

ZEBRA BROWNIES

These rich brownies with their creamy filling have been an all-time favorite.

FILLING
- 2 (3-oz.) pkg. cream cheese, softened
- ¼ cup sugar
- ½ teaspoon vanilla
- 1 egg

BROWNIES
- 1 (21.5-oz.) pkg. fudge brownie mix
- ⅓ cup water
- ⅓ cup oil
- 1 egg

Heat oven to 350°F. Grease bottom of 13x9-inch pan. In small bowl, combine all filling ingredients; beat until smooth. Set aside.

In large bowl, combine all brownie ingredients; beat 50 strokes with spoon. Spread half of brownie batter in greased pan. Pour filling mixture over brownie batter, spreading to cover. Top with spoonfuls of remaining brownie batter. To marble, pull knife through batter in wide curves; turn pan and repeat.

Bake at 350°F. for 30 to 35 minutes or until set. DO NOT OVERBAKE. Cool completely. Refrigerate at least 1 hour. Cut into bars. Store in refrigerator.
Yield: 36 bars.

HIGH ALTITUDE:
Above 3500 Feet: See package for directions.

NUTRITION PER SERVING:
Calories 110; Protein 1g; Carbohydrate 16g; Fat 5g; Sodium 70mg.

Pumpkin Patch Brownies

This whimsical special occasion treat is especially easy to make with fudge brownie mix and ready-to-spread frosting. The piped frosting can be easily done using a resealable plastic freezer bag with a corner snipped off to make a small hole.

BROWNIES
- 1   (21.5-oz.) pkg. fudge brownie mix
- 1   teaspoon cinnamon
- ½   cup water
- ½   cup oil
- 1   egg

FROSTING
- 1   can ready-to-spread chocolate fudge frosting
- 1   cup ready-to-spread vanilla frosting
- 3   to 4 drops green food color
- 24   candy pumpkins

Heat oven to 350°F. Line 13x9-inch pan with foil, leaving enough foil on sides to lift brownies out of pan. Grease foil. In large bowl, combine all brownie ingredients; beat 50 strokes by hand. Spread in foil-lined pan.

Bake at 350°F. for 28 to 35 minutes. DO NOT OVERBAKE. Cool completely. Remove brownies from pan by lifting foil edges. Invert onto serving plate, tray or heavy cardboard covered with foil. Remove foil from brownies. Frost sides and top with chocolate fudge frosting. With knife, score frosting into 24 bars.

In small bowl, combine vanilla frosting and green food color; blend well. Using decorating bag, decorating bottle, or resealable plastic bag with a small hole cut in one corner, pipe green frosting to make vine and leaf design on each bar. Place 1 candy pumpkin on each bar. Refrigerate 1 to 2 hours or until frosting is firm; cut into bars.
Yield: 24 bars.

HIGH ALTITUDE:
Above 3500 Feet: See package for directions.

NUTRITION PER SERVING:
Calories 340; Protein 2g; Carbohydrate 54g; Fat 13g; Sodium 190mg.

VARIATION:

PUMPKIN FIELD BROWNIES: Prepare brownies and frost with chocolate fudge frosting as directed above. Do not score. Prepare green frosting as directed above. Pipe vines and leaves randomly over chocolate fudge frosting. Place desired number of candy pumpkins randomly among leaves and vines.

Fruitcake Fantasy Brownies

Whether you like fruitcake or not, we think you will enjoy these fudgy, fruit-filled brownies.

- ½   cup margarine or butter
- 4   oz. semi-sweet chocolate
- 1   (14-oz.) can sweetened condensed milk (not evaporated)
- ½   teaspoon rum extract
- 2   eggs
- 1¼   cups all purpose flour
- ¾   teaspoon baking powder
- ¼   teaspoon salt
- 2   cups candied fruitcake mixture
- 1   cup chopped pecans or walnuts

Heat oven to 350°F. Grease 13x9-inch pan. In large saucepan, melt margarine and chocolate over low heat, stirring constantly. Remove from heat. Add sweetened condensed milk and rum extract; blend well. Add eggs 1 at a time, beating well after each addition. Add flour, baking powder and salt; mix well. Stir in candied fruit and pecans. Spread in greased pan.

Bake at 350°F. for 28 to 36 minutes or until toothpick inserted in center comes out clean. Cool completely. Cut into bars.
Yield: 36 bars.

HIGH ALTITUDE:
Above 3500 Feet: Increase flour to 1½ cups. Bake as directed above.

NUTRITION PER SERVING:
Calories 140; Protein 2g; Carbohydrate 20g; Fat 7g; Sodium 85mg.

WHITE CHOCOLATE CHUNK BROWNIE WEDGES

―――――――― ❧ ――――――――

These elegant brownie wedges are loaded with chunks of semi-sweet chocolate. Cover the pan tightly with foil to maintain freshness.

BROWNIES
- ½ **cup margarine or butter**
- 4 **oz. white baking bars, cut into pieces**
- 2 **eggs**
- ⅛ **teaspoon salt**
- ½ **cup sugar**
- 1½ **teaspoons vanilla**
- 1¼ **cups all purpose flour**
- 2 **oz. semi-sweet chocolate, cut into pieces**

GLAZE
- 1 **oz. semi-sweet chocolate**
- 2 **teaspoons margarine or butter**

Heat oven to 350°F. Grease and flour 9-inch round cake pan. In small saucepan, melt ½ cup margarine and 2 oz. of the white baking bar over low heat, stirring constantly until melted. Remove from heat; set aside.

In small bowl, combine eggs and salt; beat until frothy. Add sugar and continue beating for about 3 minutes or until light in color and thickened. Add melted chocolate mixture and vanilla; blend well. Stir in flour; mix well. Fold in remaining white chocolate pieces and semi-sweet chocolate pieces. Spread in greased and floured pan.

Bake at 350°F. for 23 to 28 minutes or until toothpick inserted in center comes out clean. Cool on wire rack.

In small saucepan, melt glaze ingredients until smooth, stirring constantly. Drizzle glaze over brownies. Let stand until set. Cut into wedges.
Yield: 12 wedges.

HIGH ALTITUDE:
Above 3500 Feet: Increase flour to 1⅓ cups. Bake as directed above.

NUTRITION PER SERVING:
Calories 260; Protein 3g; Carbohydrate 28g; Fat 15g; Sodium 140mg.

FUDGY ORANGE HAZELNUT BROWNIES

―――――――― ❧ ――――――――

Delicate orange frosting complements these dense brownies. Hazelnuts, also known as filberts, add a distinctive flavor.

BROWNIES
- 1 **cup sugar**
- ½ **cup margarine or butter, softened**
- ⅓ **cup unsweetened cocoa**
- 1 **tablespoon grated orange peel**
- 2 **eggs**
- 1 **cup all purpose flour**
- ½ **teaspoon baking soda**
- ¼ **teaspoon salt**
- 1 **cup coarsely chopped hazelnuts (filberts)**

FROSTING
- 1 **cup powdered sugar**
- 1 **teaspoon grated orange peel**
- 1 **to 2 tablespoons milk**

Heat oven to 350°F. Grease 9-inch square pan. In large bowl, beat sugar and margarine until light and fluffy. Add cocoa, 1 tablespoon orange peel and eggs; blend well. Add flour, baking soda and salt; mix well. Stir in hazelnuts. Spread in greased pan.

Bake at 350°F. for 23 to 33 minutes or until firm to touch. DO NOT OVERBAKE. Cool completely.

In small bowl, combine powdered sugar, 1 teaspoon orange peel and enough milk for desired spreading consistency; blend until smooth. Spread over cooled brownies. Let stand until set. Cut into bars.
Yield: 24 bars.

HIGH ALTITUDE:
Above 3500 Feet: Increase flour to 1¼ cups. Bake as directed above.

NUTRITION PER SERVING:
Calories 140; Protein 2g; Carbohydrate 19g; Fat 8g; Sodium 105mg.

GLAZED CHEESECAKE BROWNIES

Two favorites, brownies and cheesecake, are combined in this unique bar. They cut beautifully and will make an attractive addition to your holiday cookie tray.

TOPPING
- 1 (8-oz.) pkg. cream cheese, softened
- 2 tablespoons margarine or butter, softened
- ½ cup sugar
- 1 teaspoon vanilla
- 2 eggs

BROWNIES
- 4 oz. semi-sweet chocolate, cut into pieces
- 3 tablespoons margarine or butter
- ½ cup sugar
- 1 teaspoon vanilla
- 2 eggs
- ½ cup all purpose flour
- ½ teaspoon baking powder
- ¼ teaspoon salt

GLAZE
- 1 oz. semi-sweet chocolate, cut into pieces
- 2 teaspoons margarine or butter

Heat oven to 350°F. Grease and flour 9-inch square pan. In small bowl, combine all topping ingredients; blend well. Set aside.

In medium saucepan, melt 4 oz. chocolate and 3 tablespoons margarine over low heat, stirring constantly until smooth. Remove from heat; cool. Add ½ cup sugar and vanilla; blend well. Beat in 2 eggs 1 at a time, blending well after each addition. Add flour, baking powder and salt to chocolate mixture; stir just until blended. Pour into greased and floured pan. Pour topping over batter.

Bake at 350°F. for 40 to 50 minutes or until toothpick inserted in center comes out clean. Cool on wire rack.

In small saucepan, melt glaze ingredients until smooth, stirring constantly. Drizzle over brownies. Refrigerate at least 4 hours. Cut into bars. Store in refrigerator.
Yield: 24 bars.

HIGH ALTITUDE:
Above 3500 Feet: Increase flour to ½ cup plus 2 tablespoons. Bake as directed above.

NUTRITION PER SERVING:
Calories 140; Protein 2g; Carbohydrate 14g; Fat 9g; Sodium 100mg.

BRAZIL NUT BROWNIES

What could be more delicious than white chocolate frosting atop fudgy brownies?

BROWNIES
- 1 (21.5-oz.) pkg. fudge brownie mix
- ½ cup oil
- ¼ cup water
- ¼ cup coffee-flavored liqueur or strong coffee
- 1 egg
- 1 cup coarsely chopped brazil nuts

FROSTING
- 2 tablespoons margarine or butter, melted
- 1 cup powdered sugar
- 2 tablespoons coffee-flavored liqueur or strong coffee
- 1 tablespoon water
- 3 oz. white baking bars, chopped, or ½ cup vanilla milk chips
- 1 tablespoon oil

Heat oven to 350°F. Grease 13x9-inch pan. In large bowl, combine all brownie ingredients except nuts; beat 50 strokes by hand. Stir in brazil nuts. Spread in greased pan. Bake at 350°F. for 28 to 35 minutes. DO NOT OVERBAKE. Cool completely.

In medium bowl, combine margarine, powdered sugar, 2 tablespoons liqueur and 1 tablespoon water; blend well. In small saucepan over low heat, melt white baking bar and 1 tablespoon oil, stirring constantly. Add to powdered sugar mixture; beat until smooth. Spread over cooled brownies. Let stand until set. Cut into bars.
Yield: 36 bars.

HIGH ALTITUDE:
Above 3500 Feet: See package for directions.

NUTRITION PER SERVING:
Calories 170; Protein 2g; Carbohydrate 20g; Fat 9g; Sodium 70mg.

CAKES

A cake is something special! Traditionally, cakes mark the occasions of our lives, including showers, weddings, birthdays, graduations and anniversaries.

Whether you choose a layer cake topped with creamy frosting, a moist sheet cake laden with raisins and spices, or a feather-light angel food cake, we've outlined the techniques for making them all. And, we've provided tips for adding festive finishing touches like garnishes and glazes.

Pictured: **Apple Pecan Layer Cake** *p. 115,* **Black Bottom Cups** *p. 144*

CAKES

Draw ooohs and aaahs
from family and friends by baking a cake!
A snack cake takes no longer than stirring up a mix, or with some
extra time and attention, you can create an elaborate
"company's coming" cake to rival any bakery's.

KINDS OF CAKES

There are 2 main types of cakes — butter and foam cakes. Butter cakes are those made with solid shortenings and foam cakes are those made with a large number of eggs or egg whites.

BUTTER

Even though these cakes also may be made with solid shortening or margarine, most people still call them "butter" cakes. They're moist, light, tender and fine-textured. (Recipes begin on p. 113.)

FOAM

Foam cakes contain a large number of eggs or egg whites. Their light, fluffy texture comes from the air beaten into the eggs and from steam that forms in the batter during baking. The 3 types of foam cakes are angel food, chiffon and sponge. Angel food cakes contain no shortening or oil and use only egg whites. Chiffon cakes contain oil and use egg yolks and whites. Sponge cakes contain no shortening or oil and use egg yolks and whites. (Recipes begin on p. 181.)

SECRETS TO SUCCESSFUL CAKES

From a snack cake to a multi-layered birthday cake, some basic secrets will help make every cake a success!

SECERETS FOR ANY CAKES

Use shiny metal pans. Shiny aluminum pans reflect heat away from the cake and give it a tender, light-brown crust. Dark pans can cause a thick, dark crust. Insulated pans require a longer baking time.

Use the proper size of pan. When checking the size, measure from inside edge to inside edge. A cake made in a pan that is too large can be flat and overbaked, while one made in a pan that is too small may overflow during baking or take longer to bake.

Prepare the pan according to recipe directions. Pans for butter cakes are usually greased and floured. Pans for foam cakes are usually not.

Heat the oven 10 to 15 minutes before baking.

Measure ingredients accurately. Be sure to add them in the order and manner specified in the recipe.

Don't overbeat or underbeat the batter. Underbeating or overbeating will affect the texture and volume of the cake. These recipes have been tested using an electric mixer, which produces the highest volume, but they also may be mixed by hand. One minute of beating time with a mixer equals 150 strokes by hand.

Fill pans half full. This will ensure that the cake bakes evenly, and that the batter doesn't overflow the pan during baking. If you're using a special-shaped pan like a heart or Christmas tree, measure how much batter it will hold by filling it with water. Measure the amount of water and use half that amount of batter. Extra batter can be used for cupcakes.

Carefully space pans in the oven. Place single pans in the middle of the center rack. For more than 1 pan, leave at least 1 inch between the pans and the sides of the oven for good air circulation. If necessary, stagger the pans on 2 oven racks so one is not directly above the other and the air flows evenly around them.

Cool cakes completely before filling, frosting or glazing them.

Know the number of servings per cake. If you're baking for a group, here's a handy guide for knowing what size cake will serve the whole crowd:

Size of cake	Serves
8 or 9-inch layer cake	12 to16
8 or 9-inch square cake	6 to 9
13x9-inch rectangular cake	12 to 16
10x4-inch tube cake	16 to 20
12-cup bundt cake	16 to 20

SECRETS FOR BUTTER CAKES

Use butter, margarine or solid shortening. Don't substitute oil, even if the recipe calls for the shortening to be melted.

Use solid shortening to prepare the pan. Grease the bottom and sides of the pan with about 1 tablespoon of solid vegetable shortening (butter, margarine and oil don't coat as evenly) for each 8 or 9-inch round cake pan. Use a paper towel or pastry brush to spread the shortening. Then dust the greased pan with about 2 tablespoons of flour, shaking it until the bottom and sides are well coated. (If you're baking a chocolate cake, you can use cocoa instead of flour.) Tap out the excess flour. For nonstick pans, follow the manufacturer's instructions.

Instead of greasing and flouring pans, you also may use pan inserts made of parchment paper. The inserts are available at many cooking specialty stores. Use paper or foil baking cups to line cupcake pans.

Make a hollow. After filling the pans with batter, make a slight hollow in the center of the batter with the back of a spoon or spatula. This will give the cake a nicely rounded, rather than humped, top.

Cool cake in the pan. Cool cake on a wire rack for 5 to 20 minutes before removing it from the pan. To remove a cake, carefully run a knife along the edge to loosen it from the pan. Place another wire rack on top of the pan. With the pan sandwiched between the 2 racks, turn it over. Carefully lift the pan from the cake. So that the top of the cake will be facing up, once again sandwich the cake between 2 racks and turn it over. Remove the top rack.

If the cake sticks to the pan, return it to the oven and heat for 1 minute. Remove it from the pan.

Cut the cake with a thin, sharp knife. Use a sawing, back-and-forth motion. If the frosting sticks, dip the knife in hot water and wipe it with a damp towel after cutting each slice. An electric knife also works well for cutting most layer cakes.

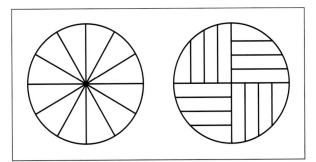

Cutting a layer cake for 12 or 16 servings

SECRETS FOR FOAM CAKES

Do not grease or flour the tube pan. During baking, the batter must be able to cling to the sides of the pan and the center tube in order to rise properly.

Beat eggs at room temperature. For the highest volume, bring egg whites to room temperature before beating them. Be sure that no egg yolk remains in the whites, and that the bowl, beaters and rubber scraper are clean and free from any oil or shortening. Even a little bit of grease will prevent the whites from beating properly.

Break bubbles in the batter. So that the cake will have an even texture, cut through the batter with a knife before baking to break large air bubbles and to seal the batter against the sides of the pan and center tube.

Bake on the bottom rack. In some ovens, cakes in tube pans bake better on the bottom rack, preventing the top from getting too brown. You may need to remove the top oven rack to leave adequate room for the pan or for the cake to expand.

Cool cake in the pan. To prevent this delicate type of cake from collapsing after baking, turn the tube or Bundt® pan upside down on a wire rack, heat-proof funnel or the neck of a bottle so the cake doesn't touch the counter.

Remove it carefully from the pan. To remove the cake, use a thin-bladed knife and, with a sawing motion, run it between the cake and the pan. Place the serving plate on top of the pan and turn it upside down. Rap one side of the pan with the flat side of the knife blade, and carefully lift the pan from the cake.

Cut it with a serrated knife. Use a smooth, gentle sawing motion. Or, use an electric knife.

Freeze leftover egg whites. If you have leftover egg whites, lightly beat them, place them in a freezer container and freeze. Thaw them in the refrigerator and use them like fresh egg whites in foam cakes, meringues and cooked frostings. One egg white equals 2 tablespoons.

How to Tell
When Cakes Are Done

Underbaked cakes are soggy, pale and raw-tasting; overbaked cakes are dry, too brown and may stick in the pan. To be sure that your cake is done just right, follow these simple steps.

Check for doneness at the minimum baking time. Then check at 1-minute intervals until the cake is done.

Butter cakes are done when . . .
- A toothpick inserted in the center comes out clean.
- The top is rounded, smooth and springs back when lightly touched in the center.

Foam cakes are done when . . .
- The top springs back when touched.
- The cracks on top look and feel dry. (If the cake is underbaked, it will pull away from the sides and tube and/or fall out of the pan when inverted).

Keeping Cakes
Fresh and Flavorful

To keep cakes at the peak of their flavor and quality:

Store when completely cooled. Cakes with frostings or fillings containing dairy products should be refrigerated.

Store under cake cover or large bowl. If a cake has a fluffy cooked frosting, insert a knife handle under an edge of the cake cover so it isn't airtight. The frosting can be totally absorbed by the cake when stored in an airtight container. If you don't have a cake cover, cakes with creamy frostings also can be covered lightly with foil, plastic wrap or waxed paper. To keep the frosting from sticking to the protective covering, insert several toothpicks halfway into the cake around the edges and in the center to support the covering.

Freeze unfrosted cakes. For unfrosted butter cakes, cool completely, wrap in heavy-duty foil and freeze. Foam cakes may be frozen in the pan to prevent crushing. Cover tightly and freeze. Unfrosted cakes may be stored in the freezer up to 6 months.

Freeze cakes with buttercream frosting. Frosted cakes can be frozen in a tightly covered plastic container. Or, place cake in freezer until frosting is frozen. Then wrap tightly in plastic wrap or foil and freeze up to 3 months. Cooked, boiled or fruit frostings and fillings don't freeze as well. Place layer cakes in a box or cake container to prevent crushing, then wrap the box in foil or plastic wrap before freezing. Foam cakes may be filled or frosted with whipped cream or whipped topping before freezing. Frosted cakes may be stored in the freezer up to 3 months.

Thaw cakes at room temperature. Thaw unfrosted cakes covered and frosted cakes loosely covered for 2 to 3 hours at room temperature.

SECRETS FOR SUCCESSFUL FROSTINGS, GARNISHES AND DECORATIONS

Easy or elaborate, frosting, garnishes, and other decorations add the crowning touch to your cake creation. (Recipes for frostings begin on p. 184.)

Create the right consistency. Frosting should have a smooth consistency that is firm enough to hold swirls and other patterns and yet soft enough to spread. Glazes should be thin enough to pour or drizzle but not so thin they run off the cake.

Make frosting patterns. Decorate a cake as you frost it by making swirls, crisscrosses, zigzags or spirals with a spatula, knife or the tines of a fork.

Tint frosting with food color. Mix enough of each color before you begin frosting or decorating. The color will darken as the frosting dries.

Add easy garnishes. A cake can be made extra-special by adding a garnish. See p. 210 for **Dessert Garnishes.** Here are just a few things that can be arranged on or sprinkled over a cake:
• Animal crackers
• Chocolate or butterscotch chips, nuts, raisins
• Coconut, colored sprinkles, sugar
• Candies such as mint wafers, jelly beans, gumdrops, peppermints or licorice strings
• Candied, fresh or dried fruit
• Fresh or artificial flowers. When using fresh flowers, choose nontoxic chemical-free blossoms such as nasturtiums, violets, roses or pansies.

Add easy decorations. Try these easy decorating ideas:
• Drizzle melted chocolate around the top edge of the cake for a border effect. Or dip a toothpick in melted chocolate to create marble or spiderweb designs.
• Sift powdered sugar or cocoa onto an unfrosted cake. For a lacy pattern, use a paper doily. Lay the doily on top of the cake. Carefully sift an even layer of powdered sugar or cocoa over it. Lift the doily straight up, leaving a pattern on the cake.
• Use a cookie cutter to mark a design on the frosting of a cake or cupcake. Fill in the design with colored sugar, sprinkles or chopped nuts.

Simple Decorating Bag
A resealable plastic freezer bag can be used as a simple decorating bag. Fill the bag with frosting and seal it. For a writing tip effect, snip off 1 corner, making a very small hole; squeeze the frosting gently through the opening. If you want to use decorative tips, snip off ¼ inch of 1 corner. Place the desired tip in the corner of the bag, fill it with frosting, seal and decorate.

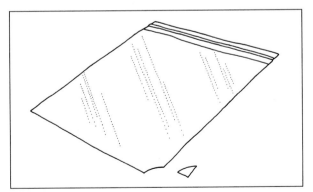

Making a simple decorating bag

NUTRITION IN THIS CHAPTER

Nutrition per serving means the calculation was done on 1 serving, 1 cupcake, 1 petits fours or 1/12 of the frosting recipe.

STEP-BY-STEP FEATURE ~
How to Frost a Two-Layer Cake

STEP 1. Cool cake layers completely on wire racks. When cooled, brush off the crumbs with a pastry brush or your fingers.

STEP 2. Place one layer, top side down, on plate. Place strips of waxed paper under cake edge. Spread with frosting; add second layer, top side up.

STEP 3. Frost sides of cake then top of cake, blending the frosting at the edges. Carefully remove waxed paper strips.

BASIC YELLOW CAKE

This cake is rich, moist and delicious. We suggest frosting it with **Chocolate Buttercream Frosting** *p. 184.*

2½ **cups all purpose flour**
  3 **teaspoons baking powder**
¼ **teaspoon salt**
1¼ **cups sugar**
¾ **cup margarine or butter, softened**
  1 **teaspoon vanilla**
  3 **eggs**
  1 **cup milk**

Heat oven to 350°F. Grease and flour two 8 or 9-inch round cake pans. In medium bowl, combine flour, baking powder and salt. In large bowl, beat sugar and margarine until light and fluffy. Add vanilla and eggs; blend well. Alternately add dry ingredients and milk, beating well after each addition. Spread batter evenly in greased and floured pans.

Bake at 350°F. for 27 to 35 minutes or until toothpick inserted in center comes out clean. Cool 10 minutes; remove from pans. Cool completely. Fill and frost as desired.

Yield: 12 servings.

TIP:
Cake can be baked in greased and floured 13x9-inch pan. Prepare as directed above. Bake at 350°F. for 33 to 40 minutes. Cool completely. Frost or top as desired.

HIGH ALTITUDE:
Above 3500 Feet: Decrease sugar to 1 cup. Bake as directed above.

NUTRITION PER SERVING:
Calories 310; Protein 5g; Carbohydrate 42g; Fat 13g; Sodium 280mg.

Basic Yellow Cake,
Chocolate Buttercream Frosting p. 184

SIMPLY WHITE CAKE

*This lovely white cake can be used anytime a basic white cake is desired. Try it with **Chocolate Cream Frosting**, p. 184, or prepare it for **Lady Baltimore Cake** (this page).*

2	cups all purpose flour
1½	cups sugar
3	teaspoons baking powder
½	teaspoon salt
1	cup milk
½	cup shortening
1	teaspoon vanilla or ½ teaspoon almond extract
5	egg whites

Heat oven to 350°F. Grease and flour two 9-inch round cake pans. In large bowl, blend flour, sugar, baking powder, salt, milk and shortening at low speed until moistened; beat 2 minutes at medium speed. Add vanilla and egg whites; continue beating an additional 2 minutes. Pour into greased and floured pans.

Bake at 350°F. for 27 to 35 minutes or until toothpick inserted in center comes out clean. Cool 10 minutes; remove from pans. Cool completely. Fill and frost as desired.
Yield: 12 servings.

TIP:
Cake can be baked in 13x9-inch pan. Grease and flour bottom only. Bake at 350°F. for 33 to 40 minutes or until toothpick inserted in center comes out clean. Cool completely. Frost or top as desired.

HIGH ALTITUDE:
Above 3500 Feet: Decrease sugar to 1¼ cups. Bake as directed above.

NUTRITION PER SERVING:
Calories 260; Protein 4g; Carbohydrate 42g; Fat 9g; Sodium 200mg.

VARIATIONS:

COCONUT CAKE: Stir 1 cup flaked coconut into batter before pouring into greased and floured pans. Sprinkle additional coconut over frosting.

POPPY SEED CAKE: Combine ¼ cup poppy seed with an additional ¼ cup milk; allow to stand 30 minutes. Add to batter with egg whites and vanilla.

LADY BALTIMORE CAKE

This fruit and nut filled layer cake with fluffy white frosting was first described in a novel by Owen Wister in 1906 titled Lady Baltimore.

LADY BALTIMORE FILLING

⅓	cup golden or dark raisins
⅓	cup chopped pitted dates or dried figs
⅓	cup chopped pecans
2	tablespoons cream sherry
1	cup White Cloud Frosting p. 188

CAKE
   Simply White Cake (this page), or 18.5-oz. pkg. pudding-included white cake mix

FROSTING
   White Cloud Frosting p. 188

In small bowl, combine raisins, dates, pecans and sherry; mix well. Cover; let stand at least 1 hour at room temperature to blend flavors, stirring occasionally.

Meanwhile, prepare and bake cake as directed in recipe or on package using two 8 or 9-inch round cake pans. Cool completely.

Prepare frosting as directed in recipe. Add 1 cup of the frosting to raisin mixture; stir until combined. Spread raisin filling between cake layers. Spread remaining frosting on sides and top of cake.
Yield: 12 servings.

HIGH ALTITUDE:
Above 3500 Feet: See recipe or package for directions.

NUTRITION PER SERVING:
Calories 390; Protein 5g; Carbohydrate 69g; Fat 11g; Sodium 280mg.

VARIATION:

LORD BALTIMORE CAKE: Omit Lady Baltimore Filling. Prepare and bake cake as directed above. Prepare White Cloud Frosting substituting ¼ cup firmly packed brown sugar for the ¼ cup sugar.

To prepare Lord Baltimore Filling, place 1 cup of the frosting in small bowl. Add ½ cup chopped pecans, ½ cup crumbled soft macaroon cookies and ¼ cup chopped candied cherries; mix well. Spread filling between cake layers. Spread remaining frosting on sides and top of cake.

APPLE PECAN LAYER CAKE

~

This layered apple cake is topped with a browned butter frosting.

CAKE
2½ cups all purpose flour
 2 cups sugar
 1 teaspoon baking powder
 1 teaspoon baking soda
 1 teaspoon salt
 1 teaspoon cinnamon
1½ cups applesauce
 ¾ cup oil
 2 eggs
 ½ cup chopped pecans

APPLE BROWN BUTTER FROSTING
 ½ cup butter (do not use margarine)
4½ cups powdered sugar
 6 to 8 tablespoons apple juice

Heat oven to 350°F. Grease and flour two 9-inch round cake pans. In large bowl, combine flour, sugar, baking powder, baking soda, salt and cinnamon. Add applesauce, oil and eggs; blend at low speed until moistened. Beat 2 minutes at high speed. Stir in pecans. Pour batter into greased and floured pans.

Bake at 350°F. for 30 to 40 minutes or until toothpick inserted in center comes out clean. Cool 10 minutes; remove from pans. Cool completely.

In small heavy saucepan over medium heat, brown butter until light golden brown, stirring constantly. Remove from heat; cool completely. In large bowl, combine browned butter, powdered sugar and 4 tablespoons of the apple juice; blend at low speed until moistened. Continue beating until well blended, adding additional apple juice for desired spreading consistency.

To assemble cake, place 1 cake layer, top side down, on serving plate; spread evenly with about ¼ of frosting. Top with remaining cake layer, top side up. Spread sides and top of cake with remaining frosting. Garnish as desired.
Yield: 12 servings.

HIGH ALTITUDE:
Above 3500 Feet: Decrease sugar to 1¾ cups. Bake at 375°F. for 25 to 35 minutes.

NUTRITION PER SERVING:
Calories 650; Protein 4g; Carbohydrate 104g; Fat 26g; Sodium 390mg.

BLACK FOREST CAKE

~

Black Forest torte originated in Germany and traditionally is chocolate cake layered with cherries, kirsch and whipped cream. **Basic Chocolate Cake** *p. 116 can be used to make the cake, if desired.*

CAKE
 1 (18.25-oz.) pkg. pudding-included dark
     chocolate cake mix
    Water
    Oil
    Eggs

FILLING
 1 (21-oz.) can cherry fruit pie filling
 ½ teaspoon almond extract

FROSTING
 1 pint (2 cups) whipping cream
 ½ cup powdered sugar
 2 tablespoons brandy
    Chocolate Curls p. 210

Heat oven to 350°F. Grease and flour two 8 or 9-inch round cake pans. Prepare and bake cake mix according to package directions. Cool completely.

In small bowl, combine filling ingredients. In medium bowl, beat whipping cream at highest speed until slightly thickened. Gradually add powdered sugar, beating until stiff peaks form. Fold in brandy.

Place 1 cake layer on serving plate; spread 1 cup filling to within 1 inch of edge. Top with second cake layer. Frost top and sides with whipped cream. Spoon remaining filling in center of top of cake; garnish with chocolate curls. Refrigerate until serving time. Store in refrigerator.
Yield: 12 servings.

HIGH ALTITUDE:
Above 3500 Feet: See package for directions.

NUTRITION PER SERVING:
Calories 500; Protein 5g; Carbohydrate 61g; Fat 27g; Sodium 360mg.

BASIC CHOCOLATE CAKE

This traditional cake is rich, chocolaty and dense.

CAKE
- 2 cups all purpose flour
- 1¼ teaspoons baking soda
- ½ teaspoon salt
- 1½ cups sugar
- ½ cup margarine or butter, softened
- 1 teaspoon vanilla
- 2 eggs
- 4 oz. unsweetened chocolate, melted
- 1 cup milk

FROSTING
- 1 cup whipping cream, whipped
- 2 tablespoons powdered sugar

Heat oven to 350°F. Grease and flour two 8 or 9-inch round cake pans. In medium bowl, combine flour, baking soda and salt. In large bowl, beat sugar and margarine until light and fluffy. Beat in vanilla and eggs. Stir in chocolate. Alternately add dry ingredients and milk, beating well after each addition. Spread batter evenly in greased and floured pans.

Bake at 350°F. for 27 to 35 minutes or until toothpick inserted in center comes out clean. Cool 10 minutes; remove from pans. Cool completely.

In small bowl, beat cream until soft peaks form. Blend in powdered sugar; beat until stiff peaks form. Fill and frost cake with whipped cream.
Yield: 12 servings.

TIP:
Cake can be baked in greased and floured 13x9-inch pan. Prepare as directed above. Bake at 350°F. for 33 to 40 minutes. Cool completely.

HIGH ALTITUDE:
Above 3500 Feet: Decrease sugar to 1¼ cups. Bake as directed above.

NUTRITION PER SERVING:
Calories 380; Protein 5g; Carbohydrate 48g; Fat 19g; Sodium 320mg.

CHOCOLATE CAKE MAKE-OVER

We've developed this cake especially for those who desire a moist cake with fewer calories and less fat.

CAKE
- 1¾ cups all purpose flour
- ½ cup unsweetened cocoa
- 1¼ teaspoons baking soda
- ½ teaspoon salt
- 1¼ cups sugar
- ½ cup margarine or butter, softened
- 1 teaspoon vanilla
- 4 egg whites
- 1 cup lowfat buttermilk

FROSTING
- 2 cups light frozen whipped topping, thawed

Heat oven to 350°F. Grease and flour two 8 or 9-inch round cake pans. In medium bowl, combine flour, cocoa, baking soda and salt. In large bowl, beat sugar and margarine until light and fluffy. Beat in vanilla and egg whites. Alternately add dry ingredients and buttermilk, beating well after each addition. Spread batter evenly in greased and floured pans.

Bake at 350°F. for 27 to 35 minutes or until toothpick inserted in center comes out clean. Cool 10 minutes; remove from pans. Cool completely. Fill and frost with whipped topping. Garnish as desired.
Yield: 12 servings.

TIP:
Cake can be baked in greased and floured 13x9-inch pan. Prepare as directed above. Bake at 350°F. for 33 to 40 minutes. Cool completely.

HIGH ALTITUDE:
Above 3500 Feet: Decrease sugar to 1 cup. Bake as directed above.

NUTRITION PER SERVING:
Calories 260; Protein 5g; Carbohydrate 40g; Fat 10g; Sodium 370mg.

Chocolate Cake Make-Over

Brown Butter Apricot Cake

This orange-flavored cake is filled with apricot preserves and topped with a frosting. It was a winner in the 32nd Pillsbury BAKE-OFF® Contest in 1986.

CAKE
- 1 (18.5-oz.) pkg. pudding-included white cake mix
- 1¼ cups water
- ⅓ cup oil
- 1 tablespoon grated orange peel
- 1 teaspoon orange extract
- 3 egg whites

FROSTING AND FILLING
- ½ cup butter (do not use margarine)
- 3 to 4 cups powdered sugar
- ⅓ cup orange juice
- ⅔ cup apricot preserves
- ⅓ cup chopped walnuts or pecans

Heat oven to 350°F. Grease and flour two 8 or 9-inch round cake pans. In large bowl, combine all cake ingredients at low speed until moistened. Beat 2 minutes at high speed. Pour batter into greased and floured pans.

Bake at 350°F. for 20 to 30 minutes or until toothpick inserted in center comes out clean. Cool 15 minutes; remove from pans. Cool completely.

Meanwhile, in small heavy saucepan over medium heat, brown butter until light golden brown, stirring constantly. Remove from heat; cool completely. In large bowl, combine browned butter, 3 cups powdered sugar and orange juice at low speed until moistened. Beat 2 minutes at medium speed or until smooth and well blended. Beat in up to 1 cup additional powdered sugar if necessary for desired spreading consistency.

To assemble cake, slice each cake layer in half horizontally; remove top half from each layer. Spread ⅓ cup of the preserves on bottom half of each layer; replace top half. Place 1 filled layer, top side down, on serving plate; spread with ½ cup of frosting. Top with second filled layer, top side up. Frost sides and top of cake with remaining frosting. Sprinkle walnuts over cake. Refrigerate until serving time. Store in refrigerator.
Yield: 12 servings.

HIGH ALTITUDE:
Above 3500 Feet: Add ¼ cup flour to dry cake mix; increase water to 1⅓ cups. Bake at 375°F. for 20 to 30 minutes.

NUTRITION PER SERVING:
Calories 500; Protein 3g; Carbohydrate 81g; Fat 20g; Sodium 360mg.

Chocolate Praline Layer Cake

This recipe won $40,000 in the 33rd Pillsbury BAKE-OFF® Contest and is one of Pillsbury's most requested recipes. It is spectacular to serve and marvelous to eat!

CAKE
- ½ cup butter or margarine
- ¼ cup whipping cream
- 1 cup firmly packed brown sugar
- ¾ cup coarsely chopped pecans
- 1 (18.25-oz.) pkg. pudding-included devil's food cake mix
- 1¼ cups water
- ⅓ cup oil
- 3 eggs

TOPPING
- 1¾ cups whipping cream
- ¼ cup powdered sugar
- ¼ teaspoon vanilla
  Pecan halves, if desired
  Chocolate Curls, if desired, p. 210

Heat oven to 325°F. In small saucepan, combine butter, ¼ cup whipping cream and brown sugar. Cook over low heat just until butter is melted, stirring occasionally. DO NOT OVERCOOK. Pour into two ungreased 9 or 8-inch round cake pans; sprinkle evenly with chopped pecans.

In large bowl, combine remaining cake ingredients at low speed until moistened. Beat 2 minutes at high speed. Carefully spoon ¼ of batter over pecan mixture around edge of one pan; fill center of pan with ¼ of batter. Repeat with remaining batter and pan.

Bake at 325°F. for 35 to 45 minutes or until top springs back when touched lightly in center. Cool 3 minutes; remove from pans. Cool completely.

In small bowl, beat 1¾ cups whipping cream until soft peaks form. Gradually add powdered sugar and vanilla; beat until stiff peaks form. To assemble cake, place 1 layer, praline side up, on serving plate. Spread top with half of whipped cream mixture. Top with remaining layer, praline side up. Spread top with remaining whipped cream. Garnish with pecans and chocolate curls. Refrigerate until serving time. Store in refrigerator.

Yield: 12 servings.

HIGH ALTITUDE:
Above 3500 Feet: Add 2 tablespoons flour to dry cake mix; increase water to 1⅓ cups. Bake at 350°F. for 30 to 35 minutes. Immediately remove from pans.

NUTRITION PER SERVING:
Calories 610; Protein 5g; Carbohydrate 56g; Fat 41g; Sodium 470mg.

Starlight Double-Delight Cake

In 1951, the $25,000 First Prize in the Pillsbury BAKE-OFF® Contest was awarded to the contestant who entered this inventive chocolate cake. First you make the frosting and then you use part of it in the cake batter.

FROSTING
- 2 (3-oz.) pkg. cream cheese, softened
- ½ cup margarine or butter, softened
- ½ teaspoon vanilla
- ½ teaspoon peppermint extract
- 6 cups (1½ lb.) powdered sugar
- ¼ cup hot water
- 4 oz. semi-sweet chocolate, melted

CAKE
- 2 cups frosting, prepared as directed
- ¼ cup margarine or butter, softened
- 3 eggs
- 2 cups all purpose flour
- 1½ teaspoons baking soda
- 1 teaspoon salt
- ¾ cup milk

Heat oven to 350°F. Grease and flour two 9-inch round cake pans. In large bowl, combine cream cheese, ½ cup margarine, vanilla and peppermint extract; blend until smooth. Add powdered sugar alternately with hot water, beating until smooth. Blend in chocolate.

In another large bowl, combine 2 cups of the frosting mixture and ¼ cup margarine; blend well. Beat in eggs 1 at a time, beating well after each addition. Add flour, baking soda, salt and milk; beat until smooth. Pour batter evenly into greased and floured pans.

Bake at 350°F. for 30 to 40 minutes or until toothpick inserted in center comes out clean. Cool 5 minutes; remove from pans. Cool completely.

To assemble cake, place 1 layer, top side down, on serving plate; spread with about ¼ of frosting. Top with second layer, top side up. Spread sides and top of cake with remaining frosting.

Yield: 12 servings.

HIGH ALTITUDE:
Above 3500 Feet: Increase flour to 2½ cups and use 1½ cups of frosting mixture in cake. Bake as directed above.

NUTRITION PER SERVING:
Calories 520; Protein 6g; Carbohydrate 79g; Fat 21g; Sodium 520mg.

Cook's Note

SOFTENING CREAM CHEESE

Cream cheese can be softened in the microwave oven for ease in spreading or blending it with other ingredients. Remove the cream cheese from its foil package and place it on a microwave-safe plate. Microwave 8 oz. of cream cheese on MEDIUM for 1 to 1½ minutes or until it has softened.

German Chocolate Cake with Coconut Pecan Frosting

Sweet baking chocolate is a blend of unsweetened chocolate, sugar and cocoa butter. It adds a light, mild flavor to this classic cake.

CAKE
   4   oz. sweet baking chocolate, cut into pieces
 ½   cup water
   2   cups sugar
   1   cup margarine or butter, softened
   4   eggs
2½ cups all purpose flour
   1   teaspoon baking soda
 ½   teaspoon salt
   1   cup buttermilk
   1   teaspoon vanilla

COCONUT PECAN FROSTING
   1   cup sugar
   1   cup evaporated milk
 ½   cup margarine or butter
   3   eggs, beaten
1⅓ cups flaked coconut
   1   cup chopped pecans or walnuts
   1   teaspoon vanilla

Heat oven to 350°F. Grease and lightly flour three 9-inch round cake pans. In small saucepan over low heat, melt chocolate with water; cool. In large bowl, beat 2 cups sugar and 1 cup margarine until light and fluffy. Add 4 eggs 1 at a time, beating well after each addition. Stir in chocolate mixture. Add flour and remaining cake ingredients; blend at low speed until well combined. Pour batter into greased and floured pans.

Bake at 350°F. for 35 to 45 minutes or until toothpick inserted in center comes out clean. Cool 5 minutes; remove from pans. Cool completely.

In medium saucepan, combine 1 cup sugar, evaporated milk, ½ cup margarine and 3 eggs. Cook over medium heat until mixture starts to bubble, stirring constantly. Stir in coconut, pecans and 1 teaspoon vanilla. Cool to room temperature. Spread frosting between cake layers and on top, leaving sides unfrosted.
Yield: 12 servings.

HIGH ALTITUDE:
Above 3500 Feet: Decrease sugar in cake to 1¾ cups; decrease baking soda to ¾ teaspoon. Bake at 375°F. for 25 to 30 minutes.

NUTRITION PER SERVING:
Calories 730; Protein 10g; Carbohydrate 85g; Fat 39g; Sodium 540mg.

Toasted Butter Pecan Cake

This yellow cake has a subtle pecan flavor in both the cake and buttery frosting. It may take a little more time to prepare, but it's worth the effort!

 ¼   cup butter, melted (do not substitute margarine)
   2   cups chopped pecans
2¾ cups all purpose flour
   2   teaspoons baking powder
 ½   teaspoon salt
   2   cups sugar
   1   cup butter or margarine, softened
   4   eggs
   1   cup milk
   2   teaspoons vanilla

FROSTING
 ¼   cup butter or margarine, softened
   4   cups powdered sugar
   1   teaspoon vanilla
   4   to 6 tablespoons half-and-half or milk

Heat oven to 350°F. Grease and flour three 8 or 9-inch round cake pans. Combine ¼ cup butter and pecans in shallow pan. Bake at 350°F. for 20 to 25 minutes or until toasted, stirring occasionally. Cool slightly.

In small bowl, combine flour, baking powder and salt. In large bowl, beat sugar and 1 cup butter until light and fluffy. Add eggs 1 at a time, beating well after each addition. Alternately add dry ingredients and milk to sugar mixture, beating well after each addition. Stir in 2 teaspoons vanilla and 1⅓ cups of the toasted pecans. Pour into greased and floured pans.

Bake at 350°F. for 20 to 30 minutes or until cake springs back when touched lightly in center. Cool 10 minutes; remove from pans. Cool completely.

In small bowl, beat ¼ cup butter until light and fluffy. Gradually add powdered sugar, 1 teaspoon vanilla and enough half-and-half for desired spreading consistency. Stir in remaining pecans. Spread frosting between cake layers and on top. **Yield: 16 servings.**

HIGH ALTITUDE:
Above 3500 Feet: Decrease sugar to 1¾ cups. Bake at 375°F. for 20 to 30 minutes.

NUTRITION PER SERVING:
Calories 570; Protein 6g; Carbohydrate 70g; Fat 30g; Sodium 310mg.

WHIPPED CREAM ORANGE MARMALADE CAKE

For the best volume, chill the bowl and beaters before beating the cream.

CAKE
- ¼ **cup frozen orange juice concentrate, thawed**
- 1¼ **cups whipping cream**
- 3 **eggs**
- 1 **teaspoon vanilla**
- 1¾ **cups all purpose flour**
- 1¼ **cups sugar**
- 2 **teaspoons baking powder**
- 2 **teaspoons grated orange peel**
- ½ **teaspoon salt**

FROSTING
- 1 **cup whipping cream**
- ¼ **cup powdered sugar**
- 1 **teaspoon orange-flavored liqueur or orange juice**

FILLING
- 2 **to 4 tablespoons orange-flavored liqueur or orange juice**
- 1 **to 1½ cups orange marmalade**

Heat oven to 350°F. Grease and flour two 9 or 8-inch round cake pans. In large bowl, gradually add ¼ cup orange juice concentrate to 1¼ cups whipping cream; beat at high speed until stiff peaks form. Set aside.

In small bowl, beat eggs and vanilla on high speed until thick and lemon-colored, about 5 to 7 minutes. Fold into whipped cream mixture.

In medium bowl, combine flour and remaining cake ingredients. Fold into whipped cream mixture until well blended. Spread batter evenly in greased and floured pans.

Bake at 350°F. for 23 to 28 minutes or until golden brown and toothpick inserted in center comes out clean. Cool 10 minutes; remove from pans. Cool completely.

In medium bowl, beat all frosting ingredients at medium speed until stiff peaks form. Set aside.

To assemble cake, place 1 layer on serving plate. Sprinkle 1 to 2 tablespoons orange-flavored liqueur evenly over top. Spread with half of the orange marmalade. Top with second layer. Sprinkle remaining 1 to 2 tablespoons of the orange-flavored liqueur over top. Spread with remaining orange marmalade. Frost sides of cake with frosting. Refrigerate 2 hours before serving. Store in refrigerator.
Yield: 12 to 16 servings.

HIGH ALTITUDE:
Above 3500 Feet: Increase flour to 2 cups. Bake as directed above.

NUTRITION PER SERVING:
Calories 350; Protein 4g; Carbohydrate 55g; Fat 13g; Sodium 135mg.

COOK'S NOTE

WHIPPED CREAM AS A FROSTING
Whipped cream can be an easy, delicious frosting for any type of cake. To make 2½ cups of whipped cream (for a 2-layer or 13x9-inch cake), begin with 1¼ cups of chilled whipping cream. Beat the whipping cream at medium speed in a chilled deep bowl with chilled beaters. Beat until soft peaks form; beat in 2 tablespoons powdered sugar. DO NOT OVERBEAT. The whipping cream can be flavored with ½ teaspoon of vanilla, ¼ teaspoon of cinnamon or 1 to 2 tablespoons of brandy, rum or flavored liqueur. Add the flavoring with the powdered sugar. Cakes frosted with whipped cream need to be stored in the refrigerator.

COOKIES 'N CREAM CAKE

Because this cake has been so popular, we've provided a tip that allows you to prepare it as a 13x9-inch sheet cake.

CAKE
- 1 (18.5-oz.) pkg. pudding-included white cake mix
- 1¼ cups water
- ⅓ cup oil
- 3 egg whites
- 1 cup coarsely crushed creme-filled chocolate sandwich cookies

FROSTING
- 3 cups powdered sugar
- ¾ cup shortening
- ¼ cup milk
- 1 teaspoon vanilla

Heat oven to 350°F. Grease and flour two 9 or 8-inch round cake pans. In large bowl, combine all cake ingredients except crushed cookies at low speed until moistened; beat 2 minutes at high speed. By hand, stir in cookies. Pour batter into greased and floured pans.

Bake at 350°F. for 25 to 35 minutes or until toothpick inserted in center comes out clean. Cool 15 minutes; remove from pans. Cool completely.

In small bowl, combine all frosting ingredients; beat until smooth. To assemble cake, place 1 cake layer, top side down, on serving plate; spread evenly with about ¼ of frosting. Top with remaining cake layer, top side up. Spread sides and top of cake with remaining frosting. Garnish as desired.

Yield: 12 servings.

TIP:
Cake can be prepared in greased and floured 13x9-inch pan. Bake at 350°F. for 30 to 40 minutes. Cool completely.

HIGH ALTITUDE:
Above 3500 Feet: Add 3 tablespoons flour to dry cake mix; increase water to 1⅓ cups. Bake at 375°F. for 20 to 30 minutes.

NUTRITION PER SERVING:
Calories 520; Protein 3g; Carbohydrate 72g; Fat 25g; Sodium 350mg.

Cookies 'n Cream Cake

CHOCOLATE SOUR CREAM CAKE

A much requested recipe.

CAKE
- 2 cups all purpose flour
- 2 cups sugar
- 1¼ teaspoons baking soda
- 1 teaspoon salt
- ½ teaspoon baking powder
- 1 cup water
- ¾ cup dairy sour cream
- ¼ cup shortening
- 1 teaspoon vanilla
- 2 eggs
- 4 oz. unsweetened chocolate, cut into pieces, melted, cooled

SOUR CREAM CHOCOLATE FROSTING
- 3 cups powdered sugar
- ¼ cup dairy sour cream
- ¼ cup margarine or butter, softened
- 3 tablespoons milk
- 1 teaspoon vanilla
- 3 oz. unsweetened chocolate, cut into pieces, melted, cooled

Heat oven to 350°F. Grease and flour two 8 or 9-inch round cake pans; line bottom of pans with waxed paper. In medium bowl, combine flour, sugar, baking soda, salt and baking powder; blend well. In large bowl, combine remaining cake ingredients; add dry ingredients. Blend at low speed until moistened; beat 3 minutes at high speed. Pour batter into greased, floured and lined pans.

Bake at 350°F. for 30 to 40 minutes or until toothpick inserted in center comes out clean. Cool 10 minutes; remove from pans. Cool completely.

In small bowl, combine all frosting ingredients at low speed until moistened; beat at high speed until smooth and creamy. To assemble cake, place 1 cake layer, top side down, on serving plate; spread evenly with about ¼ of frosting. Top with remaining cake layer, top side up. Spread sides and top of cake with remaining frosting.

Yield: 12 servings.

HIGH ALTITUDE:
Above 3500 Feet: Decrease sugar in cake to 1¾ cups; omit baking powder. Bake at 375°F. for 25 to 35 minutes.

NUTRITION PER SERVING:
Calories 540; Protein 6g; Carbohydrate 80g; Fat 22g; Sodium 400mg.

Mardi Gras Party Cake

Brown sugar whipped cream surrounds the sides of this delicate cake. It is topped and layered with a coconutty filling.

CAKE
- ⅔ cup butterscotch chips
- ¼ cup water
- 2¼ cups all purpose flour
- 1¼ cups sugar
- 1 teaspoon baking soda
- 1 teaspoon salt
- ½ teaspoon baking powder
- 1 cup buttermilk
- ½ cup shortening
- 3 eggs

FILLING
- ½ cup sugar
- 1 tablespoon cornstarch
- ½ cup half-and-half or evaporated milk
- ⅓ cup water
- ⅓ cup butterscotch chips
- 1 egg, slightly beaten
- 2 tablespoons margarine or butter
- 1 cup coconut
- 1 cup chopped nuts

SEAFOAM CREAM
- 1 cup whipping cream
- ¼ cup firmly packed brown sugar
- ½ teaspoon vanilla

Heat oven to 350°F. Generously grease and flour two 9-inch round cake pans. In small saucepan over low heat, melt ⅔ cup butterscotch chips in ¼ cup water, stirring until smooth. Cool slightly. In large bowl, combine flour, remaining cake ingredients and cooled butterscotch mixture at low speed until moistened; beat 3 minutes at medium speed. Pour batter into greased and floured pans.

Bake at 350°F. for 20 to 30 minutes or until toothpick inserted in center comes out clean. Cool 10 minutes; remove from pans. Cool completely.

In medium saucepan, combine ½ cup sugar and cornstarch; stir in half-and-half, ⅓ cup water, ⅓ cup butterscotch chips and 1 egg. Cook over medium heat until mixture thickens, stirring constantly. Remove from heat. Stir in margarine, coconut and nuts; cool slightly.

In small bowl, beat whipping cream until soft peaks form. Gradually add brown sugar and vanilla, beating until stiff peaks form.

To assemble cake, place 1 cake layer, top side down, on serving plate. Spread with half of filling mixture. Top with second layer, top side up; spread remaining filling on top to within ½ inch of edge. Frost sides and top edge of cake with seafoam cream. Refrigerate at least 1 hour before serving. Store in refrigerator.

Yield: 16 servings.

TIP:
Cake can be baked in 13x9-inch pan. Grease bottom only of pan. Bake at 350°F. for 30 to 35 minutes or until toothpick inserted in center comes out clean. Cool completely. Spread top of cooled cake with filling mixture. Serve topped with seafoam cream.

HIGH ALTITUDE:
Above 3500 Feet: Bake at 350°F. for 30 to 35 minutes. Cool 7 minutes; remove from pans. Cool completely.

NUTRITION PER SERVING:
Calories 460; Protein 6g; Carbohydrate 51g; Fat 27g; Sodium 270mg.

PRINCESS PARTY CAKE

This is an old-fashioned layer cake delicately flavored with pineapple-orange juice, pecans and coconut.

CAKE
- 3 cups all purpose flour
- 1½ cups sugar
- 4 teaspoons baking powder
- 1 teaspoon salt
- 1 cup milk
- ¾ cup shortening
- 5 eggs, reserving 3 egg whites for frosting
- ⅓ cup frozen pineapple-orange juice concentrate, thawed
- 1 teaspoon vanilla

FROSTING
- 1 cup sugar
- ¼ teaspoon cream of tartar
- ¼ teaspoon salt
- ⅓ cup light corn syrup
- ¼ cup frozen pineapple-orange juice concentrate, thawed

FILLING
- ¼ cup coconut
- ¼ cup chopped pecans
- ½ cup crushed pineapple, well drained

Heat oven to 350°F. Generously grease and flour three 8 or 9-inch round cake pans. In large bowl, combine flour, 1½ cups sugar, baking powder, 1 teaspoon salt, milk and shortening; beat at low speed for 1½ minutes. Add 2 eggs and 3 egg yolks 1 at a time, beating well after each addition. Blend in ⅓ cup juice concentrate and vanilla; beat 1½ minutes at low speed. Pour into greased and floured pans.

Bake at 350°F. for 20 to 25 minutes or until toothpick inserted in center comes out clean. Cool 10 minutes; remove from pans. Cool completely.

In top of double boiler, combine reserved egg whites and all frosting ingredients. Place over rapidly boiling water (water should not touch bottom of pan). Cook frosting, beating constantly at highest speed, about 7 minutes or until stiff peaks form. Remove from heat; continue beating until of spreading consistency. To prepare filling, combine ⅓ of frosting with coconut, pecans and pineapple; mix well.

To assemble cake, place 1 cake layer on serving plate; spread with half of filling. Place second layer over filling; spread with remaining filling. Top with remaining cake layer; frost sides and top of cake with remaining frosting.
Yield: 16 servings.

HIGH ALTITUDE:
Above 3500 Feet: Increase flour to 3 cups plus 3 tablespoons. Bake as directed above.

NUTRITION PER SERVING:
Calories 390; Protein 5g; Carbohydrate 61g; Fat 14g; Sodium 280mg.

COOK'S NOTE

MAKING FLUFFY COOKED FROSTINGS

- An electric mixer is necessary to achieve a fluffy cooked frosting. If you do not have a portable mixer, use the head from your standard mixer.
- The presence of fat will reduce the "foaming" action when beating cooked frosting containing egg whites, so make sure the whites contain no specks of yolk and the bowl and beaters are free of any oil or fat residue. Avoid using plastic bowls because they tend to retain fat.
- On damp humid days, slightly less water can be used to make the frosting because it will absorb moisture from the air.
- Beat frosting until stiff peaks form. DO NOT UNDERBEAT.
- When spreading a cooked frosting, use a wet spatula for a smoother appearance.

DARK CHOCOLATE SACHER TORTE

This Viennese classic is made with layers of chocolate cake filled with apricot jam and covered with a creamy chocolate glaze. Serve it with billows of whipped cream.

CAKE
- ½ **cup finely chopped dried apricots**
- ½ **cup rum***
- 1 **(18.25-oz.) pkg. pudding-included devil's food or dark chocolate cake mix**
- ¾ **cup water**
- ⅓ **cup oil**
- 3 **eggs**

GLAZE
- 2 **(10-oz.) jars apricot preserves**
- 2 **tablespoons rum****

FROSTING
- 1 **(6-oz.) pkg. (1 cup) semi-sweet chocolate chips**
- ¾ **cup margarine or butter**
- ½ **to 1 cup sliced almonds**

Heat oven to 350°F. Grease and flour two 9 or 8-inch round cake pans. In small bowl, combine apricots and ½ cup rum; let stand 10 minutes. In large bowl, combine apricot-rum mixture and remaining cake ingredients at low speed until moistened; beat 2 minutes at high speed. Pour into greased and floured pans.

Bake at 350°F. Bake 9-inch layers 25 to 35 minutes; bake 8-inch layers 35 to 45 minutes or until toothpick inserted in center comes out clean. Cool 15 minutes; remove from pans. Cool completely.

In small saucepan over low heat, melt glaze ingredients; strain to remove large apricot pieces. To assemble torte, carefully slice each layer in half horizontally to make 4 layers. Place 1 layer on serving plate; spread with ¼ cup glaze. Repeat with remaining layers and glaze, ending with cake layer. Spread remaining ¼ cup glaze over top of torte, allowing some to run down sides. Refrigerate 1 hour or until glaze is set.

In small saucepan over low heat, melt chocolate chips and margarine, stirring constantly until smooth. Refrigerate 30 minutes or until slightly thickened, stirring occasionally. Spread frosting over sides and top of cake. Arrange almond slices on sides of cake. Refrigerate at least 1 hour before serving. Garnish as desired. Store in refrigerator.
Yield: 16 servings.

TIPS:
* To substitute for ½ cup rum in cake, use 2 teaspoons rum extract plus water to make ½ cup.
** To substitute for 2 tablespoons rum in glaze, use 1 teaspoon rum extract plus water to make 2 tablespoons.

HIGH ALTITUDE:
Above 3500 Feet: Add 3 tablespoons flour to dry cake mix. Bake at 375°F. for 30 to 40 minutes.

NUTRITION PER SERVING:
Calories 470; Protein 5g; Carbohydrate 57g; Fat 23g; Sodium 340mg.

BANANA TORTE

Here's a moist sour cream banana cake filled with a rich vanilla custard and topped with sweetened whipped cream. One taste and you'll know it's homemade.

CAKE
- 1 **cup sugar**
- ½ **cup margarine or butter, softened**
- ¾ **cup mashed ripe bananas**
- 1 **teaspoon vanilla**
- 2 **eggs**
- 2 **cups all purpose flour**
- 1 **teaspoon baking soda**
- 1 **teaspoon baking powder**
- ½ **teaspoon salt**
- ½ **cup dairy sour cream**
- ½ **cup chopped nuts**

FILLING
- 1 **cup milk**
- ½ **cup sugar**
- 3 **tablespoons all purpose flour**
- ¼ **teaspoon salt**
- 2 **egg yolks**
- 1 **teaspoon vanilla**

TOPPING
- **Powdered sugar**
- **Whipping cream, whipped, sweetened***

Heat oven to 350°F. Grease and flour 9-inch square pan. In large bowl, beat 1 cup sugar and margarine until light and fluffy. Add bananas, 1 teaspoon vanilla and 2 eggs; mix well. Gradually add 2 cups flour, baking soda, baking powder and ½ teaspoon salt; mix well. Blend in sour cream; stir in nuts. Pour batter into greased and floured pan.

Bake at 350°F. for 40 to 45 minutes or until toothpick inserted in center comes out clean. Cool 5 minutes; remove from pan. Cool completely.

Meanwhile, in medium saucepan heat milk until very hot; do not boil. In medium bowl, combine ½ cup sugar, 3 tablespoons flour and ¼ teaspoon salt. Stir in hot milk; mix well. Return mixture to saucepan; cook over medium heat until mixture boils and thickens, about 4 to 5 minutes, stirring constantly. In small bowl, beat 2 egg yolks; gradually blend ¼ of hot milk mixture into yolks. Add egg yolk mixture to saucepan; cook 2 to 3 minutes, stirring constantly. Remove from heat; stir in 1 teaspoon vanilla. Cool.

To assemble cake, slice cooled cake horizontally into 2 layers; spread filling between layers. Sprinkle powdered sugar over top layer. Serve topped with sweetened whipped cream. Store in refrigerator.
Yield: 9 servings.

TIP:
* To prepare sweetened whipped cream, for each cup of whipping cream gradually add 2 to 4 tablespoons sugar or powdered sugar during beating.

HIGH ALTITUDE:
Above 3500 Feet: No change.

NUTRITION PER SERVING:
Calories 510; Protein 8g; Carbohydrate 65g; Fat 25g; Sodium 500mg.

MOCHA CREAM CHOCOLATE TORTE

Inspired by a Belgian dessert, this buttercream-layered torte from the 1986 BAKE-OFF® Contest is a perfect ending for a special meal. It is surprisingly easy to make.

CAKE
- 1 (18.25-oz.) pkg. pudding-included German chocolate cake mix
  Water
  Oil
  Eggs

FROSTING
- ½ cup sugar
- ¼ cup cornstarch
- 2 tablespoons instant coffee granules or crystals
- 1¼ cups milk
- 1 cup margarine or butter, softened
- ¼ cup powdered sugar
  Chocolate sprinkles, if desired
  Whole blanched almonds, if desired

Heat oven to 350°F. Grease and flour 13x9-inch pan. Prepare and bake cake mix according to package directions. Cool 15 minutes; remove from pan. Cool completely.

Meanwhile, in medium saucepan combine sugar, cornstarch and instant coffee; blend well. Gradually stir in milk. Cook over medium heat until mixture thickens and boils, stirring constantly. Remove from heat; cover with plastic wrap. Refrigerate 30 minutes or until cool. (Mixture will be very thick.) In large bowl, beat margarine and powdered sugar until well blended. Gradually add cooled coffee mixture; beat until light and fluffy.

To assemble torte, cut cooled cake in half lengthwise. Slice each half in half horizontally to make 4 layers. Place 1 layer on serving tray. Spread top with about ⅓ cup frosting. Repeat with remaining layers and frosting. Frost sides and top of cake. Sprinkle top of torte with chocolate sprinkles; garnish with almonds. Store in refrigerator.
Yield: 12 servings.

HIGH ALTITUDE:
Above 3500 Feet: See package for directions.

NUTRITION PER SERVING:
Calories 460; Protein 5g; Carbohydrate 49g; Fat 28g; Sodium 460mg.

PUMPKIN AND SPICE CREAM TORTE

Enticing cream-filled layers capture the flavors of gingerbread and pumpkin pie in one luscious dessert.

CAKE
- ½ cup firmly packed brown sugar
- ¾ cup margarine or butter, softened
- 2 eggs
- ¾ cup buttermilk
- ¾ cup molasses
- 2¼ cups all purpose flour
- 1¼ teaspoons baking soda
- 1 teaspoon baking powder
- 2 teaspoons cinnamon
- 1 teaspoon ginger
- ½ teaspoon nutmeg
- ¼ teaspoon cloves

FILLING
- 1 cup canned pumpkin
- ½ teaspoon cinnamon
- ¼ teaspoon ginger
- ⅛ teaspoon salt
- ⅛ teaspoon nutmeg
- ⅛ teaspoon cloves
- 5 cups miniature marshmallows
- 2 cups whipping cream
- ¼ cup chopped walnuts or pecans

Heat oven to 350°F. Grease and flour two 9 or 8-inch round cake pans. In large bowl, beat brown sugar, margarine and eggs until light and fluffy. Add buttermilk and molasses; mix well. Add remaining cake ingredients. Blend at low speed until moistened; beat 3 minutes at medium speed. Pour into greased and floured pans.

Bake at 350°F. for 25 to 35 minutes or until toothpick inserted in center comes out clean. Cool 10 minutes; remove from pans. Cool completely.

In large saucepan, combine pumpkin, ½ teaspoon cinnamon, ¼ teaspoon ginger, salt, ⅛ teaspoon nutmeg and ⅛ teaspoon cloves. Add marshmallows. Cook over low heat until marshmallows are melted, stirring occasionally. Remove from heat; beat until mixture is smooth. Cool completely.

In small bowl, beat whipping cream until stiff peaks form (do not overbeat). Fold into cooled pumpkin mixture. Slice each cake layer in half to make 4 layers. Place 1 layer on serving plate; spread with ¼ of filling. Repeat with remaining cake layers and filling, ending with filling; sprinkle with walnuts. Refrigerate at least 2 hours before serving. Store in refrigerator.

Yield: 16 servings.

HIGH ALTITUDE:
Above 3500 Feet: Decrease molasses to ⅔ cup; increase flour to 2¾ cups. Bake at 375°F. for 20 to 30 minutes.

NUTRITION PER SERVING:
Calories 390; Protein 4g; Carbohydrate 44g; Fat 22g; Sodium 270mg.

CANNOLI TORTE

*This is a festive white cake with maraschino cherries and chocolate chips in the filling. **Simply White Cake** p. 114 can be used to make the cake, if desired.*

CAKE
- 3 egg whites
- 1 (18.5-oz.) pkg. pudding-included white cake mix
- 1¼ cups water
- ⅓ cup oil
- 2 teaspoons almond extract

FROSTING
- 1 cup whipping cream
- 1 (15-oz.) container ricotta cheese
- 2 teaspoons vanilla
- 1 can ready-to-spread vanilla frosting
- ½ cup miniature semi-sweet chocolate chips
- ½ cup chopped maraschino cherries
- 1 tablespoon chopped walnuts
- 5 to 6 maraschino cherries, halved

Heat oven to 350°F. Grease and flour two 8 or 9-inch round cake pans. In small bowl, beat egg whites until soft peaks form, about 1 minute; set aside. In large bowl, combine remaining cake ingredients at low speed until moistened; beat 2 minutes at medium speed. Fold in egg whites. Pour batter into greased and floured pans.

Bake at 350°F. for 20 to 30 minutes or until cake springs back when touched lightly in center. Cool 15 minutes; remove from pans. Cool completely.

In small bowl, beat whipping cream until soft peaks form; set aside. In large bowl, combine ricotta cheese and vanilla; beat at medium speed until smooth. Add frosting and whipped cream; blend until smooth. Divide in half. To half of frosting, stir in chocolate chips and ½ cup chopped cherries; blend well.

To assemble cake, split each layer in half horizontally to form 4 layers. Spread cherry-chip filling between cake layers. Frost top and sides with remaining half of frosting. To garnish, sprinkle walnuts on top; place halved cherries around top edge of cake. Refrigerate at least 1 hour or until serving time. Store in refrigerator.

Yield: 16 servings.

HIGH ALTITUDE:
Above 3500 Feet: Add ¼ cup flour to dry cake mix. Bake as directed above.

NUTRITION PER SERVING:
Calories 440; Protein 6g; Carbohydrate 51g; Fat 24g; Sodium 305mg.

RASPBERRY WALNUT TORTE
―――――― ∽ ――――――

This magnificent torte looks like a delicacy you'd see in a European bakery.

CAKE
1¾ **cups all purpose flour**
 2 **teaspoons baking powder**
½ **teaspoon salt**
 1 **cup ground walnuts**
1½ **cups whipping cream**
1½ **cups sugar**
 3 **teaspoons vanilla**
 3 **eggs**

FROSTING
1½ **cups whipping cream**
 1 **(8-oz.) pkg. cream cheese, softened**
 1 **cup sugar**
⅛ **teaspoon salt**
 1 **teaspoon vanilla**
 1 **(12-oz.) jar raspberry preserves**

Heat oven to 350°F. Grease and flour two 9-inch round cake pans. In medium bowl, combine flour, baking powder, ½ teaspoon salt and ground walnuts; mix well. In small bowl, beat 1½ cups whipping cream until stiff peaks form. In large bowl, combine 1½ cups sugar, 3 teaspoons vanilla and eggs; beat 5 minutes at high speed. Fold dry ingredients and whipped cream alternately into sugar mixture, beginning and ending with flour mixture. Pour batter into greased and floured pans.

Bake at 350°F. for 25 to 30 minutes or until toothpick inserted in center comes out clean. Cool 15 minutes; remove from pans. Cool completely.

To prepare frosting, in another small bowl beat 1½ cups whipping cream until stiff peaks form. In large bowl, combine cream cheese, 1 cup sugar, ⅛ teaspoon salt and 1 teaspoon vanilla; blend well. Fold in whipped cream.

To assemble torte, split each layer in half horizontally to form 4 layers. Place 1 layer on serving plate; spread with ½ cup frosting. Top with second cake layer; spread with ½ cup of the raspberry preserves. Top with third cake layer; spread with ½ cup frosting. Top with remaining cake layer. Frost sides of cake with frosting, reserving about 1 cup for decorating. Spread remaining preserves on top of cake. Using decorating bag and star tip, pipe reserved frosting in lattice design over top of cake; pipe border around top and bottom edges of cake. Store in refrigerator.

Yield: 16 servings.

HIGH ALTITUDE:
Above 3500 Feet: Decrease baking powder to 1¾ teaspoons; decrease sugar in cake to 1⅓ cups. Bake at 375°F. for 25 to 30 minutes.

NUTRITION PER SERVING:
Calories 480; Protein 6g; Carbohydrate 59g; Fat 26g; Sodium 200mg.

CARROT CAKE WITH CREAMY COCONUT FROSTING

Pineapple not only adds an interesting flavor to this classic cake, it also helps to keep it moist. It's easy to make and is perfect for any occasion.

CAKE
2½ cups all purpose flour
2 teaspoons baking soda
1 teaspoon salt
1 teaspoon cinnamon, if desired
2 cups sugar
1 cup oil
2 teaspoons vanilla
2 eggs
2 cups shredded carrots
1 (8-oz.) can crushed pineapple, well drained
½ cup raisins
½ cup chopped nuts

CREAMY COCONUT FROSTING
1 (8¼-oz.) pkg. cream cheese, softened
2½ cups powdered sugar
6 tablespoons margarine or butter, softened
2 teaspoons vanilla
1 cup coconut
½ cup chopped nuts

Heat oven to 350°F. Grease and flour 13x9-inch pan. In medium bowl, combine flour, baking soda, salt and cinnamon; set aside. In large bowl, combine sugar, oil, 2 teaspoons vanilla and eggs; beat well. Stir in flour mixture; mix well. Stir in carrots, pineapple, raisins and ½ cup nuts. Pour batter into greased and floured pan.

Bake at 350°F. for 50 to 60 minutes or until cake springs back when touched lightly in center. Cool completely.

In large bowl, combine cream cheese, powdered sugar, margarine and 2 teaspoons vanilla; beat until smooth. Stir in coconut and ½ cup nuts. Spread over cooled cake.
Yield: 16 servings.

HIGH ALTITUDE:
Above 3500 Feet: Increase flour to 2¾ cups; decrease sugar to 1½ cups. Bake as directed above.

NUTRITION PER SERVING:
Calories 560; Protein 6g; Carbohydrate 66g; Fat 30g; Sodium 380mg.

GOLDEN CARROT PINEAPPLE CAKE

We've substantially reduced the fat and calories.

CAKE
1½ cups all purpose flour
1 cup whole wheat flour
2 teaspoons baking soda
1 teaspoon cinnamon
½ teaspoon salt
1 cup sugar
⅔ cup oil
1 (8-oz.) can crushed pineapple in its own juice, undrained
½ cup frozen cholesterol-free egg product, thawed
2 teaspoons vanilla
2 cups shredded carrots
½ cup raisins

LIGHT CREAMY FROSTING
4 oz. light cream cheese, softened
2 tablespoons margarine, softened
1 cup powdered sugar
1 teaspoon vanilla

Heat oven to 350°F. Grease and flour 13x9-inch pan. In medium bowl, combine all purpose flour, whole wheat flour, baking soda, cinnamon and salt; set aside. In large bowl, combine sugar, oil, pineapple, egg product and 2 teaspoons vanilla; beat well. Stir in flour mixture; mix well. Stir in carrots and raisins. Pour batter into greased and floured pan.

Bake at 350°F. for 30 to 40 minutes or until top springs back when touched lightly in center. Cool completely.

In small bowl, combine cream cheese and margarine; beat until smooth. Gradually beat in powdered sugar and vanilla. Spread over cooled cake.
Yield: 16 servings.

HIGH ALTITUDE:
Above 3500 Feet: Decrease sugar to ¾ cup. Bake as directed above.

NUTRITION PER SERVING:
Calories 290; Protein 4g; Carbohydrate 41g; Fat 12g; Sodium 280mg.

Golden Carrot Pineapple Cake

PINEAPPLE UPSIDE-DOWN CAKE

This pretty cake is welcome for dessert anytime — it's a small cake so there are few leftovers.

- ½ **cup firmly packed brown sugar**
- ¼ **cup margarine or butter, melted**
- 6 **canned pineapple slices, drained**
- 6 **maraschino cherries**
- 2 **eggs, separated**
- ½ **cup sugar**
- ¾ **cup all purpose flour**
- ½ **teaspoon baking powder**
- ¼ **teaspoon salt**
- ¼ **cup pineapple juice**
   Whipped cream

Heat oven to 350°F. In small bowl, combine brown sugar and margarine; blend well. Spread in bottom of ungreased 9-inch round cake pan. Arrange pineapple slices and maraschino cherries over brown sugar mixture. Set aside.

In small bowl, beat egg yolks until thick and lemon colored. Gradually add sugar; beat well. Add flour, baking powder, salt and pineapple juice to egg yolk mixture; mix well. In another small bowl, beat egg whites until stiff peaks form; fold into batter. Pour batter evenly over pineapple slices and cherries.

Bake at 350°F. for 30 to 35 minutes or until toothpick inserted in center comes out clean. Cool upright in pan 2 minutes; invert onto serving plate. Serve warm with whipped cream.
Yield: 6 servings.

HIGH ALTITUDE:
Above 3500 Feet: Increase flour to ¾ cup plus 3 tablespoons. Bake at 375°F. for 30 to 35 minutes.

NUTRITION PER SERVING:
Calories 340; Protein 4g; Carbohydrate 55g; Fat 13g; Sodium 230mg.

CRANBERRY UPSIDE-DOWN CAKE

Crimson cranberries almost glow when this dessert is turned out of the pan. Serve it warm or cool, with cream or whipped cream.

- ⅔ **cup sugar**
- 2 **cups fresh or frozen cranberries (do not thaw)**

CAKE
- 1¼ **cups all purpose flour**
- 1 **cup sugar**
- 1½ **teaspoons baking powder**
- ½ **teaspoon salt**
- 1 **teaspoon grated lemon peel**
- ⅔ **cup milk**
- ¼ **cup shortening**
- ¼ **teaspoon vanilla**
- 1 **egg**

Heat oven to 350°F. Grease 8-inch square pan. Sprinkle ⅓ cup of the sugar in pan. Arrange cranberries over sugar; sprinkle with remaining ⅓ cup sugar. Cover with foil. Bake at 350°F. for 30 minutes. Remove foil; cool.

In large bowl, combine all cake ingredients; blend at low speed until moistened. Beat 2 minutes at medium speed. Pour batter evenly over cranberries.

Bake at 350°F. for 40 to 50 minutes or until toothpick inserted in center comes out clean. For easy removal, run knife around edge of pan. Invert onto serving plate, leaving pan over cake for 2 minutes; remove pan. Serve warm or cold.
Yield: 9 servings.

HIGH ALTITUDE:
Above 3500 Feet: Decrease sugar in cake to ¾ cup. Bake as directed above.

NUTRITION PER SERVING:
Calories 290; Protein 3g; Carbohydrate 54g; Fat 7g; Sodium 190mg.

FROSTED BANANA SNACK CAKE

Well-ripened bananas are the flavor secret of this yummy cake. To hasten ripening, place bananas in a paper or plastic bag or fruit-ripening bowl.

CAKE
- ¾ cup sugar
- ⅓ cup margarine or butter, softened
- ¾ cup mashed ripe bananas
- ¼ cup buttermilk
- 1 teaspoon vanilla
- 1 egg
- 1¼ cups all purpose flour
- 1 teaspoon baking powder
- ½ teaspoon baking soda
- ½ teaspoon salt
- ½ teaspoon cinnamon
- ⅛ teaspoon cloves
- ⅛ teaspoon nutmeg
- ¼ cup chopped walnuts or pecans

FROSTING
- 2 cups powdered sugar
- 1 (3-oz.) pkg. cream cheese, softened
- 2 tablespoons margarine or butter, softened
- 1 tablespoon milk
- ½ teaspoon vanilla

Heat oven to 350°F. Grease and flour 8 or 9-inch square pan. In large bowl, beat sugar and ⅓ cup margarine until light and fluffy. Add bananas, buttermilk, vanilla and egg; mix well. Add remaining ingredients except nuts; mix well. Stir in nuts. Spread batter in greased and floured pan.

Bake at 350°F. for 25 to 30 minutes or until golden brown and toothpick inserted in center comes out clean. Cool completely.

In medium bowl, combine all frosting ingredients; beat until smooth and creamy. Spread over cooled cake. Store in refrigerator.
Yield: 9 servings.

HIGH ALTITUDE:
Above 3500 Feet: Decrease sugar to ½ cup. Bake as directed above.

NUTRITION PER SERVING:
Calories 390; Protein 4g; Carbohydrate 58g; Fat 16g; Sodium 370mg.

BANANA SNACK CAKE

This cake is perfect for after school snacking or toting to a picnic.

- 1 cup sugar
- 1 cup margarine or butter, softened
- 2 eggs
- ½ cup buttermilk
- 1 cup mashed ripe bananas
- 1 teaspoon vanilla
- 2 cups all purpose flour
- 1 cup quick-cooking rolled oats
- 1½ teaspoons baking soda
- ½ teaspoon salt
- 1 (6-oz.) pkg. (1 cup) semi-sweet chocolate chips
- ½ cup chopped nuts

Heat oven to 350°F. Grease 13x9-inch pan. In large bowl, combine sugar, margarine and eggs; mix well. Stir in buttermilk, bananas and vanilla; blend well. Stir in flour, oats, baking soda and salt; mix well. Stir in chocolate chips. Spread batter in greased pan. Sprinkle nuts evenly over top.

Bake at 350°F. for 30 to 35 minutes or until toothpick inserted in center comes out clean.
Yield: 16 servings.

HIGH ALTITUDE:
Above 3500 Feet: No change.

NUTRITION PER SERVING:
Calories 340; Protein 5g; Carbohydrate 38g; Fat 19g; Sodium 320mg.

CHOCOLATE FUDGE SNACK CAKE

Serve this rich, chocolaty cake warm with vanilla ice cream.

CAKE
- ½ cup margarine or butter
- 1 (11.75-oz.) jar hot fudge ice cream topping
- 1½ cups all purpose flour
- 1½ cups sugar
- 1 cup mashed potato flakes
- 1 teaspoon baking soda
- ¾ cup buttermilk
- 1 teaspoon vanilla
- 2 eggs
- 1 cup finely chopped walnuts
- 1 (6-oz.) pkg. (1 cup) semi-sweet chocolate chips

GLAZE
- ½ cup sugar
- ¼ cup buttermilk
- ¼ cup margarine or butter
- 1½ teaspoons light corn syrup or water
- ¼ teaspoon baking soda
- ½ teaspoon vanilla
- 2 tablespoons chopped walnuts

Heat oven to 350°F. Grease and flour 13x9-inch pan. In small saucepan over low heat, melt ½ cup margarine and fudge topping, stirring constantly until smooth. In large bowl, combine flour and remaining cake ingredients except 1 cup walnuts and chocolate chips; beat at low speed until well blended. Add fudge mixture; beat 2 minutes at medium speed. By hand, stir in 1 cup walnuts and chocolate chips. Pour batter into greased and floured pan.

Bake at 350°F. for 40 to 45 minutes or until toothpick inserted in center comes out clean.

In small saucepan, combine all glaze ingredients except vanilla and 2 tablespoons walnuts. Bring to a boil over medium heat. Reduce heat; simmer for 5 minutes or until light golden brown, stirring constantly. Remove from heat; stir in vanilla. Pour warm glaze over warm cake, spreading to cover. Sprinkle with 2 tablespoons walnuts. Serve warm or cool.

Yield: 16 servings.

HIGH ALTITUDE:
Above 3500 Feet: Increase flour to 1¾ cups; decrease sugar in cake to 1 cup. Bake as directed above. Increase simmering time for glaze to 8 minutes.

NUTRITION PER SERVING:
Calories 450; Protein 6g; Carbohydrate 57g; Fat 22g; Sodium 220mg.

CHOCOLATE CHERRY BARS

Cake mix and cherry pie filling combine to create a moist cake rich in chocolate flavor with cherries throughout.

CAKE BARS
- 1 (18.25-oz.) pkg. pudding-included devil's food cake mix
- 1 (21-oz.) can cherry fruit pie filling
- 1 teaspoon almond extract
- 2 eggs, beaten

FROSTING
- 1 cup sugar
- ⅓ cup milk
- 5 tablespoons margarine or butter
- 1 (6-oz.) pkg. (1 cup) semi-sweet chocolate chips

Heat oven to 350°F. Grease and flour 15x10x1-inch baking pan or 13x9-inch pan. In large bowl, combine all bar ingredients; stir until well blended. Pour into greased and floured pan.

Bake at 350°F. in 15x10x1-inch pan for 20 to 30 minutes or in 13x9-inch pan for 25 to 30 minutes or until toothpick inserted in center comes out clean.

In small saucepan, combine sugar, milk and margarine. Bring to a boil; boil 1 minute, stirring constantly. Remove from heat; stir in chocolate chips until smooth. Pour and spread over warm cake. Cool completely. Cut into squares. Garnish as desired.

Yield: 36 to 48 servings.

HIGH ALTITUDE:
Above 3500 Feet: Bake at 375°F. in 15x10x1-inch pan for 20 to 30 minutes or in 13x9-inch pan for 25 to 30 minutes.

NUTRITION PER SERVING:
Calories 120; Protein 1g; Carbohydrate 20g; Fat 4g; Sodium 95mg.

S'MORE SNACK CAKE

Graham crackers, chocolate chips and marshmallow creme are among the ingredients in this delightful cake, inspired by the popular picnic treat of the same name. You can be sure everyone will be back for more.

- 1   cup all purpose flour
- 2   cups graham cracker crumbs
- 1   teaspoon baking powder
- ½   teaspoon baking soda
- ½   teaspoon salt
- 1   cup firmly packed brown sugar
- ½   cup shortening
- 3   eggs
- 1   cup milk
- 1   cup miniature semi-sweet chocolate chips
- 1   (7-oz.) jar (1½ cups) marshmallow creme

Heat oven to 350°F. Grease and flour 13x9-inch pan. In medium bowl, combine flour, graham cracker crumbs, baking powder, baking soda and salt; mix well. Set aside.

In large bowl, beat brown sugar, shortening and eggs until well blended. Add dry ingredients and milk; mix at low speed until well blended. Beat at medium speed 1 minute. Stir in ⅔ cup of the chocolate chips. Spread batter evenly in greased and floured pan.

Bake at 350°F. for 25 to 35 minutes until toothpick inserted in center comes out clean. Cool 15 minutes.

Meanwhile, melt remaining ⅓ cup chocolate chips in small saucepan over low heat. Spoon teaspoonfuls of marshmallow creme onto top of warm cake; carefully spread with knife dipped in hot water. Drizzle with melted chocolate and swirl chocolate through marshmallow creme to marble. Cool completely.
Yield: 16 servings.

HIGH ALTITUDE:
Above 3500 Feet: Increase flour to 1 cup plus 2 tablespoons. Bake at 375°F. for 20 to 30 minutes.

NUTRITION PER SERVING:
Calories 290; Protein 4g; Carbohydrate 44g; Fat 12g; Sodium 220mg.

DOUBLE CHOCOLATE CREAM CHEESE CAKE

A meringue-like topping forms on this dense chocolate cake.

CAKE
- 3   cups all purpose flour
- 2   cups sugar
- ½   cup unsweetened cocoa
- 2   teaspoons baking soda
- ½   teaspoon salt
- 2   cups hot coffee
- ⅔   cup oil
- 2   tablespoons vinegar
- 2   teaspoons vanilla
- 2   eggs

TOPPING
- ⅓   cup sugar
- 1   (8-oz.) pkg. cream cheese, softened
- ½   teaspoon vanilla
- 1   egg
- 1   (6-oz.) pkg. (1 cup) semi-sweet chocolate chips
- 1   cup finely chopped nuts
- ¼   cup sugar

Heat oven to 350°F. Grease and flour bottom only of 13x9-inch pan. In large bowl, combine all cake ingredients at low speed until moistened; beat 1 minute at medium speed (batter will be thin). Pour batter into greased and floured pan.

In small bowl, beat ⅓ cup sugar, cream cheese, ½ teaspoon vanilla and 1 egg until fluffy; stir in chocolate chips and nuts. Spoon teaspoonfuls of topping evenly over batter; sprinkle with ¼ cup sugar.

Bake at 350°F. for 45 to 60 minutes or until toothpick inserted in cake portion comes out clean. Cool completely. Store in refrigerator.
Yield: 16 servings.

HIGH ALTITUDE:
Above 3500 Feet: Decrease baking soda to 1½ teaspoons. Bake at 375°F. for 60 to 70 minutes.

NUTRITION PER SERVING:
Calories 480; Protein 7g; Carbohydrate 59g; Fat 24g; Sodium 280mg.

APRICOT GOOEY CAKE

This easy-to-make snack cake is just the right size for smaller families. An apricot and coconut topping makes it special.

½ **cup dried apricots**
1½ **cups water**

CAKE
1¾ **cups all purpose flour**
½ **teaspoon baking powder**
½ **teaspoon baking soda**
½ **teaspoon salt**
1 **cup sugar**
⅓ **cup margarine or butter, softened**
½ **teaspoon vanilla**
¼ **teaspoon lemon extract**
1 **egg**
⅔ **cup water**

FROSTING
¼ **cup firmly packed brown sugar**
2 **tablespoons margarine or butter**
Reserved pureed apricots
½ **cup coconut**

In small saucepan, combine apricots and 1½ cups water. Cook over medium heat 15 to 20 minutes or until apricots are tender, stirring occasionally. Drain; puree apricots. Set aside.

Heat oven to 350°F. Grease and flour 9-inch square pan. In small bowl, combine flour, baking powder, baking soda and salt. In large bowl, beat sugar and ⅓ cup margarine until light and fluffy. Add vanilla, lemon extract and egg; beat well. Alternately add dry ingredients and ⅔ cup water to sugar mixture, beating well after each addition. Stir in 2 tablespoons of the pureed apricots. Pour batter into greased and floured pan.

Bake at 350°F. for 25 to 35 minutes or until toothpick inserted in center comes out clean. Cool slightly.

In small saucepan, combine brown sugar, 2 tablespoons margarine and remaining pureed apricots. Bring to a boil over medium heat; boil 1 minute, stirring constantly. Remove from heat; stir in coconut. Immediately spread over warm cake. Cool completely.
Yield: 9 servings.

HIGH ALTITUDE:
Above 3500 Feet: Bake at 375°F. for 25 to 35 minutes.

NUTRITION PER SERVING:
Calories 330; Protein 4g; Carbohydrate 53g; Fat 12g; Sodium 320mg.

MACAROON COOKIE CAKE

In this recipe, a quick-to-mix chocolate cake is baked with a coconut topping. It's like eating a candy bar!

CAKE
1¾ **cups all purpose flour**
1¼ **cups sugar**
1½ **teaspoons baking powder**
1 **teaspoon salt**
½ **teaspoon baking soda**
½ **cup margarine or butter, softened**
1 **cup buttermilk**
1 **teaspoon vanilla**
3 **eggs**
3 **oz. unsweetened chocolate, melted**

TOPPING
1 **(14-oz.) can sweetened condensed milk (not evaporated)**
1 **(7-oz.) pkg. (2⅔ cups) coconut**
1 **teaspoon vanilla**

Heat oven to 350°F. Grease and flour 13x9-inch pan. In large bowl, combine all cake ingredients at low speed until moistened; beat 3 minutes at medium speed. Pour batter into greased and floured pan. In small bowl, combine all topping ingredients; mix well. Carefully drop by teaspoonfuls over batter.

Bake at 350°F. for 30 to 40 minutes or until top springs back when touched lightly in center. Cool completely.
Yield: 15 servings.

HIGH ALTITUDE:
Above 3500 Feet: Increase flour to 2 cups; decrease sugar to 1 cup. Bake at 375°F. for 30 to 40 minutes.

NUTRITION PER SERVING:
Calories 370; Protein 7g; Carbohydrate 50g; Fat 17g; Sodium 350mg.

Pumpkin Gingerbread with Caramel Sauce

Although this old-time favorite is best served warm, it can be made several hours ahead and served at room temperature.

GINGERBREAD
2¼ cups all purpose flour
½ cup sugar
⅔ cup margarine or butter
¾ cup coarsely chopped pecans
1 teaspoon baking soda
1½ teaspoons ginger
½ teaspoon cinnamon
¼ teaspoon salt
¼ teaspoon cloves
¾ cup buttermilk
½ cup light molasses
½ cup canned pumpkin
1 egg

CARAMEL SAUCE
½ cup margarine or butter
1¼ cups firmly packed brown sugar
2 tablespoons light corn syrup
½ cup whipping cream

Heat oven to 350°F. In large bowl, combine flour and sugar. Using pastry blender or fork, cut in ⅔ cup margarine until mixture resembles fine crumbs. Stir in pecans. Press 1¼ cups of crumb mixture into bottom of ungreased 9-inch square pan. To remaining crumb mixture, add remaining gingerbread ingredients; mix well. Pour evenly in crust-lined pan.

Bake at 350°F. for 40 to 50 minutes or until toothpick inserted in center comes out clean.

In medium saucepan, melt ½ cup margarine; stir in brown sugar and corn syrup. Bring to a boil; cook until sugar dissolves, about 1 minute, stirring constantly. Stir in whipping cream; return to a boil. Remove from heat. Serve sauce over warm gingerbread topped with a scoop of ice cream. Garnish with chopped pecans, if desired.
Yield: 12 servings.

MICROWAVE DIRECTIONS:
To prepare sauce in microwave, place margarine in 4-cup microwave-safe measuring cup. Microwave on HIGH for 1 minute or until melted. Stir in brown sugar and corn syrup. Microwave on HIGH for 2 to 3 minutes or until sugar dissolves, stirring once halfway through cooking. Stir in whipping cream. Microwave on HIGH for 45 to 60 seconds or until mixture boils, stirring once halfway through cooking.

HIGH ALTITUDE:
Above 3500 Feet: Add 3 tablespoons flour to remaining crumb mixture. Bake as directed above.

NUTRITION PER SERVING:
Calories 510; Protein 5g; Carbohydrate 63g; Fat 27g; Sodium 360mg.

Toffee Bar Cake

You'll love this brown sugar cake with a crunchy candy bar topping.

2 cups all purpose flour
2 cups firmly packed brown sugar
½ cup shortening
1 teaspoon baking soda
½ teaspoon salt
1 cup milk
1 teaspoon vanilla
1 egg
½ cup chopped nuts
6 (1.4-oz.) chocolate covered toffee bars, broken into small pieces

Heat oven to 350°F. Grease 13x9-inch pan. In large bowl, combine flour, brown sugar and shortening until crumbly; reserve 1 cup for topping. Add baking soda, salt, milk, vanilla and egg to remaining crumb mixture; beat 3 minutes. Pour into greased pan. Sprinkle with reserved crumb mixture, nuts and toffee bars.

Bake at 350°F. for 30 to 40 minutes or until toothpick inserted in center comes out clean. Cool completely. Serve with whipped cream, if desired. 12 servings.

HIGH ALTITUDE:
Above 3500 Feet: Decrease brown sugar to 1¾ cups. Reserve ¾ cup mixture for topping. Increase eggs to 2. Bake at 375°F. for 30 to 40 minutes.

NUTRITION PER SERVING:
Calories 440; Protein 5g; Carbohydrate 58g; Fat 21g; Sodium 245mg.

Gingerbread with Raspberry Pear Sauce

Gingerbread — classic, yet classy! Experience this unique flavor combination of red raspberries and pears served over wedges of traditional gingerbread.

GINGERBREAD

- 1⅓ cups all purpose flour
- ½ cup firmly packed brown sugar
- ½ teaspoon baking powder
- ½ teaspoon baking soda
- ¼ teaspoon salt
- ¾ teaspoon cinnamon
- ½ teaspoon ginger
- ½ cup shortening or margarine
- ½ cup boiling water
- ½ cup molasses
- 1 egg, slightly beaten

RASPBERRY PEAR SAUCE

- 1 (10-oz.) pkg. frozen raspberries, thawed
- ¼ cup sugar
- 1 tablespoon lemon juice
- 3 firm pears, peeled, cut into bite-size pieces (about 3 cups)

Heat oven to 350°F. Grease bottom only of 9-inch round pan. In large bowl, combine flour, brown sugar, baking powder, baking soda, salt, cinnamon and ginger; mix well. Add remaining gingerbread ingredients; blend well. Pour into greased pan.

Bake at 350°F. for 25 to 35 minutes or until toothpick inserted in center comes out clean.

Drain raspberries, reserving ¼ cup liquid. In blender container or food processor bowl with metal blade, blend raspberries and reserved ¼ cup liquid at highest speed until smooth. Press through large strainer to remove seeds; discard seeds. In large skillet, combine raspberry puree, sugar, lemon juice and pears. Bring to a boil. Reduce heat; simmer until pears are tender. Serve sauce warm or cool over wedges of gingerbread. Garnish each serving with sweetened whipped cream, if desired. **Yield: 8 servings.**

MICROWAVE DIRECTIONS:
To prepare gingerbread, prepare batter as directed above. Pour into ungreased 8-inch (1½-quart) round microwave-safe dish. Microwave on HIGH for 5 to 7 minutes or until toothpick inserted in center comes out clean. Cool directly on counter for 10 minutes.

To prepare sauce, prepare raspberry puree as directed above. In medium microwave-safe bowl or 8-cup microwave-safe measuring cup, combine raspberry puree with sugar, lemon juice and pears. Microwave on HIGH for 5 to 6 minutes or until pears are tender, stirring twice during cooking. Serve as directed above.

HIGH ALTITUDE:
Above 3500 Feet: Increase flour to 1⅔ cups; decrease brown sugar to ¼ cup. Bake or microwave as directed above.

NUTRITION PER SERVING:
Calories 410; Protein 3g; Carbohydrate 67g; Fat 14g; Sodium 170mg.

COOK'S NOTE

PEARS

Pears come in many varieties. The Bartlett variety is best for fresh snacks, salads and poaching. Bosc, Anjou and Comice varieties are good when firm for baking and when fully ripened for snacks and salads. Since pears must be picked before they're ripe, allow them to ripen at room temperature in a paper bag or a loosely covered bowl. When ripe, pears yield to a gentle pressure of the hand.

Gingerbread with Raspberry Pear Sauce

CHOCOLATE CHIP ZUCCHINI CAKE

Sheet cakes are perfect for any occasion and they're quick and easy to make. This one is great unfrosted, or can be frosted with your favorite chocolate frosting. Choose small, firm zucchini to use in this recipe.

1½ cups sugar
½ cup margarine or butter, softened
¼ cup oil
1 teaspoon vanilla
2 eggs
2½ cups all purpose flour
¼ cup unsweetened cocoa
1 teaspoon baking soda
½ cup buttermilk
2 cups shredded zucchini
½ to 1 cup semi-sweet chocolate chips
½ cup chopped nuts

Heat oven to 350°F. Grease and flour 13x9-inch pan. In large bowl, combine sugar, margarine, oil, vanilla and eggs; beat well. Add flour, cocoa, baking soda and buttermilk; blend well. Fold in zucchini, chocolate chips and nuts. Spread in greased and floured pan.

Bake at 350°F. for 35 to 45 minutes or until toothpick inserted in center comes out clean. Cool completely. Frost as desired.
Yield: 16 servings.

HIGH ALTITUDE:
Above 3500 Feet: Bake at 375°F. for 30 to 40 minutes.

NUTRITION PER SERVING:
Calories 330; Protein 4g; Carbohydrate 42g; Fat 17g; Sodium 160mg.

CARAMEL APPLE CAKE

Brown sugar gives this cake its great caramel flavor. Raisins and apples add an interesting texture. Refer to p. 11 for suggestions on varieties of apples to use when baking.

CAKE
1¾ cups all purpose flour
1½ cups firmly packed brown sugar
1½ teaspoons cinnamon
½ teaspoon salt
½ teaspoon baking powder
½ teaspoon baking soda
1 teaspoon vanilla
¾ cup margarine or butter, softened
3 eggs
1½ cups finely chopped peeled apples
½ to 1 cup chopped nuts
½ cup raisins, if desired

FROSTING
2 cups powdered sugar
¼ teaspoon cinnamon
¼ cup margarine or butter, melted
½ teaspoon vanilla
4 to 5 teaspoons milk

Heat oven to 350°F. Grease and flour 13x9-inch pan. In large bowl, combine flour, brown sugar, cinnamon, salt, baking powder, baking soda, vanilla, margarine and eggs; beat 3 minutes at medium speed. Stir in apples, nuts and raisins. Pour into greased and floured pan.

Bake at 350°F. for 30 to 40 minutes or until toothpick inserted in center comes out clean. Cool completely.

In small bowl, blend all frosting ingredients, adding enough milk for desired spreading consistency. Spread over cooled cake.
Yield: 15 servings.

HIGH ALTITUDE:
Above 3500 Feet: Decrease brown sugar to 1 cup. Bake at 375°F. for 25 to 35 minutes.

NUTRITION PER SERVING:
Calories 390; Protein 4g; Carbohydrate 53g; Fat 18g; Sodium 280mg.

DIXIE SPICE CAKE WITH CARAMEL FROSTING

This delicious old-fashioned cake is rich with traditional spice cake flavor.

CAKE
2¼ cups all purpose flour
1¼ cups firmly packed brown sugar
½ cup sugar
1 teaspoon baking soda
½ teaspoon salt
½ teaspoon nutmeg
½ teaspoon allspice
1 cup buttermilk
⅔ cup shortening
1 teaspoon vanilla
3 eggs
1 cup chopped walnuts or pecans

CARAMEL FROSTING
½ cup margarine or butter
1 cup firmly packed brown sugar
¼ cup milk
3 cups powdered sugar
½ teaspoon vanilla

Heat oven to 350°F. Generously grease and flour bottom only of 13x9-inch pan. In large bowl, combine all cake ingredients except nuts at low speed until moistened; beat 3 minutes at medium speed. Stir in nuts. Pour batter into greased and floured pan.

Bake at 350°F. for 40 to 45 minutes or until top springs back when touched lightly in center. Cool completely.

In medium saucepan, melt margarine; add brown sugar. Cook over low heat 2 minutes, stirring constantly. Add milk; continue cooking until mixture comes to a rolling boil. Remove from heat. Gradually add powdered sugar and vanilla; mix well. If needed, add a few drops of milk for desired spreading consistency. Spread over cooled cake.
Yield: 12 servings.

HIGH ALTITUDE:
Above 3500 Feet: Increase flour to 2¼ cups plus 3 tablespoons; decrease brown sugar in cake to 1 cup. Bake at 375°F. for 35 to 40 minutes.

NUTRITION PER SERVING:
Calories 640; Protein 6g; Carbohydrate 94g; Fat 27g; Sodium 330mg.

BUTTER CRUMSHUS CAKE

Softened cream cheese adds moistness to this quick cake. The topping is baked on.

CAKE
⅓ cup butter or margarine, softened
1 (3-oz.) pkg. cream cheese, softened
1 cup all purpose flour
⅔ cup sugar
1 teaspoon baking powder
¼ teaspoon baking soda
¼ teaspoon salt
½ teaspoon vanilla
¼ cup milk
1 egg

TOPPING
¼ cup firmly packed brown sugar
3 tablespoons all purpose flour
1 tablespoon butter or margarine

Heat oven to 350°F. Generously grease and flour bottom only of 8-inch square pan. In large bowl, beat ⅓ cup butter and cream cheese until light and fluffy. Add flour and remaining cake ingredients. Blend at low speed until well combined; beat 2 minutes at medium speed. Spread batter evenly in greased and floured pan.

In small bowl, combine all topping ingredients until crumbly. Sprinkle topping evenly over batter.

Bake at 350°F. for 30 to 40 minutes or until toothpick inserted in center comes out clean. Serve warm or cool.
Yield: 6 to 8 servings.

HIGH ALTITUDE:
Above 3500 Feet: Decrease sugar to ½ cup. Bake as directed above.

NUTRITION PER SERVING:
Calories 280; Protein 4g; Carbohydrate 38g; Fat 13g; Sodium 280mg.

ORANGE KISS-ME CAKE

~

At the 1950 Pillsbury BAKE-OFF® Contest, this fresh orange cake won the $25,000 Grand Prize. For the freshest flavor, use a sweet, juicy, thin-skinned orange.

CAKE
1 orange
1 cup raisins
⅓ cup walnuts
2 cups all purpose flour
1 cup sugar
1 teaspoon baking soda
1 teaspoon salt
1 cup milk
½ cup margarine, softened, or shortening
2 eggs

TOPPING
Reserved ⅓ cup orange juice
⅓ cup sugar
1 teaspoon cinnamon
¼ cup finely chopped walnuts

Heat oven to 350°F. Grease and flour 13x9-inch pan. Squeeze orange, reserving ⅓ cup juice for topping. In blender container, food processor bowl with metal blade or food mill, grind together orange peel and pulp, raisins and ⅓ cup walnuts; set aside.

In large bowl, combine flour and remaining cake ingredients at low speed until moistened; beat 3 minutes at medium speed. Stir in orange-raisin mixture. Pour batter into greased and floured pan.

Bake at 350°F. for 35 to 45 minutes or until toothpick inserted in center comes out clean. Drizzle reserved ⅓ cup orange juice over warm cake in pan. In small bowl, combine ⅓ cup sugar and cinnamon; mix well. Stir in ¼ cup walnuts; sprinkle over cake. Cool completely.
Yield: 12 to 16 servings.

HIGH ALTITUDE:
Above 3500 Feet: Increase flour to 2 cups plus 2 tablespoons. Bake at 375°F. for 35 to 40 minutes.

NUTRITION PER SERVING:
Calories 250; Protein 4g; Carbohydrate 39g; Fat 10g; Sodium 290mg.

OLD-FASHIONED OATMEAL CAKE WITH BROILED TOPPING

~

Serve this cake for brunch, dessert or a snack.

CAKE
1½ cups quick-cooking rolled oats
1¼ cups boiling water
1 cup sugar
1 cup firmly packed brown sugar
½ cup margarine or butter, softened
1 teaspoon vanilla
3 eggs
1½ cups all purpose flour
1 teaspoon baking soda
½ teaspoon baking powder
½ teaspoon salt
1½ teaspoons cinnamon
½ teaspoon nutmeg

TOPPING
⅔ cup firmly packed brown sugar
¼ cup margarine or butter, melted
3 tablespoons half-and-half or milk
1 cup coconut
½ cup chopped nuts

Grease and flour 13x9-inch pan. In small bowl, combine rolled oats and boiling water; let stand 20 minutes.

Heat oven to 350°F. In large bowl, beat sugar, 1 cup brown sugar and ½ cup margarine until light and fluffy. Add vanilla and eggs; beat well. Add oatmeal and remaining cake ingredients; mix well. Pour batter into greased and floured pan.

Bake at 350°F. for 35 to 45 minutes or until toothpick inserted in center comes out clean.

Heat broiler. In small bowl, combine ⅔ cup brown sugar, ¼ cup margarine and half-and-half; beat at highest speed until smooth. Stir in coconut and nuts. Spoon over warm cake; spread to cover. Broil 4 to 6 inches from heat for 1 to 2 minutes or until bubbly and light golden brown. Cool completely.
Yield: 16 servings.

HIGH ALTITUDE:
Above 3500 Feet: Decrease brown sugar in cake to ¾ cup; increase flour to 1½ cups plus 3 tablespoons. Bake at 375°F. for 30 to 40 minutes.

NUTRITION PER SERVING:
Calories 360; Protein 4g; Carbohydrate 52g; Fat 15g; Sodium 270mg.

Whole Wheat Walnut Crumb Cake

This lightly spiced cake can be baked in cake layer pans or in a 13x9-inch pan. It's great for picnics.

STREUSEL
- 1 cup chopped walnuts or pecans
- 1/3 cup firmly packed brown sugar
- 1 teaspoon cinnamon

CAKE
- 2 cups whole wheat flour
- 1 cup sugar
- 3 teaspoons baking powder
- 1/2 teaspoon salt
- 1 cup milk
- 1/3 cup margarine or butter, softened
- 1 egg

GLAZE
- 3/4 cup powdered sugar
- 1 to 2 tablespoons water

Heat oven to 350°F. Grease and flour two 8 or 9-inch round cake pans. In small bowl, mix all streusel ingredients until well blended; set aside.

In large bowl, combine all cake ingredients at low speed until moistened; beat 2 minutes at medium speed. Spread about 3/4 cup of batter in each greased and floured pan; sprinkle 1/4 of streusel mixture evenly over batter in each pan. Carefully spread remaining batter over streusel in each pan; sprinkle with remaining streusel mixture.

Bake at 350°F. for 20 to 30 minutes or until toothpick inserted in center comes out clean. Cool slightly. In small bowl, combine powdered sugar and enough water for desired drizzling consistency; blend until smooth. Drizzle over warm cakes.

Yield: 2 cakes; 6 to 8 servings each.

TIP:
Cake can be baked in 13x9-inch pan. Spread half of batter in greased and floured pan; sprinkle half of streusel mixture evenly over batter. Carefully spread remaining batter over streusel; sprinkle with remaining streusel mixture. Bake at 350°F. for 25 to 35 minutes or until toothpick inserted in center comes out clean.

HIGH ALTITUDE:
Above 3500 Feet: Increase flour to 2¼ cups. Bake at 375°F. for 20 to 30 minutes.

NUTRITION PER SERVING:
Calories 220; Protein 4g; Carbohydrate 33g; Fat 9g; Sodium 180mg.

Bran Cake

This cake is especially delicious served warm from the oven. The batter can be prepared several hours ahead, refrigerated, then baked just before serving.

CAKE
- 1½ cups all purpose flour
- 1½ cups bran flakes cereal with raisins
- 1/2 cup sugar
- 1 teaspoon baking powder
- 1/2 teaspoon baking soda
- 1/2 teaspoon salt
- 1 cup buttermilk
- 1/4 cup margarine or butter, melted
- 1 egg, slightly beaten

TOPPING
- 2 tablespoons sugar
- 1/2 teaspoon cinnamon

Heat oven to 400°F. Grease bottom only of 8-inch square or 9-inch round pan. In large bowl, combine all cake ingredients; stir just until ingredients are moistened. Spread batter in greased pan. Combine topping ingredients; sprinkle over batter.*

Bake at 400°F. for 30 to 40 minutes or until toothpick inserted in center comes out clean. Serve warm.

Yield: 9 servings.

TIP:
* If desired, cover pan with plastic wrap and store in refrigerator up to 12 hours. Bake as directed above.

HIGH ALTITUDE:
Above 3500 Feet: Increase flour to 1½ cups plus 3 tablespoons. Bake at 400°F. for 20 to 30 minutes.

NUTRITION PER SERVING:
Calories 220; Protein 5g; Carbohydrate 37g; Fat 6g; Sodium 360mg.

BLACK BOTTOM CUPS

These unique cupcakes boast a filling of cream cheese and chocolate chips — delicious!

    2 (3-oz.) pkg. cream cheese, softened
  1/3 cup sugar
    1 egg
    1 (6-oz.) pkg. (1 cup) semi-sweet chocolate
        chips
 1 1/2 cups all purpose flour
    1 cup sugar
  1/4 cup unsweetened cocoa
    1 teaspoon baking soda
  1/2 teaspoon salt
    1 cup water
  1/3 cup oil
    1 tablespoon vinegar
    1 teaspoon vanilla
  1/2 cup chopped almonds, if desired
    2 tablespoons sugar, if desired

Heat oven to 350°F. Line 18 muffin cups with paper baking cups. In small bowl, combine cream cheese, 1/3 cup sugar and egg; mix well. Stir in chocolate chips; set aside.

In large bowl, combine flour, 1 cup sugar, cocoa, baking soda and salt. Add water, oil, vinegar and vanilla; beat 2 minutes at medium speed. Fill paper-lined muffin cups half full. Top each with 1 tablespoonful cream cheese mixture. Combine almonds and 2 tablespoons sugar; sprinkle evenly over cream cheese mixture.

Bake at 350°F. for 20 to 30 minutes or until cream cheese mixture is light golden brown. Cool 15 minutes; remove from pans. Cool completely. Store in refrigerator.

Yield: 18 cupcakes.

HIGH ALTITUDE:
Above 3500 Feet: No change.

NUTRITION PER SERVING:
Calories 250; Protein 3g; Carbohydrate 31g; Fat 13g; Sodium 160mg.

DOUBLE CHOCOLATE CHUNK CUPCAKES

These are great to pack in lunches.

    2 cups all purpose flour
  1/2 cup firmly packed brown sugar
  1/4 cup unsweetened cocoa
    1 teaspoon baking soda
  1/4 teaspoon salt
    1 cup buttermilk
  1/2 cup margarine or butter, melted
  1/2 teaspoon almond extract
    1 egg
  1/2 cup vanilla milk chips or 3 oz. white baking
        bars, chopped
  1/2 cup milk chocolate chips
  1/4 cup chopped slivered almonds

Heat oven to 375°F. Grease 18 muffin cups. In large bowl, combine flour, brown sugar, cocoa, baking soda and salt; blend well. Add buttermilk, margarine, almond extract and egg; blend just until dry ingredients are moistened. Fold in vanilla and milk chocolate chips and almonds. Fill greased muffin cups 3/4 full.

Bake at 375°F. for 15 to 20 minutes or until toothpick inserted in center comes out clean. Cool 3 minutes; remove from pan. Serve warm or cool.
Yield: 18 cupcakes.

HIGH ALTITUDE:
Above 3500 Feet: No change.

NUTRITION PER SERVING:
Calories 200; Protein 4g; Carbohydrate 24g; Fat 10g; Sodium 190mg.

COOK'S NOTE

CUPCAKES

Most cake batters can be baked in paper-lined muffin cups for cupcakes. A one-layer cake recipe yields 12 to 15 cupcakes; a two-layer cake recipe yields 24 to 30 cupcakes. Fill cups 2/3 full and bake at 350°F. for 15 to 20 minutes or until tops spring back when lightly touched. Immediately remove cupcakes from pan; cool. Cupcakes can be frosted by dipping the top of each cupcake in frosting; turn slightly and remove.

Peanut Butter Cups

PEANUT BUTTER CUPS

Creamy or chunky peanut butter can be used for these irresistible treat-filled cupcakes.

1³/₄ **cups all purpose flour**
1¹/₄ **cups firmly packed brown sugar**
  3 **teaspoons baking powder**
  1 **teaspoon salt**
  1 **cup milk**
 ¹/₃ **cup shortening**
 ¹/₃ **cup peanut butter**
  1 **teaspoon vanilla**
  2 **eggs**
 24 **miniature milk chocolate-covered peanut butter cups, unwrapped**

Heat oven to 350°F. Line 24 muffin cups with paper baking cups. In large bowl, combine all ingredients except peanut butter cups at low speed until moistened; beat 2 minutes at medium speed. Fill paper-lined muffin cups ²/₃ full. Press a peanut butter cup into batter until top edge is even with batter.

Bake at 350°F. for 18 to 28 minutes or until tops spring back when touched lightly in center. Serve warm or cool.

Yield: 24 cupcakes.

HIGH ALTITUDE:
Above 3500 Feet: No change.

NUTRITION PER SERVING:
Calories 170; Protein 4g; Carbohydrate 23g; Fat 7g; Sodium 185mg.

COCONUT MACAROON CAKES

When you have leftover egg whites, lightly beat the whites, place them in a freezer container or screw-top jar and freeze. When you've collected enough for these simple but special cupcakes, thaw the whites in the refrigerator and use them like fresh egg whites.

- ¾ cup all purpose flour
- 1⅓ cups sugar
- ½ teaspoon baking powder
- ¼ teaspoon salt
- 6 egg whites
- ½ teaspoon cream of tartar
- 1 teaspoon almond extract
- 1 cup coconut

Heat oven to 350°F. Line 18 muffin cups with paper baking cups. In medium bowl, combine flour, 1 cup of the sugar, baking powder and salt; set aside.

In large bowl, beat egg whites, cream of tartar and almond extract until foamy; gradually add remaining ⅓ cup sugar, beating until stiff peaks form. Gradually fold flour mixture into egg whites. Gently fold in coconut. Fill paper-lined muffin cups ⅔ full.

Bake at 350°F. for 25 to 35 minutes or until light golden brown and top crust is dry. Cool completely.

Yield: 18 cupcakes.

HIGH ALTITUDE:
Above 3500 Feet: Increase flour to ¾ cup plus 2 tablespoons. When beating egg white-sugar mixture, beat only until soft peaks form. Bake at 375°F. for 20 to 25 minutes. 21 cupcakes.

NUTRITION PER SERVING:
Calories 100; Protein 2g; Carbohydrate 20g; Fat 1g; Sodium 55mg.

RUM CROWN CAKES

These little cakes have a sponge-like texture.

SYRUP
- 1 cup sugar
- ¾ cup water
- ¼ cup orange juice
- 2 tablespoons rum

GLAZE
- ½ cup apricot preserves
- 2 tablespoons rum
- 1 tablespoon orange juice

CUPCAKES
- ⅔ cup sugar
- ½ cup margarine or butter, softened
- 4 eggs
- ¾ cup all purpose flour
- ½ cup cornstarch
- 2 teaspoons baking powder
- ¼ teaspoon salt

In small saucepan, combine 1 cup sugar and water; bring to a boil, stirring until sugar dissolves. Remove from heat. Add ¼ cup orange juice and 2 tablespoons rum; set aside. In small bowl, combine all glaze ingredients; blend well. Set aside.

Heat oven to 350°F. Grease and flour 18 fluted muffin cups.* In large bowl, beat ⅔ cup sugar and margarine until light and fluffy. Add eggs 1 at a time, beating well after each addition. In small bowl, combine flour, cornstarch, baking powder and salt. Gradually add flour mixture to sugar mixture; blend well. Spoon batter into greased and floured muffin cups, filling ⅔ full.

Bake at 350°F. for 15 to 20 minutes or until toothpick inserted in center comes out clean. With long-tined fork, immediately pierce each cake 3 times; spoon syrup over cakes in pan. Remove from pan immediately by inverting onto wire rack. Brush tops with glaze. If desired, decorate cakes with whipped cream using decorating bag.

Yield: 18 cakes.

TIP:
* Standard muffin cups can be used in place of fluted muffin cups.

HIGH ALTITUDE:
Above 3500 Feet: Bake at 375°F. for 15 to 20 minutes.

NUTRITION PER SERVING:
Calories 200; Protein 2g; Carbohydrate 32g; Fat 6g; Sodium 140mg.

CHOCOLATE POUND CAKE

~

A chocolate delight!

CAKE
- 3 cups sugar
- 1 cup margarine or butter, softened
- ½ cup shortening
- 1 teaspoon vanilla
- 5 eggs
- 3 cups all purpose flour
- ¼ cup unsweetened cocoa
- ½ teaspoon baking powder
- ½ teaspoon salt
- 1 cup milk

GLAZE
- 2 tablespoons unsweetened cocoa
- 1 tablespoon water
- 1 tablespoon light corn syrup
- 2 tablespoons margarine or butter
- ¼ teaspoon vanilla
- ½ cup powdered sugar

Heat oven to 350°F. Grease and flour 10-inch tube pan. In large bowl, combine sugar, 1 cup margarine, shortening and 1 teaspoon vanilla; beat until light and fluffy. Add eggs 1 at a time, beating well after each addition. In medium bowl, combine flour, ¼ cup cocoa, baking powder and salt. Alternately add flour mixture and milk to sugar mixture, beginning and ending with flour mixture and beating well after each addition. Pour batter into greased and floured pan.

Bake at 350°F. for 70 to 85 minutes or until toothpick inserted in center comes out clean. Cool upright in pan 25 minutes; invert onto serving plate. Cool completely.

In small saucepan, combine 2 tablespoons cocoa, water, corn syrup and 2 tablespoons margarine. Cook over low heat until mixture thickens, stirring constantly. Remove from heat. Stir in ¼ teaspoon vanilla and powdered sugar; beat until smooth. Spread glaze over top of cooled cake, allowing some to run down sides.
Yield: 16 servings.

HIGH ALTITUDE:
Above 3500 Feet: Increase flour to 3¼ cups. Bake at 375°F. for 70 to 80 minutes.

NUTRITION PER SERVING:
Calories 450; Protein 5g; Carbohydrate 62g; Fat 22g; Sodium 270mg.

ORANGE CURRANT POUND CAKE

~

Raisins can be substituted for currants in this recipe.

CAKE
- 3 cups all purpose flour
- ½ teaspoon baking powder
- ½ teaspoon salt
- 1 tablespoon grated orange peel
- 2¾ cups sugar
- 1½ cups margarine or butter, softened
- 1 teaspoon vanilla
- 6 eggs
- 1 cup dairy sour cream
- 1 cup currants

SAUCE
- ¼ cup sugar
- 1 tablespoon cornstarch
- ¾ cup orange juice
- 1 to 2 tablespoons orange liqueur

Heat oven to 350°F. Generously grease and flour 12-cup Bundt® pan. In large bowl, combine flour, baking powder, salt and orange peel; set aside. In large bowl, beat sugar and margarine until light and fluffy. Add vanilla and 1 egg at a time, beating well after each addition. Alternately add dry ingredients and sour cream to sugar mixture, beating well after each addition. Stir in currants. Pour batter into greased and floured pan.

Bake at 350°F. for 55 to 65 minutes or until toothpick inserted in center comes out clean. Cool 15 minutes; invert onto serving plate. Cool completely.

To prepare sauce, combine sugar and cornstarch in small saucepan. Stir in orange juice. Cook over medium heat until mixture boils and thickens, stirring constantly. Stir in liqueur. Serve cake with warm orange sauce.
Yield: 16 servings.

HIGH ALTITUDE:
Above 3500 Feet: Bake at 375°F. for 50 to 60 minutes.

NUTRITION PER SERVING:
Calories 480; Protein 6g; Carbohydrate 66g; Fat 22g; Sodium 310mg.

BUTTER PECAN POUND CAKE

A buttery glaze tops this rich cake.

CAKE
- 2 tablespoons ground pecans
- 1½ cups butter, softened (do not use margarine)
- 1 (3-oz.) pkg. cream cheese, softened
- 2 cups firmly packed brown sugar
- 1 cup sugar
- 5 eggs
- 3 cups all purpose flour
- ½ teaspoon baking powder
- ¼ teaspoon salt
- 1 teaspoon vanilla
- 1 teaspoon maple extract
- ¾ cup milk
- 1 cup chopped pecans, toasted, p. 23

GLAZE
- 2 tablespoons butter or margarine
- 2 tablespoons firmly packed brown sugar
- ½ cup powdered sugar
- 1 teaspoon vanilla
- 1 to 2 tablespoons hot water

Heat oven to 350°F. Grease 10-inch tube pan. Sprinkle with ground pecans, coating bottom and sides of pan. In large bowl, beat 1½ cups butter, cream cheese, 2 cups brown sugar and sugar until light and fluffy. Add eggs 1 at a time, beating well after each addition. In small bowl, combine flour, baking powder and salt; mix well. Add vanilla and maple extract to milk. Add flour mixture to butter mixture alternately with milk, beginning and ending with flour mixture. Fold in pecans. Pour batter into greased and coated pan.

Bake at 350°F. for 65 to 80 minutes or until toothpick inserted in center comes out clean. Do not open oven door for first hour of baking. Cool upright in pan 10 minutes; invert onto cooling rack. Cool completely.

In small saucepan, melt 2 tablespoons butter with 2 tablespoons brown sugar. Bring to a boil; boil until thickened, stirring constantly. Remove from heat; stir in remaining glaze ingredients, adding enough water for desired glaze consistency. Spoon over cake.

Yield: 16 to 20 servings.

HIGH ALTITUDE:
Above 3500 Feet: Decrease brown sugar in cake to 1½ cups; increase flour to 3⅓ cups. Bake as directed above.

NUTRITION PER SERVING:
Calories 420; Protein 5g; Carbohydrate 52g; Fat 22g; Sodium 230mg.

LEMON DELIGHT POUND CAKE

You'll enjoy this lemon-flavored cake — and it's so easy to make!

CAKE
- 2½ cups all purpose flour
- 1½ cups sugar
- 3 teaspoons baking powder
- ½ teaspoon salt
- ¾ cup apricot nectar or orange juice
- ¾ cup oil
- 2 teaspoons lemon extract
- 4 eggs

GLAZE
- 1½ cups powdered sugar
- ½ cup lemon juice

Heat oven to 325°F. Generously grease and flour 12-cup Bundt® pan. In large bowl, combine all cake ingredients. Blend at low speed until moistened; beat 3 minutes at medium speed. Pour batter into greased and floured pan.

Bake at 325°F. for 40 to 50 minutes or until toothpick inserted near center comes out clean. Remove cake from oven. With long-tined fork, poke deep holes every inch. In small bowl, blend glaze ingredients until smooth. Spoon half of glaze over hot cake in pan. Let stand upright in pan 10 minutes; invert onto serving plate. Spoon remaining glaze over cake. Cool completely.

Yield: 16 servings.

HIGH ALTITUDE:
Above 3500 Feet: Decrease baking powder to 2½ teaspoons. Bake at 350°F. for 40 to 50 minutes.

NUTRITION PER SERVING:
Calories 300; Protein 4g; Carbohydrate 45g; Fat 12g; Sodium 140mg.

CRANBERRY ORANGE POUND CAKE

Pound cakes were so named because the ingredients traditionally were measured by the pound. This sensational version, studded with cranberries, is a perfect buffet dessert for a party.

CAKE
2¾   cups sugar
1½   cups butter or margarine, softened
  1   teaspoon vanilla
  1   teaspoon grated orange peel
  6   eggs
  3   cups all purpose flour
  1   teaspoon baking powder
  ½   teaspoon salt
  1   (8-oz.) container dairy sour cream
1½   cups chopped fresh or frozen cranberries
      (do not thaw)

BUTTER RUM SAUCE
  1   cup sugar
  1   tablespoon all purpose flour
  ½   cup half-and-half
  ½   cup butter
  4   teaspoons light rum or ¼ teaspoon rum
      extract

Heat oven to 350°F. Generously grease and lightly flour 12-cup Bundt® pan. In large bowl, beat 2¾ cups sugar and 1½ cups butter until light and fluffy. Add vanilla and orange peel. Add eggs 1 at a time, beating well after each addition. In medium bowl, combine 3 cups flour, baking powder and salt; add alternately with sour cream, beating well after each addition. Gently stir in cranberries. Pour batter into greased and floured pan.

Bake at 350°F. for 65 to 75 minutes or until toothpick inserted in center comes out clean. Cool 15 minutes; remove from pan.

Meanwhile, in small saucepan combine 1 cup sugar and 1 tablespoon flour. Stir in half-and-half and ½ cup butter. Cook over medium heat until thickened and bubbly, stirring constantly. Remove from heat; stir in rum. Serve warm sauce over cake.
Yield: 16 servings.

TIP:
To prepare butter rum sauce in microwave, combine sugar and flour in 2-cup microwave-safe measuring cup. Stir in half-and-half and butter. Microwave on MEDIUM for 3 to 4 minutes or until thickened, stirring once halfway through cooking. Stir in rum.

HIGH ALTITUDE:
Above 3500 Feet: Decrease sugar in cake to 2½ cups. Bake as directed above.

NUTRITION PER SERVING:
Calories 550; Protein 6g; Carbohydrate 67g; Fat 29g; Sodium 360mg.

SOUR CREAM POUND CAKE

Flavored with orange peel and vanilla, this dense pound cake needs no frosting. Serve it with a dusting of powdered sugar, if desired.

2¾   cups sugar
1½   cups butter or margarine, softened
  1   teaspoon vanilla
  6   eggs
  3   cups all purpose flour
  1   teaspoon grated orange or lemon peel
  ½   teaspoon baking powder
  ½   teaspoon salt
  1   cup dairy sour cream

Heat oven to 350°F. Generously grease and flour 12-cup Bundt® pan. In large bowl, beat sugar and butter until light and fluffy. Add vanilla; add eggs 1 at a time, beating well after each addition. In medium bowl, combine flour, orange peel, baking powder and salt. Add dry ingredients alternately with sour cream, beating well after each addition. Pour batter into greased and floured pan.

Bake at 350°F. for 55 to 65 minutes or until toothpick inserted in center comes out clean. Cool 15 minutes; invert onto serving plate. Cool completely.
Yield: 16 servings.

HIGH ALTITUDE:
Above 3500 Feet: Decrease sugar to 2½ cups. Bake at 375°F. for 55 to 65 minutes.

NUTRITION PER SERVING:
Calories 440; Protein 5g; Carbohydrate 53g; Fat 23g; Sodium 290mg.

Pumpkin Pound Cake with Walnut Sauce

CAKE

2¾ cups sugar
1½ cups butter or margarine, softened
1 teaspoon vanilla
6 eggs
3 cups all purpose flour
½ teaspoon baking powder
½ teaspoon salt
¾ teaspoon cinnamon
½ teaspoon ginger
¼ teaspoon cloves
1 cup canned pumpkin

SAUCE

1 cup firmly packed brown sugar
¼ cup dark corn syrup
½ cup whipping cream
2 tablespoons butter or margarine
Dash salt
½ teaspoon vanilla
½ cup chopped walnuts or walnut halves

Heat oven to 350°F. Generously grease and lightly flour 12-cup Bundt® pan. In large bowl, beat sugar and 1½ cups butter until light and fluffy. Add 1 teaspoon vanilla; add eggs 1 at a time, beating well after each addition. In small bowl, combine flour, baking powder, ½ teaspoon salt, cinnamon, ginger and cloves; mix well. Alternately add dry ingredients and pumpkin to butter mixture, beating well after each addition. Pour batter into greased and floured pan.

Bake at 350°F. for 60 to 70 minutes or until toothpick inserted in center comes out clean. Cool 15 minutes; invert onto serving plate. Cool completely.

In medium saucepan, combine brown sugar, corn syrup, whipping cream, 2 tablespoons butter and dash of salt. Bring to a boil over medium heat, stirring constantly. Reduce heat to low; simmer 5 minutes, stirring constantly. Remove from heat; stir in ½ teaspoon vanilla and walnuts. Serve warm sauce over cake. Refrigerate any remaining sauce.
Yield: 16 servings.

TIP:
Cake can be baked in two greased and floured 9x5-inch loaf pans. Bake as directed above.

Pumpkin Pound Cake with Walnut Sauce

HIGH ALTITUDE:
Above 3500 Feet: Decrease sugar to 2½ cups. Bake at 375°F. for 50 to 60 minutes.

NUTRITION PER SERVING:
Calories 530; Protein 6g; Carbohydrate 71g; Fat 26g; Sodium 310mg.

Toffee Pound Cake

Almond brickle baking chips are available in the baking section of the grocery store.

CAKE

2½ cups all purpose flour
1½ cups sugar
1 teaspoon baking soda
½ teaspoon salt
1½ cups buttermilk
½ cup margarine or butter, softened
¼ cup shortening
1½ teaspoons vanilla
3 eggs
1 (6-oz.) pkg. almond brickle baking chips

GLAZE

⅓ cup margarine or butter
2 cups powdered sugar
1 teaspoon vanilla
2 to 3 tablespoons water

Heat oven to 350°F. Grease and flour 12-cup Bundt® or 10-inch tube pan. In large bowl, combine all cake ingredients except brickle chips at low speed until moistened; beat 3 minutes at medium speed. By hand, stir in brickle chips. Pour batter into greased and floured pan.

Bake at 350°F. for 50 to 60 minutes or until toothpick inserted in center comes out clean. Cool upright in pan 10 minutes; invert onto serving plate. Cool completely.

In medium saucepan, heat ⅓ cup margarine until light golden brown; remove from heat. Blend in powdered sugar and 1 teaspoon vanilla. Add water until glaze is smooth and of drizzling consistency. Immediately spoon over top of cooled cake, allowing some to run down sides.
Yield: 16 servings.

HIGH ALTITUDE:
Above 3500 Feet: No change.

NUTRITION PER SERVING:
Calories 400; Protein 4g; Carbohydrate 55g; Fat 19g; Sodium 295mg.

EGGNOG CAKE WITH FRUIT SAUCE

There is no eggnog in this finely textured whipped cream cake, but you'll find it captures the flavor of the holiday beverage. The fruit sauce is a delicious change of pace and makes this cake very special!

CAKE
2¾ cups all purpose flour
1⅔ cups sugar
2 teaspoons baking powder
1 teaspoon salt
1 teaspoon nutmeg
1 pint (2 cups) whipping cream (do not substitute)
2 to 3 teaspoons rum extract
4 eggs

FRUIT SAUCE
⅓ cup firmly packed brown sugar
1 tablespoon cornstarch
1 (30-oz.) can fruit cocktail or apricot halves, drained, reserving liquid
¼ cup margarine or butter
¼ teaspoon almond extract

Heat oven to 325°F. Grease and flour 12-cup Bundt® pan. In large bowl, combine all cake ingredients at low speed until moistened; beat 3 minutes at medium speed (portable mixer at highest speed). Pour batter into greased and floured pan.

Bake at 325°F. for 60 to 70 minutes or until toothpick inserted in center comes out clean. Cool upright in pan 25 minutes; invert onto serving plate. Cool completely.

In medium saucepan, combine brown sugar and cornstarch. Stir in reserved fruit liquid, margarine and almond extract. Cook over medium heat until mixture comes to a boil, stirring constantly; boil 1 minute. Remove from heat; stir in fruit. Serve fruit sauce warm or cool over cake slices.
Yield: 16 servings.

HIGH ALTITUDE:
Above 3500 Feet: Decrease sugar to 1½ cups. Bake at 350°F. for 50 to 60 minutes.

NUTRITION PER SERVING:
Calories 370; Protein 5g; Carbohydrate 53g; Fat 16g; Sodium 240mg.

APPLESAUCE FRUIT CAKE

Chockfull of spices, nuts and fruit!

1½ cups sugar
1 cup shortening
2 eggs
3¼ cups all purpose flour
1½ teaspoons baking soda
2 teaspoons cinnamon
1 teaspoon allspice
1 teaspoon cloves
½ teaspoon salt
1½ cups chopped nuts
1½ cups raisins
1½ cups coarsely chopped dates
½ cup coarsely chopped red maraschino cherries, drained, or candied cherries
2 cups applesauce
6 red maraschino cherries, halved and drained, or candied cherries
6 pecan halves

Heat oven to 325°F. Grease 10-inch tube pan; line bottom with waxed paper or foil and grease again. In large bowl, beat sugar and shortening until light and fluffy. Add eggs; blend well. Reserve ½ cup flour. Add remaining 2¾ cups flour, baking soda, cinnamon, allspice, cloves and salt to egg mixture. Blend at low speed until moistened; beat 2 minutes at medium speed.

In another large bowl, combine ½ cup reserved flour with nuts, raisins, dates and ½ cup cherries; stir until nuts and fruit are lightly coated. By hand, stir nut-fruit mixture and applesauce into batter; mix well. Pour batter into greased and waxed paper-lined pan; top with cherry halves and pecans.

Bake at 325°F. for 1¼ to 1¾ hours or until toothpick inserted in center comes out clean. Cool upright in pan 5 minutes. Remove from pan; remove waxed paper. Turn upright onto wire rack. Cool completely. Wrap cooled cake in plastic wrap or foil to keep moist. Store in refrigerator.
Yield: 20 servings.

HIGH ALTITUDE:
Above 3500 Feet: No change.

NUTRITION PER SERVING:
Calories 380; Protein 5g; Carbohydrate 58g; Fat 17g; Sodium 150mg.

Applesauce Fruit Cake

Norwegian Hazelnut Cake

Sometimes known as filberts, hazelnuts grow in clusters on the hazel tree in temperate zones around the world. They give this cake its sweet, rich flavor.

CAKE
- 2 (2½-oz.) pkg. hazelnuts (filberts) or pecans
- ½ cup margarine or butter
- 3 eggs
- 1½ cups sugar
- 1 teaspoon vanilla
- 2 cups all purpose flour
- 2 teaspoons baking powder
- ¼ teaspoon salt

GLAZE
- ½ cup whipping cream
- 1 (6-oz.) pkg. (1 cup) semi-sweet chocolate chips
- ½ teaspoon vanilla

Heat oven to 350°F. Lightly grease bottom only of 10-inch springform pan.

Reserve 8 whole nuts for garnish. In food processor bowl with metal blade or in blender container, process nuts until ground (about 1⅓ cups); reserve 1 tablespoon for garnish.

Melt margarine in small saucepan over low heat; cool. In large bowl, beat eggs, sugar and 1 teaspoon vanilla until thick and lemon colored, 2 to 3 minutes. Add flour, baking powder, salt and ground nuts; mix well. Continue beating, gradually adding cooled melted margarine until well blended. (Mixture will be thick.) Spread batter in greased pan.

Bake at 350°F. for 35 to 45 minutes or until toothpick inserted in center comes out clean. Cool 15 minutes; remove sides of pan. Run long knife under cake to loosen from pan bottom; invert onto serving plate. Cover with cloth towel; cool about 30 minutes.

To prepare glaze, in medium saucepan bring whipping cream just to a boil; remove from heat. Stir in chocolate chips until melted and smooth; add ½ teaspoon vanilla. Spread glaze over top of cake, allowing some to run down sides. Sprinkle reserved ground nuts around top edge of cake; arrange reserved whole nuts over ground nuts.
Yield: 16 servings.

Norwegian Hazelnut Cake

TIP:
A 9-inch round cake pan can be used. Line pan with foil; grease well. Bake at 350°F. for 45 to 55 minutes.

HIGH ALTITUDE:
Above 3500 Feet: Increase flour to 2 cups plus 2 tablespoons. Bake at 375°F. for 30 to 40 minutes.

NUTRITION PER SERVING:
Calories 330; Protein 5g; Carbohydrate 38g; Fat 19g; Sodium 140mg.

Delicious White Fruitcake

This traditional cake is filled with fruits and nuts and has a delicious hint of lemon.

- 1¾ cups all purpose flour
- 1 cup sugar
- ½ teaspoon salt
- ½ teaspoon baking powder
- 1½ cups margarine or butter, softened
- 1 tablespoon vanilla
- 1 tablespoon lemon extract
- 5 eggs
- 1 lb. (4 cups) pecan halves
- 1 lb. (2 cups) cut-up candied pineapple
- ¾ lb. (1½ cups) candied cherries, whole or cut up

Heat oven to 300°F. Generously grease and lightly flour two 8x4-inch loaf pans. In large bowl, blend all ingredients except nuts and fruits at low speed until moistened; beat 2 minutes at medium speed. Stir in nuts and fruits. Spoon batter into greased and floured pans.

Bake at 300°F. for 1¼ to 2 hours or until toothpick inserted in center comes out clean. Cool 15 minutes. Remove from pans; cool completely. Wrap tightly in plastic wrap or foil. Store in refrigerator up to 1 month or freeze up to 3 months.
Yield: 2 loaves; 20 servings each.

TIP:
Fruitcake can be wrapped in cheesecloth that has been soaked in brandy or fruit juice. Wrap with foil. Store in refrigerator. Moisten cloth every 2 weeks.

HIGH ALTITUDE:
Above 3500 Feet: No change.

NUTRITION PER SERVING:
Calories 270; Protein 3g; Carbohydrate 23g; Fat 19g; Sodium 170mg.

Swiss Almond Apple Cake

Serve this European-style cake for dessert or with coffee or tea. Sliced apples, a rippling of raspberry preserves and ground almonds make this an extra special delicacy.

CAKE
- ⅔ cup sugar
- ½ cup margarine or butter, softened
- 2 eggs
- 2 tablespoons lemon juice
- 2 cups all purpose flour
- 2 teaspoons baking powder
- ¼ teaspoon salt
- ¼ cup raspberry preserves
- 4 apples, peeled, thinly sliced (3½ cups)

TOPPING
- 1 cup ground almonds
- ½ cup sugar
- ½ cup dairy sour cream
- 2 eggs, beaten
- 2 tablespoons all purpose flour
- 1 teaspoon grated lemon peel

GLAZE
- ¼ cup powdered sugar
- 1 to 2 teaspoons lemon juice

Heat oven to 350°F. Grease and flour 9 or 10-inch springform pan. In large bowl, combine ⅔ cup sugar and margarine; beat until light and fluffy. Add 2 eggs and 2 tablespoons lemon juice; beat until well blended. In small bowl, combine 2 cups flour, baking powder and salt; mix well. Add to egg mixture; beat at low speed until well blended. Spread in greased and floured pan. Spoon preserves over batter; carefully spread to cover. Top with apple slices; slightly press into batter. In medium bowl, combine all topping ingredients; blend well. Pour over apples.

Bake at 350°F. for 55 to 65 minutes or until apples are tender, edges are light golden brown and toothpick inserted in center comes out clean. Cool 10 minutes. Carefully remove sides of pan. In small bowl, blend glaze ingredients until smooth; drizzle over cake. Serve warm or cool.
Yield: 16 servings.

HIGH ALTITUDE:
Above 3500 Feet: No change.

NUTRITION PER SERVING:
Calories 280; Protein 5g; Carbohydrate 39g; Fat 12g; Sodium 150mg.

Almond-Filled Cookie Cake

This $25,000 Pillsbury BAKE-OFF® Contest Grand Prize recipe is a rich almond dessert adapted from a Dutch pastry.

CRUST
- 2⅔ cups all purpose flour
- 1⅓ cups sugar
- 1⅓ cups unsalted butter, butter or margarine, softened
- ½ teaspoon salt
- 1 egg

FILLING
- 1 cup finely chopped almonds
- ½ cup sugar
- 1 teaspoon grated lemon peel
- 1 egg, slightly beaten
  Whole almonds
  Powdered sugar

Heat oven to 325°F. Grease 10 or 9-inch springform pan. In large bowl, blend all crust ingredients at low speed until dough forms. If desired, refrigerate 30 minutes for easier handling. Divide dough in half; spread half in bottom of greased pan to form crust.

In small bowl, blend all filling ingredients except whole almonds and powdered sugar; spread over crust to within ½ inch of sides of pan. Between waxed paper, press remaining dough to 10 or 9-inch circle. Remove top layer of waxed paper; place dough over filling. Remove waxed paper; press dough into place. Garnish with whole almonds.

Bake at 325°F. for 55 to 65 minutes or until light golden brown. (Place foil on rack below pan during baking to guard against spills.) Cool 15 minutes; remove sides of pan. Cool completely. If desired, sprinkle with powdered sugar.
Yield: 24 to 32 servings.

TIP:
A 9-inch round cake pan can be used. Line bottom with waxed paper; grease. Bake as directed above. Cool 30 minutes. Remove from pan.

HIGH ALTITUDE:
Above 3500 Feet: No change.

NUTRITION PER SERVING:
Calories 180; Protein 2g; Carbohydrate 19g; Fat 11g; Sodium 40mg.

Coconut Almond Cake

COCONUT ALMOND CAKE

This single-layer cake has a macaroon cookie base. Use purchased or homemade macaroons for the base.

BASE
- ½ **cup soft macaroon cookie crumbs**
- ½ **cup coconut**
- 2 **tablespoons amaretto***

CAKE
- ½ **cup sugar**
- ½ **cup margarine or butter, softened**
- 2 **eggs, separated**
- ½ **cup all purpose flour**
- ¼ **cup soft macaroon cookie crumbs**

GARNISH
    Powdered sugar
    Sliced almonds

Heat oven to 350°F. Grease 8-inch round or square cake pan. In small bowl, combine all base ingredients. Press in greased pan.

In small bowl, beat sugar and margarine until light and fluffy. Beat in egg yolks. Stir in flour and ¼ cup cookie crumbs. In another small bowl, beat egg whites until soft peaks form. Gently fold into cake batter. Spread over base.

Bake at 350°F. for 25 to 35 minutes or until toothpick inserted in center comes out clean. Cool 10 minutes. Sprinkle with powdered sugar; garnish with almonds. Cut into wedges.

Yield: 8 servings.

TIP:
* If desired, ½ teaspoon almond extract plus water to equal 2 tablespoons can be substituted for amaretto.

HIGH ALTITUDE:
Above 3500 Feet: Decrease sugar to ⅓ cup. Bake as directed above.

NUTRITION PER SERVING:
Calories 310; Protein 4g; Carbohydrate 32g; Fat 18g; Sodium 150mg.

Marzipan Cream Cake

MARZIPAN CREAM CAKE

This special cake takes a bit of extra time to prepare, but it's worth the effort!

CAKE
1¼ cups all purpose flour
¾ cup sugar
2 teaspoons baking powder
½ teaspoon salt
⅔ cup milk
¼ cup shortening
1 teaspoon vanilla
1 egg

CREAM FILLING
¼ cup sugar
1 tablespoon cornstarch
1 teaspoon unflavored gelatin
Dash salt
1¼ cups milk
2 egg yolks
1 teaspoon vanilla
¼ teaspoon almond extract
½ cup whipping cream, whipped

MARZIPAN
1 (7-oz.) pkg. almond paste
3 tablespoons light corn syrup
¼ teaspoon almond extract
1 to 1½ cups powdered sugar
½ cup apricot preserves
Food color

FROSTING

½ cup mar

1 (3-oz.) p

3 cups po

¼ teaspoo

2 to 4 teas

Heat oven to

round cake p

cording to pa

remove from

In medium s

sugar. Stir in

over mediun

stirring cons

To assemble

horizontally

Spread ⅓ of

each layer. I

layer, top si

½ cup of the

layer, top si

ture over to

In small bo

Add powde

smooth. Ac

consistency

sides of cak

Spoon rese

sired decor

1 inch apar

direction p

1 inch apar

desired, pij

of cake.

In small sa

preserves.

inside alter

serving tin

Yield: 12 s

HIGH ALT

Above 35(

NUTRITIO

Calories 510

Sodium 430

Heat oven to 350°F. Grease and flour 8 or 9-inch square pan. In large bowl, combine all cake ingredients at low speed until moistened; beat 2 minutes at medium speed. Spread batter in greased and floured pan.

Bake at 350°F. for 35 to 40 minutes or until toothpick inserted in center comes out clean. Cool 10 minutes; remove from pan. Cool completely.

In medium saucepan, combine ¼ cup sugar, cornstarch, gelatin and dash of salt. Stir in 1¼ cups milk; blend well. Cook over medium heat until mixture boils and slightly thickens, stirring constantly. In small bowl, beat 2 egg yolks; gradually blend ¼ of hot milk mixture into yolks. Add egg yolk mixture to saucepan; cook 2 to 3 minutes, stirring constantly. Remove from heat; stir in 1 teaspoon vanilla and ¼ teaspoon almond extract. Cover with plastic wrap; refrigerate until cool. Fold in whipped cream. Cover; refrigerate until firm enough to spread.

In medium bowl, break almond paste into pieces. Add corn syrup, ¼ teaspoon almond extract and ½ cup of the powdered sugar; mix until mixture forms a soft dough. Stir in enough additional powdered sugar to form a stiff dough. Knead in more powdered sugar until marzipan is firm but not sticky; set aside ⅓ cup. On pastry cloth sprinkled with powdered sugar, roll out remaining marzipan into 12-inch square. Cover with plastic wrap or waxed paper until cake is assembled.

To assemble cake, slice cooled cake horizontally into 2 layers. Place 1 layer on serving plate; spread cream filling over cake layer. Top with remaining cake layer. Brush top and sides of cake with apricot preserves. Place marzipan square over top and sides of cake, encasing cake. Make pleats with marzipan at corners; trim bottom edge. Tint reserved ⅓ cup marzipan as desired with food color. Between layers of waxed paper, roll out marzipan with rolling pin. Cut into desired shapes. Arrange on top of cake. Refrigerate at least 1 hour before serving. Store in refrigerator.

Yield: 12 servings.

HIGH ALTITUDE:
Above 3500 Feet: In cake, use 1 tablespoon less sugar and decrease baking powder to 1½ teaspoons; increase milk to ¾ cup. Bake at 375°F. for 35 to 40 minutes.

NUTRITION PER SERVING:
Calories 400; Protein 6g; Carbohydrate 62g; Fat 15g; Sodium 180mg.

BLUEBERRY POPPY SEED BRUNCH CAKE

Grated lemon peel accents this Grand Prize winner from the 1990 Pillsbury BAKE-OFF® Contest.

CAKE
⅔ cup sugar
½ cup margarine or butter, softened
2 teaspoons grated lemon peel
1 egg
1½ cups all purpose flour
2 tablespoons poppy seed
½ teaspoon baking soda
¼ teaspoon salt
½ cup dairy sour cream

FILLING
2 cups fresh or frozen blueberries, thawed, drained on paper towels
⅓ cup sugar
2 teaspoons all purpose flour
¼ teaspoon nutmeg

GLAZE
⅓ cup powdered sugar
1 to 2 teaspoons milk

Heat oven to 350°F. Grease and flour bottom and sides of 9 or 10-inch springform pan. In large bowl, beat ⅔ cup sugar and margarine until light and fluffy. Add lemon peel and egg; beat 2 minutes at medium speed. In medium bowl, combine 1½ cups flour, poppy seed, baking soda and salt; add to margarine mixture alternately with sour cream. Spread batter over bottom and 1 inch up sides of greased and floured pan, making sure batter on sides is ¼ inch thick.

In medium bowl, combine all filling ingredients; spoon over batter. Bake at 350°F. for 45 to 55 minutes or until crust is golden brown. Cool slightly. Remove sides of pan.

In small bowl, combine powdered sugar and enough milk for desired drizzling consistency. Drizzle over warm cake. Serve warm or cool.
Yield: 8 servings.

HIGH ALTITUDE:
Above 3500 Feet: Increase flour in cake to 1¾ cups. Bake as directed above.

NUTRITION PER SERVING:
Calories 380; Protein 5g; Carbohydrate 54g; Fat 17g; Sodium 290mg.

Are you
timesav
baking
the reci
develop
start wi
easy de
such as

For tho
"scratc
Simply
late Ca
cake m
vary if

As a pres
spectacu
think.

1 **pkg.**
Wat
Oil
Egg
1 **can**
6 **oz. (**
ca
¼ **cup**
Gre
Red
Edi

Grease 1
grease a
to packa
move ca
cake. C
or foil-c
cake wit

To prep
combin
over lov
constan

BLACK CAT
JAMBOREE CAKE

Follow your imagination and our easy directions to create this purr-fect Halloween theme cake. Small chocolate wafer cookies can be substituted for the mints to make the cats, or use a cookie for the body and a mint for the head. Your guests will be meowing for more.

1 **pkg. any flavor pudding-included cake mix**
   Water
   Oil
   Eggs
1 **can ready-to-spread vanilla frosting**
1 **(6-inch) black licorice twist, cut in half**
   lengthwise
2 **strands black string licorice**
6 **chocolate mints (about 1¼-inch diameter)**
1 **small black gumdrop**
2 **large orange gumdrops**

Heat oven to 350°F. Grease and flour 13x9-inch pan. Prepare and bake cake mix according to package directions. Cool completely.

Spread cake with frosting. To decorate, place licorice twist halves and 1 piece string licorice on cake to resemble fence, using twists for fence posts and string licorice for rails. To make 3 cats, use 2 mints for each cat; place on fence. Use remaining string licorice for tails and whiskers. Cut ears from black gumdrop; place on cats. On sugared surface, roll out orange gumdrops; cut into crescent moon shape. Place on cake.

Yield: 12 servings.

HIGH ALTITUDE:
Above 3500 Feet: See package for directions.

NUTRITION PER SERVING:
Not possible to calculate because of recipe variables.

Black Cat Jamboree Cake

GHOSTLY
PETITS FOURS

This recipe makes 30 petits fours — perfect for a large group.

1 **(18.5-oz.) pkg. pudding-included white cake**
   mix
   Water
   Oil
   Egg whites

MALLOW FROSTING
½ **cup sugar**
2 **tablespoons water**
2 **egg whites**
1 **(7-oz.) jar (1½ cups) marshmallow creme**
1 **teaspoon vanilla**
   Miniature semi-sweet chocolate chips

Heat oven to 350°F. Grease and flour 15x10x1-inch baking pan. Prepare cake mix according to package directions. Pour batter into greased and floured pan. Bake at 350°F. for 20 to 30 minutes or until toothpick inserted in center comes out clean. Cool completely.

Freeze cake 1 hour before cutting. Along 15-inch side, cut cake lengthwise into five 3-inch wide strips. Using sharp knife, mark and cut 6 ghost-shaped petits fours from each cake strip as shown in diagram. Return cut cake to freezer.

In double boiler over simmering water, beat sugar, 2 tablespoons water and 2 egg whites until soft peaks form. Add marshmallow creme; beat until stiff peaks form. Remove from heat; beat in vanilla. Remove petits fours from pan. Spread frosting over sides and top of each petit four to form ghosts. Use chocolate chips for eyes and mouth.

Yield: 30 petits fours.

HIGH ALTITUDE:
Above 3500 Feet: See package for directions.

NUTRITION PER SERVING:
Calories 130; Protein 1g; Carbohydrate 23g; Fat 4g; Sodium 130mg.

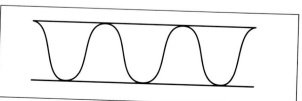

Ghostly Petits Fours

CREEPY CRAWLY CRITTER CAKE

~

Our lovable critter cake is easy to create with a cake mix baked in a Bundt® pan. Children will love to help with the decorating.

- 1 (18.5-oz.) pkg. pudding-included yellow or 18.25-oz. pkg. pudding-included devil's food cake mix
  Water
  Oil
  Eggs
- 1 can ready-to-spread vanilla frosting
- 1 can ready-to-spread chocolate fudge frosting
- 2 chocolate sandwich cookies or mints
  Assorted candies

Heat oven to 350°F. Grease and flour 12-cup Bundt® pan. Prepare and bake cake mix according to package directions. Cool 25 minutes; remove cake from pan. Cool completely.

Cover 24x16-inch board with foil. Cut cake horizontally into two layers. Cut each layer in half forming 2 half circles. Arrange cake pieces on foil-covered board forming "s" shapes as shown in diagram. Frost top and sides of cake, alternating between vanilla and chocolate frosting. Decorate cake to resemble a critter, using cookies for eyes and assorted candies for feet and antennae.

Yield: 16 servings.

HIGH ALTITUDE:
Above 3500 Feet: See package for directions.

NUTRITION PER SERVING:
Calories 390; Protein 2g; Carbohydrate 66g; Fat 13g; Sodium 330mg.

YUMMY BUNNY CAKE

~

Welcome spring with this whimsical party cake.

- 1 pkg. any flavor pudding-included cake mix
  Water
  Oil
  Eggs
- 2 cans ready-to-spread vanilla frosting
- 1 (14-oz.) pkg. (about 5 cups) coconut
  Food color
  Chocolate chips
  Jelly beans
  Red string licorice

Heat oven to 350°F. Grease and flour two 8 or 9-inch round cake pans. Prepare and bake cake mix according to package directions. Cool completely.

Cut cake as shown in diagram. Line large tray or 18x15-inch cardboard with foil. Frost sides of each cake piece. Place pieces as shown in diagram on foil-lined tray. Frost top of cake. Sprinkle about 2¾ cups coconut evenly over top and sides of cake, gently pressing coconut onto sides.

In small bowl, toss about ¾ cup coconut with 2 to 3 drops red food color until evenly colored. Repeat with 1½ cups coconut and 2 to 3 drops green food color. Sprinkle pink coconut over ears and bow tie; outline with chocolate chips. Decorate bunny face. Sprinkle green coconut evenly around cake.

Yield: 12 servings.

HIGH ALTITUDE:
Above 3500 Feet: See package for directions.

NUTRITION PER SERVING:
Not possible to calculate because of recipe variables.

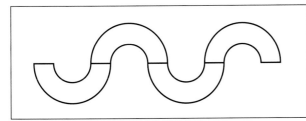

Creepy Crawly Critter Cake

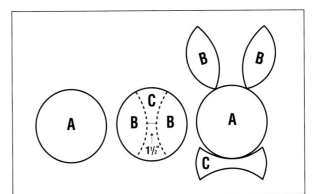

Yummy Bunny Cake

GOLDEN LEMON CAKE ROLL
〜

The lemon filling is superb.

CAKE

Powdered sugar
¾ cup all purpose flour
½ cup sugar
1½ teaspoons baking powder
½ teaspoon salt
9 egg yolks
½ cup sugar
½ cup cold water
½ teaspoon lemon extract

FILLING

½ cup sugar
⅛ teaspoon salt
3 tablespoons lemon juice
2 tablespoons margarine or butter
3 egg yolks
1 teaspoon grated lemon peel
½ cup whipping cream, whipped

Heat oven to 375°F. Lightly sprinkle clean towel with powdered sugar; set aside. Grease bottom only of 15x10x1-inch baking pan; line pan with waxed paper and grease again. In medium bowl, combine flour, ½ cup sugar, baking powder and ½ teaspoon salt; mix well.

In large bowl, beat 9 egg yolks at high speed until light lemon colored. Gradually add ½ cup sugar, beating until thickened. Add water and lemon extract; blend well. By hand, gently fold dry ingredients into egg mixture; blend well. Spread batter in greased and paper-lined baking pan.

Bake at 375°F. for 15 to 18 minutes or until top springs back when touched lightly in center. Immediately invert cake onto sugared side of towel. Quickly remove waxed paper. Starting with shortest end, roll up cake in towel; cool completely on wire rack.

In small saucepan, combine ½ cup sugar, ⅛ teaspoon salt, lemon juice, margarine and 3 egg yolks; blend well. Cook over low heat until thickened, stirring constantly. Remove from heat; stir in lemon peel. Cool to room temperature. Fold whipped cream into cooled filling mixture. Unroll cooled cake; spread filling mixture over cake. Roll up again. Cover; refrigerate 1 to 2 hours before serving. Store in refrigerator.
Yield: 12 servings.

HIGH ALTITUDE:
Above 3500 Feet: No change.

NUTRITION PER SERVING:
Calories 250; Protein 4g; Carbohydrate 34g; Fat 11g; Sodium 180mg.

JELLY ROLL
〜

The British name for jelly roll is Swiss roll. Whatever we call it, it is traditionally a light, airy cake that is rolled with a variety of fillings. We've left the choice of fillings up to you in this recipe, but any flavor of jam or jelly is delicious!

Powdered sugar
4 eggs
¾ cup sugar
¼ cup cold water
1 teaspoon vanilla
1 cup all purpose flour
1 teaspoon baking powder
¼ teaspoon salt
¾ cup favorite jelly or preserves

Heat oven to 375°F. Lightly sprinkle clean towel with powdered sugar; set aside. Generously grease and lightly flour 15x10x1-inch baking pan. In large bowl, beat eggs at highest speed until thick and lemon-colored, about 5 minutes. Gradually add sugar, beating until light and fluffy. Stir in water and vanilla. Add flour, baking powder and salt; blend at low speed just until dry ingredients are moistened. Spread batter evenly in greased and floured pan.

Bake at 375°F. for 8 to 12 minutes or until top springs back when touched lightly in center. Loosen edges; immediately invert onto sugared side of towel. Starting with shortest end, roll up cake in towel; cool completely on wire rack.

When cake is cooled, unroll; remove towel. Spread cake with jelly; roll up again, rolling loosely to incorporate filling. Wrap in foil or waxed paper. Store in refrigerator. If desired, serve sprinkled with additional powdered sugar.
Yield: 8 to 10 servings.

HIGH ALTITUDE:
Above 3500 Feet: No change.

NUTRITION PER SERVING:
Not possible to calculate because of recipe variables.

Jelly Roll

Harvest Pumpkin Cake Roll

This delicate pumpkin-flavored cake roll is filled with a complementary raisin filling and frosted with rich cream cheese frosting.

FILLING
- ¾ cup firmly packed brown sugar
- 3 tablespoons cornstarch
- ¼ teaspoon salt
- ¼ teaspoon cinnamon
- ⅛ teaspoon nutmeg
- 1 cup water
- 1 cup raisins
- 1 tablespoon margarine or butter
- 1½ teaspoons lemon juice

CAKE
- Powdered sugar
- ¾ cup all purpose flour
- 1 teaspoon baking powder
- 2 teaspoons cinnamon
- ½ teaspoon salt
- ¼ teaspoon cloves
- ¼ teaspoon ginger
- ¼ teaspoon nutmeg
- 4 eggs
- ¾ cup sugar
- ½ cup canned pumpkin

FROSTING
- ½ cup margarine or butter, softened
- 1 (3-oz.) pkg. cream cheese, softened
- ½ teaspoon vanilla
- 2 cups powdered sugar

To prepare filling, in medium saucepan combine brown sugar, cornstarch, ¼ teaspoon salt, ¼ teaspoon cinnamon and ⅛ teaspoon nutmeg. Gradually stir in water. Add raisins. Cook over medium heat until mixture boils and thickens, stirring constantly. Boil 1 minute; remove from heat. Stir in 1 tablespoon margarine and lemon juice. Refrigerate until cool.

Heat oven to 375°F. Lightly sprinkle clean towel with powdered sugar; set aside. Generously grease bottom only of 15x10x1-inch baking pan; line with waxed paper and grease again. In small bowl, combine flour, baking powder, 2 teaspoons cinnamon, ½ teaspoon salt, cloves, ginger and ¼ teaspoon nutmeg; set aside. In large bowl, beat eggs on highest speed for 5 minutes or until thick and lemon colored. Gradually beat in sugar. Stir in pumpkin. Fold flour mixture into pumpkin mixture. Spread batter evenly in greased and paper-lined pan.

Bake at 375°F. for 12 to 20 minutes or until top springs back when touched lightly in center. DO NOT OVERBAKE. Immediately invert cake onto towel; carefully remove waxed paper. Starting with shorter end, roll up hot cake in towel. Cool 30 minutes.

To prepare frosting, in small bowl combine ½ cup margarine, cream cheese and vanilla. Add powdered sugar; beat until smooth. To assemble cake roll, carefully unroll cake; remove towel. Spread evenly with raisin filling. Roll cake up again (cake may crack slightly). Place on serving plate, seam side down. Spread with frosting. If desired, garnish with additional raisins or chopped nuts. Refrigerate until serving time. Store in refrigerator.

Yield: 12 servings.

TIP:
Recipe can be made ahead and frozen. Thaw before serving.

HIGH ALTITUDE:
Above 3500 Feet: No change.

NUTRITION PER SERVING:
Calories 370; Protein 4g; Carbohydrate 61g; Fat 13g; Sodium 310mg.

Heavenly Hawaiian Cake Roll

It is important that the baking pan used in this recipe be at least 1 inch deep to prevent the batter from overflowing. Some 15x10-inch pans are not this deep.

FILLING
- ⅓ cup margarine or margarine, melted
- ½ cup firmly packed brown sugar
- 1 cup coconut
- 2 tablespoons chopped maraschino cherries
- 1 (8-oz.) can crushed pineapple in its own juice, well drained, reserving ½ cup liquid

CAKE
- Powdered sugar
- 3 eggs
- 1 cup sugar
- Reserved ½ cup pineapple liquid
- 1 cup all purpose flour
- 1 teaspoon baking powder
- ¼ teaspoon salt

TOPPING
- ½ cup whipping cream
- 2 tablespoons powdered sugar
- ½ teaspoon vanilla
- ¼ cup chopped macadamia nuts, toasted, p. 23

Heat oven to 375°F. Line 15x10x1-inch baking pan with foil. Spread margarine evenly in bottom of pan; sprinkle with brown sugar. Sprinkle coconut, maraschino cherries and pineapple evenly over brown sugar; lightly press down. Set aside.

Lightly sprinkle clean towel with powdered sugar; set aside. In small bowl, beat eggs at high speed until thick and lemon colored, about 5 minutes. Gradually add sugar; beat well. If necessary, add enough water to reserved pineapple liquid to measure ½ cup. At low speed, add reserved pineapple liquid; blend well. Add flour, baking powder and salt; beat until smooth. Spread evenly over filling mixture in pan.

Bake at 375°F. for 13 to 18 minutes or until top springs back when touched lightly in center. Invert cake onto sugared side of towel. Gently lift sides of foil from cake; carefully remove foil. Starting with shorter end and using towel to guide cake, roll up. (Do not roll towel into cake.) Wrap towel around rolled cake; cool completely on wire rack.

In small bowl, combine whipping cream, powdered sugar and vanilla; beat until stiff peaks form. Place cake roll on serving plate, seam side down. Spread topping over sides and top of cake roll; sprinkle with nuts. Store in refrigerator.

Yield: 12 servings.

TIP:
Chopped, toasted almonds or pecans can be substituted for macadamia nuts.

HIGH ALTITUDE:
Above 3500 Feet: No change.

NUTRITION PER SERVING:
Calories 300; Protein 3g; Carbohydrate 41g; Fat 14g; Sodium 140mg.

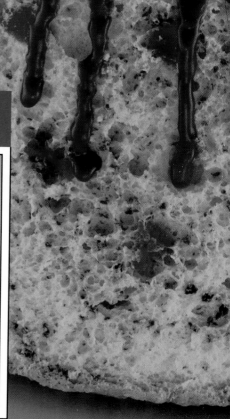

STEP-BY-STEP FEATURE ～
How to Make an Angel Food Cake

STEP 1. Beat egg whites, cream of tartar, salt, vanilla and almond extract until soft peaks form. Gradually beat in sugar until stiff peaks form.

STEP 2. Fold in flour mixture. Slide rubber scraper across bottom of bowl, bring up the side and gently fold mixture over top just until blended.

STEP 3. To prevent baked cake from collapsing, immediately invert hot cake onto bottle to cool. To remove cake, run knife around edge of pan.

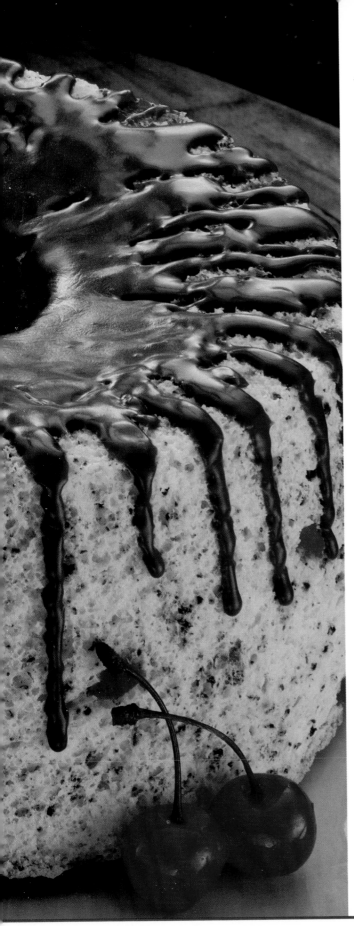

ANGEL FOOD CAKE

⁓

¾ **cup all purpose flour**
¾ **cup sugar**
1½ **cups (about 12) egg whites, room temperature**
1½ **teaspoons cream of tartar**
¼ **teaspoon salt**
1½ **teaspoons vanilla**
½ **teaspoon almond extract**
¾ **cup sugar**

Place oven rack at lowest position. Heat oven to 375°F. In small bowl, combine flour and ¾ cup sugar. In large bowl, beat egg whites, cream of tartar, salt, vanilla and almond extract until mixture forms soft peaks. Gradually add ¾ cup sugar, beating on highest speed until stiff peaks form. Spoon flour-sugar mixture ¼ cup at a time over beaten egg whites; fold in gently just until blended. Pour batter into ungreased 10-inch tube pan. With knife, cut gently through batter to remove large air bubbles.

Bake at 375°F. on lowest oven rack for 30 to 40 minutes or until crust is golden brown and cracks are very dry. Immediately invert cake onto funnel or soft drink bottle; let hang until completely cool. Remove cooled cake from pan.
Yield: 12 servings.

TIP:
To make loaves, bake in 2 ungreased 9x5-inch loaf pans for 25 to 30 minutes.

HIGH ALTITUDE:
Above 3500 Feet: Increase flour to 1 cup; increase egg whites to 1¾ cups (about 13). Bake at 400°F. for 30 to 35 minutes.

NUTRITION PER SERVING:
Calories 140; Protein 4g; Carbohydrate 31g; Fat 0g; Sodium 90mg.

VARIATION:

CHOCOLATE-CHERRY ANGEL FOOD CAKE:
Fold ⅓ cup well-drained, chopped maraschino cherries and 1 oz. grated semi-sweet chocolate into batter. Bake as directed above. In small saucepan over low heat, melt 2 tablespoons margarine or butter and 1 oz. semi-sweet chocolate with 1 table-spoon corn syrup. Stir in 1 cup powdered sugar and 2 to 3 tablespoons maraschino cherry liquid until smooth and of desired drizzling consistency. Immediately drizzle over cooled cake.

Chocolate-Cherry Angel Food Cake

CHIFFON CAKE

Chiffon cake is a foam cake that has oil added to it.

     2 cups all purpose flour
 1½ cups sugar
     3 teaspoons baking powder
   ¼ teaspoon salt
   ¾ cup cold water
   ½ cup oil
     7 egg yolks
   ½ teaspoon vanilla
     4 teaspoons finely grated lemon peel
     7 egg whites
   ½ teaspoon cream of tartar

Heat oven to 325°F. In large mixing bowl, combine flour, sugar, baking powder and salt. Add water, oil, egg yolks and vanilla. Beat on low speed until moistened; beat on high speed 5 minutes or until very smooth, scraping sides of bowl occasionally. Fold in lemon peel. Transfer to another large bowl. Thoroughly wash mixing bowl and beaters.

In large mixing bowl, beat egg whites and cream of tartar until stiff peaks form, about 3 minutes. Gradually add egg yolk mixture to egg whites, folding gently to combine. Pour into ungreased 10-inch tube pan.

Bake at 325°F. for 60 to 75 minutes or until top springs back when lightly touched. Immediately invert cake onto funnel or soft drink bottle; let hang until completely cool. To remove cake from pan, run edge of knife around outer edge of pan and tube. Remove cooled cake from pan. Glaze with **Lemon Glaze** p. 186, if desired.
Yield: 12 servings.

HIGH ALTITUDE:
Above 3500 Feet: Bake at 350°F. for 55 to 60 minutes.

NUTRITION PER SERVING:
Calories 300; Protein 6g; Carbohydrate 41g; Fat 12g; Sodium 160mg.

SPONGE CAKE

Sponge cakes do not contain shortening of any kind. They include whole eggs, as opposed to angel food cakes, which use only egg whites.

     6 eggs
   ¾ teaspoon cream of tartar
   ¾ cup sugar
 1½ cups all purpose flour
   ¾ cup sugar
     1 tablespoon grated orange peel
     1 teaspoon baking powder
   ½ teaspoon salt
   ½ cup apricot nectar or water
     1 teaspoon rum extract or vanilla

Heat oven to 350°F. Separate eggs, placing whites in large bowl and yolks in small bowl. Add cream of tartar to egg whites; beat until mixture forms soft peaks. Gradually add ¾ cup sugar, beating at highest speed until stiff peaks form. Add flour and remaining ingredients to egg yolks. Blend at low speed until moistened; beat 1 minute at medium speed. Pour over egg whites; fold in gently just until blended. Pour batter into ungreased 10-inch tube pan.

Bake at 350°F. for 35 to 45 minutes or until top springs back when touched lightly in center. Immediately invert cake on funnel or soft drink bottle; let hang until completely cool. Remove cooled cake from pan.
Yield: 12 servings.

HIGH ALTITUDE:
Above 3500 Feet: Decrease total sugar to 1¼ cups. Bake at 375°F. for 35 to 45 minutes.

NUTRITION PER SERVING:
Calories 200; Protein 5g; Carbohydrate 39g; Fat 3g; Sodium 150mg.

LEMON PLATINUM CAKE

*This luscious cake deserves a special occasion!
Layered with lemon cream filling and frosted
with billows of whipped cream, it guarantees a
grand entrance.*

CAKE
       8 egg whites
       1 teaspoon cream of tartar
      ½ teaspoon salt
       1 cup sugar
       7 egg yolks
       1 cup all purpose flour
      ⅓ cup lemon juice
       2 teaspoons grated lemon peel

FILLING
       1 cup sugar
      ¼ cup cornstarch
          Dash salt
    1¼ cups water
       2 egg yolks
       3 tablespoons lemon juice
       1 tablespoon margarine or butter
       2 teaspoons grated lemon peel

TOPPING
       2 cups whipping cream
       3 to 4 drops yellow food color, if desired
       2 kiwifruit, peeled, sliced, if desired

Heat oven to 325°F. In large bowl, beat egg whites
until foamy. Add cream of tartar and ½ teaspoon
salt; beat until soft peaks form. Gradually add
½ cup of the sugar, beating until stiff peaks form.
Set aside.

In small bowl, beat 7 egg yolks until lemon colored,
about 2 minutes. Gradually add remaining ½ cup
sugar, beating until thick and light lemon colored.
Add flour, ⅓ cup lemon juice and 2 teaspoons
lemon peel to egg yolk mixture; beat at low speed
for 1 minute. By hand, gently fold egg yolk mixture
into egg white mixture. Pour batter into ungreased
10-inch tube pan.

Bake at 325°F. for 40 to 55 minutes or until top
springs back when touched lightly in center. Immediately invert cake onto funnel or soft drink bottle;
let hang until completely cool. Remove from pan.

In small saucepan, combine 1 cup sugar, cornstarch and dash salt; mix well. Gradually stir in
water. Cook over medium heat until mixture thickens and boils, stirring constantly; remove from heat.
In small bowl, beat 2 egg yolks; gradually blend
small amount of hot mixture into egg yolks. Add
egg yolk mixture to saucepan; cook over low heat
2 to 3 minutes or until thickened, stirring constantly. Remove from heat; stir in 3 tablespoons lemon
juice, margarine and 2 teaspoons lemon peel. Cool.

In small bowl, beat whipping cream until slightly
thickened. Add ½ cup of the cooled filling mixture
and food color; beat until thickened, about
30 seconds. DO NOT OVERBEAT.

To assemble cake, slice cake horizontally to make
3 layers. Place bottom layer on serving plate; spread
with half (about ½ cup) of remaining filling mixture. Place middle layer on top; spread with
remaining filling. Top with third layer, cut side
down. Spread sides, center and top of cake with
topping. Refrigerate at least 1 hour before serving.
Just before serving, cut kiwifruit slices in half and
arrange on cake or garnish individual servings as
desired. Store in refrigerator.

Yield: 12 to 16 servings.

HIGH ALTITUDE:
Above 3500 Feet: No change.

NUTRITION PER SERVING:
Calories 290; Protein 5g; Carbohydrate 36g; Fat 15g;
Sodium 130mg.

COOK'S NOTE

SPLITTING CAKE OR CAKE LAYERS
Using toothpicks as a cutting guideline and
a long-bladed sharp knife, slice cake or cake
layers horizontally. Hold the top of the
cake or layer with the other hand to prevent
shifting of the layers as you cut. The top
layer of the cake should be placed with the
cut side against the filling and the smooth
side up.

BUTTERCREAM FROSTING

For the very creamiest results, be sure to use butter. Do not substitute margarine.

- ⅔ **cup butter, softened**
- 4 **cups powdered sugar**
- 1 **teaspoon vanilla**
- 2 **to 4 tablespoons half-and-half or milk**

In large bowl, beat butter until light and fluffy. Gradually add powdered sugar, beating well. Beat in vanilla and half-and-half, adding enough half-and-half for desired spreading consistency.

Yield: Frosts 2-layer or 13x9-inch cake.

NUTRITION PER SERVING:
Calories 250; Protein 0g; Carbohydrate 40g; Fat 11g; Sodium 105mg.

VARIATIONS:

BROWNED BUTTER FROSTING: In large saucepan over medium heat, brown butter until light golden brown, stirring constantly. Blend in remaining ingredients; beat until smooth.

CHOCOLATE BUTTERCREAM FROSTING: Blend into butter ⅓ cup unsweetened cocoa, or 2 envelopes premelted unsweetened chocolate baking flavor, or 2 oz. unsweetened chocolate, melted.

CHOCOLATE-CHERRY BUTTERCREAM FROSTING: Blend 3 tablespoons drained chopped maraschino cherries into Chocolate Buttercream Frosting.

COFFEE BUTTERCREAM FROSTING: Dissolve 1½ teaspoons instant coffee granules or crystals in 2 tablespoons of the half-and-half.

LEMON BUTTERCREAM FROSTING: Substitute 2 to 4 tablespoons lemon juice for the half-and-half and 1 teaspoon grated lemon peel for the vanilla.

NUT BUTTERCREAM FROSTING: Stir in ¼ cup chopped nuts.

ORANGE BUTTERCREAM FROSTING: Substitute 2 to 4 tablespoons orange juice for the half-and-half and 1 teaspoon grated orange peel for the vanilla.

PEANUT BUTTER FROSTING: Add 3 tablespoons peanut butter to the butter.

BUTTERY DECORATOR ICING

This delicious, creamy icing is perfect for frosting or decorating cookies, cakes or bars.

- ½ **cup butter or margarine, softened**
- ¼ **cup shortening**
- 1 **teaspoon vanilla**
- ⅛ **teaspoon salt**
- 4 **cups powdered sugar**
- 2 **to 4 tablespoons milk**

In large bowl, beat butter and shortening until light and fluffy. Add vanilla and salt. Beat in powdered sugar 1 cup at a time, scraping down sides of bowl. Add 2 tablespoons milk; beat at high speed until light and fluffy. Add enough additional milk for desired spreading consistency.

Yield: 3 cups.

TIP:
This icing can be made up to 2 weeks in advance and stored in an airtight container in the refrigerator. Bring to room temperature and beat before using.

NUTRITION PER SERVING:
Calories 220; Protein 0g; Carbohydrate 40g; Fat 8g; Sodium 105mg.

CHOCOLATE CREAM FROSTING

Whipped cream frostings such as this are always better when served immediately.

- 1 **cup whipping cream**
- ⅓ **cup chocolate syrup**

In small bowl, beat whipping cream at highest speed just until it begins to thicken. Gradually add chocolate-flavored syrup and continue beating until soft peaks form. Frost cake and serve immediately; store in refrigerator.

Yield: Frosts 2-layer or 13x9-inch cake.

NUTRITION PER SERVING:
Calories 90; Protein 1g; Carbohydrate 6g; Fat 8g; Sodium 10mg.

DECORATING TIPS AND DESIGNS

Simple to elaborate decorations can be made using a decorating bag and tips. Either whipped cream or frosting can be used to make designs on cakes and desserts. For whipped cream decorations, use a larger decorating bag and tips. After decorating, refrigerate the cake or dessert until serving time.

To decorate with frosting, use recipe for **Buttery Decorator Icing** p. 184. The following suggestions will be helpful as you begin to decorate.

- Sift the powdered sugar used in frostings. Small lumps present in unsifted powdered sugar may clog a tip.

- A frosting must be the right consistency for decorations to hold their shape. Adjust the consistency with a small amount of powdered sugar or water.

- When tinting frosting, always mix enough of each color before decorating. Frosting will darken slightly as it dries.

- Cover the frosting bowl with a damp cloth to prevent drying.

- Pack frosting to the bottom of the bag to prevent air bubbles. Squeeze out a little frosting before starting to decorate.

- Make sure the frosted surface upon which decorations will be made is smooth and even.

- Draw the design on the cake with a toothpick before beginning to decorate.

- Frosting made with butter or margarine may soften during decorating due to the heat of your hand. If frosting becomes too soft, chill for a few minutes.

- Parchment paper can be used to make a disposable decorating bag.

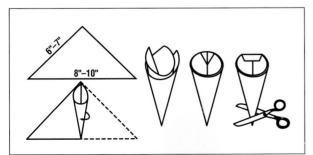

Making a Paper Decorating Bag

Petal Tip

Star Tip

Ribbon Tip

Drop Flower Tip

Writing Tip

Leaf Tip

BASIC POWDERED SUGAR GLAZE

~

For a nice even glaze, use a small plastic decorator bottle filled with the glaze to frost the cake. Or, place the frosting in a resealable plastic freezer bag and snip off 1 corner, making a very small hole. Squeeze the glaze gently through the opening.

  2 **cups powdered sugar**
  2 **tablespoons margarine or butter, softened**
  1 **teaspoon vanilla**
  3 **to 4 tablespoons milk or half-and-half**

In medium bowl, combine all ingredients, adding enough milk for desired glaze consistency. Use to glaze cakes, coffee cakes or pastries.
Yield: 1½ cups.

NUTRITION PER SERVING:
Calories 100; Protein 0g; Carbohydrate 20g; Fat 2g; Sodium 25mg.

VARIATIONS:

CHOCOLATE GLAZE: Add 2 oz. unsweetened chocolate, melted, or 2 envelopes premelted unsweetened chocolate baking flavor.

COFFEE GLAZE: Substitute hot water for milk. Dissolve 1 teaspoon instant coffee granules or crystals in the hot water.

LEMON GLAZE: Substitute 2 tablespoons lemon juice for part of milk and add 1 teaspoon grated lemon peel.

MAPLE GLAZE: Add ½ teaspoon maple extract.

ORANGE GLAZE: Substitute orange juice for milk and add 1 teaspoon grated orange peel.

SPICE GLAZE: Combine ¼ teaspoon cinnamon and ⅛ teaspoon nutmeg with powdered sugar.

COCONUT PECAN FROSTING

~

A classic frosting.

  1 **cup sugar**
  1 **cup evaporated milk**
  ½ **cup margarine or butter**
  3 **eggs, beaten**
1⅓ **cups flaked coconut**
  1 **cup chopped pecans or almonds**
  1 **teaspoon vanilla**

In medium saucepan, combine sugar, milk, margarine and eggs. Cook over medium heat until mixture starts to bubble, stirring constantly. Stir in remaining ingredients. Cool until of desired spreading consistency.
Yield: Frosts 2-layer or 13x9-inch cake.

NUTRITION PER SERVING:
Calories 317; Protein 5g; Carbohydrate 23g; Fat 24g; Sodium 135mg.

BROILED COCONUT TOPPING

~

We suggest using this topping on spice, carrot or yellow cake. It's quick and easy.

  ¼ **cup margarine or butter**
  1 **cup flaked or shredded coconut**
  ⅔ **cup firmly packed brown sugar**
  ½ **cup chopped nuts**
  3 **tablespoons half-and-half or milk**

Heat broiler. In small saucepan, melt margarine. Stir in remaining ingredients. Spread on warm cake. Broil 4 to 6 inches from heat for 1 to 2 minutes or until bubbly and light golden brown. (Watch carefully, mixture burns easily.)
Yield: Tops 13x9-inch cake.

NUTRITION PER SERVING:
Calories 150; Protein 1g; Carbohydrate 16g; Fat 10g; Sodium 50mg.

CREAM CHEESE FROSTING

~

Soften cream cheese at room temperature or in the microwave. To soften cream cheese in the microwave, remove it from the wrapper and microwave it on MEDIUM for 1 to 1½ minutes.

- 3 cups powdered sugar
- 1 (8-oz.) pkg. cream cheese, softened
- 2 tablespoons margarine or butter, melted
- 1 teaspoon vanilla

In large bowl, combine all ingredients; beat until smooth.
Yield: Frosts 2-layer or 13x9-inch cake.

NUTRITION PER SERVING:
Calories 180; Protein 1g; Carbohydrate 25g; Fat 8g; Sodium 80mg.

CHOCOLATE CREAM CHEESE FROSTING

~

Use low heat and stir constantly when melting chocolate chips.

- 1 (3-oz.) pkg. cream cheese, softened
- 2 cups powdered sugar
- 1 (6-oz.) pkg. (1 cup) semi-sweet chocolate chips, melted, cooled
- 3 tablespoons milk
- 1 teaspoon vanilla

In small bowl, combine cream cheese and powdered sugar; beat at medium speed until light and fluffy. Blend in melted chocolate, milk and vanilla at low speed until smooth. If necessary, add additional milk 1 teaspoon at a time for desired spreading consistency.
Yield: Frosts 2-layer or 13x9-inch cake.

NUTRITION PER SERVING:
Calories 170; Protein 1g; Carbohydrate 29g; Fat 7g; Sodium 25mg.

ALMOND BARK BUTTERCREAM FROSTING

~

Using low heat to melt the almond bark is the secret to making this frosting smooth and creamy. We like the frosting on chocolate cake, but it's delicious on other cake flavors too.

- 6 oz. almond bark or vanilla-flavored candy coating, cut into pieces
- 3 to 4 tablespoons chocolate-flavored liqueur
- ¾ cup butter, softened
- ¼ cup powdered sugar

In small saucepan over low heat, melt almond bark, stirring constantly. Remove from heat; stir in chocolate liqueur. Cool 30 minutes.

In small bowl, beat butter and powdered sugar until light and fluffy. Gradually beat in cooled almond bark mixture until smooth.
Yield: Frosts 2-layer or 13x9-inch cake.

NUTRITION PER SERVING:
Calories 200; Protein 1g; Carbohydrate 10g; Fat 19g; Sodium 115mg.

COOK'S NOTE

~

MELTING CHOCOLATE

Chocolate should be melted over low heat and stirred constantly to prevent scorching. Small amounts of water may cause it to "seize" or become thick, lumpy and grainy, so use utensils and equipment that are dry. Chocolate can sometimes be returned to melting consistancy by adding 1 teaspoon of solid shortening for every 2 ounces of chocolate and reheating it.

SEVEN-MINUTE FROSTING

This traditional frosting is fluffy, white and almost meringue-like in texture. It's easy to make, but takes 7 minutes to cook.

- 1½ **cups sugar**
- ¼ **teaspoon cream of tartar**
- ¼ **teaspoon salt**
- ⅓ **cup water**
- 2 **teaspoons light corn syrup**
- 2 **egg whites**
- 1 **teaspoon vanilla**

In top of double boiler, combine all ingredients except vanilla. Place over rapidly boiling water (water should not touch bottom of pan); beat at highest speed until mixture stands in peaks, about 7 minutes. DO NOT OVERCOOK. Remove from heat; add vanilla. Continue beating until frosting holds deep swirls, about 2 minutes.

Yield: Frosts 2-layer or 13x9-inch cake.

NUTRITION PER SERVING:
Calories 102; Protein 0g; Carbohydrate 26g; Fat 0g; Sodium 54mg.

VARIATIONS:

CHERRY FROSTING: Substitute ⅓ cup maraschino cherry liquid for water. Fold ⅓ cup drained chopped maraschino cherries into finished frosting.

CHOCOLATE REVEL FROSTING: Add ⅓ cup semi-sweet chocolate chips to finished frosting. Let stand 1 to 2 minutes. Chocolate will swirl through frosting when spread on cake.

LEMON FROSTING: Fold 3 teaspoons grated lemon peel into finished frosting.

MAPLE FROSTING: Substitute ½ to 1 teaspoon maple extract for vanilla.

NESSELRODE FROSTING: Substitute 1 teaspoon rum extract for vanilla. Place 1 cup frosting in small bowl; stir in ½ cup chopped mixed candied fruit and ½ cup toasted coconut. Spread between layers. Frost sides and top with remaining plain frosting.

ORANGE FROSTING: Fold 3 teaspoons grated orange peel into finished frosting.

PEPPERMINT FROSTING: Substitute 3 to 5 drops peppermint extract for vanilla. Fold ½ cup crushed hard peppermint candy into finished frosting.

WHITE CLOUD FROSTING

This delicate, airy frosting is a classic. Try it on any chocolate or white cake.

- 2 **egg whites**
- ¼ **teaspoon salt**
- 1 **teaspoon vanilla**
- ¼ **cup sugar**
- ¾ **cup light corn syrup**

In small deep bowl, beat egg whites, salt and vanilla at medium speed until foamy. Gradually add sugar 1 tablespoon at a time, beating at highest speed until soft peaks form and sugar is dissolved. In small saucepan over medium heat, bring corn syrup just to a boil. Pour in thin stream over egg whites, beating at highest speed until mixture forms stiff peaks.

Yield: Frosts 2-layer or 13x9-inch cake.

NUTRITION PER SERVING:
Calories 80; Protein 1g; Carbohydrate 20g; Fat 0g; Sodium 70mg.

GANACHE

Ganache (gahn-AHSH) is a rich combination of chocolate and cream that ranges in consistency from fudgy to light and airy, depending on the proportion of whipping cream to chocolate. This recipe makes enough ganache to frost a layer cake.

- 12 oz. semi-sweet chocolate, chopped, or 1 cup semi-sweet chocolate chips
- 1 cup whipping cream
- 2 tablespoons butter or margarine

In small saucepan, combine chocolate and whipping cream; heat over low heat until chocolate is melted and mixture is smooth and creamy, stirring constantly. Remove from heat; stir in butter. Refrigerate 30 to 45 minutes or until cold, stirring occasionally.

With wooden spoon or hand mixer, beat chilled mixture until thick and creamy and of desired spreading consistency.

Yield: Frosts 2-layer or 13x9-inch cake.

NUTRITION PER SERVING:
Calories 220; Protein 2g; Carbohydrate 19g; Fat 18g; Sodium 30mg.

COOK'S NOTE

GANACHE

Ganache is a rich mixture of chocolate and whipping cream that's used as a frosting or piped onto a dessert as a garnish. The mixture is heated over low heat until the chocolate is melted. Then it is chilled and beaten with a wire whisk or electric beater until it is thick enough to spread. Ganache sets up rather quickly, so stop and check the consistency frequently. DO NOT OVERBEAT ganache; it will thicken and resemble fudge. If ganache becomes too thick to spread, stir in 1 tablespoon of warm cream, or warm it slightly over hot water or in the microwave on LOW. The mixture will not be as glossy, but it will be spreadable.

To pipe the ganache decoratively, beat the mixture until it holds its shape when mounded. Spoon it into a decorating bag fitted with the desired tip. Pipe it directly onto the dessert.

FUDGE FROSTING

This fudgy frosting is delicious on almost any flavor of cake!

- 2 cups sugar
- ¾ cup half-and-half
- 2 oz. unsweetened chocolate or 2 envelopes premelted unsweetened chocolate baking flavor
- 2 tablespoons light corn syrup
- ⅛ teaspoon salt
- 2 tablespoons margarine or butter
- 1 teaspoon vanilla

In large saucepan, combine sugar, half-and-half, chocolate, corn syrup and salt. Cook over low heat, stirring just until sugar is dissolved. Cover; cook over medium heat for 2 minutes. Uncover; cook until candy thermometer reaches soft ball stage (234°F.), about 5 minutes. Do not stir while cooking. Remove from heat; add margarine. Cool to lukewarm (110°F.). Additional cooling may cause frosting to harden too soon.

Add vanilla; beat until frosting begins to thicken and loses its gloss. If necessary, thin with a few drops of half-and-half.

Yield: Frosts 2-layer or 13x9-inch cake.

NUTRITION PER SERVING:
Calories 210; Protein 0g; Carbohydrate 38g; Fat 7g; Sodium 55mg.

VARIATIONS:

MARSHMALLOW NUT FUDGE FROSTING: Add 1 cup miniature marshmallows and ½ cup chopped nuts to frosting just before spreading.

PEANUT BUTTER FUDGE FROSTING: Add ¼ cup creamy peanut butter with margarine.

DESSERTS

Dessert adds that sweet touch to the end of a meal or the end of a day. There's a dessert that's perfect for every occasion and in this chapter you'll find the dessert that fits yours to a "T."

The collection starts with down-home family favorites — cobblers, crisps and deep dish pies — and moves on to delicious dessert squares, creamy cheesecakes, elegant tortes . . . and more! A special section offers secrets for successful desserts, including easy tips for sensational finishing touches.

Pictured: **Chocolate Toffee Cloud** *p. 249,* **Ruby Razz Crunch** *p. 212*

DESSERTS

Dessert adds a finishing touch to any meal,
whether it is a made-in-minutes fruit cobbler or a masterpiece of many layers.
Because desserts are so versatile, you'll find ones that not only complement
your meal, but also fit your level of baking expertise.

KINDS OF DESSERTS

Desserts fall into several main categories:

BAKED AND STEAMED PUDDINGS

These moist, hearty, old-fashioned desserts are either baked in a pan, cooked in the micro-wave or steamed in a mold on the stovetop. (Recipes begin on p. 240.)

CHEESECAKES

Cheesecakes do contain cheese — most often it's cream, Neufchatel, cottage or ricotta cheese. Sometimes yogurt cheese is used. Rich and dense, cheesecakes have many flavor, crust and topping variations. (Recipes begin on p. 222.)

CRISPS, COBBLERS, BUCKLES AND PANDOWDIES

Fruit is the hallmark of these traditional desserts. They are usually topped with a pastry crust, streusel or biscuit topping. (Recipes begin on p. 196.)

CUSTARDS, FLANS AND SOUFFLES

Eggs are the main ingredient in all of these desserts. Custards and flans are baked until delicately firm and are sometimes topped with caramel or fruit. A souffle is a puffy, feather-light dessert with a reputation for elegance. (Recipes begin on p. 237.)

MERINGUES

A hard meringue is a confection of beaten egg whites, sugar and sometimes flavorings, which is shaped and then baked. These crisp, airy shells can be topped with custard, mousse, fruit or other fillings. A soft meringue is used to top desserts such as Baked Alaska. (Recipes begin on p. 248.)

SHORTCAKES

Shortcakes are drop or rolled biscuits, sponge cakes or pound cakes topped with fruit. (Recipes begin on p. 206.)

TORTES

Tortes can be made in several ways. They can be multi-layered desserts with a variety of fillings and toppings or dense confections baked in a springform pan. (Recipes begin on p. 254.)

SECRETS FOR SUCCESSFUL DESSERTS

Desserts incorporate a few basic baking techniques that will help you approach even the most elaborate confection with confidence.

SECRETS FOR STEAMED PUDDINGS

Use molds with tight-fitting lids for steamed puddings. Grease the inside of the mold with shortening and then sprinkle it with sugar.

Place molds on a wire rack or trivet in a Dutch oven. Choose a Dutch oven that is large enough to allow steam to circulate completely around the molds. Bring 1 inch of water to a boil, add the molds and cover the Dutch oven tightly. Cook at high heat until steam begins to escape, then reduce the heat to low.

Remove the mold lid after steaming. This allows the pudding to "rest," allows excess steam to escape and minimizes cracking when the pudding is unmolded.

Run a knife between the mold and the pudding to loosen the pudding for unmolding. Invert a plate over the mold. Hold the plate firmly against the mold and turn the mold upside down. The pudding should slip from the mold.

SECRETS FOR CHEESECAKES

Make the cheesecake 24 to 36 hours before serving it. This allows the cheesecake to cool and firm up completely, and allows flavors to blend and mellow. Cool the cheesecake to room temperature and then store it in the refrigerator.

Use the pan size called for in the recipe.

Have eggs and cream cheese at room temperature before mixing the batter.

Follow these tips to help prevent cracks in cheesecakes:

- **Use an electric mixer or food processor to beat the filling.** Beat at medium speed just until smooth. Overbeating or mixing at high speed can cause cracks to form in the cheesecake as it bakes.

- **Place a shallow pan half full of water on the lower rack in the oven.** The water will help minimize cracking in the top of the cheesecake.

- **Let the cheesecake "rest" after baking.** Unless other directions are specified in the recipe, when the cheesecake is done, turn off the oven and open the door. Allow the cheese-

cake to rest for 30 minutes, then transfer it to a cooling rack in a draft-free spot until it reaches room temperature. When completely cool, remove the sides of the pan and then refrigerate.

- **Do not jar the cheesecake while it is baking or cooling.**

Cut cheesecakes using a wet knife or a piece of dental floss. Dip the knife in water before each cut. To use dental floss, stretch it tightly between your hands and press firmly through the cheesecake.

SECRETS FOR CUSTARDS

Avoid overbaking custards. Because custards are made with eggs, they can curdle or become rubbery and watery if overbaked. To protect the protein in the eggs from excessive heat, bake custard in cups placed on a rack or folded towel set in a pan of hot water (about 1 inch deep).

SECRETS FOR SOUFFLES

Heat the oven 10 to 15 minutes before baking. A hot oven will allow the souffle to begin rising immediately.

Beat egg whites just until they form stiff peaks. Overbeaten egg whites will prevent the souffle from rising. Fold them gently into the batter.

Handle with care! A souffle is a delicate dessert supported by the air incorporated into the egg whites. Gently spoon the batter into the baking dish, and avoid jarring it as it is placed in or removed from the oven. Also, close and open the oven door carefully.

Serve immediately. A souffle will only hold its shape a few minutes after it's removed from the oven. As the steam escapes, it will begin to fall. Because of this, you'll want to carefully plan for the serving time.

SECRETS FOR HARD MERINGUES

Avoid making meringues on hot, humid days. High humidity will prevent meringues from reaching their full volume, and they will "weep" (beads of moisture will form on the meringue) and become sticky after baking.

Use beaters, utensils and bowls that are clean and free from grease. Even a small amount of grease (or speck of egg yolk) will prevent beaten egg whites from reaching their full volume. Use glass or stainless steel bowls rather than plastic, because plastic bowls tend to retain fat.

Egg whites should come from clean, fresh eggs with no cracks.

Bring egg whites to room temperature before beating them. Set the bowl of egg whites in a large bowl of very warm water and stir them gently for a few minutes.

Begin beating the egg whites slowly, gradually increasing speed as the egg whites begin to foam.

Beat the egg whites until they hold the desired shape, either soft or stiff peaks.

Add sugar gradually while beating. This will ensure that the sugar dissolves completely and that stiff glossy peaks will form.

Bake meringues for a long time at a low temperature. This gives meringues their crisp, melt-in-your-mouth texture. Cool completely.

Fill or top meringues just before serving to prevent them from becoming soggy.

HOW TO TELL WHEN DESSERTS ARE DONE

Just an extra minute in the oven can make a dessert overbaked. Here are some tips for telling when desserts are done:

Read the description in the recipe. The recipe provides a specific description of what a dessert looks like when it's done. It may say the top will be golden brown or cracked, or that the dessert will begin pulling away from the sides of the pan or that the filling will be bubbly around the edges.

Two common descriptions for rich, moist desserts are:

- **". . . until almost set."** About a 3-inch diameter circle in the center will be soft and will jiggle when the dessert is moved slightly. The edges of the dessert will be set and have a dry appearance. As the dessert cools, the center will become firm.

- **". . . until set."** The center of the dessert will be soft when touched lightly, but will not jiggle when moved. The center will become more firm as the dessert cools.

Check desserts at the minimum baking time. If the dessert isn't quite done, check at 1-minute increments until it meets the description in the recipe.

Baked and steamed puddings are done when . . . they are set and firm.

Baked custards and flans are done when . . . a knife inserted halfway between the center and the edge of the custard comes out clean. The center of the custard may look soft, but as it cools, it will become firm. An overbaked custard will have a porous, rubbery texture and liquid will seep from it when cut with a spoon.

A souffle is done when . . . it has doubled in volume and is firm, and the top is golden brown.

KEEPING DESSERTS FRESH AND FLAVORFUL

Many desserts have a very short lifespan — and not just because they get gobbled up! Souffles, for example, must be baked and served immediately. Hard meringues, once they're filled, will become soggy. However, other desserts such as cheesecakes, cobblers and squares can be stored or frozen with great success. Here are some tips for keeping desserts at their peak:

Store unfilled meringues, puffs and eclairs in an airtight, moisture-proof container. Meringues should be stored in a tin or other container with a tight-fitting lid in a cool, dry place to keep them crisp and to prevent droplets of moisture from forming, also known as weeping. Store up to 2 days at room temperature, or freeze them for up to 1 month. Puffs or eclairs should be stored in the refrigerator. Limit storage time to overnight. For longer storage, place unfilled puffs in an airtight container and freeze them for up to 3 months.

Store egg- or milk-based desserts in the refrigerator. Custards and flans are at their best served the day they are prepared. Baked puddings can be served warm from the oven or covered and stored in the refrigerator. They should not be frozen. Add whipped cream just before serving.

Store cobblers, dumplings and cheesecakes in the refrigerator. Cover them tightly with foil or plastic wrap. These desserts also freeze well. To freeze: allow to cool completely after baking; wrap tightly in moisture- and vapor-proof covering and freeze for 4 to 5 months. Fruit-filled dumplings may be frozen baked or unbaked. When freezing an unbaked dumpling, brush the bottom crust with egg white before filling it to prevent it from becoming soggy. Fill and shape it, but do not cut air vents in the crust. Wrap tightly and freeze. Bake the dumplings according to the recipe after thawing them at room temperature. For baked dumplings, cool completely, wrap and freeze.

SERVING DESSERTS WITH A FLAIR

One of the joys of serving a dessert is making it look pretty. Here are a few easy ideas for dressing up simple or sensational desserts.

Drizzle or pipe chocolate sauce on an individual plate before placing a wedge of cheesecake or a hard meringue on it. See diagram for Plate Painting.

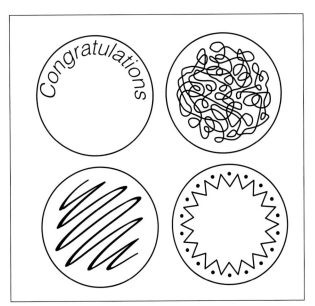

Plate Painting

Dust a serving plate or individual plate with cocoa or powdered sugar before placing the dessert on it.

Line the serving plate with a paper doily.

Make an arrangement of mint sprigs and/or edible flowers such as roses on top of the dessert or on the serving plate at the base of the dessert.

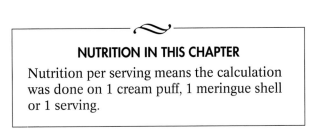

NUTRITION IN THIS CHAPTER

Nutrition per serving means the calculation was done on 1 cream puff, 1 meringue shell or 1 serving.

APPLE CRISP

A crisp is a fruit dessert that is baked with a top layer of buttered crumbs, which forms a crisp, crumbly crust as it bakes. Try the flavor variations we offer.

FRUIT MIXTURE
- 6 cups sliced peeled apples
- 1 teaspoon cinnamon, if desired
- 1 tablespoon water
- 1 teaspoon lemon juice

TOPPING
- 1 cup rolled oats
- ¾ cup all purpose flour
- ¾ cup firmly packed brown sugar
- ½ cup margarine or butter, softened

Heat oven to 375°F. Place apples in ungreased 2-quart casserole or 8-inch square (1½-quart) baking dish. Sprinkle with cinnamon, water and lemon juice. In large bowl, combine all topping ingredients; mix until crumbly. Sprinkle crumb mixture evenly over apples. Bake at 375°F. for 25 to 35 minutes or until fruit is tender and topping is golden brown. Serve warm with cream, ice cream or whipped cream, if desired.
Yield: 12 (½-cup) servings.

MICROWAVE DIRECTIONS:
Using 8-inch square (1½-quart) microwave-safe dish, prepare apple crisp as directed above. Microwave on HIGH for 12 to 14 minutes or until fruit is tender, rotating dish ¼ turn once during cooking.

NUTRITION PER SERVING:
Calories 210; Protein 2g; Carbohydrate 32g; Fat 8g; Sodium 95mg.

VARIATIONS:

APPLE CHEESE CRISP: Top baked crisp with 2 oz. (½ cup) shredded Cheddar cheese; bake an additional 2 to 3 minutes or until cheese melts.

BLUEBERRY CRISP: Substitute blueberries for the apples.

PEACH CRISP: Substitute sliced peeled peaches for the apples.

PEAR CRANBERRY CRISP: Substitute 5 cups sliced peeled pears, 1½ cups fresh or frozen cranberries, 1 cup sugar, 2 tablespoons flour and 2 teaspoons grated orange peel for fruit mixture.

PEACH BERRY CRUMBLE

This colorful fruit-laden cobbler is the perfect ending for a meal or is great for a coffee break.

TOPPING
- 1 cup all purpose flour
- ¾ cup sugar
- ¼ cup margarine or butter, softened
- 1 egg, slightly beaten

FRUIT MIXTURE
- 1 cup sugar
- 3 tablespoons cornstarch
- 1 cup water
- ¼ teaspoon almond extract
- 1 (16-oz.) pkg. frozen sliced peaches, thawed
- 1 cup fresh or frozen cranberries (do not thaw)
- 1 cup fresh or frozen blackberries (do not thaw)

Heat oven to 400°F. In medium bowl, combine flour and ¾ cup sugar. Using pastry blender or fork, cut in margarine until crumbly. Stir in egg; mix well. Set aside.

In small saucepan, combine 1 cup sugar and cornstarch; add water. Cook over medium heat until mixture boils and thickens, stirring constantly. Stir in almond extract. In ungreased 8-inch square (1½-quart) baking dish, combine peaches, cranberries and blackberries; stir in hot cornstarch mixture. Sprinkle topping over fruit mixture.

Bake at 400°F. for 40 to 45 minutes or until topping is golden brown. Serve warm. If desired, serve with sweetened sour cream, whipped cream or ice cream.
Yield: 9 servings.

NUTRITION PER SERVING:
Calories 330; Protein 3g; Carbohydrate 67g; Fat 6g; Sodium 70mg.

Apple Crisp

Simple Fruit Crisp

Select your favorite flavor of fruit filling to make this easy-to-prepare crisp.

 1 (21-oz.) can fruit pie filling (cherry, blueberry, raspberry, apricot or apple)
 1 cup all purpose flour
 ½ cup firmly packed brown sugar
 ½ teaspoon cinnamon, if desired
 ½ teaspoon nutmeg, if desired
 ⅓ cup margarine or butter, softened

Heat oven to 375°F. Spread pie filling in ungreased 8-inch square (1½-quart) baking dish. In medium bowl, combine all remaining ingredients until crumbly; sprinkle over filling. Bake at 375°F. for 25 to 30 minutes or until golden brown. If desired, serve warm with ice cream or whipped topping.
Yield: 6 to 8 servings.

NUTRITION PER SERVING:
Calories 310; Protein 2g; Carbohydrate 59g; Fat 8g; Sodium 95mg.

Individual Peach Crisp

For dessert variety, use nectarines, plums or pears instead of peaches. Serve this crisp warm with cream or ice cream.

 1½ cups (2 medium) sliced peeled peaches
 3 tablespoons all purpose flour
 3 tablespoons brown sugar
 3 tablespoons rolled oats
 3 tablespoons chopped walnuts, if desired
 ⅛ teaspoon cinnamon
 2 tablespoons margarine or butter

Heat oven to 350°F. Spoon peaches evenly into 3 ungreased 10-oz. custard cups. In small bowl, combine all remaining ingredients; blend with fork until crumbly. Sprinkle crumb mixture evenly over peaches. Bake at 350°F for 25 to 30 minutes or until fruit is tender and topping is golden brown. Serve warm.
Yield: 3 servings.

MICROWAVE DIRECTIONS:
Prepare peach crisp as directed above using 3 ungreased 6-oz. custard cups. Microwave on HIGH for 2½ to 4½ minutes or until peaches are tender, rearranging custard cups once during cooking. Serve warm.

NUTRITION PER SERVING:
Calories 260; Protein 3g; Carbohydrate 34g; Fat 13g; Sodium 95mg.

Fresh Plum Crumb

This wonderful old-fashioned dessert is flavored with nutmeg and cinnamon.

FRUIT MIXTURE
 5 cups chopped, pitted plums
 2 tablespoons quick-cooking tapioca
 3 eggs
 1½ cups sugar
 ¼ cup all purpose flour
 ½ teaspoon nutmeg
 3 tablespoons milk

TOPPING
 ¾ cup rolled oats
 ¾ cup firmly packed brown sugar
 ½ teaspoon cinnamon
 ¼ teaspoon salt
 ¼ cup margarine or butter, melted

Heat oven to 375°F. Lightly grease 13x9-inch pan. In medium bowl, combine plums and tapioca; set aside. In large bowl, lightly beat eggs; stir in sugar, flour, nutmeg and milk. Gently fold in plum mixture. Pour into greased pan. In medium bowl, combine rolled oats, brown sugar, cinnamon and salt; mix well. Stir in margarine; sprinkle over plum mixture.

Bake at 375°F. for 40 to 45 minutes or until golden brown. Serve warm.
Yield: 16 to 20 servings.

NUTRITION PER SERVING:
Calories 170; Protein 2g; Carbohydrate 32g; Fat 4g; Sodium 95mg.

BLUEBERRY PLUM CRUNCH CUPS

Dessert warm from the oven is a welcome surprise on a cool day.

FRUIT MIXTURE
2½ cups purple plums, pitted, sliced*
2½ cups blueberries*
¼ cup firmly packed brown sugar

TOPPING
1 cup all purpose flour
⅓ cup sugar
⅓ cup firmly packed brown sugar
½ teaspoon salt
¼ teaspoon nutmeg
1 egg
1 tablespoon margarine or butter, melted

Heat oven to 375°F. Grease six 6-oz. custard cups; place on cookie sheet. In medium bowl, gently combine plums, blueberries and ¼ cup brown sugar. Spoon about ½ cup fruit mixture into each greased cup.

In medium bowl, combine flour, sugar, ⅓ cup brown sugar, salt and nutmeg; mix well. Add egg; mix until crumbly. Sprinkle about ¼ cup flour mixture over each cup of fruit; drizzle each with about ½ teaspoon melted margarine. Bake at 375°F. for 25 to 30 minutes or until topping is golden brown. Serve warm with ice cream, if desired.
Yield: 6 servings.

TIP:
* Two 16-oz. cans purple plums, drained, pitted and sliced, and 2½ cups frozen blueberries, thawed and drained, can be substituted for the fresh fruit.

NUTRITION PER SERVING:
Calories 310; Protein 4g; Carbohydrate 65g; Fat 4g; Sodium 220mg.

CHOCOLATE CHERRY CRUNCH

Cherries are layered between a chocolate shortbread mixture, forming what is known as a "crunch" in this easy recipe.

CRUST AND TOPPING
1 cups all purpose flour
¾ cup firmly packed brown sugar
¾ cup quick-cooking rolled oats
¼ cup unsweetened cocoa
¼ teaspoon salt
½ cup margarine or butter, softened

FRUIT MIXTURE
1 (21-oz.) can cherry fruit pie filling
1 teaspoon brandy extract, if desired

Heat oven to 350°F. In large bowl, combine flour, brown sugar, oats, cocoa, and salt; mix well. Using pastry blender or fork, cut in margarine until crumbly. Press 1 cup crumb mixture into bottom of ungreased 8 or 9-inch square pan. In medium bowl, combine pie filling and brandy extract; spoon evenly over crust. Sprinkle remaining crumb mixture evenly over cherry filling; press lightly into filling.

Bake at 350°F. for 25 to 30 minutes or until light golden brown. Serve with ice cream or whipped cream, if desired.
Yield: 6 to 8 servings.

HIGH ALTITUDE:
Above 3500 Feet: No change.

NUTRITION PER SERVING:
Calories 410; Protein 4g; Carbohydrate 72g; Fat 13g; Sodium 230mg.

PEACHY PINEAPPLE DESSERT

Butterscotch chips add a unique richness to this deliciously sweet, quick and easy fruit cobbler.

- ¼ **cup margarine or butter, melted**
- 1 **(21-oz.) can peach fruit pie filling**
- 1 **(15.25 or 20-oz.) can crushed pineapple, undrained**
- 1 **(6-oz.) pkg. (1 cup) butterscotch chips**
- 1 **(10-oz.) can refrigerated flaky biscuits**
- ⅓ **cup chopped nuts**
  Whipped topping or ice cream, if desired

Heat oven to 400°F. In medium saucepan, combine 2 tablespoons of the melted margarine, peach filling, pineapple and butterscotch chips; heat until hot and bubbly.* Pour hot fruit mixture into ungreased 12x8-inch (2-quart) baking dish. Separate dough into 10 biscuits; cut each into 4 pieces. Dip biscuit pieces into remaining melted margarine; arrange over hot fruit mixture. Sprinkle with nuts.

Bake at 400°F. for 15 to 18 minutes or until golden brown. Serve warm or cool topped with whipped topping or ice cream.
Yield: 10 servings.

TIP:
* Fruit mixture can be heated in baking dish; heat at 400°F. for 20 minutes or until hot and bubbly. Top with biscuit pieces and nuts; bake as directed above.

NUTRITION PER SERVING:
Calories 380; Protein 3g; Carbohydrate 46g; Fat 20g; Sodium 350mg.

BLUEBERRY BUCKLE RING

Buckles are a combination of tender cake, fruit and streusel topping. Blueberries are the most common fruit used for this country dessert. Here we offer it in a non-traditional shape.

CAKE
- 1½ **cups all purpose flour**
- 2 **teaspoons baking powder**
- ¼ **teaspoon salt**
- ¾ **cup sugar**
- ¼ **cup margarine or butter, softened**
- 1 **egg**
- ½ **cup milk**
- 3 **cups fresh or frozen blueberries (do not thaw)**

TOPPING
- ⅓ **cup all purpose flour**
- ½ **cup firmly packed brown sugar**
- ½ **teaspoon cinnamon**
- ¼ **cup margarine or butter**
- ¼ **cup chopped walnuts**

Heat oven to 350°F. Grease and flour 10-inch tube pan. In medium bowl, combine 1½ cups flour, baking powder and salt; set aside. In large bowl, beat sugar and ¼ cup margarine until light and fluffy. Add egg; beat well. Alternately add dry ingredients and milk to sugar mixture, beating well after each addition. Spread ⅔ of batter into greased and floured pan; top with blueberries. Carefully spread with remaining batter.

In medium bowl, combine ⅓ cup flour, brown sugar and cinnamon. Using pastry blender or fork, cut in ¼ cup margarine until mixture is crumbly. Stir in nuts. Sprinkle over batter. Bake at 350°F. for 55 to 65 minutes or until cake is deep golden brown. Cool 10 minutes; remove from pan. Serve warm with cream, if desired.
Yield: 8 servings.

HIGH ALTITUDE:
Above 3500 Feet: No change.

NUTRITION PER SERVING:
Calories 410; Protein 5g; Carbohydrate 63g; Fat 15g; Sodium 300mg.

Blueberry Buckle Ring

BLUEBERRY PEACH COBBLER

Tender sugar-crusted biscuits sit atop a tasty blend of fruit. This cobbler is delicious warm from the oven.

FRUIT MIXTURE
- ⅓ cup sugar
- 1 tablespoon cornstarch
- ¾ cup unsweetened orange juice
- 1½ cups fresh or frozen blueberries (do not thaw)
- 1 cup fresh or frozen peach slices, cut into 1-inch pieces (do not thaw)
- 1 teaspoon grated orange peel

BISCUITS
- 1 cup all purpose flour
- 1 tablespoon sugar
- 1 teaspoon baking powder
- ¼ teaspoon baking soda
- ½ cup buttermilk
- 3 tablespoons oil
- 1 tablespoon sugar

In medium saucepan, combine ⅓ cup sugar and cornstarch. Gradually stir in orange juice. Cook over medium heat until mixture comes to a boil and is slightly thickened and clear, stirring constantly. Stir in blueberries and peach pieces; cook until fruit is hot. Stir in orange peel; set aside.

Heat oven to 375°F. In medium bowl, combine flour, 1 tablespoon sugar, baking powder and baking soda; mix well. Stir in buttermilk and oil just until dry ingredients are moistened. Pour hot fruit mixture into ungreased 1½-quart casserole. Drop dough by tablespoonfuls over fruit mixture. Sprinkle dough with 1 tablespoon sugar. Bake at 375°F. for 20 to 25 minutes or until biscuits are light golden brown.
Yield: 8 servings.

HIGH ALTITUDE:
Above 3500 Feet: No change.

NUTRITION PER SERVING:
Calories 220; Protein 3g; Carbohydrate 39g; Fat 6g; Sodium 90mg.

CALIFORNIA FRUIT COBBLER

Cobblers are fruits baked with a crust. Slices of refrigerated crescent dough form the crust for this cobbler, which calls for fresh summer fruits. The fruit can be either peeled or unpeeled.

- ¾ cup sugar
- ¼ cup cornstarch
- 2 cups sliced nectarines, cut ½ inch thick
- 2 cups sliced pears, cut ½ inch thick
- 2 cups sliced plums, cut ½ inch thick
- 1 (8-oz.) can refrigerated crescent dinner rolls
- 2 tablespoons honey
- 1 tablespoon margarine or butter, softened

TOPPING
- ½ cup dairy sour cream
- 1 tablespoon brown sugar

Heat oven to 375°F. In large saucepan, combine sugar, cornstarch and fruit. Cook over medium heat until mixture is hot and bubbly, stirring occasionally. Pour into ungreased 12x8-inch (2-quart) baking dish.

Remove dough from can in rolled sections; DO NOT UNROLL. Cut each roll into 3 slices; cut each slice in half. Arrange around edge of baking dish, placing cut side toward edge of baking dish to form a scalloped appearance.

Bake at 375°F. for 20 to 25 minutes or until crescents are deep golden brown and mixture is bubbly. In small bowl, combine honey and margarine; brush over crescents. In small bowl, combine topping ingredients. Spoon over cobbler to serve.
Yield: 6 servings.

NUTRITION PER SERVING:
Calories 440; Protein 4g; Carbohydrate 75g; Fat 14g; Sodium 340mg.

APPLE BERRY COBBLER

Refrigerated biscuits make this recipe especially quick to prepare.

- ¼ **cup sugar**
- 4 **teaspoons cornstarch**
- 1 **(10-oz.) pkg. frozen whole berries, thawed, drained, reserving ½ cup liquid**
- 2 **medium thinly sliced peeled apples**
- 1 **egg, separated**
- 1 **tablespoon water**
- 1 **(10-oz.) can refrigerated flaky biscuits**
- 2 **to 4 tablespoons sugar**

Heat oven to 400°F. In medium saucepan, combine ¼ cup sugar and cornstarch. Stir in reserved liquid. Cook over medium heat until thickened, stirring constantly. Stir in berries and apples; cook 3 to 5 minutes or until apples are just tender, stirring occasionally. Pour into ungreased 12x8-inch (2-quart) baking dish.

Beat egg yolk with water. Separate dough into 10 biscuits. Dip tops of biscuits in beaten yolk mixture; arrange, dipped side up, on top of hot fruit mixture. Bake at 400°F. for 10 to 15 minutes or until biscuits are golden brown.

Meanwhile, beat egg white until foamy; gradually add 2 to 4 tablespoons sugar, beating until stiff peaks form. Spoon meringue on top of each baked biscuit. Return to oven and bake an additional 5 to 6 minutes or until meringue is light golden brown. Serve warm. Store in refrigerator.

Yield: 10 servings.

NUTRITION PER SERVING:
Calories 170; Protein 3g; Carbohydrate 30g; Fat 4g; Sodium 300mg.

RASPBERRY PEACH COBBLER

Biscuits, made tender and moist with sour cream, top a sensational combination of raspberries and peaches. Serve it with half-and-half for a rich taste treat.

BISCUITS
- 1 **cup all purpose flour**
- ½ **cup sugar**
- 1 **teaspoon baking powder**
- ¼ **teaspoon salt**
- ¾ **cup dairy sour cream**
- 2 **tablespoons margarine or butter, melted**
- 1 **egg**

FRUIT MIXTURE
- ¾ **cup sugar**
- 3 **tablespoons cornstarch**
- 1 **(10-oz.) pkg. frozen raspberries with syrup, thawed, drained, reserving liquid**
- 1 **(16-oz.) pkg. frozen sliced peaches without syrup, thawed, drained**
- 1 **tablespoon sugar**

Heat oven to 375°F. In medium bowl, combine flour, ½ cup sugar, baking powder and salt; mix well. Stir in remaining biscuit ingredients; set aside.

In medium saucepan, combine ¾ cup sugar, cornstarch and reserved raspberry liquid. Cook over medium heat until mixture boils; boil 1 minute, stirring constantly. Add raspberries and peaches; cook 1 minute. Pour into ungreased 2-quart casserole. Spoon biscuit mixture over hot fruit mixture, forming 9 biscuits around edge of casserole. Sprinkle biscuits with 1 tablespoon sugar.

Bake at 375°F. for 35 to 45 minutes or until biscuits are golden brown. Serve warm.

Yield: 9 servings.

HIGH ALTITUDE:
Above 3500 Feet: No change.

NUTRITION PER SERVING:
Calories 330; Protein 3g; Carbohydrate 63g; Fat 8g; Sodium 140mg.

OLD-FASHIONED BERRY COBBLER

Use a heart-shaped cookie cutter to cut out the dough to top this cobbler.

FRUIT MIXTURE
- 4 cups frozen raspberries, blackberries or loganberries (do not thaw)
- ½ cup seedless raspberry jam
- 2 tablespoons quick-cooking tapioca*
- 2 tablespoons sugar
- 2 tablespoons margarine or butter

TOPPING
- 1 cup all purpose flour
- 2 tablespoons sugar
- 2 teaspoons baking powder
- ¼ teaspoon salt
- ¼ cup margarine or butter
- 2 to 4 tablespoons milk
- 1 egg
- ½ teaspoon sugar

Heat oven to 425°F. Grease 10x6-inch (1½-quart) baking dish or 1½-quart casserole. In large bowl, combine berries, jam, tapioca and 2 tablespoons sugar; mix gently. Spread in greased dish. Dot with 2 tablespoons margarine. Bake at 425°F. for 15 to 20 minutes or until mixture begins to bubble; stir.

In large bowl, combine flour, 2 tablespoons sugar, baking powder and salt; mix well. With pastry blender or fork, cut in ¼ cup margarine until crumbly. In small bowl, beat 2 tablespoons milk and egg until blended. Stir into flour mixture until blended, adding additional milk if necessary to form stiff dough. On lightly floured surface, roll out dough to ½-inch thickness. With 2-inch cookie cutter, cut out hearts, circles or diamonds. Place on top of hot fruit mixture; sprinkle with ½ teaspoon sugar.

Bake at 425°F. for 10 to 20 minutes or until fruit bubbles around edges and biscuits are light golden brown. Serve warm with cream or ice cream, if desired.
Yield: 6 to 8 servings.

TIP:
* Cornstarch can be substituted for tapioca; the fruit mixture will not be as clear.

HIGH ALTITUDE:
Above 3500 Feet: No change.

NUTRITION PER SERVING:
Calories 280; Protein 4g; Carbohydrate 45g; Fat 10g; Sodium 260mg.

WINTER FRUIT DEEP-DISH PIE

Sprinkle the pastry with sugar before baking.

FILLING
- 1 (29-oz.) can sliced peaches, undrained
- 1 (16-oz.) can purple plums, drained, pitted and quartered
- ½ cup coarsely chopped nuts
- ½ cup dark or golden raisins
- ½ cup firmly packed brown sugar
- 2 tablespoons cornstarch
- ¼ teaspoon cinnamon
- ¼ teaspoon nutmeg

BISCUIT PASTRY
- 2 cups all purpose flour
- 1 tablespoon sugar
- 3 teaspoons baking powder
- 1 teaspoon salt
- ⅓ cup shortening
- 1 cup dairy sour cream
  Milk
  Sugar

Heat oven to 400°F. In 2½-quart shallow oval or round baking dish or casserole, combine all filling ingredients.

In medium bowl, combine flour, sugar, baking powder and salt. Using pastry blender or fork, cut in shortening until mixture resembles coarse crumbs. Stir in sour cream until blended. On floured surface, toss dough lightly to coat with flour. Knead 8 to 10 times. Roll lightly into oval slightly smaller than casserole, about ½ inch thick. Trim edges. Flute edge, if desired. Using biscuit cutter, cut 1 or 2-inch circle in center of pastry or cut a decorative design using small cookie cutters. Top fruit mixture with pastry. (Edge of pastry should not touch sides of casserole.) Brush pastry lightly with milk; sprinkle with sugar.

Bake at 400°F. for 35 to 45 minutes or until pastry is dark golden brown. Cool at least 20 to 30 minutes before serving. If desired, serve with cream or ice cream.
Yield: 8 servings.

HIGH ALTITUDE:
Above 3500 Feet: Bake at 400°F. for 30 to 40 minutes.

NUTRITION PER SERVING:
Calories 490; Protein 7g; Carbohydrate 72g; Fat 20g; Sodium 410mg.

PEAR PANDOWDY

The biscuit topping will bake best if it is placed over a hot filling.

FILLING
- 4 cups sliced peeled pears (about 4 pears)
- ¼ cup firmly packed brown sugar
- ¼ teaspoon cinnamon
- ¼ teaspoon nutmeg
- 3 tablespoons margarine or butter
- 1 tablespoon lemon juice

TOPPING
- 1 cup all purpose flour
- ¼ cup sugar
- 1 teaspoon baking powder
- ¼ teaspoon salt
- ½ cup margarine or butter
- ¼ cup water
- 1 teaspoon sugar
- 2 cups whipped cream or ice cream, if desired

Heat oven to 375°F. Grease 8-inch square (1½-quart) baking dish or 2-quart casserole. In medium saucepan, combine all filling ingredients. Cook over medium heat until mixture is hot, stirring occasionally.

In small bowl, combine flour, ¼ cup sugar, baking powder and salt; mix well. Using pastry blender or fork, cut in ½ cup margarine until mixture forms coarse crumbs. Add water, stirring just until dry ingredients are moistened. Pour hot filling into greased baking dish. Drop topping by rounded tablespoonfuls onto hot filling. Sprinkle with 1 teaspoon sugar. Bake at 375°F. for 30 to 40 minutes or until golden brown. Serve warm with whipped cream.
Yield: 9 servings.

HIGH ALTITUDE:
Above 3500 Feet: No change.

NUTRITION PER SERVING:
Calories 360; Protein 2g; Carbohydrate 35g; Fat 24g; Sodium 270mg.

APPLE BROWN BETTY

Apple Brown Betty is the most traditional of betties, dating back to colonial America. A betty is a baked pudding made of layers of sugared, spiced fruit and buttered bread crumbs.

- 5 cups (5 medium) sliced peeled apples
- ½ cup firmly packed brown sugar
- 1 teaspoon grated lemon peel
- ¼ teaspoon nutmeg
- 1 tablespoon lemon juice
- 1 cup dry bread crumbs
- ½ cup margarine or butter, melted
  Whipping cream

Heat oven to 375°F. Grease 8-inch square (1½-quart) baking dish. In large bowl, combine apples, brown sugar, lemon peel, nutmeg and lemon juice; mix well. In medium bowl, combine bread crumbs and margarine; sprinkle ½ cup bread crumb mixture in greased baking dish. Spoon apple mixture over crumb mixture; top with remaining bread crumb mixture.

Cover; bake at 375°F. for 45 to 50 minutes or until apples are almost tender. Uncover; bake an additional 15 to 20 minutes or until top is crisp and golden brown. Serve warm with cream.
Yield: 8 (½-cup) servings.

NUTRITION PER SERVING:
Calories 250; Protein 2g; Carbohydrate 33g; Fat 12g; Sodium 230mg.

COOK'S NOTE

PANDOWDY

Pandowdies were first made in the 1600s. Similar to a cobbler, a pandowdy is a fruit mixture covered with a layer of soft biscuit dough. It was customary for the server to "dowdy the pan," or cut into the dessert with a spoon and stir the top and bottom together a bit before serving.

STRAWBERRY SHORTCAKE

Enjoy this classic dessert of summer — tender shortcake, warm from the oven, piled high with fresh strawberries and whipped cream.

SHORTCAKE
- 2 cups all purpose flour
- ½ cup sugar
- 3 teaspoons baking powder
- ½ teaspoon salt
- ½ cup margarine or butter
- ¾ cup milk
- 2 eggs, slightly beaten
- 4 cups sliced strawberries
- ½ cup sugar

TOPPING
- 1 cup whipping cream
- 2 tablespoons powdered sugar
- ½ teaspoon vanilla

Heat oven to 375°F. Grease and flour 8 or 9-inch round cake pan. In large bowl, combine flour, sugar, powder and salt. Using pastry blender or fork, cut in margarine until mixture resembles coarse crumbs. Add milk and eggs, stirring just until dry ingredients are moistened. Spoon into greased and floured pan.

Bake at 375°F. for 25 to 30 minutes or until toothpick inserted in center comes out clean. Cool 10 minutes; invert onto serving platter. Split layer in half, if desired.

Meanwhile, in medium bowl combine strawberries and sugar; mix well. Refrigerate 30 minutes or until serving time.

Just before serving, prepare topping. In small bowl, beat whipping cream until soft peaks form. Add powdered sugar and vanilla; beat until stiff peaks form. Serve with shortcake and sweetened strawberries. Store in refrigerator.

Yield: 8 servings.

HIGH ALTITUDE:
Above 3500 Feet: Increase flour to 2 cups plus 2 tablespoons; decrease baking powder to 2½ teaspoons. Bake at 375°F. for 30 to 35 minutes.

NUTRITION PER SERVING:
Calories 490; Protein 7g; Carbohydrate 62g; Fat 25g; Sodium 420mg.

STRAWBERRY SHORTCAKE MAKE-OVER

We've cut 200 calories and 18 grams of fat!

SHORTCAKE
- 1⅔ cups all purpose flour
- ⅓ cup sugar
- 3 teaspoons baking powder
- ½ teaspoon salt
- ½ cup evaporated skim milk
- ¼ cup margarine, melted
- 2 teaspoons vanilla
- 1 egg, slightly beaten, or ¼ cup frozen cholesterol-free egg product, thawed
- 4 cups sliced strawberries
- ¼ cup sugar

TOPPING
- ⅔ cup evaporated skim milk
- 3 tablespoons powdered sugar
- 1 teaspoon vanilla

Heat oven to 350°F. Grease and flour 8 or 9-inch round cake pan. In large bowl, combine flour, sugar, baking powder and salt. Add ½ cup evaporated skim milk, margarine, 2 teaspoons vanilla and egg, stirring just until dry ingredients are moistened. Spoon into greased and floured pan.

Bake at 350°F. for 17 to 24 minutes or until toothpick inserted in center comes out clean. Cool 10 minutes; invert onto serving platter. Split layer in half, if desired.

Meanwhile, in medium bowl combine strawberries and sugar; mix well. Refrigerate 30 minutes or until serving time.

To prepare topping, place small bowl and beaters in refrigerator to chill. Pour ⅔ cup evaporated skim milk into freezer container. Freeze until slushy, about 50 minutes.

Just before serving, spoon into small chilled bowl. Beat with chilled beaters until fluffy. Add powdered sugar and 1 teaspoon vanilla; beat until soft peaks form, scraping bowl occasionally. Serve immediately with shortcake and sweetened strawberries.* Store in refrigerator.

Yield: 8 servings.

Strawberry Shortcake Make-Over

TIP:
* Topping can be held in freezer for up to 20 minutes or in refrigerator for 10 minutes.

HIGH ALTITUDE:
Above 3500 Feet: Increase flour to 1¾ cups; decrease baking powder to 2 teaspoons. Bake at 375°F. for 18 to 25 minutes.

NUTRITION PER SERVING:
Calories 290; Protein 7g; Carbohydrate 50g; Fat 7g; Sodium 360mg.

COOK'S NOTE

LEFTOVER WHIPPED CREAM
Drop dollops of any leftover whipped cream onto a sheet of foil and freeze them uncovered until firm. Then, transfer them to an airtight freezer container and freeze for later use to top desserts. The dollops will thaw on the servings in a matter of minutes.

Chocolate Strawberry Shortcake

Old-fashioned strawberry shortcake has been updated to become a chocolate lover's delight.

SHORTCAKE
- 2 cups all purpose flour
- ½ cup sugar
- ⅓ cup unsweetened cocoa
- 3 teaspoons baking powder
- ¼ teaspoon salt
- ½ cup margarine or butter
- 1 cup milk
- 2 tablespoons sugar

FILLING
- 4 to 5 cups strawberries
- ¼ cup sugar
- 1 cup whipping cream, whipped, sweetened p. 23
- Fudge sauce, if desired

Heat oven to 400°F. Grease two 9 or 8-inch round cake pans. In large bowl, combine flour, ½ cup sugar, cocoa, baking powder and salt. Using pastry blender or fork, cut in margarine until mixture resembles coarse crumbs. Stir in milk just until moistened. Spread in greased pans. Sprinkle 2 tablespoons sugar over dough.

Bake at 400°F. for 15 to 20 minutes or until cake begins to pull away from sides of pans. Cool 15 minutes; remove from pans. Cool completely.

Reserve 5 whole strawberries for garnish. Halve remaining strawberries lengthwise. In large bowl, combine halved strawberries and ¼ cup sugar.

Place 1 shortcake, bottom side up, on serving plate. Top with half of strawberries and half of whipped cream. Place remaining shortcake on top, right side up. Top with remaining strawberries and whipped cream. Garnish with remaining whole strawberries. Drizzle with fudge sauce. Store in refrigerator.
Yield: 12 servings.

HIGH ALTITUDE:
Above 3500 Feet: No change.

NUTRITION PER SERVING:
Calories 370; Protein 5g; Carbohydrate 49g; Fat 19g; Sodium 250mg.

Apricot and Cream Shortcake

Shortcakes are usually as seasonal as the fruits that dress them.

- 1 (18.5-oz.) pkg. pudding-included yellow cake mix
- 1 (3-oz.) pkg. apricot flavor gelatin
- ⅓ cup water
- 1 (8-oz.) container vanilla or apricot yogurt
- 3 eggs
- 1 cup water
- 1 (4-oz.) container (1¾ cups) frozen whipped topping, thawed
- Apricot slices

Heat oven to 350°F. Grease 13x9-inch pan. In large bowl, combine cake mix, 2 tablespoons of the gelatin, ⅓ cup water, yogurt and eggs at low speed until moistened. Beat 2 minutes at high speed. Pour into greased pan.

Bake at 350°F. for 30 to 40 minutes or until toothpick inserted in center comes out clean. Cool cake in pan on cooling rack 15 minutes. Meanwhile, heat 1 cup water in small saucepan. Add remaining gelatin; stir to dissolve. Using long-tined fork, prick cake at ½-inch intervals. Pour gelatin mixture evenly over cake; refrigerate. Serve with whipped topping and apricot slices. Store in refrigerator.
Yield: 12 servings.

HIGH ALTITUDE:
Above 3500 Feet: Add 2 tablespoons flour to dry cake mix; increase water in cake to ½ cup. Bake at 375°F. for 25 to 30 minutes.

NUTRITION PER SERVING:
Calories 280; Protein 5g; Carbohydrate 47g; Fat 9g; Sodium 320mg.

VARIATION:

PEACHES AND CREAM SHORTCAKE: Substitute peach flavor gelatin, peach yogurt and peach slices for apricot.

PLANTATION PEACH SHORTCAKE

~

This version of shortcake was a Pillsbury BAKE-OFF® Contest finalist in 1952. The biscuit-like shortcake has brown sugar and nuts baked right in the layers. It's topped off with luscious peaches and whipped cream.

1¾ cups all purpose flour
¼ cup firmly packed brown sugar
3 teaspoons baking powder
½ teaspoon salt
½ cup margarine or butter
½ cup chopped pecans
⅔ cup half-and-half or milk
1 egg, slightly beaten
3 medium peaches, peeled, sliced
1 cup whipping cream, whipped, sweetened p. 23

Heat oven to 450°F. Generously grease two 8-inch round cake pans.* In large bowl, combine flour, brown sugar, baking powder and salt. Using pastry blender or fork, cut in margarine until mixture resembles coarse crumbs. Add pecans, half-and-half and egg; stir just until soft dough forms. Spread dough evenly in greased pans.

Bake at 450°F. for 10 to 12 minutes or until light golden brown. Remove from pans. Cool. To serve, spoon peaches and whipped cream between layers and on top. Store in refrigerator.
Yield: 8 servings.

TIP:
* For individual shortcakes, turn out dough onto well floured surface; knead gently 5 or 6 times. Roll dough to ½-inch thickness. Cut with floured 3-inch cutter. Place on ungreased cookie sheet. Bake at 450°F. for 8 to 10 minutes. To serve, split short-cakes; spoon peaches and whipped cream between layers and on top.

HIGH ALTITUDE:
Above 3500 Feet: No change.

NUTRITION PER SERVING:
Calories 470; Protein 6g; Carbohydrate 41g; Fat 31g; Sodium 410mg.

NECTARINE-BERRY SHORTCAKE

~

Refrigerated biscuits are baked in a circle in this easy shortcake. Try other fresh fruits, too.

¼ cup sugar
1 teaspoon cinnamon
1 (10-oz.) can refrigerated flaky biscuits
2 tablespoons margarine or butter, melted
3 to 4 nectarines or peaches, sliced
1 cup blueberries
½ cup sugar
1 (8-oz.) container (3½ cups) frozen whipped topping, thawed

Heat oven to 375°F. Lightly grease large cookie sheet. In small bowl, combine ¼ cup sugar and cinnamon. Separate dough into 10 biscuits; separate each biscuit into 2 layers. Dip 1 side of each biscuit piece in margarine, then in sugar-cinnamon mixture. On greased cookie sheet, arrange 9 biscuit pieces, sugared side up, in a 6-inch diameter ring, overlapping edges. Place 1 biscuit piece in center of ring. Repeat with remaining biscuit pieces to form second circle.

Bake at 375°F. for 11 to 14 minutes or until biscuits are golden brown. Cool 1 minute; remove from cookie sheet.

While biscuits are baking, combine nectarines, blueberries and ½ cup sugar. To assemble short-cake, place 1 biscuit circle on serving plate; spoon half of nectarine-blueberry mixture over biscuit layer. Top with half of the whipped topping. Repeat layers with remaining biscuit circle, fruit and whipped topping. Store in refrigerator.
Yield: 8 to 10 servings.

NUTRITION PER SERVING:
Calories 270; Protein 2g; Carbohydrate 41g; Fat 12g; Sodium 330mg.

DESSERT GARNISHES

CHOCOLATE FILIGREES

Chocolate Filigree Hearts: Trace heart pattern on white paper. Cut twelve 3x3-inch squares of waxed paper. In small saucepan over low heat, melt ¼ cup semi-sweet chocolate chips or 2 oz. semi-sweet chocolate cut into small pieces with 1½ teaspoons shortening, stirring until  melted. Pour melted chocolate into a decorating bag fitted with a small writing tip or into a small plastic freezer bag with small tip cut from 1 corner. Place a waxed paper square over the heart pattern. Pipe chocolate over the heart design, outlining heart. Carefully slip out pattern piece. Repeat, making 12 hearts. Refrigerate 5 to 10 minutes or until set.

Carefully remove from waxed paper. (For Two-Tone Chocolate Filigree Hearts continue as directed below.) Arrange on dessert as desired.

Two-Tone Chocolate Filigree Hearts: To make Two-tone Chocolate Filigree Hearts, prepare the Chocolate Filigree Hearts as  directed above. Melt vanilla-flavored candy coating or flavored chips such as butterscotch or peanut butter. Pour contrasting color/flavor of melted chips into another decorating bag. Pipe desired filigree design inside each Chocolate Filigree Heart. Refrigerate 5 to 10 minutes or until set. Carefully remove from waxed paper and arrange on dessert.

Filigree Shamrocks: Trace shamrock pattern on white paper. Melt 1 oz. white baking bar or almond bark. Stir in a small amount of  green paste food color; cool slightly. Pour mixture into a decorating bag fitted with a small writing tip, or into a small plastic freezer bag with small tip cut from 1 corner. Cut twelve 3x3-inch squares of waxed paper. Place a square over the shamrock pattern. Pipe mixture over the shamrock outlining the shamrock. Carefully slip out pattern piece. Repeat, making 12 shamrocks. Refrigerate 5 to 10 minutes or until set. Carefully remove from waxed paper. Arrange on dessert as desired.

CHOCOLATE CURLS

Small Chocolate Curls: Place 1 to 2 oz. of semi-sweet chocolate on a piece of foil. Let stand in warm place (80 to 85°F.) for 5 to 10 minutes or until slightly softened. With a vegetable peeler and using long strokes, shave chocolate from the bottom of the square. Transfer curls to dessert using a toothpick. Milk chocolate curls can be made using a thick milk chocolate bar and this method.

Large Chocolate Curls: Melt 4 oz. semi-sweet chocolate. With spatula, spread melted chocolate in thin layer on 2 inverted cookie sheets. Refrigerate until just firm but not brittle, about 10 minutes. Using metal spatula or pancake turner, scrape chocolate from pan, making curls. The width of the spatula will determine the width of the curls. Transfer curls to dessert using a toothpick.

CHOCOLATE CUTOUTS

Melt semi-sweet or sweet baking chocolate. Pour onto waxed paper-lined cookie sheet. Spread evenly to ⅛ to ¼ inch thickness. Refrigerate until slightly hardened, about 10 minutes. Press canape or small cookie cutters firmly into chocolate. Lift gently from waxed paper with spatula. Scraps of chocolate can be remelted or chopped for an easy dessert topping.

CHOCOLATE LEAVES

Melt unsweetened, semi-sweet or sweet baking chocolate, or vanilla-flavored candy coating. Brush melted chocolate evenly on underside of washed and dried nontoxic leaves (ivy, mint, lemon or rose leaves). Wipe off any chocolate that may have dripped to top side of leaf. Refrigerate leaves about 10 minutes or until chocolate is set. Apply second layer of chocolate over first layer. Refrigerate until chocolate is set. Carefully peel leaf away from chocolate. Store in refrigerator or freezer until ready to use.

CHOCOLATE-DIPPED FRUIT

Choose perfect fruits; wash and pat dry. Dip ½ to ⅔ of each fruit in melted white baking bar or dark chocolate. (One-fourth cup semi-sweet chocolate chips melted with 1 teaspoon oil will coat enough fruit to garnish most desserts.) Place on waxed paper-lined trays; refrigerate until set. Store in refrigerator.

GRATED CHOCOLATE

Let bar of chocolate (any type) stand in warm place (80 to 85°F.) until slightly softened, about 10 minutes. Using hand grater, rub bar of chocolate back and forth across grater. Clean surface frequently to prevent clogging. Sprinkle grated chocolate on dessert.

CITRUS STRIPS (ZEST)

With a lemon zester, remove strips of peel from an orange, lemon or lime. Sprinkle the strips (or zest) over the dessert. If a lemon zester is not available, remove long strips of peel with a vegetable peeler, making sure to remove only the colored part. Cut these pieces into thin julienne strips.

CITRUS TWISTS

With a sharp knife, cut an orange, lemon or lime into ⅛-inch-thick slices. On each slice, make 1 cut from the outside edge to the center. Twist the ends in opposite directions to form a twist. Or, use half of a slice and twist.

STRAWBERRY FANS

To make strawberry fans, select firm berries with stems or caps and symmetrical tips. Starting at the tip and cutting almost to the stem, cut each berry into thin slices. Gently spread the slices to form open fans.

PEANUT CHOCOLATE PARFAIT DESSERT

This peanut butter and chocolate lovers' dessert made a 1986 Pillsbury BAKE-OFF® Contest finalist $15,000 richer.

CRUST
- 1 (18.25-oz.) pkg. pudding-included devil's food cake mix
- ½ cup margarine or butter, melted
- ¼ cup milk
- 1 egg
- ¾ cup peanuts

FILLING
- ¾ cup peanut butter
- 1½ cups powdered sugar
- 1 (8-oz.) pkg. cream cheese, softened
- 2½ cups milk
- 1 (8-oz.) container (3½ cups) frozen whipped topping, thawed
- 1 (5.25-oz.) pkg. instant vanilla pudding and pie filling mix

TOPPING
- ½ cup peanuts
- 1 (1.45-oz.) bar milk chocolate, chilled, grated

Heat oven to 350°F. Grease and flour bottom only of 13x9-inch pan. In large bowl, combine all crust ingredients at medium speed until well blended. Spread evenly in greased and floured pan. Bake at 350°F. for 20 to 25 minutes. DO NOT OVERBAKE. Cool.

In small bowl, combine peanut butter and powdered sugar at low speed until crumbly; set aside. In large bowl, beat cream cheese until smooth. Add milk, whipped topping and pudding mix; beat at low speed 2 minutes until well blended.

Pour half of cream cheese mixture over cooled, baked crust. Sprinkle with half of peanut butter mixture. Repeat with remaining cream cheese and peanut butter mixtures. Sprinkle with ½ cup peanuts; gently press into filling. Sprinkle with grated chocolate. Cover; refrigerate or freeze until serving time. Store in refrigerator or freezer.
Yield: 16 servings.

HIGH ALTITUDE:
Above 3500 Feet: No change.

NUTRITION PER SERVING:
Calories 530; Protein 10g; Carbohydrate 55g; Fat 31g; Sodium 650mg.

RUBY RAZZ CRUNCH

Keep frozen rhubarb and raspberries on hand to make this delectable dessert. It's garnished with a frozen whipped cream topping.

FILLING
- 1 (10-oz.) pkg. frozen raspberries with syrup, thawed, drained, reserving liquid
- 1 (16-oz.) pkg. frozen rhubarb, thawed, drained, reserving liquid
- ½ cup sugar
- 3 tablespoons cornstarch

TOPPING*
- ½ cup whipping cream, whipped
- 2 tablespoons sugar
- 1 to 3 drops red food color, if desired

CRUST
- 1¼ cups all purpose flour
- 1 cup firmly packed brown sugar
- 1 cup quick-cooking rolled oats
- 1 teaspoon cinnamon
- ½ cup margarine or butter, melted

Heat oven to 325°F. In measuring cup, combine reserved raspberry and rhubarb liquids. If necessary, add water to make 1 cup. In medium saucepan, combine ½ cup sugar and cornstarch; stir in reserved liquids. Cook over medium heat until thickened, stirring constantly; remove from heat. Reserve 2 tablespoons raspberries for topping. Stir remaining raspberries and rhubarb into cornstarch mixture. Set aside.

Line cookie sheet with waxed paper. In small bowl, combine whipped cream, 2 tablespoons sugar, reserved raspberries and food color. Drop in 9 mounds onto waxed paper-lined cookie sheet; freeze until firm.

In large bowl, combine flour, brown sugar, rolled oats and cinnamon. Stir in margarine until crumbly. Press ⅔ of crust mixture in bottom of ungreased 9-inch square pan. Spoon filling mixture over crust, spreading evenly. Sprinkle with remaining crust mixture.

Bake at 325°F. for 45 to 55 minutes or until crust is golden brown and filling bubbles around edges. Cool slightly. To serve, cut into squares; top each serving with mound of frozen topping.
Yield: 9 servings.

MICROWAVE DIRECTIONS:
In 4-cup microwave-safe measuring cup, combine ½ cup sugar and cornstarch; mix well. Measure reserved liquids as directed above; stir into cornstarch mixture. Microwave on HIGH for 4 to 4½ minutes or until thick and bubbly, stirring once halfway through cooking. Stir in remaining raspberries and rhubarb; set aside.

Prepare topping as directed above. Place margarine in medium microwave-safe bowl. Microwave on HIGH for 45 to 60 seconds or until melted. Add remaining crust ingredients; mix until crumbly. Press ⅔ of crust mixture in bottom of 8-inch square (1½-quart) microwave-safe dish. Spoon filling mixture over crust, spreading evenly. Sprinkle with remaining crust mixture.

Microwave on MEDIUM for 10 minutes, turning dish ¼ turn halfway through cooking. Turn ¼ turn; microwave on HIGH for 4 to 5 minutes or until filling bubbles around edges. Cool at least 20 minutes before serving. To serve, cut into squares; top each serving with mound of frozen topping. Garnish as desired.

TIP:
* If desired, topping can be prepared and served without freezing.

NUTRITION PER SERVING:
Calories 440; Protein 4g; Carbohydrate 70g; Fat 16g; Sodium 220mg.

RED CHERRY DREAM SQUARES

This favorite dessert sandwiches cherry pie filling between crunchy shortbread-like layers. No potluck would be complete without it.

- 1 (18.5-oz.) pkg. pudding-included white cake mix
- 1¼ cups rolled oats
- ½ cup margarine or butter, softened
- 1 egg
- 1 (21-oz.) can cherry fruit pie filling
- ½ cup chopped nuts
- ¼ cup firmly packed brown sugar

Heat oven to 350°F. Grease 13x9-inch pan. In large bowl, combine cake mix, 1 cup of the rolled oats and 6 tablespoons of the margarine at low speed until crumbly. Reserve 1 cup crumbs for topping. To remaining crumbs, add 1 egg; mix until well blended. Press in bottom of greased pan. Spoon cherry filling over crust; spread to cover.

To reserved crumbs in large bowl, add remaining
¼ cup rolled oats, 2 tablespoons margarine,
nuts and brown sugar; mix well. Sprinkle over
cherry filling.

Bake at 350°F. for 35 to 45 minutes or until golden
brown. Cool completely. Serve with whipped
cream, if desired.
Yield: 12 servings.

HIGH ALTITUDE:
Above 3500 Feet: No change.

NUTRITION PER SERVING:
Calories 430; Protein 5g; Carbohydrate 68g; Fat 16g;
Sodium 390mg.

BERRY-BLUE PIE SQUARES

*This is a great way to serve blueberry pie to a
crowd!*

CRUST
2½ **cups all purpose flour**
 1 **tablespoon sugar**
 1 **teaspoon salt**
 1 **teaspoon grated lemon peel**
 1 **cup shortening**
 2 **egg yolks plus milk to equal ⅔ cup**

FILLING
¾ **cup finely crushed cornflakes cereal**
 1 **tablespoon lemon juice**
 6 **cups fresh or frozen blueberries (do not
      thaw)**
 1 **cup sugar**
 1 **tablespoon all purpose flour**
 1 **teaspoon cinnamon**
 3 **egg whites**

GLAZE
 1 **cup powdered sugar**
¼ **teaspoon vanilla or almond extract, if desired**
 1 **to 2 tablespoons water**

Heat oven to 375°F. In medium bowl, combine
2½ cups flour, 1 tablespoon sugar, salt and lemon
peel. Using pastry blender or fork, cut in shortening
until mixture resembles coarse crumbs. Add egg
yolk mixture; mix lightly with fork until flour mixture is moistened and soft dough forms.

Divide dough in half; shape each into ball. Flatten
balls; smooth edges. On lightly floured surface or
between sheets of waxed paper, roll 1 ball from
center to edges into 16x12-inch rectangle. Fold
dough in half; fit evenly in ungreased 15x10x1-inch
baking pan, unfolding and pressing to edges of pan.

Sprinkle cornflakes evenly over pastry. Drizzle
lemon juice over blueberries; spoon over cornflakes. In small bowl, combine 1 cup sugar,
1 tablespoon flour and cinnamon; sprinkle over
blueberries. Roll out remaining dough to
15x10-inch rectangle. Place over berries; seal edges.
Beat egg whites until foamy; brush over pastry.

Bake at 375°F. for 55 to 65 minutes or until deep
golden brown. In small bowl, combine all glaze
ingredients, adding enough water for desired drizzling consistency. Drizzle over warm crust. Serve
warm topped with ice cream, if desired.
Yield: 18 to 24 servings.

NUTRITION PER SERVING:
Calories 220; Protein 3g; Carbohydrate 32g; Fat 9g;
Sodium 125mg.

TROPICAL MACAROON DESSERT

*Experiment with the exotic — add other tropical
beauties such as mango and star fruit for a
colorful fruit dessert.*

 4 **egg whites**
 1 **teaspoon vanilla**
½ **teaspoon salt**
¾ **cup sugar**
 1 **cup coconut**
½ **cup graham cracker crumbs (about
      8 squares)**
½ **cup chopped macadamia nuts**
 1 **cup pineapple chunks**
½ **cup halved strawberries**
½ **papaya, peeled, sliced**
 2 **kiwifruit, peeled, sliced**

Heat oven to 350°F. Grease 9 or 10-inch fluted
quiche dish or 9-inch pie pan. In large bowl, beat
egg whites, vanilla and salt until foamy. Gradually
add sugar, beating until stiff peaks form. Fold in
coconut, cracker crumbs and nuts. Spread in
greased pan. Bake at 350°F. for 30 to 35 minutes or
until light golden brown. Cool completely.

Just before serving, combine fruit. Top cooled
dessert with fruit. Cut into wedges. Garnish with
whipped cream or topping, if desired.
Yield: 8 servings.

NUTRITION PER SERVING:
Calories 260; Protein 4g; Carbohydrate 38g; Fat 11g;
Sodium 200mg.

PUMPKIN PIE SQUARES

~

Butterscotch pudding flavors the crust in these hard-to-resist dessert squares.

CRUST
- ¾ cup all purpose flour
- ¾ cup rolled oats
- ½ to 1 cup chopped nuts
- ½ cup margarine or butter, softened
- 1 (3.63-oz.) pkg. butterscotch pudding and pie filling mix (not instant)

FILLING
- 1 cup coconut, if desired
- 1½ teaspoons pumpkin pie spice
- 1 (16-oz.) can (2 cups) pumpkin
- 1 (12-oz.) can sweetened condensed milk (not evaporated)
- 2 eggs

Heat oven to 350°F. In large bowl, combine all crust ingredients; mix well. Press in bottom of ungreased 13x9-inch pan. In same bowl, combine filling ingredients; blend well. Pour over crust.

Bake at 350°F. for 35 to 45 minutes or until knife inserted in center comes out clean. Cool. Cut into squares. Serve topped with whipped cream or ice cream, if desired. Store in refrigerator.

Yield: 12 to 15 squares.

NUTRITION PER SERVING:
Calories 300; Protein 6g; Carbohydrate 34g; Fat 16g; Sodium 130mg.

LEMON PIE SQUARES

~

A soft meringue covers this lemon lovers' delight.

CRUST
- 1 (18.25-oz.) pkg. pudding-included lemon cake mix
- ¼ cup margarine or butter, softened
- 3 egg yolks
- 1 cup coconut

MERINGUE
- 3 egg whites
- ½ cup sugar

FILLING
- 1 (22-oz.) can lemon pie filling

Heat oven to 350°F. In large bowl, combine all crust ingredients at low speed until crumbly. Press in bottom of ungreased 13x9-inch pan. Bake at 350°F. for 10 minutes.

Meanwhile, in small bowl beat egg whites at medium speed until soft peaks form. Gradually add sugar 1 tablespoon at a time, beating at high speed until stiff glossy peaks form and sugar is dissolved. Spread lemon filling over partially baked crust; spread meringue over lemon filling.

Bake an additional 15 to 25 minutes or until meringue is light golden brown. Cool completely; cut into squares. Garnish with **Citrus Twists** p. 211 or as desired.

Yield: 12 servings.

HIGH ALTITUDE:
Above 3500 Feet: No change.

NUTRITION PER SERVING:
Calories 370; Protein 3g; Carbohydrate 66g; Fat 11g; Sodium 390mg.

Lemon Pie Squares

RASPBERRY PRETZEL DELIGHT

This is a perfect dessert to make for a party.

CRUST
1½ **cups crushed pretzels**
¼ **cup sugar**
½ **cup margarine or butter, melted**

FILLING
1 **(12-oz.) can sweetened condensed milk (not evaporated)**
½ **cup water**
1 **(3.4-oz.) pkg. instant vanilla pudding and pie filling mix**
1 **(4-oz.) container (1¾ cups) frozen whipped topping, thawed**

TOPPING
1 **(21-oz.) can raspberry fruit pie filling**

Heat oven to 350°F. In large bowl, combine all crust ingredients; mix well. Press in bottom of ungreased 13x9-inch pan. Bake at 350°F. for 8 minutes; cool.

In same large bowl, combine condensed milk and water; blend well. Add pudding mix; beat 2 minutes. Refrigerate 5 minutes. Fold in whipped topping. Spread on cooled, baked crust. Refrigerate until filling is firm, about 1 hour.

Spoon topping over filling. Cover; refrigerate until serving time. Garnish with frozen whipped topping, fresh raspberries and mint leaves, if desired. Store in refrigerator.
Yield: 16 servings.

NUTRITION PER SERVING:
Calories 250; Protein 3g; Carbohydrate 38g; Fat 10g; Sodium 290mg.

VARIATIONS:

BLUEBERRY PRETZEL DELIGHT: Substitute 21-oz. can blueberry fruit pie filling for raspberry fruit pie filling.

CHERRY PRETZEL DELIGHT: Substitute 21-oz. can cherry fruit pie filling for raspberry fruit pie filling.

Raspberry Pretzel Delight

REFRIGERATOR PISTACHIO DESSERT

This attractive dessert can be made a day ahead of time.

CRUST
1¼ **cups all purpose flour**
½ **cup margarine or butter, softened**
½ **cup finely chopped pistachios**

FILLING
1 **(8-oz.) pkg. cream cheese, softened**
1 **cup powdered sugar**
1 **(8-oz.) container (3½ cups) frozen whipped topping, thawed**
2 **(3.75-oz.) pkg. instant pistachio pudding and pie filling mix**
3 **cups milk**

Heat oven to 350°F. Grease 13x9-inch pan. In small bowl, combine flour and margarine at low speed until crumbly. Stir in pistachios; press in bottom of greased pan. Bake at 350°F. for 18 to 22 minutes or until light golden brown; cool.

In small bowl, combine cream cheese and powdered sugar until smooth and creamy. Fold in half of the whipped topping; spread over cooled, baked crust. In large bowl, beat pudding mix and milk at medium speed until thickened, about 5 minutes. Pour mixture carefully over cheese layer. Spread with remaining whipped topping. Refrigerate several hours or overnight.
Yield: 12 servings.

TIP:
Recipe can be halved; use 9-inch square pan.

NUTRITION PER SERVING:
Calories 420; Protein 6g; Carbohydrate 45g; Fat 25g; Sodium 240mg.

STRAWBERRIES AND CREAM SQUARES

A moist and chewy macaroon-like base is topped with a fluffy whipped cream and strawberry mixture.

BASE
- 1 cup walnuts
- 16 saltine crackers
- 3 egg whites
- 1/4 teaspoon cream of tartar
- 1 cup sugar
- 1/2 teaspoon baking powder
- 1/2 teaspoon almond extract

TOPPING
- 1 cup whipping cream
- 2 tablespoons powdered sugar
- 1/2 teaspoon almond extract
- 2 cups sliced strawberries

GARNISH
- Whole strawberries, if desired

Heat oven to 300°F. Grease 8-inch square pan. In food processor bowl with metal blade or blender container, combine walnuts and crackers; process until mixture resembles coarse crumbs. In large bowl, beat egg whites and cream of tartar until foamy. Gradually add sugar, baking powder and 1/2 teaspoon almond extract, beating continuously at high speed until sugar is dissolved and stiff peaks form. Fold in crumb mixture. Spoon into greased pan, spreading evenly. Bake at 300°F. for 30 minutes or until set. Cool completely.

In small bowl, beat whipping cream until soft peaks form. Add powdered sugar and 1/2 teaspoon almond extract; beat until stiff peaks form. Fold in 2 cups strawberries. Spoon over cooled crust. Refrigerate until serving time. Garnish with whole strawberries.

Yield: 9 servings.

HIGH ALTITUDE:
Above 3500 Feet: Increase saltine crackers to 20. Bake as directed above.

NUTRITION PER SERVING:
Calories 330; Protein 5g; Carbohydrate 36g; Fat 19g; Sodium 100mg.

ALMOND FRUIT PIZZA SQUARES

Celebrate summer with this colorful and delicious dessert, made easily with refrigerated dough.

- 2 (8-oz.) cans refrigerated crescent dinner rolls
- 1 tablespoon sugar
- 1 (8-oz.) pkg. cream cheese, softened
- 1 (3½-oz.) tube almond paste
- 1/2 teaspoon almond extract
- 2 tablespoons sugar
- 2 cups strawberries, halved
- 1 cup raspberries
- 1 cup seedless green grapes, halved
- 1 (11-oz.) can mandarin orange segments, drained
- 2 kiwifruit, peeled, sliced, quartered
- 1/2 cup apricot preserves
- 1/4 cup slivered almonds, toasted, p. 23

Heat oven to 375°F. Separate dough into 4 long rectangles. Place rectangles crosswise in ungreased 15x10x1-inch baking pan; press over bottom and 1 inch up sides to form crust. Firmly press perforations to seal. Sprinkle with 1 tablespoon sugar. Bake at 375°F. for 14 to 19 minutes or until golden brown. Cool completely.

In food processor bowl with metal blade or blender container, combine cream cheese, almond paste, almond extract and 2 tablespoons sugar; process until smooth. Spread evenly over cooled crust; top with strawberries, raspberries, grapes, orange segments and kiwifruit. Heat preserves in small saucepan until melted; brush over fruit. Sprinkle with almonds. Cover; store in refrigerator.

Yield: 15 servings.

TIP:
Other fruits can be substituted. If using fruits such as bananas, apples, pears or peaches, toss with orange or lemon juice to prevent discoloration and serve within 4 hours.

NUTRITION PER SERVING:
Calories 270; Protein 5g; Carbohydrate 33g; Fat 14g; Sodium 300mg.

STREUSEL PECAN PIE SQUARES

Your turn to host the family get-together? Serve up these rich dessert squares. They're an easy version of southern pecan pie.

CRUST
- 3 cups all purpose flour
- ¾ cup firmly packed brown sugar
- 1½ cups margarine or butter, softened

FILLING
- ¾ cup firmly packed brown sugar
- 1½ cups corn syrup or maple-flavored syrup
- 1 cup milk
- ⅓ cup margarine or butter, melted
- 1 teaspoon vanilla
- 4 eggs
- 1½ cups chopped pecans

Heat oven to 400°F. In large bowl, combine all crust ingredients at low speed until crumbly. Reserve 2 cups crumb mixture for filling and topping. Press remaining crumb mixture in bottom and ¾ inch up sides of ungreased 15x10x1-inch baking pan. Bake at 400°F. for 10 minutes.

In large bowl, combine ¼ cup reserved crumb mixture and all filling ingredients except pecans; mix well. Stir in pecans. Pour over partially baked crust. Bake an additional 10 minutes.

Reduce oven temperature to 350°F. Sprinkle remaining 1¾ cups reserved crumb mixture over filling. Bake at 350°F. for 20 to 25 minutes or until filling is set and crumb topping is golden brown. Serve with whipped cream or ice cream, if desired.
Yield: 15 servings.

NUTRITION PER SERVING:
Calories 570; Protein 6g; Carbohydrate 69g; Fat 32g; Sodium 320mg.

STREUSEL RHUBARB DESSERT SQUARES

Here's a wonderful fruit dessert. Serve it warm, topped with whipped cream.

CRUST
- 1 cup all purpose flour
- ⅓ cup powdered sugar
- ⅓ cup margarine or butter

FILLING
- 1¼ cups sugar
- ¼ cup all purpose flour
- ½ teaspoon salt
- 2 eggs, slightly beaten
- 3 cups sliced fresh or frozen rhubarb (do not thaw)

TOPPING
- ¾ cup all purpose flour
- ½ cup sugar
- ¼ teaspoon cinnamon
- ⅓ cup margarine or butter

Heat oven to 350°F. In medium bowl, combine 1 cup flour and powdered sugar. Using pastry blender or fork, cut in ⅓ cup margarine until crumbly. Press in bottom of ungreased 9-inch square pan. Bake at 350°F. for 15 minutes.

In medium bowl, combine all filling ingredients; mix well. Pour over partially baked crust. In medium bowl, combine all topping ingredients except ⅓ cup margarine. Using pastry blender or fork, cut in ⅓ cup margarine until crumbly. Sprinkle over filling. Bake an additional 45 to 55 minutes or until topping is light golden brown and rhubarb is tender.
Yield: 6 to 8 servings.

NUTRITION PER SERVING:
Calories 470; Protein 5g; Carbohydrate 74g; Fat 17g; Sodium 330mg.

CHEESECAKE

Top with fresh fruit or chocolate sauce.

CRUST
- 2 **cups graham cracker crumbs (about 32 squares)**
- ½ **cup margarine or butter, melted**

FILLING
- 3 **eggs**
- 2 **(8-oz.) pkg. cream cheese, softened**
- 1 **cup sugar**
- ¼ **teaspoon salt**
- 2 **teaspoons vanilla**
- 3 **cups dairy sour cream**

Heat oven to 350°F. In medium bowl, combine crust ingredients; press over bottom and 1½ inches up sides of ungreased 10-inch springform pan. In large bowl, beat eggs. Add cream cheese, sugar, salt and vanilla; beat until smooth. Add sour cream; blend well. Pour into crust-lined pan.

Bake at 350°F. for 60 to 70 minutes or until edges are set. Center of cheesecake will be soft. Cool in pan 5 minutes; remove sides of pan. Cool completely. Store in refrigerator.

Yield: 16 servings.

NUTRITION PER SERVING:
Calories 360; Protein 6g; Carbohydrate 23g; Fat 27g; Sodium 290mg.

COOK'S NOTE

CREAM CHEESE

Cream cheese is a soft, white spreadable cheese made from cow's milk. Regular cream cheese is available in 3 and 8-ounce packages. Other forms of cream cheese include soft and whipped varieties and light cream cheese. Always use regular cream cheese in recipes (do not substitute tub varieties) unless another form is specified.

COOKIES 'N CREAM CHEESECAKE

Cookies and cream is one of the newest cheesecake flavors. Our version features chunks of chocolate sandwich cookies.

CRUST
- 1½ **cups crushed creme-filled chocolate sandwich cookies (about 15 cookies)**
- 2 **tablespoons margarine or butter, softened**

FILLING
- 3 **(8-oz.) pkg. cream cheese, softened**
- 1 **cup sugar**
- 3 **eggs**
- 1 **cup whipping cream**
- 2 **tablespoons margarine or butter, melted**
- 2 **teaspoons vanilla**
- 1 **cup coarsely chopped creme-filled chocolate sandwich cookies (about 10 cookies)**

GARNISH
- **Whipped cream**
- **Crushed creme-filled chocolate sandwich cookies**

Heat oven to 325°F. In medium bowl, combine crust ingredients; mix well. Press in bottom and up sides of ungreased 10-inch springform pan. Refrigerate 15 minutes.

In large bowl, beat cream cheese at medium speed until smooth and creamy. Gradually add sugar, beating until smooth. At low speed, add eggs 1 at a time, beating just until blended. Add whipping cream, 2 tablespoons margarine and vanilla; beat until smooth. Stir in 1 cup chopped cookies. Pour into crust-lined pan.

Bake at 325°F. for 50 to 60 minutes or until edges are set. Turn oven off; with door open at least 4 inches, let cake stand in oven for 30 minutes or until center is set. Remove from oven; cool to room temperature on wire rack. Remove sides of pan. Refrigerate overnight. To garnish, top with whipped cream; sprinkle with crushed cookies. Store in refrigerator.

Yield: 16 servings.

NUTRITION PER SERVING:
Calories 410; Protein 6g; Carbohydrate 27g; Fat 31g; Sodium 270mg.

FRUIT JEWEL CHEESECAKE

This creamy cheesecake crowned with glazed fruit makes a spectacular dessert.

CRUST
1½ cups graham cracker crumbs (about 24 squares)
¼ cup margarine or butter, melted

FILLING
3 (8-oz.) pkg. cream cheese, softened
1 cup sugar
4 eggs
1½ cups dairy sour cream
2 teaspoons grated lemon peel

CITRUS GLAZE
1 tablespoon sugar
2 teaspoons cornstarch
½ cup orange juice
¼ cup water
1 tablespoon lemon juice
¼ teaspoon grated lemon peel

TOPPING
1 pint (2 cups) strawberries, sliced
2 cups fresh or canned pineapple chunks, well drained
1 cup blueberries

Heat oven to 350°F. In medium bowl, combine crust ingredients; press in bottom of ungreased 10-inch springform pan. In large bowl, beat cream cheese and 1 cup sugar at medium speed until smooth and creamy. At low speed, add eggs 1 at a time, beating just until blended. Add sour cream and 2 teaspoons lemon peel; blend well. Pour into crust-lined pan. Bake at 350°F. for 50 to 60 minutes or until center is set. Cool. Refrigerate for several hours or overnight.

In small saucepan, combine 1 tablespoon sugar and cornstarch. Gradually add orange juice and water. Bring to a boil over medium heat, stirring constantly. Stir in lemon juice and ¼ teaspoon grated lemon peel. Cool. Just before serving, carefully remove sides of pan. Arrange fruit over cheesecake. Spoon or brush glaze over fruit. Store in refrigerator.
Yield: 16 servings.

NUTRITION PER SERVING:
Calories 360; Protein 6g; Carbohydrate 28g; Fat 25g; Sodium 240mg.

APPLESAUCE CHEESECAKE

Delicate apple flavor laced with a hint of cinnamon is a winning combination.

CRUST
1¼ cups graham cracker crumbs (about 20 squares)
½ cup chopped pecans, toasted, p. 23
¼ cup firmly packed brown sugar
¼ cup margarine or butter, melted

FILLING
3 (8-oz.) pkg. cream cheese, softened
1 cup sugar
2 tablespoons all purpose flour
3 eggs
1 cup applesauce
½ teaspoon cinnamon
⅛ teaspoon nutmeg

Heat oven to 350°F. In medium bowl, combine all crust ingredients; mix well. Press in bottom of ungreased 10-inch springform pan.

In large bowl, beat cream cheese and sugar at medium speed until smooth and creamy. Add flour; blend well. At low speed, add eggs 1 at a time, beating just until blended. Add remaining ingredients; beat until well blended. Pour into crust-lined pan.

Bake at 350°F. for 50 to 60 minutes or until center is set. Cool. Refrigerate several hours or overnight. Just before serving, carefully remove sides of pan. Store in refrigerator.
Yield: 16 servings.

NUTRITION PER SERVING:
Calories 320; Protein 5g; Carbohydrate 27g; Fat 22g; Sodium 220mg.

STEP-BY-STEP FEATURE ∼
How to Make a Decorative Cheesecake

STEP 1. Spoon chocolate batter by teaspoonfuls onto batter in pan, forming 9 drops around outside and 5 drops in center, using all the batter.

STEP 2. Starting in center of 1 outer drop, run knife through centers of outer drops; run knife through inner drops, forming 2 circles of hearts.

STEP 3. Place a shallow pan half full of water on bottom rack of oven when baking the cheesecake to help minimize cracks in the cheesecake.

CHOCOLATE ORANGE CHEESECAKE

Make this cheesecake for your sweetheart.

- 1/3 **cup graham cracker crumbs (about 5 to 6 squares)**
- 4 **(8-oz.) pkg. cream cheese, softened**
- 1 1/3 **cups sugar**
- 4 **eggs**
- 2 **tablespoons orange-flavored liqueur or orange juice**
- 1 **teaspoon grated orange peel**
- 3 **oz. semi-sweet chocolate, melted**

Heat oven to 325°F. Lightly grease bottom and sides of 9-inch springform pan. Sprinkle graham cracker crumbs over bottom and sides of pan. In large bowl, beat cream cheese at medium speed until smooth and creamy. Gradually add sugar, beating until smooth. At low speed, add eggs 1 at a time, beating just until blended. Add liqueur and orange peel; beat 2 minutes at medium speed, scraping sides of bowl occasionally.

In small bowl, reserve 1 1/2 cups of batter. Pour remaining batter into crumb-lined pan. Slowly blend melted chocolate into reserved batter. Drop spoonfuls of chocolate batter onto batter in pan. Using a table knife, swirl chocolate batter through light batter to marble.

Bake at 325°F. for 1 hour or until set. Cool for 10 minutes; remove sides of pan. Refrigerate several hours or overnight. Store in refrigerator.
Yield: 16 servings.

NUTRITION PER SERVING:
Calories 330; Protein 6g; Carbohydrate 24g; Fat 23g; Sodium 200mg.

VARIATION:

HEARTS-TO-YOU CHEESECAKE: To form heart design in top of cheesecake, spoon chocolate batter by teaspoonfuls onto batter in pan, forming a circle of 9 drops around outside and a circle of 5 drops in center; continue to spoon batter onto drops using all of chocolate batter. Starting in center of 1 outer drop, run knife through centers of outer drops; run knife through centers of inner drops, forming 2 separate rings of connected hearts.

Hearts-To-You Cheesecake

Peppermint Marble Cheesecake

PEPPERMINT MARBLE CHEESECAKE

CRUST
2 tablespoons margarine or butter, melted
1 cup crushed creme-filled chocolate sandwich cookies (about 10 cookies)
2 tablespoons sugar

FILLING
2 (8-oz.) pkg. cream cheese, softened
3/4 cup sugar
3 eggs
1/2 cup whipping cream
1 teaspoon vanilla
Dash salt
9 oz. white baking bars, melted, cooled slightly
1/4 teaspoon peppermint extract
2 to 4 drops green food color

GARNISH
Filigree Shamrocks or Chocolate Cutouts p. 210, if desired
1/2 cup whipping cream, whipped, if desired

Heat oven to 325°F. Brush bottom and sides of 9-inch springform pan with melted margarine. In small bowl, combine remaining margarine and crust ingredients; mix well. Press evenly into bottom of greased pan. Bake at 325°F. for 8 minutes. Cool.

In large bowl, beat cream cheese at medium speed until smooth and creamy. Gradually beat in 3/4 cup sugar. At low speed, add eggs 1 at a time, beating just until blended. Add whipping cream, vanilla and salt; beat until smooth. Add white baking bars; beat just until blended. Reserve 1 cup cheesecake batter; pour remaining batter over crust. Add extract and food color to reserved 1 cup batter; blend well. Drop tablespoonfuls of peppermint batter onto batter in pan, forming 5 to 6 spots. Using a table knife, swirl peppermint batter through light batter to marble.

Bake at 325°F. for 40 to 50 minutes or until edges are set and center is almost set. Turn oven off; let cheesecake stand in oven 30 minutes with door open at least 4 inches. Remove from oven. Run sharp knife around sides of pan. Cool to room temperature on wire rack. Cover; refrigerate at least 24 hours before serving.

To serve, remove sides of pan. Garnish with Filigree Shamrocks or Chocolate Cutouts and whipped cream. Store in refrigerator.
Yield: 12 servings.

NUTRITION PER SERVING:
Calories 460; Protein 7g; Carbohydrate 37g; Fat 33g; Sodium 230mg.

MINIATURE CHEESECAKES

These tasty little cheesecakes can be served as a dessert or as part of a cookie assortment.

CHEESECAKES
  2 (3-oz.) pkg. cream cheese, softened
  ¼ cup sugar
  1 egg
  ½ teaspoon almond extract

TOPPING
  ¾ cup dairy sour cream
  3 tablespoons sugar
  ¼ teaspoon almond extract

GARNISH
  ⅓ cup raspberry jam or other red jam or preserves

Heat oven to 350°F. Line 24 miniature muffin cups with paper baking cups. In medium bowl, beat cream cheese and ¼ cup sugar until smooth and creamy. Add egg and ½ teaspoon almond extract; beat until smooth. Fill paper-lined muffin cups ¾ full.

Bake at 350°F. for 15 minutes or until set. DO NOT OVERBAKE. Meanwhile, in small bowl combine all topping ingredients; blend well. Top each cheesecake with 1 heaping teaspoon topping. Bake an additional 5 to 8 minutes or until set. Cool 15 to 20 minutes.*

Spoon about ½ teaspoon jam onto each cheesecake. Refrigerate until serving time. Store in refrigerator.
Yield: 24 miniature cheesecakes.

TIP:
* At this point, cheesecakes can be covered and frozen up to 1 month. Thaw in refrigerator. Garnish just before serving.

NUTRITION PER SERVING:
Calories 70; Protein 1g; Carbohydrate 7g; Fat 4g; Sodium 30mg.

CHERRY CRESCENT CHEESECAKE CUPS

Colorful and delicious cherry-topped cheesecakes are made easily with refrigerated crescent roll dough.

FILLING
  1 (8-oz.) pkg. cream cheese, softened
  1 egg
  1 cup powdered sugar
  ¼ cup chopped almonds
  ½ to 1 teaspoon almond extract

CRUST
  1 (8-oz.) can refrigerated crescent dinner rolls

TOPPING
  1 cup cherry fruit pie filling
  1 to 2 tablespoons amaretto or cherry-flavored brandy, if desired
  1 tablespoon margarine or butter

Heat oven to 350°F. Grease 8 muffin cups. In medium bowl, combine cream cheese and egg until smooth. Add powdered sugar, almonds and extract; mix well.

Separate dough into 4 rectangles; firmly press perforations to seal. Press or roll each rectangle into an 8x4-inch rectangle. Cut each in half crosswise to form 8 squares. Press each square into bottom of greased muffin cup, leaving corners of each square extended over sides of cup. Place about ¼ cup cream cheese mixture into each cup. Bring 4 corners of each square together in center of cup and firmly press points together to seal.

Bake at 350°F. for 18 to 23 minutes or until golden brown. Immediately remove from muffin cups. In small saucepan, combine all topping ingredients; cook over low heat until bubbly and margarine melts. Serve over warm desserts. Store in refrigerator.
Yield: 8 servings.

TIP:
To reheat, wrap loosely in foil; heat at 350°F. for 20 to 25 minutes.

NUTRITION PER SERVING:
Calories 370; Protein 6g; Carbohydrate 41g; Fat 20g; Sodium 340mg.

CRESCENT CHEESECAKE TART
~

There's no need for a special tart pan in this recipe.

- 1 (8-oz.) can refrigerated crescent dinner rolls
- 1 egg white
- 1 teaspoon water
- 1 to 2 cups assorted fresh fruit (kiwifruit slices, raspberries, blueberries)

FILLING
- 2 (3-oz.) pkg. cream cheese, softened
- 2 tablespoons sugar
- 1 egg yolk
- ¼ teaspoon almond extract

Heat oven to 350°F. Separate dough into 2 long rectangles; firmly press perforations to seal. Place 1 rectangle on ungreased cookie sheet. In small bowl, combine egg white and water; brush over rectangle. Cut two 1-inch strips of dough from short side of the remaining rectangle. Cut remaining dough lengthwise into 4 long 1-inch strips. Place 1 long strip evenly on each long edge of rectangle. Place short strips on each short edge. Place remaining strips on top of first long strips. (See diagram.) Brush with remaining egg white. Bake at 350°F. for 15 minutes.

In small bowl, combine all filling ingredients; beat until smooth. Spread over crust. Bake an additional 12 to 15 minutes or until crust is deep golden brown and filling is set. Cool on wire rack. Garnish with fruit. Store in refrigerator.

Yield: 8 servings.

NUTRITION PER SERVING:
Calories 220; Protein 4g; Carbohydrate 19g; Fat 14g; Sodium 300mg.

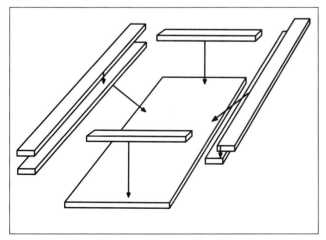

Crescent Cheesecake Tart

BLUEBERRY LEMON CHEESECAKE PIE
~

This all-American pie features red strawberry fans over blueberries and white cream cheese filling.

PASTRY
   Pastry for Two-Crust Pie p. 268
- 2 tablespoons sugar
- 2 tablespoons margarine or butter, melted
- 2 teaspoons lemon peel
   Dash nutmeg

FILLING
- 1 (8-oz.) pkg. cream cheese, softened
- ⅓ cup sugar
- 1 to 2 teaspoons grated lemon peel
- ½ cup whipping cream, whipped

TOPPING
- 1 (21-oz.) can blueberry fruit pie filling
   Strawberry Fans p. 211
   Whipping cream, whipped, sweetened p. 23

Heat oven to 450°F. Prepare pastry for Two-Crust Pie. Roll out one circle of pastry and place in 9-inch pie pan. Bake as directed for Baked Pie Shell.

Roll out remaining pastry; cut stars from pastry using a 2 to 3-inch star-shaped cookie cutter. Transfer stars to cookie sheet. In small bowl, combine 2 tablespoons sugar, margarine, 2 teaspoons grated lemon peel and nutmeg. Brush over stars just to edges. Bake at 450°F. for 6 to 8 minutes or until light golden brown. Transfer stars to wire rack.

In small bowl, beat cream cheese, ⅓ cup sugar and 1 to 2 teaspoons lemon peel until smooth and creamy. Fold in whipped cream. Spoon evenly into cooled pie shell. Spoon blueberry filling evenly over lemon filling. Refrigerate at least 1 hour before serving. Garnish with star cutouts, strawberry fans and whipped cream. Store in refrigerator.

Yield: 8 servings.

NUTRITION PER SERVING:
Calories 600; Protein 4g; Carbohydrate 61g; Fat 38g; Sodium 420mg.

ORANGE CHEESECAKE

This featherweight cheesecake is a refreshing ending for any meal.

CRUST
- 1 cup vanilla wafer crumbs (about 20 wafers)
- 2 tablespoons margarine or butter, melted

FILLING
- 2 envelopes unflavored gelatin
- 1/3 cup sugar
- 3/4 cup orange juice
- 1 (15-oz.) container light ricotta cheese
- 1 (16-oz.) container nonfat vanilla yogurt
- 2 tablespoons orange-flavored liqueur or orange juice, if desired
- 1 (11-oz.) can mandarin orange segments, well drained

Heat oven to 375°F. In small bowl, combine crust ingredients; press in bottom of ungreased 9 or 10-inch springform pan. Bake at 375°F. for 8 to 10 minutes or until light golden brown. Cool.

In small saucepan, combine gelatin, sugar and orange juice; let stand 1 minute. Stir over medium heat until dissolved. In blender container or food processor bowl with metal blade, process ricotta cheese until smooth. Add yogurt, gelatin mixture and liqueur; blend well. Stir in orange segments.

Pour into cooled, baked crust. Cover; refrigerate several hours or until firm. Before serving, carefully remove sides of pan. Garnish as desired. Store in refrigerator.

Yield: 12 servings.

NUTRITION PER SERVING:
Calories 160; Protein 7g; Carbohydrate 23g; Fat 5g; Sodium 100mg.

GLAZED ALMOND AMARETTO CHEESECAKE

A topping of glazed almonds adds a beautiful touch to this dessert.

TOPPING
- 1/2 cup sugar
- 1/4 cup water
- 1 cup sliced almonds
- 1 teaspoon amaretto

CRUST
- 2 cups graham cracker crumbs (about 32 squares)
- 1/4 cup finely chopped almonds
- 1/3 cup margarine or butter, melted

FILLING
- 2 (8-oz.) pkg. cream cheese, softened
- 1 cup sugar
- 3 eggs
- 1 cup dairy sour cream
- 1/2 cup whipping cream
- 1/4 cup amaretto
- 1/2 teaspoon almond extract

In small saucepan, combine 1/2 cup sugar and water. Bring to a boil. Boil 2 minutes; remove from heat. Stir in sliced almonds and 1 teaspoon amaretto. With slotted spoon, transfer almonds to waxed paper; separate with fork. Cool.

Heat oven to 350°F. In medium bowl, combine all crust ingredients; press in bottom and 1½ inches up sides of ungreased 10-inch springform pan. In large bowl, beat cream cheese and 1 cup sugar at medium speed until smooth and creamy. At low speed, add eggs 1 at a time, beating just until blended. Add sour cream, whipping cream, 1/4 cup amaretto and almond extract; blend well. Pour into crust-lined pan.

Bake at 350°F. for 60 to 75 minutes or until center is set. Arrange sliced almonds in 2-inch wide circle around outer edge of cheesecake during last 15 minutes of baking time. Cool 15 minutes; carefully remove sides of pan. Cool completely. Refrigerate several hours or overnight before serving. Store in refrigerator.

Yield: 16 servings.

NUTRITION PER SERVING:
Calories 390; Protein 6g; Carbohydrate 33g; Fat 26g; Sodium 220mg.

CREAMY CHOCOLATE LACE CHEESECAKE

A chocolate lover's fantasy! This cheesecake features a pretty topping.

CRUST
1½ cups chocolate wafer crumbs (about 24 wafers)
½ cup finely chopped almonds
¼ cup margarine or butter, melted

FILLING
2 (8-oz.) pkg. cream cheese, softened
⅔ cup sugar
3 eggs
1 (12-oz.) pkg. (2 cups) semi-sweet chocolate chips, melted, cooled
1 cup whipping cream
2 tablespoons margarine or butter, melted
1 teaspoon vanilla

TOPPING
1 cup dairy sour cream
1½ teaspoons vanilla
1 teaspoon sugar
½ oz. unsweetened chocolate, melted

Heat oven to 325°F. Butter or grease 9-inch spring-form pan. In large bowl, combine crust ingredients; mix well. Press in bottom and up sides of buttered pan; refrigerate.

In large bowl, beat cream cheese and ⅔ cup sugar at medium speed until smooth and creamy. At low speed, add eggs 1 at a time, beating just until blended. Add melted chocolate chips; beat well. Add whipping cream, 2 tablespoons margarine and 1 teaspoon vanilla; beat until smooth. Pour into crust-lined pan. Bake at 325°F. for 55 to 65 minutes or until edges are set. Center of cheesecake will be soft. Cool in pan 5 minutes; carefully remove sides of pan. Cool completely.

In small bowl, combine sour cream, 1½ teaspoons vanilla and 1 teaspoon sugar; stir until smooth. Spread over cooled cheesecake. Drizzle with ½ oz. melted chocolate in lace pattern. Refrigerate several hours or overnight before serving. Garnish as desired. Store in refrigerator.

Yield: 16 servings.

NUTRITION PER SERVING:
Calories 470; Protein 7g; Carbohydrate 31g; Fat 36g; Sodium 180mg.

EASY FRUIT CHEESECAKES

These scrumptious individual cheesecakes can be made ahead and frozen.

24 vanilla wafers
3 (8-oz.) pkg. cream cheese, softened
1 cup sugar
¼ teaspoon nutmeg
1 teaspoon vanilla
3 eggs
½ cup apricot preserves
3 kiwifruit, peeled, sliced

Heat oven to 325°F. Line 24 muffin cups with paper or foil baking cups. Place 1 vanilla wafer in bottom of each cup. In large bowl, beat cream cheese, sugar, nutmeg, vanilla and eggs until smooth, scraping sides of bowl occasionally. Pour mixture into paper-lined muffin cups, filling ⅔ full. Bake at 325°F. for 20 to 25 minutes or until set.*

Meanwhile, melt apricot preserves in small saucepan over low heat. Place 1 slice of kiwifruit on each cheesecake. Carefully spoon 1 teaspoon melted apricot preserves over top. Cover; refrigerate overnight. Store in refrigerator.

Yield: 24 cheesecakes.

TIPS:
* At this point, cheesecakes can be covered and frozen up to 1 month. Thaw in refrigerator. Garnish just before serving.

Other fruits, such as sliced strawberries, can be substituted for kiwifruit.

NUTRITION PER SERVING:
Calories 180; Protein 3g; Carbohydrate 18g; Fat 11g; Sodium 105mg.

Praline Cheesecake

PRALINE CHEESECAKE

Pecan halves can be pressed into the praline topping of this rich, creamy cheesecake while the topping is still warm.

CRUST
- 1 **cup graham cracker crumbs (about 16 squares)**
- ¼ **cup chopped pecans**
- ¼ **cup butter or margarine, melted**

FILLING
- 3 **(8-oz.) pkg. cream cheese, softened**
- 1 **cup firmly packed brown sugar**
- 3 **eggs**
- 1 **cup whipping cream**
- 2 **teaspoons vanilla**

TOPPING
- ½ **cup firmly packed brown sugar**
- ¼ **cup butter or margarine**

GARNISH
Pecan halves, if desired

Heat oven to 450°F. In small bowl, combine crust ingredients; press firmly in bottom of ungreased 9-inch springform pan.

In large bowl, beat cream cheese at medium speed until smooth and creamy. Gradually beat in 1 cup brown sugar. At low speed, add eggs 1 at a time, beating just until blended. Add whipping cream and vanilla; beat until smooth. Pour into crust-lined pan. Bake at 450°F. for 10 minutes. Reduce oven temperature to 250°F.; bake an additional 65 to 75 minutes or until center is set. Cool 10 minutes; carefully remove sides of pan. Cool completely.

In small saucepan, combine topping ingredients. Cook over medium heat until thick and well blended, stirring constantly. Spread evenly over top of cooled cheesecake. Garnish with pecan halves. Refrigerate at least 2 hours before serving. Store in refrigerator.
Yield: 12 to 16 servings.

FOOD PROCESSOR DIRECTIONS:
Prepare crust as directed above. To prepare filling, place cream cheese in food processor bowl with metal blade. Process until smooth. Add brown sugar and eggs; process until well combined. With machine running, pour whipping cream and vanilla through feed tube; process until mixture is smooth and creamy. Pour into crust-lined pan; continue as directed above.

NUTRITION PER SERVING:
Calories 380; Protein 5g; Carbohydrate 26g; Fat 29g; Sodium 240mg.

PUMPKIN CHEESECAKE WITH PRALINE SAUCE

This pumpkin cheesecake could compete with traditional pumpkin pie as a new holiday favorite.

CRUST
    1 tablespoon butter or margarine, softened
1¼ cups finely chopped pecans
    ¼ cup fine dry bread crumbs
    2 tablespoons sugar
    2 tablespoons butter or margarine, melted

FILLING
    4 (8-oz.) pkg. cream cheese, softened
    1 cup firmly packed brown sugar
    ⅔ cup sugar
    5 eggs
    ¼ cup all purpose flour
    2 teaspoons pumpkin pie spice
    2 tablespoons brandy, if desired
    1 (16-oz.) can (2 cups) pumpkin

PRALINE SAUCE
    ½ cup firmly packed brown sugar
    ¼ cup water
    ¼ cup butter (do not substitute margarine)
    1 egg, beaten
    ¼ cup chopped pecans
    ½ teaspoon vanilla

Heat oven to 350°F. Butter 9-inch springform pan using 1 tablespoon butter. In medium bowl, combine 1¼ cups pecans, bread crumbs and 2 tablespoons sugar. Drizzle melted butter over pecan mixture; toss to combine. Press into bottom and up sides of buttered pan; refrigerate.

In large bowl, beat cream cheese at medium speed until smooth and creamy. Gradually beat in 1 cup brown sugar and ⅔ cup sugar until smooth. At low speed, add 5 eggs 1 at a time, beating just until blended. In small bowl, combine flour, pumpkin pie spice, brandy and pumpkin; mix well. Gradually add to cream cheese mixture; beat until smooth. Pour into crust-lined pan.

Bake at 350°F. for 1 hour 20 minutes to 1 hour 30 minutes or until center is set. Turn oven off; let cake stand in oven 30 minutes with door open at least 4 inches. Remove from oven. Run sharp knife around sides of pan. Cool to room temperature on wire rack. Cover; refrigerate overnight.

In small saucepan over medium heat, combine ½ cup brown sugar, water and ¼ cup butter. Bring to a boil; boil 2 minutes. Gradually blend small amount of hot syrup into beaten egg. Return egg mixture to saucepan; cook over low heat 1 minute, stirring constantly. Remove from heat; stir in ¼ cup pecans and vanilla. Remove sides of pan from cheesecake. Serve sauce slightly warm over wedges of cheesecake. Store in refrigerator.

Yield: 16 servings.

MICROWAVE DIRECTIONS:
Prepare cheesecake as directed above. To prepare sauce, place ¼ cup butter in 4-cup microwave-safe measuring cup. Microwave on HIGH for 45 seconds to 1 minute or until melted. Stir in ½ cup brown sugar and water. Microwave on HIGH for 1 to 1½ minutes or until boiling. Boil 1 minute. Gradually blend small amount of hot syrup into beaten egg. Return egg mixture to measuring cup; blend well. Microwave on MEDIUM for 30 seconds or until slightly thickened. Stir in ¼ cup pecans and vanilla. Serve slightly warm over wedges of cheesecake.

HIGH ALTITUDE:
Above 3500 Feet: In filling, increase flour to ¼ cup plus 1 tablespoon. Bake at 350°F. for 1 hour 15 minutes to 1 hour 25 minutes.

NUTRITION PER SERVING:
Calories 500; Protein 8g; Carbohydrate 39g; Fat 35g; Sodium 260mg.

COOK'S NOTE

SPRINGFORM PAN

A springform pan is a round pan with straight sides 2½ to 3 inches in height. They are available in a number of sizes, 9 and 10-inch diameter pans being the most common. The side of the pan has a spring or clamp, which allows expansion and removal of the side from the bottom of the pan. Cheesecakes or tortes baked in this type of pan can be served easily once the side of the pan is removed.

CREME DE MENTHE CHEESECAKE SQUARES

This dessert has a chocolate wafer base topped with a mint-flavored cheesecake and is frosted with rich semi-sweet chocolate. The 13x9-inch pan makes enough to serve 20 guests.

CRUST
- 1 (8½-oz.) pkg. chocolate wafers, crushed (1¾ cups)
- ½ cup margarine or butter, melted

FILLING
- 2 (8-oz.) pkg. cream cheese, softened
- ½ cup dairy sour cream
- 4 eggs
- ⅔ cup sugar
- ½ cup creme de menthe syrup or liqueur
- ¼ teaspoon mint extract

TOPPING
- 4 oz. semi-sweet chocolate, chopped
- ½ cup dairy sour cream

Heat oven to 350°F. In medium bowl, combine crust ingredients; mix well. Press in bottom and 1 inch up sides of ungreased 13x9-inch pan. Freeze crust while preparing filling.

In large bowl, combine all filling ingredients; beat on low speed until smooth. Pour into crust-lined pan. Bake at 350°F. for 30 to 35 minutes or until knife inserted in center comes out clean. Cool on wire rack.

Melt chocolate in small saucepan over low heat, stirring constantly. Cool 5 minutes; beat in sour cream. Spread over warm cheesecake. Refrigerate 3 hours or until firm. Cut into squares. Store in refrigerator.

Yield: 20 servings.

NUTRITION PER SERVING:
Calories 300; Protein 4g; Carbohydrate 23g; Fat 20g; Sodium 160mg.

FUDGE-GLAZED CHEESECAKE WITH CARAMEL SAUCE

This cheesecake is baked in a round cake pan.

CRUST
- 1 cup crushed creme-filled chocolate sandwich cookies (about 10 cookies)*
- ¼ cup chopped pecans
- 1 tablespoon margarine or butter, melted

CHEESECAKE
- 2 (8-oz.) pkg. cream cheese, softened
- ½ cup sugar
- ¼ cup whipping cream
- 2 eggs

FUDGE GLAZE
- 2 oz. semi-sweet chocolate, chopped
- 2 tablespoons whipping cream

CARAMEL SAUCE
- 1 cup caramel ice cream topping
- ½ cup pecan halves, toasted, p. 23

Heat oven to 325°F. Line 8 or 9-inch round cake pan with foil so that foil extends over sides of pan. In large bowl, combine all crust ingredients; mix well. Press into foil-lined pan. Bake at 325°F. for 8 minutes.

In large bowl, beat cream cheese at medium speed until smooth and creamy. Gradually beat in sugar and whipping cream. At low speed, add eggs 1 at a time, beating just until blended. Pour over crust. Bake at 325°F. for 35 to 45 minutes or until center is set. Cool to room temperature on wire rack.

In small saucepan, melt chocolate with 2 tablespoons whipping cream over very low heat, stirring constantly. Spread over cheesecake. Cover; refrigerate 4 hours or overnight.

In small bowl, combine caramel topping and pecans; mix well. To serve, lift foil-lined cheesecake from pan; remove foil. Place cheesecake on serving plate; cut into wedges. Serve with caramel sauce. Store in refrigerator.

Yield: 12 to 16 servings.

TIP:
* Cookies can be crushed in food processor bowl with metal blade by processing broken cookies until uniform fine crumbs form. Or, place cookies in plastic bag; seal. Crush with rolling pin until uniform fine crumbs form.

NUTRITION PER SERVING:
Calories 310; Protein 5g; Carbohydrate 28g; Fat 20g; Sodium 180mg.

BAKED PEAR CUSTARD WITH CARAMEL SAUCE

Choose any variety of pear for this caramel-topped custard. Ripe pears should feel firm but yield to gentle pressure.

CUSTARD
- 4 pears, peeled, quartered
- ¾ cup all purpose flour
- ¾ cup sugar
- 4 eggs
- 2 cups half-and-half
- 2 tablespoons sugar

CARAMEL SAUCE
- 1 cup firmly packed brown sugar
- ¼ cup dark corn syrup
- ½ cup half-and-half
- 2 tablespoons butter or margarine
  Dash salt
- ½ teaspoon vanilla

Heat oven to 375°F. Grease 2½-quart shallow casserole. Arrange pears in greased casserole. In large bowl, combine flour and ¾ cup sugar. Add eggs; beat well. Gradually stir in 2 cups half-and-half. Pour over pears; sprinkle with 2 tablespoons sugar.

Bake at 375°F. for 40 to 50 minutes or until knife inserted near center comes out clean.

In medium saucepan, combine all sauce ingredients except vanilla. Cook over medium heat until mixture boils, stirring constantly. Reduce heat to low; simmer 5 minutes, stirring constantly. Stir in vanilla. Serve caramel sauce over warm pear custard. Store in refrigerator.

Yield: 8 to 10 servings.

NUTRITION PER SERVING:
Calories 380; Protein 5g; Carbohydrate 63g; Fat 12g; Sodium 100mg.

BAKED CUSTARD

Baked custard is done when it appears set but still jiggles slightly. The custard will firm up as it cools.

- 3 eggs, slightly beaten
- ¼ cup sugar
- ⅛ teaspoon salt
- 1 teaspoon vanilla
- 2½ cups milk
  Dash nutmeg

Heat oven to 350°F. In large bowl, combine eggs, sugar, salt and vanilla; blend well. Gradually stir in milk. Pour into 6 ungreased 6-oz. custard cups. Sprinkle with nutmeg. Place custard cups in 13x9-inch pan. Pour boiling water into pan around custard cups to a depth of 1 inch.

Bake at 350°F. for 45 to 55 minutes or until knife inserted near center comes out clean. Serve warm or cold. Store in refrigerator.

Yield: 6 servings.

TIP:
If desired, pour mixture into 1 to 1½-quart casserole. Place in 13x9-inch pan; pour boiling water into pan around casserole to a depth of 1 inch. Bake at 350°F. for 50 to 60 minutes.

NUTRITION PER SERVING:
Calories 120; Protein 7g; Carbohydrate 13g; Fat 4g; Sodium 125mg.

CUSTARD WITH RASPBERRY PUREE

For a colorful presentation, top this cholesterol-reduced custard with fresh fruit and mint leaves.

CUSTARD
- 2 tablespoons brown sugar
- 1/8 teaspoon salt
- 1 cup evaporated skim milk
- 1/2 cup frozen cholesterol-free egg product, thawed
- 1/2 teaspoon vanilla
  Nutmeg

RASPBERRY PUREE
- 1 (10-oz.) pkg. frozen raspberries with syrup, thawed

GARNISH
  Fresh fruit, if desired
  Mint leaves, if desired

Heat oven to 325°F. In 2-cup measuring cup, combine brown sugar, salt, milk, egg product and vanilla; blend well. Place 4 ungreased 5-oz. custard cups in 9-inch square pan on oven rack. Pour custard mixture into custard cups. Pour boiling water into pan around custard cups to a depth of 1 inch.

Bake at 325°F. for 30 to 35 minutes or until knife inserted in center comes out clean. To unmold, loosen edges with knife. Invert dessert plate on top of each custard cup. Quickly invert to release hot custard onto plate. Sprinkle with nutmeg.

Pour raspberries into food processor bowl with metal blade or blender container. Cover; process until smooth. Strain to remove seeds. Spoon 2 tablespoons sauce on each plate around warm custard. Garnish with fresh fruit and mint leaves. Serve with additional sauce. Store in refrigerator.

Yield: 4 servings.

NUTRITION PER SERVING:
Calories 210; Protein 9g; Carbohydrate 34g; Fat 4g; Sodium 200mg.

CARAMEL FLAN

Serve fresh fruit in the center of this custard dessert ring.

- 1/2 cup sugar
- 5 eggs
- 2 1/2 cups milk
- 1/2 cup sugar
- 1 teaspoon vanilla
- 3 cups fresh fruit (strawberry halves or slices, seedless grapes, pineapple cubes or peeled and sliced kiwifruit)

In small heavy skillet over medium heat, caramelize 1/2 cup sugar, stirring constantly until sugar melts and turns rich golden brown. Pour into 8-inch ring mold; holding pan with pot holders, swirl so sugar coats bottom and sides.

Heat oven to 325°F. In large bowl, slightly beat eggs. Stir in milk, 1/2 cup sugar and vanilla. Place caramel-coated ring mold in shallow baking pan on oven rack. Pour egg mixture over caramel in mold. Pour hot water into pan around mold to a depth of 1 inch.

Bake at 325°F. for 55 to 60 minutes or until a knife inserted halfway between center and edge comes out clean. Remove mold from hot water; cool on wire rack. Refrigerate at least 3 1/2 hours.

To unmold, loosen edges with spatula. Invert mold onto serving plate. Spoon any caramel that remains in mold over custard. Serve with fruit. Store in refrigerator.

Yield: 8 servings.

NUTRITION PER SERVING:
Calories 210; Protein 7g; Carbohydrate 34g; Fat 5g; Sodium 80mg.

CARAMEL-TOPPED CHOCOLATE FLAN

The caramel runs down the sides of the custard forming a sauce when unmolded. It's wonderful warm or cold.

CARAMEL
- ⅓ **cup sugar**
- 2 **tablespoons water**
- ⅛ **teaspoon cream of tartar**

FLAN
- 1⅓ **cups half-and-half**
- 3 **oz. sweet baking chocolate, chopped**
- 2 **tablespoons sugar**
- 3 **eggs**
- ½ **teaspoon vanilla**

In small heavy saucepan over medium heat, combine ⅓ cup sugar, water and cream of tartar until mixture comes to a boil, stirring constantly. Let boil without stirring until mixture begins to caramelize, about 10 to 12 minutes. If it darkens in one spot, swirl pan around gently. Stir until mixture is a medium caramel color. Immediately pour caramel into bottom of 6 ungreased 6-oz. custard cups; set aside.

In small saucepan over low heat, combine half-and-half, chocolate and 2 tablespoons sugar, stirring constantly until smooth. Remove from heat. In small bowl, beat eggs and vanilla until light and lemon colored. Gradually add chocolate mixture; blend well. Carefully pour custard over caramel in custard cups. Place cups in 13x9-inch pan. Pour very hot water into pan to within ½-inch of tops of custard cups. Bake at 325°F. for 50 minutes or until knife inserted in center comes out clean. Unmold and serve warm or refrigerate in custard cups and serve cold. Garnish with whipped cream and fresh fruit, if desired. Store in refrigerator.

Yield: 6 servings.

NUTRITION PER SERVING:
Calories 300; Protein 6g; Carbohydrate 31g; Fat 17g; Sodium 65mg.

CHOCOLATE SOUFFLE

Always bake a souffle on the middle oven rack in a preheated oven. Do not open the oven door for at least the first 25 minutes of baking or the souffle may fall.

- ½ **cup sugar**
- 2 **tablespoons cornstarch**
- ¼ **teaspoon salt**
- ¾ **cup milk**
- 2 **oz. unsweetened chocolate or 2 envelopes premelted unsweetened chocolate baking flavor**
- 3 **tablespoons margarine or butter**
- 1 **teaspoon vanilla**
- 4 **eggs, separated**
- ¼ **teaspoon cream of tartar**
  Whipped cream or topping, if desired

Heat oven to 350°F. Prepare 4 to 5-cup souffle dish or casserole with foil band by cutting 3-inch strip of foil to go around top of dish. Lightly grease dish and strip of foil. With greased side toward inside of dish, secure foil band around top of dish, letting it extend 2 inches above edge of dish.

In medium saucepan, combine sugar, cornstarch and salt; stir in milk. Cook over medium heat until mixture boils and thickens, stirring constantly. Remove from heat; stir in chocolate and margarine until melted. Stir in vanilla. Add egg yolks 1 at a time, beating well after each addition. In large bowl, beat egg whites with cream of tartar until soft peaks form. Gently fold in chocolate mixture. Pour into greased souffle dish.*

Bake at 350°F. for 45 to 50 minutes or until knife inserted near center comes out clean. Remove foil band; immediately serve souffle with whipped cream or topping.

Yield: 10 servings.

TIP:
* Souffle can stand at room temperature, loosely covered, up to 1 hour before baking.

NUTRITION PER SERVING:
Calories 170; Protein 4g; Carbohydrate 15g; Fat 11g; Sodium 130mg.

APRICOT SOUFFLE

This delicate, melt-in-your-mouth souffle is enhanced with a luscious apricot sauce.

- 2 **tablespoons cornstarch**
- 2 **tablespoons sugar**
- ¾ **cup evaporated skim milk**
- ¼ **cup apricot preserves**
- 3 **tablespoons apricot nectar**
- 1 **teaspoon vanilla**
- 6 **egg whites**
- ½ **teaspoon cream of tartar**

SAUCE
- ⅓ **cup apricot preserves**
- 2 **tablespoons apricot nectar**

Spray 2½-quart souffle dish with nonstick cooking spray. In small saucepan, combine cornstarch and sugar. Add milk, ¼ cup apricot preserves and 3 tablespoons apricot nectar. Cook over medium heat until mixture boils and thickens, stirring constantly. Pour into large bowl; stir in vanilla. Cover surface with plastic wrap; set aside. Cool to room temperature.

Heat oven to 425°F. In large bowl, beat egg whites and cream of tartar until stiff peaks form, about 2 to 3 minutes. Gently fold egg white mixture into cooled apricot mixture. Spoon into spray-coated souffle dish. Place souffle dish in 13x9-inch pan. Pour boiling water into pan around souffle dish to a depth of 1 inch. Place in 425°F. oven. Immediately reduce heat to 350°F.; bake 25 minutes or until puffy, set and golden brown.

Meanwhile, in small saucepan combine sauce ingredients. Cook over medium heat until thoroughly heated. Serve souffle immediately with sauce.

Yield: 6 to 8 servings.

HIGH ALTITUDE:
Above 3500 Feet: No change.

NUTRITION PER SERVING:
Calories 120; Protein 4g; Carbohydrate 25g; Fat 0g; Sodium 70mg.

GRANDMA'S RICE PUDDING

Short-grain rice works well in cooked puddings. The pudding will set up slightly when cool.

- ½ **cup uncooked white rice (not instant)**
- ½ **cup sugar**
- 2 **cups milk**
- 1 **tablespoon margarine or butter**
  Cinnamon, nutmeg or raisins, if desired

Heat oven to 300°F. Grease 1½-quart casserole. In greased casserole, combine rice, sugar and milk; dot with margarine. Bake at 300°F. for 1¾ to 2 hours until rice is tender and pudding is creamy, stirring occasionally. Cool; sprinkle each serving with cinnamon. Store in refrigerator.

Yield: 4 (½-cup) servings.

NUTRITION PER SERVING:
Calories 270; Protein 6g; Carbohydrate 49g; Fat 5g; Sodium 95mg.

QUICK RICE PUDDING

This recipe starts with cooked rice.

- 2 **cups milk**
- 1½ **cups cooked white rice**
- ½ **cup raisins, if desired**
- ⅓ **cup sugar**
- 1 **teaspoon cinnamon**
- 1 **teaspoon vanilla**
- 2 **eggs, beaten**

Heat oven to 350°F. In medium saucepan, heat milk to very warm. DO NOT BOIL. Remove from heat; add remaining ingredients; mix well. Pour into ungreased 1½-quart casserole. Place casserole in 13x9-inch pan. Pour boiling water in pan around casserole to a depth of 1 inch. Bake at 350°F. for 30 minutes. Carefully stir pudding; bake an additional 15 to 20 minutes or until knife inserted near center comes out clean. Serve warm or cold with cream, if desired.

Yield: 12 (½-cup) servings.

NUTRITION PER SERVING:
Calories 100; Protein 3g; Carbohydrate 19g; Fat 2g; Sodium 35mg.

CREAM CHEESE BREAD PUDDINGS WITH RUM SAUCE

Bread pudding has graduated from "the poor man's dessert" of years past. This exceptional microwave version is served warm with a marvelous buttery rum sauce.

BREAD PUDDINGS
- 1/3 cup raisins
- 2 tablespoons water
- 1 (3-oz.) pkg. cream cheese, softened
- 1/4 cup sugar
- 2 eggs
- 1 1/2 cups milk
- 1 teaspoon vanilla
- 5 (1-oz.) slices oatmeal bread or whole wheat bread, cut into 1/2-inch cubes

RUM SAUCE
- 1/4 cup butter or margarine
- 1/2 cup firmly packed brown sugar
- 2 tablespoons milk
- 1 tablespoon dark rum or 1/2 teaspoon rum extract
- Nutmeg or cinnamon

MICROWAVE DIRECTIONS:
In large microwave-safe bowl, combine raisins and water; microwave on HIGH for 1 to 1 1/2 minutes or until mixture boils. Set aside.

Butter four 1-cup souffle dishes or 10-oz. custard cups. In small bowl, beat cream cheese and sugar until smooth. Add eggs 1 at a time, beating well after each addition. Slowly beat in 1 1/2 cups milk and vanilla. Add bread to raisins; stir. Pour milk mixture over bread, stirring well. Spoon mixture evenly into buttered dishes.

Arrange dishes in circle in microwave oven. Cover with waxed paper; microwave on MEDIUM for 10 to 14 minutes or until knife inserted near center comes out clean, rotating dishes once halfway through cooking. Let stand while preparing sauce.

To prepare sauce, in 4-cup microwave-safe measuring cup, microwave butter on HIGH for 45 to 60 seconds or until melted. Stir in brown sugar and 2 tablespoons milk. Microwave on HIGH for 1 to 1 1/2 minutes or until boiling; stir. Microwave on HIGH an additional minute; stir in rum. To serve, sprinkle nutmeg over puddings; serve with sauce.

Yield: 4 servings; 2/3 cup sauce.

NUTRITION PER SERVING:
Calories 550; Protein 12g; Carbohydrate 72g; Fat 25g; Sodium 450mg.

FRUIT AND RICE PUDDING

This is an old favorite tastefully tailored for healthier eating. Fruit bits are added for a new flavor twist.

- 1 1/2 cups skim milk
- 2 cups cooked brown rice
- 1/2 cup dried fruit bits
- 1/4 cup firmly packed brown sugar
- 1/4 teaspoon cinnamon
- 1/2 cup frozen cholesterol-free egg product, thawed
- 1 teaspoon vanilla

Heat milk in small saucepan until very warm. Heat oven to 350°F. In ungreased 1 1/2-quart casserole, combine all ingredients. Place casserole in 13x9-inch pan. Pour boiling water into pan around casserole to a depth of 1 inch.

Bake at 350°F. for 35 to 45 minutes. Carefully stir pudding; bake an additional 15 to 25 minutes or until knife inserted in center comes out clean. Serve warm.

Yield: 6 servings.

NUTRITION PER SERVING:
Calories 190; Protein 6g; Carbohydrate 36g; Fat 3g; Sodium 75mg.

CRANBERRY PUDDING WITH BUTTER SAUCE

The perfect holiday dessert for a small gathering.

PUDDING
1½ cups finely crushed dry bread crumbs
 1 cup sugar
 1 tablespoon all purpose flour
1½ teaspoons baking powder
 ¼ teaspoon salt
 ¼ teaspoon ginger
 ¼ teaspoon cinnamon
 ⅛ to ¼ teaspoon allspice
 ⅓ cup butter or margarine, melted
 ⅓ cup milk
 1 cup coarsely chopped fresh or frozen cranberries (do not thaw)
 1 egg, slightly beaten

BUTTER SAUCE
 ½ cup sugar
 1 teaspoon cornstarch
 ½ cup whipping cream
 ¼ cup butter or margarine, melted
 ½ teaspoon vanilla

MICROWAVE DIRECTIONS:
Grease bottom only of 4-cup microwave-safe measuring cup; line bottom with microwave-safe waxed paper and grease again. In large bowl, combine bread crumbs, 1 cup sugar, flour, baking powder, salt, ginger, cinnamon and allspice. Stir in ⅓ cup butter, milk, cranberries and egg; mix well. (Batter will be stiff.) Spoon batter into greased and lined measuring cup; press down slightly. Cover tightly with microwave-safe plastic wrap. Microwave on MEDIUM for 11 to 14 minutes, rotating measuring cup ½ turn halfway through cooking. Pudding is done when it starts to pull away from sides of measuring cup. Uncover; let stand on flat surface 5 minutes. Loosen pudding from sides of measuring cup; invert onto serving plate. Remove waxed paper; cool slightly.

In 4-cup microwave-safe measuring cup, combine ½ cup sugar and cornstarch. Stir in whipping cream and ¼ cup butter. Microwave on HIGH for 1½ to 2 minutes or until mixture boils, stirring once during cooking. Microwave on HIGH for 1 minute.

Stir in vanilla. Cut pudding into wedges. Serve warm sauce over warm pudding.
Yield: 6 servings; 1 cup sauce.

HIGH ALTITUDE:
Above 3500 Feet: No change.

NUTRITION PER SERVING:
Calories 490; Protein 4g; Carbohydrate 62g; Fat 27g; Sodium 450mg.

STEAMED PLUM PUDDING

This moist pudding has been England's traditional Christmas dessert for nearly 300 years.

 1 cup all purpose flour
 3 tablespoons brown sugar
 1 teaspoon cinnamon
 ½ teaspoon baking powder
 ½ teaspoon allspice
 ½ teaspoon cloves
 ¼ teaspoon baking soda
 ½ cup milk
 3 tablespoons oil
 2 tablespoons molasses
 1 egg
 1 cup candied fruit
 ½ cup raisins
 ½ cup chopped nuts

Using solid shortening, generously grease 1-quart mold or casserole. In medium bowl, combine all ingredients except fruit, raisins and nuts. Mix until dry ingredients are moistened. Fold in fruit, raisins and nuts. Spoon into greased mold. Cover with lid or foil. Place on wire rack in large steamer or Dutch oven. Pour boiling water, 3 to 4 inches deep, into steamer; cover. Keep water boiling gently over low heat. If necessary, add water to maintain steam.

Steam 1½ to 2 hours or until pudding springs back when touched lightly in center. Cut into slices. If desired, serve hot with **Rum Hard Sauce** p. 245.
Yield: 6 to 8 servings.

HIGH ALTITUDE:
Above 3500 Feet: No change.

NUTRITION PER SERVING:
Calories 290; Protein 4g; Carbohydrate 47g; Fat 11g; Sodium 105mg.

Cranberry Pudding with Butter Sauce

Chocolate Bread Pudding with Cherry Raspberry Sauce

This spectacular souffle-like bread pudding is a chocolate lover's fantasy.

BREAD PUDDING
1 (6-oz.) pkg. (1 cup) semi-sweet chocolate chips
1 cup whipping cream
2/3 cup firmly packed brown sugar
5 eggs, separated
1/2 cup margarine or butter, cut into pieces
1 teaspoon vanilla
4 cups soft bread cubes

CHERRY RASPBERRY SAUCE
2 tablespoons sugar
4 teaspoons cornstarch
1 (16-oz.) can pitted dark sweet cherries, drained, reserving liquid
1 (10-oz.) pkg. frozen raspberries in syrup, thawed, drained, reserving liquid

Heat oven to 350°F. Grease 12x8-inch (2-quart) baking dish. In large saucepan, combine chocolate chips and whipping cream. Heat over medium-low heat until chips are melted, stirring occasionally. Stir in 1/3 cup of the brown sugar. Add egg yolks 1 at a time, blending well after each addition. Continue cooking until slightly thickened, stirring constantly. Add margarine and vanilla; stir until smooth. Remove from heat; stir in bread cubes.

In large bowl, beat egg whites at medium speed until soft peaks form. Gradually add remaining 1/3 cup brown sugar, beating at high speed until stiff peaks form. Fold egg white mixture into chocolate mixture. Pour into greased baking dish. Place baking dish in 13x9-inch or larger pan. Pour boiling water into pan around baking dish to a depth of 1 inch. Bake at 350°F. for 35 to 40 minutes or until center is set.

In medium saucepan, combine sugar and cornstarch. Gradually stir in reserved liquids from fruits. Cook over medium-high heat until mixture boils and thickens, stirring constantly. Cool slightly; stir in fruit. Serve over warm bread pudding. Store any remaining bread pudding and sauce in refrigerator.
Yield: 10 to 12 servings; 1 1/3 cups sauce.

NUTRITION PER SERVING:
Calories 390; Protein 6g; Carbohydrate 45g; Fat 22g; Sodium 220mg.

Old-Fashioned Bread Pudding with Brandy Hard Sauce

Bread pudding, a simple, thrifty pudding of the past, has been rediscovered today as a delicious custard embellished with raisins and nuts and served with hard sauce.

BREAD PUDDING
2 1/2 cups white and whole wheat bread cubes
1 1/4 cups warm milk
1/4 cup sugar
1/2 teaspoon cinnamon
1/2 teaspoon nutmeg
1/2 teaspoon vanilla
2 eggs, beaten
1/2 cup raisins
1/4 cup chopped nuts, if desired

BRANDY HARD SAUCE
1 cup powdered sugar
1/4 cup butter or margarine, softened
2 teaspoons hot water
1 tablespoon brandy or bourbon or 1 teaspoon brandy extract

Heat oven to 350°F. Grease 1-quart casserole. In greased casserole, combine bread cubes and milk. In medium bowl, combine sugar, cinnamon, nutmeg, vanilla and eggs; mix well. Stir in raisins and nuts. Add egg mixture to bread cube mixture; mix well. Bake at 350°F. for 45 to 50 minutes or until pudding is set.

In small bowl, combine all hard sauce ingredients. Beat at high speed until well blended. Cover; refrigerate until serving time. Serve sauce with warm pudding. Store any remaining bread pudding and sauce in refrigerator.
Yield: 4 to 5 servings; 3/4 cup sauce.

NUTRITION PER SERVING:
Calories 370; Protein 6g; Carbohydrate 55g; Fat 14g; Sodium 250mg.

Old-Fashioned Bread Pudding with Brandy Hard Sauce

STEP-BY-STEP FEATURE ～
How to Make Meringue Shells (Tartlets)

STEP 1. Begin with egg whites that contain no specks of yolk. Beat until soft peaks form. Soft peaks will curl down when the beaters are lifted.

STEP 2. Gradually add sugar, 1 tablespoon at a time, beating until the sugar is almost dissolved. Continue beating until stiff peaks form.

STEP 3. Line a cookie sheet with parchment paper or foil. Pipe meringue onto paper-lined cookie sheet in spirals.

STRAWBERRY LEMON MERINGUE TARTLETS

Some like meringues with an almost marshmallow-like center, while others prefer meringues dry and crisp throughout. We have provided directions for both.

  4 **egg whites**
  ½ **teaspoon cream of tartar**
  1 **cup sugar**
  1 **(8-oz.) container lemon yogurt**
  1 **pint (2 cups) strawberries, halved or sliced**
     Citrus Strips, if desired p. 211

Heat oven to 275°F. Line cookie sheet with parchment paper or foil. In large bowl, beat egg whites and cream of tartar at medium speed until soft peaks form. Add sugar 2 tablespoons at a time, beating at high speed until stiff glossy peaks form and sugar is almost dissolved.

Fill large decorating bag with large star tip.* Pipe meringue onto paper-lined cookie sheet in spirals to form 6 round bases about 3 inches in diameter. Pipe a border of rosettes around each base.

Bake at 275°F. for 35 minutes. For s*ofter meringues*, remove pan from oven immediately. Cool on wire rack. For *dry crisp meringues*, turn oven off and leave meringues in oven with door closed for 2 hours or overnight.

Carefully remove meringues from paper; place on serving plates. Just before serving, spoon yogurt into center of each meringue; top with strawberries. Garnish with citrus strips. Store in refrigerator.
Yield: 6 servings.

TIP:
* A large resealable plastic freezer bag with a corner snipped off can be used instead of a decorating bag and tip.

NUTRITION PER SERVING:
Calories 190; Protein 5g; Carbohydrate 42g; Fat 1g; Sodium 60mg.

Strawberry Lemon Meringue Tartlets

CHOCOLATE PASSION TORTE

Enjoy the fabulous cookies 'n cream combination in both the brownie and mousse layers of this dessert. Vary the candy in the mousse according to personal preferences.

BROWNIE
- 1 (21.5-oz.) pkg. fudge brownie mix
- ½ cup water
- ½ cup oil
- 2 eggs
- 1 cup coarsely chopped creme-filled chocolate sandwich cookies (about 10 cookies)

MOUSSE
- 6 tablespoons water
- 1½ teaspoons unflavored gelatin
- ½ cup sugar
- ¼ cup unsweetened cocoa
- 1 cup whipping cream
- 1 (5-oz.) creamy white bar with almonds, chopped (1 cup)
- ½ cup chopped pecans, toasted, p. 23
- 4 creme-filled chocolate sandwich cookies, chopped

GLAZE
- ½ oz. unsweetened chocolate or white baking bar, melted

Heat oven to 350°F. Lightly grease 10-inch spring-form pan. In large bowl, combine brownie mix, water, oil and eggs; beat 50 strokes by hand. Stir in 1 cup chopped cookies. Spread in greased pan. Bake at 350°F. for 43 to 53 minutes or until center is almost set. Cool 1 hour.

Place 2 tablespoons of the water in small bowl; add gelatin and let stand 1 minute to soften. Meanwhile, in small heavy saucepan combine remaining 4 tablespoons water, sugar and cocoa. Cook over medium-low heat for 2 to 3 minutes or until sugar dissolves, stirring occasionally. Reduce heat to low; add gelatin mixture. Cook and stir until gelatin is completely dissolved. Cool to room temperature.

In small bowl, beat whipping cream at medium speed until stiff peaks form; add gelatin mixture and beat at low speed until well blended. Fold in white bar, pecans and 4 chopped cookies. Spoon mousse over cooled brownie. Drizzle glaze over mousse in lattice pattern. Cover; refrigerate at least 2 hours. Remove sides of pan. Store in refrigerator.
Yield: 16 servings.

HIGH ALTITUDE:
Above 3500 Feet: Add ¼ cup flour to dry brownie mix. Bake as directed above.

NUTRITION PER SERVING:
Calories 430; Protein 5g; Carbohydrate 50g; Fat 24g; Sodium 210mg.

TAMPICO TORTE

This dessert combines bananas and caramel with a creamy orange-flavored topping — all favorite Mexican flavors.

CRUST
- 1 cup all purpose flour
- ¼ cup firmly packed brown sugar
- ½ cup margarine or butter

FILLING
- ¾ cup caramel ice cream topping
- ¼ cup all purpose flour
- 2 medium bananas

TOPPING
- 1 (8-oz.) pkg. cream cheese, softened
- ¼ cup sugar
- 1 tablespoon grated orange peel
- 1 cup whipping cream, whipped
- ¼ cup slivered almonds, toasted, p. 23

Heat oven to 350°F. Grease 10-inch tart pan with removable bottom. In medium bowl, combine 1 cup flour and brown sugar. Using pastry blender or fork, cut in margarine until mixture resembles coarse crumbs. Press in bottom of greased pan. Bake at 350°F. for 14 to 19 minutes or until light golden brown.

In small saucepan over medium heat, combine caramel topping and ¼ cup flour; bring just to a boil. Cool; refrigerate until very cold.

Just before serving, spread caramel mixture over crust. Slice bananas; arrange over caramel. In small bowl, beat cream cheese and sugar until fluffy. Fold in orange peel and whipped cream. Spread over sliced bananas. Sprinkle with slivered almonds. Remove torte from pan. Serve immediately.
Yield: 10 servings.

NUTRITION PER SERVING:
Calories 410; Protein 6g; Carbohydrate 46g; Fat 23g; Sodium 230mg.

Tampico Torte

CHOCOLATE CARAMEL CHEESECAKE TORTE

Serve this memorable treat at a dessert buffet.

CRUST
- ¾ cup shortening or butter-flavored shortening
- ½ cup sugar
- ¼ cup firmly packed brown sugar
- 1 teaspoon vanilla
- 2 eggs
- 1½ cups all purpose flour
- ½ teaspoon baking powder

FILLING
- 30 caramels, unwrapped
- ¼ cup evaporated milk
- ½ cup semi-sweet chocolate chips

TOPPING
- 1 (8-oz.) pkg. light cream cheese (Neufchatel) or cream cheese, softened
- ½ cup sugar
- 2 tablespoons powdered sugar
- 1 egg

GLAZE
- ¼ cup semi-sweet chocolate chips, melted

Heat oven to 350°F. Grease bottom and sides of 9 or 10-inch springform pan. In large bowl, combine shortening, ½ cup sugar and brown sugar; beat until light and fluffy. Add vanilla and 2 eggs; beat until creamy. Add flour and baking powder; mix well. Spread in greased pan. Bake at 350°F. for 15 to 25 minutes or until light golden brown.

Meanwhile, in small saucepan combine caramels and evaporated milk. Cook and stir over low heat until caramels are melted and mixture is smooth. Pour over partially baked crust; spread to within ¼ inch of edges. Sprinkle with ½ cup chocolate chips. In small bowl, combine all topping ingredients; beat until smooth. Pour over chocolate chips; spread evenly.

Bake at 350°F. for 25 to 35 minutes or until filling is set and edges are light golden brown. Drizzle with glaze. Cool to room temperature on wire rack. Remove sides of pan. Refrigerate at least 2 to 3 hours before serving. Store in refrigerator.
Yield: 16 servings.

HIGH ALTITUDE:
Above 3500 Feet: No change.

NUTRITION PER SERVING
Calories 340; Protein 5g; Carbohydrate 43g; Fat 17g; Sodium 140mg.

CHOCO-PEANUT MOUSSE TORTE

A thin slice of this layered dessert is sure to satisfy your sweet tooth. Salted peanuts in the crust and topping add a special flavor that complements the chocolate.

CRUST
- 1½ cups crushed shortbread cookies
- ⅓ cup finely chopped salted peanuts
- ¼ cup margarine or butter, melted
- 2 tablespoons sugar

CHOCOLATE LAYER
- 1⅓ cups semi-sweet chocolate chips
- 1 cup hot milk

PEANUT BUTTER LAYER
- 1 cup peanut butter chips
- ½ cup hot milk
- 1 cup whipping cream, whipped
- 2 tablespoons powdered sugar
- ⅓ cup chopped salted peanuts

Heat oven to 350°F. In medium bowl, combine all crust ingredients; mix well. Press in bottom and 1½ inches up sides of ungreased 9-inch springform pan. Bake at 350°F. for 9 to 11 minutes or until light golden brown. Cool completely.

In blender container or food processor bowl with metal blade, combine chocolate chips and 1 cup hot milk. Cover; blend until smooth. Pour into small bowl; cover with plastic wrap. In blender container or food processor bowl with metal blade, combine peanut butter chips and ½ cup hot milk. Cover; blend until smooth. Pour mixture into large bowl; cover with plastic wrap. Refrigerate chocolate mixture and peanut butter mixture 1 hour or until slightly thickened.

Spread chocolate mixture in cooled crust. Fold whipped cream and powdered sugar into peanut butter mixture; spread evenly over chocolate layer. Sprinkle with ⅓ cup chopped peanuts. Refrigerate until firm. Store in refrigerator.

Yield: 12 servings.

NUTRITION PER SERVING:
Calories 430; Protein 8g; Carbohydrate 33g; Fat 30g; Sodium 180mg.

Viennese Almond Torte

—⌐∿⌐—

Serve this pretty European-style dessert for special occasions.

CRUST
- 2 **cups all purpose flour**
- ½ **cup firmly packed brown sugar**
- ½ **to 1 teaspoon cardamom**
- ½ **cup margarine or butter**

FILLING
- ⅔ **cup sugar**
- ½ **cup margarine or butter, melted**
- 3 **eggs**
- ½ **teaspoon almond extract**
- 1 **cup vanilla milk chips or 6-oz. pkg. white baking bars, coarsely chopped**
- 1½ **cups sliced almonds**
  Powdered sugar, if desired

Heat oven to 400°F. In medium bowl, combine flour, brown sugar and cardamom; mix well. Using pastry blender or fork, cut in ½ cup margarine until mixture is crumbly.* (Mixture will be dry.) Press 1¾ cups of the crumbs in bottom and 1 inch up sides of ungreased 9 or 10-inch springform pan.

Bake at 400°F. for 10 to 12 minutes or until light golden brown. Meanwhile, in large bowl combine sugar, ½ cup margarine, eggs and almond extract; blend well. Stir in vanilla milk chips and 1 cup of the almonds; mix well.

Reduce oven temperature to 350°F. Pour filling over partially baked crust. Sprinkle with remaining crumbs; sprinkle remaining ½ cup almonds around edge of torte.

Bake at 350°F. for 40 to 55 minutes or until golden brown and nuts are lightly toasted. (Place foil or cookie sheet on lowest rack during baking to guard against spills.) Cool 10 minutes. Run knife around edge of pan to loosen; remove sides of pan. Sprinkle lightly with powdered sugar. Serve warm or cool.

Yield: 12 servings.

TIP:
* To prepare crust in food processor, combine all crust ingredients in food processor bowl with metal blade. Process 10 to 15 seconds or until mixture is crumbly.

HIGH ALTITUDE:
Above 3500 Feet: Decrease sugar in filling to ½ cup. Bake at 350°F. for 45 to 55 minutes.

NUTRITION PER SERVING:
Calories 450; Protein 7g; Carbohydrate 47g; Fat 27g; Sodium 190mg.

Raspberry Cream Brownie Wedges

Two delicious brownie layers separated by a raspberry cream filling make a gourmet chocolate dessert. Serve it with a flavored coffee topped with whipped cream.

FILLING
- 1 (8-oz.) pkg. cream cheese, softened
- ½ cup seedless raspberry preserves
- 1 tablespoon all purpose flour
- 1 egg
- 2 to 3 drops red food color*

BROWNIE
- ¾ cup margarine or butter
- 4 oz. unsweetened chocolate
- ¾ cup sugar
- 3 eggs
- 1 cup all purpose flour
- ½ teaspoon baking powder
- ¼ teaspoon salt
- 3 tablespoons raspberry-flavored liqueur or water

GLAZE
- 1 oz. white baking bar
- 2 teaspoons oil

Heat oven to 350°F. Lightly grease 9-inch springform pan. In small bowl, combine all filling ingredients. Beat 1 minute at medium speed; set aside.

In medium saucepan, melt margarine and chocolate over low heat, stirring constantly. Remove from heat; cool slightly. Add sugar and 3 eggs; beat well. Stir in flour, baking powder and salt; blend well. Stir in raspberry liqueur; blend well. Spread half of chocolate mixture in bottom of greased pan. Spread filling evenly over chocolate. Spread remaining chocolate mixture evenly over filling.

Bake at 350°F. for 37 to 42 minutes or until center is set. Cool on wire rack 5 minutes; run knife around edge of pan to loosen. Cool completely; remove from pan.

In small saucepan, melt glaze ingredients over low heat, stirring constantly until smooth. Drizzle glaze over top of brownie; allow to set. Cut into wedges.
Yield: 12 servings.

TIP:
* Use paste food color for more vivid color.

HIGH ALTITUDE:
Above 3500 Feet: Decrease sugar to ⅔ cup. Bake as directed above.

NUTRITION PER SERVING:
Calories 410; Protein 6g; Carbohydrate 38g; Fat 26g; Sodium 280mg.

Frozen Raspberry Macadamia Dessert

This is a quick-to-make, spectacular dessert for a special occasion!

CRUST
- 1 cup crushed vanilla wafers (about 20 wafers)
- ½ cup finely chopped macadamia nuts or almonds
- ¼ cup margarine or butter, melted

FILLING
- 1 (14-oz.) can sweetened condensed milk (not evaporated)
- 3 tablespoons lemon juice
- 3 tablespoons orange-flavored liqueur or orange juice
- 1 (10-oz.) pkg. frozen raspberries with syrup, thawed
- 1 cup whipping cream, whipped
  Chocolate Filigree Hearts p. 210

Heat oven to 375°F. In small bowl, combine all crust ingredients; mix well. Press firmly in bottom of ungreased 8-inch springform pan. Bake at 375°F. for 8 to 10 minutes. Cool.

In large bowl, combine sweetened condensed milk, lemon juice and liqueur; beat until smooth. Add raspberries; beat at low speed until well blended. Fold in whipped cream. Pour over cooled, baked crust. Freeze until firm. Just before serving, let stand at room temperature about 15 minutes. Garnish with Chocolate Filigree Hearts. Store in freezer.
Yield: 12 servings.

NUTRITION PER SERVING:
Calories 310; Protein 4g; Carbohydrate 30g; Fat 20g; Sodium 115mg.

LEMON STRAWBERRY PIE TORTE

A perfect dessert for a summer luncheon.

CRUST
- ⅔ **cup all purpose flour**
- 3 **tablespoons finely chopped nuts**
- 2 **tablespoons brown sugar**
- ⅓ **cup margarine or butter, softened**

FILLING
- 1 **(8-oz.) pkg. cream cheese, softened**
- 1⅓ **cups milk**
- 1 **(3.75-oz.) pkg. instant lemon pudding and pie filling mix**
- 3 **to 4 cups halved or whole strawberries, reserving 1 large whole berry for garnish**

TOPPING
- 1 **(3-oz.) pkg. strawberry flavor gelatin**
- ¾ **cup boiling water**
- ¾ **cup cold water**

Heat oven to 350°F. In medium bowl, combine flour, nuts and brown sugar. Using pastry blender or fork, cut in margarine until crumbly. Press in bottom of ungreased 9 or 10-inch springform pan. Bake at 350°F. for 15 to 22 minutes or until light golden brown. Cool completely.

In small bowl, beat cream cheese at medium speed until smooth and creamy. Gradually blend in milk until smooth. Add pudding mix; beat at low speed 1 minute or until thickened. Pour over cooled, baked crust. Arrange strawberry halves, cut side up and pointing outward, on top of filling in circular pattern, starting at outside edge of pie. (Whole berries can be set pointed end up in circular pattern, starting at outside edge of pie.) Place reserved strawberry in center of pie. Refrigerate pie while preparing topping.

In small bowl, dissolve gelatin in boiling water. Stir in cold water. Refrigerate until mixture is cooled, about 15 minutes. Slowly pour gelatin mixture over strawberries. (Berries may not be completely covered.) Refrigerate at least 3 hours or until set.

Just before serving, run knife, dipped in hot water, around edge of pan to loosen. Carefully remove sides of pan.

Yield: 10 servings.

NUTRITION PER SERVING:
Calories 310; Protein 6g; Carbohydrate 33g; Fat 17g; Sodium 220mg.

STREAMLINED HUNGARIAN TORTE

This pastry torte is a Pillsbury BAKE-OFF® Contest classic. Feathery-light meringue tops flaky pastry layers filled with nuts and apricot preserves. It is not as time-consuming as you might think.

- 1 **pkg. active dry yeast**
- ¼ **cup warm water**
- 1⅓ **cups margarine or butter**
- 3½ **cups all purpose flour**
- ½ **cup dairy sour cream**
- 4 **eggs, separated**
- 1¾ **cups chopped walnuts**
- ¾ **cup sugar**
- 1 **teaspoon cinnamon**
- 1 **(10-oz.) jar (¾ cup) apricot preserves***
- ½ **cup sugar**

Heat oven to 350°F. Grease 13x9-inch pan. In small bowl, dissolve yeast in warm water (105 to 115°F.). In large bowl, using pastry blender or fork cut margarine into flour until mixture resembles coarse crumbs. Stir in sour cream, egg yolks and dissolved yeast just until soft dough forms.

Shape dough into a ball; divide into 3 equal parts. On well floured surface, roll each part to 13x9-inch rectangle. Place 1 rectangle in bottom of greased pan. Reserve ¼ cup of the walnuts. Combine remaining walnuts, ¾ cup sugar and cinnamon; sprinkle over dough in pan. Top with second dough rectangle; spread evenly with preserves. Top with remaining dough rectangle. Bake at 350°F. for 40 to 50 minutes or until light golden brown.

In large bowl, beat egg whites until foamy. Gradually add ½ cup sugar, 1 tablespoon at a time, beating until stiff peaks form, about 3 minutes. Cover baked pastry with egg white mixture; sprinkle with reserved walnuts. Bake an additional 10 to 15 minutes or until golden brown. Cool.

Yield: 16 servings.

TIP:
* Other flavors of preserves can be substituted.

HIGH ALTITUDE:
Above 3500 Feet: No change.

NUTRITION PER SERVING:
Calories 460; Protein 7g; Carbohydrate 50g; Fat 26g; Sodium 200mg.

PIES AND PASTRIES

P ie. It's an all-time favorite that even defines the spirit of our country: "As American as apple pie." Whether topped with streusel or baked in a deep dish, then crowned with a scoop of ice cream or dollop of whipped cream, it's little wonder Americans love their pie.

In this chapter, choose from glorious fruit pies, sumptuous cream pies or light meringues. Or indulge in the art of making pastries — cream-filled puffs, fruit tarts, strudels, puff pastry confections and more.

*Pictured: **Eclairs** p. 333, **Lemon Meringue Pie** p. 314, **Winter Fruit Phyllo Tarts** p. 325*

PIES AND PASTRIES

Flaky-crusted pies have always been prized by pie lovers and
pie bakers, not just because they're the perfect complement to a steaming
cup of coffee, but because they're a yardstick by which a pie baker's skill is measured.
In this chapter, you'll learn how to make flaky pie crust,
as well as pastries and delectable fillings.

KINDS OF PIES AND PASTRIES

*Although the fillings are countless, there are only
a few main types of pies and pastries:*

FRUIT PIES

These are made with 1 or 2 crusts; the top crust
can be plain or decorative, such as a lattice.
Use fresh, frozen, canned or dried fruit for
fillings or use canned pie filling when time's
short. (Recipes begin on p. 271.)

CUSTARD PIES

These are 1-crust pies that have a filling made
with milk and egg which bakes with the pastry.
This type includes pecan and pumpkin pies.
(Recipes begin on p. 288.)

CREAM PIES

This category includes 1-crust (pastry or
crumb) pies filled with custard or pudding and
crowned with meringue or whipped topping.
The crust is baked first and then the filling and
toppings are added. (Recipes begin on p. 300.)

MERINGUE PIES

Meringue pies are 1-crust custard or cream pies
topped with a soft meringue. (Recipes begin on
p. 314.)

TARTS

These are 1-crust or crumb-crust shallow or
miniature pies. They may be fruit, custard or
cream-filled and are crowned with toppings

such as whipped cream, streusel or meringue.
(Recipes begin on p. 317.)

PASTRIES

This category includes a wide range of desserts
made with different kinds of pastry, such as
buttery dough, flaky phyllo (FEE-low) and airy
puff pastry. The pastries can be filled with fruit
and/or nuts, custard or whipped cream. (Recipes begin on p. 333.)

CREAM PUFFS AND ECLAIRS

These egg-rich crisp, hollow pastries are filled
with whipped cream, pudding or custard.
(Recipes are on p. 333.)

SECRETS FOR SUCCESSFUL PIES AND PASTRIES

*Pies and pastries require a light touch and a bit of
patience, but the results are well worth the effort!
Here are some secrets for making your pies and
pastries a success:*

SECRETS FOR ANY PIES

**Use only the ingredients called for in the
recipe.** Do not substitute oil, butter or margarine when shortening is called for. Shortening
refers to solid vegetable shortening. In the
past, lard was commonly used for pie crust.
Lard makes a tender, flaky crust, has a
distinctive flavor and can be substituted for
the shortening.

Measure and blend ingredients carefully. Careful measurement and thorough blending will yield the highest quality pastries and fillings.

Stir flour and salt together thoroughly. Then add the shortening and liquid.

Use a pastry blender or fork to cut in the shortening. Using a pastry blender or fork will distribute the shortening evenly to give the pastry its flaky texture.

Use ice-cold water. Cold water contributes to a flaky crust. Add an ice cube to the water, removing it before adding the water to the flour/shortening mixture.

Avoid overmixing. Overmixing can toughen the pastry. Use a light touch.

Refrigerate the dough before rolling. For easier handling, the dough can be refrigerated for 30 minutes before rolling it out.

Flour the surface for rolling. A floured surface is essential for rolling out dough without sticking, but the less flour used, the flakier the pastry will be. For best results, roll dough on a lightly floured pastry cloth using a cloth-covered rolling pin. Rub the flour into the pastry cloth and cloth-covered rolling pin. You can anchor the corners of the cloth with tape to a flat surface. OR, chilled dough can be placed between 2 large sheets of waxed paper or plastic wrap before rolling it out.

Choose dull-finished aluminum or glass pie pans. Shiny pie pans can give your pie a soggy bottom. Nine-inch pie pans are the standard size used in the recipes in this chapter.

Do not grease the pie pan. Because of the high proportion of fat in pastry dough, there is no need to grease the pan before baking, unless it is specified in the recipe.

When placing the pastry in the pan:
- Fold the pastry in half or quarters and place it in the pie pan. Unfold it gently.

- Firmly press the dough against the sides and bottom without stretching it. If the dough is stretched, the crust will shrink as it bakes.

- Mend any cracks by lightly wetting your fingers and pressing the edges together.

- With a kitchen shears or knife, trim uneven edges of dough that may be hanging over the pan, then flute or decorate the edges.

- For 2-crust pies, trim the bottom pastry even with the pan edge. Add filling and cover with top pastry, allowing a 1-inch overlap of top pastry around the edge. Press edges well to seal. Form a standing rim of pastry and flute. For other finishing touches see p. 266.

Prick an unfilled pastry shell before baking. If the pastry shell is to be baked before it's filled, prick the bottom and sides with a fork to keep it from puffing during baking. If it does begin to puff, reprick the crust. Don't prick the bottom of an unbaked pastry before you pour in the filling, or the filling will seep under the pastry.

If you're making a 2-crust pie, try:
- Brush the top pastry with a slightly beaten egg white to make it shiny. If desired, sprinkle it with sugar.

- Brush the top pastry with milk, cream, or a mixture of 1 egg yolk and 1 tablespoon water to make the crust golden brown. If desired, sprinkle it with sugar.

Cut vents in the top crust of a 2-crust pie. Vents allow the steam that forms during baking to escape and minimize bubbling over of the filling. They can be cut before or after the pastry is placed over the filling, and can be plain or fancy.

If the crust is baking unevenly:
- If the edges are browning before the center is done, cover those edges with 2-inch-wide strips of foil. Gently fold the strips over the edges.

- If the whole top is getting too brown, loosely drape a sheet of foil over the pie.

- For more information, see the Cook's Note on p. 281 to learn how to make a special foil cover.

If you're making a crumb crust (see chart p. 269):

- Finely crush the crumbs using a food processor, or place broken cookies or crackers in a plastic bag and crush them with a rolling pin.

- Press the crumbs evenly over the bottom and up the sides of the pan, then press another pie pan of the same size firmly into the crust to make it smooth.

- If the crust is baked, it will release from the pan easily when the pie is cut. If the crust has been chilled to set it, press a warm towel around the outside of the pan to soften the margarine and make cutting and serving easier.

If time is extra short . . . In this cookbook, all pie recipes call for homemade crusts, but if time is short, you can use convenience products such as refrigerated rolled-out pie crusts, sticks of pie crust dough, frozen unbaked pie crusts or purchased crumb crusts.

If you have some extra time . . . Make 2 pies at the same time. Freeze the extra pie for a future use.

SECRETS FOR MERINGUE PIES

Place soft meringue over a hot filling. When topping a pie, spread the meringue over the pie until it touches the crust. This will create a tight seal and prevent shrinkage during baking.

Cool the pie completely after baking and before refrigerating it.

Dip a knife in water before making each cut when slicing the finished pie.

SECRETS FOR PASTRIES

Two popular types of pastry dough are phyllo and puff pastry. Here are tips for using them successfully:

Phyllo (filo)

- Phyllo dough is a delicate, thinly rolled wheat dough used as a wrapper for a variety of fillings. It's used frequently in Greek and Middle Eastern pastries. The paper-thin dough can be found in the freezer section of the supermarket. A 1-pound box usually contains about 22 pastry sheets, each about 18x14 inches.

- Thaw phyllo dough in the refrigerator for 8 to 12 hours before using it.

- Have all other ingredients ready before opening the phyllo package. Cover the sheets with plastic wrap to prevent them from drying out.

- Brush the phyllo sheets with either margarine or butter to produce the characteristic flakiness and to help prevent sticking. See our Step-By-Step Feature on p. 336.

Puff pastry

- Elegant and airy, puff pastry is used for special desserts such as palmiers. Because the technique involved with making puff pastry requires some skill and time, you may choose to purchase already-made puff pastry. You'll find it in the freezer section of your supermarket. See our Cook's Note on Making Puff Pastry on p. 334.

- Purchase the freshest pastry dough.

- Store pastry in the freezer for several months or in the refrigerator for 1 week.

- Thaw puff pastry in the refrigerator so that it remains cold.

- Keep the pastry cold during preparation of the recipe. The colder the pastry, the better it will rise, puff and separate into layers.

- Lightly flour the rolling pin and rolling surface.

- After cutting and shaping, refrigerate the dough to chill it before baking.

- Heat the oven for 10 to 15 minutes before baking.

SECRETS FOR CREAM PUFFS

Heat the oven 10 to 15 minutes before baking. The oven must be hot so that the pastry puffs up immediately. Puffs will double in size.

Bake until properly done. Cream puffs that have been baked to the proper doneness (golden brown and firm to the touch) will retain their shape and won't collapse.

Cut a slit in the side of each puff after baking. The slit lets the steam escape, allowing the inside of the puff to dry so that it won't become soggy.

Fill puffs as close to serving time as possible. This will prevent the puffs from becoming soggy.

HOW TO TELL WHEN PIES AND PASTRIES ARE DONE

As with any baked good, knowing when a pie or pastry is done is key to the success of your baking experience.

A pie crust is done when . . . it is evenly light golden brown.

Fruit pies are done when . . . the crust is golden brown and the filling is bubbly.

Custard pies are done when . . . a knife inserted in the center comes out clean.

Meringue pies are done when . . . the meringue has a golden glow and the tips of the meringue are light golden brown.

Puffs and eclairs are done when . . . they are golden brown and firm to the touch.

KEEPING PIES AND PASTRIES FRESH AND FLAVORFUL

Pies and pastries can be refrigerated or frozen to keep them at their just-baked best. See Freezing Guidelines p. 25.

Refrigerate pies containing dairy products or eggs. Pies made with eggs, milk, dairy sour cream, whipped cream, whipped topping, yogurt or cream cheese should be refrigerated as soon as possible after they've been prepared. Custard and cream pies, or pies with meringue topping do not freeze well.

Store fruit pies at room temperature, in the refrigerator or freezer. A fruit pie can be stored at room temperature for up to 2 days. If the room is very warm, the pie should be refrigerated. Fruit pies can be frozen baked or unbaked.

Refrigerate or freeze pumpkin and pecan pies. Pumpkin and pecan pies keep well in the refrigerator, or can be frozen after they are baked.

Freeze pie dough or unbaked shells. Keeping pie dough or unbaked pie shells in the freezer will give you a jump on pie baking when time is short. To freeze dough, form it into a flattened ball and wrap it tightly in moisture- and vapor-proof wrap. Freeze shells in the pan (a disposable foil pie pan works well for freezing). If freezing more than 1 shell, stack them and then wrap tightly.

Store baked puff pastries in the freezer. They don't hold up well in the refrigerator, so wrap puff pastries tightly in moisture- and vapor-proof wrap and freeze.

Store unfilled puffs and eclairs in an airtight, moisture-proof container. Puffs and eclairs should be kept in a container with a tight-fitting lid and stored in the refrigerator. Limit storage time to overnight. For longer storage, place unfilled puffs in an airtight container and freeze for up to 3 months.

NUTRITION IN THIS CHAPTER

Nutrition per serving means calculation was done on 1 serving, 1 cream puff/pastry, 1 individual tart or 1 dumpling.

FINISHING TOUCHES FOR PIES

Make pies extra-special with fancy edges and crusts. With tools as simple as a knife, a fork or your fingertips, you can dress up your pies. For finishing touches from lattice-work crusts to herringbone edges, just follow the easy step-by-step instructions and illustrations on these pages.

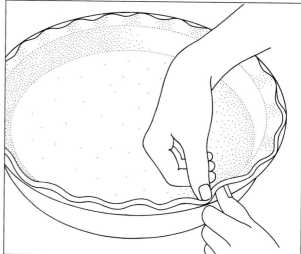

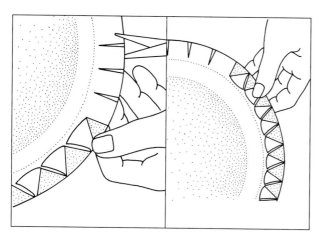

STARBURST EDGE

Trim dough even with edge of pan. Cut edge of crust at about ½-inch intervals, making each cut ½ inch long. Fold each piece in half diagonally to form a triangle, pressing lightly to seal dough.

SCALLOPED EDGE

Trim dough even with edge of pan. Form a stand-up rim. Place left thumb and index finger about ¾ inch apart on outside of raised edge. With right thumb, push pastry toward outside to form a scalloped edge.

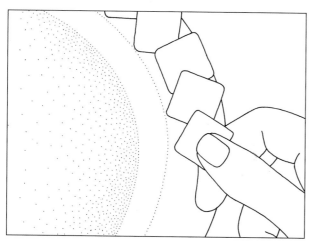

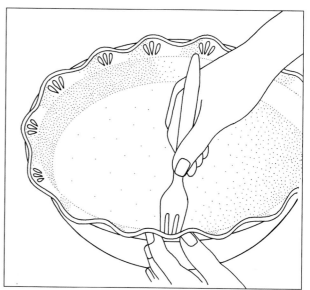

CUT-OUT EDGE

Trim dough even with edge of pan. Using canape cutter of desired shape, cut shapes from additional dough. Brush edge of crust with egg white. Overlap cutouts on edge of crust, pressing lightly to secure.

SCALLOPED EDGE VARIATION

Complete a scalloped edge, making scallops wide enough to accommodate width of fork. Dip fork in flour; press fork tines in center of each scallop, but do not press tines through the pastry.

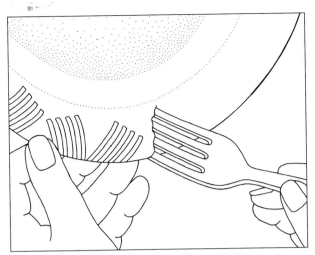

HERRINGBONE EDGE

Trim dough even with edge of pan. Dip fork tines in flour; press fork tines diagonally onto edge of dough. Rotate tines and press next to first set of marks, creating herringbone pattern. Continue around rim.

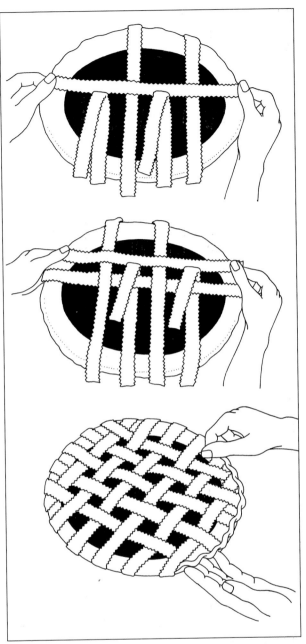

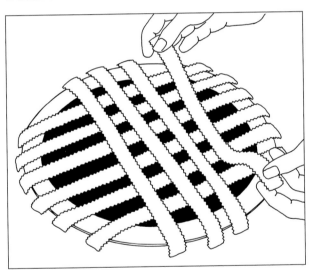

EASY LATTICE

Follow directions for Woven Lattice but do not weave lattice strips. Lay half the strips in 1 direction. Rotate pan 1 quarter turn and lay remaining strips at right angles directly over first strips. Trim ends even with edge of dough. Form a stand-up rim; flute.

WOVEN LATTICE

Prepare crust for 2-crust pie, leaving 1/2 inch of bottom crust extending beyond edge of pan. Cut remaining dough into about 1/2-inch-wide strips (for a decoative edge, use a pastry wheel). Lay part of strips across filling in parallel rows about 3/4 inch apart, twisting if desired. Use longest strips for the center and shortest strips on the sides. Add strips at right angles, lifting every other strip as the cross strips are added to form a woven lattice. Trim ends even with edge of dough. Form a stand-up rim; flute.

PASTRY FOR PIES AND TARTS

ONE-CRUST PIE
   1 cup all purpose flour
   ½ teaspoon salt
   ⅓ cup shortening
   2 to 4 tablespoons ice water

In medium bowl, combine flour and salt. Using pastry blender or fork, cut shortening into flour until mixture resembles coarse crumbs. Sprinkle flour mixture with water 1 tablespoon at a time, while tossing and mixing lightly with fork. Add water until dough is just moist enough to form a ball when lightly pressed together. (Too much water causes dough to become sticky and tough; too little water causes edges to crack and pastry to tear easily while rolling.)

Shape dough into ball. Flatten ball to ½-inch thickness, rounding and smoothing edges. On floured surface, roll lightly from center to edge into 11-inch circle. Fold pastry in half; place in 9-inch pie pan or 9 or 10-inch tart pan. Unfold; gently press in bottom and up sides of pan. Do not stretch.

If using pie pan, fold edge under to form a standing rim; flute edges. If using tart pan, trim pastry edges if necessary.

- **For Filled One-crust Pie**: Fill and bake as directed in recipe.
- **For Baked Pie Shell (Unfilled)**: Prick bottom and sides of pastry generously with fork. Bake at 450°F. for 9 to 12 minutes or until light golden brown; cool. Continue as directed in recipe.

Yield: One-Crust pastry.

TIPS:
See Variations in next column; use half of the ingredient amounts specified.

See p. 273 for food processor directions.

NUTRITION PER SERVING:
Calories 130; Protein 2g; Carbohydrate 12g; Fat 8g; Sodium 130mg.

TWO-CRUST PIE
   2 cups all purpose flour
   1 teaspoon salt
   ⅔ cup shortening
   5 to 7 tablespoons ice water

In medium bowl, combine flour and salt. Using pastry blender or fork, cut shortening into flour until mixture resembles coarse crumbs. Sprinkle flour mixture with water 1 tablespoon at a time, while tossing and mixing lightly with fork. Add water until dough is just moist enough to form a ball when lightly pressed together. (Too much water causes dough to become sticky and tough; too little water causes edges to crack and pastry to tear easily while rolling.)

Shape dough into 2 balls. Flatten 1 ball to ½-inch thickness, rounding and smoothing edges. On lightly floured surface, roll from center to edge into 11-inch circle. Fold pastry in half; place in 9-inch pie pan, or 9 or 10-inch tart pan. Unfold; gently press in bottom and up sides of pan. Do not stretch.

Trim pastry even with pan edge. Roll out remaining pastry; set aside. Continue as directed in recipe.
Yield: Two-crust pastry.

TIP:
See p. 273 for food processor directions.

NUTRITION PER SERVING:
Calories 260; Protein 3g; Carbohydrate 24g; Fat 17g; Sodium 270mg.

VARIATIONS:

CHEESE PASTRY: Add ½ to 1 cup shredded Cheddar or American cheese to flour. Omit salt.

EXTRA FLAKY PASTRY: Add 2 teaspoons sugar with flour and 2 teaspoons vinegar with water.

WHOLE WHEAT PASTRY: Substitute up to 1 cup whole wheat flour for all purpose flour. Additional water may be necessary.

Press-in-the-Pan Oil Pastry

If you have avoided making pies because you do not like to roll out pastry, try this easy recipe.

1¾ **cups all purpose flour**
1 **teaspoon sugar**
1 **teaspoon salt**
½ **cup oil**
¼ **cup milk**

Heat oven to 425°F. In medium bowl, combine flour, sugar and salt. In small bowl, combine oil and milk; pour over flour mixture. Stir with fork until well mixed. Press in bottom and up sides of 9-inch pie pan; flute edge. If desired, crust can be rolled out between 2 sheets of waxed paper. Prick bottom and sides of pastry generously with fork. Bake at 425°F. for 12 to 17 minutes or until light golden brown. Cool completely. Fill with desired filling.

Yield: 9-inch baked pie shell.

MICROWAVE DIRECTIONS:
Prepare pastry as directed above using 9-inch microwave-safe pie pan; flute edge. Prick bottom and sides of pastry generously with fork. Microwave on HIGH for 6 to 8 minutes, rotating pan ½ turn every 2 minutes. Crust is done when surface appears dry and flaky. Cool completely.

NUTRITION PER SERVING:
Calories 230; Protein 3g; Carbohydrate 22g; Fat 14g; Sodium 270mg.

Crumb Pie Crusts

Cookie crumb crusts are easy because there is no rolling of dough.
Fill these crusts with ice cream or creamy pudding fillings.
See the easy directions below.

Kind of Cookie	Amounts of Crumbs	Sugar	Margarine or Butter, Melted
Chocolate Wafer	1¼ cups (20 wafers)	¼ cup	¼ cup
Creme-Filled Choco/Vanilla Cookie	1½ cups (15 cookies)	none	¼ cup
Crisp Macaroon Cookie	1½ cups	none	¼ cup
Gingersnap Cookie	1½ cups	none	¼ cup
Graham Cracker*	1½ cups (24 squares)	¼ cup	⅓ cup
Granola (coarsely crushed)	1½ cups	none	¼ cup
Pretzel**	1¼ cups	¼ cup	½ cup
Vanilla Wafer	1½ cups (30 wafers)	none	¼ cup

Heat oven to 375°F. In medium bowl, combine crumbs, sugar and melted margarine; blend well. Press mixture firmly in bottom and up sides of 8- or 9-inch pie pan or in bottom of 9-inch springform pan. Bake at 375°F. for 8 to 10 minutes. Cool; fill with ice cream or pudding. Freeze or refrigerate.

TIPS:
  * One-half teaspoon cinnamon can be added, if desired.
** For easier serving, butter pan before preparing crust.

STEP 1. After shortening is cut evenly into flour, add ice water 1 tablespoon at a time; toss lightly with a fork until dough forms.

STEP 2. With light strokes, roll pastry into an 11-inch circle. Fold dough in half or quarters; transfer to pan and unfold without stretching.

STEP 3. For two-crust pie, trim bottom pastry even with pan edge; add filling. Cover with top pastry, allowing 1-inch overlap; fold over. Seal and flute.

RASPBERRY CHERRY PIE

Adding another fruit to a can of prepared fruit pie filling makes a filling that is doubly delicious.

CRUST
> **Pastry for Two-Crust Pie p. 268**

FILLING
- 2 **cups fresh or frozen whole raspberries (do not thaw)**
- ¼ **to ½ cup sugar**
- 1 **tablespoon all purpose flour**
- 1 **(21-oz.) can cherry fruit pie filling**

Prepare pastry for Two-Crust Pie using 9-inch pie pan.

Heat oven to 400°F. In large bowl, combine all filling ingredients; stir gently. Spoon into pastry-lined pan. Top with remaining pastry; fold edge of top pastry under bottom pastry.* Press together to seal; flute edge. Cut slits or shapes in several places in top pastry.

Bake at 400°F. for 40 to 45 minutes or until crust is golden brown and filling is bubbly. (Place foil or cookie sheet on lowest oven rack during baking to guard against spills.)
Yield: 8 servings.

TIP:
* If desired, top with lattice crust p. 267.

NUTRITION PER SERVING:
Calories 440; Protein 3g; Carbohydrate 74g; Fat 15g; Sodium 200mg.

COOK'S NOTE

BAKING FRUIT PIES

When baking a fruit pie, a cookie sheet or baking pan can be placed under the pie to catch any juice that might otherwise over-flow onto the bottom of the oven.

Raspberry Cherry Pie

PERFECT APPLE PIE

~

Tart apples, such as Granny Smith and Pippin, make the best pie. This delicious apple pie, a Pillsbury favorite, has stood the test of time.

CRUST
   Pastry for Two-Crust Pie p. 268

FILLING*
   6   **cups thinly sliced peeled apples**
   ¾   **cup sugar**
   2   **tablespoons all purpose flour**
   ¾   **teaspoon cinnamon**
   ¼   **teaspoon salt**
   ⅛   **teaspoon nutmeg**
   1   **tablespoon lemon juice**

Prepare pastry for Two-Crust Pie using 9-inch pie pan.

Heat oven to 425°F. In large bowl, combine all filling ingredients; toss lightly. Spoon into pastry-lined pan. Top with remaining pastry; fold edge of top pastry under bottom pastry. Press together to seal; flute edge. Cut slits or shapes in several places in top pastry.

Bake at 425°F. for 40 to 45 minutes or until apples are tender and crust is golden brown.
Yield: 8 servings.

TIP:
* Two 21-oz. cans apple fruit pie filling can be substituted for filling.

NUTRITION PER SERVING:
Calories 370; Protein 2g; Carbohydrate 57g; Fat 15g; Sodium 270mg.

VARIATIONS:

CARAMEL PECAN APPLE PIE: Immediately after removing pie from oven, drizzle with ⅓ cup caramel ice cream topping. Sprinkle with 2 to 4 tablespoons chopped pecans.

CHEESE CRUST APPLE PIE: Substitute Cheese Pastry p. 268 for Pastry for Two-Crust Pie.

APPLE COBBLESTONE PIE

~

Coconut adds texture to this pie topping.

CRUST
   Pastry for Filled One-Crust Pie p. 268
FILLING
   6   **to 10 medium apples, peeled, quartered**
   ½   **cup sugar**
   3   **tablespoons all purpose flour**
   ½   **teaspoon cinnamon**
   ¼   **teaspoon nutmeg**
   1   **tablespoon lemon juice**

TOPPING
   ⅔   **cup coconut**
   ¼   **cup all purpose flour**
   ¼   **cup sugar**
   2   **tablespoons margarine or butter, softened**

Prepare pastry for Filled One-Crust Pie using 9-inch pie pan.

Heat oven to 375°F. In large bowl, combine all filling ingredients until apples are well coated. Arrange apples, rounded side up, in pastry-lined pan, placing close together to resemble cobblestones. Sprinkle any remaining sugar mixture over apples.

In medium bowl, combine all topping ingredients until crumbly; sprinkle over apples. Bake at 375°F. for 40 to 50 minutes or until apples are tender.
Yield: 8 servings.

TIP:
Large apples can be substituted for medium apples; cut each into 6 pieces.

NUTRITION PER SERVING:
Calories 390; Protein 3g; Carbohydrate 62g; Fat 15g; Sodium 170mg.

COOK'S NOTE

BAKING APPLES

Apple varieties good for baking and cooking have tart flavor and firm texture. For successful results, choose Jonathan, McIntosh, Winesap, Granny Smith, Rhode Island Greening, Rome Beauty or Northern Spy varieties. One pound of apples is equivalent to 3 medium apples and yields 3 cups of sliced apples.

WHOLE WHEAT APPLE MINCEMEAT PIE

Old-time mincemeat included ground meat in the mixture. Modern versions do not contain meat but are combinations of spicy chopped fruit. Prepared mincemeat is available in most large supermarkets.

CRUST
- 1 cup all purpose flour
- 1 cup whole wheat flour
- 2 tablespoons sugar
- ½ teaspoon salt
- ½ cup shortening
- ½ cup cold water

FILLING
- 4 cups sliced peeled apples
- 1⅓ cups prepared mincemeat
- ½ cup sugar
- 2 tablespoons all purpose flour
- ½ teaspoon grated lemon peel
- 1 tablespoon lemon juice

TOPPING
- 1 egg white
- 2 tablespoons water
- 1 to 2 teaspoons sugar

Heat oven to 375°F. In medium bowl, combine 1 cup all purpose flour, whole wheat flour, 2 tablespoons sugar and salt; blend well. Using pastry blender or fork, cut in shortening until mixture resembles coarse crumbs. Sprinkle flour mixture with cold water 1 tablespoon at a time, while tossing and mixing lightly with fork. Add water until dough is just moist enough to form a ball when lightly pressed together.

Shape dough into 2 balls. Flatten balls; smooth edges. Roll 1 ball lightly on floured surface from center to edge into 10 ½-inch circle. Fold dough in half; place in 9-inch pie pan. Unfold; fit evenly in pan. Do not stretch. Trim bottom pastry even with pan edge. Roll out remaining dough; set aside.

In large bowl, combine all filling ingredients; spoon into pastry-lined pan. Top with remaining pastry; fold edge of top pastry under bottom pastry. Flute edge. Cut slits in several places in top pastry. Combine egg white and 2 tablespoons water; brush over top. Sprinkle lightly with 1 to 2 teaspoons sugar.

Bake at 375°F. for 40 to 50 minutes or until apples are tender.
Yield: 8 servings.

NUTRITION PER SERVING:
Calories 430; Protein 5g; Carbohydrate 72g; Fat 14g; Sodium 140mg.

COOK'S NOTE

MIXING PASTRY WITH A FOOD PROCESSOR

If you have a food processor, you can try using it to mix pastry dough. It's easy and reliable and makes a high-quality crust. To mix pastry dough:

- Place the dry ingredients in the food processor and process for 20 seconds.
- Mix all liquid ingredients together. You can place the mixture in the refrigerator or add an ice cube to chill it thoroughly.
- Cut the margarine or butter into small pieces and distribute it evenly over the top of the dry ingredients. Or drop spoonfuls of shortening evenly over the dry ingredients. Process for 15 to 20 seconds or until the mixture looks like coarse crumbs.
- Take the liquid mixture out of the refrigerator or remove the ice cube. Add the liquid in a slow, steady stream to the flour/shortening mixture as the food processor is running. Process until the liquid is just distributed throughout the dough and the dough holds together. Pinch a marble-sized piece of dough between your thumb and index finger. If it doesn't hold together, add more liquid.

EASY APPLE PIE FOLDOVER

Smaller families will enjoy this easy version of apple pie.

FILLING

1½ **cups (2 medium) thinly sliced peeled apples**
¼ **cup firmly packed brown sugar**
 1 **tablespoon water**
 1 **teaspoon lemon juice**
 1 **tablespoon all purpose flour**
 1 **tablespoon sugar**
¼ **teaspoon salt**
½ **teaspoon vanilla**
 1 **tablespoon margarine or butter**

CRUST

Pastry for One-Crust Pie p. 268
 1 **tablespoon water**
 1 **egg**

In medium saucepan, combine apples, brown sugar, 1 tablespoon water and lemon juice. Cook over medium heat until bubbly, stirring occasionally. Reduce heat to low; cover and cook 6 to 8 minutes or until apples are tender, stirring occasionally. In small bowl, combine flour, sugar and salt; stir into apple mixture. Cook until mixture thickens, stirring constantly. Remove from heat; stir in vanilla and margarine. Cool 15 to 20 minutes.

Meanwhile, prepare pastry for One-Crust Pie. Heat oven to 375°F. Place circle of pastry on ungreased cookie sheet. Spoon fruit mixture evenly on half of pastry to within ½ inch of edge. In small bowl, beat 1 tablespoon water and egg; brush over edges of pastry. Fold remaining side of pastry over fruit, turnover fashion; press edges to seal firmly.* Flute edge; cut small slits in top of pastry. Brush surface with egg mixture.

Bake at 375°F. for 25 to 35 minutes or until crust is golden brown.

Yield: 4 servings.

TIP:

* If desired, cut out decorative shapes from remaining side of pastry before folding pastry over fruit. Omit slits.

NUTRITION PER SERVING:
Calories 380; Protein 4g; Carbohydrate 48g; Fat 19g; Sodium 370mg.

TOPSY TURVY APPLE PIE

This fun-to-serve upside-down pie features traditional apple filling baked between two flaky pie crusts and topped with a rich pecan glaze.

GLAZE

¼ **cup firmly packed brown sugar**
 1 **tablespoon margarine or butter, melted**
 1 **tablespoon corn syrup**
¼ **cup pecan halves**

CRUST

Pastry for Two-Crust Pie p. 268

FILLING

⅔ **cup sugar**
 2 **tablespoons all purpose flour**
½ **teaspoon cinnamon**
 4 **cups sliced peeled apples**

GARNISH

Whipped cream or ice cream, if desired

In 9-inch pie pan, combine brown sugar, margarine and corn syrup; mix well. Spread mixture evenly in bottom of pan; arrange pecans over mixture. Prepare pastry for Two-Crust Pie. Place bottom pastry over mixture in pan, gently pressing pastry to fit pan.

Heat oven to 425°F. In small bowl, combine sugar, flour and cinnamon; mix well. Arrange half of apple slices in pastry-lined pan; sprinkle with half of sugar mixture. Repeat with remaining apple slices and sugar mixture. Top with remaining pastry; fold edge of top pastry under bottom pastry. Press together to seal and flute edge. Cut slits in several places in top pastry.

Bake at 425°F. for 8 minutes. Reduce oven temperature to 325°F.; bake an additional 25 to 35 minutes or until apples are tender and crust is golden brown. (Place pan on foil or cookie sheet during last 15 minutes of baking to guard against spills.)

Loosen edge of pie; carefully invert onto serving plate. Serve warm or cold with whipped cream or ice cream.

Yield: 8 servings.

NUTRITION PER SERVING:
Calories 440; Protein 2g; Carbohydrate 59g; Fat 22g; Sodium 350mg.

Topsy Turvy Apple Pie

Maple Frosted Apple Pan-Tart

You don't even need a pie pan to bake this new version of apple pie. It's quickly shaped, then baked on a cookie sheet.

CRUST
    Pastry for Two-Crust Pie p. 268

FILLING
1½ cups cornflakes cereal
6 cups thinly sliced, peeled apples
1 cup sugar
1 teaspoon cinnamon
1 egg white, beaten

GLAZE
½ cup powdered sugar
3 tablespoons maple-flavored syrup

Prepare pastry for Two-Crust Pie.

Heat oven to 350°F. Place 1 circle of pastry on ungreased cookie sheet. Sprinkle cornflakes over pastry to within ½ inch of edge. Top with apples; sprinkle with sugar and cinnamon. Brush edge of pastry with egg white. Place remaining circle of pastry over filling. Fold edge of bottom pastry over top pastry; pinch and flute edges to seal. Cut several slits in top pastry; brush with beaten egg white.

Bake at 350°F. for 45 to 55 minutes or until apples are tender and crust is golden brown.

In small bowl, combine glaze ingredients. Drizzle over warm crust. To serve, cut into wedges. Serve warm or cool.

Yield: 8 servings.

NUTRITION PER SERVING:
Calories 460; Protein 2g; Carbohydrate 76g; Fat 16g; Sodium 380mg.

Apple Raspberry Streusel Pie

Enjoy this pie warm from the oven with a scoop of ice cream.

CRUST
    Pastry for Filled One-Crust Pie p. 268

FILLING
1 tablespoon lemon juice
5 cups sliced, peeled apples
¼ cup sugar
2 tablespoons cornstarch
½ teaspoon cinnamon
1 (10-oz.) pkg. frozen raspberries in syrup, thawed, drained, reserving ½ cup liquid

TOPPING
¾ cup all purpose flour
½ cup firmly packed brown sugar
½ teaspoon cinnamon
⅓ cup margarine or butter, softened

Prepare pastry for Filled One-Crust Pie using 9-inch pie pan. Heat oven to 375°F. In medium bowl, sprinkle lemon juice over sliced apples; toss. Set aside.

In large saucepan, combine sugar, cornstarch and ½ teaspoon cinnamon. Stir in raspberry liquid. Cook over medium heat until mixture thickens, stirring constantly. Remove from heat; fold in drained raspberries and apples. Pour mixture into pastry-lined pan.

In medium bowl, combine all topping ingredients until crumbly; sprinkle over fruit mixture.

Bake at 375°F. for 40 to 50 minutes or until apples are tender and crust is golden brown.

Yield: 8 servings.

NUTRITION PER SERVING:
Calories 390; Protein 3g; Carbohydrate 62g; Fat 15g; Sodium 190mg.

CRANBERRY APPLE PIE

~

For a special dessert, serve this tart and tangy pie with cinnamon ice cream.

CRUST
> **Pastry for Two-Crust Pie p. 268**

FILLING
- 4 cups sliced peeled tart apples
- 2 cups fresh or frozen cranberries
- 1 cup sugar
- 2 tablespoons cornstarch
- 2 tablespoons margarine or butter

Prepare pastry for Two-Crust Pie using 9-inch pie pan.

Heat oven to 425°F. In large bowl, combine apples and cranberries. In small bowl, combine sugar and cornstarch. Sprinkle sugar mixture over fruit; toss lightly. Spoon into pastry-lined pan. Dot with margarine. Top with remaining pastry; fold edge of top pastry under bottom pastry. Press together to seal; flute edge. Cut slits in several places in top pastry.

Bake at 425°F. for 35 to 45 minutes or until apples are tender and crust is golden brown.

Yield: 8 servings.

NUTRITION PER SERVING:
Calories 420; Protein 2g; Carbohydrate 62g; Fat 18g; Sodium 240mg.

COOK'S NOTE

~

CRANBERRIES

These shiny scarlet berries grow in huge, sandy bogs on low trailing vines. They are cultivated primarily in Massachusetts, Wisconsin, Washington and Oregon. Cranberries also grow wild in northern Europe and in northern regions of North America. Cranberries are harvested between Labor Day and Halloween, so the peak market time is from October through December. When buying fresh cranberries, select plump, firm berries that are bright in color and free of discolorations or punctures. They can be refrigerated, tightly wrapped, for 2 months or frozen for up to a year. Cranberries are a good source of vitamin C.

FROSTED CRANBERRY CHERRY PIE

~

A glazed topping and two favorite crimson berries make this pretty pie unique and delicious.

CRUST
> **Pastry for Two-Crust Pie p. 268**

FILLING
- 1 (21-oz.) can cherry fruit pie filling
- 1 (16-oz.) can whole berry cranberry sauce
- 3 tablespoons cornstarch
- ¼ teaspoon cinnamon

GLAZE
- ½ cup powdered sugar
- 1 tablespoon light corn syrup
- 3 to 4 teaspoons water
- ¼ cup almond slices

Prepare pastry for Two-Crust Pie using 9-inch pie pan.

Heat oven to 400°F. In large bowl, combine all filling ingredients. Spoon into pastry-lined pan. Top with remaining pastry; fold edge of top pastry under bottom pastry. Press together to seal; flute edge. Cut slits in several places in top pastry. Bake at 400°F. for 40 to 50 minutes or until crust is golden brown.

Remove pie from oven. Immediately combine powdered sugar, corn syrup and enough water for drizzling consistency. Drizzle over hot pie; decorate or sprinkle with almonds. Cool at least 1 hour before serving.

Yield: 8 servings.

NUTRITION PER SERVING:
Calories 540; Protein 3g; Carbohydrate 91g; Fat 18g; Sodium 350mg.

CHERRY PIE

This versatile recipe gives you the option of using canned tart cherries, fresh tart cherries or cherry fruit pie filling.

CRUST
>   Pastry for Two-Crust Pie p. 268

FILLING*
>   2 (16-oz.) cans pitted red tart cherries, drained**
> 1¼ cups sugar
>   ¼ cup all purpose flour
>   2 tablespoons margarine or butter

Prepare pastry for Two-Crust Pie using 9-inch pie pan.

Heat oven to 425°F. In large bowl, combine cherries, sugar and flour; toss lightly to mix. Spoon into pastry-lined pan. Dot with margarine. Top with remaining pastry.*** Fold edge of top pastry under bottom pastry. Press together to seal; flute edge. Cut slits in several places in top pastry.

Bake at 425°F. for 35 to 45 minutes or until juice begins to bubble through slits in crust.
Yield: 8 servings.

TIPS:
* Two 21-oz. cans cherry fruit pie filling can be substituted for filling.
** Four cups pitted fresh red tart cherries can be substituted for canned cherries. If desired, sprinkle cherries with ¼ teaspoon almond extract before dotting with margarine.
*** If desired, top with lattice crust p. 267; brush with beaten egg white and sprinkle with sugar.

NUTRITION PER SERVING:
Calories 470; Protein 5g; Carbohydrate 68g; Fat 20g; Sodium 310mg.

FRESH RASPBERRY LATTICE PIE

*For an elegant presentation, garnish this lattice-topped pie with **Chocolate Leaves** p. 211.*

FILLING
> 4½ cups raspberries*
> 1¼ cups sugar
>   5 tablespoons cornstarch
>   Dash salt
>   1 tablespoon margarine or butter

CRUST
>   Pastry for Two-Crust Pie p. 268

GARNISH
>   Powdered sugar
>   Chocolate Leaves p. 211, if desired

In medium saucepan, combine raspberries, sugar, cornstarch and salt. Cook over medium heat, stirring constantly until mixture boils and thickens, about 15 minutes. Refrigerate for 1 hour or until mixture comes to room temperature.

Prepare pastry for Two-Crust Pie using 9-inch pie pan. Heat oven to 425°F. Pour filling into pastry-lined pan; dot with margarine.

To make lattice top, cut remaining pastry into ½-inch-wide strips. Arrange strips in lattice design over filling as shown on p. 267. Trim edges and flute. With any remaining pastry, form small pea-sized balls and place over the crossings in lattice pattern.

Bake at 425°F. for 35 to 45 minutes or until golden brown. Sprinkle with powdered sugar before serving. Garnish with Chocolate Leaves.
Yield: 6 to 8 servings.

TIP:
* Frozen whole raspberries, thawed and well drained, can be substituted for fresh raspberries.

NUTRITION PER SERVING:
Calories 480; Protein 2g; Carbohydrate 72g; Fat 20g; Sodium 360mg.

FRESH BLUEBERRY PIE

Fresh blueberries make this succulent fruit pie extra special.

CRUST
Pastry for Two-Crust Pie p. 268

FILLING
- 4 cups fresh or frozen blueberries, thawed, well drained
- ¾ cup sugar
- ¼ cup all purpose flour
- ¼ teaspoon cinnamon
- 2 teaspoons lemon juice
- 2 tablespoons margarine or butter

TOPPING
- Milk
- Sugar
- Cinnamon
- Cinnamon ice cream, if desired

Prepare pastry for Two-Crust Pie using 9-inch pie pan.

Heat oven to 425°F. In large bowl, combine blueberries, ¾ cup sugar, flour, ¼ teaspoon cinnamon and lemon juice; mix lightly. Spoon into pastry-lined pan. Dot with margarine. Top with remaining pastry; fold edge of top pastry under bottom pastry. Press together to seal; flute edge. Cut slits in several places in top pastry. Brush pastry with milk; sprinkle with sugar and cinnamon.

Bake at 425°F. for 45 to 55 minutes or until golden brown. Serve warm or cool with cinnamon ice cream.

Yield: 6 to 8 servings.

NUTRITION PER SERVING:
Calories 460; Protein 3g; Carbohydrate 63g; Fat 22g; Sodium 390mg.

CRUNCHY CRUST BLUEBERRY SWIRL PIE

This delicious Pillsbury BAKE-OFF® Contest recipe features a press-in-the-pan pie crust of nuts and rolled oats with a blueberry-lemon filling that is swirled with sour cream.

CRUST
- ¾ cup all purpose flour
- ½ cup rolled oats
- ½ cup chopped nuts
- 2 tablespoons sugar
- ½ cup margarine or butter, melted

FILLING
- 1 (3-oz.) pkg. lemon flavor gelatin
- ½ cup boiling water
- 1 (21-oz.) can blueberry fruit pie filling
- ½ cup dairy sour cream

Heat oven to 400°F. Grease 9-inch pie pan. In medium bowl, combine flour, rolled oats, nuts and sugar. Add melted margarine; mix well. Press mixture evenly in bottom and up to top edge of greased 9-inch pie pan.

Bake at 400°F. for 11 to 14 minutes or until golden brown. Cool.

In medium bowl, dissolve gelatin in boiling water; stir in pie filling. Refrigerate until thickened. Pour into cooled, baked crust. Spoon sour cream by teaspoonfuls onto filling. With spatula, swirl sour cream into filling. Refrigerate until serving time. If desired, top with whipped cream. Store in refrigerator.

Yield: 8 servings.

NUTRITION PER SERVING:
Calories 390; Protein 5g; Carbohydrate 50g; Fat 21g; Sodium 180mg.

FRESH STRAWBERRY PIE

Use the recipe and variations below to make wonderful fresh fruit pies when your favorite fruit is at its peak.

CRUST
Pastry for One-Crust Pie p. 268

FILLING
3 pints (6 cups) strawberries
1 cup sugar
3 tablespoons cornstarch
½ cup water
4 to 5 drops red food color, if desired

TOPPING
Whipped cream

Prepare and bake pastry as directed for Baked Pie Shell using 9-inch pie pan.

In small bowl, crush enough strawberries to make 1 cup. In medium saucepan, combine sugar and cornstarch. Add crushed strawberries and water. Cook until mixture boils and thickens, stirring constantly; stir in food color. Cool.

Spoon remaining whole or sliced strawberries into cooled, baked pie shell; pour cooked strawberry mixture over top. Refrigerate 3 hours or until set. To serve, top with whipped cream. Store in refrigerator.
Yield: 6 to 8 servings.

NUTRITION PER SERVING:
Calories 300; Protein 2g; Carbohydrate 47g; Fat 12g; Sodium 139mg.

VARIATIONS:

FRESH PEACH PIE: Substitute sliced peaches for strawberries. Omit red food color.

FRESH RASPBERRY PIE: Substitute raspberries for strawberries.

FRESH STRAWBERRY RHUBARB PIE

You'll enjoy this version of a midwestern favorite. It's wonderful served with whipped cream or vanilla ice cream.

CRUST
Pastry for Two-Crust Pie p. 268

FILLING
1 pint (2 cups) strawberries
3 cups chopped rhubarb*
1 cup sugar
¼ cup cornstarch

Prepare pastry for Two-Crust Pie using 9-inch pie pan.

Heat oven to 400°F. In large bowl, combine all filling ingredients; mix lightly. Spoon into pastry-lined pan; top with remaining pastry. Fold edge of top pastry under bottom pastry. Press together to seal; flute edge. Cut slits in several places in top pastry.

Bake at 400°F. for 45 to 60 minutes or until golden brown. (Place pan on foil or cookie sheet during last 15 minutes of baking to guard against spills.) If desired, serve with whipped cream and additional strawberries.
Yield: 8 servings.

TIP:
* One 16-oz. pkg. frozen sliced rhubarb, thawed and well drained, can be substituted for fresh rhubarb.

NUTRITION PER SERVING:
Calories 380; Protein 2g; Carbohydrate 57g; Fat 16g; Sodium 330mg.

COOK'S NOTE

RHUBARB

There are two types of rhubarb: outdoor (garden) and indoor (hothouse). Outdoor rhubarb becomes available in spring and lasts until fall. Hothouse rhubarb is available January through June. When buying rhubarb, look for crisp, plump, medium-sized stalks. The stalks will vary in color from green tinged with pink to pink or red. If there are any leaves, they should be fresh looking, not wilted or damaged.

OLD-FASHIONED
PINEAPPLE RHUBARB PIE

Fresh rhubarb can be stored, unwashed, in the crisper section of the refrigerator for up to a week. Wash it just before using.

CRUST
   Pastry for Filled One-Crust Pie p. 268

FILLING
   3 **cups chopped fresh rhubarb or 16-oz. pkg. frozen sliced rhubarb**
   ¾ **cup sugar**
   ¼ **cup all purpose flour**
   1 **(8 ¼-oz.) can crushed pineapple, drained**

TOPPING
   ½ **cup all purpose flour**
   ½ **cup sugar**
   ¼ **cup margarine or butter**

Prepare pastry for Filled One-Crust Pie using 9-inch pie pan.

Heat oven to 425°F. In large bowl, combine all filling ingredients; toss to combine. Spoon into pastry-lined pan. In small bowl, combine all topping ingredients until crumbly; sprinkle over fruit mixture.

Bake at 425°F. for 15 minutes. Reduce oven temperature to 400°F.; bake an additional 25 minutes or until filling is hot and bubbly.

Yield: 8 servings.

NUTRITION PER SERVING:
Calories 350; Protein 3g; Carbohydrate 57g; Fat 13g; Sodium 170mg.

FIRESIDE FRUIT
PIE

A beautiful medley of apricots, apples and dates.

CRUST
   Pastry for Two-Crust Pie p. 268

FILLING
   1 **(17-oz.) can apricot halves, drained, reserving liquid**
   ½ **cup sugar**
   2 **tablespoons cornstarch**
   3 **cups chopped peeled tart apples**
   1 **cup chopped dates**
   1 **tablespoon lemon juice**

Prepare pastry for Two-Crust Pie using 9-inch pie pan.

Heat oven to 425°F. In large saucepan, combine reserved apricot liquid, sugar, cornstarch, apples, dates and lemon juice. Cover; cook gently until apples are soft, stirring occasionally. Remove from heat; fold in apricot halves. Spoon into pastry-lined pan.

To make decorative top crust, use canape cutter (about 1 inch) to cut out center of dough. Repeat cutouts in an evenly spaced pattern, working from center to within 1½ inches of edge. Arrange pastry over filling; fold edge of top pastry under bottom pastry. Press together to seal; flute edge.

Bake at 425°F. for 25 to 35 minutes or until crust is golden brown and filling bubbles.

Yield: 8 servings.

NUTRITION PER SERVING:
Calories 450; Protein 2g; Carbohydrate 74g; Fat 16g; Sodium 330mg.

COOK'S NOTE

MAKING A FOIL COVER FOR A PIE CRUST EDGE

- Using 12-inch-wide foil, cut a piece 4 inches longer than the diameter of the pie pan.
- Cut a circle from the center of the foil that is 2 inches smaller than the diameter of the pie pan.

- Center the foil over the partially baked pie after about 15 to 20 minutes of baking and gently fold it around the fluted edge.
- Another idea for making a foil cover is to cut a 7-inch-diameter circle from the center of a 12-inch disposable foil pizza pan. It can be reused over and over again!

STREUSEL-TOP PEACH PIE

Fresh peaches grown in the United States are available from May through October.

CRUST
> **Pastry for Filled One-Crust Pie p. 268**

FILLING
- 4 **cups sliced peeled peaches***
- ½ **cup powdered sugar**
- ⅓ **cup all purpose flour**
- ½ **teaspoon cinnamon**

TOPPING
- ¾ **cup all purpose flour**
- ½ **cup firmly packed brown sugar**
- ½ **teaspoon cinnamon**
- ⅓ **cup margarine or butter**

Prepare pastry for Filled One-Crust Pie using 9-inch pie pan.

Heat oven to 375°F. In large bowl, combine all filling ingredients; toss gently. Spoon into pastry-lined pan. In medium bowl, combine all topping ingredients until crumbly; sprinkle over filling.

Bake at 375°F. for 40 to 45 minutes or until peaches are tender and topping is golden brown. **Yield: 8 servings.**

TIP:
* Two 29-oz. cans peach slices, well drained, or 4 cups frozen sliced peaches, thawed and well drained, can be substituted for the fresh peaches.

NUTRITION PER SERVING:
Calories 370; Protein 3g; Carbohydrate 53g; Fat 15g; Sodium 190mg.

VARIATIONS:

STREUSEL-TOP APRICOT PIE: Substitute 4 cups fresh apricot halves or 2 (29-oz.) cans apricot halves, well drained, for the peaches.

STREUSEL-TOP BLUEBERRY PIE: Substitute 4 cups fresh or unsweetened frozen blueberries, partially thawed and drained, for the peaches. Well drained, canned blueberries can also be used.

STREUSEL-TOP PEACH BLUEBERRY PIE:
Substitute 1 cup blueberries for 1 cup of the peaches.

STREUSEL-TOP PEACH RASPBERRY PIE:
Substitute 1 cup raspberries for 1 cup of the peaches.

GEORGIA PEACH 'N PECAN PIE

Native Georgian pecans paired with homegrown peaches make this pie a matchless creation.

CRUST
> **Pastry for Filled One-Crust Pie p. 268**

FILLING
- ¼ **cup sugar**
- 3 **tablespoons all purpose flour**
- ¼ **teaspoon nutmeg**
  Dash salt
- ½ **cup light corn syrup**
- 3 **eggs**
- 3 **cups cubed peeled peaches***
- ¼ **cup margarine or butter, melted**

TOPPING
- ½ **cup coarsely chopped pecans**
- ¼ **cup all purpose flour**
- ¼ **cup firmly packed brown sugar**
- 2 **tablespoons margarine or butter, softened**

Prepare pastry for Filled One-Crust Pie using 9-inch pie pan.

Heat oven to 400°F. In large bowl, combine sugar, 3 tablespoons flour, nutmeg, salt, corn syrup and eggs; beat at medium speed 1 minute. Stir in peaches and ¼ cup margarine. Spoon into pastry-lined pan.

In small bowl, combine all topping ingredients; mix well. Sprinkle over peach filling.

Bake at 400°F. for 35 to 45 minutes or until center is set. Serve warm or cool with whipped cream, if desired.
Yield: 8 servings.

TIP:
* One 29-oz. can peach slices, well drained and cubed, can be substituted for the fresh peaches.

NUTRITION PER SERVING:
Calories 450; Protein 5g; Carbohydrate 53g; Fat 24g; Sodium 325mg.

Georgia Peach 'n Pecan Pie,
Streusel-Top Peach Blueberry Pie

CHOCOLATE SILK PECAN PIE

Sink your teeth into a chocolate layer that's as smooth as silk, followed by a sweetened, crunchy pecan layer.

CRUST
  Pastry for Filled One-Crust Pie p. 268

PECAN FILLING
  ⅓ **cup sugar**
  ½ **cup dark corn syrup**
  3 **tablespoons margarine or butter, melted**
  ⅛ **teaspoon salt, if desired**
  2 **eggs**
  ½ **cup chopped pecans**

CHOCOLATE FILLING
  1 **cup hot milk**
  ¼ **teaspoon vanilla**
  1⅓ **cups semi-sweet chocolate chips**

TOPPING
  1 **cup whipping cream**
  2 **tablespoons powdered sugar**
  ¼ **teaspoon vanilla**
  Chocolate Curls, if desired, p. 210

Prepare pastry for Filled One-Crust Pie using 9-inch pie pan.

Heat oven to 350°F. In small bowl, combine sugar, corn syrup, margarine, salt and eggs; beat 1 minute at medium speed. Stir in pecans. Pour into pastry-lined pan.

Bake at 350°F. for 40 to 55 minutes or until center of pie is puffed and golden brown. Cool 1 hour.

While filled crust is cooling, combine all chocolate filling ingredients in blender container or food processor bowl with metal blade; blend 1 minute or until smooth. Refrigerate about 1½ hours or until mixture is slightly thickened but not set. Gently stir; pour into cooled, filled crust. Refrigerate until firm, about 1 hour.

In small bowl, beat whipping cream, powdered sugar and ¼ teaspoon vanilla until stiff peaks form. Spoon or pipe over filling. Garnish with Chocolate Curls. Store in refrigerator.
Yield: 8 to 10 servings.

NUTRITION PER SERVING:
Calories 490; Protein 5g; Carbohydrate 46g; Fat 32g; Sodium 240mg.

CHOCOLATE PECAN PIE

This rich chocolate version of pecan pie is topped with whipped cream and chocolate-dipped nuts.

CRUST
  Pastry for Filled One-Crust Pie p. 268

FILLING
  1 **cup light corn syrup**
  ½ **cup sugar**
  ¼ **cup margarine or butter, melted**
  1 **teaspoon vanilla**
  3 **eggs**
  1 **(6-oz.) pkg. (1 cup) semi-sweet chocolate chips**
  1½ **cups pecan halves**

TOPPING
  2 **tablespoons reserved semi-sweet chocolate chips**
  10 **pecan halves**
  Whipped cream

Prepare pastry for Filled One-Crust Pie using 9-inch pie pan.

Heat oven to 325°F. In large bowl, combine corn syrup, sugar, margarine, vanilla and eggs; beat well. Reserve 2 tablespoons chocolate chips for topping. Stir in remaining chocolate chips and 1½ cups pecans. Spread evenly in pastry-lined pan.

Bake at 325°F. for 55 to 65 minutes or until deep golden brown and filling is set. Cool completely.

Line cookie sheet with waxed paper. Melt 2 tablespoons reserved chocolate chips in small saucepan over low heat. Dip each of 10 pecan halves into chocolate. Place on paper-lined cookie sheet. Refrigerate 15 to 20 minutes or until chocolate is set.

Garnish pie with whipped cream and chocolate-dipped nuts. Store in refrigerator.
Yield: 10 servings.

NUTRITION PER SERVING:
Calories 570; Protein 5g; Carbohydrate 60g; Fat 34g; Sodium 180mg.

Chocolate Pecan Pie

TEXAS OSGOOD PECAN PIE

A thin, crisp meringue forms during the baking of this rich pecan pie, a traditional pie in Texas.

CRUST
Pastry for Filled One-Crust Pie p. 268

FILLING
- 1 cup sugar
- ½ cup margarine or butter, softened
- ¼ teaspoon cinnamon
- ¼ teaspoon cloves
- 1 teaspoon vinegar
- 1 teaspoon vanilla
- 4 eggs, separated
- 1 cup chopped pecans
- 1 cup raisins or chopped dates

TOPPING
- ¾ cup whipping cream, whipped

Prepare pastry for Filled One-Crust Pie using 9-inch pie pan.

Heat oven to 325°F. In large bowl, beat sugar and margarine at medium speed until light and fluffy. Add cinnamon, cloves, vinegar, vanilla and egg yolks; blend well. Stir in pecans and raisins.

In small bowl, beat egg whites until stiff peaks form; fold into pecan-raisin mixture. Spoon into pastry-lined pan.

Bake at 325°F. for 35 to 45 minutes or until golden brown and center is set. Cool. Serve with whipped cream.
Yield: 8 servings.

NUTRITION PER SERVING:
Calories 580; Protein 6g; Carbohydrate 56g; Fat 39g; Sodium 270mg.

GOLDEN PECAN PIE

Even the most ardent calorie watchers find it hard to resist the sweet seduction of pecan pie.

CRUST
Pastry for Filled One-Crust Pie p. 268

FILLING
- ⅓ cup firmly packed brown sugar
- 1½ teaspoons all purpose flour
- 1¼ cups light corn syrup
- 1¼ teaspoons vanilla
- 3 eggs
- 1½ cups pecan halves or broken pecans
- 2 tablespoons margarine or butter, melted

Prepare pastry for Filled One-Crust Pie using 9-inch pie pan.

Heat oven to 375°F. In large bowl, combine brown sugar, flour, corn syrup, vanilla and eggs; beat well. Stir in pecans and margarine. Pour into pastry-lined pan.

Bake at 375°F. for 40 to 50 minutes or until center of pie is puffed and golden brown. Cool.
Yield: 8 servings.

NUTRITION PER SERVING:
Calories 490; Protein 5g; Carbohydrate 64g; Fat 25g; Sodium 190mg.

VARIATION:

ORANGE PECAN PIE: Add ½ teaspoon grated orange peel to filling. Garnish with candied orange peel, if desired.

COOKS NOTE

CANDIED ORANGE PEEL

To prepare candied orange peel, use a vegetable peeler to remove the colored outer peel of 2 oranges. Cut the peel into thin strips. In small saucepan, combine ¾ cup sugar, ½ cup water and orange peel. Bring to a boil; reduce heat, cover and simmer for 15 minutes. Drain. Spread orange peel on waxed paper; cool 10 minutes. Roll pieces of peel in 3 tablespoons of sugar until well coated. Let dry overnight. Store in an airtight container in the refrigerator up to 3 months. Use the peel as a garnish for desserts.

FUDGY BROWNIE PIE

You'll love this brownie in a crust! It has an indulgent whipped cream topping that's irresistible.

CRUST
Pastry for Filled One-Crust Pie p. 268

FILLING
- ½ **cup sugar**
- ⅓ **cup unsweetened cocoa**
- ½ **cup light corn syrup**
- 1 **teaspoon vanilla**
- 3 **eggs**
- ¾ **cup chopped nuts**
- ¼ **cup margarine or butter, melted**

TOPPING
- 1 **cup whipping cream**
- 2 **tablespoons powdered sugar**
- 1½ **teaspoons orange extract**
- 2 **tablespoons orange marmalade**
- 1 **to 2 teaspoons orange juice or water**

Prepare pastry for Filled One-Crust Pie using 9-inch pie pan.

Heat oven to 350°F. In large bowl, combine sugar and cocoa. Add corn syrup, vanilla and eggs; beat well using wire whisk or rotary beater. Stir in nuts and margarine. Pour into pastry-lined pan. Bake at 350°F. for 30 to 40 minutes or until center is set. Cool completely.

In small bowl, beat whipping cream until soft peaks form. Add powdered sugar and orange extract; beat until stiff peaks form. Spread or pipe over cooled filling. In small bowl, combine orange marmalade and enough orange juice for drizzling consistency. Drizzle marmalade mixture over whipped cream. Refrigerate at least 30 minutes before serving. Store in refrigerator.
Yield: 8 servings.

NUTRITION PER SERVING:
Calories 540; Protein 6g; Carbohydrate 50g; Fat 35g; Sodium 280mg.

SWEET CHOCOLATE PIE

A wire whisk works well to mix ingredients in this recipe.

CRUST
Pastry for Filled One-Crust Pie p. 268

FILLING
- 1 **cup sugar**
- ⅓ **cup margarine or butter**
- 4 **oz. sweet baking chocolate, chopped**
- ½ **cup evaporated milk or half-and-half**
- 1 **teaspoon vanilla**
- 4 **eggs**
- 1 **cup coconut**
- ½ **cup chopped pecans or walnuts**

TOPPING
Whipped cream, if desired

Prepare pastry for Filled One-Crust Pie using 9-inch pie pan.

Heat oven to 350°F. In medium saucepan, combine sugar, margarine and chocolate. Cook over low heat, stirring constantly until smooth. Remove from heat; cool 5 minutes. Add evaporated milk, vanilla and eggs; beat until well blended. Sprinkle coconut and pecans in bottom of pastry-lined pan; slowly pour chocolate mixture over coconut and pecans.

Bake at 350°F. for 35 to 45 minutes or until center is set. Cool completely. Serve with whipped cream.
Yield: 8 to 10 servings.

NUTRITION PER SERVING:
Calories 450; Protein 5g; Carbohydrate 42g; Fat 29g; Sodium 250mg.

PEANUT BUTTER LOVERS' PIE

Use either chunky or creamy peanut butter for the baked filling. The pie is sumptuous when topped with hot fudge sauce and a sprinkling of chopped peanuts.

CRUST
   Pastry for Filled One-Crust Pie p. 268

FILLING
   2 **eggs, separated, at room temperature**
   ½ **cup firmly packed brown sugar**
   ¾ **cup peanut butter**
   ¼ **cup dark corn syrup**
   1 **(5-oz.) can (⅔ cup) evaporated milk or milk**
   1 **teaspoon vanilla**

Prepare pastry for Filled One-Crust Pie using 9-inch pie pan.

Heat oven to 350°F. In small bowl, beat egg whites until stiff peaks form. In large bowl, beat egg yolks and brown sugar until mixture is light in color and thickened. Blend in peanut butter and corn syrup. Gradually beat in milk and vanilla. Fold egg whites into peanut butter mixture. Pour into pastry-lined pan.

Bake at 350°F. for 30 to 35 minutes or until filling is set. Serve warm or at room temperature. Store in refrigerator.

Yield: 8 to 10 servings.

NUTRITION PER SERVING:
Calories 320; Protein 9g; Carbohydrate 31g; Fat 18g; Sodium 240mg.

APRICOT DELIGHT PIE

Apricot flavor wonderfully complements this simple custard. Other fresh or canned fruits could be easily substituted.

CRUST
   Pastry for Filled One-Crust Pie p. 268

FILLING
   1 **(14-oz.) can sweetened condensed milk (not evaporated)**
   ½ **cup dairy sour cream**
   1 **egg**
   1 **(17-oz.) can apricot halves, well drained**
   ¼ **cup apricot preserves, melted**

Prepare pastry for Filled One-Crust Pie using 9-inch pie pan.

Heat oven to 375°F. In small bowl, combine sweetened condensed milk, sour cream and egg; mix well. Pour into pastry-lined pan.

Bake at 375°F. for 25 to 35 minutes or until just set. Cool 10 minutes.

Arrange well-drained apricot halves over cooled filling. Brush with apricot preserves. Refrigerate until serving time. Store in refrigerator.

Yield: 8 servings.

MICROWAVE DIRECTIONS:
Prepare pastry for One-Crust Pie using 9-inch microwave-safe pie pan. Prick crust generously with fork. Microwave on HIGH for 6 to 8 minutes, rotating pan ½ turn every 2 minutes. Crust is done when surface appears dry and flaky. In 4-cup microwave-safe measuring cup, combine sweetened condensed milk, sour cream and egg; mix well. Microwave on HIGH for 2½ to 3 minutes, stirring with wire whisk once during cooking. Cook until mixture starts to thicken. Pour into cooked crust. Microwave on MEDIUM for 3 to 4 minutes or until just set in center. Cool 10 minutes. Continue as directed above.

NUTRITION PER SERVING:
Calories 370; Protein 7g; Carbohydrate 50g; Fat 17g; Sodium 220mg.

Peanut Butter Lovers' Pie

Praline Creme Pumpkin Pie

Praline and creamy orange-flavored layers top this sensational pumpkin pie.

CRUST
>   **Pastry for Filled One-Crust Pie p. 268**

FILLING
>   ½ **cup sugar**
>   1½ **teaspoons pumpkin pie spice**
>   ¼ **teaspoon salt**
>   1 **(16-oz.) can (2 cups) pumpkin**
>   1 **(12-oz.) can (1½ cups) evaporated milk**
>   2 **eggs, slightly beaten**

PRALINE LAYER
>   ¼ **cup firmly packed brown sugar**
>   2 **tablespoons all purpose flour**
>   ¼ **cup margarine or butter**
>   ½ **cup chopped pecans**

TOPPING
>   1 **(3-oz.) pkg. cream cheese, softened**
>   2 **teaspoons milk**
>   1 **teaspoon grated orange peel**
>   1 **(8-oz.) container (3½ cups) frozen whipped topping, thawed**

Prepare pastry for Filled One-Crust Pie using 9-inch pie pan.

Heat oven to 425°F. In large bowl, combine all filling ingredients; beat until well blended. Pour into pastry-lined pan. Bake at 425°F. for 15 minutes.

Meanwhile, in small bowl combine brown sugar and flour. Using pastry blender or fork, cut in margarine until mixture resembles coarse crumbs. Stir in pecans. Sprinkle pecan mixture over pumpkin filling. Reduce oven temperature to 350°F.; bake an additional 30 to 35 minutes or until knife inserted near center comes out clean. Cool completely.

In small bowl, combine cream cheese, milk and orange peel; mix until smooth. Gently fold whipped topping into cream cheese mixture. Spoon over cooled pie. Refrigerate until serving time. Store in refrigerator.
Yield: 10 to 12 servings.

NUTRITION PER SERVING:
Calories 340; Protein 6g; Carbohydrate 34g; Fat 21g; Sodium 270mg.

Old-Fashioned Pumpkin Pie

For lovers of this traditional Thanksgiving dessert, all the familiar flavors and smooth creamy texture are here.

CRUST
>   **Pastry for Filled One-Crust Pie p. 268**

FILLING
>   ¾ **cup sugar**
>   1½ **teaspoons pumpkin pie spice**
>   ½ **teaspoon salt**
>   1 **(16-oz.) can (2 cups) pumpkin**
>   1 **(12-oz.) can (1½ cups) evaporated milk**
>   2 **eggs, beaten**

TOPPING
>   ½ **cup whipping cream, whipped**

Prepare pastry for Filled One-Crust Pie using 9-inch pie pan.

Heat oven to 425°F. In large bowl, combine all filling ingredients; blend well. Pour into pastry-lined pan. Bake at 425°F. for 15 minutes. Reduce oven temperature to 350°F.; bake an additional 40 to 50 minutes or until knife inserted near center comes out clean. Cool; refrigerate until serving time. Serve with whipped cream. Store in refrigerator.
Yield: 8 servings.

NUTRITION PER SERVING:
Calories 320; Protein 7g; Carbohydrate 42g; Fat 14g; Sodium 310mg.

VARIATION:

MAPLE PUMPKIN PIE: Substitute ½ cup maple-flavored syrup for ½ cup of the evaporated milk.

Cook's Note

PUMPKIN PIE SPICE

To make pumpkin pie spice, combine 4 teaspoons cinnamon, 1 teaspoon ginger, ½ teaspoon allspice, ½ teaspoon nutmeg and ½ teaspoon cloves. Store in a tightly sealed container in a cool, dark place.

Old-Fashioned Pumpkin Pie

HONEY PUMPKIN PIE

You'll enjoy the honey flavor in this classic holiday pie.

CRUST
Pastry for Filled One-Crust Pie p. 268

FILLING
- 1 (16-oz.) can (2 cups) pumpkin
- ¾ cup honey
- ½ teaspoon salt
- 1¼ teaspoons cinnamon
- ½ teaspoon ginger
- ¼ teaspoon cloves
- ¼ teaspoon nutmeg
- 3 eggs, slightly beaten
- 1 (12-oz.) can (1½ cups) evaporated milk

Prepare pastry for Filled One-Crust Pie using 9-inch pie pan.

Heat oven to 425°F. In large bowl, combine pumpkin, honey, salt, cinnamon, ginger, cloves and nutmeg; mix well. Add eggs; blend well. Gradually add milk, beating at low speed until well blended. Pour into pastry-lined pan.

Bake at 425°F. for 15 minutes. Reduce oven temperature to 350°F.; bake an additional 45 to 55 minutes or until knife inserted near center comes out clean. Cool completely before serving. Store in refrigerator.
Yield: 8 servings.

NUTRITION PER SERVING:
Calories 290; Protein 6g; Carbohydrate 48g; Fat 9g; Sodium 360mg.

SWEET POTATO PIE

Dry sherry adds a smooth sweet taste to this traditional southern pie.

CRUST
Pastry for Filled One-Crust Pie p. 268

FILLING
- 1½ cups mashed canned sweet potatoes
- ⅔ cup firmly packed brown sugar
- 1 cup half-and-half
- 1 teaspoon cinnamon
- ½ teaspoon allspice
- 1 tablespoon dry sherry or lemon juice
- 2 eggs, beaten

TOPPING
- 1 cup whipping cream
- 2 tablespoons sugar
- 1 teaspoon vanilla
  Pecan halves

Prepare pastry for Filled One-Crust Pie using 9-inch pie pan.

Heat oven to 425°F. In blender container or food processor bowl with metal blade, combine all filling ingredients; blend well. Pour into pastry-lined pan.

Bake at 425°F. for 15 minutes. Reduce oven temperature to 350°F.; bake an additional 30 to 40 minutes or until pie is set in center. Cool completely.

In small bowl, beat whipping cream, sugar and vanilla until soft peaks form. Garnish pie with whipped cream and pecan halves. Store in refrigerator.
Yield: 6 to 8 servings.

NUTRITION PER SERVING:
Calories 450; Protein 5g; Carbohydrate 53g; Fat 24g; Sodium 190mg.

COOK'S NOTE

PUMPKIN

Pumpkin, a member of the squash family, is rich in vitamin A and contains a fair amount of vitamins B and C. It also provides such minerals as calcium, iron, potassium, and phosphorus.

There are 2 types of canned pumpkin available. Read the label carefully to make certain you are buying the type of canned pumpkin that is called for in your recipe. *Canned pumpkin* contains unseasoned pumpkin puree. It is used in most pumpkin recipes. *Canned pumpkin pie filling* has sugar and seasonings added to the pulp during processing. Usually only eggs and milk are necessary to complete this pie filling.

French Silk Chocolate Pie

FRENCH SILK CHOCOLATE PIE

This classic pie originated in Pillsbury's 3rd BAKE-OFF® Contest. We've replaced the raw eggs in the original recipe with pasteurized cholesterol-free egg product to eliminate the possibility of salmonella.

CRUST
    Pastry for One-Crust Pie p. 268

FILLING
  3 **oz. unsweetened chocolate, chopped**
  ¾ **cup butter, softened (do not substitute margarine)**
  1 **cup sugar**
  ½ **teaspoon vanilla**
  ¾ **cup frozen cholesterol-free egg product, thawed**

TOPPING
  ½ **cup sweetened whipped cream**
    Chocolate Curls, if desired, p. 210

Prepare and bake pastry as directed for Baked Pie Shell using 9-inch pie pan; cool.

Melt chocolate in small saucepan over low heat; cool. In small bowl, beat butter until fluffy; add sugar gradually, beating until light and fluffy. Blend in cooled chocolate and vanilla. Add egg product ¼ cup at a time, beating at high speed 2 minutes after each addition. Beat until mixture is smooth and fluffy. Pour into cooled, baked pie shell. Refrigerate at least 2 hours before serving. Garnish with whipped cream and Chocolate Curls. Store in refrigerator.
Yield: 8 to 10 servings.

NUTRITION PER SERVING:
Calories 400; Protein 5g; Carbohydrate 34g; Fat 28g; Sodium 270mg.

VARIATION:

FRENCH SILK CHOCOLATE TARTLETS:
Prepare and roll pastry for Two-Crust Pie. Cut pastry into 8 quarters. Place 1 quarter of pastry in bottom and up sides of each of 8 tartlet pans. Trim edges. Generously prick crust with fork. Bake at 450°F. for 8 to 10 minutes until lightly browned; cool. Divide filling evenly into cooled, baked crusts.
Yield: 8 tartlets.

MAPLE BANANA CREAM PIE

A unique crust treatment and complementary maple flavor transform ordinary banana cream pie into something special.

FILLING
- 1 (3-oz.) pkg. vanilla pudding and pie filling mix (not instant)
- 1½ cups milk
- ½ cup maple-flavored syrup
- 2 medium bananas, sliced

CRUST
- Pastry for Two-Crust Pie p. 268

TOPPING
- 1 cup whipping cream
- 2 tablespoons maple-flavored syrup
- Maple leaf cutouts, if desired*

Prepare pudding according to package directions using 1½ cups milk and ½ cup syrup. Cover surface with plastic wrap; cool 1 hour.

Prepare and bake half of pastry as directed in One-Crust Pie recipe for Baked Pie Shell, using 9-inch pie pan; cool. Meanwhile, roll out remaining pastry; place on ungreased cookie sheet. Cut pastry into 8-inch circle, reserving scraps for cutouts.* Generously prick circle with fork. Bake at 450°F. for 8 minutes or until lightly browned; cool completely.

Arrange banana slices over bottom of cooled, baked pie shell. Spoon half of cooled filling over bananas; top with cooled 8-inch crust. Spoon remaining filling over crust. Refrigerate 5 hours or until set.

In small bowl, combine whipping cream and 2 tablespoons syrup; beat until soft peaks form. Pipe or spoon over pie. Garnish with maple leaf cutouts.

Yield: 8 servings.

TIP:
* To make cutouts, use maple leaf-shaped cookie cutter or desired shape. Cut shapes from pastry; transfer to cookie sheet. Sprinkle with sugar. Bake at 450°F. for 6 to 8 minutes or until lightly browned. Cool on wire rack.

NUTRITION PER SERVING:
Calories 500; Protein 4g; Carbohydrate 61g; Fat 27g; Sodium 280mg.

STRAWBERRIES AND CREAM PIE

Neufchatel cheese, a reduced-fat cream cheese, can be substituted for the cream cheese in this luscious pie.

CRUST
- Pastry for One-Crust Pie p. 268

FILLING
- 1 (8-oz.) pkg. cream cheese, softened
- ⅓ cup sugar
- ¼ to ½ teaspoon almond extract
- 1 cup whipping cream, whipped
- 4 cups strawberries

TOPPING
- ½ cup semi-sweet chocolate chips
- 1 tablespoon shortening

Prepare and bake pastry as directed for Baked Pie Shell using 9-inch pie pan or 10-inch tart pan with removable bottom; cool.

In large bowl, beat cream cheese until fluffy. Gradually add sugar and almond extract; blend well. Fold in whipped cream. Spoon into cooled, baked pie shell. Arrange strawberries, points up, over filling. Refrigerate.

In small saucepan over low heat, melt chocolate chips and shortening, stirring constantly until smooth. Drizzle over strawberries and filling. Refrigerate until set. Store in refrigerator.

Yield: 10 to 12 servings.

NUTRITION PER SERVING:
Calories 290; Protein 3g; Carbohydrate 23g; Fat 22g; Sodium 150mg.

COOK'S NOTE

BRAIDED CRUST

To prepare braided edge, place the pastry in the pan; trim pastry even with edge of pan. Brush edge of crust with egg white. Using second crust, cut crust into twelve ¼ to ⅜-inch strips. Braid 3 strips together and place on edge of crust, pressing lightly to secure. Repeat with remaining strips.

Strawberries and Cream Pie

RASPBERRY ANGEL CREAM PIE

Walnuts are pressed into the crust before baking.

CRUST
Pastry for One-Crust Pie p. 268
¼ cup chopped walnuts or pecans

FILLING
25 large marshmallows
½ cup milk
1 cup whipping cream, whipped

TOPPING
⅓ cup sugar
2 tablespoons cornstarch
¾ cup water
1 teaspoon lemon juice
1 teaspoon orange-flavored liqueur, if desired
1 teaspoon red food color, if desired
2 cups fresh or frozen whole raspberries, thawed, drained

GARNISH
Whipped cream
Whole raspberries

Heat oven to 450°F. Prepare pastry for One-Crust Pie using 9-inch pie pan. Press walnuts into bottom of pastry-lined pan. Generously prick pastry with fork. Bake at 450°F. for 9 to 12 minutes or until light golden brown. Cool completely.

In large saucepan, combine marshmallows and milk. Cook over medium heat until marshmallows are melted, stirring constantly. Cover; refrigerate until thickened but not set, 35 to 45 minutes. (Mixture may separate as it cools.)

Fold in whipped cream. Spread over bottom of cooled, baked crust. Refrigerate until thoroughly chilled, about 1 hour.

In medium saucepan, combine sugar and cornstarch; mix well. Gradually stir in water, lemon juice, liqueur and food color. Cook over medium heat 10 minutes, stirring occasionally. Stir in 1 cup of the raspberries. Continue cooking until thickened and clear, stirring constantly. Cover surface with plastic wrap. Refrigerate until just cool, about 1 hour.

Fold in remaining 1 cup raspberries. Spoon evenly over cooled filling. Refrigerate 1 to 2 hours or until set. Garnish with whipped cream and whole raspberries. Store in refrigerator.
Yield: 8 servings.

NUTRITION PER SERVING:
Calories 400; Protein 3g; Carbohydrate 44g; Fat 24g; Sodium 160mg.

QUICK HAWAIIAN CREAM PIE

Favorite flavors of the tropics, banana, pineapple and coconut, are highlighted in this cream pie.

CRUST
Pastry for One-Crust Pie p. 268

FILLING
1 cup whipping cream
½ cup milk
1 tablespoon rum or 1 teaspoon rum extract
1 (3.4-oz.) pkg. instant vanilla pudding and pie filling mix
½ cup whipping cream, whipped
⅓ cup (1 small) mashed ripe banana
1 (8-oz.) can crushed pineapple, well drained

TOPPING
½ cup coconut
¼ to ½ cup chopped pecans, toasted, p. 23

Prepare and bake pastry as directed for Baked Pie Shell using 9-inch pie pan; cool.

In small bowl, combine 1 cup whipping cream, milk, rum and pudding mix; beat at high speed until thick. Fold in whipped cream, banana and pineapple. Spoon into cooled, baked pie shell. Top with coconut and pecans. Refrigerate about 3 hours or until set. Store in refrigerator.
Yield: 8 servings.

NUTRITION PER SERVING:
Calories 420; Protein 3g; Carbohydrate 32g; Fat 31g; Sodium 340mg.

Orange Kist Coconut Cream Pie

This light, creamy pie from the 1990 Pillsbury BAKE-OFF® Contest has a mild orange flavor and is topped with almonds and coconut.

CRUST
   Pastry for One-Crust Pie p. 268

FILLING
   1 **cup sugar**
   3 **tablespoons cornstarch**
   1 **cup water**
   ¼ **cup orange juice**
   ¼ **cup margarine or butter**
   1 **tablespoon grated orange peel**
   3 **egg yolks**
   ½ **cup coconut, toasted, p. 23**
   ½ **cup dairy sour cream**
   ½ **cup whipping cream, whipped**

TOPPING
   ½ **cup whipping cream**
   2 **tablespoons powdered sugar**
   ¼ **cup coconut, toasted, p. 23**
   2 **tablespoons sliced almonds, toasted, p. 23**

Prepare and bake pastry as directed for Baked Pie Shell using 9-inch pie pan; cool.

In medium saucepan, combine sugar and cornstarch; mix well. Stir in water, orange juice, margarine, orange peel and egg yolks. Cook over medium heat until mixture thickens and boils, about 5 minutes, stirring constantly. Cover surface with plastic wrap. Refrigerate until just cool, about 1 hour. Stir in ½ cup toasted coconut and sour cream. Fold in whipped cream. Spoon into cooled, baked pie shell.

In small bowl, beat ½ cup whipping cream and powdered sugar until stiff peaks form. Spread over filling. Garnish with ¼ cup toasted coconut and almonds. Refrigerate 1 to 2 hours. Store in refrigerator.
Yield: 8 servings.

NUTRITION PER SERVING:
Calories 490; Protein 4g; Carbohydrate 46g; Fat 32g; Sodium 220mg.

Cranberry Cream Pie

Creme de cassis, a black currant liqueur, is the flavoring in the topping of this quick and easy pie.

CRUST
   Pastry for One-Crust Pie p. 268

FILLING
   1 **(3-oz.) pkg. raspberry flavor gelatin**
   ¾ **cup boiling water**
   1 **(16-oz.) can whole berry cranberry sauce**
   1 **(3.4-oz.) pkg. vanilla instant pudding and pie filling mix**
   ¾ **cup milk**
   1 **(8-oz.) container (3½ cups) frozen whipped topping, thawed**
   1 **tablespoon creme de cassis, if desired**

Prepare and bake pastry as directed for Baked Pie Shell using 9-inch pie pan; cool.

In medium bowl, combine gelatin and boiling water; stir to dissolve. Stir in cranberry sauce. Refrigerate just until cool, 10 to 15 minutes.

In large bowl, prepare pudding mix with ¾ cup milk as directed on package; let stand about 2 minutes. Blend in gelatin mixture. Fold in 2½ cups of the whipped topping. Spoon into cooled, baked pie shell. Refrigerate until set, about 2 hours.

In small bowl, fold creme de cassis into remaining 1 cup whipped topping. Pipe or spoon dollops on top of pie. Garnish as desired. Store in refrigerator.
Yield: 10 servings.

NUTRITION PER SERVING:
Calories 220; Protein 8g; Carbohydrate 33g; Fat 6g; Sodium 170mg.

CANTALOUPE CREAM PIE

This refreshing dessert is best served the same day and is an excellent source of vitamins A and C.

CRUST
    Pastry for One-Crust Pie p. 268

FILLING
- 1 envelope unflavored gelatin
- ½ cup orange juice
- 1 large (1½ lb.) cantaloupe, halved, seeded
- ¼ cup sugar
- 2 teaspoons grated orange peel
- 1 cup whipping cream

TOPPING
- ⅓ cup apricot jam
- 2 tablespoons orange-flavored liqueur or orange juice

Prepare and bake pastry as directed for Baked Pie Shell using 9-inch pie pan; cool.

In small saucepan, combine gelatin and orange juice; let stand 1 minute. Cook and stir over low heat until gelatin is dissolved. Scoop melon into balls (about 2 cups); reserve. Remove remaining melon from rind; cut into pieces. In blender container or food processor bowl with metal blade, puree melon pieces, sugar and orange peel until smooth. Add gelatin mixture and whipping cream; blend well. Refrigerate until slightly thickened, about 10 minutes. Pour into cooled, baked pie shell; spread evenly. Refrigerate until set, 45 to 60 minutes. Top with melon balls. Refrigerate 1 hour or until set.

Just before serving, heat jam in small saucepan until melted; stir in liqueur. Spoon over pie.
Yield: 8 servings.

NUTRITION PER SERVING:
Calories 330; Protein 3g; Carbohydrate 38g; Fat 19g; Sodium 125mg.

LEMON FUDGE RIBBON PIE

A contemporary microwave pie from the 1986 Pillsbury BAKE-OFF® Contest.

CRUST
    Pastry for One-Crust Pie p. 268
- ½ teaspoon unsweetened cocoa

FILLING
- 1 (8-oz.) pkg. cream cheese, cut into 2 pieces
- 1 cup sugar
- ¼ cup lemon juice
- 1 teaspoon vanilla
- 3 eggs, beaten
- ½ oz. unsweetened chocolate or 1 oz. semi-sweet chocolate

TOPPING
- 1 cup whipping cream
- 1 tablespoon powdered sugar
    Grated Chocolate, if desired, p. 210

MICROWAVE DIRECTIONS:
Prepare pastry for One-Crust Pie using 9-inch microwave-safe pie pan. Prick crust generously with fork. Sprinkle edge of pastry with cocoa; rub in gently with finger tips before fluting. Microwave on HIGH for 6 to 8 minutes, rotating pan ½ turn every 2 minutes. Crust is done when surface appears dry and flaky. Cool completely.

In medium microwave-safe bowl, microwave cream cheese on HIGH for 1 to 1½ minutes to soften. Stir in sugar until smooth. Add lemon juice, vanilla and eggs; blend well. Microwave on HIGH for 2 minutes; stir. Microwave on HIGH for an additional 3 to 5 minutes, stirring every 2 minutes, until smooth and thickened.

In small microwave-safe bowl, microwave unsweetened chocolate on HIGH for 2 minutes or until melted; blend in ½ cup of the lemon filling. Pour into cooled, baked crust; spread evenly. Carefully spread remaining lemon filling over chocolate filling. Cover with waxed paper; refrigerate 3 to 4 hours or until firm.

In small bowl, beat whipping cream until soft peaks form. Blend in powdered sugar; beat until stiff peaks form. Spoon or pipe over filling. Garnish with Grated Chocolate. Store in refrigerator.
Yield: 8 servings.

NUTRITION PER SERVING:
Calories 490; Protein 6g; Carbohydrate 43g; Fat 33g; Sodium 290mg.

SOUR CREAM RAISIN PIE

In this rich pie, plump raisins are surrounded by a spicy sour cream filling.

CRUST
Pastry for One-Crust Pie p. 268

FILLING
1½ cups raisins
¾ cup sugar
¼ cup cornstarch
½ teaspoon cinnamon
¼ teaspoon salt
¼ teaspoon nutmeg
2 cups milk
3 egg yolks, beaten
1 cup dairy sour cream
1 tablespoon lemon juice
1 cup whipping cream, whipped

Prepare and bake pastry as directed for Baked Pie Shell using 9-inch pie pan; cool.

In medium saucepan, combine raisins, sugar, cornstarch, cinnamon, salt and nutmeg; mix well. Stir in milk, blending until smooth. Cook over medium heat until mixture boils, stirring constantly. Boil 1 minute; remove from heat. Blend small amount of hot raisin mixture into egg yolks; add yolk mixture to hot mixture. Add sour cream; mix well. Cook just until mixture starts to bubble, stirring constantly. Remove from heat; stir in lemon juice. Cool slightly; pour into cooled, baked pie shell. Refrigerate 2 hours or until set. Top with whipped cream. Store in refrigerator.
Yield: 8 servings.

NUTRITION PER SERVING:
Calories 530; Protein 7g; Carbohydrate 61g; Fat 29g; Sodium 260mg.

VARIATION:

SOUR CREAM RAISIN MERINGUE PIE: Heat oven to 350°F. Substitute meringue for 1 cup whipping cream. In small bowl, beat 3 egg whites and ¼ teaspoon cream of tartar at medium speed until soft peaks form, about 1 minute. Gradually add ¼ cup sugar, 1 tablespoon at a time, beating at highest speed until stiff peaks form and sugar is dissolved. Spoon meringue over filling. Seal to edge of crust. Bake at 350°F. for 10 to 15 minutes or until lightly browned. Cool completely. Store in refrigerator.

SWEET CHERRITY PIE

In this pie from the 1976 Pillsbury BAKE-OFF® Contest, a cream cheese layer is topped with a pink fluffy cherry layer. It's best when refrigerated overnight before serving.

CRUST
1 cup all purpose flour
½ to 1 cup finely chopped nuts
¼ cup firmly packed brown sugar
½ cup margarine or butter, softened

FILLING
1 (8-oz.) pkg. cream cheese, softened
½ teaspoon almond extract
1 cup powdered sugar
1 cup whipping cream*
1 (21-oz.) can cherry fruit pie filling

Heat oven to 375°F. In ungreased 13x9-inch pan, combine all crust ingredients; mix well. Bake at 375°F. for 15 to 20 minutes or until golden brown, stirring once during baking. Reserve ½ cup of the crumb mixture for topping. Firmly press remaining warm crumb mixture in bottom and up sides of ungreased 9 or 10-inch pie pan. Refrigerate 15 minutes.

In small bowl, combine cream cheese, almond extract and powdered sugar; blend until smooth. Spread over cooled, baked crust. In medium bowl, beat whipping cream until stiff peaks form. Fold in pie filling. Spoon over cream cheese layer. Sprinkle with reserved ½ cup crumb mixture. Refrigerate 2 to 3 hours or until thoroughly chilled before serving. Store in refrigerator.
Yield: 8 to 10 servings.

TIP:
* Do not use frozen whipped topping; a curdled appearance will result.

NUTRITION PER SERVING:
Calories 540; Protein 6g; Carbohydrate 57g; Fat 34g; Sodium 190mg.

Blueberry Lemon Mousse Pie

A layer of spiced, glazed blueberries tucked under a blanket of chilled lemon chiffon makes this pie cool and refreshing.

CRUST
    Pastry for One-Crust Pie p. 268

FILLING
    1 (16½-oz.) can blueberries
    ¼ cup sugar
    2 tablespoons cornstarch
    1 teaspoon grated lemon peel
    ½ teaspoon nutmeg
    ⅛ teaspoon ground cardamom, if desired
    1 tablespoon margarine or butter

TOPPING
    1 (3-oz.) pkg. lemon flavor gelatin
    1 cup boiling water
    ½ cup cold water
    1 teaspoon grated lemon peel
    1 cup whipping cream, whipped

Prepare and bake pastry as directed for Baked Pie Shell using 9-inch pie pan; cool.

Drain blueberries, reserving ½ cup liquid. In small saucepan, combine sugar and cornstarch; stir in blueberry liquid. Cook over medium heat until mixture boils and thickens, stirring constantly. Boil slowly 1 minute; remove from heat. Stir in blueberries and remaining filling ingredients. Set aside to cool while preparing topping.

In large bowl, dissolve gelatin in boiling water. Stir in cold water and lemon peel. Refrigerate until mixture begins to thicken and is of syrupy consistency, about 30 to 45 minutes. Beat thickened gelatin at highest speed about 3 to 4 minutes or until light and fluffy; gelatin should about double in volume. Fold whipped cream thoroughly into gelatin. Pour blueberry filling into cooled, baked pie shell; spoon lemon topping over cooled filling. Refrigerate at least 1 hour before serving. Store in refrigerator.

Yield: 8 servings.

NUTRITION PER SERVING:
Calories 390; Protein 4g; Carbohydrate 46g; Fat 21g; Sodium 195mg

White Chocolate Pecan Mousse Pie

This light and fluffy mousse pie flavored with buttered pecans will melt in your mouth! It's best served well chilled.

CRUST
    Pastry for One-Crust Pie p. 268

FILLING
    2 tablespoons butter
    2 cups chopped pecans
    1 cup vanilla milk chips or 6-oz. pkg. white baking bars, chopped
    ¼ cup milk
    2 cups whipping cream
    ⅓ cup sugar
    1 teaspoon vanilla

GARNISH
    1 tablespoon Grated Chocolate p. 210, or ¼ cup chocolate syrup, if desired

Heat oven to 450°F. Prepare pastry for One-Crust Pie using 10-inch springform pan or 9-inch pie pan. Place pastry in pan; press in bottom and up sides of pan. With fork dipped in flour, press top edge of pastry to sides of pan. Generously prick pastry with fork. Bake at 450°F. for 9 to 11 minutes or until light golden brown. Cool completely.

Melt butter in 10-inch skillet over medium heat. Stir in pecans. Cook until pecans are golden brown, about 6 minutes, stirring constantly. Cool at room temperature 1 hour.

In small saucepan over low heat, melt vanilla milk chips with milk, stirring constantly with wire whisk. Cool at room temperature 1 hour.

In large bowl, beat whipping cream until stiff peaks form. Fold in sugar, vanilla, pecans and melted vanilla milk chips. Spoon into cooled, baked crust. Refrigerate 4 hours before serving. Just before serving, garnish with Grated chocolate. Store in refrigerator.

Yield: 10 to 12 servings.

TIP:
Pie can be frozen. Let stand at room temperature 30 to 45 minutes before serving.

NUTRITION PER SERVING:
Calories 470; Protein 4g; Carbohydrate 27g; Fat 39g; Sodium 140mg.

CHOCOLATE CARAMEL MOUSSE PIE

Candy fans will love the classic flavors of caramel, pecans and chocolate in a pie from the 1992 Pillsbury BAKE-OFF® Contest.

CRUST
   Pastry for One-Crust Pie p. 268

FILLING
   1 **cup evaporated milk**
   6 **oz. semi-sweet chocolate, chopped**
   1 **envelope unflavored gelatin**
   3 **tablespoons water**
   1 **cup powdered sugar**
   1 **teaspoon vanilla**
   1 **(14-oz.) pkg. caramels, unwrapped**
   ⅓ **cup evaporated milk**
   1 **cup chopped pecans**

TOPPING
   1 **cup whipping cream**
   2 **tablespoons powdered sugar**
   ½ **teaspoon vanilla**
   ⅓ **cup pecan halves**

Prepare and bake pastry as directed for Baked Pie Shell using 9-inch pie pan or 10-inch tart pan with removable bottom; cool.

In heavy saucepan, combine 1 cup evaporated milk and chocolate. Cook over medium heat until chocolate melts, stirring constantly. In small bowl, dissolve gelatin in water. Add to chocolate mixture; beat until well blended. Add 1 cup powdered sugar and 1 teaspoon vanilla; beat until mixture is smooth. Refrigerate until mixture is slightly thickened, 15 to 20 minutes.

In medium saucepan, combine caramels and ⅓ cup evaporated milk. Cook over medium heat until caramels are melted, stirring constantly. Reserve ⅓ cup of the caramel mixture; set aside. Spread remaining caramel mixture over bottom of cooled, baked pie shell. Sprinkle with 1 cup chopped pecans.

In small bowl, beat whipping cream, 2 tablespoons powdered sugar and ½ teaspoon vanilla until stiff peaks form. Beat chilled chocolate mixture on high speed until mixture is light in color, about 2 minutes. Fold in 1 cup of the whipped cream, reserving remaining whipped cream for garnish. Refrigerate chocolate mixture for 15 to 30 minutes or until thickened. Spoon and spread chocolate mixture over chopped pecans. Pipe or spoon reserved whipped cream around edge of pie. If necessary, slightly heat reserved ⅓ cup caramel mixture. Drizzle over pie; garnish with pecan halves. Refrigerate 2 hours or until set. Store in refrigerator.
Yield: 8 to 10 servings.

NUTRITION PER SERVING:
Calories 630; Protein 8g; Carbohydrate 71g; Fat 38g; Sodium 220mg.

COOK'S NOTE

MOUSSE

The term mousse refers to a light airy mixture that can be either sweet or savory. The characteristic light fluffy texture of mousse is made by folding beaten egg whites or whipped cream into a gelatin or custard mixture. Dessert mousses are often flavored with chocolate or pureed fruit.

LEMON LUSCIOUS PIE

Garnish this velvety smooth sour cream lemon pie with whipped cream and walnuts.

CRUST
   Pastry for One-Crust Pie p. 268

FILLING
   1 **cup sugar**
   3 **tablespoons cornstarch**
   1 **cup milk**
   ¼ **cup lemon juice**
   3 **egg yolks, slightly beaten**
   ¼ **cup margarine or butter**
   1 **tablespoon grated lemon peel**
   1 **cup dairy sour cream**

Prepare and bake pastry as directed for Baked Pie Shell using 9-inch pie pan; cool.

In medium saucepan, combine sugar and cornstarch; mix well. Stir in milk, lemon juice and egg yolks; cook over medium heat until thick, stirring constantly. Remove from heat; stir in margarine and lemon peel. Cool. Fold in sour cream. Spoon into cooled, baked pie shell. Refrigerate at least 2 hours or until set. Store in refrigerator.
Yield: 8 servings.

NUTRITION PER SERVING:
Calories 430; Protein 4g; Carbohydrate 44g; Fat 27g; Sodium 270mg.

LEMON TRUFFLE PIE

White chocolate and lemon are featured in this heavenly pie.

CRUST
   Pastry for One-Crust Pie p. 268

FILLING
   1 **cup sugar**
   2 **tablespoons cornstarch**
   2 **tablespoons all purpose flour**
   1 **cup water**
   2 **egg yolks, beaten**
   1 **tablespoon margarine or butter**
   ½ **teaspoon grated lemon peel**
   ¼ **cup lemon juice**
   1 **cup vanilla milk chips or 6-oz. pkg. white baking bars, chopped**
   1 **(8-oz.) pkg. light cream cheese (Neufchatel), softened**
   ½ **cup whipping cream**
   1 **tablespoon sliced almonds, toasted, p. 23**

Prepare and bake pastry as directed for Baked Pie Shell using 9-inch pie pan; cool.

In medium saucepan, combine sugar, cornstarch and flour; mix well. Gradually stir in water until smooth. Cook over medium heat until mixture thickens and boils, stirring constantly. Reduce heat; cook 2 minutes, stirring constantly. Remove from heat. Blend about ¼ cup of hot mixture into egg yolks. Gradually stir yolk mixture into hot mixture in saucepan. Cook over low heat until mixture comes to a boil, stirring constantly. Cook 2 minutes, stirring constantly. Remove from heat; stir in margarine, lemon peel and lemon juice. Place ⅓ cup of hot lemon mixture in small saucepan; cool remaining mixture 15 minutes. Add vanilla milk chips to hot lemon mixture in small saucepan. Stir over low heat just until chips are melted.

In small bowl, beat cream cheese until fluffy. Add vanilla milk chip mixture; beat until well blended. Spread over bottom of cooled, baked pie shell. Spoon remaining lemon mixture over cream cheese layer. Refrigerate 2 to 3 hours or until set.

In small bowl, beat whipping cream until stiff peaks form. Pipe or spoon over pie. Garnish with toasted almonds. Store in refrigerator.
Yield: 8 to 10 servings.

NUTRITION PER SERVING:
Calories 400; Protein 5g; Carbohydrate 44g; Fat 23g; Sodium 230mg.

Lemon Truffle Pie, Apricot Tea Tart p. 321

MOCHA FRAPPE PIE

For tender flaky pie crust, add just enough cold water to moisten the flour mixture, tossing it gently with a fork. Once the mixture is moistened, stop mixing.

CRUST
- 1 cup all purpose flour
- 2 tablespoons sugar
- ½ teaspoon salt
- ⅓ cup shortening
- 1 egg yolk
- 2 to 3 tablespoons water

FILLING
- 4¼ cups miniature marshmallows
- ¼ cup sugar
- 1 (5-oz.) can (⅔ cup) evaporated milk
- 2 teaspoons instant coffee granules or crystals
- 1 (6-oz.) pkg. (1 cup) semi-sweet chocolate chips
- 1 cup whipping cream, whipped

TOPPING
Chocolate Curls, if desired, p. 210

Heat oven to 375°F. In medium bowl, combine flour, 2 tablespoons sugar and salt; mix well. Using pastry blender or fork, cut in shortening until mixture resembles coarse crumbs. In small bowl, combine egg yolk and 2 tablespoons water. Stir egg yolk mixture into flour mixture with fork until mixture forms a ball. Add additional water, if necessary, until dough is moist enough to hold together.

Shape dough into a ball. Flatten ball; smooth edges. On lightly floured surface, roll ball lightly from center to edge to form a 10½-inch circle. Fold pastry in half; place in 9-inch pie pan. Unfold; fit evenly in pan. Do not stretch. Fold edge under to form standing rim; flute. Prick bottom and sides of crust with fork. Bake at 375°F. for 12 to 17 minutes or until light golden brown. Cool completely.

In large saucepan over low heat, melt marshmallows, ¼ cup sugar, milk and coffee until mixture is smooth, stirring occasionally. Stir in chocolate chips until melted. Cool slightly. Spread ¾ cup of chocolate mixture in bottom of cooled, baked pie shell. Refrigerate remaining chocolate mixture until thoroughly cooled, about 15 minutes. Fold whipped cream into remaining chocolate mixture. Spoon over chocolate layer; spread evenly.

Refrigerate 2 to 3 hours. Garnish with Chocolate Curls. Store in refrigerator.
Yield: 8 servings.

NUTRITION PER SERVING:
Calories 490; Protein 5g; Carbohydrate 55g; Fat 28g; Sodium 180mg

WHITE CHRISTMAS PIE

This creamy white filling in a chocolate crust is topped with bright red raspberry sauce. It's a treat for your eyes as well as your taste buds.

CRUST
- 1 cup all purpose flour
- ¼ cup firmly packed brown sugar
- 2 tablespoons unsweetened cocoa
- ¼ teaspoon salt
- ⅓ cup shortening
- 3 to 4 tablespoons cold water

FILLING
- ¼ cup sugar
- ¼ cup cornstarch
- 1½ cups milk
- 1 (6-oz.) pkg. white baking bars, chopped, or 1 cup vanilla milk chips
- 1 teaspoon vanilla
- ¾ cup whipping cream
- 2 tablespoons powdered sugar

RASPBERRY SAUCE AND GARNISH
- 1 (10-oz.) pkg. frozen raspberries in syrup, thawed
- 1 tablespoon cornstarch
  Chocolate Cutouts, if desired, p. 210

Heat oven to 450°F. In medium bowl, combine flour, brown sugar, cocoa and salt; mix well. Using pastry blender or fork, cut in shortening until mixture resembles coarse crumbs. Sprinkle flour mixture with water 1 tablespoon at a time, while tossing and mixing lightly with fork. Add water until dough is just moist enough to hold together.

Shape dough into a ball. Flatten ball; smooth edges. On lightly floured surface, roll ball lightly from center to edge to form 10½-inch circle. Fold pastry in half; place in 9-inch pie pan. Unfold; fit evenly in pan. Do not stretch. Fold edge under to form standing rim; flute. Prick bottom and sides of crust generously with fork. Bake at 450°F. for 8 to

11 minutes or until crust appears dry and flaky. Cool completely.

In medium saucepan, combine sugar and ¼ cup cornstarch. Add milk gradually, stirring over medium heat until mixture boils; boil 1 minute, stirring constantly. Add baking bar and vanilla, stirring until baking bar is melted and mixture is smooth. Pour into large bowl; cover top with plastic wrap. Cool to room temperature.

In small bowl, beat whipping cream with powdered sugar until soft peaks form. Beat cooled baking bar mixture at medium speed until light and fluffy, about 1 minute. Fold whipped cream into mixture. Spoon evenly into cooled, baked pie shell. Refrigerate 2 to 3 hours or until set.

In small saucepan over medium heat, combine raspberries and 1 tablespoon cornstarch. Bring to boil, stirring constantly. Boil 1 minute, stirring constantly. Cool. Serve pie with raspberry sauce. Garnish with Chocolate Cutouts. Store in the refrigerator.

Yield: 8 servings.

NUTRITION PER SERVING:
Calories 500; Protein 6g; Carbohydrate 61g; Fat 27g; Sodium 130mg.

COOK'S NOTE

UNFLAVORED GELATIN

Unflavored gelatin is used to thicken or set a liquid mixture. In recipes, the unflavored gelatin is sprinkled over cold water or liquid and allowed to stand about 2 minutes to soften. The softened gelatin is combined with hot water or a hot liquid. The mixture is then refrigerated to set. Some fresh foods contain an enzyme that prevents the gelatin from setting up. These foods, fresh pineapple, kiwifruit, figs, guava, papaya and gingerroot, can be used successfully with gelatin only after they've been cooked or canned.

CARAMEL CANDY PIE

Caramel candies are melted into a smooth and luscious filling in this winning recipe from the 4th Pillsbury BAKE-OFF® Contest. Caramelized almonds add the finishing touch.

CRUST
   Pastry for One-Crust Pie p. 268

FILLING
   1   **envelope unflavored gelatin**
   ¼   **cup cold water**
   1   **(14-oz.) pkg. vanilla caramels, unwrapped**
   1   **cup milk**
1½   **cups whipping cream, whipped**

TOPPING
   2   **tablespoons sugar**
   ¼   **cup slivered almonds**

Prepare and bake pastry as directed for Baked Pie Shell using 9-inch pie pan; cool.

In small bowl, sprinkle gelatin over water; let stand to soften. In medium saucepan, combine caramels and milk. Cook over low heat until caramels are melted and mixture is smooth, stirring occasionally. Stir in softened gelatin. Refrigerate 45 to 60 minutes or until slightly thickened. Fold thickened caramel mixture into whipped cream. Spoon into cooled crust. Refrigerate 2 hours or until set.

Line cookie sheet with foil. In small skillet, combine sugar and almonds. Cook over low heat until sugar is melted and almonds are golden brown, stirring constantly. Immediately spread on foil-lined cookie sheet. Cool completely; break apart. Just before serving, garnish pie with caramelized almonds. Store in refrigerator.

Yield: 8 servings.

NUTRITION PER SERVING:
Calories 530; Protein 6g; Carbohydrate 55g; Fat 32g; Sodium 280mg.

LEMON MERINGUE PIE

Egg whites should be brought to room temperature for fluffy meringue with more volume.

CRUST
    Pastry for One-Crust Pie p. 268

FILLING
1¼ cups sugar
⅓ cup cornstarch
½ teaspoon salt
1½ cups cold water
3 egg yolks
2 tablespoons margarine or butter
1 tablespoon grated lemon peel
½ cup fresh lemon juice

MERINGUE
3 egg whites
¼ teaspoon cream of tartar
½ teaspoon vanilla
¼ cup sugar

Prepare and bake pastry as directed for Baked Pie Shell using 9-inch pie pan; cool.

In medium saucepan, combine 1¼ cups sugar, cornstarch and salt; mix well. Gradually stir in cold water until smooth. Cook over medium heat, stirring constantly, until mixture boils; boil 1 minute, stirring constantly. Remove from heat. In small bowl, beat egg yolks; stir about ¼ cup of hot mixture into egg yolks. Gradually stir yolk mixture into hot mixture. Cook over low heat, stirring constantly, until mixture boils. Boil 1 minute, stirring constantly. Remove from heat; stir in margarine, lemon peel and lemon juice. Cool slightly, about 15 minutes. Pour into cooled, baked pie shell.

Heat oven to 350°F. In small deep bowl, beat egg whites, cream of tartar and vanilla at medium speed until soft peaks form, about 1 minute. Add sugar 1 tablespoon at a time, beating at high speed until stiff glossy peaks form and sugar is dissolved. Spoon meringue onto hot filling; spread to edge of crust to seal well and prevent shrinkage. Bake at 350°F. for 12 to 15 minutes or until light golden brown. Cool completely. Refrigerate 3 hours or until filling is set. Store in refrigerator.
Yield: 8 servings.

NUTRITION PER SERVING:
Calories 320; Protein 4g; Carbohydrate 48g; Fat 13g; Sodium 320mg.

LEMON PUFF PEACH PIE

CRUST
1 cup all purpose flour
½ teaspoon salt
⅓ cup shortening
3 to 4 tablespoons milk

FILLING
½ cup sugar
3 tablespoons cornstarch
¼ teaspoon nutmeg
4 cups sliced peeled peaches
¼ teaspoon grated lemon peel

TOPPING
½ cup sugar
1 tablespoon all purpose flour
1 tablespoon lemon juice
3 eggs, separated
¼ teaspoon grated lemon peel
¼ teaspoon cream of tartar

Heat oven to 450°F. In medium bowl, combine 1 cup flour and salt. Using pastry blender or fork, cut in shortening until mixture resembles coarse crumbs. Sprinkle mixture with milk 1 tablespoon at a time, while tossing and mixing lightly with fork. Add milk until dough is moist enough to form a ball when lightly pressed together.

Shape dough into ball. Flatten ball to ½-inch thickness, rounding and smoothing edges. Roll lightly on floured surface from center to edge into 10½-inch circle. Fold pastry in half; place in 9-inch pie pan. Unfold; fit evenly in pan. Do not stretch. Turn edge under to form a standing rim; flute. Prick bottom and sides of pastry generously with fork. Bake at 450°F. for 10 to 12 minutes or until light golden brown; cool.

Reduce oven temperature to 325°F.; place oven rack at lowest position. In medium saucepan, combine ½ cup sugar, cornstarch, nutmeg and peaches. Cook over medium heat until mixture boils and thickens, stirring constantly. Remove from heat. Stir in lemon peel; keep warm while preparing topping.

In small saucepan, combine ½ cup sugar, 1 tablespoon flour, lemon juice and egg yolks; beat until well blended. Cook over medium heat just until mixture comes to a boil, stirring constantly. Remove from heat. Stir in lemon peel; set aside. Cool while preparing egg whites. In small bowl, beat egg whites and cream of tartar until stiff peaks form. Stir about ¼ of egg white mixture into warm

egg yolk mixture; fold in remaining egg whites. Spoon peach filling into cooled, baked pie shell. Lightly spoon topping onto peaches; spread to edge of crust to seal well and prevent shrinkage. Bake on lowest oven rack at 325°F. for 25 to 30 minutes or until golden brown. Cool completely. Store in refrigerator.
Yield: 8 servings.

NUTRITION PER SERVING:
Calories 310; Protein 5g; Carbohydrate 49g; Fat 11g; Sodium 160mg.

RHUBARB CREAM PIE

CRUST
Pastry for Filled One-Crust Pie p. 268

FILLING
2 cups diced fresh rhubarb (do not use frozen rhubarb)
3 egg yolks
½ cup half-and-half
1 cup sugar
2 tablespoons all purpose flour
½ teaspoon salt

MERINGUE
3 egg whites
¼ teaspoon cream of tartar
½ teaspoon vanilla
6 tablespoons sugar

Prepare pastry for Filled One-Crust Pie using 9-inch pie pan.

Heat oven to 400°F. Place rhubarb in pastry-lined pan. In small bowl, beat egg yolks until thick and lemon colored. Stir in half-and-half. Add remaining filling ingredients; blend well. Pour egg mixture over rhubarb.

Bake at 400°F. for 10 minutes. Reduce oven temperature to 350°F.; bake an additional 40 minutes.

In small deep bowl, beat egg whites, cream of tartar and vanilla at medium speed until soft peaks form. Gradually add 6 tablespoons sugar 1 tablespoon at a time, beating at high speed until stiff glossy peaks form and sugar is dissolved. Spoon meringue onto hot filling; spread to edge of crust to seal well and prevent shrinkage.

Bake at 350°F. for 15 to 20 minutes or until light golden brown.
Yield: 8 servings.

NUTRITION PER SERVING:
Calories 310; Protein 4g; Carbohydrate 50g; Fat 11g; Sodium 260mg.

SOUTHERN-STYLE LEMON MERINGUE PIE

A layer of preserves makes this pie unique.

CRUST
Pastry for One-Crust Pie p. 268

FILLING
½ cup blackberry or raspberry preserves
1 cup sugar
¼ cup cornstarch
½ teaspoon salt
1⅔ cups water
3 egg yolks
2 tablespoons margarine or butter
1½ teaspoons grated lemon peel
⅓ cup lemon juice

MERINGUE
3 egg whites
¼ teaspoon cream of tartar
6 tablespoons sugar

Prepare and bake pastry as directed for Baked Pie Shell using 9-inch pie pan; cool. Spread preserves in bottom of cooled, baked pie shell.

In medium saucepan, combine 1 cup sugar with cornstarch and salt; mix well. Stir in water; blend until smooth. Cook over medium heat until mixture boils and thickens, stirring constantly. Boil 1 minute, stirring constantly. Remove from heat. In small bowl, beat egg yolks; stir about ¼ cup of hot mixture into egg yolks. Gradually stir yolk mixture into hot mixture. Cook over low heat, stirring constantly, just until mixture begins to bubble. Remove from heat; stir in margarine, lemon peel and lemon juice. Cool slightly, about 15 minutes. Pour over preserves in crust.

Heat oven to 400°F. In small bowl, beat egg whites and cream of tartar until soft peaks form, about 1 minute. Add 6 tablespoons sugar 1 tablespoon at a time, beating at high speed until stiff glossy peaks form and sugar is dissolved. Spoon meringue onto hot filling; spread to edge of crust to seal well and prevent shrinkage.

Bake at 400°F. for 10 to 18 minutes or until light golden brown. Cool completely. Refrigerate 3 hours or until filling is set. Store in refrigerator.
Yield: 8 servings.

NUTRITION PER SERVING:
Calories 390; Protein 4g; Carbohydrate 65g; Fat 13g; Sodium 325mg.

GRAPEFRUIT MERINGUE PIE

In the 1930s Pillsbury had a monthly publication called the Cookery Club Bulletin. This recipe was a favorite published in 1935.

CRUST
Pastry for One-Crust Pie p. 268

FILLING
- ¾ cup sugar
- ¼ cup cornstarch
- 3 tablespoons all purpose flour
- ½ teaspoon salt
- 1¼ cups cold water
- ½ cup fresh grapefruit juice
- 3 egg yolks
- 2 tablespoons margarine or butter
- 1 teaspoon grated grapefruit peel

MERINGUE
- 3 egg whites
- ¼ teaspoon cream of tartar
- ¼ cup sugar

Prepare and bake pastry as directed for Baked Pie Shell using 9-inch pie pan; cool.

In medium saucepan, combine ¾ cup sugar, cornstarch, flour and salt; mix well. Gradually stir in cold water and grapefruit juice until smooth. Cook over medium heat, stirring constantly, until mixture boils; boil 1 minute, stirring constantly. Remove from heat. In small bowl, beat egg yolks; stir about ¼ cup of hot mixture into egg yolks. Gradually stir yolk mixture into hot mixture. Cook over low heat, stirring constantly, until mixture boils. Boil 1 minute, stirring constantly. Remove from heat; stir in margarine and grapefruit peel. Cool slightly, about 15 minutes. Pour into cooled, baked pie shell.

Heat oven to 350°F. In small deep bowl, beat egg whites and cream of tartar at medium speed until soft peaks form, about 1 minute. Add ¼ cup sugar 1 tablespoon at a time, beating at high speed until stiff glossy peaks form and sugar is dissolved. Spoon meringue onto hot filling; spread to edge of crust to seal well and prevent shrinkage. Bake at 350°F. for 12 to 15 minutes or until light golden brown. Cool completely. Refrigerate 3 hours or until filling is set. Store in refrigerator.
Yield: 8 servings.

NUTRITION PER SERVING:
Calories 350; Protein 4g; Carbohydrate 57g; Fat 12g; Sodium 290mg.

MAGIC MERINGUE PIE

This pie features a pineapple filling.

CRUST
Pastry for One-Crust Pie p. 268

FILLING
- ¾ cup sugar
- 2 tablespoons all purpose flour
- ⅛ teaspoon salt
- 1 cup dairy sour cream
- 1 tablespoon lemon juice
- 3 egg yolks
- 1 (20-oz.) can crushed pineapple, drained, reserving ½ cup liquid

MERINGUE
- 2 tablespoons sugar
- 1 tablespoon cornstarch
- ½ cup water
- 3 egg whites
- ⅛ teaspoon salt
- ½ teaspoon vanilla
- 6 tablespoons sugar

Prepare and bake pastry as directed for Baked Pie Shell using 9-inch pie pan; cool.

In medium saucepan, combine ¾ cup sugar, 2 tablespoons flour and ⅛ teaspoon salt; mix well. Stir in sour cream, lemon juice, egg yolks, drained pineapple and reserved liquid. Cook over medium heat until mixture boils and thickens, stirring constantly. Cover surface with plastic wrap. Refrigerate just until cool, about 1 hour. Pour into cooled, baked pie shell.

Heat oven to 350°F. In small saucepan, combine 2 tablespoons sugar and cornstarch; mix well. Gradually stir in water until smooth. Cook over medium heat until mixture boils and thickens, stirring constantly. Cool.

In small bowl, beat egg whites, ⅛ teaspoon salt and vanilla at medium speed until soft peaks form. Gradually add cornstarch mixture and 6 tablespoons sugar 1 tablespoon at a time, beating at high speed until stiff peaks form and sugar is dissolved. Spoon meringue onto filling; spread to edge of crust to seal well and prevent shrinkage.

Bake at 350°F. for 10 to 15 minutes or until light golden brown. Cool completely. Store in refrigerator.
Yield: 8 servings.

NUTRITION PER SERVING:
Calories 370; Protein 5g; Carbohydrate 54g; Fat 16g; Sodium 240mg.

CRANBERRY ORANGE FROZEN TART

Only 3 ingredients are in the filling!

CRUST
>   **Pastry for One-Crust Pie p. 268**

FILLING
>   1   **(14-oz.) can sweetened condensed milk (not evaporated)**
>   1   **(10-oz.) pkg. (1¼ cups) frozen cranberry-orange sauce, thawed**
>   1   **cup frozen whipped topping, thawed**

Prepare and bake pastry as directed for Baked Pie Shell using 10-inch tart pan with removable bottom or 9-inch pie pan; cool.

In medium bowl, combine sweetened condensed milk and cranberry-orange sauce; blend well. Fold in 1 cup whipped topping. Spoon mixture evenly into cooled, baked tart shell. Freeze overnight or until firm. Garnish as desired.

Yield: 12 servings.

NUTRITION PER SERVING:
Calories 250; Protein 3g; Carbohydrate 38g; Fat 9g; Sodium 140mg.

CHERRY BERRY TART

A simple filling makes this tart a quick dessert.

CRUST
>   **Pastry for One-Crust Pie p. 268**

FILLING
>   1   **(21-oz.) can cherry fruit pie filling**
>   1   **cup halved strawberries**
>   1   **cup blueberries**

GARNISH
>   **Whipped cream, if desired**

Prepare and bake pastry as directed for Baked Pie Shell using 9-inch tart pan with removable bottom or 9-inch pie pan; cool. In large bowl, gently combine all filling ingredients. Spoon into cooled, baked tart shell. Refrigerate at least 1 hour. Remove sides of pan. Garnish with whipped cream.

Yield: 8 servings.

NUTRITION PER SERVING:
Calories 310; Protein 2g; Carbohydrate 50g; Fat 11g; Sodium 170mg.

ZESTY ORANGE PUMPKIN TART

Orange marmalade flavors this elegant variation of pumpkin pie.

CRUST
>   **Pastry for Filled One-Crust Pie p. 268**

FILLING
>   1   **(16-oz.) can (2 cups) pumpkin**
>   1   **(12-oz.) can (1½ cups) evaporated milk**
>   ½   **cup sugar**
>   ⅓   **cup orange marmalade**
>   2   **eggs, slightly beaten**
>   1   **teaspoon pumpkin pie spice**
>   ½   **teaspoon salt**

TOPPING
>   1   **cup whipping cream**
>   2   **tablespoons powdered sugar**
>   ½   **teaspoon grated orange peel, if desired**

Prepare pastry for Filled One-Crust Pie using 10-inch tart pan with removable bottom or 9-inch pie pan.

Heat oven to 425°F. In large bowl, combine all filling ingredients; blend well. Pour into pastry-lined pan.

Bake at 425°F. for 45 to 55 minutes or until knife inserted in center comes out clean. Cool; remove sides of pan.

In small bowl, beat whipping cream until soft peaks form. Blend in powdered sugar and orange peel; beat until stiff peaks form. Spoon or pipe topping over filling. Store in refrigerator.

Yield: 8 servings.

NUTRITION PER SERVING:
Calories 460; Protein 8g; Carbohydrate 53g; Fat 24g; Sodium 380mg.

TANGY CRESCENT NUT TART

This 32nd Pillsbury BAKE-OFF® Contest winner uses refrigerated crescent rolls to form the easy crust for this tangy lemon tart.

CRUST
1 (8-oz.) can refrigerated crescent dinner rolls

FILLING
1 cup sugar
¼ cup all purpose flour
2 to 3 teaspoons grated lemon peel
3 to 4 tablespoons lemon juice
1 teaspoon vanilla
4 eggs
1 cup coconut
1 cup finely chopped hazelnuts (filberts) or walnuts

GARNISH
1 to 2 tablespoons powdered sugar

Heat oven to 350°F. Lightly grease 10-inch tart pan with removable bottom. Separate dough into 8 triangles. Place in greased pan; press in bottom and up sides to form crust. Firmly press perforations to seal.

Bake at 350°F. for 5 minutes. Cool 5 minutes; gently press sides of warm crust to top of pan.

In large bowl, combine sugar, flour, lemon peel, lemon juice, vanilla and eggs; beat 3 minutes at medium speed. Stir in coconut and hazelnuts. Pour filling into partially baked crust.

Bake an additional 25 to 30 minutes or until filling is set and crust is golden brown. Cool completely. Sprinkle with powdered sugar. Store in refrigerator.
Yield: 8 to 12 servings.

TIP:
A 10-inch round pizza pan can be substituted for the tart pan. Bake crust at 350°F. for 5 minutes; bake filled crust an additional 20 to 25 minutes.

NUTRITION PER SERVING:
Calories 230; Protein 5g; Carbohydrate 23g; Fat 14g; Sodium 180mg.

CHERRY CREAM CHEESE CRESCENT TARTS

Refrigerated crescent rolls form a quick and easy tart shell for these festive hand-held desserts. A fabulous filling of cream cheese, cherries, chocolate and almonds gives them flavor appeal for all ages.

CRUST
2 (8-oz.) cans refrigerated crescent dinner rolls

FILLING
1 (8-oz.) pkg. cream cheese, softened
1 cup powdered sugar
1 egg
½ teaspoon almond extract
½ cup miniature semi-sweet chocolate chips
¼ cup chopped almonds
1 tablespoon finely chopped maraschino cherries, well drained

GLAZE
⅓ cup powdered sugar
1 tablespoon finely chopped maraschino cherries, well drained
2 to 2½ teaspoons maraschino cherry liquid

Heat oven to 350°F. Lightly grease 16 muffin cups. Separate dough into 8 rectangles; firmly press perforations to seal. Press or roll each rectangle into 8x4-inch rectangle; cut in half crosswise to form 16 squares. Place squares in greased muffin cups. Gently press each square in center to cover bottom and sides of cup, leaving corners of dough extended.

In small bowl, combine cream cheese, 1 cup powdered sugar, egg and almond extract; beat well. Stir in remaining filling ingredients. Place about 2 tablespoons filling in each pastry-lined cup.

Bake at 350°F. for 15 to 20 minutes or until golden brown. Cool 5 minutes; remove from muffin cups.

In small bowl, combine all glaze ingredients, adding enough cherry liquid for desired drizzling consistency. Drizzle over warm or cool tarts. Store lightly covered in refrigerator.
Yield: 16 tarts.

NUTRITION PER SERVING:
Calories 240; Protein 4g; Carbohydrate 24g; Fat 14g; Sodium 280mg.

Pear Tart Elegante

A glistening topping of red currant jelly highlights the fruit in this show-off dessert.

CRUST
- ¼ cup margarine or butter, softened
- 2 tablespoons sugar
- Dash salt
- ½ teaspoon grated lemon peel
- ½ teaspoon vanilla
- 1 egg yolk
- ¾ cup all purpose flour
- ¼ cup finely ground blanched almonds

FILLING
- 4 tablespoons red currant jelly
- ½ cup all purpose flour
- 3 tablespoons sugar
- ¼ cup margarine or butter, softened
- ½ teaspoon grated lemon peel
- ½ teaspoon almond extract
- 1 (3-oz.) pkg. cream cheese, softened
- 1 egg
- 5 canned pear halves, well drained
- 1 cup fresh or frozen whole raspberries or strawberries, slightly thawed

Heat oven to 375°F. In small bowl, combine ¼ cup margarine, 2 tablespoons sugar and salt; beat at medium speed until light and fluffy. Add ½ teaspoon lemon peel, vanilla and egg yolk; beat until smooth. Stir in ¾ cup flour and almonds; blend well. Press mixture in bottom and up sides of 10-inch tart pan or 9-inch springform pan. Bake at 375°F. for 10 minutes; cool.

Brush baked crust with 2 tablespoons of the currant jelly. In small bowl, combine ½ cup flour, 3 tablespoons sugar, ¼ cup margarine, ½ teaspoon grated lemon peel, almond extract, cream cheese and egg; beat 1 minute at medium speed. Pour filling over crust. Arrange pear halves on filling, rounded sides up and narrow ends pointing toward center. If desired, score pears making cuts ⅛-inch deep crosswise at ¼-inch intervals on each side of pear half. Bake at 375°F. for 25 to 35 minutes or until center is set.

In small saucepan, heat remaining 2 tablespoons currant jelly over medium heat until melted. Arrange berries in rows between pear halves. Brush jelly lightly over pears, berries and filling. Garnish as desired.
Yield: 8 servings.

NUTRITION PER SERVING:
Calories 320; Protein 5g; Carbohydrate 35g; Fat 19g; Sodium 195mg.

Caramel Pear Pastry

Pears are ripe when they yield to gentle pressure around the stem. Buy them a few days ahead, if necessary, to allow time for ripening at room temperature. See Cook's Note p. 139.

- 1 (8-oz.) can refrigerated crescent dinner rolls
- 2 ripe pears, thinly sliced
- 1 tablespoon sugar
- ¼ cup firmly packed brown sugar
- ¼ cup whipping cream or half-and-half

Heat oven to 375°F. Unroll dough into 2 long rectangles. On ungreased cookie sheet, overlap long sides ½ inch; firmly press perforations and edges to seal. Press or roll out to form 14x9-inch rectangle. Arrange pear slices in 2 rows lengthwise down center of rectangle leaving 1-inch edge on each side. Fold long sides 1 inch over filling; fold short ends over filling. Pinch slightly to seal corner folds. Sprinkle dough and pears with 1 tablespoon sugar.

Bake at 375°F. for 20 to 30 minutes or until crust is deep golden brown.

Meanwhile, in small saucepan over medium heat bring brown sugar and whipping cream to a boil. Boil gently 5 minutes, stirring constantly. Remove from heat; brush over pears. Serve warm or cool.
Yield: 8 servings.

NUTRITION PER SERVING:
Calories 180; Protein 2g; Carbohydrate 25g; Fat 8g; Sodium 240mg.

APRICOT TEA TART

This apricot and cream cheese tart is topped with an easy lattice crust.

CRUST
Pastry for Two-Crust Pie p. 268

APRICOT FILLING
1½ **cups chopped dried apricots**
 ½ **cup orange juice**
 2 **eggs**
 ½ **cup sugar**
 2 **tablespoons all purpose flour**
 ½ **cup light corn syrup**
 2 **tablespoons margarine or butter, melted**
 1 **teaspoon vanilla**

CREAM CHEESE FILLING
 1 **(3-oz.) pkg. cream cheese, softened**
 ¼ **cup sugar**
 1 **tablespoon all purpose flour**
 ⅓ **cup dairy sour cream**
 1 **egg**

TOPPING
 1 **teaspoon orange juice**
 1 **teaspoon sugar**

Prepare pastry for Two-Crust Pie using 10-inch tart pan with removable bottom or 9-inch pie pan.

Heat oven to 375°F. In medium saucepan, combine apricots and ½ cup orange juice; bring to a boil. Reduce heat to low; simmer uncovered for 1 to 2 minutes. Cool slightly. Reserve 1 tablespoonful apricot mixture for cream cheese filling.

Beat 2 eggs in small bowl; reserve 1 teaspoon for topping. Stir remaining beaten eggs, ½ cup sugar, 2 tablespoons flour, corn syrup, margarine and vanilla into apricot mixture in saucepan; mix well. Spoon into pastry-lined pan.

In small bowl, combine all cream cheese filling ingredients and reserved 1 tablespoonful apricot mixture; beat at medium speed until well blended. Spoon over apricot filling. Heat cookie sheet in oven for 10 minutes.

Meanwhile, to make lattice top cut remaining pastry into ½-inch wide strips. Arrange strips in lattice design over filling. Trim and seal edges. In small bowl, combine 1 teaspoon orange juice and reserved 1 teaspoon beaten egg; blend well. Gently brush over lattice crust; sprinkle with 1 teaspoon sugar.

Place tart on preheated cookie sheet. Bake at 375°F. for 45 to 55 minutes or until crust is golden brown. Cool; remove sides of pan. Store in refrigerator.
Yield: 10 to 12 servings.

NUTRITION PER SERVING:
Calories 380; Protein 4g; Carbohydrate 53g; Fat 17g; Sodium 200mg.

COUNTRY RHUBARB TART

An easy shaping of the pastry in this recipe results in the appearance of a tart in a 9-inch pie pan.

CRUST
Pastry for Filled One-Crust Pie p. 268

FILLING
1¼ **cups sugar**
 3 **tablespoons all purpose flour**
 ½ **teaspoon grated orange peel**
 3 **eggs, slightly beaten**
 ½ **cup dairy sour cream**
3½ **cups sliced rhubarb**

TOPPING
 ¼ **cup sugar**
 ¼ **cup all purpose flour**
 2 **tablespoons margarine or butter, softened**

Prepare pastry for Filled One-Crust Pie. Ease pastry into 9-inch pie pan; gently press toward center to avoid stretching. Press firmly against sides and bottom. Do not flute.

Heat oven to 375°F. In medium bowl, combine 1¼ cups sugar, 3 tablespoons flour and orange peel; stir in eggs and sour cream; mix well. Add rhubarb; toss gently. Spoon filling into pastry-lined pan. Fold edges of pastry over filling, ruffling decoratively.

In small bowl, combine all topping ingredients until crumbly. Sprinkle over filling. Bake at 375°F. for 50 to 60 minutes or until crust is light golden brown. Store in refrigerator.
Yield: 8 servings.

NUTRITION PER SERVING:
Calories 360; Protein 4g; Carbohydrate 53g; Fat 15g; Sodium 220mg.

FRESH FRUIT TARTS

Look for strawberry glaze by the fresh fruit in the produce section of your grocery store. It brings out the natural luster of these fruit-filled tarts.

CRUST
> **Pastry for Two-Crust Pie p. 268**

FILLING
> 5 cups assorted fresh fruit (blueberries, straw-berries, bananas)
> 1 (16-oz.) jar strawberry glaze
> ½ cup frozen whipped topping, thawed, or whipped cream

Prepare pastry for Two-Crust Pie. Heat oven to 450°F. Using fluted round cookie cutter, cut five 4-inch circles from each circle of pastry. Fit circles over backs of ungreased muffin cups. Pinch 5 equally spaced pleats around sides of each cup. Prick each pastry generously with fork.

Bake at 450°F. for 9 to 13 minutes or until light golden brown. Cool completely; remove from muffin cups.

In large bowl, combine fruit and strawberry glaze. Refrigerate until thoroughly chilled. Before serving, spoon ½ cup fruit mixture into each cooled tart shell; top with whipped topping.

Yield: 10 tarts.

NUTRITION PER SERVING:
Calories 320; Protein 2g; Carbohydrate 48g; Fat 13g; Sodium 180mg.

COUNTRY FRUIT TART

Now that fresh fruit can be shipped around the world, we can enjoy luscious fruit year-round. Use the fruits suggested or your own combination for a variety of colors and shapes.

CRUST
> **Pastry for One-Crust Pie p. 268**
> **Sugar**

FILLING
> 1 (3½-oz.) tube almond paste*
> 2 tablespoons margarine or butter, softened
> 1½ to 2 cups small strawberries, raspberries, sliced apricots, nectarines or peaches
> 2 to 4 tablespoons apple jelly
> Whipped cream, if desired

Prepare pastry for One-Crust Pie. Place pastry on large ungreased cookie sheet. Using paper pattern or salad plate as guide, cut 8-inch circle from center of pastry; reserve remaining pastry.

Heat oven to 450°F. In small bowl, combine almond paste and margarine; beat until smooth. Spread evenly on pastry circle to within 1 inch of edge. From remaining pastry, cut as many 1-inch circles or decorative shapes as possible, about 35. Moisten uncovered edge of pastry with water. Arrange small circles on edge of pastry, overlapping slightly. Sprinkle with sugar.

Bake at 450°F. for 9 to 11 minutes or until lightly browned. Cool completely on cookie sheet. Place on serving plate. Just before serving, arrange fresh fruit over filling, overlapping cut pieces slightly. In small saucepan, heat jelly just until warm; brush over fruit. Serve with whipped cream.

Yield: 6 to 8 servings.

TIP:
* The following almond paste made in the food processor can be substituted for the 3½-oz. tube almond paste. Place ½ cup toasted whole or slivered almonds in food processor bowl with metal blade. Process until finely ground. Add ⅔ cup powdered sugar and 1 tablespoon water along with the 2 tablespoons margarine from above. Process until smooth. Continue as directed above.

NUTRITION PER SERVING:
Calories 260; Protein 2g; Carbohydrate 27g; Fat 17g; Sodium 230mg.

Fresh Fruit Tarts

FUDGE CROSTATA WITH RASPBERRY SAUCE

A beautiful lattice crust bakes into the chocolate fudge filling in this decadent pie. The raspberry sauce adds the finishing touch.

CRUST
> **Pastry for Two-Crust Pie p. 268**

FILLING
- 1 **(6-oz.) pkg. (1 cup) semi-sweet chocolate chips**
- ½ **cup margarine or butter, softened**
- ⅔ **cup sugar**
- 1 **cup ground almonds**
- 1 **egg**
- 1 **egg, separated**

SAUCE
- 1 **(12-oz.) pkg. frozen whole raspberries, thawed**
- ¾ **cup sugar**
- 1 **teaspoon lemon juice**

GARNISH, if desired
> **Sweetened whipped cream**
> **Chocolate Curls p. 210**
> **Whole raspberries**

Prepare pastry for Two-Crust Pie using 10-inch tart pan with removable bottom or 9-inch pie pan.

Heat oven to 425°F. In small saucepan over low heat, melt chocolate chips and 2 tablespoons of the margarine, stirring constantly until smooth. In medium bowl, beat remaining 6 tablespoons margarine and ⅔ cup sugar until light and fluffy. Add almonds, 1 egg, egg yolk and melted chocolate; blend well. Spread mixture evenly over bottom of pastry-lined pan.

To make lattice top, cut remaining pastry into ½-inch wide strips. Arrange strips in lattice design over chocolate mixture. Trim and seal edges. In small bowl, beat egg white until foamy; gently brush over lattice.

Bake at 425°F. for 10 minutes. Reduce oven temperature to 350°F.; bake an additional 30 to 35 minutes or until crust is golden brown. Cool; remove sides of pan.

In blender container or food processor bowl with metal blade, blend raspberries at highest speed until smooth. Press through strainer to remove seeds; discard seeds. In small saucepan, combine raspberry puree, ¾ cup sugar and lemon juice; mix well. Bring mixture to a boil over medium-low heat. Boil 3 minutes, stirring constantly. Cool.

Garnish pie with whipped cream, Chocolate Curls and whole raspberries. Serve with raspberry sauce. Store in refrigerator.
Yield: 10 to 12 servings.

NUTRITION PER SERVING:
Calories 480; Protein 5g; Carbohydrate 50g; Fat 29g; Sodium 270mg.

MINI GRAPE TARTS

These delectable single-serving tarts are topped with colorful red and green grapes.

CRUST
> **Pastry for Two-Crust Pie p. 268**

FILLING
- ½ **cup whipping cream**
- 1 **(8-oz.) pkg. cream cheese, softened**
- ⅓ **cup sugar**
- 1 **teaspoon grated lemon peel**
- 1½ **cups red and green seedless grapes**
- ¼ **cup apple or currant jelly**

Prepare pastry for Two-Crust Pie. Heat oven to 425°F. Using round cookie cutter, cut five 4-inch circles from each circle of pastry. Fit circles over backs of ungreased muffin cups; press gently to mold over cups. Generously prick bottom of crusts with fork. Bake at 425°F. for 7 to 10 minutes or until light golden brown. Cool completely; remove from muffin cups.

In small bowl, combine whipping cream, cream cheese, sugar and lemon peel; beat until smooth and fluffy. Spoon into cooled tart shells, spreading evenly. Arrange grapes over filling to cover surface. Melt jelly in small saucepan over low heat; brush over grapes. Store in refrigerator. If desired, serve with additional whipped cream.
Yield: 10 tarts.

NUTRITION PER SERVING:
Calories 330; Protein 3g; Carbohydrate 32g; Fat 21g; Sodium 190mg.

Fudge Crostata with Raspberry Sauce

TIN ROOF FUDGE TART

Flavors of a popular ice cream treat team up for this tasty pie.

CRUST
    Pastry for One-Crust Pie p. 268
- 2 oz. dark chocolate candy bar or semi-sweet baking chocolate, chopped
- 1 tablespoon margarine or butter

PEANUT LAYER
- 20 caramels, unwrapped
- ⅓ cup whipping cream
- 1½ cups Spanish peanuts

MOUSSE LAYER
- 8 oz. dark chocolate candy bar or semi-sweet baking chocolate, chopped
- 2 tablespoons margarine or butter
- 1 cup whipping cream
- 2 teaspoons vanilla

TOPPING
- 5 caramels, unwrapped
- 3 tablespoons whipping cream
- 1 teaspoon margarine or butter

GARNISH
    Whipped cream, if desired
    Spanish peanuts, if desired

Prepare and bake pastry as directed for Baked Pie Shell using 10-inch tart pan with removable bottom or 9-inch pie pan.

In small, heavy saucepan over very low heat, melt 2 oz. dark chocolate and 1 tablespoon margarine, stirring constantly until smooth. Spread over bottom and sides of cooled, baked tart shell. Refrigerate until chocolate is set.

In medium saucepan over low heat, melt 20 caramels with ⅓ cup whipping cream until mixture is smooth, stirring frequently. Stir in 1½ cups peanuts until well coated; immediately spoon into chocolate-lined tart shell.

In small, heavy saucepan over very low heat, melt 8 oz. dark chocolate and and 2 tablespoons margarine, stirring constantly until smooth. Cool slightly, about 10 minutes. In small bowl, combine 1 cup whipping cream and vanilla; beat until soft peaks form. Fold ⅓ of the whipped cream into chocolate mixture; fold in remaining whipped cream. Spread over peanut layer. Refrigerate 2 hours or until set. Remove sides of pan.

In small saucepan over very low heat, melt all topping ingredients until smooth, stirring frequently. To garnish, pipe or spoon whipped cream around edge of chilled pie. Just before serving, drizzle with topping and sprinkle with peanuts. Store in refrigerator.
Yield: 12 servings.

NUTRITION PER SERVING:
Calories 560; Protein 10g; Carbohydrate 39g; Fat 45g; Sodium 250mg.

COOK'S NOTE

LINING TART PANS WITH PARCHMENT PAPER

Parchment paper is grease- and moisture-resistant. It is available in many supermarkets and kitchenware stores.

To line the removable bottom of a tart pan, trace the bottom onto a piece of parchment paper and cut out the parchment piece. Place it in the pan and grease it lightly. Prepare the dessert as directed.

At serving time, slip a pancake turner between the parchment paper and the removable bottom and carefully transfer the dessert to a serving plate.

CREAM PUFFS

This egg-rich dough depends on steam as the leavening agent. Fill the tender puff with your favorite sweet or savory fillings.

- ½ **cup water**
- ¼ **cup margarine or butter**
- ½ **cup all purpose flour**
- ¼ **teaspoon salt**
- 2 **eggs**

Heat oven to 400°F. Grease cookie sheet. In medium saucepan, combine water and margarine; bring to a boil over medium heat. Stir in flour and salt; cook, stirring vigorously, until mixture leaves sides of pan in smooth ball. Remove from heat. Add eggs 1 at a time, beating vigorously after each addition until mixture is smooth and glossy.* Spoon 6 mounds of dough (about ¼ cup each) 3 inches apart onto greased cookie sheet.

Bake at 400°F. for 30 to 40 minutes or until golden brown. Remove from oven; prick puffs with sharp knife to allow steam to escape. Remove from cookie sheet; cool completely. Split; if desired, remove any filaments of soft dough. Fill with ice cream, whipped cream or pudding. If desired, top with chocolate sauce.

Yield: 6 cream puffs.

TIPS:

* An electric mixer at medium speed can be used to beat in eggs 1 at a time. Beat for 1 minute after each addition until smooth and glossy. DO NOT OVERBEAT.

Recipe can be doubled to yield 12 puffs. Bake as directed above.

NUTRITION PER SERVING:
Calories 136; Protein 4g; Carbohydrate 8g; Fat 10g; Sodium 206mg.

VARIATIONS:

ECLAIRS: Pipe or spoon cream puff dough into 12 ovals about 3 to 3½-inches long. Bake as directed above. When cool, fill with prepared vanilla pudding and glaze with **Chocolate Glaze** p. 186.

SNACK CREAM PUFFS: Drop by tablespoons, making 20 small cream puffs. Bake as directed for 13 to 17 minutes.

PRALINE CREAM PUFFS: Prepare and bake 6 cream puffs as directed above. Fill with 2 cups vanilla ice cream. Drizzle with a combination of 1¼ cups warm caramel ice cream topping and ½ cup chopped pecans, toasted, p. 23

FRUIT AND CREAM PASTRY

Phyllo dough, found in your grocer's freezer, makes it possible to easily prepare this many-layered pastry.

- 10 **(18x14-inch) frozen phyllo (filo) pastry sheets, thawed**
- ½ **cup margarine or butter, melted**
- 1 **(3.5-oz.) pkg. instant vanilla pudding and pie filling mix**
- 1 **cup cold milk**
- 1 **cup frozen whipped topping, thawed**
- 1 **cup thinly sliced fresh or canned peaches**
- 1 **cup fresh or frozen blueberries, thawed**
  Powdered sugar

Heat oven to 375°F. Cover large cookie sheet with foil. Unroll phyllo sheets; do not separate. Cut stack of phyllo sheets in half; cover with plastic wrap or towel. Working with 1 stack of phyllo sheets, place 1 phyllo square on 1 end of foil-lined cookie sheet. Brush with melted margarine. Continue layering and brushing with margarine the remaining 9 squares phyllo dough. Repeat with remaining stack of phyllo sheets, forming 2 pastries.

Bake at 375°F. for 10 to 15 minutes or until golden brown. Cool completely.

In small bowl, combine pudding mix and milk; blend at low speed until smooth. Fold in whipped topping. Carefully remove baked pastries from foil. Place 1 cooled pastry on serving plate. Spread with pudding mixture; arrange fruit on pudding. Top with remaining pastry, pressing gently. Sprinkle with powdered sugar. Refrigerate until serving. Cut into squares.

Yield: 9 servings.

NUTRITION PER SERVING:
Calories 220; Protein 2g; Carbohydrate 23g; Fat 14g; Sodium 230mg.

Easy-Method Puff Pastry

In contrast to the classic method of using a solid layer of butter, this recipe uses the method of tossing the butter with the flour. Cold butter and ice water are essential to the success of this recipe.

    4 **cups all purpose flour**
  ½ **teaspoon salt**
    2 **cups cold butter**
  1¼ **cups ice water**
    1 **teaspoon lemon juice**

In large bowl, combine flour and salt. Cut butter into approximately 1x1x½-inch slices; add to flour mixture. Toss until butter is thoroughly coated with flour and slices are separated. In small bowl, combine ice water and lemon juice; pour over flour mixture. Using large spoon, quickly mix together (butter will remain in slices and flour will not be completely moistened).

On lightly floured surface, knead dough 10 to 15 times or until a very rough ball forms. Shape dough into a rectangle (dough will be dry in some areas). Flatten dough slightly, making corners square.

On well floured surface, roll dough to a 15x12-inch rectangle, keeping corners square. Fold dough crosswise into thirds forming a 12x5-inch rectangle. Give dough a quarter turn and repeat folding crosswise into thirds forming a 5x4-inch rectangle. Cover tightly with plastic wrap; refrigerate 20 minutes.

Repeat the rolling, folding, turning and folding steps, forming a 5x4-inch rectangle. Cover tightly with plastic wrap; refrigerate 20 minutes.

Repeat the rolling, folding, turning and folding steps forming a 5x4-inch rectangle. Cover tightly with plastic wrap; refrigerate at least 20 minutes.

To use dough in a recipe, cut dough crosswise in half. Wrap and refrigerate unused portion. Shape and bake puff pastry as directed in the following recipes: **Palmiers** (this page), **Cheesy Pastry Strips** p. 335 and **Patty Shells** p. 335.
Yield: 2 portions

Cook's Note

MAKING PUFF PASTRY

Try these easy tips to create layers of rich buttery pastry.

- For classic puff pastry, use butter. Butter needs to be cold but soft enough to be "moldable." It should not be hard or too soft.
- Dough needs to be chilled to handle it. Don't make puff pastry on a hot humid day.
- To achieve maximum layering, be sure to roll the rectangle to the exact size specified, making sure corners are very square.
- Use a sharp knife to cut straight down through the dough. Always leave the cut edge untreated — don't brush with egg or the edges won't puff. To cut patty shells, flour the cutter each time.
- Line the cookie sheets with parchment paper. Cut the paper to fit the cookie sheet.
- Be sure oven is heated to the proper temperature. To achieve maximum puffing, pastry should go from the refrigerator to a hot oven. Always refrigerate dough while the first sheet is baking.
- If you want to reuse dough scraps, layer them before rerolling. Rolling them into a ball will not allow for puffing during baking.

Palmiers

A swirl of cinnamon and sugar flavors this rich pastry.

  1 **portion Easy-Method Puff Pastry (this page)**
  ½ **cup sugar**
  1 **teaspoon cinnamon**

Line cookie sheets with parchment paper. With sharp knife, cut dough crosswise in half. Cover half of dough with plastic wrap; return to refrigerator.

Heat oven to 375°F. In small bowl, combine sugar and cinnamon; mix well. On lightly floured surface, roll remaining half of dough to 14x10-inch rectangle. Sprinkle with half of the sugar-cinnamon mixture; press lightly into dough. Starting from 2 shortest sides, roll sides to meet in center. With sharp knife, cut into about 3/8-inch slices. Place 2 inches apart on paper-lined cookie sheets.

Bake at 375°F. for 15 to 20 minutes or until golden brown. Remove from paper; cool on wire rack. Repeat with remaining piece of dough and cinnamon sugar mixture. Serve with coffee, tea or as a dessert.

Yield: 56 palmiers.

NUTRITION PER SERVING:
Calories 50; Protein 1g; Carbohydrate 5g; Fat 3g; Sodium 45mg.

PATTY SHELLS

Fill these with fruit yogurt and fresh fruit for a special dessert.

1   portion Easy-Method Puff Pastry p. 334

Line cookie sheets with parchment paper. With sharp knife, cut the portion of dough crosswise in half. Cover half of dough with plastic wrap; return to the refrigerator.

Heat oven to 425°F. On lightly floured surface, roll remaining half of dough into a 12-inch square. Cut dough with floured 3½-inch round-shaped cookie cutter. Do not twist cutter. Dip cutter in flour between cuts. With floured 2½-inch round-shaped cutter, cut into centers of 3½-inch circles by cutting to but not completely through pastry. (This will create center portion to be removed after baking.) Place 2 inches apart on paper-lined cookie sheets.

Bake at 425°F. for 15 to 20 minutes or until golden brown. Remove from paper. Using fork, remove centers from patty shells; cool on wire rack. Repeat with remaining piece of dough.

Yield: 18 patty shells.

TIP:
Three 10-oz. pkg. frozen puff pastry shells can be substituted for recipe.

NUTRITION PER SERVING:
Calories 130; Protein 1g; Carbohydrate 10g; Fat 9g; Sodium 120mg.

CHEESY PASTRY STRIPS

These are a wonderful accompaniment to soup or salad.

1   portion Easy-Method Puff Pastry p. 334
¼   cup grated Parmesan cheese
¾   teaspoon dried basil leaves
¼   teaspoon garlic powder
1   egg, beaten

Line cookie sheets with parchment paper. Heat oven to 425°F. In small bowl, combine Parmesan cheese, basil and garlic powder; mix well. On lightly floured surface, roll dough to 14x10-inch rectangle. Brush with egg; sprinkle with cheese mixture. With sharp knife, cut into two 14x5-inch rectangles. Cut each rectangle into twenty eight 5x½-inch strips. Place strips 2 inches apart on paper-lined cookie sheets.*

Bake at 425°F. for 15 to 20 minutes or until golden brown. Remove from paper; cool on wire rack.

Yield: 56 pastry strips.

TIP:
* Strips of dough can be twisted 3 or 4 times before placing on paper-lined cookie sheets. Press ends of dough down on paper.

NUTRITION PER SERVING:
Calories 50; Protein 1g; Carbohydrate 3g; Fat 4g; Sodium 55mg.

COOK'S NOTE

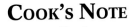

PURCHASED PUFF PASTRY

Purchased puff pastry can be substituted in these recipes. Be sure to purchase the freshest pastry possible. Thaw the puff pastry in the refrigerator and keep it cold during the preparation of the recipe. Be sure the oven is heated to the proper temperature. To achieve maximum puffing, pastry should go from the refrigerator to a hot oven. Always refrigerate dough while the first sheet is baking.

STEP-BY-STEP FEATURE ～
How to Handle Phyllo Dough for Strudel

STEP 1. Prepare filling ingredients. After unwrapping the phyllo dough, cover it with plastic wrap. Separate the sheets as you need them, leaving remaining sheets covered.

STEP 2. Working quickly, top the pastry sheets with filling to within 2 inches of edges. Fold the shorter sides of phyllo over filling. Starting with longer side and using plastic wrap to lift, carefully roll up.

APPLE MINCEMEAT STRUDEL

Thaw phyllo in the refrigerator and keep it cold until ready to use. Unused phyllo pastry can be stored tightly wrapped in the refrigerator for up to 1 week, or it can be refrozen.

1	medium apple, chopped
2	tablespoons brown sugar
1/2	teaspoon grated orange peel
1/4	teaspoon cinnamon
1	cup prepared mincemeat
8	(18x14-inch) frozen phyllo (filo) pastry sheets, thawed
1/3	cup margarine or butter, melted
4	tablespoons dry bread crumbs

Heat oven to 375°F. Grease cookie sheet. In medium bowl, combine apple, brown sugar, orange peel and cinnamon. Stir in mincemeat; set aside.

Unroll phyllo sheets; cover with plastic wrap or towel. Place 1 phyllo sheet on sheet of plastic wrap; brush with margarine and sprinkle with 1 tablespoon bread crumbs. Repeat layering with remaining phyllo and margarine, sprinkling 1 tablespoon bread crumbs on every other sheet. (Top phyllo sheet should be brushed with margarine only.) Spoon mincemeat mixture over phyllo to within 2 inches of edges; press lightly. Fold shorter sides of phyllo up over filling. Starting with longer side and using plastic wrap, lift phyllo and carefully roll up jelly-roll fashion. Place seam side down on greased cookie sheet. Make several crosswise slits in top of roll. Brush with margarine.

Bake at 375°F. for 20 to 25 minutes or until golden brown. Cool completely. To serve, cut into slices.
Yield: 12 servings.

NUTRITION PER SERVING:
Calories 130; Protein 1g; Carbohydrate 21g; Fat 6g; Sodium 170mg.

Apple Mincemeat Strudel

MINIATURE CUSTARD CREAM PUFFS

Cluster these dainty cream puffs on your favorite dessert plates and drizzle them with a rich chocolate glaze.

CREAM PUFFS
- 1 cup water
- ½ cup margarine or butter
- 1 cup all purpose flour
- ½ teaspoon salt
- 4 eggs

FILLING
- 1 (3.5-oz.) pkg. instant vanilla pudding and pie filling mix
- 1¾ cups milk
- ¾ cup whipping cream, whipped

GLAZE
- 3 oz. semi-sweet chocolate
- 1 oz. unsweetened chocolate
- 1 tablespoon shortening

Heat oven to 425°F. Grease cookie sheets. In medium saucepan, combine water and margarine; bring to a boil over medium heat. Stir in flour and salt; cook, stirring constantly, until mixture leaves sides of pan in smooth ball. Remove from heat. Add eggs 1 at a time, beating vigorously after each addition until smooth and glossy.* Spoon 32 to 40 scant tablespoons of dough onto greased cookie sheets.

Bake at 425°F. for 13 to 17 minutes or until golden brown. Prick puffs with sharp knife to allow steam to escape. Remove from cookie sheets; cool completely.

In large bowl, combine pudding mix and milk. Beat at low speed until well blended, about 2 minutes; let stand 5 minutes. Fold in whipped cream until well blended.

In small saucepan over low heat, melt glaze ingredients; stir until smooth. To assemble, cut off top of each puff; if desired, remove any filaments of soft dough. Fill with pudding mixture; replace tops. Arrange 4 to 5 puffs on each dessert plate; drizzle with glaze. Serve immediately. Store in refrigerator.
Yield: 8 servings.

TIP:
* An electric mixer at medium speed can be used to beat in eggs 1 at a time. Beat for 1 minute after each addition until smooth and glossy. DO NOT OVER-BEAT.

NUTRITION PER SERVING:
Calories 430; Protein 8g; Carbohydrate 34g; Fat 31g; Sodium 390mg.

VARIATION:

MINIATURE AMARETTO CREAM PUFFS:
Prepare recipe as directed above except substitute ¼ cup amaretto for ¼ cup of the milk in filling.

LITTLE JACK HORNER PIES

These hand-held pies are a great casual dessert.

- Pastry for Two-Crust Pie p. 268
- ⅔ cup plum, strawberry or peach preserves
- 2 tablespoons sugar
- ¼ teaspoon cinnamon

Heat oven to 400°F. Prepare pastry for Two-Crust Pie. Cut each circle of pastry into 5 rounds with 4-inch cookie cutter; spoon about 1 tablespoon preserves onto half of each pastry round. Fold pastry over filling; press edges with fork to seal.

In small bowl, combine sugar and cinnamon; sprinkle over pies. Place on ungreased cookie sheets. Bake at 400°F. for 8 to 10 minutes or until light golden brown.
Yield: 10 pies.

TIP:
To make pie crust cookies from trimmings, cut pastry into shapes; sprinkle with remaining sugar and cinnamon. Bake on ungreased cookie sheet at 400°F. for 5 to 8 minutes or until light golden brown.

NUTRITION PER SERVING:
Calories 240; Protein 1g; Carbohydrate 34g; Fat 11g; Sodium 140mg.

COUNTRY FRENCH APPLE CRESCENT CASSEROLE

This recipe for apple dumplings in custard won $10,000 in the 34th Pillsbury BAKE-OFF® Contest. It is reminiscent of an Old World specialty and is a delicious addition to any menu.

DUMPLINGS
- 2 tablespoons sugar
- ½ to 1 teaspoon cinnamon
- 1 (8-oz.) can refrigerated crescent dinner rolls
- 1 large apple, peeled, cut into 8 slices

SAUCE
- ½ cup sugar
- ½ cup whipping cream
- 1 tablespoon almond extract or amaretto
- 1 egg

TOPPING
- ½ cup sliced almonds
- Cinnamon

Heat oven to 375°F. In small bowl, combine 2 tablespoons sugar and ½ teaspoon cinnamon; blend well. Separate dough into 8 triangles; sprinkle sugar mixture evenly over each. Gently press sugar mixture into each triangle, flattening each slightly. Place apple slice on wide end of each triangle; tuck in edges around apple slice. Roll up, starting at wide end; roll to opposite point. Seal all seams. Place, tip side down, in ungreased 9-inch round baking dish or pie pan, placing long side of 7 filled crescents around outside edge of dish and 1 in center.

Bake at 375°F. for 15 to 20 minutes or until golden brown.

In small bowl using wire whisk, combine all sauce ingredients until well blended. Spoon sauce mixture evenly over partially baked rolls. Sprinkle with almonds and cinnamon.

Bake an additional 13 to 18 minutes or until deep golden brown. Cover top of pan with foil during last 5 minutes of baking time if necessary to prevent excessive browning. Serve warm. Store in refrigerator.
Yield: 8 servings.

NUTRITION PER SERVING:
Calories 270; Protein 4g; Carbohydrate 31g; Fat 15g; Sodium 250mg.

APPLE CROUSTADE

Tender, flaky pastry desserts like this are easy to create with frozen phyllo dough found in your supermarket freezer section.

- 1 (21-oz.) can apple fruit pie filling
- ½ teaspoon cinnamon
- 10 (18x14-inch) frozen phyllo (filo) pastry sheets, thawed
- ½ cup margarine or butter, melted

Heat oven to 375°F. In small bowl, combine pie filling and cinnamon; set aside. Unroll phyllo sheets; cover with plastic wrap or towel. Brush each phyllo sheet lightly with margarine; fold lengthwise into thirds. Brush top of each generously with margarine. Arrange strips, margarine side up, in spoke-fashion in ungreased 12-inch pizza pan, allowing 1 end of each strip to overlap others in center and other end to extend about 10 inches over side of pan. Spread pie filling in 8-inch circle in center of phyllo . Loosely twist each strip; coil to form a roll. (Phyllo may tear slightly as twisted.) Lay roll over edge of filling, leaving a 3-inch circle of filling uncovered in center.

Bake at 375°F. for 20 to 30 minutes or until golden brown. Serve warm or cool, cut into wedges.
Yield: 8 servings.

TIP:
If phyllo dries out while arranging in spoke fashion, brush with additional melted margarine.

NUTRITION PER SERVING:
Calories 220; Protein 1g; Carbohydrate 26g; Fat 13g; Sodium 190mg.

Mom's Apple Dumplings

For the best results, use firm baking apples. See p. 11 for examples.

SAUCE

1½ cups sugar
1½ cups water
¼ cup red cinnamon candies
¼ teaspoon cinnamon
¼ teaspoon nutmeg

DUMPLINGS

2 cups all purpose flour
2 teaspoons baking powder
1 teaspoon salt
⅔ cup shortening
½ to ⅔ cup cold milk
6 small (2½-inch diameter) baking apples, peeled and cored
3 tablespoons margarine or butter
1 egg white, beaten
1 tablespoon sugar
   Half-and-half, if desired

In medium saucepan, combine all sauce ingredients. Bring mixture to a full rolling boil, stirring occasionally. Set aside.

Heat oven to 375°F. In large bowl, combine flour, baking powder and salt. Using pastry blender or fork, cut in shortening until mixture resembles coarse crumbs. Sprinkle flour mixture with milk while tossing and mixing lightly with fork, adding enough milk until soft dough forms. Shape dough into ball. Roll on lightly floured surface into 18x12-inch rectangle. Cut rectangle into 6 squares.* Place an apple in center of each pastry square; dot with margarine. Bring corners of pastry squares up to top of apple; press edges to seal. Repeat with remaining apples. Place in ungreased 13x9-inch pan. Pour sauce in pan evenly around dumplings. Brush dumplings with egg white; sprinkle with 1 tablespoon sugar.

Bake at 375°F. for 40 to 50 minutes or until dumplings are light golden brown and apples are tender. Serve warm or cool with half-and-half.
Yield: 6 dumplings.

TIP:
* If desired, prepare 5 dumplings, reserving remaining pastry square for decorative cutouts. Garnish sealed dumplings with cutouts. Bake as directed above.

Mom's Apple Dumplings

HIGH ALTITUDE:
Above 3500 Feet: No change.
NUTRITION PER SERVING:
Calories 780; Protein 7g; Carbohydrate 114g; Fat 33g; Sodium 580mg.

Pear Dumplings

In this recipe, whole pears are wrapped in dough and baked until golden and tender.

DUMPLINGS

   Pastry for Two-Crust Pie p. 268
4 medium, firm, ripe whole pears
1 egg
1 tablespoon milk

SAUCE

½ cup sugar
1 teaspoon cornstarch
1 cup white Zinfandel wine
2 tablespoons margarine or butter
½ to 1 teaspoon cinnamon

Grease cookie sheet. Prepare pastry for Two-Crust Pie. Heat oven to 425°F. Cut four 4½-inch rounds from 1 circle of pastry. Cut remaining pastry into ¾-inch wide strips. Peel pears leaving stem intact. Using apple corer, remove core from bottom half of each pear. Dry surface of pears with paper towels. Place 1 pear in center of pastry round. Press pastry up around base of pear as far as it will go; then attach pastry strips, overlapping each ¼ inch, to completely wrap pear. Press to seal edges. Repeat to wrap remaining pears. Place wrapped pears on greased cookie sheet. In small bowl, beat egg and milk; brush over pastry on each pear.

Bake at 425°F. for 30 to 40 minutes or until golden brown, brushing with egg mixture once halfway through baking.

Meanwhile, in small saucepan combine sugar and cornstarch; mix well. Stir in wine, margarine and cinnamon. Bring to a boil; boil 1 minute, stirring constantly. Reduce heat; simmer until serving time, stirring occasionally. Serve warm dumplings with warm sauce.
Yield: 4 dumplings.

NUTRITION PER SERVING:
Calories 790; Protein 5g; Carbohydrate 96g; Fat 40g; Sodium 740mg.

QUICK BREADS

∼

Q uick breads are a welcome addition to breakfast, lunch and dinner. Flaky biscuits fresh from the oven round out a breakfast of fruit and coffee. Enjoy warm herb muffins with soup for a special lunch, or impress dinner guests with a basket of tender golden brown popovers.

Quick breads, like popovers, biscuits, breads and muffins, can be prepared in just minutes because they don't require the time and techniques that yeast breads do. Quick breads are an easy way to deliver fresh-from-the-oven baked goods to meals from everyday to elegant.

Pictured: **Cherry Nut Bread** *p. 379,* **Caramel Biscuit Ring-a-Round** *p. 398,* **Magic Marshmallow Crescent Puffs** *p. 406*

STEP-BY-STEP FEATURE ~
How to Make Baking Powder Biscuits

STEP 1. Using pastry blender, cut shortening into flour mixture until consistency of coarse crumbs. Add milk; stir with fork until soft dough forms.

STEP 2. Dust a rolling pin and smooth surface with flour. Roll out dough to ½-inch thickness. Cut dough with floured 2-inch cutter.

BAKING POWDER BISCUITS

Tossing or kneading biscuit dough lightly helps distribute leavening for even baking and rising. These traditional biscuits are great served with any meal. For variety, try the delicious variations.

- **2 cups all purpose flour**
- **3 teaspoons baking powder**
- **½ teaspoon salt**
- **½ cup shortening**
- **¾ to 1 cup milk**

Heat oven to 450°F. In large bowl, combine flour, baking powder and salt. Using pastry blender or fork, cut in shortening until mixture resembles coarse crumbs. Stirring with fork, add enough milk until mixture leaves sides of bowl and forms a soft, moist dough.

On floured surface, toss dough lightly until no longer sticky. Roll or press out to ½-inch thickness; cut with floured 2-inch round cutter. Place biscuits on ungreased cookie sheet.

Bake at 450°F. for 8 to 12 minutes or until light golden brown. Serve warm.
Yield: 12 to 14 biscuits.

FOOD PROCESSOR DIRECTIONS:
In food processor bowl with metal blade, combine flour, baking powder and salt. Process with 5 on-off pulses to mix. Add shortening to flour mixture. Process until mixture resembles coarse crumbs. Add *½ to ⅔ cup* milk; process with on-off pulses just until ball starts to form. On lightly floured surface, roll or press out to ½-inch thickness; cut with floured 2-inch round cutter. Continue as directed above.

HIGH ALTITUDE:
Above 3500 Feet: No change.

NUTRITION PER SERVING:
Calories 140; Protein 2g; Carbohydrate 14g; Fat 8g; Sodium 155mg.

(Recipe continued on next page.)

Baking Powder Biscuits

CARROT AND HERB DINNER BISCUITS

Biscuits are at their best when served warm from the oven and these are no exception. The herb and vegetable flavor is a delicious change of pace.

- 1¼ cups all purpose flour
- ¾ cup cornmeal
- ¼ cup sugar
- 3 teaspoons baking powder
- 1 teaspoon dried basil leaves
- 1 teaspoon dried parsley flakes
- ½ teaspoon salt
- ¾ cup margarine or butter
- ½ cup shredded carrots
- ⅓ cup milk
- 1 egg

Heat oven to 400°F. In medium bowl, combine flour, cornmeal, sugar, baking powder, basil, parsley flakes and salt; blend well. Using pastry blender or fork, cut in margarine until mixture resembles coarse crumbs. Stir in carrots. Add milk and egg, stirring just until moistened. To form each biscuit, drop ¼ cup of dough onto ungreased cookie sheet.

Bake at 400°F. for 12 to 14 minutes or until light golden brown. Serve warm.
Yield: 12 biscuits.

HIGH ALTITUDE:
Above 3500 Feet: No change.

NUTRITION PER SERVING:
Calories 210; Protein 3g; Carbohydrate 21g; Fat 12g; Sodium 310mg.

CHEDDAR CHIVE DROP BISCUITS

For tender biscuits, stir gently and work quickly. Stirring just until all the dry ingredients are moistened helps keep biscuits from becoming tough.

- 2 cups all purpose flour
- 3 teaspoons baking powder
- 1 teaspoon salt
- ½ cup shortening
- 1¼ cups plain yogurt
- 4 oz. (1 cup) shredded Cheddar cheese
- ¼ cup chopped fresh chives

Heat oven to 450°F. Grease cookie sheets. In large bowl, combine flour, baking powder and salt; blend well. Using pastry blender or fork, cut in shortening until mixture resembles coarse crumbs. Add yogurt, cheese and chives; stir just until moistened. Drop dough by generous tablespoonfuls onto greased cookie sheets.

Bake at 450°F. for 9 to 12 minutes or until light golden brown. Serve warm.
Yield: 18 biscuits.

HIGH ALTITUDE:
Above 3500 Feet: No change.

NUTRITION PER SERVING:
Calories 140; Protein 4g; Carbohydrate 12g; Fat 8g; Sodium 220mg.

Carrot and Herb Dinner Biscuits,
Cheddar Chive Drop Biscuits

CURRANT SCONES

The original scones from Scotland were made with oats and griddle-baked. This updated version is made with flour and is slightly sweet. Serve them warm with butter and jam.

- 2 cups all purpose flour
- ¼ cup sugar
- 3 teaspoons baking powder
- ¼ teaspoon salt
- ¼ cup margarine or butter
- ⅔ cup dried currants
- 1 (5-oz.) can (⅔ cup) evaporated milk
- 1 egg
  Sugar

Heat oven to 400°F. In medium bowl, combine flour, sugar, baking powder and salt; blend well. Using pastry blender or fork, cut in margarine until mixture is crumbly. Stir in currants. In small bowl, combine evaporated milk and egg; add all at once, stirring just until moistened.

On well floured surface, gently knead dough 5 or 6 times. Place on ungreased cookie sheet; press into 8-inch circle, about 1 inch thick. Cut into 8 wedges; do not separate. Sprinkle with sugar.

Bake at 400°F. for 15 to 20 minutes or until golden brown. Cut into wedges; serve warm.

Yield: 8 scones.

HIGH ALTITUDE:
Above 3500 Feet: No change.

NUTRITION PER SERVING:
Calories 250; Protein 6g; Carbohydrate 43g; Fat 7g; Sodium 280mg.

COOK'S NOTE

CLOTTED CREAM

Clotted cream, also known as Devonshire cream, is made by gently heating unpasteurized cream until a layer of thick cream forms on the surface. The thickened cream is removed when it has cooled.

SCOTTISH SCONES

In England or Scotland, scones are split in half and served with butter, preserves and clotted cream.

SCONES
- 1½ cups all purpose flour
- ¾ cup rolled oats
- ¼ cup firmly packed brown sugar
- 2 teaspoons baking powder
- ½ teaspoon salt
- ½ teaspoon cinnamon
- ½ cup margarine or butter
- ½ cup milk

TOPPING
- 1 tablespoon margarine or butter, melted
- 1 tablespoon sugar
- ¼ teaspoon cinnamon

Heat oven to 375°F. Lightly grease cookie sheet. In medium bowl, combine flour, oats, brown sugar, baking powder, salt and ½ teaspoon cinnamon; blend well. Using pastry blender or fork, cut in ½ cup margarine until mixture is crumbly. Add milk all at once, stirring just until moistened.

On floured surface, gently knead dough 5 or 6 times. Place on greased cookie sheet; press into 6-inch circle, about 1 inch thick. Brush top of dough with melted margarine. In small bowl, combine sugar and ¼ teaspoon cinnamon; sprinkle over top. Cut dough into 8 wedges; separate slightly.

Bake at 375°F. for 20 to 30 minutes or until golden brown. Serve warm.

Yield: 8 scones.

HIGH ALTITUDE:
Above 3500 Feet: No change.

NUTRITION PER SERVING:
Calories 270; Protein 4g; Carbohydrate 32g; Fat 14g; Sodium 370mg.

WHOLE WHEAT DATE SCONES

Try this updated version of a traditional English teatime biscuit wedge.

1¼ **cups all purpose flour**
 ¾ **cup whole wheat flour**
 2 **tablespoons sugar**
2½ **teaspoons baking powder**
 ½ **teaspoon salt**
 6 **tablespoons margarine or butter**
 ½ **cup chopped dates**
 ½ **cup milk**
 2 **eggs**

Heat oven to 425°F. Grease cookie sheet. In medium bowl, combine flour, whole wheat flour, sugar, baking powder and salt; mix well. Using pastry blender or fork, cut in margarine until mixture resembles coarse crumbs. Stir in dates. In small bowl, combine milk and eggs; reserve 2 tablespoons. Add remaining egg mixture all at once, stirring just until moistened.

On floured surface, gently knead dough to make a smooth ball. Place on greased cookie sheet. With floured hands, press dough into 8-inch circle. Cut into 8 wedges; do not separate. Brush with reserved egg mixture.

Bake at 425°F. for 13 to 15 minutes or until golden brown. Cut into wedges; serve warm.

Yield: 8 scones.

HIGH ALTITUDE:
Above 3500 Feet: No change.

NUTRITION PER SERVING:
Calories 260; Protein 6g; Carbohydrate 35g; Fat 11g; Sodium 350mg.

MINI-CHIP ORANGE SCONE DROPS

Since they require no kneading, you can make these scone drops even when you're in a time crunch.

SCONES
 2 **cups all purpose flour**
 ⅓ **cup sugar**
 2 **teaspoons baking powder**
 ½ **teaspoon salt**
 ¼ **teaspoon baking soda**
 ⅓ **cup margarine or butter**
 ⅓ **cup orange juice**
 ⅓ **cup milk**
 2 **tablespoons grated orange peel**
 ½ **cup miniature semi-sweet chocolate chips**

TOPPING
 3 **tablespoons sugar**
 ½ **teaspoon cinnamon**

Heat oven to 375°F. Grease cookie sheets. In large bowl, combine flour, ⅓ cup sugar, baking powder, salt and baking soda; blend well. Using pastry blender or fork, cut in margarine until mixture resembles coarse crumbs. Add orange juice, milk and orange peel; stir just until dry ingredients are moistened. Stir in chocolate chips. Drop by heaping teaspoonfuls 2 inches apart onto greased cookie sheets.

In small bowl, combine topping ingredients; sprinkle over scones. Bake at 375°F. for 8 to 10 minutes or until light golden brown. Immediately remove from cookie sheets. Serve warm.

Yield: 30 scones.

HIGH ALTITUDE:
Above 3500 Feet: No change.

NUTRITION PER SERVING:
Calories 80; Protein 1g; Carbohydrate 12g; Fat 3g; Sodium 90mg.

Bacon Biscuit Wedges

BACON BISCUIT WEDGES

This easy-to-make version of a southern favorite is flavored with bacon.

- 2 **cups all purpose flour**
- ¼ **cup (about 4 slices) crumbled cooked bacon**
- 2 **teaspoons baking powder**
- ½ **teaspoon salt**
- ¼ **cup shortening**
- ⅔ **to 1 cup milk**
- 1 **tablespoon margarine or butter, melted**

Heat oven to 400°F. Grease cookie sheet. In large bowl, combine flour, bacon, baking powder and salt. Using pastry blender or fork, cut in shortening until mixture resembles coarse crumbs. Stirring with fork, add enough milk until mixture leaves sides of bowl and forms a soft, moist dough. On floured surface, gently knead dough 5 or 6 times or until no longer sticky. Shape dough into ball. Place on greased cookie sheet; flatten into 8-inch circle. With sharp knife, score top surface into 8 wedges.

Bake at 400°F. for 21 to 26 minutes or until golden brown. Brush with margarine. Cut into wedges; serve warm.

Yield: 8 biscuit wedges.

HIGH ALTITUDE:
Above 3500 Feet: No change.

NUTRITION PER SERVING:
Calories 220; Protein 5g; Carbohydrate 25g; Fat 10g; Sodium 300mg.

ORANGE PRUNE DROP SCONES

Next time you are looking for a breakfast bread, try these fiber-rich, tender scones.

2¼ **cups all purpose flour**
 ½ **cup sugar**
  3 **teaspoons baking powder**
 ½ **teaspoon salt**
  2 **teaspoons grated orange peel**
 ¼ **cup margarine or butter**
  1 **egg**
  1 **to 1¼ cups buttermilk**
  1 **cup finely chopped dried, pitted prunes**
     Sugar

Heat oven to 375°F. Grease cookie sheet. In large bowl, combine flour, ½ cup sugar, baking powder, salt and orange peel; blend well. Using pastry blender or fork, cut in margarine until mixture is crumbly. Add egg and enough buttermilk until mixture leaves sides of bowl and forms a moist dough. Stir in prunes. To form each scone, drop ¼ cup of dough onto greased cookie sheets. Sprinkle with sugar.

Bake at 375°F. for 13 to 16 minutes or until edges are light golden brown. Serve warm.

Yield: 14 scones.

HIGH ALTITUDE:
Above 3500 Feet: Increase flour to 2½ cups; decrease buttermilk to ¾ to 1 cup. Bake as directed above.

NUTRITION PER SERVING:
Calories 180; Protein 4g; Carbohydrate 31g; Fat 4g; Sodium 210mg.

DOUBLE ORANGE SCONES

Scones are generally richer than biscuits because they contain eggs, cream or milk, and butter. These are highlighted with orange flavor.

  2 **cups all purpose flour**
  3 **tablespoons sugar**
2½ **teaspoons baking powder**
  2 **teaspoons grated orange peel**
 ⅓ **cup margarine or butter**
 ½ **cup chopped canned mandarin orange segments, drained**
 ¼ **cup milk**
  1 **egg, slightly beaten**
  1 **tablespoon sugar**

Heat oven to 400°F. Lightly grease cookie sheet. In large bowl, combine flour, 3 tablespoons sugar, baking powder and orange peel. Using pastry blender or fork, cut in margarine until mixture resembles coarse crumbs. Add orange segments, milk and egg. With fork, stir just until mixture leaves sides of bowl and soft dough forms.

On floured surface, gently knead dough 10 times. Place on greased cookie sheet; roll or pat into 6-inch circle. Sprinkle dough with 1 tablespoon sugar. Cut dough into 8 wedges; separate slightly.

Bake at 400°F. for 15 to 20 minutes or until golden brown. Serve warm.

Yield: 8 scones.

HIGH ALTITUDE:
Above 3500 Feet: Increase flour to 2¼ cups. Bake as directed above.

NUTRITION PER SERVING:
Calories 220; Protein 4g; Carbohydrate 32g; Fat 9g; Sodium 200mg.

Basil Parmesan Scones

These rich savory scones get their texture from gentle handling and whipping cream rather than butter or shortening.

1¼ to 1½ cups all purpose flour
3 tablespoons oat bran
2 tablespoons grated Parmesan cheese
2 teaspoons baking powder
1 teaspoon dried basil leaves
½ teaspoon salt
1 cup whipping cream
1 teaspoon oat bran

Heat oven to 425°F. Grease cookie sheet. In large bowl, combine 1¼ cups flour, 3 tablespoons oat bran, cheese, baking powder, basil and salt; blend well. Reserve 1 teaspoon whipping cream. Add remaining cream to flour mixture, stirring just until soft dough forms. If dough is too wet, stir in flour 1 tablespoon at a time.

On floured surface, gently knead dough to form smooth ball. Place on greased cookie sheet; pat or roll to 6-inch circle. Cut into 8 wedges; do not separate. Brush with reserved 1 teaspoon whipping cream; sprinkle with 1 teaspoon oat bran.

Bake at 425°F. for 15 to 18 minutes or until lightly browned. Cut into wedges; serve warm.

Yield: 8 scones.

HIGH ALTITUDE:
Above 3500 Feet: No change.

NUTRITION PER SERVING:
Calories 200; Protein 4g; Carbohydrate 21g; Fat 12g; Sodium 250mg.

Fresh Herb Scones

Three popular herbs combine in this savory supper scone.

2 cups all purpose flour
¼ cup chopped fresh parsley
1 tablespoon sugar
1 tablespoon chopped fresh thyme or
    1 teaspoon dried thyme leaves
3 teaspoons baking powder
1 teaspoon chopped fresh rosemary or
    ¼ teaspoon dried rosemary leaves, crushed
½ teaspoon salt
⅓ cup margarine or butter
½ cup milk
1 egg, slightly beaten

Heat oven to 400°F. Lightly grease cookie sheet. In large bowl, combine flour, parsley, sugar, thyme, baking powder, rosemary and salt. Using pastry blender or fork, cut in margarine until mixture resembles coarse crumbs. Stir in milk and egg just until moistened.

On floured surface, gently knead dough 10 times. Place on greased cookie sheet; roll or pat dough into 6-inch circle. Cut into 8 wedges; separate slightly.

Bake at 400°F. for 15 to 20 minutes or until golden brown. Cut into wedges; serve warm.

Yield: 8 scones.

HIGH ALTITUDE:
Above 3500 Feet: Decrease baking powder to 2 teaspoons. Bake as directed above.

NUTRITION PER SERVING:
Calories 210; Protein 5g; Carbohydrate 27g; Fat 9g; Sodium 350mg.

POTATO SCONES

Scones can be made in various shapes including rounds, squares, triangles and diamonds.

- 1¼ **cups all purpose flour**
- ½ **cup mashed potato flakes**
- 1 **tablespoon sugar**
- 2½ **teaspoons baking powder**
- ½ **teaspoon baking soda**
- ½ **teaspoon onion salt**
- ¼ **cup margarine or butter**
- ½ **cup buttermilk**
- 1 **egg, slightly beaten**
- 1 **tablespoon milk**

Heat oven to 375°F. In large bowl, combine flour, potato flakes, sugar, baking powder, baking soda and onion salt; blend well. Using pastry blender or fork, cut in margarine until mixture is crumbly. Add buttermilk and egg; stir just until moistened.

On well floured surface, gently knead dough 5 or 6 times. Place on ungreased cookie sheet; press into 7-inch circle, about 1 inch thick. Brush with milk.

Bake at 375°F. for 15 to 25 minutes or until golden brown. Cut into wedges; serve warm.
Yield: 8 scones.

HIGH ALTITUDE:
Above 3500 Feet: No change.

NUTRITION PER SERVING:
Calories 160; Protein 3g; Carbohydrate 20g; Fat 7g; Sodium 360mg.

BLACK PEPPER AND ONION SCONES

For optimum flavor, use freshly ground black pepper and adjust the level to suit your taste buds.

- ¾ **cup chopped onions**
- ¼ **cup margarine or butter**
- 2 **cups all purpose flour**
- 2 **tablespoons sugar**
- 3 **teaspoons baking powder**
- ½ **teaspoon salt**
- ½ **to 1 teaspoon coarsely ground black pepper**
- ½ **cup whipping cream**
- 1 **egg**
   Margarine or butter, melted

Heat oven to 400°F. In small skillet, cook onions in ¼ cup margarine until crisp-tender; set aside. Cool slightly.

In medium bowl, combine flour, sugar, baking powder, salt and pepper; blend well. Add whipping cream, egg and onions; stir just until moistened.

On floured surface, gently knead dough 5 or 6 times. Place on ungreased cookie sheet; press into 8-inch circle, about ½ inch thick. Cut into 8 wedges; separate slightly.

Bake at 400°F. for 12 to 16 minutes or until very light brown. Brush with melted margarine. Cut into wedges; serve warm.
Yield: 8 scones.

HIGH ALTITUDE:
Above 3500 Feet: Decrease baking powder to 2 teaspoons. Bake at 425°F. for 12 to 15 minutes.

NUTRITION PER SERVING:
Calories 240; Protein 4g; Carbohydrate 29g; Fat 12g; Sodium 330mg.

How to Make Blueberry Muffins

STEP 1. Combine dry ingredients and blueberries; push up sides of bowl to form well. Combine liquid ingredients; pour into well.

STEP 2. Stir just until dry ingredients are moistened (about 12 to 15 strokes). Batter will remain lumpy. Do not overmix.

STEP 3. Lightly grease or line muffin cups with paper baking cups. Fill each cup ⅔ full. Bake at 400°F. for 20 to 25 minutes.

MUFFINS

≈

2 cups all purpose flour
½ cup sugar
3 teaspoons baking powder
½ teaspoon salt
¾ cup milk
⅓ cup oil
1 egg, beaten

Heat oven to 400°F. Grease bottoms only of 12 muffin cups or line with paper baking cups. In medium bowl, combine flour, sugar, baking powder and salt; mix well. In small bowl, combine milk, oil and egg; blend well. Add to dry ingredients all at once; stir just until dry ingredients are moistened (Batter will be lumpy.) Fill greased muffin cups ⅔ full.

Bake at 400°F. for 20 to 25 minutes or until toothpick inserted in center comes out clean. Cool 1 minute before removing from pan. Serve warm.
Yield: 12 muffins.

MICROWAVE DIRECTIONS:
Prepare muffin batter as directed above. Using 6-cup microwave-safe muffin pan, line each cup with 2 paper baking cups to absorb moisture during cooking. Fill cups ⅔ full. Microwave 6 muffins on HIGH for 2 to 2½ minutes or until toothpick inserted in center comes out clean, rotating pan ½ turn halfway through cooking. Remove muffins from pan and immediately discard outer baking cups. Repeat with remaining batter.

HIGH ALTITUDE:
Above 3500 Feet: No change.

NUTRITION PER SERVING:
Calories 180; Protein 3g; Carbohydrate 25g; Fat 7g; Sodium 180mg.

VARIATIONS:

APPLE MUFFINS: Decrease sugar to ¼ cup. Add 1 teaspoon cinnamon and 1 cup finely chopped, peeled apple to dry ingredients. Substitute apple juice for milk. Bake at 400°F. for 18 to 22 minutes.

BLUEBERRY MUFFINS: Stir 1 cup fresh or frozen blueberries (do not thaw) and 1 teaspoon grated lemon or orange peel into dry ingredients.

(Recipe continued on next page.)

Blueberry Muffins

(Recipe continued from previous page.)

CHOCOLATE CHIP MUFFINS: Add ¾ cup miniature chocolate chips to dry ingredients. Sprinkle tops of muffins before baking with a combination of 3 tablespoons sugar and 2 tablespoons brown sugar.

JAM MUFFINS: Place ½ teaspoon any flavor jam on each muffin before baking; press into batter. If desired, sprinkle with finely chopped nuts.

LEMON MUFFINS: Add 1 tablespoon grated lemon peel to dry ingredients.

ORANGE MUFFINS: Add 1 tablespoon grated orange peel to dry ingredients and substitute orange juice for milk.

STREUSEL-TOPPED MUFFINS: In small bowl, blend ¼ cup firmly packed brown sugar, 1 tablespoon margarine or butter, softened, ½ teaspoon cinnamon and ¼ cup chopped nuts or flaked coconut with fork until crumbly. Sprinkle over muffins before baking.

SUGAR-COATED MUFFINS: Brush tops of hot muffins with 2 tablespoons melted margarine or butter; dip in mixture of ¼ cup sugar and ½ teaspoon cinnamon.

WHOLE WHEAT MUFFINS: Use 1 cup all purpose flour and 1 cup whole wheat flour.

BRAN MUFFINS

A batch of these wholesome refrigerator muffins is great to have on hand for hurried mornings.

2	cups shreds of whole bran cereal
2½	cups buttermilk
½	cup oil
2	eggs
2½	cups all purpose flour
1½	cups sugar
1¼	teaspoons baking soda
1	teaspoon baking powder
½	teaspoon salt
¾	cup raisins, if desired

In large bowl, combine cereal and buttermilk; let stand 5 minutes until cereal is softened. Add oil and eggs; blend well. Stir in flour and remaining ingredients; mix well. Batter can be baked immediately or stored in tightly covered container in refrigerator for up to 2 weeks.

When ready to bake, heat oven to 400°F. Grease desired number of muffin cups or line with paper baking cups. Stir batter; fill greased muffin cups ¾ full.

Bake at 400°F. for 18 to 20 minutes or until toothpick inserted in center comes out clean. Immediately remove from pan. Serve warm.
Yield: 24 to 30 muffins.

MICROWAVE DIRECTIONS:
Prepare muffin batter as directed above. Using 6-cup microwave-safe muffin pan, line each cup with 2 paper baking cups to absorb moisture during cooking. Fill cups ½ full. Microwave on HIGH as directed below or until toothpick inserted in center comes out clean, rotating pan ½ turn halfway through cooking. Remove muffins from pan and immediately discard outer baking cups.

4 muffins - 2 to 2½ minutes
2 muffins - 1¼ to 1¾ minutes

HIGH ALTITUDE:
Above 3500 Feet: Increase flour to 2¾ cups; decrease sugar to 1¼ cups. Bake as directed above.

NUTRITION PER SERVING:
Calories 150; Protein 3g; Carbohydrate 25g; Fat 4g; Sodium 160mg.

REFRIGERATOR APPLE BRAN MUFFINS

There are only 4 grams of fat in each muffin.

  2   cups shreds of whole bran cereal
1½   cups buttermilk
  1   cup unsweetened applesauce
  ½   cup oil
  4   egg whites
  2   cups all purpose flour
  ½   cup whole wheat flour
  1   cup sugar
  1   teaspoon baking powder
  1   teaspoon baking soda
  1   teaspoon cinnamon
  1   teaspoon ginger
  ¼   teaspoon salt
  ½   cup raisins

In large bowl, combine cereal and buttermilk; let stand 5 minutes or until cereal is softened. Add applesauce, oil and egg whites; blend well. Stir in all purpose flour, whole wheat flour and remaining ingredients; mix well. Batter can be baked immediately or stored in tightly covered container in refrigerator for up to 1 week.

When ready to bake, heat oven to 400°F. Grease desired number of muffin cups or line with paper baking cups. Stir batter; fill greased muffin cups ¾ full. Sprinkle with sugar, if desired.

Bake at 400°F. for 15 to 20 minutes or until toothpick inserted in center comes out clean. Immediately remove from pan. Serve warm.
Yield: 30 muffins.

MICROWAVE DIRECTIONS:
Prepare muffin batter as directed above. Using 6-cup microwave-safe muffin pan, line each cup with 2 paper baking cups to absorb moisture during cooking. Fill cups ½ full. Sprinkle with sugar, if desired. Microwave on HIGH as directed below or until toothpick inserted in center comes out clean, rotating pan ½ turn halfway through cooking. Remove muffins from pan and immediately discard outer baking cups.

  6 muffins - 3 to 3½ minutes
  4 muffins - 2½ to 2¾ minutes
  2 muffins - 2 to 2¼ minutes

HIGH ALTITUDE:
Above 3500 Feet: Increase all purpose flour to 2¼ cups. Bake as directed above.

NUTRITION PER SERVING:
Calories 120; Protein 3g; Carbohydrate 21g; Fat 4g; Sodium 125mg.

REFRIGERATOR SWEET MUFFINS

4½   cups all purpose flour
  1   cup firmly packed brown sugar
  ½   cup sugar
  4   teaspoons baking powder
  1   teaspoon baking soda
  1   teaspoon salt
  2   cups buttermilk
  ¾   cup oil
1½   teaspoons vanilla
  3   eggs

In large bowl, combine flour, brown sugar, sugar, baking powder, baking soda and salt; blend well. Add buttermilk, oil, vanilla and eggs; stir just until dry ingredients are moistened. Batter can be baked immediately or stored in tightly covered container in refrigerator for up to 5 days.

When ready to bake, heat oven to 375°F. Grease bottoms only of desired number of muffin cups or line with paper baking cups. Stir batter; fill greased muffin cups ⅔ full.

Bake at 375°F. for 20 to 25 minutes or until toothpick inserted in center comes out clean. Immediately remove from pan. Serve warm.
Yield: 24 muffins.

MICROWAVE DIRECTIONS:
Prepare muffin batter as directed above. Using 6-cup microwave-safe muffin pan, line each cup with 2 paper baking cups to absorb moisture during cooking. Fill cups ½ full. Microwave on HIGH as directed below or until toothpick inserted in center comes out clean, rotating pan ½ turn halfway through cooking. Remove muffins from pan and immediately discard outer baking cups. Cool 1 minute on wire rack before serving.

  6 muffins - 3 to 3½ minutes
  4 muffins - 2½ to 2¾ minutes
  2 muffins - 2 to 2¼ minutes

HIGH ALTITUDE:
Above 3500 Feet: Decrease brown sugar to ¾ cup. Bake as directed above.

NUTRITION PER SERVING:
Calories 210; Protein 4g; Carbohydrate 32g; Fat 8g; Sodium 220mg.

BANANA BRAN MUFFINS

~

These monster muffins will delight after-school snackers.

- ½ **cup margarine or butter, softened**
- ½ **cup firmly packed brown sugar**
- 1½ **cups (3 medium) mashed ripe bananas**
- ¼ **cup milk**
- 1 **teaspoon vanilla**
- 2 **eggs**
- 1½ **cups all purpose flour**
- ½ **cup unprocessed bran or wheat germ**
- 1 **teaspoon baking powder**
- 1 **teaspoon baking soda**
- ¼ **teaspoon salt**
- 1 **cup chopped walnuts**

Heat oven to 375°F. Grease eight 6-oz. custard cups or 18 muffin cups; place custard cups on 15x10x1-inch baking pan. In large bowl, beat margarine and brown sugar until fluffy. Add bananas, milk, vanilla and eggs; blend well. Stir in flour, bran, baking powder, baking soda and salt just until dry ingredients are moistened; stir in walnuts. Fill greased custard cups ⅔ full.

Bake at 375°F. for 20 to 25 minutes or until toothpick inserted in center comes out clean. Cool 5 minutes; remove from custard cups. Serve warm. **Yield: 8 jumbo or 18 regular-sized muffins.**

HIGH ALTITUDE:
Above 3500 Feet: No change.

NUTRITION PER SERVING:
Calories 430; Protein 8g; Carbohydrate 47g; Fat 23g; Sodium 410mg.

BANANA BRAN MUFFINS MAKE-OVER

~

Now these jumbo muffins are better for you as well as delicious. We've reduced the fat by almost 50 percent.

- ⅓ **cup margarine or butter, softened**
- ½ **cup firmly packed brown sugar**
- 1½ **cups (3 medium) mashed ripe bananas**
- ½ **cup frozen cholesterol-free egg product, thawed, or 2 eggs, slightly beaten**
- ¼ **cup skim milk**
- 1 **teaspoon vanilla**
- ¾ **cup all purpose flour**
- ¾ **cup whole wheat flour**
- ½ **cup unprocessed bran or wheat germ**
- 1 **teaspoon baking powder**
- 1 **teaspoon baking soda**
- 3 **tablespoons chopped walnuts**

Heat oven to 375°F. Grease eight 6-oz. custard cups or 18 muffin cups; place custard cups on 15x10x1-inch baking pan. In large bowl, beat margarine and brown sugar until fluffy. Add bananas, egg product, milk and vanilla; blend well. Stir in all purpose flour, whole wheat flour, wheat germ, baking powder and baking soda just until dry ingredients are moistened. Fill greased custard cups ⅔ full. Sprinkle batter with walnuts.

Bake at 375°F. for 22 to 27 minutes or until toothpick inserted in center comes out clean. Cool 5 minutes; remove from pan. Serve warm. **Yield: 8 jumbo or 18 regular-sized muffins.**

HIGH ALTITUDE:
Above 3500 Feet: Increase all purpose flour to 1 cup. Bake as directed above.

NUTRITION PER SERVING:
Calories 310; Protein 7g; Carbohydrate 44g; Fat 12g; Sodium 310mg.

Banana Bran Muffins Make-Over

HONEY-GLAZED BANANA MUFFINS

These muffins are delicious!

MUFFINS
- 2 cups shreds of whole bran cereal
- 1 cup buttermilk
- ½ cup (1 medium) mashed ripe banana
- ¼ cup oil
- ¼ cup honey
- 1 egg, slightly beaten
- 1 cup whole wheat flour
- 1 teaspoon baking soda
- ⅛ teaspoon salt

GLAZE
- 2 tablespoons margarine or butter, softened
- 2 tablespoons honey

Heat oven to 400°F. Line 16 muffin cups with paper baking cups. In large bowl, combine cereal and buttermilk; let stand 10 minutes or until cereal is softened. Add banana, oil, honey and egg to cereal mixture; mix well. Add flour, baking soda and salt; blend well. Fill paper-lined muffin cups ⅔ full. In small bowl, blend glaze ingredients until smooth; set aside.

Bake at 400°F. for 18 to 22 minutes or until toothpick inserted in center comes out clean. Brush muffins with glaze. Serve warm.

Yield: 16 muffins.

HIGH ALTITUDE:
Above 3500 Feet: No change.

NUTRITION PER SERVING:
Calories 130; Protein 3g; Carbohydrate 20g; Fat 6g; Sodium 200mg.

TOPSY-TURVY TROPICAL MUFFINS

The sweet taste of the tropics is packed into these mouth-watering muffins.

TOPPING
- ½ cup firmly packed brown sugar
- ½ cup coconut
- ⅓ cup finely chopped macadamia nuts or almonds
- ¼ cup margarine or butter, melted

MUFFINS
- 2½ cups all purpose flour
- ⅓ cup firmly packed brown sugar
- 1 teaspoon baking soda
- ½ teaspoon salt
- 1 cup dairy sour cream
- ⅓ cup oil
- 1 egg
- 1 (8-oz.) can crushed pineapple in its own juice, undrained

Heat oven to 400°F. Generously grease 24 muffin cups. In small bowl, combine all topping ingredients; mix well. Spoon scant tablespoonful into bottom of each greased muffin cup.

In large bowl, combine flour, ⅓ cup brown sugar, baking soda and salt; mix well. In small bowl, combine sour cream, oil, egg and pineapple; blend well. Add to dry ingredients; stir just until dry ingredients are moistened. Spoon 1 heaping tablespoonful batter over topping in each muffin cup.

Bake at 400°F. for 12 to 15 minutes or until toothpick inserted in center comes out clean. Loosen edges with knife; immediately invert onto wire rack set on sheet of waxed paper. Serve warm.

Yield: 24 muffins.

HIGH ALTITUDE:
Above 3500 Feet: Increase flour to 2½ cups plus 2 tablespoons. Bake as directed above.

NUTRITION PER SERVING:
Calories 170; Protein 2g; Carbohydrate 20g; Fat 9g; Sodium 125mg.

QUICK PUMPKIN ORANGE MINI-MUFFINS

1 medium orange
½ cup sugar
1¾ cups all purpose flour
2 teaspoons baking powder
½ teaspoon baking soda
½ teaspoon salt
½ teaspoon cinnamon
¼ teaspoon cloves
⅓ cup shortening
½ cup chopped dates
½ cup chopped nuts
2 eggs
1 cup canned pumpkin
⅓ cup orange juice

FOOD PROCESSOR DIRECTIONS:
Heat oven to 375°F. Grease 36 miniature muffin cups. Using vegetable peeler, peel strips of rind from orange. In food processor bowl with metal blade, process rind with sugar until finely grated, about 60 to 90 seconds. Add flour, baking powder, baking soda, salt, cinnamon and cloves. Process with 3 long pulses; scrape down sides of bowl. Add shortening; process 10 to 15 seconds or until mixture resembles cornmeal. Add dates and nuts; process just to distribute. In small bowl, slightly beat eggs; stir in pumpkin and orange juice. Add to processor bowl; process 6 to 8 seconds to combine thoroughly. Fill greased muffin cups ¾ full.

Bake at 375°F. for 14 to 17 minutes or until very light golden brown and toothpick inserted in center comes out clean.
Yield: 36 mini-muffins.

CONVENTIONAL DIRECTIONS:
In large bowl, beat shortening and sugar until light and fluffy. Add pumpkin, orange juice, *2 teaspoons grated orange peel* and eggs; blend well. Add flour, baking powder, baking soda, salt, cinnamon and cloves; stir just until dry ingredients are moistened. Fold in dates and nuts. Bake as directed above.

TIP:
Recipe can be baked in 12 greased regular-sized muffin cups. Bake at 400°F. for 18 to 22 minutes.

HIGH ALTITUDE:
Above 3500 Feet: No change.

NUTRITION PER SERVING:
Calories 70; Protein 1g; Carbohydrate 10g; Fat 3g; Sodium 65mg.

PUMPKIN STREUSEL MUFFINS

Streusel topping and cream cheese filling make these muffins special.

MUFFINS
1 egg, beaten
½ cup milk
½ cup canned pumpkin
⅓ cup oil
1¾ cups all purpose flour
½ cup sugar
3 teaspoons baking powder
½ teaspoon cinnamon
¼ teaspoon salt
¼ teaspoon nutmeg
1 (3-oz.) pkg. cream cheese

TOPPING
¼ cup firmly packed brown sugar
½ teaspoon cinnamon
1 tablespoon margarine or butter
¼ cup finely chopped nuts

Heat oven to 400°F. Grease bottoms only of 12 muffin cups or line with paper baking cups. In medium bowl, combine egg, milk, pumpkin and oil; mix well. Stir in flour, sugar, baking powder, ½ teaspoon cinnamon, salt and nutmeg just until dry ingredients are moistened. (Batter will be lumpy.) Fill greased muffin cups about ½ full (reserve remaining batter). Divide cream cheese into 12 equal pieces. Place 1 piece on batter in each cup; top with reserved batter, filling each cup about ¾ full. Combine all topping ingredients; mix well. Sprinkle evenly over each muffin.

Bake at 400°F. for 18 to 22 minutes or until golden brown. Immediately remove from pan. Serve warm. Store in refrigerator.
Yield: 12 muffins.

HIGH ALTITUDE:
Above 3500 Feet: No change.

NUTRITION PER SERVING:
Calories 230; Protein 4g; Carbohydrate 29g; Fat 12g; Sodium 160mg.

GOLDEN HARVEST MUFFINS

Make and freeze a batch of these muffins. Warm them in the microwave for breakfast on the run.

    1   cup all purpose flour
    1   cup whole wheat flour
    1   cup sugar
    2   teaspoons baking soda
    2   teaspoons cinnamon
    ½   teaspoon salt
    ¼   teaspoon cloves
    2   cups shredded peeled apples
    ½   cup shredded carrots
    ½   cup coconut
    ½   cup raisins
    ½   cup chopped walnuts or pecans
    ¾   cup oil
    ¼   cup milk
    2   teaspoons vanilla
    2   eggs, beaten

Heat oven to 350°F. Line with paper baking cups or grease bottoms and sides of 18 muffin cups. In large bowl, combine all purpose flour, whole wheat flour, sugar, baking soda, cinnamon, salt and cloves. Add apples, carrots, coconut, raisins and walnuts; mix well. Add oil, milk, vanilla and eggs; stir just until moistened. Fill paper-lined muffin cups ¾ full.

Bake at 350°F. for 20 to 25 minutes or until toothpick inserted in center comes out clean. Immediately remove from pan. Serve warm.
Yield: 18 muffins.

HIGH ALTITUDE:
Above 3500 Feet: Increase all purpose flour to 1¼ cups; decrease oil to ½ cup. Bake as directed above.

NUTRITION PER SERVING:
Calories 230; Protein 3g; Carbohydrate 29g; Fat 13g; Sodium 200mg.

MAPLE OATMEAL MUFFINS

Maple syrup and oatmeal — what a tempting breakfast combination! Serve the muffins warm from the oven.

    1   cup quick-cooking rolled oats
    ½   cup milk
    ¾   cup maple-flavored syrup
    ¼   cup margarine or butter, melted
    1   egg
    1   cup all purpose flour
    2   teaspoons baking powder
    ¼   teaspoon cinnamon
    ½   cup chopped walnuts

Heat oven to 400°F. Grease bottoms only of 12 muffins cups or line with paper baking cups. In large bowl, combine oats and milk; let stand 5 minutes. Add syrup, margarine and egg; blend well. Add flour, baking powder, cinnamon and walnuts; stir just until dry ingredients are moistened. Fill greased muffin cups ⅔ full.

Bake at 400°F. for 15 to 20 minutes or until toothpick inserted in center comes out clean. Immediately remove from pan. Serve warm.
Yield: 12 muffins.

MICROWAVE DIRECTIONS:
Prepare muffin batter as directed above. Using 6-cup microwave-safe muffin pan, line each cup with 2 paper baking cups to absorb moisture during cooking. Fill cups ½ full. Sprinkle tops with a mixture of *1½ tablespoons sugar* and *½ teaspoon cinnamon*. Microwave on HIGH for 2½ to 2¾ minutes or until toothpick inserted in center comes out clean, rotating pan ½ turn halfway through cooking. Remove muffins from pan and immediately discard outer baking cups. Cool 1 minute on wire rack before serving. Repeat with remaining batter.

HIGH ALTITUDE:
Above 3500 Feet: Decrease maple-flavored syrup to ½ cup. Bake as directed above.

NUTRITION PER SERVING:
Calories 190; Protein 4g; Carbohydrate 27g; Fat 8g; Sodium 110mg.

Maple Oatmeal Muffins

DILLY ZUCCHINI RICOTTA MUFFINS

~

For a summer harvest taste treat, serve these savory muffins warm from the oven!

- 1½ **cups all purpose flour**
- 2 **tablespoons sugar**
- 3 **teaspoons baking powder**
- ½ **teaspoon salt**
- ¾ **teaspoon dried dill weed**
- ¼ **cup milk**
- ½ **cup margarine or butter, melted**
- 2 **eggs**
- ⅔ **cup ricotta cheese**
- ½ **cup shredded unpeeled zucchini**

Heat oven to 400°F. Line with paper baking cups or grease 12 muffin cups. In large bowl, combine flour, sugar, baking powder, salt and dill weed; mix well. In medium bowl, combine milk, margarine and eggs. Stir in ricotta cheese and zucchini; beat well. Add to dry ingredients, stirring just until moistened. (Batter will be stiff.) Fill paper-lined muffin cups ⅔ full.

Bake at 400°F. for 20 to 25 minutes or until toothpick inserted in center comes out clean. Immediately remove from pan. Serve warm.
Yield: 12 muffins.

HIGH ALTITUDE:
Above 3500 Feet: No change.

NUTRITION PER SERVING:
Calories 170; Protein 5g; Carbohydrate 15g; Fat 10g; Sodium 280mg.

BACON-JACK CHEESE MUFFINS

~

- 2 **cups all purpose flour**
- 3 **teaspoons sugar**
- 3 **teaspoons baking powder**
- ⅛ **to ¼ teaspoon cayenne pepper**
- 1¼ **cups milk**
- 2 **tablespoons bacon drippings or oil***
- 1 **egg**
- 6 **slices bacon, crisply cooked, crumbled**
- 3 **oz. (¾ cup) shredded Monterey Jack cheese**

***Dilly Zucchini Ricotta Muffins,
Parmesan Herb Muffins p. 376***

Heat oven to 400°F. Generously grease 12 muffin cups. In large bowl, combine flour, sugar, baking powder and cayenne pepper; blend well. Add milk, bacon drippings and egg; stir just until dry ingredients are moistened. Stir in bacon and cheese. Fill greased muffin cups ⅔ full.

Bake at 400°F. for 20 to 25 minutes or until golden brown. Cool 1 to 2 minutes before removing from pan. Serve warm.
Yield: 12 muffins.

TIP:
* If using oil, add ¼ teaspoon salt with dry ingredients.

HIGH ALTITUDE:
Above 3500 Feet: No change.

NUTRITION PER SERVING:
Calories 170; Protein 6g; Carbohydrate 18g; Fat 7g; Sodium 230mg.

ONION RYE MUFFINS

~

Caraway seed adds special flavor.

- ¾ **cup chopped onions**
- ½ **cup margarine or butter**
- 1¼ **cups all purpose flour**
- ¾ **cup medium rye flour**
- 2 **tablespoons sugar**
- 3 **teaspoons baking powder**
- ¾ **teaspoon salt**
- ½ **teaspoon caraway seed, crushed**
- ½ **cup milk**
- 2 **eggs**

Heat oven to 400°F. Line with paper baking cups or grease 12 muffin cups. In small skillet, cook onions in margarine until soft; set aside. In large bowl, combine all purpose flour, rye flour, sugar, baking powder, salt and caraway seed; mix well. Add milk, eggs and cooked onion; stir just until dry ingredients are moistened. Fill paper-lined muffin cups ⅔ full.

Bake at 400°F. for 15 to 20 minutes or until toothpick inserted in center comes out clean. Immediately remove from pan. Serve warm.
Yield: 12 muffins.

HIGH ALTITUDE:
Above 3500 Feet: No change.

NUTRITION PER SERVING:
Calories 170; Protein 4g; Carbohydrate 20g; Fat 9g; Sodium 270mg.

MEXICALI CORN MUFFINS

~

We've added green chiles to corn muffins creating a flavor combination that's hard to beat. They are a great addition to a chili supper.

1¼ **cups all purpose flour**
¾ **cup cornmeal**
2 **tablespoons sugar**
4 **teaspoons baking powder**
½ **teaspoon salt**
¾ **cup milk**
¼ **cup dairy sour cream**
¼ **cup oil**
1 **egg**
1 **(4-oz.) can chopped green chiles, drained**

Heat oven to 400°F. Line with paper baking cups or grease 12 muffin cups. In large bowl, combine flour, cornmeal, sugar, baking powder and salt; mix well. In medium bowl, combine milk, sour cream, oil, egg and chiles; beat well. Add to dry ingredients, stirring just until moistened. Fill paper-lined muffin cups ⅔ full.

Bake at 400°F. for 18 to 22 minutes or until toothpick inserted in center comes out clean. Immediately remove from pan. Serve warm.
Yield: 12 muffins.

MICROWAVE DIRECTIONS:
Prepare muffin batter as directed above. Using 6-cup microwave-safe muffin pan, line each cup with 2 paper baking cups to absorb moisture during cooking. Fill cups ½ full. Microwave 6 muffins on HIGH for 2½ to 3 minutes or until toothpick inserted in center comes out clean, rotating pan ½ turn halfway through cooking. Remove muffins from pan and immediately discard outer baking cups. Cool 1 minute on wire rack before serving. Repeat, making 6 additional muffins. With remaining batter, make 3 muffins; microwave 3 muffins on HIGH for 1½ to 2 minutes. Serve warm.
Yield: 15 muffins.

HIGH ALTITUDE:
Above 3500 Feet: No change.

NUTRITION PER SERVING:
Calories 150; Protein 3g; Carbohydrate 20g; Fat 7g; Sodium 200mg.

PARMESAN HERB MUFFINS

~

Flecks of parsley and sage flavor these cheesy muffins. Serve them warm with butter.

2 **cups all purpose flour**
1 **tablespoon sugar**
1½ **teaspoons baking powder**
½ **teaspoon baking soda**
½ **teaspoon dried sage leaves, crushed**
½ **cup chopped fresh parsley**
¾ **cup grated Parmesan cheese**
1¼ **cups buttermilk**
¼ **cup margarine or butter, melted**
1 **egg**

Heat oven to 400°F. Grease bottoms only of 12 muffin cups or line with paper baking cups. In large bowl, combine flour, sugar, baking powder, baking soda, sage, parsley and cheese; blend well. Add buttermilk, margarine and egg; stir just until dry ingredients are moistened. Fill greased muffin cups ⅔ full.

Bake at 400°F. for 15 to 20 minutes or until toothpick inserted in center comes out clean. Immediately remove from pan. Serve warm.
Yield: 12 muffins.

MICROWAVE DIRECTIONS:
Prepare muffin batter as directed above. Using 6-cup microwave-safe muffin pan, line each cup with 2 paper baking cups to absorb moisture during cooking. Fill cups ½ full. If desired, sprinkle top of each muffin with *cornflake crumbs*. Microwave 6 muffins on HIGH for 2½ to 3 minutes or until toothpick inserted in center comes out clean, rotating pan ½ turn halfway through cooking. Remove muffins from pan and immediately discard outer baking cups. Cool 1 minute on wire rack before serving. Repeat with remaining batter.

HIGH ALTITUDE:
Above 3500 Feet: No change.

NUTRITION PER SERVING:
Calories 160; Protein 6g; Carbohydrate 19g; Fat 7g; Sodium 280mg.

RAISIN, WHEAT AND RYE MUFFINS

Sweet spices and raisins flavor these muffins. They are sensational served anytime!

- 1 **cup all purpose flour**
- ½ **cup whole wheat flour**
- ½ **cup medium rye flour**
- ¼ **cup sugar**
- 3 **teaspoons baking powder**
- ½ **teaspoon salt**
- ½ **teaspoon cinnamon**
- ¼ **teaspoon nutmeg**
- ½ **cup raisins**
- 1 **cup milk**
- ½ **cup oil**
- 1 **egg, slightly beaten**

Heat oven to 375°F. Grease bottoms only of 12 muffin cups or line with paper baking cups. In large bowl, combine all purpose flour, whole wheat flour, rye flour, sugar, baking powder, salt, cinnamon, nutmeg and raisins; blend well. Add milk, oil and egg; stir just until dry ingredients are moistened. Fill greased muffin cups ⅔ full.

Bake at 375°F. for 15 to 20 minutes or until very light brown and toothpick inserted in center comes out clean. Immediately remove from pan. Serve warm.
Yield: 12 muffins.

MICROWAVE DIRECTIONS:
Prepare muffin batter as directed above. Using 6-cup microwave-safe muffin pan, line each cup with 2 paper baking cups to absorb moisture during cooking. Fill cups ½ full. Microwave 6 muffins on HIGH for 2 to 2½ minutes or until toothpick inserted in center comes out clean, rotating pan ½ turn halfway through cooking. Remove muffins from pan and immediately discard outer baking cups. Cool 1 minute on wire rack before serving. Repeat, making 6 additional muffins. With remaining batter, make 3 muffins; microwave 3 muffins on HIGH for 1½ to 1¾ minutes, rotating once.
Yield: 15 muffins.

HIGH ALTITUDE:
Above 3500 Feet: Decrease baking powder to 2 teaspoons. Bake at 400°F. for 15 to 20 minutes.

NUTRITION PER SERVING:
Calories 170; Protein 3g; Carbohydrate 17g; Fat 10g; Sodium 220mg.

THE GIANT'S CORN MUFFINS

These picture perfect muffins were a finalist in the 33rd BAKE-OFF® Contest in 1988.

MUFFINS
- 1 **cup cornmeal**
- ½ **cup all purpose flour**
- ½ **cup whole wheat flour**
- 1 **teaspoon baking powder**
- 1 **teaspoon baking soda**
- ½ **teaspoon salt**
- ¼ **teaspoon nutmeg**
- 1 **cup plain yogurt or buttermilk**
- ¼ **cup margarine or butter, melted**
- 3 **tablespoons honey**
- 1 **egg**
- 1 **green onion, sliced, including green top**
- 1 **(11-oz.) can whole kernel corn with red and green peppers, drained**

TOPPING
- 1 **tablespoon all purpose flour**
- 1 **tablespoon cornmeal**
- 2 **teaspoons sugar**
  Dash salt
- 4 **teaspoons margarine or butter**

Heat oven to 400°F. Grease bottoms only of six 6-oz. custard cups or 12 muffin cups; place custard cups on 15x10x1-inch baking pan. In large bowl, combine 1 cup cornmeal, ½ cup all purpose flour, whole wheat flour, baking powder, baking soda, ½ teaspoon salt and nutmeg; blend well. In medium bowl, combine yogurt, ¼ cup margarine, honey, egg, onion and corn; mix well. Add to dry ingredients; stir just until dry ingredients are moistened. Spoon batter evenly into greased custard cups. (Cups will be full.) In small bowl, combine all topping ingredients; mix well. Crumble evenly over muffins.

Bake at 400°F. for 20 to 30 minutes or until toothpick inserted in center comes out clean. Cool 1 minute; remove from custard cups. Serve warm.
Yield: 6 muffins.

HIGH ALTITUDE:
Above 3500 Feet: No change.

NUTRITION PER SERVING:
Calories 380; Protein 9g; Carbohydrate 56g; Fat 13g; Sodium 760mg.

BANANA BREAD

~

For optimum flavor, use well-ripened bananas to make this family-favorite bread.

³/₄ **cup sugar**
¹/₂ **cup margarine or butter, softened**
2 **eggs**
1 **cup (2 medium) mashed ripe bananas**
¹/₃ **cup milk**
1 **teaspoon vanilla**
2 **cups all purpose flour**
¹/₂ **cup chopped nuts, if desired**
1 **teaspoon baking soda**
¹/₂ **teaspoon salt**

Heat oven to 350°F. Grease bottom only of 9x5 or 8x4-inch loaf pan. In large bowl, beat sugar and margarine until light and fluffy. Beat in eggs. Add bananas, milk and vanilla; blend well. In small bowl, combine flour, nuts, baking soda and salt; mix well. Add to banana mixture; stir just until dry ingredients are moistened. Pour into greased pan.

Bake at 350°F. for 50 to 60 minutes or until toothpick inserted in center comes out clean. Cool 5 minutes; remove from pan. Cool completely. Wrap tightly and store in refrigerator.
Yield: 1 (16-slice) loaf.

HIGH ALTITUDE:
Above 3500 Feet: Increase flour to 2 cups plus 1 tablespoon. Bake at 375°F. for 45 to 55 minutes.

NUTRITION PER SERVING:
Calories 190; Protein 3g; Carbohydrate 26g; Fat 9g; Sodium 210mg.

VARIATION:

APPLESAUCE BREAD: Substitute 1 cup applesauce for mashed bananas and add ³/₄ teaspoon cinnamon with flour.

NUT BREAD

~

Try the flavorful variations, too.

³/₄ **cup sugar**
¹/₂ **cup margarine or butter, softened**
1 **cup buttermilk**
2 **eggs**
2 **cups all purpose flour**
1 **cup chopped nuts**
¹/₂ **teaspoon baking powder**
¹/₂ **teaspoon baking soda**
¹/₂ **teaspoon salt**

Heat oven to 350°F. Grease bottom only of 9x5 or 8x4-inch loaf pan. In large bowl, beat sugar and margarine until light and fluffy. Add buttermilk and eggs; blend well. In small bowl, combine flour, nuts, baking powder, baking soda and salt; mix well. Add to buttermilk mixture; stir just until dry ingredients are moistened. Pour into greased pan.

Bake at 350°F. for 55 to 65 minutes or until toothpick inserted in center comes out clean. Cool 15 minutes; remove from pan. Cool completely. Wrap tightly and store in refrigerator.
Yield: 1 (16-slice) loaf.

HIGH ALTITUDE:
Above 3500 Feet: Increase flour to 2 cups plus 1 tablespoon. Bake at 375°F. for 50 to 60 minutes.

NUTRITION PER SERVING:
Calories 210; Protein 4g; Carbohydrate 23g; Fat 11g; Sodium 200mg.

VARIATIONS:

DATE BREAD: Prepare batter as directed above, substituting brown sugar for sugar and decreasing nuts to ¹/₂ cup. Stir in 1 cup chopped dates and 1 teaspoon grated orange peel after flour addition.

POCKET OF STREUSEL BREAD: For filling, in small bowl, combine ¹/₂ cup firmly packed brown sugar, ¹/₂ cup chopped walnuts, 1 teaspoon cinnamon and 1 tablespoon margarine or butter, melted; mix well. Prepare batter as directed above, substituting brown sugar for sugar and decreasing nuts to ¹/₂ cup. Spread half of batter in greased and floured 9x5-inch loaf pan. Spoon filling down center of batter and spread to within ¹/₂ inch of all sides. Carefully spoon remaining batter over filling, spreading gently to cover. Bake at 350°F. for 50 to 55 minutes.

CHERRY NUT BREAD

This eye-catching quick bread is perfect for party trays or gift-giving.

- 2 **cups all purpose flour**
- 2/3 **cup sugar**
- 2 **teaspoons baking powder**
- 1/2 **teaspoon salt**
- 3/4 **cup milk**
- 1/2 **cup margarine or butter, melted**
- 1 **teaspoon almond extract**
- 2 **eggs**
- 1/2 **cup slivered almonds**
- 1 **(10-oz.) jar (3/4 cup) maraschino cherries, drained, chopped**

Heat oven to 350°F. Grease bottom only of 8x4 or 9x5-inch loaf pan. In large bowl, combine flour, sugar, baking powder and salt; mix well. In small bowl, combine milk, margarine, almond extract and eggs; blend well. Add to flour mixture in large bowl; stir just until dry ingredients are moistened. Stir in almonds and cherries. Pour into greased pan.

For 8x4-inch pan, bake at 350°F. for 65 to 75 minutes or until toothpick inserted in center comes out clean. For 9x5-inch pan, bake 60 to 70 minutes. Cool 10 minutes; remove from pan. Cool completely. Wrap tightly and store in refrigerator.

Yield: 1 (12-slice) loaf.

HIGH ALTITUDE:
Above 3500 Feet: Increase flour to 2¼ cups. For 8x4-inch pan, bake at 375°F. for 55 to 65 minutes. For 9x5-inch pan, bake at 375°F. for 50 to 60 minutes.

NUTRITION PER SERVING:
Calories 250; Protein 5g; Carbohydrate 33g; Fat 12g; Sodium 250mg.

BANANA BLUEBERRY MINI LOAVES

Mini-loaves are an ideal size for singles or small families. For convenience, use the disposable foil mini-loaf pans available in supermarkets.

- 1 **cup sugar**
- 1/2 **cup oil**
- 1 **cup (2 medium) mashed ripe bananas**
- 1/2 **cup plain yogurt**
- 1 **teaspoon vanilla**
- 2 **eggs**
- 2 **cups all purpose flour**
- 1 **teaspoon baking soda**
- 1/2 **teaspoon salt**
- 1 **cup fresh or frozen blueberries (do not thaw)**

Heat oven to 350°F. Grease and flour bottoms only of three 6x3½-inch loaf pans. In large bowl, beat together sugar and oil. Add bananas, yogurt, vanilla and eggs; blend well. Add flour, baking soda and salt; stir just until dry ingredients are moistened. Gently stir in blueberries. Pour into greased and floured pans.

Bake at 350°F. for 40 to 50 minutes or until toothpick inserted in center comes out clean. Cool 5 minutes; remove from pans. Cool completely. Wrap tightly and store in refrigerator.

Yield: 3 (12-slice) loaves.

TIP:
Recipe can be baked in 9x5-inch loaf pan. Grease and flour bottom only of pan. Bake at 350°F. for 60 to 70 minutes.

HIGH ALTITUDE:
Above 3500 Feet: Increase flour to 2¼ cups. Bake 6x3½-inch pans at 375°F. for 30 to 40 minutes. Bake 9x5-inch pan at 375°F. for 50 to 60 minutes.

NUTRITION PER SERVING:
Calories 90; Protein 1g; Carbohydrate 13g; Fat 4g; Sodium 65mg.

Chocolate Chip Banana Bread

Best when served the next day, this bread is an easy make-ahead. It also can be frozen for later use.

- ¾ **cup sugar**
- ½ **cup margarine or butter, softened**
- 1 **cup (2 medium) mashed ripe bananas**
- ½ **cup dairy sour cream**
- 2 **eggs**
- 2 **cups all purpose flour**
- 1 **teaspoon baking soda**
- ½ **teaspoon salt**
- ¾ **cup miniature semi-sweet chocolate chips**
- ½ **cup chopped nuts**

Heat oven to 350°F. Grease and flour bottom only of one 9x5 or two 8x4-inch loaf pans. In large bowl, combine sugar and margarine; beat until light and fluffy. Add bananas, sour cream and eggs; blend well. Stir in flour, baking soda and salt; blend well. Fold in chocolate chips and nuts. Pour into greased and floured pan.

Bake at 350°F. for 55 to 65 minutes or until toothpick inserted in center comes out clean. Cool 15 minutes; remove from pan. Cool completely. Wrap tightly and store in refrigerator.

Yield: 1 (16-slice) loaf.

HIGH ALTITUDE:
Above 3500 Feet: Bake at 375°F. for 50 to 60 minutes.

NUTRITION PER SERVING:
Calories 250; Protein 4g; Carbohydrate 30g; Fat 13g; Sodium 220mg.

Zucchini Orange Bread

This recipe makes 2 loaves.

BREAD
- 4 **eggs**
- 1½ **cups sugar**
- ¾ **cup oil**
- ⅔ **cup orange juice**
- 2 **cups shredded unpeeled zucchini**
- 3¼ **cups all purpose flour**
- 1½ **teaspoons baking powder**
- 1½ **teaspoons baking soda**
- 1 **teaspoon salt**
- 2½ **teaspoons cinnamon**
- ½ **teaspoon cloves**
- 2 **teaspoons grated orange peel**
- ½ **cup chopped nuts, if desired**

GLAZE
- 1 **cup powdered sugar**
- 2 **to 3 teaspoons orange juice**

Heat oven to 350°F. Grease and flour bottoms only of two 8x4 or two 9x5-inch loaf pans. In large bowl, beat eggs until thick and lemon colored; gradually beat in sugar. Stir in oil, ⅔ cup orange juice and zucchini. Stir in remaining bread ingredients; mix well. Pour batter into greased and floured pans.

Bake at 350°F. for 45 to 55 minutes or until toothpick inserted in center comes out clean. Cool 10 minutes; remove from pans. Cool slightly.

In small bowl, blend glaze ingredients, adding enough orange juice for desired spreading consistency. Spread over warm loaves. Cool completely. Wrap tightly and store in refrigerator.

Yield: 2 (16-slice) loaves.

HIGH ALTITUDE:
Above 3500 Feet: Increase flour to 3¼ cups plus 3 tablespoons. Bake at 350°F. for 45 to 50 minutes.

NUTRITION PER SERVING:
Calories 170; Protein 2g; Carbohydrate 24g; Fat 7g; Sodium 140mg.

Chocolate Chip Banana Bread,
Zucchini Orange Bread

HOLIDAY CRANBERRY BREAD

Flavors of orange and cranberry go well together in this festive quick bread.

- 1 cup sugar
- 1 tablespoon grated orange peel
- ¾ cup water
- ⅓ cup orange juice
- 2 tablespoons oil
- 1 egg
- 2 cups all purpose flour
- 1½ teaspoons baking powder
- 1 teaspoon salt
- ½ teaspoon baking soda
- 1 cup halved fresh or frozen whole cranberries (do not thaw)
- 1 cup chopped nuts

Heat oven to 350°F. Grease bottom only of 9x5-inch loaf pan. In large bowl, combine sugar, orange peel, water, orange juice, oil and egg; blend well. Add flour, baking powder, salt and baking soda; stir just until dry ingredients are moistened. Stir in cranberries and nuts. Pour into greased pan.

Bake at 350°F. for 50 to 60 minutes or until toothpick inserted in center comes out clean. Cool 10 minutes; remove from pan. Cool completely. Wrap tightly and store in refrigerator.

Yield: 1 (12-slice) loaf.

HIGH ALTITUDE:
Above 3500 Feet: No change.

NUTRITION PER SERVING:
Calories 240; Protein 4g; Carbohydrate 36g; Fat 9g; Sodium 270mg.

CRANBERRY SURPRISE LOAF

A cream cheese layer highlights this easy-to-make quick bread.

- 2 (3-oz.) pkg. cream cheese, softened
- 1 egg
- 2 cups all purpose flour
- 1 cup sugar
- 1½ teaspoons baking powder
- ½ teaspoon baking soda
- ½ teaspoon salt
- ¾ cup apple juice
- ¼ cup margarine or butter, melted
- 1 egg, beaten
- 1½ cups coarsely chopped fresh cranberries*
- ½ cup chopped nuts

Heat oven to 350°F. Grease and flour bottom only of 9x5-inch loaf pan. In small bowl, beat cream cheese until light and fluffy. Add 1 egg; blend well. Set aside.

In large bowl, combine flour, sugar, baking powder, baking soda and salt. Stir in apple juice, margarine and beaten egg. Fold in cranberries and nuts. Spoon half of batter into greased and floured pan. Spoon cream cheese mixture evenly over batter. Top with remaining batter.

Bake at 350°F. for 65 to 75 minutes or until top springs back when lightly touched in center. Cool 15 minutes; remove from pan. Cool completely. Wrap tightly and store in refrigerator.

Yield: 1 (16-slice) loaf.

TIP:
* To chop cranberries in food processor, add about 2 cups fresh cranberries to food processor bowl with metal blade. Process with 10 on-off pulses or until all berries are coarsely chopped.

HIGH ALTITUDE:
Above 3500 Feet: Increase flour to 2 cups plus 3 tablespoons; decrease sugar to ½ cup. Bake at 375°F. for 55 to 65 minutes.

NUTRITION PER SERVING:
Calories 220; Protein 4g; Carbohydrate 28g; Fat 10g; Sodium 200mg.

Cranberry Surprise Loaf

PECAN PUMPKIN BREAD

This sweetly spiced harvest quick bread is flavored with cinnamon and nutmeg.

- 2½ cups all purpose flour
- 1 cup whole wheat flour
- 3 cups sugar
- 2 teaspoons baking soda
- 1½ teaspoons salt
- 2 teaspoons cinnamon
- 1 teaspoon nutmeg
- 1 cup oil
- ⅔ cup water
- 4 eggs
- 1 (16-oz.) can pumpkin (2 cups)
- 1 cup chopped pecans

Heat oven to 350°F. Grease bottom only of two 9x5-inch loaf pans or three 8x4-inch loaf pans. In large bowl, combine all purpose flour, whole wheat flour, sugar, baking soda, salt, cinnamon and nutmeg; mix well. In medium bowl, combine oil, water, eggs and pumpkin; blend well. Add to flour mixture; beat 1 minute at medium speed. Fold in pecans. Pour batter into greased pans.

Bake at 350°F. for 60 to 70 minutes or until toothpick inserted in center comes out clean. Cool 10 minutes; remove from pans. Cool completely.
Yield: 2 (16-slice) loaves.

HIGH ALTITUDE:
Above 3500 Feet: No change.

NUTRITION PER SERVING:
Calories 230; Protein 3g; Carbohydrate 31g; Fat 10g; Sodium 180mg.

PINEAPPLE PECAN QUICK BREAD

Lemon and pineapple flavor this cake-like bread. It's a great choice for breakfast, brunch or dessert.

BREAD
- 2 cups sugar
- 1 cup margarine or butter, softened
- 4 eggs
- 3 cups all purpose flour
- ½ teaspoon baking powder
- ½ teaspoon baking soda
- ½ teaspoon salt
- 1 cup buttermilk
- 1 to 2 tablespoons grated lemon peel
- ½ teaspoon lemon or pineapple extract
- ½ cup chopped pecans
- 1 (20-oz.) can crushed pineapple, drained, reserving liquid

GLAZE
- ½ cup sugar
- 3 tablespoons reserved pineapple liquid
- ½ teaspoon vanilla

Heat oven to 350°F. Grease and flour bottom only of two 8x4 or two 9x5-inch loaf pans. In large bowl, beat sugar and margarine until light and fluffy. Add eggs 1 at a time, beating well after each addition. Add flour, baking powder, baking soda, salt, buttermilk, lemon peel and lemon extract; mix until smooth. Stir in pecans and pineapple. Pour into greased and floured pans.

Bake at 350°F. for 50 to 65 minutes or until toothpick inserted in center comes out clean. In small bowl, blend all glaze ingredients until smooth; spoon over warm loaves. Cool 10 minutes; remove from pans. Cool completely. Wrap tightly and store in refrigerator.
Yield: 2 (16-slice) loaves.

HIGH ALTITUDE:
Above 3500 Feet: Increase flour to 3 cups plus 3 tablespoons. Bake as directed above.

NUTRITION PER SERVING:
Calories 200; Protein 3g; Carbohydrate 29g; Fat 8g; Sodium 145mg.

EGGNOG QUICK BREAD

This eggnog-flavored quick bread is perfect for the holidays!

- 2 eggs
- 1 cup sugar
- 1 cup dairy eggnog (not canned)
- ½ cup margarine or butter, melted
- 2 teaspoons rum extract
- 1 teaspoon vanilla
- 2¼ cups all purpose flour
- 2 teaspoons baking powder
- ½ teaspoon salt
- ¼ teaspoon nutmeg

Heat oven to 350°F. Grease bottom only of 9x5-inch loaf pan. Beat eggs in large bowl. Add sugar, eggnog, margarine, rum extract and vanilla; blend well. Add flour, baking powder, salt and nutmeg; stir just until dry ingredients are moistened. Pour into greased pan.

Bake at 350°F. for 45 to 50 minutes or until toothpick inserted in center comes out clean. Cool 10 minutes; remove from pan. Cool completely. Wrap tightly and store in refrigerator.

Yield: 1 (16-slice) loaf.

HIGH ALTITUDE:
Above 3500 Feet: No change.

NUTRITION PER SERVING:
Calories 190; Protein 3g; Carbohydrate 28g; Fat 8g; Sodium 190mg.

BROWN BREAD

Serve this sweet, traditional, round-shaped bread with sausage and baked beans.

- 2 cups raisins
  Boiling water
- ½ cup firmly packed brown sugar
- ¼ cup margarine or butter, softened
- 1 cup cornmeal
- ½ cup molasses
- 2 cups buttermilk
- 1 egg
- 3 cups all purpose flour
- 2 teaspoons baking soda

Heat oven to 350°F. Grease and flour bottoms only of two 1-quart casseroles or two 8x4-inch loaf pans. In small bowl, cover raisins with boiling water and let stand 5 minutes; drain.

In large bowl, beat brown sugar and margarine until light and fluffy. Add cornmeal, molasses, buttermilk and egg; blend well. Stir in flour and baking soda. Fold in raisins. Pour batter into greased and floured casseroles.

Bake at 350°F. for 40 to 50 minutes or until toothpick inserted in center comes out clean. Cool 10 minutes; remove from pans. Cool completely. Wrap tightly and store in refrigerator.

Yield: 2 (16-slice) loaves.

HIGH ALTITUDE:
Above 3500 Feet: No change.

NUTRITION PER SERVING:
Calories 130; Protein 3g; Carbohydrate 26g; Fat 2g; Sodium 110mg.

SOUR CREAM COFFEE CAKE

Rich, sweet cake-like breads served for breakfast or brunch are called coffee cakes. This version is quick to make and is filled and topped with a nutty brown sugar mixture.

COFFEE CAKE

- ¾ **cup sugar**
- ½ **cup margarine or butter, softened**
- 1 **teaspoon vanilla**
- 3 **eggs**
- 2 **cups all purpose flour**
- 1 **teaspoon baking powder**
- 1 **teaspoon baking soda**
- ⅛ **teaspoon salt**
- 1 **cup dairy sour cream**

FILLING AND TOPPING

- 1¼ **cups firmly packed brown sugar**
- 1 **cup chopped walnuts**
- 2 **teaspoons cinnamon**
- 3 **tablespoons margarine or butter, melted**

Heat oven to 350°F. Grease and lightly flour 10-inch tube pan. In large bowl, beat sugar and ½ cup margarine until light and fluffy. Add vanilla and eggs; mix well. In small bowl, combine flour, baking powder, baking soda and salt. Stir flour mixture and sour cream alternately into sugar mixture, beginning and ending with flour mixture.

In small bowl, combine all filling and topping ingredients; mix well. Spread half of batter in greased pan; sprinkle with half of the brown sugar mixture. Repeat with remaining batter and brown sugar mixture.

Bake at 350°F. for 35 to 40 minutes or until toothpick inserted in center comes out clean. Cool upright in pan 15 minutes. Invert onto large plate or cookie sheet, then invert again onto serving plate, streusel side up.
Yield: 16 servings.

TIP:
Recipe can be baked in greased and floured 13x9-inch pan. Prepare recipe as directed above. Spread half of batter in bottom of pan; sprinkle with half of the brown sugar mixture. Repeat with remaining batter and brown sugar mixture. Bake at 350°F. for 30 to 40 minutes or until toothpick inserted in center comes out clean.

HIGH ALTITUDE:
Above 3500 Feet: No change.

NUTRITION PER SERVING:
Calories 330; Protein 4g; Carbohydrate 40g; Fat 17g; Sodium 225mg.

APPLE STREUSEL COFFEE CAKE

Leaving the peel on the apples adds color to this delicious coffee cake.

COFFEE CAKE

- 1 **cup all purpose flour**
- 1 **teaspoon baking powder**
- ¼ **teaspoon baking soda**
- ⅛ **teaspoon salt**
- ¼ **cup margarine or butter, softened**
- ½ **cup sugar**
- ¼ **cup frozen cholesterol-free egg product, thawed, or 1 egg**
- 1 **teaspoon vanilla**
- 3 **tablespoons nonfat plain yogurt**
- 2 **cups thinly sliced unpeeled apples**

TOPPING

- ¼ **cup all purpose flour**
- 2 **tablespoons brown sugar**
- ½ **teaspoon cinnamon**
- 2 **tablespoons margarine or butter**

Heat oven to 350°F. Grease 9-inch round cake pan or 8-inch square pan. In small bowl, combine 1 cup flour, baking powder, baking soda and salt; mix well. Set aside.

In large bowl, beat ¼ cup margarine and sugar until light and fluffy. Add egg product and vanilla; blend well. Alternately add dry ingredients and yogurt to sugar mixture, beating well after each addition. Spread batter in greased pan; arrange apple slices over batter.

In small bowl, combine all topping ingredients except margarine. Using pastry blender or fork, cut in 2 tablespoons margarine until crumbly. Sprinkle topping evenly over apples.

Bake at 350°F. for 30 to 35 minutes or until toothpick inserted in center comes out clean. Cool 10 minutes; if desired, remove from pan.
Yield: 8 servings.

HIGH ALTITUDE:
Above 3500 Feet: No change.

NUTRITION PER SERVING:
Calories 230; Protein 3g; Carbohydrate 36g; Fat 9g; Sodium 220mg.

Apple Coffee Cake Supreme

Savor the down-home goodness of apples in this delicious coffee cake. Baking the cake in a tart pan gives it an elegant look.

COFFEE CAKE
- ½ cup sugar
- 2 eggs
- 1 to 2 teaspoons grated lemon peel
- ½ cup plain yogurt
- 3 tablespoons margarine or butter, melted
- 1⅓ cups all purpose flour
- 2 teaspoons baking powder
- ½ teaspoon salt
- 3 to 4 cups thinly sliced peeled apples
- 2 tablespoons sugar
- ½ to 1 cup sliced almonds

GLAZE
- ⅓ cup sugar
- ⅓ cup margarine or butter, melted
- 1 egg, beaten

Heat oven to 375°F. Grease 10-inch tart pan with removable bottom or 8-inch square pan. In small bowl, beat ½ cup sugar and 2 eggs; stir in lemon peel, yogurt and 3 tablespoons margarine. Add flour, baking powder and salt to egg mixture; blend well. Pour into greased pan. Arrange apple slices on top of dough, overlapping slightly. Sprinkle with 2 tablespoons sugar and almonds.

Bake at 375°F. for 35 to 45 minutes or until golden brown and toothpick inserted in center comes out clean.*

Meanwhile, in small bowl combine all glaze ingredients; blend well. Slowly pour over almonds and allow mixture to soak into hot cake. Broil 5 to 6 inches from heat for 1 to 2 minutes or until bubbly. Serve warm. Store in refrigerator.
Yield: 6 to 8 servings.

TIP:
* If using 8-inch square pan, increase baking time 5 minutes.

HIGH ALTITUDE:
Above 3500 Feet: No change.

NUTRITION PER SERVING:
Calories 400; Protein 8g; Carbohydrate 49g; Fat 21g; Sodium 380mg.

Country Apple Coffee Cake

Refrigerated flaky biscuits mean quick preparation for this delicious breakfast treat.

COFFEE CAKE
- 2 tablespoons margarine or butter, softened
- 1½ cups chopped peeled apples
- 1 (10-oz.) can refrigerated flaky biscuits
- ⅓ cup firmly packed brown sugar
- ¼ teaspoon cinnamon
- ⅓ cup light corn syrup
- 1 egg
- ½ cup pecan halves or pieces

GLAZE
- ⅓ cup powdered sugar
- ¼ teaspoon vanilla
- 1 to 2 teaspoons milk

Heat oven to 350°F. Using 1 tablespoon of the margarine, generously grease 9-inch round cake pan or 8-inch square pan. Spread 1 cup of the apples in greased pan. Separate dough into 10 biscuits; cut each into quarters. Arrange biscuit pieces, points up, over apples. Top with remaining ½ cup apples. In small bowl, combine remaining 1 tablespoon margarine, brown sugar, cinnamon, corn syrup and egg; beat 2 to 3 minutes or until sugar is partially dissolved. Stir in pecans; spoon over biscuit pieces and apples.

Bake at 350°F. for 35 to 45 minutes or until deep golden brown. Cool 5 minutes. In small bowl, blend all glaze ingredients, adding enough milk for desired drizzling consistency. Drizzle over warm cake. Serve warm or cool. Store in refrigerator.
Yield: 6 to 8 servings.

NUTRITION PER SERVING:
Calories 290; Protein 3g; Carbohydrate 44g; Fat 12g; Sodium 430mg.

Raspberry Cream Cheese Coffee Cake

This indulgent coffee cake is easy to make, and impressive to serve.

- 2¼ **cups all purpose flour**
- ¾ **cup sugar**
- ¾ **cup margarine or butter**
- ½ **teaspoon baking powder**
- ½ **teaspoon baking soda**
- ¼ **teaspoon salt**
- ¾ **cup dairy sour cream**
- 1 **teaspoon almond extract**
- 1 **egg**
- 1 **(8-oz.) pkg. cream cheese, softened**
- ¼ **cup sugar**
- 1 **egg**
- ½ **cup raspberry preserves**
- ½ **cup sliced almonds**

Heat oven to 350°F. Grease and flour bottom and sides of 9 or 10-inch springform pan. In large bowl, combine flour and ¾ cup sugar. Using pastry blender or fork, cut in margarine until mixture resembles coarse crumbs. Reserve 1 cup of crumb mixture. To remaining crumb mixture, add baking powder, baking soda, salt, sour cream, almond extract and 1 egg; blend well. Spread batter over bottom and 2 inches up sides of greased and floured pan. (Batter should be about ¼ inch thick on sides.)

In small bowl, combine cream cheese, ¼ cup sugar and 1 egg; blend well. Pour into batter-lined pan. Carefully spoon preserves evenly over cream cheese mixture. In small bowl, combine reserved crumb mixture and sliced almonds. Sprinkle over preserves.

Bake at 350°F. for 45 to 55 minutes or until cream cheese filling is set and crust is deep golden brown. Cool 15 minutes. Remove sides of pan. Serve warm or cool, cut into wedges. Store in refrigerator.
Yield: 16 servings.

HIGH ALTITUDE:
Above 3500 Feet: No change.

NUTRITION PER SERVING:
Calories 320; Protein 5g; Carbohydrate 34g; Fat 18g; Sodium 230mg.

Marbled Raspberry Coffee Cake

This cake, flavored with lemon and swirled with raspberry preserves, is perfect for a Valentine's Day brunch.

COFFEE CAKE
- 1 **cup all purpose flour**
- ½ **cup sugar**
- 1 **teaspoon baking powder**
- ¼ **teaspoon baking soda**
- ¼ **teaspoon salt**
- 1 **(3-oz.) pkg. cream cheese, softened**
- ¼ **cup margarine or butter, softened**
- ¼ **cup milk**
- 1 **teaspoon grated lemon peel**
- 1 **egg**
- ¼ **cup raspberry preserves**

FROSTING
- ½ **cup powdered sugar**
- 1 **tablespoon lemon juice**
- 2 **teaspoons margarine or butter, softened**
- ¼ **cup sliced almonds**

Heat oven to 350°F. Grease and flour 8-inch square pan. In small bowl, combine all coffee cake ingredients except preserves; blend at low speed until moistened. Beat 2 minutes at medium speed. Spread batter in greased and floured pan. Spoon preserves by teaspoonfuls over batter. Using knife, swirl preserves over top of batter to marble.

Bake at 350°F. for 25 to 30 minutes or until toothpick inserted in center comes out clean. Cool slightly.

In small bowl, combine all frosting ingredients except almonds; beat until smooth. Frost warm cake; sprinkle with almonds. Serve warm.
Yield: 9 servings.

HIGH ALTITUDE:
Above 3500 Feet: No change.

NUTRITION PER SERVING:
Calories 250; Protein 4g; Carbohydrate 34g; Fat 11g; Sodium 230mg.

Raspberry Cream Cheese Coffee Cake

BLUEBERRY BRUNCH CAKE

Any flavor fruit pie filling can be used to make this glazed coffee cake.

COFFEE CAKE
- 1 cup margarine or butter, softened
- 1¾ cups sugar
- 1 teaspoon vanilla
- 4 eggs
- 3 cups all purpose flour
- 1½ teaspoons baking powder
- ½ teaspoon salt
- ¼ teaspoon nutmeg
- 1 (21-oz.) can blueberry fruit pie filling

GLAZE
- 1¼ cups powdered sugar
- 1 tablespoon margarine or butter, softened
- 2 to 3 tablespoons lemon juice
  Few drops yellow food color

Heat oven to 350°F. Grease and flour 15x10x1-inch baking pan. In large bowl, combine 1 cup margarine, sugar and vanilla. Add eggs 1 at a time, beating well after each addition. By hand, stir in flour, baking powder and salt; mix well. Spread half of batter in greased pan. Stir nutmeg into blueberry filling; spread filling evenly over batter. Drop remaining batter by teaspoonfuls over filling.

Bake at 350°F. for 30 to 40 minutes or until toothpick inserted in center comes out clean and top is golden brown.

In small bowl, blend all glaze ingredients, adding enough lemon juice for desired drizzling consistency. Drizzle over warm cake.

Yield: 24 servings.

HIGH ALTITUDE:
Above 3500 Feet: No change.

NUTRITION PER SERVING:
Calories 250; Protein 3g; Carbohydrate 41g; Fat 10g; Sodium 170mg.

BLUEBERRY MUFFIN CAKE

Serve this for brunch on the patio.

TOPPING
- ¼ cup all purpose flour
- ¼ cup sugar
- ½ teaspoon cinnamon
- 3 tablespoons margarine or butter

COFFEE CAKE
- 2 tablespoons fine dry bread crumbs
- 2 cups all purpose flour
- 1 cup sugar
- 3 teaspoons baking powder
- ½ teaspoon baking soda
- ½ teaspoon salt
- ½ teaspoon cinnamon
- 1 cup fresh or frozen blueberries, thawed, drained
- 2 eggs
- ⅓ cup orange-flavored liqueur or orange juice
- ¼ cup margarine or butter, melted, cooled
- 1 (8-oz.) container dairy sour cream
- 1 teaspoon grated orange peel

In small bowl, combine all topping ingredients except margarine; mix well. Using pastry blender or fork, cut in 3 tablespoons margarine until mixture resembles coarse crumbs. Set aside.

Heat oven to 375°F. Grease 10-inch springform pan or 9-inch square pan. Sprinkle with bread crumbs; set aside. In large bowl, combine 2 cups flour, 1 cup sugar, baking powder, baking soda, salt and ½ teaspoon cinnamon; mix well. Stir in blueberries. Beat eggs in medium bowl. Stir in orange liqueur, ¼ cup margarine, sour cream and orange peel. Add to blueberry mixture, stirring just until dry ingredients are moistened. Spoon batter into greased pan; sprinkle with topping.

Bake at 375°F. for 35 to 45 minutes or until toothpick inserted in center comes out clean. Cool 10 minutes; remove sides of pan. Serve warm or cool.

Yield: 12 servings.

HIGH ALTITUDE:
Above 3500 Feet: Decrease baking powder to 2 teaspoons. Bake as directed above.

NUTRITION PER SERVING:
Calories 320; Protein 4g; Carbohydrate 48g; Fat 12g; Sodium 320mg.

Blueberry Muffin Cake

PUMPKIN DATE COFFEE CAKE

Pumpkin and orange are an unbeatable flavor combination in this date and nut-studded coffee cake.

TOPPING
- ¼ cup all purpose flour
- ¼ cup sugar
- ½ teaspoon cinnamon
- 3 tablespoons margarine or butter

COFFEE CAKE
- 2 cups all purpose flour
- 1 cup sugar
- 3 teaspoons baking powder
- 1 teaspoon pumpkin pie spice
- ½ teaspoon baking soda
- ½ teaspoon salt
- 2 eggs
- 1 cup canned pumpkin
- ⅓ cup orange juice
- ¼ cup margarine or butter, melted, cooled
- 1 teaspoon grated orange peel
- 1 cup chopped nuts
- ½ cup chopped dates

GLAZE
- ½ cup powdered sugar
- 1 teaspoon grated orange peel
- 1 to 2 tablespoons orange juice

In small bowl, combine all topping ingredients except margarine; mix well. Using pastry blender or fork, cut in 3 tablespoons margarine until mixture resembles coarse crumbs. Set aside.

Heat oven to 375°F. Grease 10-inch tube pan. In large bowl, combine 2 cups flour, 1 cup sugar, baking powder, pumpkin pie spice, baking soda and salt; mix well. Beat eggs in small bowl. Stir in pumpkin, ⅓ cup orange juice, ¼ cup margarine and 1 teaspoon orange peel. Add to dry ingredients, stirring just until dry ingredients are moistened. Stir in nuts and dates. Spoon batter into greased pan; sprinkle with topping.

Bake at 375°F. for 40 to 45 minutes or until toothpick inserted in center comes out clean. Cool 30 minutes; remove from pan.

In small bowl, blend all glaze ingredients, adding enough orange juice for desired drizzling consistency. Drizzle over warm cake. Serve warm or cool.
Yield: 12 servings.

HIGH ALTITUDE:
Above 3500 Feet: No change.

NUTRITION PER SERVING:
Calories 360; Protein 5g; Carbohydrate 53g; Fat 14g; Sodium 300mg.

CARAMEL BISCUIT RING-A-ROUND

The easiest way to cut the refrigerated biscuits into quarters is to use a kitchen scissors.

- ¾ cup firmly packed brown sugar
- ½ cup chopped nuts
- ⅓ cup margarine or butter
- 2 tablespoons water
- 2 (7.5-oz.) cans refrigerated biscuits

Heat oven to 400°F. Generously grease 12-cup Bundt® pan. In small saucepan, combine brown sugar, nuts, margarine and water; heat until margarine melts, stirring occasionally. Separate dough into 20 biscuits. Cut each biscuit into quarters; place in large bowl. Pour brown sugar mixture over biscuits; toss lightly to coat evenly. Spoon coated biscuit pieces into greased pan.

Bake at 400°F. for 20 to 30 minutes or until golden brown. Let stand in pan 3 minutes; invert onto serving plate. Serve warm.
Yield: 10 servings.

NUTRITION PER SERVING:
Calories 260; Protein 4g; Carbohydrate 37g; Fat 11g; Sodium 430mg.

WINTER FRUIT COFFEE CAKE

This coffee cake featuring fresh winter fruits also can be served for dessert with whipped cream.

COFFEE CAKE

1½ cups all purpose flour
2 teaspoons baking powder
¾ cup sugar
¼ cup margarine or butter, softened
2 eggs
½ cup buttermilk
2 teaspoons grated orange peel
½ cup golden raisins
1 cup thinly sliced apples
1 orange, peeled, thinly sliced

TOPPING

¼ cup sugar
½ teaspoon cinnamon
2 tablespoons margarine or butter, melted
½ cup chopped pecans

Heat oven to 350°F. Grease and flour 9-inch springform pan. In medium bowl, combine flour and baking powder; set aside. In large bowl, beat ¾ cup sugar and ¼ cup margarine until light and fluffy. Add eggs; blend well. Alternately add dry ingredients and buttermilk to sugar mixture, beating well after each addition. Stir in orange peel and raisins. Pour into greased pan. Arrange apple and orange slices decoratively over top of batter.

In small bowl, combine all topping ingredients; sprinkle over fruit.

Bake at 350°F. for 40 to 50 minutes or until golden brown. Cool 10 minutes; remove sides of pan. Serve warm.
Yield: 8 to 10 servings.

HIGH ALTITUDE:
Above 3500 Feet: No change.

NUTRITION PER SERVING:
Calories 300; Protein 4g; Carbohydrate 45g; Fat 12g; Sodium 170mg.

CARAMEL
STICKY BUNS

Nothing could be easier to make or more tempting to eat than these caramel rolls made with refrigerated biscuit dough.

TOPPING
¼ cup margarine or butter, melted
¼ cup firmly packed brown sugar
2 tablespoons light corn syrup
¼ cup chopped pecans

COATING
1 tablespoon sugar
½ teaspoon cinnamon

BUNS
1 (10-oz.) can refrigerated flaky biscuits

Heat oven to 375°F. Grease 12 muffin cups. In small bowl, combine all topping ingredients; mix well. Spoon scant tablespoon topping into each greased muffin cup.

In medium bowl, combine coating ingredients; mix well. Separate dough into 10 biscuits. Cut each biscuit into 6 pieces. Toss pieces in coating mixture. Place 5 coated pieces of dough in each greased muffin cup. Place pan on cookie sheet to guard against spills.

Bake at 375°F. for 15 to 20 minutes or until golden brown. Cool in pan 1 minute; invert onto waxed paper. Serve warm.

Yield: 12 rolls.

NUTRITION PER SERVING:
Calories 150; Protein 2g; Carbohydrate 19g; Fat 8g; Sodium 300mg.

DANISH ALMOND
CREAM ROLLS

We've simplified the traditional layering process used to make Danish pastry by using refrigerated crescent rolls. You'll be delighted with the creamy almond filling.

ROLLS
2 (3-oz.) pkg. cream cheese, softened
½ to 1 teaspoon almond extract
½ cup powdered sugar
½ cup finely chopped almonds
2 (8-oz.) cans refrigerated crescent dinner rolls
1 egg white
1 teaspoon water
¼ cup sliced almonds

GLAZE
⅔ cup powdered sugar
¼ to ½ teaspoon almond extract
3 to 4 teaspoons milk

Heat oven to 350°F. In small bowl, beat cream cheese, ½ teaspoon almond extract and ½ cup powdered sugar until fluffy. Stir in ½ cup chopped almonds.

Separate 1 can of dough into 4 rectangles; firmly press perforations to seal. Press or roll each to form a 7x4-inch rectangle; spread each with about 2 tablespoons of the cream cheese filling to within ¼ inch of edges. Starting at longer side, roll up each rectangle, firmly pinching edges and ends to seal. Gently stretch each roll to 10 inches. Coil each roll into a spiral with the seam on the inside, tucking ends under. Place on ungreased cookie sheets. Repeat with remaining can of dough and cream cheese filling.

In small bowl, combine egg white and water; brush over rolls. Sprinkle with ¼ cup sliced almonds.

Bake at 350°F. for 17 to 23 minutes or until deep golden brown. In small bowl, blend all glaze ingredients, adding enough milk for desired drizzling consistency; drizzle over warm rolls. Serve warm.

Yield: 8 rolls.

NUTRITION PER SERVING:
Calories 410; Protein 8g; Carbohydrate 42g; Fat 24g; Sodium 540mg.

Caramel Sticky Buns

QUICK CRESCENT CINNAMON CRISPS

Here's a fast and easy version of the ever popular "elephant ears."

- 1 (8-oz.) can refrigerated crescent dinner rolls
- 2 tablespoons margarine or butter, melted
- ⅓ cup sugar
- 1 teaspoon cinnamon
- ¼ cup finely chopped pecans

Heat oven to 375°F. Unroll dough into 2 long rectangles; firmly press perforations to seal. Brush with margarine. In small bowl, combine sugar and cinnamon; blend well. Sprinkle half of mixture over dough; sprinkle with pecans. Starting at shorter side, roll up each rectangle. Cut each roll crosswise into 4 slices. On ungreased cookie sheet, pat or roll out each slice to a 4-inch circle; sprinkle each with remaining sugar-cinnamon mixture.

Bake at 375°F. for 10 to 15 minutes or until golden brown.

Yield: 8 rolls.

NUTRITION PER SERVING:
Calories 180; Protein 2g; Carbohydrate 20g; Fat 11g; Sodium 260mg.

COOK'S NOTE

CINNAMON

Cinnamon comes from the bark of a tropical evergreen tree. When the bark is dried, it curls and is cut into lengths which are sold as cinnamon sticks. Ground cinnamon is used in baked recipes. Cinnamon sold in bulk at the supermarket or food co-op is less expensive than prepackaged forms.

MAGIC MARSHMALLOW CRESCENT PUFFS

In 1969, this recipe was the grand prize winner in the 20th Pillsbury BAKE-OFF® Contest. The cinnamon-sugar coated marshmallows melt during baking, forming tender crescent dough puffs with sweet centers.

PUFFS
- ¼ cup sugar
- 2 tablespoons all purpose flour
- 1 teaspoon cinnamon
- 2 (8-oz.) cans refrigerated crescent dinner rolls
- 16 large marshmallows
- ¼ cup margarine or butter, melted

GLAZE
- ½ cup powdered sugar
- ½ teaspoon vanilla
- 2 to 3 teaspoons milk
- ¼ cup chopped nuts, if desired

Heat oven to 375°F. In small bowl, combine sugar, flour and cinnamon. Separate dough into 16 triangles. Dip 1 marshmallow in margarine; roll in sugar mixture. Place marshmallow on wide end of triangle. Roll up starting at wide end of triangle and rolling to opposite point. Completely cover marshmallow with dough; firmly pinch edges to seal. Dip 1 end in remaining margarine; place margarine side down in ungreased large muffin cup or 6-oz. custard cup. Repeat with remaining marshmallows.

Bake at 375°F. for 12 to 15 minutes or until golden brown. (Place foil or cookie sheet on rack below muffin cups to guard against spills.) Immediately remove from muffin cups; cool on wire racks.

In small bowl, blend powdered sugar, vanilla and enough milk for desired drizzling consistency. Drizzle over warm rolls. Sprinkle with nuts.

Yield: 16 rolls.

NUTRITION PER SERVING:
Calories 190; Protein 2g; Carbohydrate 24g; Fat 10g; Sodium 270mg.

MAPLE CREAM COFFEE TREAT

For breakfast, brunch or dessert, these cream-filled, caramel-topped finger rolls will surely bring rave reviews. Use your favorite nuts or those you might have on hand, such as pecans, almonds or walnuts.

- 1 **cup firmly packed brown sugar**
- ½ **cup chopped nuts**
- ⅓ **cup maple-flavored syrup or dark corn syrup**
- ¼ **cup margarine or butter, melted**
- 1 **(8-oz.) pkg. cream cheese, softened**
- ¼ **cup powdered sugar**
- 2 **tablespoons margarine or butter, softened**
- ½ **cup coconut**
- 2 **(10-oz.) cans refrigerated flaky biscuits**

Heat oven to 350°F. In ungreased 13x9-inch pan, combine brown sugar, nuts, syrup and ¼ cup margarine; spread evenly in bottom of pan.

In small bowl, blend cream cheese, powdered sugar and 2 tablespoons margarine until smooth; stir in coconut.

Separate dough into 20 biscuits. Press or roll each to a 4-inch circle. Spread tablespoonfuls of cream cheese mixture down center of each circle to within ¼ inch of edge. Overlap sides of dough over filling, forming finger-shaped rolls. Arrange rolls, seam side down, in 2 rows of 10 rolls each over brown sugar mixture in pan.

Bake at 350°F. for 25 to 30 minutes or until deep golden brown. Cool 3 to 5 minutes; invert onto foil, waxed paper or serving platter.

Yield: 20 rolls.

NUTRITION PER SERVING:
Calories 250; Protein 3g; Carbohydrate 29g; Fat 14g; Sodium 370mg.

PEANUT BUTTER AND JELLY BISCUIT TREATS

Enjoy these tempting rolls warm from the oven.

ROLLS
- 1 **(10-oz.) can refrigerated flaky biscuits**
- 10 **tablespoons peanut butter**
- 8 **to 10 tablespoons strawberry preserves**

GLAZE
- ¼ **cup powdered sugar**
- 1 **to 2 teaspoons milk**

Heat oven to 375°F. Separate dough into 10 biscuits; separate each biscuit into 2 layers. Spoon 1 tablespoon peanut butter on center of half of biscuit pieces. Top with remaining biscuit pieces; pinch edges to seal. Place biscuits in ungreased 9-inch round cake pan or 8-inch square pan. With thumb, make imprint in center of each roll; fill each with about 1 tablespoon preserves.

Bake at 375°F. for 23 to 28 minutes or until golden brown. In small bowl, blend powdered sugar and enough milk for desired glaze consistency. Drizzle over warm rolls.

Yield: 10 rolls.

NUTRITION PER SERVING:
Calories 250; Protein 6g; Carbohydrate 31g; Fat 12g; Sodium 370mg.

CORN BREAD

You'll enjoy this version of the all-American quick bread.

- 1 cup all purpose flour
- 1 cup cornmeal
- 2 tablespoons sugar
- 3 teaspoons baking powder
- ½ teaspoon salt
- 1 cup milk
- ¼ cup oil or melted shortening
- 1 egg, slightly beaten

Heat oven to 425°F. Grease 8 or 9-inch square pan. In medium bowl, combine flour, cornmeal, sugar, baking powder and salt; mix well. Stir in remaining ingredients just until smooth. Pour batter into greased pan. Bake at 425°F. for 18 to 22 minutes or until toothpick inserted in center comes out clean. **Yield: 9 servings.**

HIGH ALTITUDE:
Above 3500 Feet: Decrease baking powder to 2 teaspoons. Bake as directed above.

NUTRITION PER SERVING:
Calories 190; Protein 4g; Carbohydrate 25g; Fat 8g; Sodium 240mg.

VARIATIONS:

BACON CORN BREAD: Cook 4 to 5 slices bacon until crisp; drain on paper towel. Substitute bacon drippings for oil. Sprinkle batter with crumbled bacon before baking.

CORN BREAD RING: Bake in greased 1½-quart (6-cup) ring mold for 15 to 20 minutes. Immediately remove from mold.

CORN MUFFINS: Spoon batter into greased muffin cups and bake 15 to 20 minutes. Immediately remove from muffin cups.
Yield: 12 muffins.

CORN STICKS: Bake in well-greased, hot corn stick pans, filling ⅔ full. Bake 12 to 15 minutes. Immediately remove from pan.
Yield: 18 corn sticks.

MEXICAN CORN BREAD: Prepare batter using 2 eggs, slightly beaten. Stir in 2 oz. (½ cup) shredded Cheddar cheese, ¼ cup chopped green chiles and ¼ cup finely chopped onion. Bake 20 to 25 minutes.

PERFECT POPOVERS

Popovers are a big, puffy, steam-raised quick bread made from an egg-rich batter. They are delicious served plain, with butter and jam, or filled with your favorite sandwich mixture.

- 3 eggs, room temperature
- 1¼ cups milk, room temperature
- 1¼ cups all purpose flour
- ¼ teaspoon salt

Heat oven to 450°F. Generously grease 10 popover cups or 6-oz. custard cups.* In small bowl, beat eggs with rotary beater until lemon-colored and foamy. Add milk; blend well. Add flour and salt; beat with rotary beater just until batter is smooth and foamy on top. Pour batter into greased cups, filling about ⅔ full.

Bake at 450°F. for 15 minutes. (DO NOT OPEN OVEN.) Reduce heat to 350°F.; bake an additional 25 to 35 minutes or until popovers are high, hollow and deep golden brown. Remove from oven; insert sharp knife into each popover to allow steam to escape. Remove from pan. Serve warm.
Yield: 10 popovers.

TIP:
* Standard muffin pans can be used. Fill alternating greased cups with batter to prevent sides of popovers from touching.

HIGH ALTITUDE:
Above 3500 Feet: Increase flour to 1¼ cups plus 2 tablespoons. Bake at 450°F. for 15 minutes. Reduce heat to 350°F.; bake an additional 20 to 30 minutes.

NUTRITION PER SERVING:
Calories 90; Protein 4g; Carbohydrate 14g; Fat 2g; Sodium 90mg.

VARIATION:

DILL PARMESAN POPOVERS: Add 2 tablespoons grated Parmesan cheese and 1 teaspoon dried dill weed with flour.

SPOONBREAD

Baked in a casserole and served with a spoon, spoonbread is usually served in place of bread, potatoes or rice.

- 2 cups water
- 1 cup white cornmeal
- 1 teaspoon seasoned salt
- 1 cup buttermilk
- 2 tablespoons margarine or butter, melted
- 2 teaspoons baking powder
- 3 eggs, separated
  Margarine or butter, if desired

Heat oven to 375°F. Grease 2-quart casserole. In medium saucepan, bring water to a boil. Slowly stir in cornmeal and salt. Reduce heat to medium; cook about 5 minutes or until very thick, stirring constantly. Remove from heat; stir in buttermilk. Cool 5 minutes. Gradually beat in 2 tablespoons margarine, baking powder and egg yolks. In small bowl, beat egg whites until stiff but not dry. Fold into cornmeal mixture. Pour batter into greased casserole.

Bake at 375°F. for 40 to 50 minutes or until golden brown and knife inserted near center comes out clean. Serve immediately with margarine.
Yield: 8 (½-cup) servings.

NUTRITION PER SERVING:
Calories 120; Protein 5g; Carbohydrate 14g; Fat 6g; Sodium 370mg.

PATIO SKILLET BREAD

Try this southern-style version of corn bread baked in a skillet. You'll enjoy the combination of vegetable and herb flavors.

- 1½ cups all purpose flour
- 1½ cups yellow cornmeal
- 2 tablespoons sugar
- 4 teaspoons baking powder
- 2½ teaspoons salt
- ¼ to ½ teaspoon dried sage leaves
- ¼ teaspoon dried thyme leaves
- 1 cup finely chopped celery
- 1 cup finely chopped onions
- 1 (2-oz.) jar chopped pimiento, drained
- 1½ cups milk
- ⅓ cup margarine or butter, melted
- 3 eggs, slightly beaten

Heat oven to 400°F. Line 10-inch ovenproof skillet or 9-inch square pan with foil; grease foil. In large bowl, combine flour, cornmeal, sugar, baking powder, salt, sage, thyme, celery, onions and pimiento; blend well. Add milk, margarine and eggs; stir just until dry ingredients are moistened. Pour into foil-lined skillet. Bake at 400°F. for 30 to 35 minutes or until deep golden brown. Serve immediately. Store in refrigerator.
Yield: 12 servings.

HIGH ALTITUDE:
Above 3500 Feet: No change.

NUTRITION PER SERVING:
Calories 210; Protein 6g; Carbohydrate 29g; Fat 8g; Sodium 640mg.

COOK'S NOTE

HOW TO TEST BAKING POWDER FOR FRESHNESS

The shelf life of baking powder is short, about 6 to 8 months. Check the bottom of the can for its expiration date. If none is available, determine if yours is active by pouring ⅓ cup hot tap water over 1 teaspoon of baking powder. Watch for active bubbling. If few bubbles result, the baking powder will not leaven your baked product.

RASPBERRY NECTARINE PANCAKE PUFF

Serve this warm from the oven, before the pancake loses its "puff."

PANCAKE
- ½ cup all purpose flour
- 1 tablespoon sugar
- ¼ teaspoon salt
- ½ cup milk
- 3 eggs
- 2 tablespoons margarine or butter

SAUCE
- 1 (10-oz.) pkg. frozen raspberries in light syrup, thawed
- ⅓ cup red currant jelly
- 1 tablespoon cornstarch

FRUIT
- 1½ cups sliced nectarines or peaches

Heat oven to 425°F. In medium bowl, combine all pancake ingredients except margarine. Beat with rotary beater until smooth. Place margarine in 10-inch ovenproof, nonstick skillet. Melt in 425°F. oven just until margarine sizzles, about 2 to 3 minutes. Remove skillet from oven; tilt to coat bottom with melted margarine. Immediately pour batter into hot skillet.

Bake at 425°F. for 14 to 18 minutes or until puffed and golden brown.

Meanwhile, drain raspberries; reserve syrup. Set raspberries aside. Add water to syrup to make ¾ cup. In small saucepan, combine syrup, jelly and cornstarch; stir to dissolve cornstarch. Cook and stir over medium heat until thickened and clear. Stir in raspberries. Arrange nectarine slices over pancake; drizzle with some of the raspberry sauce. Cut into wedges. Serve with additional raspberry sauce.

Yield: 4 servings.

HIGH ALTITUDE:
Above 3500 Feet: No change.

NUTRITION PER SERVING:
Calories 350; Protein 9g; Carbohydrate 54g; Fat 11g; Sodium 280mg.

Raspberry Nectarine Pancake Puff

PUFFED FRUIT-TOPPED PANCAKE

This popover-like pancake boasts a delectable fruit topping.

PANCAKE
- ¾ cup all purpose flour
- ¼ cup whole wheat flour
- ½ teaspoon grated orange peel
- ¼ teaspoon nutmeg
- ⅛ teaspoon allspice
  Dash salt
- 1 cup milk
- 3 eggs

TOPPING
- 2 tablespoons margarine or butter
- 1 (16-oz.) can sliced pears in lite syrup, drained, reserving ½ cup liquid
- 1 (6-oz.) pkg. (1 cup) dried apricots
- ¼ cup firmly packed brown sugar

Heat oven to 450°F. Grease bottom only of 13x9-inch pan. In medium bowl, combine all pancake ingredients. Beat with rotary beater until smooth. Pour into greased pan.

Bake at 450°F. for 15 minutes. (DO NOT OPEN OVEN.) Reduce heat to 350°F.; bake an additional 14 to 17 minutes or until dark golden brown.

Meanwhile, melt margarine in medium skillet over medium heat. Add pear slices, apricots, brown sugar and reserved ½ cup pear liquid. Bring to a boil. Reduce heat to low; simmer 5 to 10 minutes or until apricots are tender, stirring occasionally. Serve pancake immediately with warm fruit topping.

Yield: 6 servings.

TIP:
To microwave topping, place margarine in 1-quart microwave-safe casserole. Microwave on HIGH for 30 to 60 seconds or until melted. Stir in apricots, brown sugar and reserved ½ cup pear liquid; cover tightly. Microwave on HIGH for 4 to 6 minutes or until apricots are tender, stirring once halfway through cooking. Add pear slices; cover tightly. Microwave on HIGH for 1 to 2 minutes or until hot.

HIGH ALTITUDE:
Above 3500 Feet: No change.

NUTRITION PER SERVING:
Calories 330; Protein 8g; Carbohydrate 56g; Fat 8g; Sodium 130mg.

Puffy Surprise Oven Pancakes

Serve these tender oven pancakes with your favorite fresh fruit.

- 2 eggs
- ½ cup all purpose flour
- ½ cup milk
- 2 tablespoons margarine or butter
- 4 cups sliced fruit*
- ½ cup firmly packed brown sugar
- 1 (8-oz.) container dairy sour cream

Heat oven to 425°F. In medium bowl, beat eggs slightly. Add flour and milk; beat with rotary beater until combined. In oven, melt 1 tablespoon margarine in each of two 9-inch glass pie plates; spread to cover bottom. Pour batter over margarine in pie plates.

Bake at 425°F. for 10 to 15 minutes or until golden brown. (Pancakes will form a well in the center and edges will puff up.) Spoon fruit into center of pancakes. Sprinkle with brown sugar and top with sour cream. Serve immediately.

Yield: 4 servings.

TIP:
* Any of the following fruits can be used: strawberries, bananas, pineapple, raspberries, peaches and blueberries.

HIGH ALTITUDE:
Above 3500 Feet: No change.

NUTRITION PER SERVING:
Calories 490; Protein 9g; Carbohydrate 65g; Fat 22g; Sodium 155mg.

Orange Oven French Toast

This recipe is great for large groups and can be easily made ahead. Plan to serve it for your next brunch.

- ½ cup margarine or butter, melted
- ¼ cup honey
- 2 teaspoons cinnamon
- 6 eggs
- 1 cup milk
- 1 cup orange juice
- ¼ cup sugar
- 2 teaspoons grated orange peel
- ½ teaspoon salt
- ½ teaspoon cinnamon
- 16 slices whole wheat or white bread
- 2 oranges, sliced

Heat oven to 400°F. In small bowl, combine margarine, honey and 2 teaspoons cinnamon; mix well. Pour mixture evenly into 2 ungreased 15x10x1-inch baking pans. In medium bowl, slightly beat eggs. Add milk, orange juice, sugar, orange peel, salt and ½ teaspoon cinnamon; mix well. Dip bread in egg mixture. Place on margarine mixture in pans. Pour any remaining egg mixture over bread.*

Bake at 400°F. for 10 minutes; turn slices over. Bake an additional 10 minutes or until golden brown. Arrange on serving platter with orange slices.

Yield: 16 slices.

TIP:
* At this point, bread can be covered and refrigerated overnight. Uncover; bake as directed above.

NUTRITION PER SERVING:
Calories 200; Protein 6g; Carbohydrate 24g; Fat 9g; Sodium 300mg.

Crunchy Oven French Toast

CRUNCHY OVEN FRENCH TOAST

Minimum last-minute preparation makes this a perfect recipe for company. Make it ahead of time and freeze it for up to 2 weeks.

3   eggs
1   cup half-and-half
2   tablespoons sugar
1   teaspoon vanilla
¼   teaspoon salt
3   cups cornflakes cereal, crushed to 1 cup
8   diagonally-cut slices French bread
      (¾ inch thick)
      Strawberry syrup
      Fresh strawberries

Grease 15x10x1-inch baking pan. In shallow bowl, combine eggs, half-and-half, sugar, vanilla and salt; mix well. Place crushed cereal in shallow bowl. Dip bread in egg mixture, making sure all egg mixture is absorbed. Dip bread into crumbs. Place in single layer in greased pan; cover. Freeze 1 to 2 hours or until firm.

Heat oven to 425°F. Bake 15 to 20 minutes or until golden brown, turning once. Serve with syrup and strawberries. Garnish with whipped topping, if desired.

Yield: 8 slices.

NUTRITION PER SERVING:
Calories 200; Protein 6g; Carbohydrate 30g; Fat 6g; Sodium 340mg.

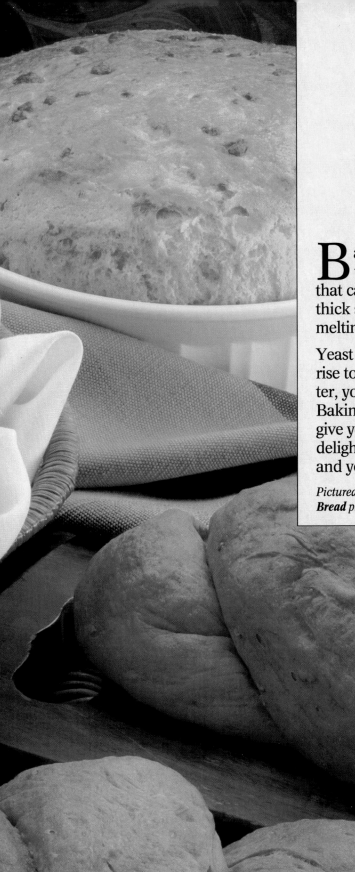

YEAST BREADS

~

B aking bread fills the home — and the heart — with an aroma and warmth that can't be topped. What can compare to a thick slice of still-warm bread spread with melting butter or homemade jam?

Yeast is the magician that makes these breads rise to their golden-crusted best. In this chapter, you'll learn how to put that magic to work. Baking yeast bread is a simple skill that will give you hours of pleasure and produce delightful breads that will warm your home and your heart.

*Pictured: **Two-Tone Rye Twist Loaves** p. 433, **Easy Cheese Batter Bread** p. 440, **Basic Dinner Rolls** p. 452*

YEAST BREADS

Baking yeast bread is one of those basic skills that people
have mastered throughout the centuries and throughout the world.
Whether you're baking a hearty loaf or a good-morning pan of sweet rolls,
the techniques are simple and easy to learn. Fine-tuning your
yeast bread-baking skills may take a little longer,
but practicing is half the fun!

KINDS OF YEAST BREADS

*These breads all have something in common —
the leavening agent is yeast. Yeast is a
microorganism that is activated with "food"
(sugar and flour), "water" (liquid ingredients)
and warmth. As the yeast grows and multiplies,
it creates gas bubbles that cause bread dough
to rise. Yeast breads can be divided into
2 main categories:*

BATTER

Batter breads could be called short-cut
breads because they don't require kneading.
The dough contains less flour and is stickier.
Instead of kneading, the dough is beaten with
an electric mixer after the first addition of flour,
placed in the pan rather than shaped, and rises
only once, not twice. Batter breads have a
coarse texture and pebbly surface. (Recipe
examples include: **Cornmeal Sesame Batter
Rolls** p. 456 and **English Muffin Batter Bread**
p. 442.)

KNEADED

Kneading dough distributes ingredients
evenly and develops the gluten in flour, which
provides strength, elasticity and structure to the
bread. Kneading gives bread an even texture
and a smooth rounded top. Kneading can be
done by hand, by using a heavy-duty mixer
with bread hooks or with a heavy-duty food
processor. Kneaded breads are usually shaped
and usually require 2 risings. (Recipe examples
include: **Quick Sourdough French Bread**
p. 429, **Sweet Potato Rolls** p. 455 and **Herb
Cheese Pretzels** p. 467.)

SECRETS FOR BAKING WITH YEAST

*There's a lot of mystique surrounding yeast
because how it is handled will affect the results of
baked goods. Here are some tips that will help
take the mystery out of baking with yeast:*

Check the expiration date on the package.
Outdated yeast won't become active and the
bread won't rise.

**To substitute 1 form of yeast for another form
of yeast, use these equivalents:** One envelope
of active dry yeast equals 2¼ teaspoons of bulk
active dry yeast or ⅓ of a 2-ounce cake of
compressed fresh yeast.

**To substitute fast-acting yeast for regular
yeast, reduce the rise time in the recipe by
about half.**

Test the yeast before beginning. If you're
concerned that your yeast may not be active,
dissolve 1 teaspoon of sugar in ½ cup of warm
water (110 to 115°F.). Slowly sprinkle 1 packet
of yeast into the water. Stir the mixture and set
a timer for 10 minutes. In 3 to 4 minutes, the

yeast should have absorbed enough liquid to activate and will come to the surface.

If at the end of 10 minutes, the yeast has multiplied to the 1-cup mark and has a rounded crown, it's still very active and fresh and can be used in your recipe. Remember to deduct the ½ cup of water used for the test from the total liquid used in the recipe. If the yeast has not multiplied, it will not provide satisfactory results in the recipe. This process is sometimes referred to as "proofing the yeast."

Use a yeast or candy thermometer to accurately determine the temperature of liquids. If the liquid in which the dry yeast is dissolved is too hot, it will kill the yeast cells. If it's too cold, they won't be activated. Use very warm liquid (120 to 130°F.) if the active dry yeast will be added to dry ingredients. If it's to be added to liquid ingredients, use warm liquid (110 to 115°F).

Place dough in a warm spot to rise. Yeast doughs rise or "proof" best when the temperature is 80 to 85°F. To make sure the dough is warm enough:

- Cover the bowl loosely with plastic wrap and/or a cloth towel.

- Place the bowl on a wire rack over a pan of hot water in a draft-free spot.

- OR place the bowl on the top rack of an unheated oven. Put a pan of hot water on the rack below it.

- OR turn the oven on at 400°F. for 1 minute, then turn it off. Place the bowl on the center rack of the oven and close the door.

Test the dough to make sure that it has risen sufficiently. When you think the dough has doubled in size, lightly poke 2 fingers about ½ inch into the dough. If the indentations remain, the dough has risen enough.

SECRETS FOR SUCCESSFUL YEAST BREADS

Although the techniques for making yeast breads are simple, a few "secrets" will ensure that even your first efforts will be attractive and great-tasting.

SECERETS FOR ALL YEAST BREADS
What to do if . . .

- **You forget to add the yeast.** Dissolve it in a small amount of warm liquid and work it into the dough.

- **The dough doesn't rise.** The yeast may have been old, or the liquid may have been too hot or too cold, or you may have added too much salt. Try placing the dough in a warmer spot or waiting longer to give it more time to rise.

- **The dough rises too quickly.** Punch down the dough and let it rise again. If it rises before you're ready to bake it, move the dough to a cooler spot to slow down the action of the yeast.

Use aluminum pans. They give breads and rolls well-browned crusts. Uncoated aluminum pans give the most even browning and uniform results. Dark metal pans and glass pans absorb more heat and will produce a darker crust.

Grease the pan(s) as directed in the recipe.

To make dough a day ahead, cover and refrigerate it up to 24 hours, if desired. The dough is ready to bake when it has doubled in size. If it has not doubled in size in the refrigerator, let it stand at room temperature for 30 to 45 minutes or until it has doubled.

Create a variety of crusts:

- For a crisp crust, gently brush the bread dough with water before baking it.

- For a hard crust, place a pan of water in the bottom of the oven.

- For a shiny crust, beat 1 egg with 1 tablespoon of water and brush it gently on the bread before baking. Sprinkle the bread with sesame or poppy seeds, if desired.

- For a soft, tender crust, gently brush the bread with milk just before baking, or with melted butter just after baking.

Remove the bread from the pan immediately after baking it. Cool the bread on a wire rack to prevent the crust from becoming soggy.

Cool breads away from drafts. This will help prevent the bread from shrinking and the crust from cracking.

Cool breads before slicing them. Slicing a too-warm loaf or coffee cake will cause crumbling and tearing.

Cut breads with a sharp knife or electric knife. Use a back-and-forth sawing motion rather than pressing straight down.

SECRETS FOR BATTER BREADS

Use the same pan for rising and baking. Most batter breads require only 1 rising, so let them rise and bake in the same pan.

Watch for small, unbroken bubbles during rising. Their appearance is an indication that the bread has risen sufficiently. (If large air pockets appear under the baked crust, it is an indication that the dough rose too quickly. Next time proof in a cooler place.)

SECRETS FOR KNEADED BREADS

Practice makes perfect. The more you knead bread, the better technique you'll develop. If a dough is not kneaded enough, the bread will be dry, heavy and have a crumbly texture. Using a dough hook on a standard mixer will result in bread with a slightly lower volume, while a heavy-duty mixer will create loaves with higher volume. Avoid over-kneading the dough. Dough that is kneaded too long (more than 10 minutes) can become dry and coarse because too much flour may be added.

Add flour gradually during kneading. As you knead the dough, add just enough flour so that the dough is no longer sticky. In the recipes, a range is given for the amount of flour because flour can gain or lose moisture depending on weather conditions and how it is stored. Too much flour added during kneading may produce streaks and uneven grain.

Prepare pans while the dough rests. Grease them or leave them ungreased according to the recipe directions.

Shape loaves and rolls to fit the pan. The shaped dough should be large enough so that it will touch the sides of the pan as the dough rises. The pan helps provide support for the dough.

Cover loaves with foil during baking if they become too brown before they're done.

HOW TO TELL WHEN YEAST BREADS ARE DONE

Sound plays a key role in determining if yeast breads are done, so listen carefully!

Yeast breads are done when . . .

- They are golden brown.

- They pull away from the sides of the pan.

- Tapping on the top crust of a loaf produces a hollow sound.

Keeping Yeast Breads Fresh and Flavorful

Breads can become moldy or stale soon after baking. Proper storage is essential in preserving their freshness and flavor.

Cool breads completely before storing.

Store bread in an airtight container in a cool, dry place. Or, wrap it in foil or plastic wrap. Bread should be stored at room temperature no longer than 5 days.

Refrigerate bread to slow the growth of mold. Refrigeration is necessary, especially for moist breads or during hot, humid weather. However, refrigeration won't preserve freshness and can cause bread to dry out. To store bread for a longer period of time, freeze it.

To freeze bread, see the chart on p. 25.

To freeze rolls:

- Bake and cool completely.
- Place the rolls on foil-wrapped cardboard and seal in a large plastic freezer bag. Label and date the bag.
- Freeze for up to 1 month.

Use stale bread for croutons or crumbs.

Using Bread Flour

Bread flour is made from the finest hard spring wheat available, and contains more protein strength than all purpose flour. Its higher protein content gives the dough more structure and allows it to have more elasticity, resulting in loaves with better texture and higher volume.

Bread flour performs well in all yeast bread baking.

Bread flour can be directly substituted in any traditional bread recipe calling for all purpose flour. When substituting bread flour for all purpose flour, knead the dough for 10 to 15 minutes, let it rest 15 minutes before shaping, and allow for a slightly longer rise time.

Store bread flour in an airtight container in a cool, dry place. Bread flour should be used within 18 to 24 months of purchase.

Baking with a Bread Machine

Bread machines that mix, knead and bake bread have become popular appliances. Here are a few tips for making the most of your bread machine:

- **Read and follow manufacturer's directions.**
- **Use only recipes specifically developed for your bread machine.**
- **Always use bread flour.**
- **For a whole grain loaf, whole grain flour can be substituted for up to half of the bread flour.** The volume of a whole grain loaf will be less than a regular loaf.
- **Measure ingredients accurately.** This should be done with all baked recipes, but it is especially important when using these appliances.
- **Bring ingredients to room temperature before placing them in the machine.** However, don't use perishable ingredients such as yogurt, eggs or milk if you're using the delayed-time bake cycle. The ingredients can spoil before baking begins.

NUTRITION IN THIS CHAPTER

Nutrition per serving means the calculation was done on 1 slice, 1 serving, 1 roll, 1 bread stick or 1 pretzel.

STEP-BY-STEP FEATURE ∽
How to Make Yeast Bread

STEP 1. To knead dough, push dough down and away with heels of hands. Give dough a quarter turn. Repeat until dough is smooth and elastic.

STEP 2. Let dough rise until doubled in size. To test for doubled size, poke 2 fingers into dough. It is doubled when indentations remain.

STEP 3. Roll dough to 14x7-inch rectangle. Starting with 7-inch side, roll up. Pinch edges and ends to seal. Place, seam side down, in pan.

DELICIOUS WHITE BREAD

Use this basic recipe with its many variations to bake your family favorites.

> 5 **to 6 cups all purpose flour**
> 3 **tablespoons sugar**
> 2 **teaspoons salt**
> 2 **pkg. active dry yeast**
> 2 **cups water**
> ¼ **cup oil or shortening**
> 1 **tablespoon margarine or butter, melted**

In large bowl, combine 2 cups flour, sugar, salt and yeast; blend well. In small saucepan, heat water and oil until very warm (120 to 130°F.). Add warm liquid to flour mixture. Blend at low speed until moistened; beat 3 minutes at medium speed. By hand, stir in an additional 2½ to 3 cups flour until dough pulls cleanly away from sides of bowl.

On floured surface, knead in ½ to 1 cup flour until dough is smooth and elastic, about 5 minutes. Place dough in greased bowl; cover loosely with plastic wrap and cloth towel. Let rise in warm place (80 to 85°F.) until light and doubled in size, 45 to 60 minutes.

Grease two 8x4 or two 9x5-inch loaf pans. Punch down dough several times to remove all air bubbles. Divide dough into 2 parts; shape into loaves. Place in greased pans. Cover; let rise in warm place until dough fills pans and tops of loaves are about 1 inch above pan edges, 30 to 35 minutes.

Heat oven to 375°F. Uncover dough. Bake 40 to 50 minutes or until loaves sound hollow when lightly tapped. Immediately remove from pans; cool on wire racks. Brush with melted margarine.
Yield: 2 (18-slice) loaves.

HIGH ALTITUDE:
Above 3500 Feet: No change.

NUTRITION PER SERVING:
Calories 100; Protein 2g; Carbohydrate 17g; Fat 2g; Sodium 125mg.

(Recipe continued on next page.)

Delicious White Bread

(Recipe continued from previous page.)

VARIATIONS:

BREAD STICKS: After first rise time, punch down dough. Divide dough in half. Cut each half into 32 pieces; shape each into 8-inch long breadstick. Place on greased cookie sheets. Brush with beaten egg white; sprinkle with sesame seed. Cover; let rise in warm place about 30 minutes or until doubled in size. Bake at 400°F. for about 14 minutes.
Yield: 64 bread sticks.

BUTTER-TOPPED MINI-LOAVES: Prepare dough as directed above. After allowing dough to rest, divide into 12 pieces. Shape each piece into a 7-inch oblong loaf; taper ends. Place loaves 3 inches apart on greased cookie sheets. Cover; let rise in warm place until doubled in size, about 45 minutes. Make ¼-inch deep slit down center of each loaf; drizzle with 1 teaspoon melted butter. Sprinkle with sesame seed or poppy seed, if desired. Bake at 375°F. for 20 to 25 minutes or until loaves sound hollow when lightly tapped.
Yield: 12 mini-loaves.

CINNAMON SWIRL BREAD: Divide dough into 2 parts. Roll each to 14x7-inch rectangle of dough. Brush each with melted margarine or butter; sprinkle each with mixture of ¼ cup sugar and 1 teaspoon cinnamon. Starting with 7-inch side, roll up. Seal edges and place seam side down in greased loaf pans. Let rise and bake as directed above.
Yield: 2 (18-slice) loaves.

HAMBURGER BUNS: After first rise time, punch down dough. Divide dough in half; shape each half into eight 2-inch balls. If desired, flatten slightly. Place on greased cookie sheets. Let rise in warm place about 30 minutes. Bake at 400°F. for about 15 minutes.
Yield: 16 buns.

RAISIN BREAD: Add ½ teaspoon cinnamon with the salt and stir in 1 cup raisins after beating step. Shape and bake as directed above.
Yield: 2 (18-slice) loaves.

WHOLE WHEAT BREAD

The nut-like flavor of whole wheat comes through in these flavorful loaves.

  2 **pkg. active dry yeast**
  ¼ **cup warm water**
  ½ **cup firmly packed brown sugar or honey**
  3 **teaspoons salt**
2½ **cups hot water**
  ¼ **cup margarine or butter**
4½ **cups whole wheat flour**
2¾ **to 3¾ cups all purpose flour**

In small bowl, dissolve yeast in warm water (105 to 115°F.). In large bowl, combine brown sugar, salt, hot water and margarine; cool slightly. To cooled mixture, add 3 cups whole wheat flour. Blend at low speed until moistened; beat 3 minutes at medium speed. Add remaining whole wheat flour and dissolved yeast; mix well. By hand, stir in an additional 2¼ to 2¾ cups all purpose flour until dough pulls cleanly away from sides of bowl.

On floured surface, knead in ½ to 1 cup all purpose flour until dough is smooth and elastic, about 10 to 15 minutes. Place dough in greased bowl; cover loosely with plastic wrap and cloth towel. Let rise in warm place (80 to 85°F.) until light and doubled in size, about 30 to 45 minutes.

Generously grease two 8x4 or 9x5-inch loaf pans. Punch down dough several times to remove all air bubbles. Divide dough into 2 parts; shape into loaves. Place in greased pans. Cover; let rise in warm place until light and doubled in size, about 30 to 45 minutes.

Heat oven to 375°F. Uncover dough. Bake 30 minutes. Reduce oven temperature to 350°F.; bake an additional 10 to 15 minutes or until loaves sound hollow when lightly tapped. Immediately remove from pans; cool on wire racks.
Yield: 2 (16-slice) loaves.

HIGH ALTITUDE:
Above 3500 Feet: No change.

NUTRITION PER SERVING:
Calories 140; Protein 4g; Carbohydrate 27g; Fat 2g; Sodium 220mg.

RYE BREAD

Dense and hearty, this classic bread makes wonderful sandwiches or provides a satisfying accompaniment to robust soups.

- 2 pkg. active dry yeast
- 1 cup warm water
- 1 cup warm milk
- ½ cup molasses
- ¼ cup shortening, melted
- 2 teaspoons salt
- 3 to 3½ cups all purpose flour
- 3 cups medium rye flour
- 1 tablespoon water
- 1 egg yolk

In small bowl, dissolve yeast in warm water (105 to 115°F.). In large bowl, combine warm milk (105 to 115°F.), molasses, shortening and salt; blend well. Add dissolved yeast. Add 2 cups all purpose flour. Blend at low speed until moistened. Beat 3 minutes at medium speed. By hand, stir in 3 cups rye flour and an additional ¾ to 1 cup all purpose flour until dough pulls cleanly away from sides of bowl.

On floured surface, knead in ¼ to ½ cup all purpose flour until dough is smooth and elastic, about 5 minutes. Place dough in greased bowl; cover loosely with plastic wrap and cloth towel. Let rise in warm place (80 to 85°F.) until light and doubled in size, about 45 to 60 minutes.

Grease 2 cookie sheets. Punch down dough several times to remove all air bubbles. Divide dough into 2 parts; shape into balls. Shape dough into two 12-inch oblong loaves; round ends. Place on greased cookie sheets. With sharp knife, make four ¼-inch deep diagonal slashes on top of each loaf. Cover; let rise in warm place until doubled in size, about 20 to 30 minutes.

Heat oven to 350°F. Uncover dough. Combine water and egg yolk; brush on loaves. Bake at 350°F. for 35 to 45 minutes or until loaves sound hollow when lightly tapped. Immediately remove from pans; cool on wire racks.
Yield: 2 (22-slice) loaves.

HIGH ALTITUDE:
Above 3500 Feet: Decrease first rise time by 15 to 30 minutes. Decrease second rise time by 10 minutes. Bake as directed above.

NUTRITION PER SERVING:
Calories 80; Protein 2g; Carbohydrate 17g; Fat 1g; Sodium 175mg.

BUTTERMILK BREAD

Serve this simply delicious bread with butter and jam.

- 5 to 6 cups all purpose flour
- ¼ cup sugar
- 2 teaspoons salt
- ½ teaspoon baking soda
- 2 pkg. active dry yeast
- 1½ cups buttermilk
- ½ cup water
- ½ cup margarine or butter
- 1 tablespoon margarine or butter, melted

In large bowl, combine 2 cups flour, sugar, salt, baking soda and yeast; blend well. In small saucepan, heat buttermilk, water and ½ cup margarine until very warm (120 to 130°F.). (Mixture will look curdled.) Add warm liquid to flour mixture. Blend at low speed until moistened; beat 3 minutes at medium speed. By hand, stir in an additional 2½ to 3 cups flour until dough pulls cleanly away from sides of bowl.

On floured surface, knead in ½ to 1 cup flour until dough is smooth and elastic, about 10 minutes. Place dough in greased bowl; cover loosely with plastic wrap and cloth towel. Let rise in warm place (80 to 85°F.) until light and doubled in size, 30 to 45 minutes.

Grease two 8x4 or 9x5-inch loaf pans. Punch down dough several times to remove all air bubbles. Divide dough into 4 parts; shape into balls. Shape into 4 rolls by rolling out each ball into a 10x7-inch rectangle. Starting with shorter side, roll up; pinch edges firmly to seal. Place 2 rolls side by side, seam side down, in each greased pan. Cover; let rise in warm place until dough fills pans and tops of loaves are about 1 inch above pan edges, 15 to 30 minutes.

Heat oven to 375°F. Uncover dough. Bake 30 to 40 minutes or until loaves sound hollow when lightly tapped. Immediately remove from pans; brush with 1 tablespoon melted margarine. Cool on wire racks.
Yield: 2 (14-slice) loaves.

HIGH ALTITUDE:
Above 3500 Feet: No change.

NUTRITION PER SERVING:
Calories 140; Protein 3g; Carbohydrate 22g; Fat 4g; Sodium 230mg.

VIENNA BREAD

Vienna bread traditionally is an oval yeast bread with a crisp, shiny crust. You will be pleased with this sesame seed-topped version.

  1 **pkg. active dry yeast**
  1 **cup warm water**
5½ **to 6 cups all purpose flour**
  3 **tablespoons sugar**
  1 **cup milk**
  2 **tablespoons oil**
  2 **teaspoons salt**
  1 **egg white, slightly beaten**
    Sesame seed

In large bowl, dissolve yeast in warm water (105 to 115°F.). Stir in 2 cups flour and sugar. Cover; let rise in warm place (80 to 85°F.) for 1 hour.

In small saucepan, heat milk and oil until warm (105 to 115°F.). Add warm liquid to flour mixture. Stir in salt and an additional 2½ to 2¾ cups flour until dough pulls cleanly away from sides of bowl.

On floured surface, knead in 1 to 1¼ cups flour until dough is smooth and elastic, 8 to 10 minutes. Place dough in greased bowl; cover loosely with plastic wrap and cloth towel. Let rise in warm place until light and doubled in size, about 1 to 1¼ hours. Punch down dough. Cover; let rise a second time until light and doubled in size, about 50 to 60 minutes.

Generously grease large cookie sheet. Punch down dough several times to remove all air bubbles. Divide dough into 2 parts. Shape into two 14-inch oblong loaves. Place loaves on greased cookie sheet. With scissors, cut five 1-inch deep slits on tops of loaves. Cover; let rise in warm place until light and doubled in size, about 30 to 40 minutes.

Heat oven to 350°F. Uncover dough. Brush tops and sides of loaves with beaten egg white; sprinkle with sesame seed. Bake 40 to 50 minutes or until loaves sound hollow when lightly tapped. Immediately remove from cookie sheet; cool on wire racks.
Yield: 2 (18-slice) loaves.

HIGH ALTITUDE:
Above 3500 Feet: No change.

NUTRITION PER SERVING:
Calories 90; Protein 3g; Carbohydrate 17g; Fat 1g; Sodium 125mg.

FRENCH BREAD BRAIDS

French bread is a light, crusty yeast-raised bread made with water instead of milk. This braided version of the classic is a welcome addition to any meal.

4¾ **to 5¾ cups all purpose flour**
  3 **teaspoons salt**
  1 **tablespoon sugar**
  2 **pkg. active dry yeast**
  2 **cups water**
  2 **tablespoons shortening**
  1 **tablespoon water**
  1 **egg white**

In large bowl, combine 3 cups flour, salt, sugar and yeast; blend well. In small saucepan, heat 2 cups water and shortening until very warm (120 to 130°F.). Add warm liquid to flour mixture. Blend at low speed until moistened; beat 3 minutes at medium speed. By hand, stir in an additional 1½ to 2¼ cups flour to form a stiff dough.

On floured surface, knead in ¼ to ½ cup flour until dough is smooth and elastic, about 8 minutes. Place dough in greased bowl; cover loosely with plastic wrap and cloth towel. Let rise in warm place (80 to 85°F.) until light and doubled in size, about 1 hour.

Grease large cookie sheet. Punch down dough several times to remove all air bubbles. Divide dough in half; divide each half into 3 equal parts. Roll each part into 14-inch rope. Braid 3 ropes together; seal ends. Place on greased cookie sheet. Repeat with other half of dough. In small bowl, combine 1 tablespoon water and egg white; beat slightly. Carefully brush over loaves. Cover loosely with greased plastic wrap and cloth towel; let rise in warm place until light and doubled in size, 20 to 30 minutes.

Heat oven to 375°F. Uncover dough. Brush loaves again with egg white mixture. Bake 25 to 30 minutes or until golden brown. Immediately remove from cookie sheet; cool on wire racks.
Yield: 2 (18-slice) loaves.

HIGH ALTITUDE:
Above 3500 Feet: No change.

NUTRITION PER SERVING:
Calories 80; Protein 2g; Carbohydrate 16g; Fat 1g; Sodium 180mg.

CHALLAH

This rich egg bread is a Jewish tradition. It is served on the Sabbath and holidays.

4½ **to 5½ cups all purpose flour**
2 **tablespoons sugar**
1 **teaspoon salt**
2 **pkg. active dry yeast**
1 **cup water**
⅓ **cup margarine or butter**
4 **eggs**
1 **egg white**
1 **tablespoon water**
Poppy seed

In large bowl, combine 2 cups flour, sugar, salt and yeast; blend well. In small saucepan, heat 1 cup water and margarine until very warm (120 to 130°F.). Add warm liquid and 4 eggs to flour mixture. Blend at low speed until moistened; beat 3 minutes at medium speed. By hand, stir in an additional 2 to 2½ cups flour until dough pulls cleanly away from sides of bowl.

On floured surface, knead in ½ to 1 cup flour until dough is smooth and elastic, about 5 minutes. Place dough in greased bowl; cover loosely with plastic wrap and cloth towel. Let rise in warm place (80 to 85°F.) until light and doubled in size, about 35 to 45 minutes.

Grease large cookie sheet. Punch down dough several times to remove all air bubbles. Divide dough in half; divide each half into 3 equal parts. Roll each part into 14-inch rope. Braid 3 ropes together; seal ends. Place on greased cookie sheet. Repeat with other half of dough. Cover; let rise in warm place until doubled in size, about 15 to 25 minutes.

Heat oven to 400°F. Uncover dough. Bake 10 minutes. Brush with mixture of egg white and 1 tablespoon water; sprinkle with poppy seed. Return to oven; bake an additional 5 to 10 minutes or until loaves sound hollow when lightly tapped. Immediately remove from cookie sheet; cool on wire racks.
Yield: 2 (15-slice) loaves.

HIGH ALTITUDE:
Above 3500 Feet: Decrease each rise time by 10 to 15 minutes.

NUTRITION PER SERVING:
Calories 120; Protein 4g; Carbohydrate 20g; Fat 3g; Sodium 105mg.

GOLDEN PARTY LOAVES

Carrots add color, texture and flavor to these party perfect mini-loaves.

4½ **to 5½ cups all purpose flour**
1½ **cups finely shredded carrots**
1 **teaspoon salt**
1 **pkg. active dry yeast**
¾ **cup apricot nectar**
½ **cup plain yogurt**
¼ **cup honey**
¼ **cup margarine or butter**
1 **egg**
Margarine or butter, softened

In large bowl, combine 2 cups flour, carrots, salt and yeast; blend well. In small saucepan, heat apricot nectar, yogurt, honey and ¼ cup margarine until very warm (120 to 130°F.). Add warm liquid and egg to flour mixture. Blend at low speed until moistened; beat 3 minutes at medium speed. By hand, stir in an additional 2 to 2½ cups flour to form a stiff dough.

On floured surface, knead in ½ to 1 cup flour until dough is smooth and elastic, about 5 minutes. Place dough in greased bowl; cover loosely with plastic wrap and cloth towel. Let rise in warm place (80 to 85°F.) until light and doubled in size, about 1 hour.

Grease and flour two 9x5 or 8x4-inch loaf pans. Punch down dough several times to remove all air bubbles. Divide dough in half. Work dough with hands to remove large air bubbles. Divide each half into thirds. Shape each third into a small loaf. Spread sides of loaves with softened margarine. Place 3 loaves crosswise in greased and floured pans. Repeat with remaining dough. Cover; let rise in warm place until light and doubled in size, about 45 minutes.

Heat oven to 375°F. Uncover dough. Bake 30 to 35 minutes or until deep golden brown and loaves sound hollow when lightly tapped. Immediately remove from pans; cool on wire racks. Brush warm loaves with softened margarine.
Yield: 6 (7-slice) mini-loaves.

HIGH ALTITUDE:
Above 3500 Feet: No change.

NUTRITION PER SERVING:
Calories 90; Protein 2g; Carbohydrate 16g; Fat 2g; Sodium 70mg.

QUICK SOURDOUGH FRENCH BREAD

In this recipe, we've kept the traditional sourdough flavor but streamlined the method using fast-acting yeast, sour cream and vinegar.

    4 to 5 cups all purpose flour
    2 tablespoons wheat germ
    1 tablespoon sugar
    2 teaspoons salt
  ½ teaspoon ginger
    2 pkg. fast-acting dry yeast
    1 cup very warm water
    1 cup dairy sour cream, room temperature
    2 tablespoons vinegar
    1 egg white
    1 tablespoon water
    2 teaspoons poppy seed

In large bowl, combine 1½ cups flour, wheat germ, sugar, salt, ginger and yeast; blend well. Add 1 cup very warm water (120 to 130°F.), sour cream and vinegar to flour mixture. Blend at low speed until moistened; beat 3 minutes at medium speed. By hand, stir in an additional 2 to 2½ cups flour until dough pulls cleanly away from sides of bowl.

On floured surface, knead in ½ to 1 cup flour until dough is smooth and elastic, about 3 minutes. Place dough in greased bowl; cover loosely with plastic wrap and cloth towel. Let rise in warm place (80 to 85°F.) until light and doubled in size, 25 to 30 minutes.

Grease large cookie sheet. Punch down dough several times to remove all air bubbles. Divide dough in half; roll each half into 14x8-inch rectangle. Starting with 14-inch side, roll up; pinch edges firmly to seal. Place, seam side down, on greased cookie sheet; taper ends to a point. With sharp knife, make five ¼-inch deep diagonal slashes on top of each loaf. Cover; let rise in warm place until light and doubled in size, about 15 minutes.

Heat oven to 375°F. Uncover dough. Bake 25 minutes. In small bowl, beat egg white and 1 tablespoon water. Brush top of loaves with egg white mixture. Sprinkle with poppy seed. Bake an additional 5 to 10 minutes or until golden brown and loaves sound hollow when lightly tapped. Immediately remove from cookie sheet; cool on wire racks.

Yield: 2 (17-slice) loaves.

HIGH ALTITUDE:
Above 3500 Feet: No change.

NUTRITION PER SERVING:
Calories 90; Protein 3g; Carbohydrate 16g; Fat 2g; Sodium 130mg.

COOK'S NOTE

YEAST

Yeast is a living single-cell organism used for making bread. Healthy yeast cells feed on sugar or starch in a moist environment, causing fermentation which produces carbon dioxide and alcohol that leaven the bread. During baking, the yeast cells finally reach a temperature that kills them, the bread sets in its risen form, the alcohol evaporates and carbon dioxide is driven off. To determine if your yeast is fresh, refer to Secrets for Baking with Yeast p. 418.

Quick Sourdough French Bread

Sourdough Bread

This delicious bread has a slightly sour, tangy flavor created by using a yeast or sourdough starter as the leavener. Since the starter takes 5 days to develop, you'll need to plan ahead to make this bread.

STARTER
- 1 pkg. active dry yeast
- 2 cups warm water
- 3½ cups all purpose flour
- 1 tablespoon sugar or honey

BREAD
- 1 cup starter
- 5½ to 6 cups all purpose flour
- ¼ cup sugar
- 1 tablespoon salt
- 1⅔ cups warm water
- ⅓ cup oil

In large nonmetal bowl, dissolve yeast in 2 cups warm water (105 to 115°F.); let stand 5 minutes. Add 3½ cups flour and 1 tablespoon sugar; blend well. Cover loosely with plastic wrap and cloth towel. Let stand in warm place (80 to 85°F.) for 5 days, stirring at least once each day. When the starter is ready for use, it is bubbly and may have a yellow liquid layer on top. Stir well before using.*

Place 1 cup starter in large bowl.** Add 2 cups flour, ¼ cup sugar, salt, 1⅔ cups warm water (105 to 115°F.) and oil; blend well. Stir in 2½ to 2¾ cups flour until dough pulls cleanly away from sides of bowl.

On floured surface, knead in remaining 1 to 1¼ cups flour until dough is smooth and elastic, about 5 minutes. Place dough in greased bowl; cover loosely with plastic wrap and cloth towel. Let rise in warm place 8 to 10 hours or overnight.

Grease 3 cookie sheets or 9-inch round cake pans.*** Uncover dough. Punch down dough several times to remove air bubbles. Divide dough into 3 parts. Work dough with hands to remove all air bubbles. Shape into round loaves. Place on greased cookie sheets. Cover; let rise in warm place until doubled in size, 2 to 3 hours.

Heat oven to 400°F. With sharp knife, make three ¼-inch deep slits on top of each loaf. Bake 20 to 25 minutes or until loaves sound hollow when lightly tapped. Immediately remove from cookie sheets; cool on wire racks.
Yield: 3 (16-slice) loaves.

TIPS:
* If starter will not be used immediately, cover and refrigerate until ready to use. Return to room temperature before using.

** If desired, starter can be replenished for future use. After removing 1 cup starter, add to remaining starter 1 cup flour, ⅔ cup warm water (105 to 115°F.) and 1 teaspoon sugar or honey; blend well. Cover loosely with plastic wrap and cloth towel. Let stand in warm place (80 to 85°F.) 10 to 12 hours or overnight. The starter will become bubbly and rise. Stir, cover and store in refrigerator. Repeat this process each time the starter is used. If starter is used once a week, it will remain active. If not used, stir in 1 teaspoon sugar or honey weekly.

*** Three 8x4-inch loaf pans can be used. Bake at 400°F. for 25 to 30 minutes.

HIGH ALTITUDE:
Above 3500 Feet: No change.

NUTRITION PER SERVING:
Calories 100; Protein 3g; Carbohydrate 18g; Fat 2g; Sodium 135mg.

Cook's Note

YEAST STARTER

Before yeast was commercially available, yeast starters were used as the leavening agent for making breads. The starters were made with a combination of flour, water, sugar and airborne yeast. The airborne yeast served as the catalyst for the starter. The starter was put in a warm place until the yeast fermented and the mixture became foamy. A portion of this starter was used to leaven a batch of bread, and the remaining starter was "fed" with flour, water and sugar to be kept "alive" for future baking. Today yeast starters are often used for sourdough bread.

Oat Bran French Bread

You'll enjoy this updated, contemporary version of French bread.

2¼ to 2¾ cups all purpose flour
⅓ cup oat bran hot cereal, uncooked
1 pkg. active dry yeast
1 teaspoon salt
1 cup water
1 tablespoon honey
1 tablespoon cornmeal
½ teaspoon cornstarch
¼ cup water

In large bowl, combine 1 cup flour, cereal, yeast and salt; blend well. In small saucepan, heat 1 cup water and honey until very warm (120 to 130°F.). Add warm liquid to flour mixture. Blend at low speed until moistened; beat 3 minutes at medium speed. By hand, stir in an additional 1 to 1¼ cups flour to form a stiff dough.

On floured surface, knead in ¼ to ½ cup flour until dough is smooth and elastic, about 5 minutes. Place dough in greased bowl; cover loosely with plastic wrap and cloth towel. Let rise in warm place (80 to 85°F.), about 30 minutes.

Grease cookie sheet; sprinkle with cornmeal. Punch down dough several times to remove all air bubbles. Shape dough by rolling back and forth on counter into a 15-inch long loaf. Place on greased cookie sheet. Cover; let rise in warm place until almost doubled in size, about 15 minutes.

Heat oven to 400°F. In small saucepan, combine cornstarch and ¼ cup water; mix well. Bring to a boil; cook until mixture is thickened and clear. Remove from heat; cool, stirring occasionally. Uncover dough. With very sharp knife, cut four ½-inch deep diagonal slashes on top of loaf. Brush loaf with thin layer of cornstarch mixture. Bake at 400°F. for 10 minutes. Brush with cornstarch mixture again. Bake an additional 15 to 20 minutes or until golden brown and loaf sounds hollow when lightly tapped. Immediately remove from cookie sheet; cool on wire rack.

Yield: 1 (15-slice) loaf.

FOOD PROCESSOR DIRECTIONS:
Grease cookie sheet; sprinkle with cornmeal. Sprinkle yeast over ¼ *cup water heated to 105 to 115°F.* Stir in honey. Let stand until foamy, about 5 minutes. In food processor bowl with metal blade, combine 2¼ cups flour, cereal and salt; process to blend. Stir ⅔ cup water heated to 105 to 115°F. into yeast mixture. With motor running, pour yeast mixture through feed tube in a steady stream as fast as flour absorbs it. When dough forms a ball, stop machine. Dough should feel slightly sticky. If dough is too wet, add flour by tablespoons with motor running; if too dry, add water by teaspoons until well blended. Knead by processing continuously for 45 seconds. Continue as directed above.

TIP:
A French bread pan can be substituted for a cookie sheet. Grease pan; sprinkle with cornmeal. To shape bread, divide dough in half. Gently elongate each half by rolling back and forth to 1 inch shorter than length of pan. Place in greased pan. Continue as directed above.

HIGH ALTITUDE:
Above 3500 Feet: No change.

NUTRITION PER SERVING:
Calories 90; Protein 3g; Carbohydrate 19g; Fat 0g; Sodium 140mg.

SPEEDY CARAWAY RYE BREAD

This bread can be ready to serve in less than 2 hours.

3 to 4 cups all purpose flour
1 tablespoon caraway seed
2 teaspoons salt
1½ teaspoons onion powder
3 pkg. active dry yeast
2¼ cups water
3 tablespoons brown sugar
3 tablespoons margarine or butter
2½ cups medium rye flour
　　Egg white, beaten
　　Coarse salt, if desired

In large bowl, combine 2 cups all purpose flour, caraway seed, salt, onion powder and yeast; blend well. In small saucepan, heat water, brown sugar and margarine until very warm (120 to 130°F.). Add warm liquid to flour mixture. Blend at low speed until moistened; beat 3 minutes at medium speed. Stir in rye flour and an additional ¾ to 1½ cups all purpose flour until dough pulls cleanly away from sides of bowl.

On floured surface, knead in ¼ to ½ cup all purpose flour until dough is smooth and elastic, about 5 minutes. Place dough in greased bowl; cover loosely with plastic wrap and cloth towel. Place bowl in pan of warm water (about 95°F.); let rise 15 minutes.

Grease large cookie sheet. Punch down dough several times to remove all air bubbles. Divide dough into 2 parts; shape into two 12-inch oblong loaves. Place on greased cookie sheet. With sharp knife, make ⅛-inch deep slash down center of each loaf. Brush with egg white. Cover; let rise in warm place 15 minutes.

Heat oven to 375°F. Uncover dough. Sprinkle loaves with coarse salt, if desired. Bake 25 to 35 minutes or until loaves sound hollow when lightly tapped. Immediately remove from cookie sheet; cool on wire racks.
Yield: 2 (16-slice) loaves.

HIGH ALTITUDE:
Above 3500 Feet: No change.

NUTRITION PER SERVING:
Calories 90; Protein 3g; Carbohydrate 16g; Fat 1g; Sodium 150mg.

SPEEDY WHOLE WHEAT BREAD

Toasted sesame seed tops these quick-to-prepare round loaves.

2½ to 3 cups all purpose flour
3 tablespoons sesame seed, toasted, p. 23
2 teaspoons salt
3 pkg. active dry yeast
2¼ cups water
¼ cup honey
3 tablespoons margarine or butter
3 cups whole wheat flour
1 egg white, beaten
　　Sesame seed, toasted, p. 23

In large bowl, combine 2 cups all purpose flour, 3 tablespoons sesame seed, salt and yeast; blend well. In small saucepan, heat water, honey and margarine until very warm (120 to 130°F.). Add warm liquid to flour mixture. Blend at low speed until moistened; beat 3 minutes at medium speed. By hand, stir in whole wheat flour and an additional ¼ to ½ cup all purpose flour until dough pulls cleanly away from sides of bowl.

On floured surface, knead in ¼ to ½ cup all purpose flour until dough is smooth and elastic, about 5 to 8 minutes. Place dough in greased bowl; cover loosely with plastic wrap and cloth towel. Place bowl in pan of warm water (about 95°F.); let rise 15 minutes.

Grease large cookie sheet or 15x10x1-inch baking pan. Punch down dough several times to remove all air bubbles. Divide dough into 2 parts; shape into round balls. Place 3 inches apart on greased cookie sheet. With sharp knife, make three ⅛-inch deep slashes on top of each loaf. Carefully brush loaves with egg white; sprinkle with sesame seed. Cover; let rise in warm place until light and doubled in size, about 15 minutes.

Heat oven to 375°F. Uncover dough. Bake 25 to 35 minutes or until loaves sound hollow when lightly tapped. Immediately remove from cookie sheet; cool on wire racks.
Yield: 2 (16-slice) loaves.

HIGH ALTITUDE:
Above 3500 Feet: No change.

NUTRITION PER SERVING:
Calories 110; Protein 3g; Carbohydrate 19g; Fat 2g; Sodium 150mg.

SPEEDY WHITE BREAD

These homey loaves are filled with old-fashioned goodness — and we've streamlined the method for convenience.

    5 to 6 cups all purpose flour
    3 tablespoons sugar
 2¼ teaspoons salt
    3 pkg. active dry yeast
 2¼ cups water
    3 tablespoons margarine or butter

In large bowl, combine 2 cups flour, sugar, salt and yeast; blend well. In small saucepan, heat water and margarine until very warm (120 to 130°F.). Add warm liquid to flour mixture. Blend at low speed until moistened; beat 3 minutes at medium speed. Stir in an additional 2½ to 3 cups flour until dough pulls cleanly away from sides of bowl.

On floured surface, knead in ½ to 1 cup flour until dough is smooth and elastic, about 5 minutes. Place dough in greased bowl; cover loosely with plastic wrap and cloth towel. Place bowl in pan of warm water (about 95°F.); let rise 15 minutes.

Grease large cookie sheet. Punch down dough several times to remove all air bubbles. Divide dough into 2 parts; shape into round balls. Place on greased cookie sheet. With sharp knife, slash ¼-inch deep lattice design on top of each loaf. Cover; let rise in warm place 15 minutes.

Heat oven to 400°F. Uncover dough. Bake 20 to 30 minutes or until loaves sound hollow when lightly tapped. Immediately remove from cookie sheet; cool on wire racks.
Yield: 2 (16-slice) loaves.

HIGH ALTITUDE:
Above 3500 Feet: Bake at 375°F. for 25 to 30 minutes.

NUTRITION PER SERVING:
Calories 110; Protein 3g; Carbohydrate 21g; Fat 1g; Sodium 165mg.

COOK'S NOTE

BRAIDING BREAD DOUGH

For ease in braiding, place the strips of dough side by side on a greased cookie sheet. Braid from the center to the ends. Press and pinch the ends of the strips together; tuck ends under to seal.

TWO-TONE RYE TWIST LOAVES

 2½ cups all purpose flour
 2½ cups medium rye flour
    1 tablespoon salt
    1 tablespoon grated orange peel
    2 pkg. active dry yeast
    2 cups milk
  ¼ cup molasses
  ¼ cup margarine or butter
    2 teaspoons unsweetened cocoa
    1 to 2 teaspoons anise seed
    1 teaspoon instant coffee granules or crystals
    1 to 1½ cups all purpose flour

In large bowl, combine 2½ cups each all purpose and rye flour; mix well. In another large bowl, combine 2 cups of the flour mixture, salt, orange peel and yeast; blend well. In medium saucepan, heat milk, molasses and margarine until very warm (120 to 130°F.). Add warm liquid to flour-yeast mixture. Blend at low speed until moistened; beat 3 minutes at medium speed. Pour half of batter into another bowl; set aside. To remaining batter, stir in cocoa, anise seed, instant coffee and 1 to 1½ cups flour mixture to form a stiff dough. On floured surface, knead in ½ to 1 cup flour mixture until dough is smooth and elastic, about 5 minutes.

To reserved batter, stir in remaining flour mixture and ½ to ¾ cup all purpose flour to make a stiff dough. On floured surface, knead in ½ to ¾ cup additional all purpose flour until dough is smooth and elastic, about 5 minutes. Place doughs in greased bowls; cover loosely with plastic wrap and cloth towels. Let rise in warm place (80 to 85°F.) until light and doubled in size, about 1 hour.

Grease 2 cookie sheets. Punch down doughs. Divide each dough into 2 parts. Roll each part into 14-inch rope. For each loaf, twist a dark and a light rope together, pinching ends to seal. Place on greased cookie sheets. Cover; let rise until doubled in size, about 1 hour.

Heat oven to 350°F. Uncover dough. Bake 25 to 30 minutes or until loaves sound hollow when lightly tapped. Immediately remove from cookie sheets; cool on wire racks.
Yield: 2 (12-slice) loaves.

HIGH ALTITUDE:
Above 3500 Feet: No change.

NUTRITION PER SERVING:
Calories 150; Protein 4g; Carbohydrate 28g; Fat 3g; Sodium 300mg.

THREE GRAIN BREAD

A healthy, hearty loaf — great for sandwiches!

3½ to 4 cups all purpose flour
1¾ cups medium rye flour
1¾ cups whole wheat flour
  2 teaspoons salt
  3 pkg. active dry yeast
1¾ cups milk
  ¾ cup water
  ⅔ cup honey
  3 tablespoons margarine or butter
  2 tablespoons molasses
  ½ cup shelled sunflower seeds
  ¼ cup wheat germ
  ¼ cup shreds of whole bran cereal

Combine 2 cups all purpose flour, the rye flour and whole wheat flour. In large bowl, combine 3 cups flour mixture, salt and yeast. In small saucepan, heat milk, water, honey, margarine and molasses until very warm (120 to 130°F.). Add warm liquid to flour mixture. Blend at low speed until moistened; beat 3 minutes at medium speed. By hand, stir in sunflower nuts, wheat germ, bran cereal, remaining flour mixture and an additional 1¼ to 1½ cups all purpose flour until dough pulls cleanly away from sides of bowl.

On floured surface, knead in ¼ to ½ cup all purpose flour until smooth and elastic, about 5 minutes. Place dough in greased bowl; cover loosely with plastic wrap and cloth towel. Let rise in warm place (80 to 85°F.) until light and doubled in size, about 45 minutes.

Grease two 8x4-inch loaf pans. Punch down dough several times to remove all air bubbles. Divide dough into 2 parts; shape into loaves. Place in greased pans. Cover; let rise in warm place until dough fills pans and tops of loaves are about 1 inch above pan edges, about 20 to 30 minutes.

Heat oven to 350°F. Uncover dough. Bake 40 to 45 minutes or until loaves sound hollow when lightly tapped. Immediately remove from pans; cool on wire racks.
Yield: 2 (16-slice) loaves.

HIGH ALTITUDE:
Above 3500 Feet: No change.

NUTRITION PER SERVING:
Calories 150; Protein 4g; Carbohydrate 29g; Fat 2g; Sodium 160mg.

CRACKED WHEAT RAISIN BREAD

Try this wholesome bread toasted — it's great!

1½ cups cracked wheat
  1 cup raisins
  ½ cup firmly packed brown sugar
  2 teaspoons salt
  3 tablespoons margarine or butter
  2 cups boiling water
  2 pkg. active dry yeast
  ⅔ cup warm water
  5 to 6 cups all purpose flour
    Beaten egg

In large bowl, combine cracked wheat, raisins, brown sugar, salt, margarine and 2 cups boiling water. Mix well and allow to cool to 105 to 115°F. In small bowl, dissolve yeast in warm water (105 to 115°F.). Add to cooled cracked wheat mixture. Add 2 cups flour to cracked wheat mixture. Blend at low speed until moistened; beat 2 minutes at medium speed. By hand, stir in an additional 2½ to 3 cups flour until dough pulls cleanly away from sides of bowl.

On floured surface, knead in ½ to 1 cup flour until dough is smooth and elastic, about 10 minutes. Place dough in greased bowl; cover loosely with plastic wrap and cloth towel. Let rise in warm place (80 to 85°F.) until light and doubled in size, about 45 to 60 minutes.

Grease large cookie sheet. Punch down dough several times to remove all air bubbles. Divide dough into 2 parts; shape into balls. Place on greased cookie sheet. Cover; let rise in warm place until light and doubled in size, about 45 to 60 minutes.

Heat oven to 350°F. Uncover dough. With sharp knife, slash a ½-inch deep lattice design on top of each loaf. Brush with beaten egg. Bake at 350°F. for 35 to 45 minutes or until loaves sound hollow when lightly tapped. Immediately remove from cookie sheet; cool on wire racks.
Yield: 2 (20-slice) loaves.

HIGH ALTITUDE:
Above 3500 Feet: No change.

NUTRITION PER SERVING:
Calories 110; Protein 3g; Carbohydrate 23g; Fat 1g; Sodium 120mg.

Cracked Wheat Raisin Bread

Swiss Braided Raisin Loaf

Swiss cheese and raisins are featured in this pretty braided loaf.

- 3½ to 4 cups all purpose flour
- 1 tablespoon sugar
- 1 teaspoon salt
- 2 pkg. active dry yeast
- ⅔ cup milk
- ⅓ cup margarine or butter
- 3 eggs
- ½ to 1 cup golden raisins or dark raisins
- 2 oz. (½ cup) shredded Swiss cheese
  Margarine or butter, melted

In large bowl, combine 1½ cups flour, sugar, salt and yeast; blend well. In small saucepan, heat milk and margarine until very warm (120 to 130°F.). Add warm liquid and eggs to flour mixture. Blend at low speed until moistened; beat 3 minutes at medium speed. By hand, stir in raisins, cheese and an additional 1½ to 1¾ cups flour until dough pulls cleanly away from sides of bowl.

On floured surface, knead in ½ to ¾ cup flour until dough is smooth and elastic, about 5 minutes. Place dough in greased bowl; cover loosely with plastic wrap and cloth towel. Let rise in warm place (80 to 85°F.) until light and doubled in size, about 45 to 55 minutes.

Grease large cookie sheet. Punch down dough several times to remove all air bubbles. Divide dough into 4 parts. Roll each part into 20-inch rope. Place the 4 ropes, side by side, on greased cookie sheet, pinching together at l end to seal. Braid by weaving far right rope over and under other ropes to far left, then weave next far right rope over and under; repeat until ropes are completely braided. Pinch ends together and tuck both ends under to seal. Cover; let rise in warm place until light and doubled in size, about 30 minutes.

Heat oven to 375°F. Uncover dough. Bake 20 to 30 minutes or until golden brown and loaf sounds hollow when lightly tapped. Immediately remove from cookie sheet; cool on wire rack. While warm, brush with melted margarine.
Yield: 1 (17-slice) loaf.

HIGH ALTITUDE:
Above 3500 Feet: No change.

NUTRITION PER SERVING:
Calories 210; Protein 6g; Carbohydrate 31g; Fat 7g; Sodium 230mg.

Whole Wheat Raisin Loaf

If you like whole wheat bread, you'll enjoy this raisin-studded, slightly sweet loaf. Serve it toasted with your favorite jam.

- 3 to 3¾ cups all purpose flour
- ½ cup sugar
- 3 teaspoons salt
- 1 teaspoon cinnamon
- ½ teaspoon nutmeg
- 2 pkg. active dry yeast
- 2 cups milk
- ¾ cup water
- ¼ cup oil
- 4 cups whole wheat flour
- 1 cup rolled oats
- 1 cup raisins
  Margarine or butter, melted
  Sugar, if desired

In large bowl, combine 1½ cups all purpose flour, ½ cup sugar, salt, cinnamon, nutmeg and yeast; blend well. In small saucepan, heat milk, water and ¼ cup oil until very warm (120 to 130°F.). Add warm liquid to flour mixture. Blend at low speed until moistened; beat 3 minutes at medium speed. By hand, stir in whole wheat flour, rolled oats, raisins and an additional 1 to 1½ cups all purpose flour until dough pulls cleanly away from sides of bowl.

On floured surface, knead in ½ to ¾ cup all purpose flour until dough is smooth and elastic, about 5 minutes. Place dough in greased bowl; cover loosely with plastic wrap and cloth towel. Let rise in warm place (80 to 85°F.) until light and doubled in size, about 20 to 30 minutes.

Grease two 9x5 or 8x4-inch loaf pans. Punch down dough several times to remove all air bubbles. Divide dough into 2 parts; shape into loaves. Place in greased pans; brush tops with oil. Cover; let rise in warm place until light and doubled in size, 30 to 45 minutes.

Heat oven to 375°F. Uncover dough. Bake 40 to 50 minutes or until deep golden brown and loaves sound hollow when lightly tapped. Cover with foil last 10 minutes of baking if necessary to avoid excessive browning. Immediately remove from pans; cool on wire racks. Brush tops of loaves with margarine; sprinkle with sugar.
Yield: 2 (16-slice) loaves.

NUTRITION PER SERVING:
Calories 170; Protein 5g; Carbohydrate 32g; Fat 3g;
Sodium 210mg.

WHOLE WHEAT BUBBLE LOAF
—————————— ❧ ——————————

*This pull-apart loaf is great to serve with any
meal. It has terrific nutty whole wheat flavor.*

2	to 2½ cups all purpose flour
2	tablespoons sugar
1½	teaspoons salt
1	pkg. active dry yeast
1¼	cups milk
2	tablespoons margarine or butter
1	egg
1½	cups whole wheat flour
¼	cup margarine or butter, melted
4	teaspoons sesame seed

In large bowl, combine 1 cup all purpose flour,
sugar, salt and yeast; blend well. In small saucepan,
heat milk and 2 tablespoons margarine until very
warm (120 to 130°F.). Add warm liquid and egg to
flour mixture. Blend at low speed until moistened;
beat 3 minutes at medium speed. By hand, stir in
whole wheat flour until dough pulls cleanly away
from sides of bowl.

On floured surface, knead in 1 to 1½ cups all
purpose flour until dough is smooth and elastic,
about 5 minutes. Place in greased bowl; cover
loosely with plastic wrap and cloth towel. Let rise
in warm place (80 to 85°F.) until light and doubled
in size, about 45 to 60 minutes.

Generously grease one 2-quart deep casserole.
Punch down dough several times to remove all air
bubbles. Using sharp knife or scissors, cut dough
into 30 to 40 walnut-size pieces. Place half of
dough pieces in greased casserole. Drizzle with
2 tablespoons melted margarine; sprinkle with
2 teaspoons sesame seed. Repeat with remaining
dough pieces, margarine and sesame seed. Cover;
let rise in warm place until light and doubled in
size, about 30 to 45 minutes.

Heat oven to 400°F. Uncover dough. Bake 25 to
35 minutes or until loaf sounds hollow when lightly
tapped. Cool 5 minutes; remove from casserole.
Pull apart to serve.
Yield: 1 loaf; 20 servings.

HIGH ALTITUDE:
Above 3500 Feet: Decrease first rise time to 30 to
45 minutes.

NUTRITION PER SERVING:
Calories 140; Protein 4g; Carbohydrate 21g; Fat 5g;
Sodium 210mg.

COOK'S NOTE
—————————— ❧ ——————————

WHOLE WHEAT FLOUR
Whole wheat or graham flour is milled from
the entire wheat kernel. It has a higher
nutritional value and contains more fiber
than other flours. Baked products made
with whole wheat flour will have a heavier,
more compact texture. Because whole
wheat flour has less baking strength than all
purpose flour, it should be used in combination with all purpose or bread flour.

HI-PROTEIN HONEY WHEAT BREAD

This wholesome bread is delicious by itself or for sandwiches. In this recipe, use creamed cottage cheese, which has cream added to it.

  4 **to 5 cups all purpose flour**
  2 **teaspoons salt**
  2 **pkg. active dry yeast**
  1 **cup water**
  ½ **cup honey**
  ¼ **cup margarine or butter**
  1 **cup creamed cottage cheese**
  2 **eggs**
  1 **cup whole wheat flour**
  ½ **cup rolled oats**
  1 **cup chopped nuts**

In large bowl, combine 2 cups all purpose flour, salt and yeast; blend well. In medium saucepan, heat water, honey, margarine and cottage cheese until very warm (120 to 130°F.). (Margarine does not need to melt completely.) Add warm liquid and eggs to flour mixture. Blend at low speed until moistened; beat 3 minutes at medium speed. By hand, stir in whole wheat flour, oats, nuts and enough all purpose flour to form a soft dough.

On floured surface, knead dough until smooth and elastic, about 10 minutes. Place in greased bowl; cover loosely with plastic wrap and cloth towel. Let rise in warm place (80 to 85°F.) until light and doubled in size, about 1 hour.

Generously grease two 8x4 or 9x5-inch loaf pans or two 8 or 9-inch round cake pans. Punch down dough. Divide dough into 2 parts; shape into loaves. Place in greased pans. Cover; let rise in warm place until light and doubled in size, about 1 hour.

Heat oven to 375°F. Uncover dough. Bake 35 to 40 minutes or until loaves sound hollow when lightly tapped. Immediately remove from pans; cool on wire racks. For softer crusts, brush tops of loaves with melted margarine, if desired.
Yield: 2 (16-slice) loaves.

HIGH ALTITUDE:
Above 3500 Feet: No change.

NUTRITION PER SERVING:
Calories 150; Protein 5g; Carbohydrate 22g; Fat 5g; Sodium 170mg.

HONEY GRANOLA BREAD

Whole wheat flour, honey and granola make this a tasty sandwich bread for the school lunch box.

  5 **to 5½ cups all purpose flour**
  1 **cup granola cereal**
  2 **teaspoons salt**
  2 **pkg. active dry yeast**
  1½ **cups water**
  1 **cup plain yogurt**
  ½ **cup honey**
  ¼ **cup oil or shortening**
  2 **eggs**
  2 **cups whole wheat flour**

In large bowl, combine 3 cups all purpose flour, granola, salt and yeast; blend well. In medium saucepan, heat water, yogurt, honey and oil until very warm (120 to 130°F.). Add warm liquid and eggs to flour mixture. Blend at low speed until moistened; beat 3 minutes at medium speed. By hand, stir in whole wheat flour and an additional 1 cup all purpose flour to form a stiff dough.

On floured surface, knead in 1 to 1½ cups all purpose flour until dough is smooth and elastic, about 10 minutes. Place dough in greased bowl; cover loosely with plastic wrap and cloth towel. Let rise in warm place (80 to 85°F.) until light and doubled in size, about 1 hour.

Generously grease two 9x5 or 8x4-inch loaf pans. Punch down dough several times to remove all air bubbles. Divide dough into 2 parts; shape into loaves. Place in greased pans. Cover; let rise in warm place until light and doubled in size, 30 to 45 minutes.

Heat oven to 350°F. Uncover dough. Bake 30 to 40 minutes or until loaves sound hollow when lightly tapped. Immediately remove from pans; cool on wire racks. If desired, brush loaves with melted margarine.
Yield: 2 (17-slice) loaves.

HIGH ALTITUDE:
Above 3500 Feet: Bake at 350°F. for 40 to 50 minutes.

NUTRITION PER SERVING:
Calories 150; Protein 4g; Carbohydrate 27g; Fat 3g; Sodium 135mg.

TOASTED OAT BREAD

Rolled oats are sprinkled over the dough before baking.

BREAD
5½ to 6 cups all purpose flour
1 cup rolled oats, toasted*
½ cup sugar
2 teaspoons salt
2 pkg. active dry yeast
2 cups milk
¼ cup margarine or butter
1 egg

TOPPING
1 tablespoon water
1 egg white
1 tablespoon rolled oats

In large bowl, combine 2 cups flour, 1 cup rolled oats, sugar, salt and yeast; blend well. In small saucepan, heat milk and margarine until very warm (120 to 130°F.). Add warm liquid and egg to flour mixture. Blend at low speed until moistened; beat 3 minutes at medium speed. By hand, stir in an additional 3¼ to 3½ cups flour until dough pulls cleanly away from sides of bowl.

On floured surface, knead in ¼ to ½ cup flour until dough is smooth and elastic, about 5 minutes. Place dough in greased bowl; cover loosely with plastic wrap and cloth towel. Let rise in warm place (80 to 85°F.) until light and doubled in size, about 30 to 45 minutes.

Grease two 8x4 or 9x5-inch loaf pans. Punch down dough several times to remove all air bubbles. Divide dough into 2 parts; shape into loaves. Place in greased pans. Cover; let rise in warm place until dough fills pans and tops of loaves are about 1 inch above pan edges, about 20 to 30 minutes.

Heat oven to 375°F. Uncover dough. In small bowl, combine water and egg white; beat slightly. Carefully brush on loaves; sprinkle with 1 tablespoon rolled oats.

Bake at 375°F. for 25 to 35 minutes or until loaves sound hollow when lightly tapped. Cover with foil during last 10 minutes of baking if necessary to avoid excessive browning. Immediately remove from pans; cool on wire racks.
Yield: 2 (16-slice) loaves.

TIP:
* To toast rolled oats, spread on 15x10x1-inch baking pan; place in oven at 375°F. for 10 to 15 minutes or until light brown. (Oats brown rapidly.)

HIGH ALTITUDE:
Above 3500 Feet: No change.

NUTRITION PER SERVING:
Calories 130; Protein 4g; Carbohydrate 24g; Fat 2g; Sodium 160mg.

COOK'S NOTE

BUTTER CUTOUTS
Slice chilled butter about ¼ inch thick. Cut out small shapes with canape cutters or small cookie cutters. (Open top cutters are necessary to push out the shapes; simple shapes work best.) Refrigerate until served. Arrange the cutouts on individual bread and butter plates, on a butter serving plate or on a bed of crushed ice in a shallow bowl. (Margarine does not work well for cutouts.)

Easy Cheese Batter Bread

Batter breads are among the simplest to prepare because they aren't kneaded or shaped. This moist version is even better the second day.

2½ cups all purpose flour
 2 teaspoons sugar
1½ teaspoons salt
 1 pkg. active dry yeast
 4 oz. (1 cup) shredded Cheddar cheese
 ¾ cup milk
 ½ cup margarine or butter
 3 eggs

In large bowl, combine 1½ cups flour, sugar, salt and yeast; blend well. Stir in cheese. In small saucepan, heat milk and margarine until very warm (120 to 130°F.). Add warm liquid and eggs to flour mixture. Blend at low speed until moistened; beat 3 minutes at medium speed. By hand, stir in remaining 1 cup flour. Cover loosely with plastic wrap and cloth towel. Let rise in warm place (80 to 85°F.) until light and doubled in size, 45 to 60 minutes.

Generously grease 1½ or 2-quart casserole or 9x5-inch loaf pan. Stir down dough to remove all air bubbles. Turn into greased casserole. Cover; let rise in warm place until light and doubled in size, 20 to 25 minutes.

Heat oven to 350°F. Uncover dough. Bake 40 to 45 minutes or until deep golden brown. Immediately remove from casserole; cool on wire rack.

Yield: 1 (18-slice) loaf.

HIGH ALTITUDE:
Above 3500 Feet: Bake at 375°F. for 40 to 45 minutes.

NUTRITION PER SERVING:
Calories 150; Protein 5g; Carbohydrate 15g; Fat 8g; Sodium 290mg.

Italian Cheese Bread Ring

Try this exceptional cheese-filled loaf whenever you're in the mood for something special. It's almost like a sandwich in a loaf!

BREAD
4½ to 5¼ cups all purpose flour
 ¼ cup sugar
1½ teaspoons salt
 2 pkg. active dry yeast
 1 cup milk
 1 cup water
 ½ cup margarine or butter
 2 eggs
 2 tablespoons sesame seed

FILLING
 4 oz. (1 cup) shredded mozzarella cheese
 ½ teaspoon dried Italian seasoning
 ¼ teaspoon garlic powder
 ¼ cup margarine or butter, softened

In large bowl, combine 2½ cups flour, sugar, salt and yeast; blend well. In small saucepan, heat milk, water and ½ cup margarine until very warm (120 to 130°F.). Add warm liquid and eggs to flour mixture. Blend at low speed until moistened; beat 3 minutes at medium speed. By hand, stir in remaining 2 to 2¾ cups all purpose flour to form a stiff batter.

Generously grease 12-cup Bundt® or 10-inch tube pan; sprinkle with sesame seed. In small bowl, combine all filling ingredients; mix well. Spoon half of batter into greased pan; spoon filling mixture evenly over batter to within ½ inch of sides of pan. Spoon remaining batter over filling. Cover loosely with plastic wrap and cloth towel. Let rise in warm place (80 to 85°F.) until light and doubled in size, about 30 minutes.

Heat oven to 350°F. Uncover dough. Bake 30 to 40 minutes or until golden brown and loaf sounds hollow when lightly tapped. Immediately remove from pan; cool on wire rack. Serve warm or cool.

Yield: 1 (24-slice) loaf.

HIGH ALTITUDE:
Above 3500 Feet: No change.

NUTRITION PER SERVING:
Calories 190; Protein 5g; Carbohydrate 24g; Fat 8g; Sodium 240mg.

Italian Cheese Bread Ring

This
pun

1
1¼
1
1
¾
½
2
2
1
1½
1
1

In l
115
coff
Add
at lo
mec
pos
batt
tow
ligh

Ger
dov
grea
rise
abo

Hea
35
sou
rem
Yie

HIG
Abo
1¾

NU
Calo
Sod

Dilly Casserole Bread

DILLY CASSEROLE BREAD

The next time you want to impress family or friends, bake them a loaf of this easy bread. It is a BAKE-OFF® Contest grand prize winner and one of Pillsbury's most requested recipes.

    2 to 2²/₃ cups all purpose flour
    2 tablespoons sugar
    2 to 3 teaspoons instant minced onion
    2 teaspoons dill seed
    1 teaspoon salt
    ¼ teaspoon baking soda
    1 pkg. active dry yeast
    ¼ cup water
    1 tablespoon margarine or butter
    1 cup creamed cottage cheese
    1 egg
    2 teaspoons margarine or butter, melted
    ¼ teaspoon coarse salt, if desired

In large bowl, combine 1 cup flour, sugar, onion, dill seed, 1 teaspoon salt, baking soda and yeast; blend well. In small saucepan, heat water, 1 tablespoon margarine and cottage cheese until very warm (120 to 130°F.). Add warm liquid and egg to flour mixture. Blend at low speed until moistened; beat 3 minutes at medium speed. By hand, stir in remaining 1 to 1²/₃ cups flour to form a stiff batter. Cover loosely with plastic wrap and cloth towel. Let rise in warm place (80 to 85°F.) until light and doubled in size, 45 to 60 minutes.

Generously grease 1½ or 2-quart casserole. Stir down dough to remove all air bubbles. Turn into greased casserole. Cover; let rise in warm place until light and doubled in size, 30 to 45 minutes.

Heat oven to 350°F. Uncover dough. Bake 30 to 40 minutes or until deep golden brown and loaf sounds hollow when lightly tapped. Immediately remove from casserole; cool on wire rack. Brush warm loaf with melted margarine; sprinkle with coarse salt.
Yield: 1 (18-slice) loaf.

FOOD PROCESSOR DIRECTIONS:

In small bowl, soften yeast in ¼ cup warm water (105 to 115°F.). In food processor bowl with metal blade, combine 2 cups flour, sugar, onion, dill seed, 1 teaspoon salt, baking soda and 1 tablespoon margarine. Cover; process 5 seconds. Add cottage cheese and egg. Cover; process about 10 seconds or until blended. With machine running, pour yeast mixture through feed tube. Continue processing until blended, about 20 seconds or until mixture pulls away from sides of bowl and forms a ball, adding additional flour if necessary. Carefully scrape dough from blade and bowl; place in lightly greased bowl. Cover loosely with plastic wrap and cloth towel. Let rise in warm place (80 to 85°F.) until light and doubled in size, 45 to 60 minutes. Continue as directed above.

HIGH ALTITUDE:

Above 3500 Feet: Bake at 375°F. for 35 to 40 minutes.

NUTRITION PER SERVING:

Calories 100; Protein 4g; Carbohydrate 16g; Fat 2g; Sodium 125mg.

SAVORY BUBBLE LOAF

This loaf is best served warm from the oven.

BREAD
- 3 to 3½ cups all purpose flour
- 2 tablespoons sugar
- 1 teaspoon salt
- 1 pkg. active dry yeast
- 1¼ cups milk
- 2 tablespoons oil
- 1 egg
- ⅓ cup margarine or butter, melted

TOPPING
- 2 tablespoons grated Parmesan cheese
- 1 tablespoon sesame seed
- ½ to 1 teaspoon garlic salt
- ½ teaspoon paprika

In large bowl, combine 1½ cups flour, sugar, salt and yeast; blend well. In small saucepan, heat milk and oil until very warm (120 to 130°F.). Add warm liquid and egg to flour mixture. Blend at low speed until moistened; beat 3 minutes at medium speed. By hand, stir in an additional 1¼ to 1½ cups flour until dough pulls cleanly away from sides of bowl.

On floured surface, knead in ¼ to ½ cup flour until dough is smooth and elastic, about 2 minutes. Place dough in greased bowl; cover loosely with plastic wrap and cloth towel. Let rise in warm place (80 to 85°F.) until light and doubled in size, about 45 to 60 minutes.

Punch down dough several times to remove all air bubbles. Divide dough into 16 equal pieces; shape into balls. Dip each into melted margarine. Place half of balls in ungreased 12-cup Bundt® pan, forming 1 layer. Combine topping ingredients; sprinkle half over layer of balls. Form second layer with remaining balls. Pour any remaining margarine over balls. Sprinkle with remaining topping. Cover; let rise in warm place until light and doubled in size, about 30 to 45 minutes.

Heat oven to 375°F. Uncover dough. Bake 25 to 30 minutes or until golden brown and loaf sounds hollow when lightly tapped. Cool 5 minutes; remove from pan. Serve warm.

Yield: 1 (16-slice) loaf.

HIGH ALTITUDE:

Above 3500 Feet: No change.

NUTRITION PER SERVING:

Calories 180; Protein 4g; Carbohydrate 24g; Fat 7g; Sodium 315mg.

COOK'S NOTE

MILK IN YEAST BREADS

Milk can be used in place of water when baking bread. It will give the bread a browner crust, a yellower grain and a sweeter flavor.

DANISH SESAME BRAN BREAD

Sesame seed highlights these loaves.

- 1 cup boiling water
- 1 cup yellow cornmeal
- 2½ to 3 cups all purpose flour
- 3 cups whole wheat flour
- ½ cup shreds of whole bran cereal
- ½ cup sesame seed, toasted, p. 23
- 2 teaspoons salt
- 2 pkg. active dry yeast
- 1 cup milk
- ¼ cup oil
- ¼ cup molasses
- ¼ cup honey
- ½ cup plain yogurt, room temperature

In small bowl, combine 1 cup boiling water and cornmeal. In large bowl, combine 1 cup all purpose flour, 1 cup whole wheat flour, cereal, sesame seed, salt and yeast; blend well. In small saucepan, heat milk, oil, molasses and honey until very warm (120 to 130°F.). (Mixture will look curdled.) Add warm liquid, cornmeal mixture and yogurt to flour mixture. Blend at low speed until moistened; beat 3 minutes at medium speed. By hand, stir in remaining 2 cups whole wheat flour and about ½ cup all purpose flour until dough pulls cleanly away from sides of bowl.

On floured surface, knead in 1 to 1½ cups all purpose flour until dough is smooth and elastic, about 8 minutes. Place in greased bowl; cover loosely with plastic wrap and cloth towel. Let rise in warm place (80 to 85°F.) until light and doubled in size, about 1 to 1½ hours.

Grease two 9x5 or 8x4-inch loaf pans. Punch down dough several times to remove all air bubbles. Divide dough into 2 parts; shape into loaves. Place in greased pans. Cover; let rise in warm place until dough fills pans and tops of loaves are about 1 inch above pan edges, about 45 to 60 minutes.

Heat oven to 350°F. Uncover dough. Bake 30 to 40 minutes or until golden brown and loaves sound hollow when lightly tapped. Immediately remove from pans; cool on wire racks.

Yield: 2 (14-slice) loaves.

HIGH ALTITUDE:
Above 3500 Feet: No change.

NUTRITION PER SERVING:
Calories 160; Protein 5g; Carbohydrate 29g; Fat 4g; Sodium 170mg.

ONION LOVER'S TWIST

Savory onions and Parmesan cheese are rolled inside the braided strips of dough in these no-knead loaves.

BREAD
- 3½ to 4½ cups all purpose flour
- ¼ cup sugar
- 1½ teaspoons salt
- 1 pkg. active dry yeast
- ¾ cup water
- ½ cup milk
- ¼ cup margarine or butter
- 1 egg

FILLING
- ¼ cup margarine or butter
- 1 cup finely chopped onions or ¼ cup instant minced onion
- 1 tablespoon grated Parmesan cheese
- 1 tablespoon sesame or poppy seed
- ½ to 1 teaspoon garlic salt
- 1 teaspoon paprika

In large bowl, combine 2 cups flour, sugar, salt and yeast; blend well. In small saucepan, heat water, milk and ¼ cup margarine until very warm (120 to 130°F.). Add warm liquid and egg to flour mixture. Blend at low speed until moistened; beat 3 minutes at medium speed. By hand, stir in remaining 1½ to 2½ cups flour to form a soft dough. Cover loosely with plastic wrap and cloth towel. Let rise in warm place (80 to 85°F.) until light and doubled in size, 45 to 60 minutes.

Grease large cookie sheet. Melt ¼ cup margarine in small saucepan; stir in remaining filling ingredients. Set aside. Stir down dough to remove all air bubbles. On floured surface, toss dough until no longer sticky. Roll dough into 18x12-inch rectangle; spread with filling. Cut rectangle in half crosswise to make two 12x9-inch rectangles. Cut each rectangle into three 9x4-inch strips. Starting with 9-inch side, roll up each strip; pinch edges and ends to seal. On greased cookie sheet, braid 3 rolls together; pinch ends to seal. Repeat with remaining 3 rolls for second loaf. Cover; let rise in warm place until light and doubled in size, 25 to 30 minutes.

Heat oven to 350°F. Uncover dough. Bake 27 to 35 minutes or until golden brown and loaves sound hollow when lightly tapped. Immediately remove from cookie sheet; cool on wire racks.

Yield: 2 (16-slice) loaves.

Above 3500 Feet: No change.

NUTRITION PER SERVING:
Calories 100; Protein 2g; Carbohydrate 16g; Fat 3g; Sodium 200mg.

Hawaiian Potato Bread

Spread slices of this pineapple-flavored loaf with butter and pineapple preserves. Serve them with coffee or tea.

BREAD
- 5 to 6 cups all purpose flour
- 2 teaspoons salt
- 2 pkg. active dry yeast
- 1 cup pineapple juice
- 1½ cups water
- ¼ cup margarine or butter
- 2 eggs
- 2 cups mashed potato flakes

TOPPING
- 1 tablespoon margarine or butter, melted
- ¼ cup sugar
- 3 tablespoons all purpose flour
- ¼ teaspoon nutmeg

In large bowl, combine 1½ cups flour, salt and yeast; blend well. In medium saucepan, heat pineapple juice, water and ¼ cup margarine until very warm (120 to 130°F.). Add warm liquid and eggs to flour mixture. Blend at low speed until moistened; beat 4 minutes at medium speed. Add potato flakes, beating only until thoroughly moistened. Stir in an additional 3 to 3½ cups flour until dough pulls cleanly away from sides of bowl.

On floured surface, knead in ½ to 1 cup flour until dough is smooth and elastic, about 10 minutes. Place dough in greased bowl; cover loosely with plastic wrap and cloth towel. Let rise in warm place (80 to 85°F.) until light and doubled in size, about 1 hour.

Grease two 8 or 9-inch round cake pans. Punch down dough several times to remove all air bubbles. With floured hands, divide dough into 2 parts; shape into 2 round loaves. Place in greased pans. Cover; let rise in warm place until light and doubled in size, about 30 to 45 minutes.

Heat oven to 350°F. Uncover dough. Brush loaves with melted margarine. Combine remaining topping ingredients until crumbly; sprinkle evenly over loaves. Bake at 350°F. for 35 to 45 minutes or until loaves sound hollow when lightly tapped. Immediately remove from pans by loosening sides and placing loaves on wire racks; cool.
Yield: 2 (24-slice) loaves.

HIGH ALTITUDE:
Above 3500 Feet: Decrease first rise time to 40 to 45 minutes.

NUTRITION PER SERVING:
Calories 90; Protein 2g; Carbohydrate 16g; Fat 2g; Sodium 110mg.

Cook's Note

USING POTATO FLAKES IN RECIPES
To measure potato flakes, lightly pour them into a measuring cup and level them off with the straight edge of a spatula or knife.

HEARTY PESTO BREAD

We've flavored this bread with classic pesto ingredients — basil and garlic. It's wonderful!

BREAD
2½ to 3½ cups all purpose flour
 ¾ cup rolled oats
 ½ cup wheat germ
 1 to 3 tablespoons chopped fresh basil or
    1 to 3 teaspoons dried basil leaves
 2 teaspoons salt
 3 pkg. active dry yeast
2¼ cups water
 ¼ cup oil
 2 tablespoons honey
 2 cups whole wheat flour
 1 tablespoon cornmeal

FILLING
 ½ cup margarine or butter, softened
 2 to 4 tablespoons chopped fresh basil or
    2 to 4 teaspoons dried basil leaves
 2 tablespoons dried parsley flakes
 2 teaspoons garlic powder
 2 teaspoons chopped fresh chives

In large bowl, combine 1¼ cups all purpose flour, rolled oats, wheat germ, 1 to 3 tablespoons basil, salt and yeast; blend well. In small saucepan, heat water, oil and honey until very warm (120 to 130°F.). Add warm liquid to flour mixture. Blend at low speed until moistened; beat 3 minutes at medium speed. By hand, stir in whole wheat flour and an additional 1 to 1¾ cups all purpose flour until dough pulls cleanly away from sides of bowl.

On floured surface, knead in ¼ to ½ cup all purpose flour until dough is smooth and elastic, about 10 minutes. Place dough in greased bowl; cover loosely with plastic wrap and cloth towel. Let rise in warm place (80 to 85°F.) until light and doubled in size, about 45 minutes.

Grease large cookie sheet; sprinkle with cornmeal. In small bowl, combine all filling ingredients; blend well. Punch down dough several times to remove all air bubbles. Divide dough into 2 parts. Roll each part into 15x12-inch rectangle; spread half of filling over each rectangle to within 1 inch of edges. Starting with 12-inch side, roll up each tightly; pinch edges firmly to seal. Place, seam side down, on greased cookie sheet. With sharp knife, make two ⅛-inch deep diagonal slashes on top of each loaf. Cover; let rise in warm place until light and doubled in size, 45 to 60 minutes.

Heat oven to 375°F. Uncover dough. Bake 30 to 35 minutes or until loaves sound hollow when lightly tapped. Immediately remove from cookie sheet; cool on wire racks.
Yield: 2 (24-slice) loaves.

HIGH ALTITUDE:
Above 3500 Feet: Decrease each rise time by about 15 minutes.

NUTRITION PER SERVING:
Calories 90; Protein 2g; Carbohydrate 13g; Fat 3g; Sodium 120mg.

COOK'S NOTE

WHEAT GERM

Wheat germ is the embryo or sprouting section of the wheat kernel. It contributes a nutty flavor and crunchy texture to baked goods. In addition, it is a good source of thiamine, vitamin E, folic acid, phosphorus, magnesium and zinc. Two tablespoons of wheat germ contain 2 grams of dietary fiber. Because wheat germ contains oil, it can turn rancid quickly. Store it in the refrigerator up to 3 months. Wheat germ is available in both raw and toasted varieties.

Hearty Pesto Bread

BRAIDED HOLIDAY STOLLEN

Stollen, Germany's traditional Christmas bread, is a rich, dried fruit-filled loaf. This tempting bread can be decorated with candied cherries.

BREAD
5½ to 6½ cups all purpose flour
1 cup sugar
1 teaspoon salt
2 pkg. active dry yeast
1 cup water
1 cup milk
1 cup margarine or butter
2 eggs
1½ cups golden raisins
1½ cups slivered almonds

FROSTING
½ cup powdered sugar
2 teaspoons milk

In large bowl, combine 2 cups flour, sugar, salt and yeast; blend well. In small saucepan, heat water, 1 cup milk and margarine until very warm (120 to 130°F.). Add warm liquid and eggs to flour mixture. Blend at low speed until moistened; beat 2 minutes at medium speed. By hand, stir in raisins, almonds and remaining 3½ to 4½ cups flour until dough pulls away from sides of bowl. Cover tightly and refrigerate overnight.

Grease 3 cookie sheets. Remove dough from refrigerator. On lightly floured surface, divide dough into 3 equal parts. Divide each part into 3 pieces. Roll each piece into a rope 16 inches long. Place 3 ropes lengthwise on each greased cookie sheet. Braid ropes loosely from center to each end. Pinch ends together; tuck under to seal. Cover loosely with plastic wrap and cloth towel. Let rise in warm place (80 to 85°F.) until doubled in size, about 1½ to 2 hours.

Heat oven to 350°F. Uncover dough. Bake 25 to 35 minutes or until light golden brown.* Immediately remove from cookie sheets; cool on wire racks. In small bowl, combine frosting ingredients. Drizzle over cooled loaves.
Yield: 3 (16-slice) loaves.

TIP:
* If baking only 1 loaf at a time, cover and refrigerate remaining loaves until ready to bake. If baking 2 loaves, alternate cookie sheet positions halfway through baking.

HIGH ALTITUDE:
Above 3500 Feet: No change.

NUTRITION PER SERVING:
Calories 160; Protein 3g; Carbohydrate 23g; Fat 7g; Sodium 95mg.

JULEKAKE

Scandinavian for "Christmas cake," Julekake is a fragrant yeast loaf flavored with fruits and sweet spices. This recipe makes 3 loaves.

BREAD
5½ to 6½ cups all purpose flour
½ cup sugar
1 teaspoon salt
1 teaspoon cardamom
½ teaspoon cinnamon
2 pkg. active dry yeast
1 cup milk
½ cup water
⅔ cup margarine or butter
3 eggs
½ cup candied green cherries, halved
½ cup candied red cherries, halved
½ cup raisins

GLAZE
1½ cups powdered sugar
¼ teaspoon almond extract
2 to 3 tablespoons milk

In large bowl, combine 2 cups flour, sugar, salt, cardamom, cinnamon and yeast; blend well. In small saucepan, heat 1 cup milk, water and margarine until very warm (120 to 130°F.). Add warm liquid and eggs to flour mixture. Blend at low speed until moistened; beat 3 minutes at medium speed. By hand, stir in an additional 3 to 3½ cups flour, cherries and raisins to form a soft dough.

On floured surface, knead in ½ to 1 cup flour until smooth and elastic, about 8 minutes. Place dough in greased bowl; cover loosely with plastic wrap and cloth towel. Let rise in warm place (80 to 85°F.) until light and doubled in size, about 55 to 60 minutes.

Grease 2 large cookie sheets. Punch down dough several times to remove all air bubbles. Divide dough into 3 equal parts; shape into round balls. Place on greased cookie sheets; flatten slightly.

Cover; let rise in warm place until light and doubled in size, about 45 minutes.

Heat oven to 350°F. Uncover dough. Bake 30 to 35 minutes or until golden brown. Immediately remove from cookie sheets; cool on wire racks. In small bowl, combine all glaze ingredients, adding enough milk for desired drizzling consistency. Drizzle over cooled loaves. Garnish as desired.

Yield: 3 (16-slice) loaves.

HIGH ALTITUDE:
Above 3500 Feet: No change.

NUTRITION PER SERVING:
Calories 130; Protein 2g; Carbohydrate 22g; Fat 3g; Sodium 80mg.

RICH CHOCOLATE YEAST BREAD

A cinnamon-nut filling is surrounded by rich chocolate dough in this indulgent bread.

BREAD
- 1 cup milk
- ½ cup water
- 2 pkg. active dry yeast
- 6 to 7 cups all purpose flour
- ½ cup sugar
- ¼ cup unsweetened cocoa
- 2 teaspoons salt
- 3 eggs
- ½ cup margarine or butter, melted
- ½ cup dairy sour cream
- 2 teaspoons vanilla

FILLING
- ⅓ cup sugar
- 1 teaspoon cinnamon
- 2 tablespoons margarine or butter, softened
- ¼ cup chopped pecans

GLAZE
- 1 cup powdered sugar
- 3 tablespoons unsweetened cocoa
- 2 tablespoons margarine or butter, softened
- 1 teaspoon vanilla
- 2 tablespoons milk

In small saucepan, heat 1 cup milk and water until warm (105 to 115°F.). Dissolve yeast in liquid. In large bowl, combine 2 cups flour, ½ cup sugar, ¼ cup cocoa and salt; blend well. Add warm liquid, eggs, melted margarine, sour cream and 2 teaspoons vanilla to flour mixture. Blend at low speed until moistened; beat 3 minutes at medium speed. By hand, stir in 3 cups additional flour to form a stiff dough.

On floured surface, knead in 1 to 2 cups flour until dough is smooth and elastic, about 10 minutes. Place dough in greased bowl; cover loosely with plastic wrap and cloth towel. Let rise in warm place (80 to 85°F.) until light and doubled in size, about 1 to 1½ hours.

Grease 2 cookie sheets. Punch down dough several times to remove all air bubbles. Divide dough into 2 equal parts; shape into balls. In small bowl, combine ⅓ cup sugar and cinnamon.

On lightly floured surface, roll each half into a 12x9-inch rectangle. Spread each rectangle with 1 tablespoon margarine; sprinkle each with half of the sugar-cinnamon mixture and 2 tablespoons of the pecans. Starting with longer side, roll up tightly, pressing edges and ends to seal. Place each roll, seam side down, on greased cookie sheet, joining ends to form circle; pinch to seal. With scissors or sharp knife, make cuts at 1½-inch intervals to within ½ inch of inside of ring. Turn each slice on side, cut side up. Cover; let rise in warm place until light and doubled in size, about 1 to 1½ hours.

Heat oven to 350°F. Uncover dough. Bake 25 to 30 minutes or until loaves sound hollow when lightly tapped. Immediately remove from cookie sheets; cool on wire racks. In small bowl, combine all glaze ingredients; mix until smooth. Spoon glaze over cooled loaves.

Yield: 2 (12-slice) loaves.

HIGH ALTITUDE:
Above 3500 Feet: No change.

NUTRITION PER SERVING:
Calories 290; Protein 7g; Carbohydrate 44g; Fat 10g; Sodium 265mg.

BASIC DINNER ROLLS

Each variation uses half of the dough so you can try 2 different shapings.

- 5¾ **to 6¾ cups all purpose flour**
- ¼ **cup sugar**
- 2 **teaspoons salt**
- 2 **pkg. active dry yeast**
- 1 **cup water**
- 1 **cup milk**
- ½ **cup margarine or butter**
- 1 **egg**
  Melted margarine or butter, if desired

In large bowl, combine 2 cups flour, sugar, salt and yeast; blend well. In small saucepan, heat water, milk and ½ cup margarine until very warm (120 to 130°F.). Add warm liquid and egg to flour mixture. Blend at low speed until moistened; beat 3 minutes at medium speed. By hand, stir in an additional 2½ to 3 cups flour until dough pulls cleanly away from sides of bowl.

On floured surface, knead in 1¼ to 1¾ cups flour until dough is smooth and elastic, about 8 to 10 minutes. Place dough in greased bowl; cover loosely with plastic wrap and cloth towel. Let rise in warm place (80 to 85°F.) until light and doubled in size, about 45 to 60 minutes.

Punch down dough several times to remove all air bubbles. Divide dough in half. To make **Pan Rolls**, lightly grease two 13x9-inch pans. Divide each half of dough into 16 equal pieces. Shape each into a ball, pulling edges under to make a smooth top. Place balls, smooth side up, in greased pans. Cover; let rise in warm place until light and doubled in size, about 20 to 30 minutes.

Heat oven to 400°F. Uncover dough. Bake at 400°F. for 16 to 20 minutes or until golden brown. Remove rolls from pans immediately; cool on wire racks. Brush with melted margarine.

Yield: 32 rolls

TIP:

To make dough a day ahead, after first rise time, punch down dough, cover and refrigerate dough overnight. Shape dough as directed in recipe; let rise a second time until light and doubled in size, about 25 to 35 minutes.

HIGH ALTITUDE:

Above 3500 Feet: No change.

NUTRITION PER SERVING:
Calories 280; Protein 7g; Carbohydrate 46g; Fat 8g; Sodium 360mg.

VARIATIONS:

BOW KNOT ROLLS: Lightly grease cookie sheets. Using half of dough, divide dough into 16 equal pieces. On lightly floured surface, roll each piece into a 9-inch rope. Tie each into a loose knot. Place 2 to 3 inches apart on greased cookie sheets. After rising, bake 12 to 15 minutes or until golden brown.
Yield: 16 rolls.

CLOVERLEAF ROLLS: Lightly grease 12 muffin cups. Using half of dough, divide dough into 12 equal pieces; divide each into thirds. Shape each into a ball, pulling edges under to make a smooth top. Place 3 balls, smooth side up, in each greased muffin cup. After rising, bake 14 to 18 minutes or until golden brown.
Yield: 12 rolls.

CRESCENT ROLLS: Lightly grease cookie sheets. Using half of dough, divide dough in half again; shape each half into a ball. On lightly floured surface, roll each ball into a 12-inch circle. Spread each with 1 tablespoon softened margarine or butter. Cut each circle into 12 wedges. Beginning at wide end of wedge, roll toward point. Place, point side down, 2 to 3 inches apart on greased cookie sheets. Curve ends to form a crescent shape. After rising, bake 12 to 15 minutes or until golden brown.
Yield: 24 rolls.

CROWN ROLLS: Lightly grease 12 muffin cups. Using half of dough, divide dough into 12 equal pieces. Shape each into a ball, pulling edges under to make a smooth top. Place 1 ball, smooth side up, in each greased muffin cup. Using kitchen shears dipped in flour, cut balls of dough into quarters almost to bottom. After rising, bake 14 to 18 minutes or until golden brown.
Yield: 12 rolls.

SWIRL ROLLS: Lightly grease cookie sheets. Using half of dough, divide dough into 16 equal pieces. On lightly floured surface, roll each piece into an 8-inch rope. Beginning at center, make a loose swirl or coil with each rope; tuck end under. Place 2 to 3 inches apart on greased cookie sheets. After rising, bake 12 to 15 minutes or until golden brown.
Yield: 16 rolls.

HOW TO SHAPE DINNER ROLLS

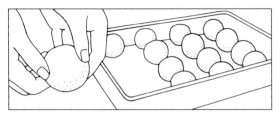

Pan Rolls

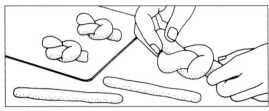

Bow Knot Rolls

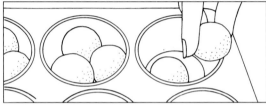

Cloverleaf Rolls

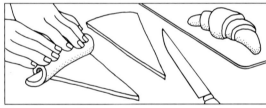

Crescent Rolls

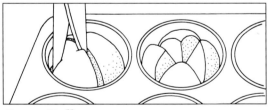

Crown Rolls

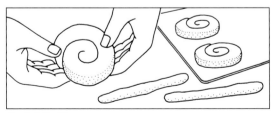

Swirl Rolls

OATS 'N WHEAT DINNER ROLLS

Full of nutritious ingredients, these tasty rolls are excellent to serve with soup.

ROLLS
1¾ to 2¾ cups all purpose flour
⅓ cup rolled oats
¼ cup sugar
1 teaspoon salt
1 pkg. active dry yeast
1 cup milk
3 tablespoons margarine or butter
1 egg
¾ cup whole wheat flour

TOPPING
1 egg white
1 tablespoon water
1 tablespoon rolled oats

In large bowl, combine 1 cup all purpose flour, ⅓ cup rolled oats, sugar, salt and yeast; blend well. In small saucepan, heat milk and margarine until very warm (120 to 130°F.). Add warm liquid and egg to flour mixture. Blend at low speed until moistened; beat 2 minutes at medium speed. By hand, stir in whole wheat flour and an additional ½ to 1¼ cups all purpose flour until dough pulls cleanly away from sides of bowl.

On floured surface, knead in ¼ to ½ cup all purpose flour until dough is smooth and elastic, about 5 minutes. Place dough in greased bowl; cover loosely with plastic wrap and cloth towel. Let rise in warm place (80 to 85°F.) until light and doubled in size, about 1 hour.

Grease 9-inch square pan. Punch down dough several times to remove all air bubbles. Divide dough into 16 pieces; shape into balls. Place in greased pan. Cover; let rise in warm place until light and doubled in size, about 35 to 45 minutes.

Heat oven to 375°F. Uncover dough. In small bowl, combine egg white and water; beat slightly. Carefully brush over rolls; sprinkle with 1 tablespoon rolled oats. Bake at 375°F. for 20 to 30 minutes or until golden brown. Immediately remove from pan. Serve warm.
Yield: 16 rolls.

HIGH ALTITUDE:
Above 3500 Feet: No change.

NUTRITION PER SERVING:
Calories 150; Protein 5g; Carbohydrate 26g; Fat 3g; Sodium 170mg.

ROSEMARY FRENCH ROLLS

Fast-acting yeast shortens the rise time in this recipe.

  2 **to 2½ cups all purpose flour**
  1 **teaspoon sugar**
  1 **teaspoon salt**
  1 **pkg. fast-acting yeast**
  1 **cup water**
  1 **egg white, beaten**
  3 **teaspoons dried rosemary leaves, crushed**

In large bowl, combine 1 cup flour, sugar, salt and yeast; mix well. In small saucepan, heat water until very warm (120 to 130°F.). Add warm water to flour mixture. Blend at low speed until moistened; beat 2 minutes at medium speed. By hand, stir in an additional ½ to 1 cup flour until dough pulls cleanly away from sides of bowl.

On floured surface, knead in ½ cup flour until dough is smooth and elastic, about 5 minutes. Place dough in greased bowl; cover loosely with plastic wrap. Let rise in warm place (80 to 85°F.) until light and doubled in size, about 30 minutes.

Grease large cookie sheet. Punch down dough several times to remove all air bubbles. Divide dough into 12 pieces; shape into balls. Place on greased cookie sheet. Cover with greased plastic wrap. Let rise in warm place until doubled in size, about 15 minutes.

Place shallow pan half full of hot water on lower oven rack. Heat oven to 425°F. Uncover dough. Brush rolls with egg white; sprinkle with rosemary. Bake at 425°F. for 14 to 21 minutes or until light golden brown. Immediately remove from cookie sheet; cool on wire rack.
Yield: 12 rolls.

FOOD PROCESSOR DIRECTIONS:
Grease large cookie sheet. In food processor bowl with metal blade, combine 2½ cups flour, sugar, salt and yeast. Cover; process 5 seconds. With machine running, pour hot water through feed tube; continue processing until dough forms a ball. (If dough does not form a ball, add additional flour 1 tablespoon at a time.) Process an additional 40 to 60 seconds. Do not knead dough; place in greased bowl and continue as directed above.

HIGH ALTITUDE:
Above 3500 Feet: No change.

Rosemary French Rolls

NUTRITION PER SERVING:
Calories 100; Protein 3g; Carbohydrate 21g; Fat 0g; Sodium 180mg.

SWEET POTATO ROLLS

Sweet potatoes add a southern twist to these wonderful dinner rolls.

  3¾ **to 4 cups all purpose flour**
  ¼ **cup sugar**
  1 **teaspoon salt**
  1 **pkg. active dry yeast**
  1 **cup milk**
  ¼ **cup margarine or butter**
  ¾ **cup mashed canned sweet potatoes**
  1 **egg**
      Melted margarine or butter, if desired

In large bowl, combine 1 cup flour, sugar, salt and yeast; blend well. In small saucepan, heat milk and margarine until very warm (120 to 130°F.). Add warm liquid, sweet potatoes and egg to flour mixture. Blend at low speed until moistened; beat 2 minutes at medium speed. By hand, stir in remaining 2¾ to 3 cups flour to form a soft dough. (Dough will be somewhat sticky.)

On floured surface, knead dough until smooth and elastic, about 2 minutes. Place dough in greased bowl; cover loosely with plastic wrap and cloth towel. Let rise in warm place (80 to 85°F.) until light and doubled in size, about 45 to 55 minutes.

Grease 2 large cookie sheets. Punch down dough several times to remove all air bubbles. On floured surface, toss dough lightly until no longer sticky. Divide dough into 18 pieces; shape into balls. Place 2 inches apart on greased cookie sheets. Cover; let rise in warm place until light and doubled in size, about 30 to 40 minutes.

Heat oven to 375°F. Uncover dough. Bake 15 to 20 minutes or until golden brown. Immediately remove from cookie sheets; cool on wire racks. Brush with melted margarine.
Yield: 18 rolls.

HIGH ALTITUDE:
Above 3500 Feet: No change.

NUTRITION PER SERVING:
Calories 170; Protein 4g; Carbohydrate 28g; Fat 4g; Sodium 170mg.

HERBED OATMEAL PAN BREAD

A unique shaping method highlights these herb topped rolls.

BREAD
- 2 cups water
- 1 cup rolled oats
- 3 tablespoons margarine or butter
- 3¾ to 4¾ cups all purpose flour
- ¼ cup sugar
- 2 teaspoons salt
- 2 pkg. active dry yeast
- 1 egg

HERB BUTTER
- 1 tablespoon grated Parmesan cheese
- ½ teaspoon dried basil leaves
- ¼ teaspoon dried oregano leaves
- ¼ teaspoon garlic powder
- 6 tablespoons margarine or butter, melted

Bring water to a boil in medium saucepan; stir in rolled oats. Remove from heat; stir in 3 tablespoons margarine. Cool to 120 to 130°F. In large bowl, combine 1½ cups flour, sugar, salt and yeast; blend well. Add rolled oats mixture and egg. Blend at low speed until moistened; beat 3 minutes at medium speed. By hand, stir in an additional 1¾ cups to 2½ cups flour to form stiff dough.

On floured surface, knead in ½ to ¾ cup flour until dough is smooth and elastic, about 5 minutes. Shape dough into ball; cover with large bowl. Let rest 15 minutes. Grease 13x9-inch baking pan. Punch down dough several times to remove all air bubbles; press into greased pan. Using very sharp knife, cut diagonal lines 1½ inches apart, cutting completely through dough. Repeat in opposite direction creating diamond pattern. Cover loosely with greased plastic wrap and cloth towel.* Let rise in warm place (80 to 85°F.) until light and doubled in size, about 45 minutes.

Heat oven to 375°F. Uncover dough. Redefine cuts by poking tip of knife into cuts until knife hits bottom of pan; do not pull knife through dough. In small bowl, combine Parmesan cheese, basil, oregano and garlic powder; mix well. Set aside. Spoon 4 tablespoons of the butter over cut dough.

Bake at 375°F. for 15 minutes. Brush remaining 2 tablespoons of butter over bread. Sprinkle with Parmesan cheese-herb mixture. Bake for an additional 10 to 15 minutes or until golden brown. Serve warm or cool.

Yield: 16 rolls.

TIPS:

* To bake at a later time, at this point let stand at room temperature for 20 minutes. Remove cloth towel. Refrigerate 2 to 24 hours. Remove plastic wrap from dough; let stand at room temperature 30 minutes. Bake as directed above.

Two 8 or 9-inch square pans or one 8-inch and one 9-inch square pan can be substituted for 13x9-inch pan. When using 2 square pans, one pan can be baked and the other pan refrigerated for baking the next day.

HIGH ALTITUDE:
Above 3500 Feet: No change.

NUTRITION PER SERVING:
Calories 240; Protein 6g; Carbohydrate 35g; Fat 8g; Sodium 350mg.

COOK'S NOTES

ROLLED OATS

Rolled oats can be purchased in 3 varieties: old-fashioned, quick-cooking and instant. Old-fashioned rolled oats are whole oats that have been hulled, steamed and flattened by rollers into flakes. Quick-cooking rolled oats have been cut into smaller pieces before rolling, yielding thinner flakes that cook more quickly. Instant oats have been cut into even smaller pieces, precooked and dried so that they cook very fast.

Old-fashioned and quick-cooking rolled oats usually can be used interchangeably in our recipes unless we specify a variety. However, old-fashioned rolled oats will result in a firmer textured end product. Instant oats are not usually used for baking; most instant oat products include sugar, salt or flavorings and are meant to be used primarily as breakfast cereal.

Herbed Oatmeal Pan Bread

POTATO CHIVE ROLLS

These light and tender dinner rolls are mildly flavored with sour cream and chives.

4½ to 5 cups all purpose flour
  1 cup mashed potato flakes
  1 tablespoon sugar
  3 to 4 teaspoons chopped fresh or freeze-dried chives
  2 teaspoons salt
  2 pkg. active dry yeast
  2 cups milk
  ½ cup dairy sour cream
  2 eggs

In large bowl, combine 1½ cups flour, potato flakes, sugar, chives, salt and yeast; blend well. In small saucepan, heat milk and sour cream until very warm (120 to 130°F.). Add warm liquid and eggs to flour mixture. Blend at low speed until moistened; beat 3 minutes at medium speed. By hand, stir in remaining 3 to 3½ cups flour to form a stiff dough. Cover loosely with plastic wrap and cloth towel. Let rise in warm place (80 to 85°F.) until light and doubled in size, about 45 to 55 minutes.

Generously grease 13x9-inch pan. On floured surface, knead dough gently until no longer sticky. Divide dough into 24 pieces; shape into balls. Place in greased pan. Cover; let rise in warm place until light and doubled in size, 30 to 35 minutes.

Heat oven to 375°F. Uncover dough. Bake 25 to 35 minutes or until golden brown. Remove from pan immediately; cool on wire rack. If desired, lightly dust tops of rolls with flour.
Yield: 24 rolls.

HIGH ALTITUDE:
Above 3500 Feet: No change.

NUTRITION PER SERVING:
Calories 130; Protein 4g; Carbohydrate 24g; Fat 2g; Sodium 200mg.

WHOLE WHEAT PARTY BUNS

The goodness of whole wheat makes these dinner rolls delicious anytime.

3¾ to 4¼ cups all purpose flour
  3 cups whole wheat flour
  ½ cup sugar
  2 teaspoons salt
  2 pkg. active dry yeast
  2 cups water
  ¾ cup shortening or oil
  2 tablespoons molasses
  2 eggs, beaten

In large bowl, combine 2 cups all purpose flour, 1 cup whole wheat flour, sugar, salt and yeast; blend well. In small saucepan, heat water, shortening and molasses until very warm (120 to 130°F.). Add warm liquid to flour mixture; blend at low speed until moistened. Add eggs; beat 3 minutes at medium speed. By hand, stir in remaining whole wheat flour and enough all purpose flour (about 1¼ cups) to make a stiff dough.

On floured surface, knead in ½ to 1 cup all purpose flour until dough is smooth and elastic, about 5 minutes. Place in greased bowl; cover loosely with plastic wrap and cloth towel. Let rise in warm place (80 to 85°F.) until light and doubled in size, about 45 to 60 minutes.

Generously grease two 15x10x1-inch baking pans or cookie sheets. Punch down dough. Divide into 36 pieces; shape into balls. Arrange 18 balls in each greased pan. Cover; let rise in warm place (80 to 85°F.) until doubled in size, about 30 to 45 minutes.

Heat oven to 375°F. Uncover dough. Bake 15 to 20 minutes or until golden brown. If desired, brush with melted butter. Remove from pans immediately; cool on wire racks. Serve warm or cool.
Yield: 36 rolls.

HIGH ALTITUDE :
Above 3500 Feet: No change.

NUTRITION PER SERVING:
Calories 140; Protein 3g; Carbohydrate 22g; Fat 5g; Sodium 125mg.

FLAKY BUTTER BRIOCHES

A brioche is a tender French roll, rich in butter and eggs, distinguished by its top knot.

4¼ to 4¾ cups all purpose flour
⅓ cup sugar
1 teaspoon salt
2 pkg. active dry yeast
1¼ cups milk
½ cup butter or margarine
3 eggs

In large bowl, combine 2 cups flour, sugar, salt and yeast; blend well. In small saucepan, heat milk and butter until very warm (120 to 130°F.). Add warm liquid and 2 of the eggs to flour mixture. Blend at low speed until moistened; beat 3 minutes at medium speed. By hand, stir in an additional 2 to 2¼ cups flour until dough pulls cleanly away from sides of bowl.

Generously grease 24 individual brioche pans or muffin cups. On floured surface, knead in ¼ to ½ cup flour until dough is smooth, about 2 to 3 minutes. Divide dough into 4 equal parts. Shape 3 dough parts into 8 balls each. Place 1 ball in each greased pan. Shape remaining dough into 24 small balls. With finger, make a deep indentation in center of each large ball. Place 1 small ball in each indentation, pressing down slightly. Cover; let rise in warm place (80 to 85°F.) until light and doubled in size, about 45 minutes.

Heat oven to 350°F. Uncover dough. Beat remaining egg; carefully brush over rolls. Bake at 350°F. for 15 to 20 minutes or until golden brown. Immediately remove from pans; cool on wire racks.
Yield: 24 rolls.

HIGH ALTITUDE:
Above 3500 Feet: No change.

NUTRITION PER SERVING:
Calories 150; Protein 4g; Carbohydrate 23g; Fat 5g; Sodium 140mg.

BUTTERHORN CRESCENTS

Serve these impressive looking rolls for your next dinner party.

1 pkg. active dry yeast
1 cup warm milk
3¾ cups all purpose flour
1 teaspoon salt
1 cup butter or margarine
¼ cup sugar
1 egg

In small bowl, dissolve yeast in warm milk (105 to 115°F.). In large bowl, combine flour and salt. Using pastry blender or fork, cut in butter until mixture is crumbly. Beat sugar and egg together; add yeast mixture and sugar-egg mixture to flour mixture, mixing well. (Dough will be stiff.) Cover; refrigerate overnight.

Divide dough into 3 parts. On lightly floured surface, roll each part into a 12-inch circle; cut each circle into 12 wedges. Roll up starting with wide end. Place, point side down, on ungreased cookie sheets. Curve ends to form a crescent shape. Cover loosely with plastic wrap and cloth towel. Let rise in warm place (80 to 85°F.) until light and doubled in size, about 30 to 45 minutes.

Heat oven to 375°F. Uncover dough. Bake 10 to 15 minutes or until light golden brown. Immediately remove from cookie sheets; cool on wire racks.
Yield: 36 rolls.

HIGH ALTITUDE :
Above 3500 Feet: No change.

NUTRITION PER SERVING:
Calories 100; Protein 2g; Carbohydrate 12g; Fat 6g; Sodium 115mg.

VARIATION:

FROSTED BUTTERHORN CRESCENTS:
In small bowl, combine 2 cups powdered sugar, ½ teaspoon almond extract and 2 to 3 tablespoons milk, adding enough milk for desired spreading consistency. Spread over cooled rolls.

Basic Pizza Crust

If you make pizza often, you may want to double this recipe. The crusts can be prebaked and frozen for tasty homemade pizza anytime.

2¼ to 2¾ cups all purpose flour
 1 teaspoon sugar
 1 teaspoon salt
 1 pkg. fast-acting yeast
 1 cup water
 2 tablespoons olive oil or oil

In large bowl, combine 1½ cups flour, sugar, salt and yeast; mix well. In small saucepan, heat water until very hot (120 to 130°F.). Add warm water and oil to flour mixture. Blend at low speed until well moistened; beat 2 minutes at medium speed. By hand, stir in an additional ½ to ¾ cup flour until dough pulls cleanly away from sides of bowl.

On floured surface, knead in ¼ to ½ cup flour until dough is smooth and elastic, about 3 to 5 minutes. Cover loosely with plastic wrap and cloth towel. Let rise in warm place (80 to 85°F.) until light and doubled in size, about 30 minutes.

Place oven rack at lowest position; heat oven to 425°F. Grease two 12-inch pizza pans. Punch down dough several times to remove air bubbles. Divide dough in half; press into greased pizza pans. Bake at 425°F. on lowest oven rack for 15 minutes. Top as desired with favorite pizza toppings. Bake an additional 15 to 20 minutes or until crust is golden brown and toppings are thoroughly heated.
Yield: 2 crusts; 8 servings each.

FOOD PROCESSOR DIRECTIONS:
In food processor bowl with metal blade, combine 2¼ cups flour, sugar, salt and yeast. Cover; process 5 seconds. With machine running, pour 1 cup water heated to 120 to 130°F. and oil through feed tube; continue processing until dough forms a ball. (If dough does not form a ball, add an additional ½ cup flour, 1 tablespoon at a time.) Process an additional 40 to 60 seconds. Cover; let rise. Continue as directed above.

TIP:
To freeze 1 pizza crust, prepare as directed above. Grease 12-inch pizza pan. Press half of dough in greased pan. Bake at 425°F. for 15 minutes. Cool. Place in moisture-proof freezer bag. Freeze for up to 2 months. Thaw before using and top with favorite pizza toppings. Bake at 425°F. on lowest oven rack for 18 to 22 minutes or until crust is golden brown and toppings are thoroughly heated.

HIGH ALTITUDE:
Above 3500 Feet: No change.

NUTRITION PER SERVING:
Calories 100; Protein 2g,; Carbohydrates 17g; Fat 2g; Sodium 135mg.

Cornmeal Bread Sticks

The use of fast-acting yeast and the food processor will save you time in the preparation of these bread sticks.

1¾ to 2¼ cups all purpose flour
 1 cup cornmeal
 ¼ cup sugar
 1 teaspoon salt
 1 pkg. fast-acting dry yeast
 1 cup water
 ¼ cup margarine or butter
   Margarine or butter, melted
   Cornmeal

In large bowl, combine 1 cup flour, 1 cup cornmeal, sugar, salt and yeast; blend well. In small saucepan, heat water and ¼ cup margarine until very warm (120 to 130°F.). Add warm liquid to flour mixture. Blend at low speed until moistened; beat 2 minutes at medium speed. By hand, stir in an additional ½ to 1 cup flour until dough pulls cleanly away from sides of bowl.

On floured surface, knead in ¼ cup flour until dough is smooth and elastic, about 2 minutes. Place in greased bowl; cover loosely with plastic wrap and cloth towel. Let rise in warm place (80 to 85°F.) until light and doubled in size, about 10 minutes.

Grease 2 large cookie sheets; sprinkle with corn-meal. Punch down dough several times to remove all air bubbles. Divide dough into 24 parts; roll each into 10-inch rope. Place on greased cookie sheets. Cover; let rise in warm place until light and doubled in size, about 10 minutes.

Heat oven to 375°F. Uncover dough. Carefully brush sticks with melted margarine; sprinkle with cornmeal. Bake at 375°F. for 12 to 16 minutes or until bottoms are golden brown. Immediately remove from pans; cool on wire racks.

Yield: 24 bread sticks.

FOOD PROCESSOR DIRECTIONS:
In food processor bowl with metal blade, combine 1¼ cups flour, 1 cup cornmeal, sugar, salt, yeast and ¼ cup margarine. Cover; process 5 seconds. With machine running, pour 1 cup water heated to 120 to 130°F. through feed tube; continue processing until blended, about 20 seconds. Add ½ to 1 cup flour; process 10 to 20 seconds longer or until stiff dough forms. With rubber scraper, carefully pull dough from blade and bowl; place in lightly greased bowl. Continue as directed above.

HIGH ALTITUDE:
Above 3500 Feet: No change.

NUTRITION PER SERVING:
Calories 110; Protein 2g; Carbohydrate 17g; Fat 4g; Sodium 130mg.

COOK'S NOTE

CORNMEAL

By definition, cornmeal is ground dried corn kernels. Commercial cornmeal has the tough outer hull (bran) or the corn kernel steamed away in the milling process. Once the germ is removed, the endosperm is ground by steel rollers into granules. The granules are separated by size; the largest are grits, the medium size are used as cornmeal and the small ones are used as corn flour.

The color of cornmeal can be yellow, white or blue depending on the variety of corn. All are generally interchangeable in recipes. However, when blue cornmeal is used in baking, it turns grayish blue. Much of the blue cornmeal available is grown organically without chemicals or fertilizers in New Mexico. It is abundant in the Southwest and is sold in specialty stores or in food co-ops.

EASY ENGLISH MUFFINS

These fantastic English muffins are baked on the griddle, then toasted to perfection.

>   2 **pkg. active dry yeast**
>   2 **cups warm water**
>   5 **to 6 cups all purpose flour**
>   1 **tablespoon sugar**
>   3 **teaspoons salt**
> ½ **cup shortening**
>   **Cornmeal**
>   **Margarine or butter**

In large bowl, dissolve yeast in warm water (105 to 115°F.). Add 3 cups flour, sugar, salt and shortening to yeast mixture, stirring by hand until moistened. Stir vigorously by hand until smooth. Gradually add remaining 2 to 3 cups flour to form a stiff dough, beating well after each addition. On floured surface, gently knead dough 5 to 6 times until no longer sticky. Roll dough to ¼ to ⅜-inch thickness; cut with floured 3 to 4-inch round cutter. Sprinkle cornmeal evenly over 2 ungreased cookie sheets. Place cut-out dough on cornmeal; sprinkle with additional cornmeal. Cover loosely with plastic wrap and cloth towel. Let rise in warm place until light, about 30 to 45 minutes.

Heat griddle to 350°F. With wide spatula, invert dough onto ungreased griddle. Bake 5 to 6 minutes on each side or until light golden brown; cool. Split in half and toast before serving. Spread with margarine.

Yield: 18 to 26 muffins.

HIGH ALTITUDE:
Above 3500 Feet: No change.

NUTRITION PER SERVING:
Calories 149; Protein 3g; Carbohydrate 23g; Fat 4g; Sodium 250mg.

HERB FOCACCIA

This large, flat, round Italian bread is topped with olive oil and rosemary.

3½ **cups all purpose flour**
1 **teaspoon sugar**
1 **teaspoon salt**
1 **pkg. fast-acting yeast**
1 **cup water**
2 **tablespoons oil**
1 **egg**
3 **to 4 tablespoons olive oil**
1 **teaspoon dried rosemary or basil leaves, crushed**

Grease cookie sheet. In large bowl, combine 1 cup flour, sugar, salt and yeast; mix well. In small saucepan, heat water and oil until very warm (120 to 130°F.). Add warm liquid and egg to flour mixture. Blend at low speed until moistened; beat 2 minutes at medium speed. By hand, stir in an additional 1¾ cups flour until dough pulls away from sides of bowl. On floured surface, knead in ¾ cup flour until dough is smooth and elastic, about 5 minutes. Cover with large bowl; let rest 5 minutes.

Place dough on greased cookie sheet. Roll or press to 12-inch circle. Cover loosely with greased plastic wrap and cloth towel. Let rise in warm place (80 to 85°F.) until light and doubled in size, about 30 minutes.

Heat oven to 400°F. Uncover dough. With fingers or handle of wooden spoon, poke holes in dough at 1 inch intervals. Drizzle 3 to 4 tablespoons olive oil over top of dough. Sprinkle evenly with rosemary.

Bake at 400°F. for 17 to 27 minutes or until golden brown. Immediately remove from cookie sheet; cool on wire rack.

Yield: 1 (16-slice) loaf.

TIPS:

For two smaller loaves, grease 2 cookie sheets. Divide dough in half. Roll or press each half into an 8-inch circle. Continue as directed above. Bake for 10 to 20 minutes.

To freeze focaccia, wrap in plastic wrap or foil and store up to 3 months in freezer.

HIGH ALTITUDE:
Above 3500 Feet: No change.

NUTRITION PER SERVING:
Calories 150; Protein 3g; Carbohydrate 21g; Fat 6g; Sodium 140mg.

ITALIAN BREAD STICKS

These garlic-flavored sticks of bread are a perfect accompaniment to Italian entrees.

1 **pkg. active dry yeast**
⅔ **cup warm water**
2 **to 2¼ cups all purpose flour**
1½ **teaspoons sugar**
1 **teaspoon garlic salt**
¼ **cup shortening**
1 **tablespoon water**
1 **egg white**
  Sesame or poppy seed

In large bowl, dissolve yeast in ⅔ cup warm water (105 to 115°F.). Add 1 cup flour, sugar, garlic salt and shortening. Blend at low speed until moistened; beat 3 minutes at medium speed. By hand, stir in an additional 1 to 1¼ cups flour to form a soft dough.

Place dough in greased bowl; cover loosely with plastic wrap and cloth towel. Let rise in warm place (80 to 85°F.) until light and doubled in size, about 30 to 40 minutes.

Grease 15x10x1-inch baking pan. On lightly floured surface, knead dough about 10 times, or until no longer sticky. Roll into 15x10-inch rectangle; place in greased pan. Starting with 10-inch side, cut dough into 12 strips. Cut strips in half forming 24 sticks. Combine 1 tablespoon water and egg white; blend well. Brush on sticks; sprinkle with sesame seed. Cover; let rise in warm place, about 15 to 20 minutes.

Heat oven to 375°F. Uncover dough. Bake 18 to 22 minutes or until golden brown. Immediately remove from pan; cool on wire rack.

Yield: 24 bread sticks.

TIP:
For softer bread sticks, dough can be baked in greased 13x9-inch pan. Cut into 20 bread sticks.

HIGH ALTITUDE:
Above 3500 Feet: No change.

NUTRITION PER SERVING:
Calories 60; Protein 1g; Carbohydrate 9g; Fat 2g; Sodium 80mg.

Herb Focaccia, Italian Bread Sticks

CHEWY BREAD RINGS

These will remind you of bagels in flavor and texture, but they are much easier to make.

2½ to 3½ cups all purpose flour
  2 teaspoons sugar
  1 teaspoon salt
  1 pkg. active dry yeast
 ¾ cup water
 ½ cup milk
  2 teaspoons oil
  1 egg, beaten
    Poppy seed, sesame seed or caraway seed,
      if desired
    Water

In large bowl, combine 1½ cups flour, sugar, salt and yeast. In small saucepan, heat water, milk and oil until very warm (120 to 130°F.). Add warm liquid to flour mixture. Blend at low speed until moistened; beat 2 minutes at medium speed. By hand, stir in an additional ¾ to 1½ cups flour until dough pulls cleanly away from sides of bowl.

On floured surface, knead in ¼ to ½ cup flour until dough is smooth and elastic, about 5 minutes. Place dough in greased bowl; cover loosely with plastic wrap and cloth towel. Let rise in warm place (80 to 85°F.) until light and doubled in size, about 40 to 50 minutes.

Grease 2 cookie sheets. Punch down dough several times to remove all air bubbles. Divide dough into 18 pieces. Roll each into 8-inch rope. Form rings, overlapping ends; press to seal. Place on greased cookie sheets. Cover; let rise in warm place until light and doubled in size, about 15 to 25 minutes.

Heat oven to 400°F. Uncover dough. Gently brush rings with egg; sprinkle with poppy seed. Place 13x9-inch pan of hot water on lowest oven rack. Place cookie sheet on middle oven rack over baking pan. Bake at 400°F. for 18 to 22 minutes or until golden brown and rings sound hollow when lightly tapped. Remove from oven; immediately brush with water. Cool on cookie sheet.

Yield: 18 bread rings.

HIGH ALTITUDE:
Above 3500 Feet: No change.

NUTRITION PER SERVING:
Calories 100; Protein 3g; Carbohydrate 19g; Fat 1g; Sodium 125mg.

BAGEL STICKS

The bagel sticks are cooked in water before baking.

3½ to 4½ cups all purpose flour
  2 tablespoons sugar
 ½ teaspoon salt
  2 pkg. active dry yeast
1½ cups water
  1 egg, separated
  2 quarts water
  1 tablespoon sugar
  1 tablespoon water
  2 tablespoons sesame seed

In large bowl, combine 1½ cups flour, 2 tablespoons sugar, salt and yeast; blend well. In small saucepan, heat 1½ cups water until hot (120 to 130°F.). Add hot water and egg white to flour mixture. Blend at low speed until moistened; beat 3 minutes at medium speed. By hand, stir in 1¾ to 2¼ cups flour to form a stiff dough.

On floured surface, knead in ¼ to ¾ cup flour until dough is smooth and elastic, about 7 minutes. Place dough in greased bowl; cover loosely with plastic wrap and cloth towel. Let rise in warm place (80 to 85°F.) until light and doubled in size, about 30 minutes.

Grease 2 cookie sheets. Punch down dough several times to remove all air bubbles. Divide dough into 16 equal pieces; shape into 6-inch sticks. Place on greased cookie sheets. Cover loosely with greased plastic wrap and cloth towel; let rise in warm place until light and doubled in size, about 10 minutes.

Heat oven to 375°F. In Dutch oven, or large kettle combine 2 quarts water and 1 tablespoon sugar. Bring to a boil. Cook 2 bagel sticks at a time in boiling water for 30 seconds, turning once; drain with slotted spoon. Return to greased cookie sheets. In small bowl, combine egg yolk and 1 tablespoon water. Brush over bagel sticks; sprinkle with sesame seed. Bake at 375°F. for 20 to 24 minutes or until light golden brown. Immediately remove from cookie sheets.

Yield: 16 sticks.

HIGH ALTITUDE:
Above 3500 Feet: No change.

NUTRITION PER SERVING:
Calories 150; Protein 5g; Carbohydrate 29g; Fat 1g; Sodium 75mg.

SOFT PRETZELS

Enjoy these with mustard.

    3 to 3½ cups all purpose flour
    1 tablespoon sugar
    1 teaspoon salt
    1 pkg. active dry yeast
    1 cup water
    1 tablespoon shortening
    6 cups water
    ¼ cup baking soda
    1 tablespoon water
    1 egg white
      Coarse salt or sesame seed

In large bowl, combine 1 cup flour, sugar, salt and yeast; blend well. In small saucepan, heat 1 cup water and shortening until very warm (120 to 130°F.). Add warm liquid to flour mixture. Blend at low speed until moistened; beat 3 minutes at medium speed. Stir in an additional 1½ to 1¾ cups flour until dough pulls cleanly away from sides of bowl.

On floured surface, knead in ½ to ¾ cup flour until dough is smooth and elastic, about 5 minutes. Place dough in greased bowl; cover loosely with plastic wrap and cloth towel. Let rise in warm place (80 to 85°F.) until light and doubled in size, about 45 to 60 minutes.

Grease cookie sheets. Punch down dough several times to remove all air bubbles. Shape dough into ball. Divide dough into 12 pieces. Roll each into 16-inch rope; form pretzel shape. Place on greased cookie sheets. Cover; let rise in warm place until light, about 15 to 20 minutes.

Heat oven to 400°F. In large non-aluminum saucepan, combine 6 cups water and baking soda; bring to a boil. Drop pretzels in water that is just boiling, one at a time, cooking 5 seconds on each side. Remove from water with slotted spoon; place on greased cookie sheet. Combine 1 tablespoon water and egg white; brush on pretzels. Sprinkle with coarse salt.

Bake at 400°F. for 8 to 10 minutes or until golden brown. Immediately remove from cookie sheet; cool on wire racks. Serve warm.

Yield: 12 pretzels.

HIGH ALTITUDE:
Above 3500 Feet: No change.

NUTRITION PER SERVING:
Calories 140; Protein 5g; Carbohydrate 27g; Fat 1g; Sodium 185mg.

HERB CHEESE PRETZELS

A flavorful soft pretzel — perfect to serve with soup or salad.

    2 cups all purpose flour
    2 teaspoons sugar
    1 pkg. active dry yeast
    1 teaspoon salt
    ½ teaspoon Italian seasoning
    ¼ teaspoon onion powder
    ¼ teaspoon garlic powder
  1½ cups water
    3 tablespoons oil
    2 tablespoons grated Parmesan cheese
    3 oz. (¾ cup) shredded Cheddar cheese
  1½ to 2 cups whole wheat flour
    1 tablespoon water
    1 egg white

In large bowl, combine all purpose flour, sugar, yeast, salt, Italian seasoning, onion powder and garlic powder. In small saucepan, heat 1½ cups water and oil until very warm (120 to 130°F.). Add warm mixture to flour mixture. Blend at low speed until moistened; beat 3 minutes at medium speed. Add Parmesan cheese and Cheddar cheese. Stir in 1½ to 2 cups whole wheat flour until dough pulls cleanly away from sides of bowl.

On floured surface, knead dough until smooth and elastic, about 3 to 5 minutes. Place dough in greased bowl; cover loosely with plastic wrap and cloth towel. Let rise in warm place (80 to 85°F.) about 30 minutes.

Heat oven to 400°F. Generously grease 2 cookie sheets. Punch down dough several times to remove all air bubbles. Divide dough into 12 pieces. Roll each piece into a pencil-shaped 20-inch rope; tie in loose pretzel shape. Place on greased cookie sheets. In small bowl, combine 1 tablespoon water and egg white; blend well. Brush over pretzels.

Bake for 20 to 25 minutes or until golden brown. Immediately remove from cookie sheets; cool on wire racks.

Yield: 12 pretzels.

HIGH ALTITUDE:
Above 3500 Feet: Bake at 400°F. for 15 to 20 minutes.

NUTRITION PER SERVING:
Calories 210; Protein 8g; Carbohydrate 31g; Fat 7g; Sodium 250mg.

REFRIGERATED COFFEE CAKE DOUGH

This easy no-knead dough is made ahead and refrigerated, then shaped into any of the following coffee cakes. By changing the shape and adding your favorite filling, you can create your own specialties.

- 3¾ to 4 cups all purpose flour
- ¼ cup sugar
- 1 teaspoon salt
- 2 pkg. active dry yeast
- 1 cup milk
- ¼ cup water
- ½ cup margarine or butter
- 2 eggs

In large bowl, combine 1½ cups flour, sugar, salt and yeast; blend well. In small saucepan, heat milk, water and margarine until very warm (120 to 130°F.). Add warm liquid and eggs to flour mixture. Blend at low speed until moistened; beat 3 minutes at medium speed. By hand, stir in 2¼ to 2½ cups flour to make a stiff dough. Cover tightly; refrigerate overnight. Shape and bake as directed in the following recipes.

HIGH ALTITUDE:
Above 3500 Feet: No change.

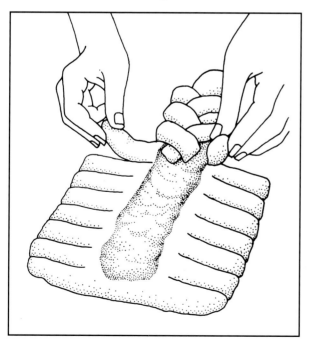

Making an easy braid

PINEAPPLE NUT COFFEE CAKE

This coffee cake features a braided look that is easy to create.

COFFEE CAKES
- ¼ cup sugar
- 1 tablespoon cornstarch
- 1 (8¼-oz.) can crushed pineapple, undrained
- 2 tablespoons margarine or butter
- ½ cup chopped nuts
- ½ cup raisins, if desired
- 1 recipe Refrigerated Coffee Cake Dough (this page)

TOPPING
- ¼ cup sugar
- 2 tablespoons all purpose flour
- 1 tablespoon margarine or butter, softened

In small saucepan, combine ¼ cup sugar, cornstarch and pineapple; blend well. Cook over medium heat until thickened, stirring constantly, about 3 minutes. Remove from heat; stir in 2 tablespoons margarine, nuts and raisins. Cool. Set aside.

Grease 2 cookie sheets. Turn dough onto lightly floured surface; divide in half. Roll half of dough into 12x6-inch rectangle; place on greased cookie sheet. Spread half of prepared filling lengthwise down center ⅓ of rectangle. Cut 1-inch wide strips on each side of rectangle just to edge of filling. To give braided appearance, fold strips of dough at an angle across filling, alternating from side to side as shown in diagram. Repeat with second half of dough. Cover loosely with plastic wrap and cloth towel. Let rise in warm place (80 to 85°F.) until light and doubled in size, about 30 to 40 minutes.

Heat oven to 375°F. Uncover dough. In small bowl, combine all topping ingredients; blend well. Sprinkle half of mixture on top of each coffee cake. Bake at 375°F. for 20 to 25 minutes or until golden brown. Immediately remove from cookie sheets; cool on wire racks.

Yield: 2 (12-slice) coffee cakes.

NUTRITION PER SERVING:
Calories 200; Protein 4g; Carbohydrate 29g; Fat 8g; Sodium 160mg.

STREUSEL COFFEE CAKE

There's no special shaping required for this easy coffee cake.

- **1 recipe Refrigerated Coffee Cake Dough p. 468**
- **½ cup all purpose flour**
- **⅓ cup firmly packed brown sugar**
- **1 teaspoon cinnamon**
- **¼ cup margarine or butter**
- **½ cup chopped nuts**

Grease 13x9-inch pan. Press dough in greased pan. Cover loosely with plastic wrap and cloth towel. Let rise in warm place (80 to 85°F.) until light and doubled in size, about 45 to 60 minutes.

In small bowl, combine flour, brown sugar and cinnamon; mix well. Using pastry blender or fork, cut in margarine until mixture is crumbly. Stir in nuts. Set aside.

Heat oven to 375°F. Uncover dough. Sprinkle brown sugar mixture over dough. Bake at 375°F. for 20 to 25 minutes or until golden brown. Serve warm.

Yield: 15 servings.

NUTRITION PER SERVING:
Calories 190; Protein 4g; Carbohydrate 25g; Fat 9g; Sodium 150mg.

FRESH APPLE COFFEE CAKE

Rows of apples sprinkled with cinnamon and sugar top this wonderful bread.

- **1 recipe Refrigerated Coffee Cake Dough p. 468**
- **4 cups sliced peeled apples**
- **¾ cup sugar**
- **3 tablespoons all purpose flour**
- **½ teaspoon cinnamon**
- **2 tablespoons margarine or butter**
- **½ cup powdered sugar**
- **3 to 4 teaspoons milk**

Generously grease 13x9-inch pan. Press dough in greased pan. Arrange apple slices in rows on top of dough. In small bowl, combine sugar, flour and cinnamon; mix well. Using pastry blender or fork, cut in margarine until mixture is crumbly. Sprinkle evenly over apples. Cover loosely with plastic wrap and cloth towel. Let rise in warm place (80 to 85°F.) until light and doubled in size, about 40 to 45 minutes.

Heat oven to 375°F. Uncover dough. Bake 30 to 40 minutes or until golden brown around edges and apples are tender. In small bowl, blend powdered sugar and enough milk for desired drizzling consistency. Drizzle over warm coffee cake. Serve warm.

Yield: 15 servings.

NUTRITION PER SERVING:
Calories 310; Protein 6g; Carbohydrate 51g; Fat 9g; Sodium 250mg.

FANNED PRUNE COFFEE CAKE

Use a kitchen shears to cut the slices for this beautiful coffee cake.

- **2 cups cooked chopped prunes**
- **3 tablespoons sugar**
- **2 tablespoons lemon juice**
- **1 recipe Refrigerated Coffee Cake Dough p. 468**
- **¼ cup honey**
- **2 tablespoons margarine or butter, melted**

In medium saucepan, combine prunes, sugar and lemon juice; bring to a boil. Boil 1 minute, stirring occasionally; cool. Grease 2 cookie sheets. On lightly floured surface, divide dough in half. Roll half into 18x9-inch rectangle. Spread half of prepared filling crosswise on two-thirds of dough. Fold dough over half of filling. Fold again, forming 3 layers of dough and 2 layers of filling. Seal edges well. Place on greased cookie sheet. With scissors or sharp knife, make 8 cuts at 1-inch intervals, to within 1 inch of opposite side. Separate strips slightly; twist so filling shows. Repeat with second half of dough. Cover loosely with plastic wrap and cloth towel. Let rise in warm place (80 to 85°F.) until light and doubled in size, about 30 to 40 minutes.

Heat oven to 375°F. Uncover dough. Bake 15 to 25 minutes or until golden brown. In small bowl, combine honey and margarine. Brush mixture over hot coffee cakes to glaze. Serve warm.

Yield: 2 (16-slice) coffee cakes.

NUTRITION PER SERVING:
Calories 140; Protein 3g; Carbohydrate 22g; Fat 4g; Sodium 120mg.

APRICOT COFFEE CAKE

A tea ring shape shows off the apricot filling.

 1 **(6-oz.) pkg. (1 cup) dried apricots, finely chopped**
 1 **cup water**
 3 **tablespoons brown sugar**
 2 **teaspoons orange juice**
 ¼ **cup chopped nuts**
 1 **recipe Refrigerated Coffee Cake Dough p. 468**
 1 **cup powdered sugar, if desired**
 2 **to 3 tablespoons milk, if desired**

In small saucepan, combine apricots and water. Cook over medium heat, stirring occasionally, until water is absorbed and apricots are soft, about 20 to 25 minutes. Add brown sugar, orange juice and nuts; cool.

Grease 2 cookie sheets. On lightly floured surface, divide dough in half. Roll half of dough into 18x12-inch rectangle; spread with half of filling. Starting with 18-inch side, roll up tightly, pressing edges to seal. Place seam side down on greased cookie sheet. Join ends to form ring; pinch ends to seal. With scissors or sharp knife, cut from outside edge of ring to within ½ inch of inside of ring, making cuts 1 inch apart. Repeat with second half of dough. Cover loosely with plastic wrap and cloth towel. Let rise in warm place (80 to 85°F.) until light and doubled in size, about 30 to 40 minutes.

Heat oven to 375°F. Uncover dough. Bake 20 to 25 minutes or until golden brown. Immediately remove from cookie sheets; cool on wire racks. In small bowl, combine powdered sugar and enough milk for desired drizzling consistency. Drizzle over warm coffee cakes.

Yield: 2 (16-slice) coffee cakes.

NUTRITION PER SERVING:
Calories 140; Protein 3g; Carbohydrate 24g; Fat 4g; Sodium 115mg.

TROPICAL TREAT COFFEE CAKE

Peach or apricot preserves, coconut and nuts top this special coffee cake.

 1 **recipe Refrigerated Coffee Cake Dough p. 468**
 1 **(10-oz.) jar peach or apricot preserves**
 2 **tablespoons margarine or butter, melted**
 ½ **cup coconut**
 ¼ **cup chopped nuts, if desired**

Grease 13x9-inch pan. Press dough in greased pan. In small bowl, combine preserves and margarine; spread over dough. Sprinkle with coconut and nuts. Cover loosely with greased plastic wrap and cloth towel. Let rise in warm place (80 to 85°F.) until light and doubled in size, about 40 to 45 minutes.

Heat oven to 375°F. Uncover dough. Bake 30 to 40 minutes or until golden brown around edges. Serve warm.

Yield: 15 servings.

NUTRITION PER SERVING:
Calories 200; Protein 3g; Carbohydrate 31g; Fat 7g; Sodium 135mg.

BUTTER ALMOND COFFEE CAKE

Serve this buttery almond delicacy warm or cool. It's indescribable!

TOPPING
 ⅓ **cup butter or margarine, melted**
 ½ **cup sliced almonds**
 ½ **cup sugar**
 2 **tablespoons light corn syrup**
 ½ **teaspoon almond extract**

COFFEE CAKE
 1¾ **to 2 cups all purpose flour**
 ¼ **cup sugar**
 ½ **teaspoon salt**
 1 **pkg. active dry yeast**
 ½ **cup milk**
 ¼ **cup butter or margarine**
 1 **egg**

Grease 8 or 9-inch square pan. In small bowl, combine all topping ingredients; blend well. Spread evenly in bottom of greased pan; set aside.

In large bowl, combine 1 cup flour, ¼ cup sugar, salt and yeast; blend well. In small saucepan, heat milk and ¼ cup butter until very warm (120 to 130°F.). Add warm liquid and egg to flour mixture. Blend at low speed until moistened; beat 3 minutes at medium speed. By hand, stir in an additional ¾ to 1 cup flour to make a stiff batter. Spoon evenly over topping mixture in pan. Cover loosely with plastic wrap and cloth towel. Let rise in warm place (80 to 85°F.) until light and doubled in size, about 1½ hours.

Heat oven to 375°F. Uncover dough. Bake 20 to 25 minutes or until golden brown. Immediately turn onto serving platter or foil.

Yield: 9 servings.

HIGH ALTITUDE:
Above 3500 Feet: No change.

NUTRITION PER SERVING:
Calories 340; Protein 5g; Carbohydrate 43g; Fat 16g; Sodium 280mg.

Orange Butter Coffee Cake
———— ∽ ————

Enjoy the aroma of yeast dough when you bake this delightful coffee cake — it has a mouth-watering orange and coconut filling and glaze.

COFFEE CAKE
- 1 pkg. active dry yeast
- ¼ cup warm water
- 2¾ to 3 cups all purpose flour
- ¼ cup sugar
- 1 teaspoon salt
- ⅔ cup dairy sour cream
- 6 tablespoons butter or margarine, melted
- 2 eggs

FILLING
- ¾ cup sugar
- ¾ cup coconut, toasted, p. 23
- 2 tablespoons grated orange peel
- 2 tablespoons butter or margarine, melted

GLAZE
- ¾ cup sugar
- ⅓ cup dairy sour cream
- ¼ cup butter or margarine
- 3 tablespoons orange juice
- ¼ cup coconut, toasted, p. 23

In large bowl, dissolve yeast in warm water (105 to 115°F.). Add 1¾ cups flour and remaining coffee cake ingredients to yeast mixture. Beat 2 minutes at medium speed. By hand, stir in remaining 1 to 1¼ cups flour to form a soft dough. Cover with plastic wrap and cloth towel. Let rise in warm place (80 to 85°F.) until light and doubled in size, about 45 to 60 minutes.

Generously grease 13x9-inch pan. In small bowl, combine all filling ingredients except butter; set aside. On floured surface, knead dough about 15 times. Divide dough in half; roll half of dough into 12-inch circle. Brush with 1 tablespoon of the melted butter. Sprinkle with half of filling mixture. Cut into 12 wedges. Roll up each wedge starting with wide end. Repeat with second half of dough. Place rolls, point side down, in 3 lengthwise rows in greased pan. Cover; let rise in warm place until light and doubled in size, about 45 to 60 minutes.

Heat oven to 350°F. Uncover dough. Bake 25 to 30 minutes or until golden brown. Leave in pan. Meanwhile, in small saucepan combine all glaze ingredients except coconut. Bring to a boil; boil 3 minutes, stirring occasionally. Pour glaze over warm coffee cake. Sprinkle with ¼ cup toasted coconut.

Yield: 24 servings.

HIGH ALTITUDE:
Above 3500 Feet: Bake at 350°F. for 20 to 25 minutes.

NUTRITION PER SERVING:
Calories 220; Protein 3g; Carbohydrate 29g; Fat 10g; Sodium 160mg.

Cook's Note
———— ∽ ————

SOUR CREAM
Sour cream lasts longer if you turn the original container, tightly sealed, upside down in the refrigerator. This prevents air from filling the top.

STEP-BY-STEP FEATURE ～
How to Shape Tannenbaum Coffee Cakes

STEP 1. Roll half of the dough into a triangle with two 15-inch sides and a 12-inch base. Brush with melted margarine; sprinkle with filling.

STEP 2. Fold 15-inch sides of triangle toward center, covering filling. Press all seams to seal. Invert, seam side down, onto greased pan.

STEP 3. Make 12 slits (1 inch apart) along outside edges to within ½ inch of center of dough. Twist each strip so cut side is up to show filling.

TANNENBAUM COFFEE CAKES

Tannenbaum, the German word for pine tree, is a fitting name for these Christmas tree-shaped loaves.

COFFEE CAKES
- 5 to 6 cups all purpose flour
- ½ cup sugar
- 2 teaspoons salt
- 2 pkg. active dry yeast
- 1½ cups milk
- ½ cup margarine or butter
- 2 eggs

FILLING
- ¼ cup margarine or butter, melted
- 1 cup sugar
- ½ cup chopped nuts
- 1 tablespoon cinnamon

TOPPING
- 1 cup powdered sugar
- 2 to 3 tablespoons milk
- Candied cherries

In large bowl, combine 2 cups flour, ½ cup sugar, salt and yeast; blend well. In medium saucepan, heat 1½ cups milk and ½ cup margarine until very warm (120 to 130°F.). Add warm liquid and eggs to flour mixture. Blend at low speed until moistened; beat 3 minutes at medium speed. By hand, stir in an additional 2 to 2½ cups flour to form a stiff dough.

On floured surface, knead in 1 to 1½ cups flour until dough is smooth and elastic, about 5 to 8 minutes. Place dough in greased bowl; cover loosely with plastic wrap and cloth towel. Let rise in warm place (80 to 85°F.) until light and doubled in size, about 1 to 1¼ hours.

Generously grease two 15x10x1-inch baking pans. Punch down dough several times to remove all air bubbles. Divide dough into 2 parts. On lightly floured surface, roll one part into a triangle with two 15-inch sides and a 12-inch base.* Brush with 1 tablespoon of the melted margarine. In small bowl, combine 2 tablespoons melted margarine, 1 cup sugar, nuts and cinnamon; mix well. Sprinkle ½ of filling mixture evenly over dough.

(Recipe continued on next page.)

Tannenbaum Coffee Cakes

(Recipes continued from previous page.)

To shape tree, starting at top point of dough triangle, fold 15-inch sides to meet in center, pressing all seams to seal. Invert, seam side down, onto greased pan. With scissors or sharp knife, make 12 slits about 1 inch apart along each long outside edge of tree, cutting to within ½ inch of center of dough. Starting at bottom of tree, twist each strip so cut side is up to show filling. Cover; let rise in warm place until light and doubled in size, about 30 to 40 minutes. Repeat with remaining dough and filling.

Heat oven to 350°F. Uncover dough. Bake 20 to 30 minutes or until golden brown. Cool 5 minutes; remove from pans. Cool on wire racks. In small bowl, blend powdered sugar and enough milk for desired drizzling consistency. Drizzle over coffee cakes. Garnish with candied cherries.

Yield: 2 (24-slice) coffee cakes.

TIP:
* For easier shaping of each coffee cake, roll dough on lightly floured cookie sheet. When ready to place on baking pan, invert baking pan over tree on cookie sheet. Invert again; remove cookie sheet.

HIGH ALTITUDE:
Above 3500 Feet: No change.

NUTRITION PER SERVING:
Calories 140; Protein 2g; Carbohydrate 22g; Fat 4g; Sodium 130mg.

POTICA
❦

This rich Yugoslavian coffee cake ring is rolled and filled with nuts and dates.

COFFEE CAKE
- 1 pkg. active dry yeast
- ½ cup warm water
- 2 cups all purpose flour
- 2 tablespoons sugar
- ¼ teaspoon salt
- ½ cup margarine or butter
- 1 egg

FILLING
- ¼ cup sugar
- ¼ teaspoon cinnamon
- ¼ cup milk
- ¼ cup honey
- ½ cup ground walnuts
- ½ cup chopped dates

In small bowl, dissolve yeast in warm water (105 to 115°F.). In large bowl, combine flour, 2 tablespoons sugar and salt. With pastry blender or fork, cut in margarine until mixture is crumbly. Add yeast mixture and egg to flour mixture; mix well. Cover tightly and refrigerate overnight.

In large saucepan, combine all filling ingredients. Bring to a boil, stirring constantly. Remove from heat; cool 10 minutes. Set aside.

Grease 6½-cup ring mold. On well floured surface, toss dough until no longer sticky. Roll dough into 20x10-inch rectangle; spread filling evenly over dough. Starting with 20-inch side, roll up tightly, pressing edges to seal. Place seam side down in greased ring mold. Pinch ends to seal. Cover; let rise in warm place (80 to 85°F.) until light and doubled in size, about 1 to 2 hours.

Heat oven to 350°F. Uncover dough. Bake 30 to 40 minutes or until light golden brown. Immediately remove from pan; cool on wire rack.

Yield: 1 (16-slice) coffee cake.

HIGH ALTITUDE:
Above 3500 Feet: No change.

NUTRITION PER SERVING:
Calories 190; Protein 3g; Carbohydrate 26g; Fat 8g; Sodium 105mg.

RUM PECAN RING
❦

Pretty shaping plus an irresistible nut filling make this coffee cake a winner!

COFFEE CAKE
- 3 to 3¼ cups all purpose flour
- ¼ cup sugar
- ½ teaspoon salt
- 1 pkg. active dry yeast
- 1 cup milk
- ½ cup margarine or butter
- 1 egg

FILLING
- ⅔ cup firmly packed brown sugar
- ¼ cup margarine or butter, softened
- ½ cup ground pecans
- ½ teaspoon rum extract

GLAZE
- 1 cup powdered sugar
- ¼ teaspoon rum extract
- 3 to 5 teaspoons milk
  Pecan halves

In large bowl, combine 1½ cups flour, sugar, salt and yeast; mix well. In medium saucepan, heat 1 cup milk and ½ cup margarine until very warm (120 to 130°F.). Add warm liquid and egg to flour mixture. Blend at low speed until moistened; beat 3 minutes at medium speed. By hand, gradually stir in remaining flour until dough pulls cleanly away from sides of bowl.

On floured surface, knead dough until smooth and elastic, about 3 to 5 minutes. Place dough in greased bowl; cover loosely with plastic wrap and cloth towel. Let rise in warm place (80 to 85°F.) until light and doubled in size, about 50 to 60 minutes.

To prepare filling, in small bowl, combine brown sugar and ¼ cup margarine. Stir in ground pecans and ½ teaspoon rum extract.

Grease large cookie sheet. Punch down dough several times to remove all air bubbles. Turn dough onto lightly floured surface. Roll dough into 18x12-inch rectangle. Spread with filling to within ½ inch of edges. Starting with 18-inch side, roll up tightly, pressing edges to seal. Place seam side down on greased cookie sheet. Join ends to form ring; pinch ends to seal. With scissors or sharp knife, cut from outside edge of ring to within ½ inch of inside of ring, making cuts 2 inches apart. Using wooden spoon handle, crease middle of each 2-inch section until dough fans out on either side of crease. Cover; let rise in warm place until light and doubled in size, about 30 to 40 minutes.

Heat oven to 350°F. Uncover dough. Bake 25 to 35 minutes or until golden brown. Immediately remove from cookie sheet; cool on wire rack. In small bowl, blend all glaze ingredients except pecans, adding enough milk for desired drizzling consistency. Drizzle over ring. Garnish with pecan halves.
Yield: 16 servings.

HIGH ALTITUDE:
Above 3500 Feet: No change.

NUTRITION PER SERVING:
Calories 280; Protein 4g; Carbohydrate 41g; Fat 12g; Sodium 180mg.

RICH DANISH RING

From Denmark, famous for its Danish pastry, comes this melt-in-your-mouth coffee cake.

COFFEE CAKE
- 1 pkg. active dry yeast
- 1 cup warm milk
- 3½ cups all purpose flour
- ½ cup sugar
- 1 teaspoon salt
- ½ cup margarine or butter
- 2 eggs, slightly beaten

FILLING
- ¼ cup margarine or butter, softened
- ½ cup raisins or dried currants, if desired
  Powdered sugar

In small bowl, dissolve yeast in warm milk (105 to 115°F.). In large bowl, combine flour, sugar and salt; blend well. Using pastry blender or fork, cut in ½ cup margarine until mixture is crumbly. Add yeast mixture and eggs; stir well. Cover loosely with plastic wrap and cloth towel. Let rise in warm place (80 to 85°F.) until light and doubled in size, about 1 hour.

Grease 12-cup Bundt® pan or 10-inch tube pan. On well floured surface, toss dough lightly until no longer sticky. Roll dough into 20x10-inch rectangle; spread with ¼ cup margarine and raisins. Starting with 20-inch side, roll up tightly, pressing edges to seal. Place, seam side down, in greased pan. Join ends to form ring; pinch ends to seal. Cover; let rise in warm place until light and doubled in size, about 45 to 50 minutes.

Heat oven to 350°F. Uncover dough. Bake 40 to 50 minutes or until golden brown. Immediately remove from pan; cool on wire rack. Sprinkle with powdered sugar.
Yield: 16 servings.

HIGH ALTITUDE:
Above 3500 Feet: No change.

NUTRITION PER SERVING:
Calories 230; Protein 4g; Carbohydrate 32g; Fat 10g; Sodium 255mg.

APRICOT CHERRY POINSETTIA COFFEE CAKE

Impressive to serve — delicious to eat!

COFFEE CAKE
- 2 to 2½ cups all purpose flour
- ¼ cup sugar
- 1 teaspoon salt
- 1 pkg. active dry yeast
- ⅔ cup milk
- 2 tablespoons shortening or margarine
- 1 egg
- ½ teaspoon grated orange peel

FILLING
- 1 tablespoon margarine or butter, melted
- ½ cup chopped red candied cherries
- ½ cup chopped dried apricots
- 2 tablespoons sugar

ICING AND TOPPING
- ½ cup powdered sugar
- 2 to 3 teaspoons milk
- ½ to 1 teaspoon grated orange peel

In large bowl, combine 1 cup flour, ¼ cup sugar, salt and yeast; mix well. In small saucepan, heat ⅔ cup milk and shortening until very warm (120 to 130°F.). Add warm liquid, egg and ½ teaspoon grated orange peel to flour mixture. Blend at low speed until moistened; beat 3 minutes at medium speed. By hand, stir in an additional ¾ to 1 cup flour to form a moderately stiff dough.

On floured surface, knead in ¼ to ½ cup flour until dough is smooth and elastic, about 5 minutes. Place dough in greased bowl; cover loosely with plastic wrap and cloth towel. Let rise in warm place (80 to 85°F.) until light and doubled in size, about 1 to 1¼ hours.

Grease cookie sheet. Punch down dough several times to remove all air bubbles. On lightly floured surface, roll dough into 16x12-inch rectangle. Brush with melted margarine. In small bowl, combine cherries, apricots and 2 tablespoons sugar. Sprinkle evenly over dough.

Starting with 12-inch side, roll up tightly, pressing edges to seal. Cut into 12 slices. Reserve 2 end pieces for center. Arrange remaining slices, slightly overlapping, in circle on greased cookie sheet, leaving a 2-inch space in center. Divide each reserved end piece in half; shape into balls. Place balls in center. Cover; let rise in warm place until light and doubled in size, 30 to 40 minutes.

Heat oven to 350°F. Uncover dough. Pinch outer half of each slice to form a petal tip. Bake at 350°F. for 15 to 25 minutes or until very light brown. Loosely cover with foil during last few minutes of baking if necessary to avoid excessive browning. Cool 5 minutes. Remove from cookie sheet; cool on wire rack.

In small bowl, blend powdered sugar and enough milk for desired drizzling consistency. Drizzle over coffee cake. Sprinkle center with ½ to 1 teaspoon grated orange peel.
Yield: 10 to 12 servings.

HIGH ALTITUDE:
Above 3500 Feet: No change.

NUTRITION PER SERVING:
Calories 220; Protein 4g; Carbohydrate 41g; Fat 4g; Sodium 200mg.

COOK'S NOTE

GIFT SUGGESTIONS FOR BREAD BAKERS

- Patterned or foil muffin cups
- Printed or patterned foil for wrapping bread
- Rolls of fancy ribbon or cording
- Roll cozies or covers
- Baskets
- Cast-iron molds in animal or corn shapes
- Canister set or large decorative flour container
- Muffin tins of various sizes
- Bread pans of various sizes
- Bread knife
- Cutting board
- Butter dish
- Butter stamp or curler
- Assortment of jams, jellies or honey

Apricot Cherry Poinsettia Coffee Cake

CHEESE-FILLED TEA RINGS

This delectable ring-shaped coffee cake boasts a lemony cream cheese filling.

COFFEE CAKES
3½ to 4½ cups all purpose flour
¼ cup sugar
1 teaspoon salt
½ teaspoon grated lemon peel
2 pkg. active dry yeast
½ cup milk
½ cup water
¼ cup margarine or butter
2 eggs

FILLING
2 (8-oz.) pkg. cream cheese, softened
½ cup sugar
1 tablespoon lemon juice
½ cup raisins
2 tablespoons margarine or butter, melted

GLAZE
1 cup powdered sugar
3 to 4 teaspoons lemon juice
1 drop yellow food color, if desired

In large bowl, combine 1½ cups flour, ¼ cup sugar, salt, lemon peel and yeast; blend well. In small saucepan, heat milk, water and ¼ cup margarine until very warm (120 to 130°F.). Add warm liquid and eggs to flour mixture. Blend at low speed until moistened; beat 3 minutes at medium speed. By hand, stir in an additional 1½ to 2 cups flour until dough pulls cleanly away from sides of bowl.

On floured surface, knead in ½ to 1 cup flour until dough is smooth and elastic, about 5 minutes. Place dough in greased bowl; cover loosely with plastic wrap and cloth towel. Let rise in warm place (80 to 85°F.) until light and doubled in size, about 45 to 60 minutes.

Grease 2 cookie sheets. In small bowl, combine cream cheese, ½ cup sugar and 1 tablespoon lemon juice; blend at medium speed until smooth. Stir in raisins. Punch down dough several times to remove all air bubbles. Divide dough in half. Roll half of dough into 15x10-inch rectangle; spread half of filling over dough. Starting with 15-inch side, roll up tightly, pressing edges to seal. Place seam side down on greased cookie sheet. Join ends to form ring; pinch ends of dough to seal. With scissors or sharp knife cut from inside edge of ring to within ¼ inch of outer edge of ring, making 16 cuts. Re-

peat with second half of dough. Cover; let rise in warm place until light and doubled in size, about 20 to 30 minutes.

Heat oven to 375°F. Uncover dough. Bake 20 to 25 minutes or until golden brown. Immediately remove from pans; brush with melted margarine. Cool on wire racks. In small bowl, blend glaze ingredients adding enough lemon juice for desired drizzling consistency; drizzle over cooled rings.
Yield: 2 (12-slice) coffee cakes.

HIGH ALTITUDE:
Above 3500 Feet: Decrease first rise time 10 to 15 minutes.

NUTRITION PER SERVING:
Calories 240; Protein 5g; Carbohydrate 31g; Fat 11g; Sodium 180mg.

CASSEROLE DATE BREAD

This date-filled, layered, casserole bread is topped with a crunchy streusel topping.

FILLING
1 cup chopped dates
⅓ cup water
1 tablespoon sugar
¼ cup chopped nuts, if desired

TOPPING
¼ cup sugar
3 tablespoons all purpose flour
⅛ teaspoon nutmeg
2 tablespoons margarine or butter

BREAD
2⅓ cups all purpose flour
2 tablespoons sugar
1 pkg. active dry yeast
½ teaspoon salt
¼ teaspoon nutmeg
1 cup milk
2 tablespoons margarine or butter
1 egg

In small saucepan, cook filling ingredients over medium heat for 3 to 5 minutes or until mixture is thickened; cool. Set aside.

In small bowl, combine all topping ingredients except margarine. Using pastry blender or fork, cut in 2 tablespoons margarine until mixture is crumbly. Set aside.

Grease 1½-quart casserole or 9x5-inch loaf pan. In large bowl, combine 1 cup flour, 2 tablespoons sugar, yeast, salt and ¼ teaspoon nutmeg; blend well. In small saucepan, heat milk and 2 tablespoons margarine until very warm (120 to 130°F.). Add warm liquid and egg to flour mixture. Blend at low speed until moistened; beat 3 minutes at medium speed. By hand, stir in remaining 1⅓ cups flour. Spread half of dough in greased pan. Spread filling evenly over dough. Spread remaining dough evenly on top of filling. Sprinkle topping evenly over dough. Cover loosely with plastic wrap and cloth towel. Let rise in warm place (80 to 85°F.) until ½ inch from top of casserole, about 15 to 25 minutes.

Heat oven to 350°F. Uncover dough. Bake 30 to 35 minutes or until golden brown. Remove from pans immediately by loosening sides and placing loaf on wire rack. Serve warm.

Yield: 16 servings.

HIGH ALTITUDE:
Above 3500 Feet: Bake at 350°F. for 35 to 40 minutes.

NUTRITION PER SERVING:
Calories 190; Protein 4g; Carbohydrate 32g; Fat 5g; Sodium 115mg.

APRICOT DANISH SQUARES

COFFEE CAKE
- 2 pkg. active dry yeast
- ¼ cup warm water
- 3 tablespoons sugar
- ¾ teaspoon salt
- ¼ cup orange juice
- ¼ cup margarine or butter, softened
- ½ teaspoon grated orange peel
- 2 eggs
- 2 to 2½ cups all purpose flour

TOPPING
- ½ cup sliced almonds
- 3 tablespoons margarine or butter
- 2 tablespoons brown sugar
- ½ teaspoon cinnamon
- ¼ teaspoon grated orange peel
- ¾ cup apricot preserves

GLAZE
- ¾ cup powdered sugar
- 1 to 2 tablespoons orange juice

In large bowl, dissolve yeast in warm water (105 to 115°F.). Blend in sugar, salt, ¼ cup orange juice, ¼ cup margarine, ½ teaspoon orange peel and eggs. Add 1 cup flour to yeast mixture. Blend at low speed until moistened; beat 3 minutes at medium speed. By hand, stir in remaining flour to form a soft, sticky batter. Cover loosely with plastic wrap and cloth towel. Let rise in warm place (80 to 85°F.) until light and doubled in size, about 30 to 45 minutes.

Grease 15x10x1-inch baking pan. In small saucepan, cook and stir almonds in 3 tablespoons margarine until almonds are light golden brown. Remove from heat; blend in remaining topping ingredients. Stir down dough; spread in greased pan. Spoon topping over batter; spread gently. Cover; let rise in warm place until light and doubled in size, about 30 minutes.

Heat oven to 350°F. Uncover dough. Bake 25 to 35 minutes or until golden brown. In small bowl, blend powdered sugar and enough orange juice for desired drizzling consistency. Drizzle over warm coffee cake.

Yield: 18 servings.

HIGH ALTITUDE:
Above 3500 Feet: No change.

NUTRITION PER SERVING:
Calories 200; Protein 3g; Carbohydrate 32g; Fat 7g; Sodium 150mg.

COOK'S NOTE

DATES

Dates are oval, glossy, thin-skinned fruits that can range from golden to dark mahogany in color. They grow on date palm trees in California, Arizona and the Middle East.

Fresh dates can be found in large supermarkets and specialty markets from late summer through the winter, with peak supplies in November. Dried dates are available year-round. You'll find them whole (pitted or unpitted) or chopped. Fresh and dried dates are interchangeable in most recipes.

APPLE KUCHEN

Kuchen is a German yeast-raised cake, filled with fruit or cheese. This recipe has a delectable apple filling and sugar-cinnamon topping.

KUCHEN
- 2 to 3 cups all purpose flour
- 1/3 cup sugar
- 1/2 teaspoon salt
- 1 pkg. active dry yeast
- 1/2 cup milk
- 1/4 cup margarine or butter
- 2 eggs
- 4 to 5 medium apples, peeled, cut into 1/2-inch slices (4 cups)

TOPPING
- 3/4 cup sugar
- 3 tablespoons all purpose flour
- 1/2 teaspoon cinnamon
- 2 tablespoons margarine or butter, softened

In large bowl, combine 1 cup flour, 1/3 cup sugar, salt and yeast; blend well. In small saucepan, heat milk and 1/4 cup margarine until very warm (120 to 130°F.). Add warm liquid and eggs to flour mixture. Blend at low speed until moistened; beat 3 minutes at medium speed. By hand, stir in remaining 1 to 2 cups flour until dough pulls cleanly away from sides of bowl.

Generously grease 13x9-inch pan. On floured surface, toss dough lightly until no longer sticky; press in greased pan. Arrange apple slices in rows on top of dough. In small bowl, combine all topping ingredients; blend well. Sprinkle topping evenly over apples. Cover loosely with plastic wrap and cloth towel. Let rise in warm place (80 to 85°F.) until light, about 45 to 60 minutes.

Heat oven to 375°F. Uncover dough. Bake 30 to 40 minutes or until golden brown and apples are tender. Serve warm.

Yield: 15 servings.

TIP:
To reheat, wrap loosely in foil. Heat at 350°F. for 8 to 10 minutes or until warm.

HIGH ALTITUDE:
Above 3500 Feet: No change.

NUTRITION PER SERVING:
Calories 230; Protein 4g; Carbohydrate 41g; Fat 6g; Sodium 140mg.

CHERRY SQUARES

This flavorful coffee cake requires no kneading and is conveniently baked in a 13x9-inch pan.

COFFEE CAKE
- 2 1/2 to 3 cups all purpose flour
- 1/4 cup sugar
- 1 teaspoon salt
- 1 pkg. active dry yeast
- 1/2 cup milk
- 1/2 cup water
- 1/2 cup margarine or butter
- 2 eggs
- 1 (21-oz.) can cherry fruit pie filling

GLAZE
- 1/2 cup powdered sugar
- 1/4 teaspoon almond extract
- 3 to 4 teaspoons milk

In large bowl, combine 1 1/2 cups flour, sugar, salt and yeast; blend well. In small saucepan, heat 1/2 cup milk, water and margarine until very warm (120 to 130°F.). Add warm liquid and eggs to flour mixture. Blend at low speed until moistened; beat 3 minutes at medium speed. By hand, stir in an additional 1 to 1 1/2 cups flour to make a stiff batter. Cover loosely with plastic wrap and cloth towel. Let rise in warm place (80 to 85°F.) until light and doubled in size, about 45 to 60 minutes.

Generously grease 13x9-inch pan. Stir batter; spoon 2/3 of batter into greased pan. Top with cherry filling. Spoon remaining batter by tablespoonfuls over filling. Cover; let rise in warm place until light, about 20 to 30 minutes.

Heat oven to 350°F. Uncover dough. Bake 35 to 40 minutes or until golden brown. In small bowl, blend all glaze ingredients adding anough milk for desired drizzling consistency. Drizzle over warm coffee cake.

Yield: 15 servings.

HIGH ALTITUDE:
Above 3500 Feet: Decrease first rise time to 10 to 15 minutes.

NUTRITION PER SERVING:
Calories 260; Protein 4g; Carbohydrate 44g; Fat 8g; Sodium 230mg.

Cherry Squares

BASIC SWEET ROLL DOUGH

This is a versatile, sweet yeast dough that can be refrigerated overnight or baked the same day. All of the following variations use a half recipe of the dough, so you can make 2 scrumptious kinds at once.

- 6 **to 7 cups all purpose flour**
- ½ **cup sugar**
- 2 **teaspoons salt**
- 2 **pkg. active dry yeast**
- 1 **cup water**
- 1 **cup milk**
- ½ **cup margarine or butter**
- 1 **egg**

In large bowl, combine 2 cups flour, sugar, salt and yeast; blend well. In small saucepan, heat water, milk and margarine until very warm (120 to 130°F.). Add warm liquid and egg to flour mixture. Blend at low speed until moistened; beat 3 minutes at medium speed. By hand, stir in an additional 3 cups flour until dough pulls cleanly away from sides of bowl.

On floured surface, knead in 1 to 2 cups flour until dough is smooth and elastic, about 8 to 10 minutes. Place dough in greased bowl; cover loosely with plastic wrap and cloth towel. Let rise in warm place (80 to 85°F.) until light and doubled in size, about 45 to 60 minutes.

Punch down dough several times to remove all air bubbles. Divide dough in half. Shape and bake each half as directed in the following recipes.

TIP:
To make dough a day ahead, after first rise time, punch down dough, cover and refrigerate dough overnight. Shape dough and let rise as directed in recipe.

HIGH ALTITUDE:
Above 3500 Feet: No change.

ORANGE ROLLS

Serve these delightful rolls at a spring brunch.

ROLLS
- ½ **recipe Basic Sweet Roll Dough (this page)**
- 2 **tablespoons margarine or butter, melted**
- ⅓ **cup sugar**
- 2 **teaspoons grated orange peel**

ORANGE FROSTING
- ½ **cup powdered sugar**
- 1 **tablespoon margarine or butter, softened**
- 1 **to 2 tablespoons orange juice**

Generously grease 18 muffin cups. On lightly floured surface, roll dough into 18x12-inch rectangle. Spread with 2 tablespoons melted margarine. In small bowl, combine sugar and orange peel; blend well. Sprinkle over dough. Starting with 18-inch side, roll up tightly, pressing edges to seal. Cut into 18 slices; place cut side down in greased muffin cups. Cover loosely with greased plastic wrap and cloth towel. Let rise in warm place (80 to 85°F.) until light and almost doubled in size, about 30 to 45 minutes.

Heat oven to 350°F. Uncover dough. Bake 15 to 20 minutes or until golden brown. Immediately remove from pan; cool slightly on wire rack.

In small bowl, combine frosting ingredients, adding enough orange juice for desired spreading consistency. Frost warm rolls. Serve warm.
Yield: 18 rolls.

NUTRITION PER SERVING:
Calories 170; Protein 3g; Carbohydrate 29g; Fat 5g; Sodium 180mg.

Orange Rolls, Kolachy

KOLACHY

These fruit-filled sweet rolls hail from Eastern Europe.

- ½ **recipe Basic Sweet Roll Dough p. 482**
- ½ **cup prepared prune or apricot filling**
- 2 **tablespoons margarine or butter, melted**
  Sugar

Grease 2 large cookie sheets. On lightly floured surface, roll dough into 18x12-inch rectangle. Cut into 24 (3-inch) squares. Place 1 teaspoonful filling in center of each square. Gently pull opposite corners of square over filling. Repeat with other 2 corners, wrapping top corner around kolachy and tucking it under. Place 2 inches apart on greased cookie sheets. Cover loosely with greased plastic wrap and cloth towel. Let rise in warm place (80 to 85°F.) until light and almost doubled in size, about 30 to 45 minutes.

Heat oven to 350°F. Uncover dough. Bake 15 to 20 minutes or until golden brown. Immediately remove from cookie sheets; cool slightly on wire racks. Brush with margarine; roll tops in sugar. Serve warm.
Yield: 24 rolls.

NUTRITION PER SERVING:
Calories 100; Protein 2g; Carbohydrate 16g; Fat 2g; Sodium 115mg.

FRUIT-FILLED SWEET ROLLS

Use your favorite fruit preserve to fill these "thumbprint" rolls.

- ½ **recipe Basic Sweet Roll Dough p. 482**
- 1 **to 2 tablespoons margarine or butter, melted**
- ⅓ **cup any flavor fruit preserves**
- 1 **to 2 tablespoons margarine or butter, melted**
- ¾ **cup powdered sugar**
- 1 **tablespoon margarine or butter, softened**
- ¼ **teaspoon vanilla**
- 1 **to 2 tablespoons milk**

Lightly grease cookie sheets. On lightly floured surface, divide dough into 16 parts. Roll each into 15-inch rope. On greased cookie sheet, starting at center, make a loose swirl with each rope; tuck end under. Cover; let rise in warm place until light and doubled in size, about 20 to 25 minutes.

Heat oven to 375°F. Uncover dough. Carefully brush rolls with 1 to 2 tablespoons melted margarine. Make deep thumbprint in center of each roll; fill with about 1 teaspoon preserves.

Bake at 375°F. for 12 to 16 minutes or until light golden brown. Immediately remove from pans; brush with 1 to 2 tablespoons melted margarine. In small bowl, blend powdered sugar, 1 tablespoon margarine, vanilla and enough milk for desired drizzling consistency. Drizzle over warm rolls. Serve warm.

Yield: 16 rolls.

NUTRITION PER SERVING:
Calories 220; Protein 4g; Carbohydrate 35g; Fat 7g; Sodium 220mg.

CARAMEL NUT STICKY ROLLS

After removing the rolls from the oven, cool them upright 1 minute, then invert onto a wire rack.

- ½ **cup firmly packed brown sugar**
- ½ **cup margarine or butter, softened**
- 2 **tablespoons light corn syrup**
- ¼ **cup chopped nuts**
- ½ **recipe Basic Sweet Roll Dough p. 482**
- 2 **tablespoons margarine or butter, softened**
- ¼ **cup sugar**
- 1 **teaspoon cinnamon**

Generously grease 13x9-inch pan. In small bowl, combine brown sugar, ½ cup margarine and corn syrup; blend well. Drop mixture by spoonfuls into greased pan; spread evenly. Sprinkle with nuts. On lightly floured surface, roll out dough into 18x12-inch rectangle. Spread with 2 tablespoons margarine. In small bowl, combine sugar and cinnamon; blend well. Sprinkle over dough. Starting with 18-inch side, roll up tightly, pressing edges to seal. Cut into 18 slices; place cut side down in greased pan. Cover; let rise in warm place (80 to 85°F.) until light and doubled in size, about 35 to 45 minutes.

Heat oven to 375°F. Uncover dough. Bake 25 to 30 minutes or until deep golden brown. Cool in pan 1 minute; invert onto wire rack. Serve warm.
Yield: 18 rolls.

NUTRITION PER SERVING:
Calories 240; Protein 3g; Carbohydrate 33g; Fat 10g; Sodium 230mg.

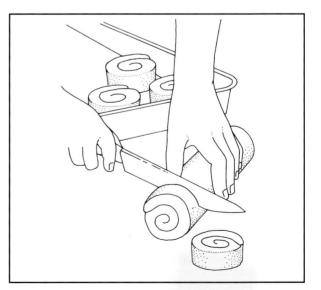

Cutting Cinnamon Rolls

CINNAMON ROLLS

~

Everyone's favorite!

- ½ **recipe Basic Sweet Roll Dough p. 482**
- ¼ **cup margarine or butter, softened**
- ½ **cup sugar or firmly packed brown sugar**
- 2 **teaspoons cinnamon**
- ¾ **cup powdered sugar**
- 1 **tablespoon margarine or butter, softened**
- ¼ **teaspoon vanilla**
- 1 **to 2 tablespoons milk**

Generously grease 13x9-inch pan. On lightly floured surface, roll out dough into 18x12-inch rectangle. Spread with ¼ cup margarine. In small bowl, combine sugar and cinnamon; blend well. Sprinkle over dough. Starting with 18-inch side, roll up tightly, pressing edges to seal. Cut into 18 slices; place slices, cut side down, in greased pan. Cover; let rise in warm place until light and doubled in size, about 35 to 45 minutes.

Heat oven to 375°F. Uncover dough. Bake 25 to 30 minutes or until golden brown. Immediately remove from pan; place on wire racks. In small bowl, blend powdered sugar, 1 tablespoon margarine, vanilla and enough milk for desired drizzling consistency. Drizzle over warm rolls. Serve warm.
Yield: 18 rolls.

NUTRITION PER SERVING:
Calories 200; Protein 3g; Carbohydrate 33g; Fat 6g; Sodium 190mg.

RECIPE MAKE-OVER

LIGHT CINNAMON ROLLS

~

We've kept the flavor, but reduced the fat and calories in these luscious rolls.

ROLLS
- 3½ **cups all purpose flour**
- 1 **teaspoon sugar**
- 1 **teaspoon salt**
- 1 **pkg. fast-acting yeast**
- 1 **cup water**
- 2 **tablespoons reduced-calorie margarine or regular margarine**
- 2 **egg whites**

- 2 **tablespoons apple juice**
- ⅓ **cup sugar or firmly packed brown sugar**
- 2 **teaspoons cinnamon**

GLAZE
- ¼ **cup powdered sugar**
- 2 **to 3 teaspoons skim milk**

In large bowl, combine 1 cup of the flour, 1 teaspoon sugar, salt and yeast; blend well. In small saucepan, heat water and margarine until very warm (120 to 130°F.). Add warm liquid and egg whites to flour mixture. Blend at low speed until moistened; beat 2 minutes at medium speed. By hand, stir in an additional 1¾ cups flour until dough pulls cleanly away from sides of bowl. On floured surface, knead in ¾ cup flour until dough is smooth and elastic, about 5 minutes. Cover with large bowl; let rest 5 minutes.

Grease two 9 or 8-inch square pans. On lightly floured surface, roll dough into 18x10-inch rectangle. Brush with apple juice. In small bowl, combine ⅓ cup sugar and cinnamon; mix well. Sprinkle evenly over dough. Starting with 18-inch side, roll up tightly, pressing edges to seal. Cut into 18 slices; place cut side down in greased pans. Cover; let rise in warm place (80 to 85°F.) until light and doubled in size, about 30 minutes.

Heat oven to 375°F. Uncover dough. Bake 25 to 30 minutes or until light golden brown. In small bowl, blend powdered sugar and enough milk for desired glaze consistency. Drizzle over warm rolls. Serve warm.
Yield: 18 rolls.

HIGH ALTITUDE:
Above 3500 Feet: No change.

NUTRITION PER SERVING:
Calories 120; Protein 3g; Carbohydrate 25g; Fat 1g; Sodium 135mg.

WHOLE WHEAT CARAMEL ROLLS

These sensational whole wheat rolls form their own caramel topping as they bake.

- 1 to 2 cups all purpose flour
- 1 cup whole wheat flour
- 3 tablespoons sugar
- 1 teaspoon salt
- 1 pkg. active dry yeast
- ¾ cup milk
- ¼ cup water
- 2 tablespoons shortening
- 1 cup firmly packed brown sugar
- ⅓ cup margarine or butter, melted
- ½ cup chopped nuts

In large bowl, combine ½ cup all purpose flour, whole wheat flour, sugar, salt and yeast; blend well. In small saucepan, heat milk, water and shortening until very warm (120 to 130°F.). Add warm liquid to flour mixture. Stir by hand until moistened. Stir in an additional ¼ to ¾ cup all purpose flour to form a stiff dough.

On floured surface, knead in ¼ to ¾ cup all purpose flour until dough is smooth and elastic, about 5 minutes. Place dough in greased bowl; cover loosely with plastic wrap and cloth towel. Let rise in warm place (80 to 85°F.) until light and doubled in size, about 1¼ hours.

Grease 9-inch square pan. Punch down dough several times to remove all air bubbles. On lightly floured surface, roll into 16x12-inch rectangle. In small bowl, combine brown sugar and margarine; blend well. Spread evenly over dough; sprinkle with nuts. Starting with 16-inch side, roll up tightly, pressing edge to seal. Cut into 16 slices; place cut side down in greased pan. Cover; let rise in warm place until light and doubled in size, about 45 to 60 minutes.

Heat oven to 350°F. Uncover dough. Bake 25 to 30 minutes or until golden brown. Cool 2 minutes; turn onto serving plate or foil.
Yield: 16 rolls.

HIGH ALTITUDE :
Above 3500 Feet: Bake at 375°F. for 25 to 30 minutes.

NUTRITION PER SERVING:
Calories 210; Protein 3g; Carbohydrate 31g; Fat 8g; Sodium 190mg.

ONE-RISE CARAMEL ROLLS

Wonderfully gooey through and through, these rolls are at their best served warm.

TOPPING
- 1 cup firmly packed brown sugar
- 1 cup whipping cream (do not substitute)

ROLLS
- 3½ cups all purpose flour
- ¼ cup sugar
- 1 teaspoon salt
- 1 pkg. active dry yeast
- 1 cup water
- 2 tablespoons margarine or butter
- 1 egg

FILLING
- ½ cup sugar
- 2 teaspoons cinnamon
- ½ cup margarine or butter, softened

In ungreased 13x9-inch pan, combine topping ingredients. Set aside.

In large bowl, combine 1½ cups flour, ¼ cup sugar, salt and yeast; blend well. In small saucepan, heat water and 2 tablespoons margarine until very warm (120 to 130°F.). Add warm liquid and egg to flour mixture. Blend at low speed until moistened; beat 3 minutes at medium speed. By hand, stir in remaining 2 cups flour to form a stiff dough.

On floured surface, knead 2 to 3 minutes. Press or roll dough into 15x7-inch rectangle. In small bowl, combine filling ingredients; spread over dough. Starting with 15-inch side, roll up tightly, pressing edges to seal. Cut into 15 rolls; place, cut side down, over topping in pan. Cover; let rise in warm place (80 to 85°F.) until light and doubled in size, about 35 to 45 minutes.

Heat oven to 400°F. Uncover dough. Bake 20 to 25 minutes or until golden brown. Cool in pan 10 to 15 minutes. Invert onto serving platter or foil.
Yield: 15 rolls.

HIGH ALTITUDE:
Above 3500 Feet: No change.

NUTRITION PER SERVING:
Calories 340; Protein 5g; Carbohydrate 49g; Fat 14g; Sodium 250mg.

Jumbo Pineapple Caramel Rolls

Be ready for a pineapple and caramel treat when you make these giant sweet rolls.

ROLLS
- 1 (8-oz.) can crushed pineapple in its own juice, drained, reserving liquid
  Water
- 2 tablespoons margarine or butter
- 2½ to 3 cups all purpose flour
- 1 teaspoon salt
- 1 pkg. active dry yeast
- 1 egg
- 1 cup mashed potato flakes

TOPPING
- ¼ cup margarine or butter
- ½ cup firmly packed brown sugar
- 2 tablespoons corn syrup
  Reserved crushed pineapple
- ½ cup coconut, if desired

FILLING
- 2 tablespoons margarine or butter, softened
- ¼ cup firmly packed brown sugar
- ½ teaspoon cinnamon

Measure out ⅓ cup pineapple liquid; add water to measure 1¼ cups. Reserve crushed pineapple. In small saucepan, heat liquid and 2 tablespoons margarine until very warm (120 to 130°F.). In large bowl, combine 1½ cups flour, salt and yeast. Add warm liquid and egg. Blend at low speed until moistened; beat 3 minutes at medium speed. Add potato flakes, beating just until moistened. By hand, stir in an additional ½ to ¾ cup flour until dough pulls cleanly away from sides of bowl.

On floured surface, knead in ½ to ¾ cup flour until dough is smooth and elastic, about 5 minutes. Place dough in greased bowl; cover loosely with plastic wrap and cloth towel. Let rise in warm place (80 to 85°F.) until light and doubled in size, about 45 to 60 minutes.

To prepare topping, melt ¼ cup margarine in 13x9-inch pan. Stir in remaining topping ingredients. Set aside.

Punch down dough. On floured surface, roll dough into 16x10-inch rectangle. Spread with 2 tablespoons margarine. In small bowl, combine ¼ cup brown sugar and cinnamon; sprinkle evenly over dough. Starting with 16-inch side, roll up tightly, pressing edges to seal. Cut into 12 slices; place, cut side down, over topping in pan. Cover; let rise in warm place until doubled in size, about 30 to 45 minutes.

Heat oven to 375°F. Uncover dough. Bake 25 to 30 minutes or until golden brown. Immediately invert onto serving platter or foil.
Yield: 12 rolls.

HIGH ALTITUDE:
Above 3500 Feet: No change.

NUTRITION PER SERVING:
Calories 300; Protein 5g; Carbohydrate 48g; Fat 10g; Sodium 280mg.

COOK'S NOTE

BUTTER BALLS
Using the large end of a melon baller dipped in hot water, cut balls out of hard butter, then refrigerate them. For best results, use a 1-pound block of butter.

QUICK PRALINE ROLLS

Yeast and baking powder give these rolls a biscuit-like texture.

FILLING
- ¾ **cup firmly packed brown sugar**
- ⅓ **cup margarine or butter, softened**
- ½ **cup chopped walnuts**

ROLLS
- 1¾ **to 2¾ cups all purpose flour**
- 2 **tablespoons sugar**
- 1 **teaspoon baking powder**
- ½ **teaspoon salt**
- 1 **pkg. active dry yeast**
- ⅓ **cup milk**
- ¼ **cup water**
- ⅓ **cup margarine or butter**
- 1 **egg**
- ¼ **cup chopped walnuts**

In small bowl, combine brown sugar and ⅓ cup margarine; beat until light and fluffy. Stir in ½ cup nuts; set aside.

In large bowl, combine 1 cup flour, sugar, baking powder, salt and yeast; blend well. In small saucepan, heat milk, water and ⅓ cup margarine until very warm (120 to 130°F.). Add warm liquid and egg to flour mixture. Blend at low speed until moistened; beat 3 minutes at medium speed. By hand, stir in remaining ¾ to 1¾ cups flour to form a soft dough.

Grease cookie sheet. On floured surface, toss dough until no longer sticky. Roll into 15x10-inch rectangle; spread with half of filling mixture. Starting with 15-inch side, roll up tightly, pressing edges to seal. Cut into 15 slices. Place cut side down on greased cookie sheet; flatten to ½ inch. Spread tops of rolls with remaining filling. Sprinkle with ¼ cup nuts. Cover loosely with greased plastic wrap and cloth towel. Let rise in warm place (80 to 85°F.) until light, about 45 minutes.

Heat oven to 400°F. Uncover dough. Bake 10 to 12 minutes or until light golden brown. Immediately remove from cookie sheet; place on wire racks. Serve warm.
Yield: 15 rolls.

HIGH ALTITUDE :
Above 3500 Feet: No change.

NUTRITION PER SERVING:
Calories 260; Protein 4g; Carbohydrate 32g; Fat 13g; Sodium 200mg.

ORANGE GLORY ROLLS

These scrumptious marmalade-topped rolls will melt in your mouth!

TOPPING
- ¾ **cup orange marmalade**
- 1 **tablespoon margarine or butter**

ROLLS
- 4¼ **to 5¼ cups all purpose flour**
- ½ **cup sugar**
- 1 **teaspoon salt**
- 2 **pkg. active dry yeast**
- 1 **cup milk**
- ½ **cup water**
- ¼ **cup margarine or butter**
- 2 **eggs**
- 2 **tablespoons margarine or butter, softened**

Generously grease 24 muffin cups. In small saucepan, combine topping ingredients. Cook over low heat until melted, stirring frequently. Place heaping teaspoonful of topping in each greased muffin cup; set aside.

In large bowl, combine 1½ cups flour, sugar, salt and yeast; blend well. In small saucepan, heat milk, water and ¼ cup margarine until very warm (120 to 130°F.). Add warm liquid and eggs to flour mixture. Blend at low speed until moistened; beat 2 minutes at medium speed. By hand, stir in remaining 2¾ to 3¾ cups flour to form a stiff dough.

On floured surface, toss dough until no longer sticky. Divide dough in half. Roll half into 12x10-inch rectangle; spread with 1 tablespoon of the softened margarine. Starting with 12-inch side, roll up tightly, pressing edges to seal. Cut into 12 slices; place cut side down over marmalade mixture in muffin cups. Repeat with second half of dough. Cover loosely with plastic wrap and cloth towel. Let rise in warm place (80 to 85°F.) until light and doubled in size, about 35 to 45 minutes.

Heat oven to 375°F. Uncover dough. Bake 15 to 20 minutes or until light golden brown. (Place foil or cookie sheet on rack below pan during baking to guard against spills.) Immediately invert onto foil or waxed paper.
Yield: 24 rolls.

HIGH ALTITUDE :
Above 3500 Feet: No change.

NUTRITION PER SERVING:
Calories 180; Protein 4g; Carbohydrate 33g; Fat 4g; Sodium 140mg.

GLAZED CHEESECAKE ROLLS

These feather-light yeast rolls have a lemon-flavored cheesecake filling.

ROLLS
- 1 pkg. active dry yeast
- ¼ cup warm water
- 1 teaspoon sugar
- 3½ to 4½ cups all purpose flour
- ⅓ cup sugar
- ½ teaspoon salt
- ½ cup water
- ½ cup margarine or butter
- 2 eggs
- 2 tablespoons margarine or butter, melted

FILLING
- 2 tablespoons sugar
- 1 tablespoon all purpose flour
- ¼ cup dairy sour cream
- 1 (3-oz.) pkg. cream cheese, softened
- 1 tablespoon lemon juice
- ¼ teaspoon vanilla
- 1 egg white

GLAZE
- 2 cups powdered sugar
- 1 tablespoon margarine or butter, softened
- ½ teaspoon vanilla
- 3 to 4 tablespoons milk

Dissolve yeast in ¼ cup warm water (105 to 115°F.); add 1 teaspoon sugar. Let stand 10 minutes. In large bowl, blend 1½ cups flour, ⅓ cup sugar and salt. In small saucepan, heat ½ cup water and ½ cup margarine until very warm (120 to 130°F.). Add warm liquid, yeast mixture and eggs to flour mixture. Blend at low speed until moistened; beat 2 minutes at medium speed. By hand, stir in an additional 1 to 1½ cups flour to form a soft, sticky batter. Cover loosely with plastic wrap and cloth towel. Let rise in warm place (80 to 85°F.) until light and doubled in size, about 1 hour.

On floured surface, knead in 1 to 1½ cups flour until dough is smooth and elastic, about 5 minutes.

Grease 2 cookie sheets. With floured hands, divide dough into 16 parts; shape each into smooth ball. Place 3 inches apart on greased cookie sheets. Brush with melted margarine. Cover; let rise in warm place until light and doubled in size, about 1 hour.

Heat oven to 375°F. In small bowl, blend all filling ingredients until smooth. Uncover dough. With thumb, make 1½-inch deep indentation in center of each roll; fill with 1 tablespoon filling.

Bake at 375°F. for 10 to 15 minutes or until light golden brown. Immediately remove from cookie sheets; cool slightly on wire racks. In small bowl, combine all glaze ingredients, adding enough milk for desired drizzling consistency. Drizzle glaze over warm rolls. Store in refrigerator.

Yield: 16 rolls.

HIGH ALTITUDE:
Above 3500 Feet: No change.

NUTRITION PER SERVING:
Calories 290; Protein 5g; Carbohydrate 40g; Fat 12g; Sodium 190mg.

COOK'S NOTES

ENRICHED FLOUR

Flour is enriched to restore the natural iron and B vitamins that are lost in the milling process. Enrichment causes no change in the flour's taste, color, texture, quality or caloric value.

RASPBERRY SWEET ROLLS

What could be more inviting than a tender sweet roll filled with preserves, then topped with a creamy glaze?

ROLLS
3½ to 4 cups all purpose flour
½ cup sugar
1 teaspoon salt
2 pkg. active dry yeast
1 cup milk
½ cup margarine or butter
2 eggs

TOPPING
¼ cup margarine or butter, melted
½ cup red raspberry preserves

GLAZE
1 cup powdered sugar
2 to 3 tablespoons milk

In large bowl, combine 1½ cups flour, sugar, salt and yeast; blend well. In small saucepan, heat 1 cup milk and ½ cup margarine until very warm (120 to 130°F.). Add warm liquid and eggs to flour mixture. Blend at low speed until moistened; beat 3 minutes at medium speed. By hand, stir in an additional 1¾ to 2 cups flour until dough pulls cleanly away from sides of bowl.

On floured surface, knead in ¼ to ½ cup flour until dough is smooth and elastic, about 3 to 5 minutes. Place dough in greased bowl; cover loosely with plastic wrap and cloth towel. Let rise in warm place (80 to 85°F.) until light and doubled in size, about 45 to 60 minutes.

Grease 3 cookie sheets. Punch down dough several times to remove all air bubbles. Turn dough onto lightly floured surface; divide into 24 pieces. Roll each piece into 15-inch rope. On greased cookie sheet, loosely coil each rope into a circle, tucking ends under. Cover; let rise in warm place until light and doubled in size, about 15 to 20 minutes.

Heat oven to 350°F. Uncover dough. Carefully brush rolls with half of the melted margarine. Make deep thumbprint in center of each roll; fill with 1 teaspoon preserves.

Bake at 350°F. for 10 to 20 minutes or until golden brown. Immediately remove from pan; brush a second time with half of the melted margarine. Cool slightly on wire rack.

In small bowl, blend powdered sugar and enough milk for desired drizzling consistency. Drizzle over warm rolls.
Yield: 24 rolls.

HIGH ALTITUDE:
Above 3500 Feet: No change.

NUTRITION PER SERVING:
Calories 190; Protein 3g; Carbohydrate 30g; Fat 7g; Sodium 170mg.

Raspberry Sweet Rolls

Sugar 'n Spice Puffs

The delicious taste of a raised doughnut comes to mind when you eat this tender fluffy sweet roll.

ROLLS

3¼ to 3½ cups all purpose flour
1 cup rolled oats
½ cup sugar
1¼ teaspoons salt
1 teaspoon grated orange peel
1 pkg. active dry yeast
1 cup milk
½ cup water
¼ cup dairy sour cream
3 tablespoons shortening or oil
1 egg

TOPPING

¾ cup sugar
2 teaspoons cinnamon
½ cup margarine or butter, melted

In large bowl, combine 1½ cups flour, ½ cup oats, ¼ cup sugar, salt, orange peel and yeast; blend well. In medium saucepan, heat milk, water, sour cream and shortening until very warm (120 to 130°F.). Add warm liquid and egg to flour mixture. Blend at low speed until moistened; beat 3 minutes at medium speed. By hand, stir in ½ cup oats and 1½ cups flour to form a stiff dough.

On floured surface, knead in remaining ¼ to ½ cup flour until smooth and elastic, about 5 minutes. Place in greased bowl; cover loosely with plastic wrap and cloth towel. Let rise in warm place (80 to 85°F.) until light and doubled in size, about 1 hour.

Generously grease 18 muffin cups. Punch down dough; shape into ball. Divide dough into 18 pieces; shape into balls. Place in greased muffin cups. Cover; let rise in warm place until light and doubled in size, about 45 minutes.

Heat oven to 375°F. Uncover dough. Bake 15 to 20 minutes or until golden brown. Cool 5 minutes; remove from muffin cups. In small bowl, combine ¾ cup sugar and cinnamon. Roll warm rolls in melted margarine, then in cinnamon-sugar mixture. **Yield: 18 rolls.**

HIGH ALTITUDE :
Above 3500 Feet: No change.

NUTRITION PER SERVING:
Calories 240; Protein 5g; Carbohydrate 35g; Fat 9g; Sodium 225mg.

Overnight Mini Sweet Rolls

This recipe makes smaller size rolls so guests can try both flavors.

ROLLS

3 to 3¾ cups all purpose flour
¼ cup sugar
½ teaspoon salt
1 pkg. active dry yeast
1 cup milk
¼ cup margarine or butter
1 egg

BLUEBERRY FILLING

¼ cup all purpose flour
¼ cup sugar
½ teaspoon cinnamon
3 tablespoons margarine or butter
¾ cup fresh blueberries

CHERRY FILLING

1 (3½-oz.) tube almond paste
1 tablespoon margarine or butter, softened
1 tablespoon light corn syrup
1 (6-oz.) jar maraschino cherries, drained, halved

In large bowl, combine 1½ cups flour, ¼ cup sugar, salt and yeast; blend well. In small saucepan, heat milk and ¼ cup margarine until very warm (120 to 130°F.). Add warm liquid and egg to flour mixture. Blend at low speed until moistened; beat 2 minutes at medium speed. By hand, stir in an additional 1¼ to 1¾ cups flour until dough pulls cleanly away from sides of bowl.

On floured surface, knead in ¼ to ½ cup flour until dough is smooth and elastic, about 5 minutes. Place in greased bowl; cover loosely with plastic wrap and cloth towel. Let rise in warm place (80 to 85°F.) until light and doubled in size, about 45 minutes.

Grease two 9-inch round pans. Punch down dough several times to remove all air bubbles. Divide dough in half. On lightly floured surface, roll out half of dough into 16x6-inch rectangle. In small bowl, combine all blueberry filling ingredients except blueberries; mix well. Sprinkle evenly over dough; top with blueberries. Starting with 16-inch side, roll up tightly, pressing edges to seal. Cut into 16 slices; place cut side down in 1 greased pan. Cover with greased plastic wrap; refrigerate overnight.

On lightly floured surface, roll out remaining half of dough into 16x6-inch rectangle. In small bowl, combine all cherry filling ingredients except cherries; beat well. Spread evenly over dough; top with cherries. Starting with 16-inch side, roll up tightly, pressing edges to seal. Cut into 16 slices; place cut side down in other greased pan. Cover with greased plastic wrap; refrigerate overnight.

When ready to bake, let rolls stand at room temperature 1 hour. Heat oven to 375°F. Uncover rolls. Bake 22 to 27 minutes or until deep golden brown. Immediately remove from pan; cool on wire racks. If desired, drizzle with powdered sugar glaze.* **Yield: 32 rolls.**

TIP:
* To make powdered sugar glaze, in small bowl combine 1 cup powdered sugar and enough water for desired drizzling consistency (about 4 to 6 teaspoons); blend well.

HIGH ALTITUDE:
Above 3500 Feet: No change.

NUTRITION PER SERVING:
Calories 130; Protein 3g; Carbohydrate 19g; Fat 4g; Sodium 65mg.

PEANUT BUTTER AND JELLY ROLLS

A peanut lover's dream — chopped peanuts are swirled into a peanut butter dough and topped with peanut butter frosting.

ROLLS
4½ to 5 cups all purpose flour
  ½ cup sugar
  2 teaspoons salt
  2 pkg. active dry yeast
  2 cups milk
  ½ cup peanut butter

FILLING
  1 cup chopped peanuts
  6 tablespoons grape jelly

GLAZE
  1 cup powdered sugar
  2 tablespoons peanut butter
  1 to 2 tablespoons milk

In large bowl, combine 2 cups flour, sugar, salt and yeast; blend well. In small saucepan, heat 2 cups milk until very warm (120 to 130°F.). Add warm milk and ½ cup peanut butter to flour mixture. Blend at low speed until moistened; beat 3 minutes at medium speed. By hand, stir in an additional 2 to 2¼ cups flour until dough pulls cleanly away from sides of bowl.

On floured surface, knead in ½ to ¾ cup flour until dough is smooth and elastic, about 5 minutes. Place dough in greased bowl; cover loosely with plastic wrap and cloth towel. Let rise in warm place (80 to 85°F.) until light and doubled in size, about 1 hour.

Grease two 9-inch square or round cake pans. Punch down dough several times to remove all air bubbles. Shape into ball. Roll into 18x12-inch rectangle; sprinkle with peanuts. Starting with 18-inch side, roll up tightly, pressing edges to seal. Cut into 18 slices; place in greased pans. Make deep thumbprint in center of each roll; fill each with 1 teaspoon grape jelly. Cover; let rise in warm place until light and doubled in size, about 30 to 45 minutes.

Heat oven to 350°F. Uncover dough. Bake 25 to 35 minutes or until golden brown. Cool in pans about 5 minutes. Carefully remove from pans; cool on wire racks.

In small bowl, blend all glaze ingredients, adding enough milk for desired drizzling consistency. Drizzle over rolls. **Yield: 18 rolls.**

HIGH ALTITUDE:
Above 3500 Feet: No change.

NUTRITION PER SERVING:
Calories 320; Protein 10g; Carbohydrate 48g; Fat 10g; Sodium 305mg.

BEEHIVE BUNS

These honey-flavored raisin buns are shaped like miniature beehives. Serve them warm with butter.

ROLLS
- 2 cups whole wheat flour
- 2 pkg. active dry yeast
- 1 teaspoon salt
- 1 cup raisins
- 1 cup very hot water
- 1 cup milk
- ⅓ cup honey
- ⅓ cup margarine or butter
- 2 eggs
- 2 to 3¼ cups all purpose flour

GLAZE
- 3 tablespoons honey
- 3 tablespoons margarine or butter
- 1¼ cups powdered sugar
- 1 teaspoon vanilla

In large bowl, combine whole wheat flour, yeast and salt; set aside. Cover raisins with water for 1 minute; drain. In small saucepan, heat milk, ⅓ cup honey and ⅓ cup margarine until very warm (120 to 130°F.). Add warm mixture to flour mixture. Beat in eggs 1 at a time; stir in drained raisins. By hand, stir in 1½ to 2 cups of the all purpose flour until dough pulls cleanly away from sides of bowl.

On floured surface, knead in remaining ½ to 1¼ cups of the all purpose flour until dough is smooth and elastic, about 5 minutes. Place dough in greased bowl; cover loosely with plastic wrap and cloth towel. Let rise in warm place (80 to 85°F.) until light and doubled in size, about 45 to 60 minutes.

Grease 24 muffin cups. Punch down dough several times to remove all air bubbles. Divide dough into 24 pieces. (Cover dough pieces with inverted bowl to prevent drying out.) Using 1 piece of dough at a time, roll to form 10 to 12-inch rope. Coil rope in muffin cup, tucking end into top center to form beehive shape. Repeat with remaining pieces. Cover; let rise in warm place until light and doubled in size, about 30 to 45 minutes.

Heat oven to 350°F. Uncover dough. Bake 15 to 20 minutes or until golden brown. Immediately remove from muffin cups; place on wire racks. In small saucepan, heat 3 tablespoons each honey and margarine. Stir in powdered sugar and vanilla until smooth. Drizzle over warm rolls.
Yield: 24 rolls.

HIGH ALTITUDE:
Above 3500 Feet: No change.

NUTRITION PER SERVING:
Calories 210; Protein 4g; Carbohydrate 37g; Fat 5g; Sodium 150mg.

STREUSEL PUMPKIN SWEET ROLLS

For convenience, follow our easy tip to prepare these rolls, refrigerate overnight, then pop them in the oven in the morning.

ROLLS
- 4¾ to 5¾ cups all purpose flour
- ½ cup sugar
- 2 teaspoons grated lemon peel
- 1½ teaspoons salt
- 1 pkg. active dry yeast
- 1¼ cups milk
- 1 cup canned pumpkin
- ½ cup margarine or butter

CRUMB TOPPING
- 1½ cups all purpose flour
- 1 cup firmly packed brown sugar
- 1 teaspoon cinnamon
- ½ teaspoon allspice
- ¾ cup margarine or butter
- ½ cup chopped nuts

GLAZE
- 1 cup powdered sugar
- ½ teaspoon vanilla
- 1 to 2 tablespoons milk

In large bowl, combine 1½ cups flour, sugar, lemon peel, salt and yeast; mix well. In small saucepan, heat 1¼ cups milk, pumpkin and ½ cup margarine until very warm (120 to 130°F.). Add warm mixture to flour mixture. Blend at low speed until moistened; beat 3 minutes at medium speed. By hand, stir in an additional 2½ to 3 cups flour until dough pulls cleanly away from sides of bowl.

Streusel Pumpkin Sweet Rolls

On floured surface, knead in ¾ to 1¼ cups flour until dough is smooth and elastic, about 5 to 8 minutes. Place dough in greased bowl; cover loosely with plastic wrap and cloth towel. Let rise in warm place (80 to 85°F.) until light and doubled in size, about 1 hour.

Grease 15x10x1-inch baking pan.* In medium bowl, combine 1½ cups flour, brown sugar, cinnamon and allspice. With fork or pastry blender, cut in ¾ cup margarine until mixture is crumbly. Punch dough down several times to remove all air bubbles. On lightly floured surface, roll into 20x15-inch rectangle. Spoon 2½ cups of the crumb topping evenly over dough; sprinkle with nuts. Starting with 20-inch side, roll up tightly, pressing edges to seal. Cut into 20 slices; place cut side down in greased pan. Cover loosely with plastic wrap and cloth towel.** Let rise in warm place until light and doubled in size, about 45 minutes.

Heat oven to 350°F. Uncover dough. Sprinkle with remaining crumb topping. Bake at 350°F. for 35 to 50 minutes or until golden brown.

In small bowl, blend all glaze ingredients, adding enough milk for desired drizzling consistency. Drizzle over warm rolls.

Yield: 20 rolls.

TIPS:
* Rolls can be baked in two 13x9-inch baking pans. Decrease baking time to 25 to 35 minutes. Place on separate oven racks and stagger for more even heat distribution.

** At this point, dough can be refrigerated overnight. Dough may rise in the refrigerator. If necessary, let dough stand at room temperature until almost double original size. Bake as directed above.

HIGH ALTITUDE :
Above 3500 Feet: No change.

NUTRITION PER SERVING:
Calories 380; Protein 6g; Carbohydrate 59g; Fat 14g; Sodium 310mg.

DELICIOUS HOT CROSS BUNS

These cinnamon-flavored, currant-filled rolls had their origin in England and were traditionally served on Good Friday.

ROLLS
- 4 to 4½ **cups all purpose flour**
- ⅓ **cup sugar**
- ½ **teaspoon salt**
- ½ **teaspoon cinnamon**
- 2 **pkg. active dry yeast**
- ¾ **cup milk**
- ½ **cup oil**
- 3 **eggs**
- ½ **cup dried currants or raisins**
- 1 **egg white, beaten**

FROSTING*
- 1½ **cups powdered sugar**
- 2 **tablespoons margarine or butter, softened**
- ½ **teaspoon vanilla**
- 1 to 2 **tablespoons milk**

In large bowl, combine 1½ cups flour, sugar, salt, cinnamon and yeast; blend well. In small saucepan, heat ¾ cup milk and oil until very warm (120 to 130°F.). Add warm liquid and eggs to flour mixture. Blend at low speed until moistened; beat 3 minutes at medium speed. By hand, stir in currants and an additional 2¼ to 2½ cups flour until dough pulls cleanly away from sides of bowl.

On floured surface, knead in ¼ to ½ cup flour until dough is smooth and elastic, about 5 minutes. Place dough in greased bowl; cover loosely with plastic wrap and cloth towel. Let rise in warm place (80 to 85°F.) until light and doubled in size, about 30 to 45 minutes.

Grease 15x10x1-inch baking pan. Punch down dough several times to remove all air bubbles. Divide dough into 35 parts; shape into balls. Place in greased pan; brush with egg white. Cover; let rise in warm place until light and doubled in size, about 20 to 30 minutes.

Heat oven to 375°F. Uncover dough. Bake 15 to 20 minutes or until golden brown. Cool slightly. In small bowl, combine all frosting ingredients, adding enough milk for desired piping consistency; beat well. Using decorating bag or spoon, make crosses on each roll.

Yield: 35 rolls.

TIP:
* If frosting is not desired, before brushing with egg white, carefully cut cross on each roll with sharp knife.

HIGH ALTITUDE:
Above 3500 Feet: No change.

NUTRITION PER SERVING:
Calories 140; Protein 3g; Carbohydrate 21g; Fat 4g; Sodium 50mg.

COOK'S NOTE

RAISINS AND DRIED CURRANTS

Raisins are grapes that are harvested and sun-dried for 3 to 5 weeks. Golden raisins, known for their amber color and moist texture, are not sun-dried and are sent for processing immediately after harvest. Golden raisins are dipped in hot water and treated with sulfur dioxide to retain color, then dried in dehydrators. Most raisins come from Thompson seedless grapes, but Muscat and Sultana varieties are also used. Most grapes for raisins are grown in California.

Dried currants resemble tiny, dark raisins. They are dried, seedless Zante grapes. Dried currants are often used interchanegably with raisins.

LUCIA BUNS

These delicately saffron-flavored rolls are served in Sweden on December 13, St. Lucia Day.

ROLLS
- ¾ **cup milk**
- ½ **teaspoon dried saffron threads or cardamom**
- 1 **pkg. active dry yeast**
- ¼ **cup warm water**
- 3¾ **to 4¾ cups all purpose flour**
- ½ **cup margarine or butter, softened**
- ½ **cup sugar**
- 1 **teaspoon salt**
- 2 **eggs**
- 40 **raisins (2 tablespoons)**

GLAZE
- 1 **egg**
- 1 **tablespoon water**

In small saucepan, heat milk and saffron until milk is bright yellow; cool. In large bowl, dissolve yeast in warm water (105 to 115°F.). Strain milk into yeast mixture. Add 1½ cups flour, margarine, sugar, salt and 2 eggs to yeast mixture. Blend at low speed until moistened; beat 3 minutes at medium speed. By hand, stir in an additional 2 to 2¾ cups flour until dough pulls cleanly away from sides of bowl.

On floured surface, knead in ¼ to ½ cup flour until dough is smooth and elastic, about 5 minutes. Place dough in greased bowl; cover loosely with plastic wrap and cloth towel. Let rise in warm place (80 to 85°F.) until light, about 2 hours. (Dough does not double in size.)

Lightly grease 2 cookie sheets. Punch down dough several times to remove all air bubbles. Divide dough into 20 equal pieces. Roll each piece to make a 10-inch rope; shape into "S." Repeat with remaining dough. Place on greased cookie sheets. Cover with greased plastic wrap and cloth towel. Let rise in warm place until light, about 30 to 45 minutes.

Heat oven to 375°F. Uncover dough. Firmly press 1 raisin into center of each coil of each "S." Combine glaze ingredients; brush carefully over rolls. Bake at 375°F. for 10 to 15 minutes or until light golden brown. Immediately remove from cookie sheets; cool on wire racks.
Yield: 20 rolls.

HIGH ALTITUDE :
Above 3500 Feet: No change.

NUTRITION PER SERVING:
Calories 180; Protein 4g; Carbohydrate 28g; Fat 6g; Sodium 180mg.

VARIATION:

LUCIA COFFEE CAKES: Prepare dough as directed above. When ready to shape dough, divide dough in half. Cut each half into 9 equal pieces. Roll each piece into a 7-inch rope. Curl one end of each of 8 of the ropes into a coil. Arrange in a sunburst pattern on greased cookie sheet, fitting the uncurled ends together. Coil the 9th rope and place in the center of sunburst. Repeat with remaining half of dough. Cover with greased plastic wrap and cloth towel. Let rise in warm place until light, about 1 hour. Heat oven to 375°F. Firmly press 1 raisin in center of each coil. Combine glaze ingredients; brush carefully over coffee cakes. Bake at 375°F. for 15 to 20 minutes or until light golden brown. Immediately remove from cookie sheets; cool on wire racks.
Yield: 2 (16-slice) coffee cakes.

No-Knead Water-Rising Twists

This recipe was a winner in the 1st Pillsbury BAKE-OFF® Contest in 1949. In the original recipe, the dough was wrapped in a towel and placed in water to rise. We've streamlined the recipe with conventional rising directions.

2½ to 3½ cups all purpose flour
½ cup sugar
1 teaspoon salt
1 pkg. active dry yeast
¾ cup milk
½ cup margarine or butter
1 teaspoon vanilla
2 eggs
½ cup chopped nuts
½ cup sugar
1 teaspoon cinnamon

In large bowl, combine 1 cup flour, ½ cup sugar, salt and yeast; blend well. In small saucepan, heat milk and margarine until very warm (120 to 130°F.). Add warm liquid, vanilla and eggs to flour mixture. Blend at low speed until moistened; beat 2 minutes at medium speed. By hand, stir in remaining 1½ to 2½ cups flour to form a soft dough. Cover loosely with plastic wrap and cloth towel. Let rise in warm place (80 to 85°F.) until light and doubled in size, about 30 to 40 minutes. (Dough will be sticky.)

Grease 2 large cookie sheets. In small bowl, combine nuts, ½ cup sugar and cinnamon; blend well. Drop about ¼ cup dough into nut-sugar mixture; thoroughly coat. Stretch dough to about 8 inches in length; twist into desired shape. Place on greased cookie sheet. Repeat with remaining dough. Cover; let rise in warm place, about 15 minutes.

Heat oven to 375°F. Uncover dough. Bake 8 to 16 minutes or until light golden brown. Immediately remove from cookie sheet; cool on wire racks. Serve warm.
Yield: 12 rolls.

HIGH ALTITUDE :
Above 3500 Feet: No change.

NUTRITION PER SERVING:
Calories 320; Protein 6g; Carbohydrate 47g; Fat 12g; Sodium 290mg.

Apple Cinnamon Twists

Raisins, nuts and fresh apples are featured in this twisted sweet roll.

ROLLS
4½ to 5½ cups all purpose flour
1½ teaspoons salt
2 pkg. active dry yeast
1 cup milk
½ cup water
¼ cup margarine or butter
¼ cup honey
2 eggs
1 cup raisins

FILLING
1½ cups sugar
1½ teaspoons cinnamon
1 cup finely chopped peeled apples
¼ cup margarine or butter, melted
1 cup finely chopped nuts

GLAZE
1 cup powdered sugar
4 to 6 teaspoons water

In large bowl, combine 2 cups flour, salt and yeast; blend well. In small saucepan, heat milk, ½ cup water, ¼ cup margarine and honey until very warm (120 to 130°F.). Add warm liquid and eggs to flour mixture. Blend at low speed until moistened; beat 3 minutes at medium speed. By hand, stir in raisins and an additional 2¼ to 2¾ cups flour until dough pulls cleanly away from sides of bowl.

On floured surface, knead in remaining ¼ to ¾ cup flour until dough is smooth and elastic, about 10 minutes. Cover loosely with plastic wrap and cloth towel; let rest 20 minutes.

Generously grease two 9 or 8-inch square pans. In medium bowl, combine 1½ cups sugar, cinnamon and apples. Punch down dough to remove all air bubbles. Divide dough into 2 parts. Roll out half of dough to 12-inch square; brush with half of the melted margarine. Spoon ¼ of apple mixture on center ⅓ of dough; sprinkle with ¼ cup of the nuts.

Fold ⅓ of dough over nuts. Spoon an additional ¼ of apple mixture and ¼ cup of the nuts over dough. Fold remaining ⅓ of dough over nuts. Cut crosswise into 1-inch strips. Twist each strip. Place in greased pan. Repeat with remaining dough and filling. Cover with plastic wrap. Refrigerate 2 to 24 hours.

Heat oven to 375°F. Uncover dough. Let stand at room temperature 10 minutes. Bake at 375°F. for 30 to 40 minutes or until deep golden brown. Cover with foil last 10 minutes of baking if necessary to avoid excessive browning. Immediately remove from pans; invert onto wire rack. In small bowl, blend powdered sugar and enough water for desired drizzling consistency. Drizzle over warm rolls.

Yield: 24 rolls.

HIGH ALTITUDE :
Above 3500 Feet: Bake at 375°F. for 45 to 55 minutes.

NUTRITION PER SERVING:
Calories 290; Protein 5g; Carbohydrate 49g; Fat 8g; Sodium 190mg.

MAPLE BREAKFAST BUNS

These delicious oat rolls can be prepared and refrigerated overnight, then baked and served warm the next morning.

ROLLS
2 pkg. active dry yeast
1¼ cups warm milk
3½ to 4 cups all purpose flour
½ cup rolled oats
¼ cup sugar
¼ cup firmly packed brown sugar
½ teaspoon salt
¼ cup oil

FILLING
2 tablespoons margarine or butter, softened
½ cup firmly packed brown sugar
½ teaspoon maple extract

GLAZE
½ cup powdered sugar
⅛ teaspoon maple extract
2 to 3 teaspoons milk

In small bowl, dissolve yeast in warm milk (105 to 115°F.). In large bowl, combine 1 cup flour, rolled oats, sugar, ¼ cup brown sugar and salt; blend well. Add warm mixture and oil to flour mixture. Blend at low speed until moistened; beat 3 minutes at medium speed. By hand, stir in an additional 2¼ to 2½ cups flour until dough pulls cleanly away from sides of bowl.

Generously grease 13x9-inch pan. On floured surface, knead in ¼ to ½ cup flour until dough is smooth and elastic, about 5 minutes. Place dough in greased bowl; cover loosely with plastic wrap and cloth towel. Let rest at room temperature 25 minutes.

Roll dough into 16x12-inch rectangle; spread with margarine. Combine ½ cup brown sugar and ½ teaspoon maple extract; sprinkle over dough. Starting with 12-inch side, roll up tightly, pressing edges to seal. Cut into 12 slices; place cut side up in greased pan. Cover with greased plastic wrap; refrigerate overnight.

One and one-half hours before baking, remove rolls from refrigerator; cover with cloth towel. Let rise in warm place (80 to 85°F.) until light, about 1½ hours.

Heat oven to 350°F. Uncover dough. Bake 20 to 30 minutes or until golden brown. Cool 1 minute; remove from pan. Cool slightly on wire rack. In small bowl, blend all glaze ingredients, adding enough milk for desired glaze consistency. Drizzle glaze over warm rolls.

Yield: 12 rolls.

HIGH ALTITUDE :
Above 3500 Feet: No change.

NUTRITION PER SERVING:
Calories 330; Protein 6g; Carbohydrate 58g; Fat 8g; Sodium 130mg.

NUTRITION INFORMATION

NUTRITION INFORMATION

Pillsbury provides information for each recipe as a guideline for making food choices. Recipe analysis is based on the most current nutritional values available from the United States Department of Agriculture (USDA) and food manufacturers. For each recipe, you'll find calories per serving, plus grams of protein, carbohydrate and fat, and milligrams of sodium.

CALCULATING NUTRITION INFORMATION:

The recipe nutrition calculations are based on:

- a single unit (1 cookie), or the largest number of servings when a range is given (1/10 of recipe when 8 to 10 servings are listed).

- the first ingredient listed when an option is given.

- the larger amount of an ingredient when a range is given.

- 'if desired' or garnishing ingredients when they are included in the ingredient listing.

USING NUTRITION INFORMATION:

The amount of nutrients a person needs is determined by one's age, sex, size and activity level. The following are general guidelines to use for evaluating daily food intake. These numbers will increase or decrease according to individual needs.

Calories:	2350
Protein:	45 to 65 grams
Carbohydrates:	325 grams
Fat:	75 grams or less
Sodium:	2400 milligrams

REDUCING FAT IN BAKED GOODS

Ingredients high in fat, such as margarine, butter, shortening, oil, whipping cream, cream cheese, sour cream and chocolate, add flavor to recipes but also add calories and grams of fat to our diet. In addition to enhancing flavor, fat makes pastry flaky, cakes moist and tender, and cookies crisp. Decreasing fat in a baked item can create a drier, coarser, denser texture and reduce overall flavor. If you would like to try reducing the fat in baked recipes, here are some suggestions:

- Reduce the amount of margarine, butter, shortening or oil in a recipe by 1/4 to 1/3.

- Substitute skim milk for 2% or whole milk.

- Substitute lowfat yogurt, light sour cream and light cream cheese in place of the regular products. Although nonfat counterparts are available, they are not always as successful in baked recipes.

- Limit the use of nuts. For example, sprinkle 2 table-spoons chopped nuts over a frosted cake instead of adding 1/2 cup of them to the batter.

- Use cholesterol-free, fat-free egg product or egg whites in place of whole eggs in recipes.

- Use evaporated skimmed milk instead of whipping cream in dessert sauces.

- Substitute or add flavorings and/or seasonings to replace the flavor lost from fat. For example, add chocolate and rum flavoring to a cocoa sauce for more intense flavor.

- Serve lowfat baked items such as muffins and coffee cakes warm from the oven. The texture change is not as noticeable when they're eaten warm.

- See our Recipe Make-Overs section in the Index, p. 511.

INDEX

MW = Microwave Option